AUDACIOUS PLAN AND PROFILE 1914.

At the outbreak of war in August 1914 all British battleships were wearing a dark slate grey paintwork scheme. So dark was the shade of grey that photographic film sometimes had trouble in recording the ships without losing detail in the shadows. White (some red) recognition bands on funnels stood out boldly but these were quickly painted out on the outbreak of hostilities.

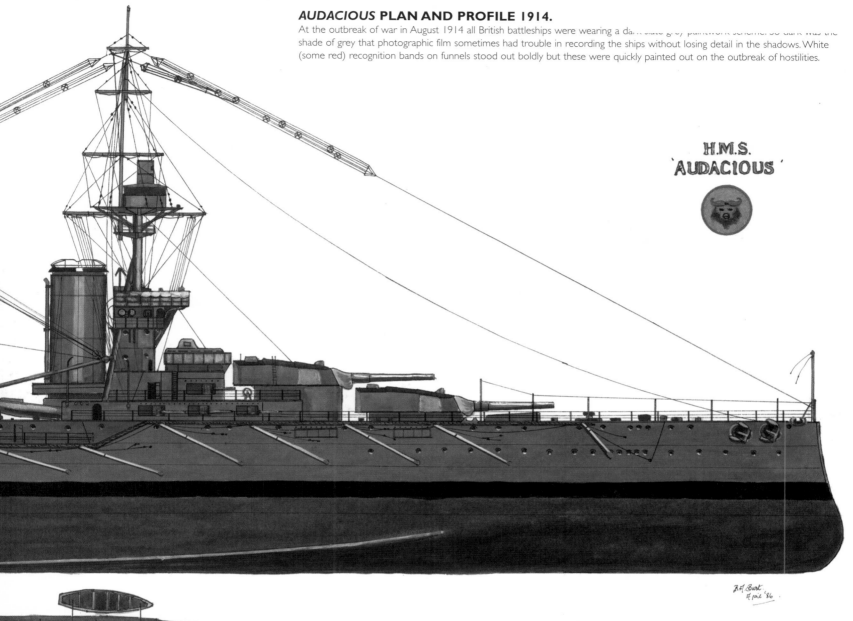

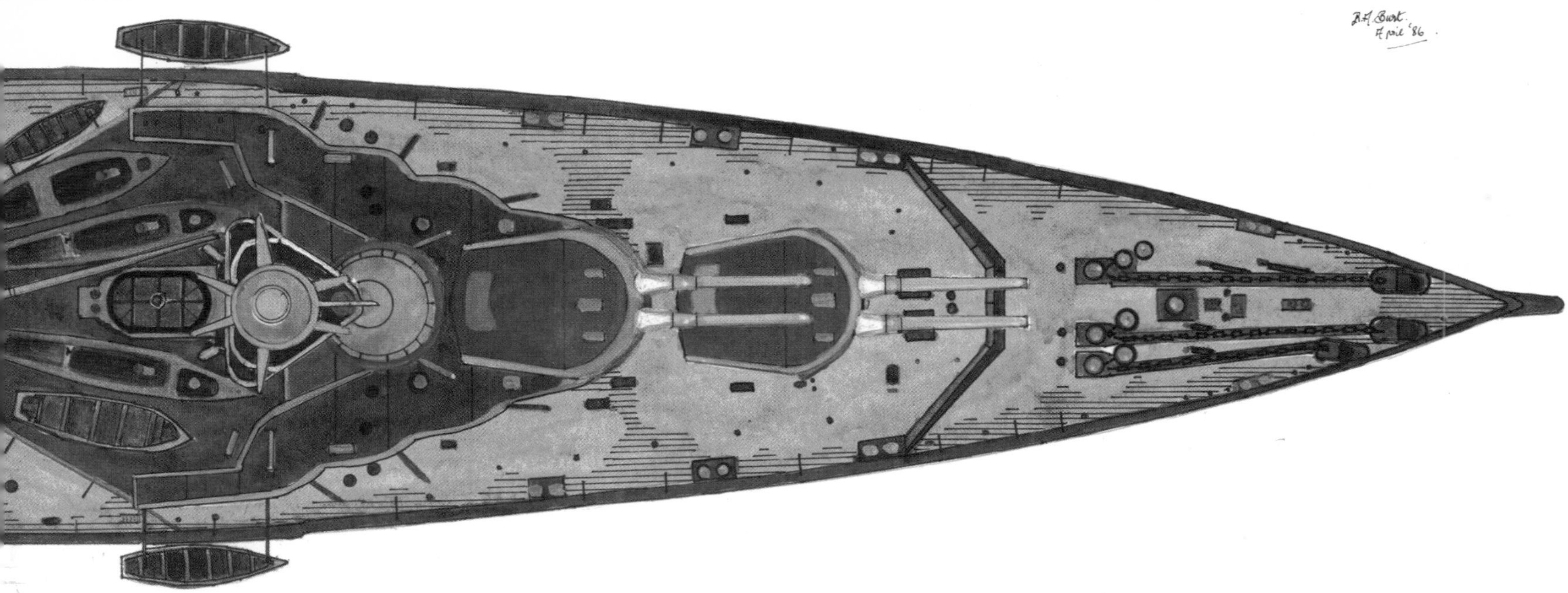

BRITISH BATTLESHIPS OF WORLD WAR ONE

BRITISH BATTLESHIPS OF WORLD WAR ONE

R A BURT

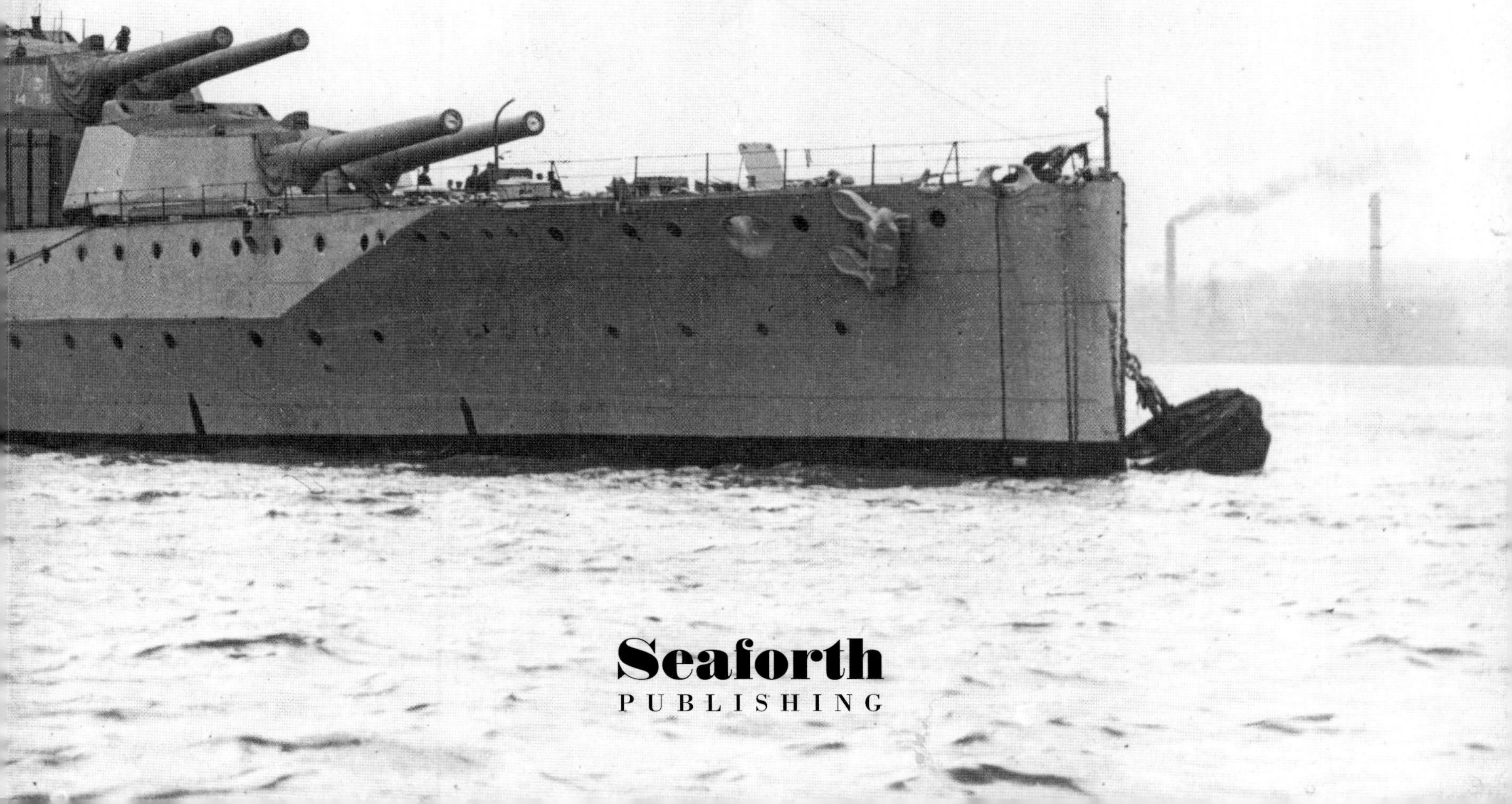

Seaforth
PUBLISHING

Overleaf: *Queen Elizabeth* at anchor in the Firth of Forth just a few days after the surrender of the High Seas Fleet (Nov 1918), the conference for the surrender being held in her wardroom between Admiral David Beatty and Rear Admiral Meurer.

Acknowledgements

During the six years this book has been in preparation, the author has been indebted to the following persons and establishments. In particular, I should like to extend sincere thanks to David Lyon, Michael Dandridge and Mrs Pilkington of the Draught Room at the National Maritime Museum, Greenwich; to David Brown and his staff at the Naval Historical Library; to D. W. Robinson, Press Officer, and to P. H. Judd, Chief Naval Architect, both of Vickers Shipbuilding Group. I must also acknowledge the help received from A. M. Ingham of the Naval Ordnance Museum, Priddy's Hard, and appreciation is also due to my editor, Michael Boxall, J. A. Roberts, A. S. Norris, the late P. A. Vicary and, especially, the late W. P. Trotter M.C., who gave me much sound advice and great encouragement throughout the years I knew him. Much gratitude is expressed to my publishers; in particular to David Gibbons and Anthony A. Evans, both of whom pointed out items I might otherwise have missed. Finally, to my wife Janice and our two children must go special mention for their patience and encouragement; indeed, if it were not for their making sacrifices to their lifestyle and enjoyment, I doubt if the work could have been completed. The photographs are all from the author's collection; the drawings are based on the official shipbuilding draughts now held at the National Maritime Museum, Greenwich.

R.A.B.

This edition first published in Great Britain in 2012 by
Seaforth Publishing, an imprint of Pen & Sword Books Ltd,
47 Church Street, Barnsley S70 2AS

www.seaforthpublishing.com

British Library Cataloguing in Publication Data
A catalogue record for this book is available from the British Library

ISBN 978 1 84832 147 2

Typeset and designed by Stephen Dent
Printed and bound in China through Printworks International.

Contents

Preface

Right: Dr Oscar Parkes in his Mediterranean outfit during his service in the Navy at the Dardanelles campaign, 1915.

In general, collectors of historical warship photographs and naval enthusiasts and historians are a pretty mixed group of people. They come from all walks of life and range from motor mechanics to Members of Parliament; for some strange reason there is usually a heavy sprinkling of doctors and solicitors. But what starts a person's enthusiasm off? Be it serious research or gathering collectables on yesterday's navies, it is an enthusiasm that usually turns into an obsession (in the nicest possible way). The reasons are many, but in most cases cannot be explained very easily. At the turn of the century, it was not at all common for anyone other than naval personnel to gather ships' statistics or indeed collect photographs of warships. In fact, other than a few resident photographers such as West, Hopkins, Cribb, Long and Symonds, who sold their photographs commercially, pictures of many warships of the day were extremely difficult to procure.

One of the more notable characters of the time was F. T. Jane, a journalist and correspondent during the Boer War, who turned his attention toward warship design and construction. He became deeply involved in naval affairs, and one could read his biting remarks in most of the naval periodicals as well as in the daily newspapers. His brainchild was, of course, that now famous album *All the World's Fighting Ships*, which appeared for the first time in 1897, the year of Queen Victoria's Diamond Jubilee. Throughout the initial preparation for the book, Jane was involved in making a series of small sketches of all major warships then in existence, and for help he turned to one of the more notable photograph collectors of the day, W. A. Beiber, who in turn was kind enough to lend Jane scores and scores of rare prints for reference. It took Jane eighteen months to complete the work and, in his own words, 'it nearly gave me brain fever'. The book was to become more popular with both the Service and the public than any major naval reference work previously published.

There were no photographs in that first edition, nor indeed for the next few years, but for the 1903 edition it was found possible to include a few 'real' views. This was very well received, and it was only a matter of time before the annual featured photographs

Right: Arrival of the dreadnoughts within the British Fleet. Anchored here at Scapa Flow, *Dreadnought* and *Bellerophon* lie alongside the pre-dreadnoughts *Implacable*, *Lord Nelson*, *Irresistible* and *Bulwark*.

Left: *Inflexible* leads units of the pre-dreadnought *King Edward VII* class during manoeuvres in 1909.

for the majority of ships within its pages. To supply the increase in views needed, naval photographers were suddenly in great demand: and names such as Cribb, Seward, Bekan, Abrahams, Cozens, Gregory, Hopkins and Symonds were soon familiar to the ever-growing number of warship enthusiasts. In short, Jane's famous annual went a long way to encourage many to start becoming involved in naval matters.

One of the greatest warship historians of the twentieth century was soon to become actively involved with Jane; and Dr Oscar Parkes, who was deeply concerned in naval affairs, showed an enthusiasm found in few people. One can do no better than relate his own jottings on how he became a collector and enthusiast:

> 'How long have you been interested in warships?' is a common enough question between ship lovers, usually to be met with a full account of how the interest came about. My own goes back to a very early age – in fact, as far back as memory can reach, and that is to an infant's high folding chair. This, when broken, provided a play table upon which was displayed strange composite pictures flanked on each side by a row of large coloured wooden beads on a rod. These latter may have helped in teaching one to count; to the former I owe my love of ships and locomotives because it displayed both warships and a train. Of the train I remember nothing except that it 'symbolised' the real thing which sometimes could be seen from my pram when one of our several 'walks' took us across the bridge below which ran the branch L&NWR line. But the ship! she was indeed a strange misshapen thing, which afterwards I knew to be the *Devastation* – and in the middle of the eighties she and her sister *Thunderer* were still regarded by the man in the street as the symbols of Britain's greatness afloat.
>
> With attention focused upon engine and ship every day, it did not require any family or environmental background to germinate a ship or engine lover with the desire to see a real ship as I had already seen a real engine. But it was to be some years before that wish was satisfied, and in the meantime I had to be content with ship pictures. And here may I add that throughout boyhood, until well into the nineteen hundreds, none of my friends had the least interest in ships; never once did I have the opportunity to 'talk ship'. It was without the help of periodicals, societies, picture postcards and recognition books, which are so familiar to the enthusiast today – thus it was a lonely hobby.
>
> Hence, while the engine love could be satisfied by the near-by railways, the ship side was more difficult. Even if I did demand pictures, none were forthcoming – we never took in any paper which showed them; and so my memories of those early years must be confined to the isolated occasions when special pictures and naval occasions served to keep interest alive until a wider field discovered in the local library provided what was necessary to develop that side of life which was to mean so much. The *Naval Annual* came to notice, and they were sporting a range of *Brassey's* on their shelves. I felt a wonderful storehouse had been opened, but unfortunately these were in the reference library and could not be taken away, so much of my spare time as could be managed was spent trying to understand the plans and reading about new ships. The many pages giving details of the world's fighting ships delighted me, but at the age of ten I was not tempted into becoming a compiler of lists by copying out sections of *Brassey's*. About this time, Newnes had brought out *The Army and Navy Illustrated*, a fine glossy six-penny-worth, half of which was devoted to the Navy. It raised a new standard in photograph reproduction, which has never been surpassed, and we got splendid pictures of the naval manoeuvres, visits to dockyards, and big shipbuilding establishments with photos of their famous productions, accounts of past naval battles, mostly illustrated by Chas de Lacy, and portraits of our leading commanding officers, as well as every new ship. One grudged space to life and scenes on board of the 'cooks of the galley' sort, and especially when a whole page was

Above: *King George V* and *Marlborough* in attendance at the Fleet Review for HM King George V in July 1914.

taken up by 'Jack Ashore' – kissing a nursemaid or wheeling a pram. Presumably the Editor, Commander C. N. Robinson, considered such sentimental relief held some publicity value – sailors were not always at sea – but I know they evoked my youthful scorn.

Special numbers showing the Channel, Mediterranean and Reserve Fleets were almost too good to be true, and in years to come were in much demand. A special delight was a magnificent view of the battleship *Benbow*, then port guard ship at Greenock, showing her 110-ton gun elevated in silent menace, and Symonds' well-known view of the *Devastation* passing the old training ship *St Vincent* at Portsmouth. The joyous excitements from those special issues were very rarely surpassed.

It was during afternoon school at Berkhamsted that my father came into the classroom and announced that he was taking my brother and myself to see the Naval Review at Spithead. The form master thought it only proper to ask the Headmaster for permission, and so I proceeded toward the VII Form, where the formidable grey-bearded Dr Fry was instructing, to make my request. 'Certainly not!' he thundered (or seemed to), 'I won't have the term interrupted in such a manner. Go tell your Father that if every boy's parent did the same the School would be emptied. Off you go.' 'Rubbish, of course you can. Come along and get your things packed,' and without anymore ado we went and got Matron to make us parcels of what was wanted, and I had the rare delight of leaving school in mid-term with wonderful prospects ahead – my brother, because we should see thousands of different soldiers during the processions, and myself anticipated the supreme joy of seeing real warships for the first time.

Oscar Parkes went on to see active service with the Royal Navy in the First World War, and when demobilized in 1919 became the Editor of Jane's *All the World's Fighting Ships* and later Director of Naval Photographs at the Imperial War Museum. Dr Parkes, who wrote profoundly on naval affairs for many years, was considered to be the most knowledgeable person on warships throughout the whole of the British Empire. Every warship enthusiast and collector of today owes much to Dr Parkes and F. T. Jane – and that certainly includes the author of this book, who became deeply interested in the Royal Navy's battleships after reading Parkes's famous book *British Battleships*, published in 1957, as well as the Jane's annuals when visiting the local library. Being primarily interested in battleships and battlecruisers, I noticed that, apart from a few publications currently available, the subject was not that well treated, and this applied in particular to the 1906–18 period. For many years I have anticipated putting this situation in order, and with the publication of this book comes an ambition fulfilled. I hope it will not only fill a gap in naval literature but will give as much pleasure to the reader as it has given to me while writing it.

R. A. Burt

Introduction

Design Procedure

The designs for British capital ships were generally governed by certain requirements intended to ensure the ship's capability for survival. Layouts had to conform to 'standard Admiralty practice', which took into account four features that were deemed essential:

1. Safety (stability, structural strength, etc.)
2. Potential foreign opponents
3. Time and cost
4. Docking facilities.

On any design committee would sit not only constructors but ship's officers, engineers, ordnance experts, dockyard controllers and other specialist personnel experienced in warship construction. Each participant would be given a hearing and all opinions taken into consideration. This procedure meant more often than not that some essential features of the design could not necessarily be reconciled with others, and compromises would have to be reached, sacrifices being made in an endeavour to achieve a balance that would suit all the members of the committee. In most cases, this resulted in an 'ideal' warship being marred, usually because of the constant displacement restriction that was always of prime concern. Faced with innumerable problems, the British constructors not only came up with adequate designs, but more often than not with innovatory ideas that placed British ships well ahead of their rivals.

The British capital ship was expected to go anywhere and to operate as effectively in the Pacific Ocean as in the North Sea. Furthermore, they were expected to counter effectively any challenge from foreign navies, all of whose ships had differing features: the devotion to compartmentation and heavy armour plating of the German Navy; the prime importance of machinery and speed in Italian ships; and the 'one-off' experimental types of the French and Russians, which usually followed current trends in naval architecture and had no homogeneity among their respective fleets. Abroad, there was a strong tendency to design ships for the waters in which they would serve, and for the majority of powers, this meant home waters. The British warship, however, had to be a compromise of all these features and still be able to bring any antagonist to battle without being outclassed.

Builders

Ten yards were responsible for the construction of the battleships and battlecruisers that served in the Royal Navy during the First World War.

Armstrong An engineering firm founded in 1847, and a constructor of warships since 1882; in 1897 took over the firm of Joseph Whitworth; main yards at Elswick and Walker on the Tyne; other factories included ammunition works at Scotswood on the Tyne, Erith Engineering Works and an ordnance factory at Pozzuoli, near Naples.

Beardmore Warship constructors since the beginning of the twentieth century; also armour and ordnance manufacturers; yard at Dalmuir.

John Brown Sheffield steelworks; initially supplier of plates for warships; took over Thompson Shipyard on the upper Clyde in 1897 to become John Brown Construction Co.

Cammell Laird William Laird & Son were constructors in the 1840s of some of the very earliest iron vessels; became large warship builders from 1885; amalgamated with Charles Cammell Co., steel manufacturers of Sheffield, in 1903; yard at Birkenhead.

Devonport H.M. Dockyard, Devonport; warship construction here began in the last decades of the eighteenth century; the last

Below: *Hercules* at the Fleet Review, Spithead, in July 1914. This photograph was taken from the Royal Yacht by Mr Stephen Cribb, the official photographer.

battleship built here was *Royal Oak*, completed in May 1916.

Fairfield Founded 1864 by John Elder and Charles Randolph; 1869 carried on by W. Pierce and became Fairfield Shipbuilding and Engineering Co. in 1885; constructors of machinery, merchant ships and warships of all sizes; yard at Govan on the Clyde.

Harland & Wolff E. J. Harland bought Robert Hickson & Co. in 1859, and was joined by G. W. Wolff two years later; builders of great liners and merchant vessels as well as major warships; yard at Belfast.

Palmer Founded 1852; built early iron warships including *Defence*, *Triumph* and *Swiftsure* in the 1860s; yard at Jarrow on the Tyne.

Portsmouth H.M. Dockyard, Portsmouth, the oldest of the Royal dockyards; major dry dock facilities, repair shops, etc., as well as construction yards; the last battleship built there was *Royal Sovereign*, which was completed in May 1916.

Scotts Founded in 1711; builders of cargo vessels, then turned to marine engineering in 1823; began warship construction in 1849 at Greenoch.

12in 45cal Mk X Gun

as mounted in *Lord Nelson* class, *Dreadnought*, *Bellerophon*, *Invincible* and *Indefatigable* classes
Weight without breech: 56 tons 16 cwt
Length: 557.55in
Bore: 45cal (length 540in)
Material: wire wound construction (steel)
Chamber length: 81in
Rifling system: polygroove plain section
Twist: uniform one turn in 30 calibres
Muzzle velocity: 2,725/2,821ft sec
Muzzle energy: 47,800ft tons
Elevation in turret: 13½°
Weight of shell: 850lb
Weight of charge: 258lb MD Cordite
Range: 16,400 yards
Rate of fire: approx. 2 rounds per minute.

12in 50cal Mk XI and XI* Gun

as mounted in *St Vincent*, *Neptune* and *Colossus* classes
Weight: 66.7 tons
Length: 617in
Bore: 50cal
Material: wire wound construction (steel)
Chamber length: 112in
Rifling system: polygroove plain section
Twist: uniform one turn in 30 calibres
Muzzle velocity: 2,850ft sec
Muzzle energy: 52,200ft tons
Elevation in turret: 15°
Weight of shell: 850lb
Weight of charge: 306lb
Range: 21,000 yards at 20° (approx.).

12in 45cal Mk XIII Gun

as mounted in *Agincourt*
Weight with breech: 60 tons (approx.)
Length: 557.55in
Bore: 45cal (length 540in)
Material: wire wound construction (steel)
Chamber length: 82in
Rifling system: polygroove plain section
Twist: uniform one turn in 30 calibres
Muzzle velocity: 2,700ft sec
Muzzle energy: 47,800ft tons
Weight of shell: 850lb
Weight of charge: 280lb
Elevation in turret: 15°
Range: 20,000 yards (approx.).

13.5in 45cal Mk V Gun

as mounted in *Orion*, *King George V*, *Lion*, *Iron Duke* class and *Tiger*
Weight: 76 tons
Length: 625.9in
Bore: 45cal
Capacity 92,000cu in
Material: wire wound construction (steel)
Chamber length: 92.13in
Chamber diameter: 16.85in
Rifling system: polygroove plain section
Length of rifling: 509.57in
Twist: uniform one turn in 30 calibres
Number of grooves: 68
Depth of grooves: 0.12in
Width of grooves: 0.445in
Muzzle velocity: 2,582/2,491ft sec
Muzzle energy: 63,190ft tons
Elevation in turret: 20°
Weight of shell: 1,250lb/1,400lb
Weight of charge: 293lb
Range at 20° elevation: 23,800 yards.

13.5in Mk VI Gun

as mounted in *Erin*
Weight: 77 tons
Length: 625.9in
Bore: 45cal
Capacity 92,000cu in
Material: wire wound construction (steel)
Chamber length: 95in
Chamber diameter: 15in
Rifling system: polygroove plain section
Length of rifling: 506.743in
Twist: uniform one turn in 30 calibres
Number of grooves: 68
Depth of grooves: 0.12in
Width of grooves: 0.445in
Muzzle velocity: 2,445ft sec
Muzzle energy: 60,600ft tons
Elevation in turret: 20°

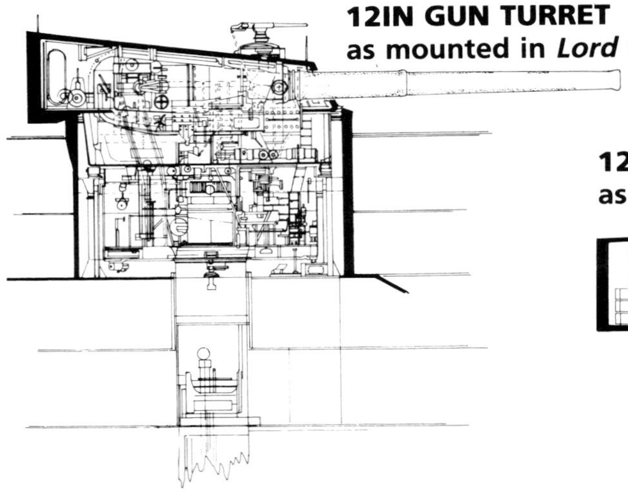

12IN GUN TURRET
as mounted in *Lord Nelson* and *Dreadnought*

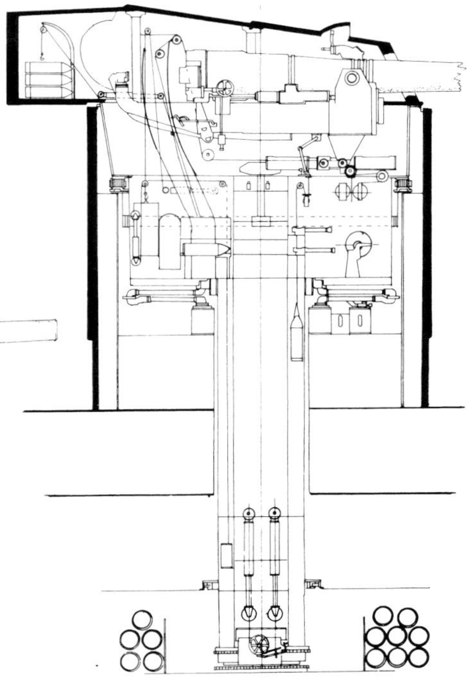

12IN GUN TURRET
as mounted in *St Vincent*

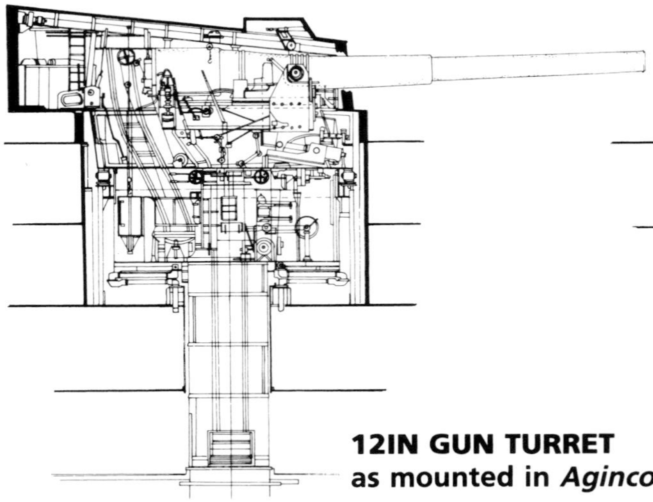

12IN GUN TURRET
as mounted in *Agincourt*

Thames Iron Works Warship builders since the beginning of the nineteenth century; constructed *Warrior*, the first iron-hulled sea-going warship in 1859; yard at Blackwall; the firm went into liquidation in 1912 on completion of *Thunderer*, which was the last major warship to be built on the Thames.

Vickers Originally a steel firm, based in Sheffield; amalgamated with Maxim in 1883 and began the manufacture of guns; subsequently manufacturer of warships, weapons, ammunition and aircraft; yard at Barrow in Furness.

Armament

The primary raison d'être of a battleship or battlecruiser was to carry her armament and use it successfully against an enemy. The change from mixed calibres to an all-big-gunned ship in 1906 (as described on page 20) certainly brought no shortage of problems. *Dreadnought* adopted an echelon system of turret layout, with one turret forward and one aft, one amidships and one staggered on each beam, port and starboard. At the time, however, many authorities still looked upon the mixed calibre as the better method of arming a battleship, and hailed the *Lord Nelson* class as

Weight of shell: 1,400lb
Weight of charge: 297lb.

14in 45cal Mk I Gun

as mounted in *Canada*
Weight loaded: 85 tons 4cwt
Length: 648.4in
Bore: 45cal
Material: wire wound construction (steel)
Chamber length: 94.165in
Chamber diameter: 15–18.5in
Rifling system: polygroove plain section
Length of rifling: 529.82in
Twist: uniform one turn in 30 calibres
Number of grooves: 84
Depth of grooves: 0.12in
Width of grooves: 0.349in
Muzzle velocity: 2,507ft sec
Muzzle energy: 65,790ft tons
Elevation in turret: 20°
Weight of shell: 1,586lb
Weight of charge: 344lb MD Cordite
Range: 24,300 yards at 20°.

15in 42cal Mk I Gun

as mounted in *Queen Elizabeth, Royal Sovereign, Renown, Repulse* and *Courageous* classes
Weight without breech: 97 tons 3cwt
Weight with breech: 100 tons
Length: 650.4in
Bore: 42cal
Rifling system: polygroove plain section
Length of rifling: 516.33in
Twist: uniform one turn in 30 calibres
Muzzle velocity: 2,450ft sec
Muzzle energy: 79,890ft tons
Weight of shell: 1,920lb
Weight of charge: 428lb
Elevation in turret: 20°
Range: 23,734 yards at 20°
Rate of fire: approx. 2 rounds per minute.

18in 40cal Mk I Gun

as mounted in *Furious*
Weight: 150 tons (approx.)
Length: 720in
Bore: 40cal
Material: wire wound construction (steel)
Rifling system: polygroove plain section
Muzzle velocity: 2,400ft sec
Weight of shell: 3,320lb
Weight of charge: 630lb
Range: 30,000 yards (approx.)
Rate of fire: 1 per minute (average).

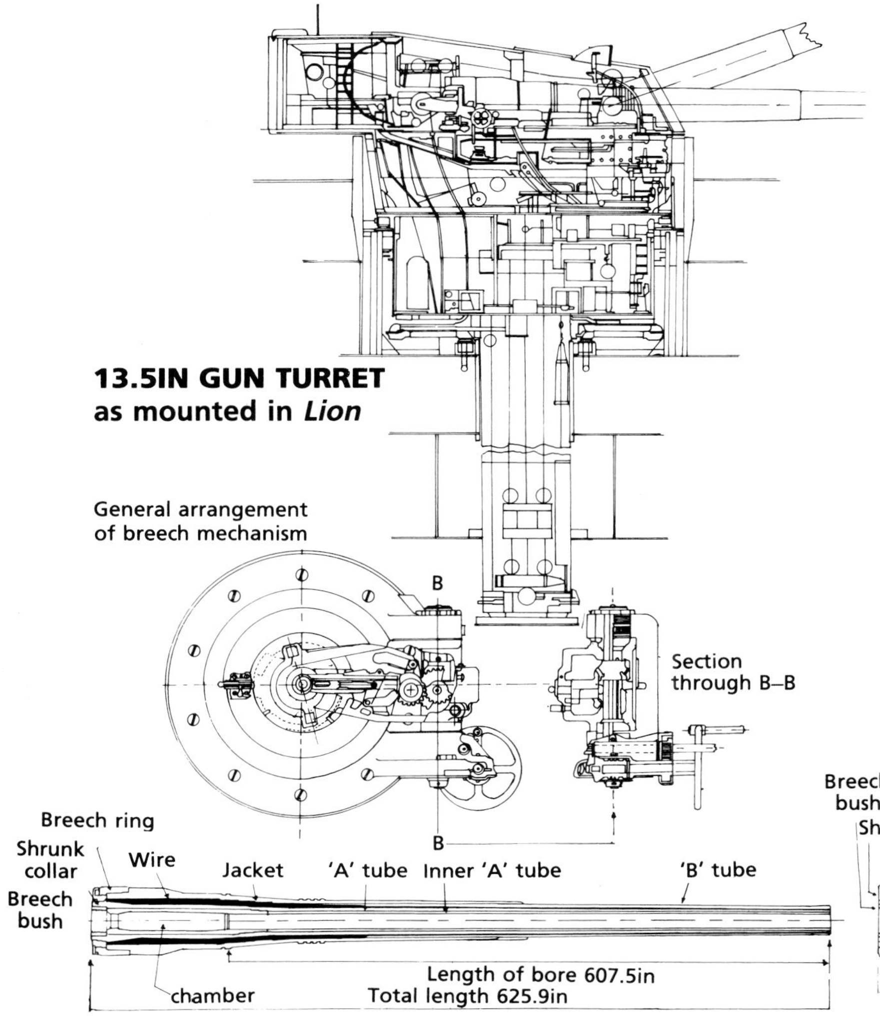

13.5IN GUN TURRET
as mounted in *Lion*

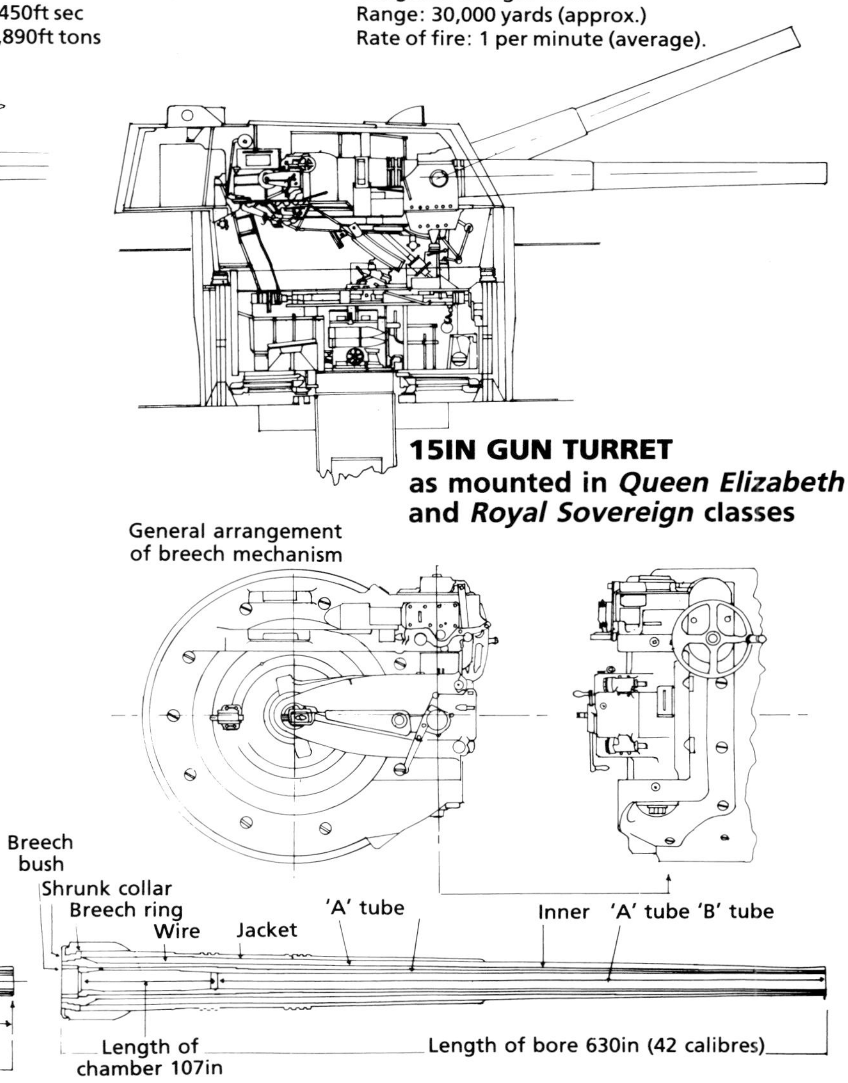

15IN GUN TURRET
as mounted in *Queen Elizabeth* and *Royal Sovereign* classes

Right: *Marlborough* looking aft from the forecastle showing forward 13.5in turrets and bridgework, summer 1914.

the final answer. There was indeed something to be said for mixed calibres: the most telling argument in favour of including a weapon of approximately 9.2in calibre (as in the *Lord Nelson* and *King Edward VII* classes) was the effective amount of metal that could be thrown per minute compared with fewer numbers of 12in guns:

	12in gun of 1906	Contemporary 9.2in gun
Hits per minute	0.81	2.84
Weight of shell	850lb	380lb
Weight of shell striking per minute	688.5lb	1,079.2lb

If the smaller gun could be judged by these figures, the discharge at any given time would have been more than half as much more metal than from the 12in. It was inevitable that those who considered the 9.2in battery ought not to have been abandoned could strengthen their argument with facts such as these. Moreover, although *Dreadnought* carried ten big guns, she could fire only eight on either broadside because of the disposition of her echelon turrets.

Such deficiencies in the design were outweighed by the advantage gained in fitting all large-calibre guns – a necessity given the greatly increased ranges at which engagements were now being fought as shown by the Russo-Japanese War of 1904–5. The call for a main armament of eight or more guns of uniform heavy calibre was prompted by the need for maximum destructive effect and to facilitate long-range fire control by means of salvo firing and spotting the fall of shot.

The adverse criticism of those opposed to the new system did not deter the other major naval powers from following Britain's lead, and all but the USA gave their early dreadnoughts the echelon fashion of mounting the big guns. The main armaments of the early dreadnoughts, both British and German, were adequate for the job and there was little to choose between them. But when the *Queen Elizabeth* class with their 15in guns were constructed, the lead in firepower and turret technology went to the Royal Navy. In fact, this gun and turret arrangement of four guns forward and four aft became 'standard' fitting for many successive warships.

Little good can be said of the British secondary batteries, which plainly lacked the punch required of them; they most certainly were not on a par with their German and French counterparts. From *Dreadnought* to the *King George V* class of 1910, the secondary battery of 4in guns was the subject of constant severe criticism, to which the Admiralty would not bend. The Board's Victorian attitude was responsible for the major weakness in all British battleships and battlecruiser designs from 1906 to 1910, when the 6in gun was introduced in *Tiger* and the *Iron Dukes*.

Fire Control

At the turn of the century, the quality of big guns in warships was improving rapidly, with increasing accuracy and longer ranges. However, to shoot the guns to good effect and obtain an adequate percentage of hits on any given target efficient rangefinding equipment was vital. This applied in particular at ranges over 8,000 or 9,000 yards.

Optical rangefinders of various types were fitted in all warships, and many experiments took place to obtain a suitable system. By the time *Dreadnought* had arrived in 1906, rangefinders had evolved into a practical standard type of instrument; the best known, and most widely used in the world's warships, was the Barr and Stroud 'coincidence' system, which was a short-base, split-image rangefinder of varying length (depending on position, between 3ft 6in and 9ft). The largest of these was quite capable of taking ranges accurately up to 8,000 yards. This system of improved rangefinding, however, did not give provision for passing information to the gunlayers within the turrets in order to modify ranges relative to the target's course and speed. Electro-mechanical equipment had been introduced for this purpose some years earlier (basically an electrical transmitter that conveyed information from the rangefinders to the guns), but it did not prove successful. Later Captain J. S. Dumaresq and Sir Percy Scott developed improved types, while the fitting of Vickers rate-of-change clocks provided some further answers. A follow-the-pointer system was introduced in 1908; in this the range and deflection were transmitted from the fire control position direct to the sights of the guns by means of electrically-controlled pointers, which were rotated in front of the respective dials and indicated the point to which the dials had to be set for correction.

By 1916, the Royal Navy was using what was considered a highly elaborate 'director control' to back up a first class armament, a combination quite unmatched in foreign navies. Witness progress aboard *Bellerophon*, for example: she was fitted with a revolving tower aloft in which was located a 9ft Barr and Stroud rangefinder and a Vickers fire control table. Personnel in the tower consisted of the control officer, the rangefinder and rate keeper. This method was relatively new within the Royal Navy, but quickly became standard procedure. Most of the Grand Fleet's battleships and battlecruisers were fitted with similar equipment, backed up by extra rangefinders in the turrets and bridgework. Doubts among contemporary fire control staff can be ascribed to inefficient training and hunting arrangements within the electro-mechanical gear. The principle itself was sound enough, allowing as it did the personnel to retain the same position regardless of the angle of the target; but the director towers in all British battleships afforded a restricted view because of the tripod masts.

After Jutland, in May 1916, director control came under close examination. It was now fully realized that this was one of the most important departments of a fighting ship, and certain aspects of the systems then in use had failed during the battle – the Barr and Stroud rangefinders had not given the required results because of the poor lighting conditions during the action. It was generally known that the Germans had Zeiss stereoscopic rangefinders, and a different method of fire control; the former was slightly superior to that used in British ships, but the latter, according to intelligence reports, was inferior to British equipment, and not up to requirements laid down by the Admiralty. This was borne out in 1919 after tests had been carried out in the captured battleship *Baden*: although much of the equipment had been sabotaged by the Germans, the fire control gear was examined and found to be relatively primitive.

From 1917, the Admiralty strove for a balanced and adequate fire control system, but an ideal layout was not in service until the middle of 1918. The war was nearly at an end by the time inclinometers were introduced, and highly trained staff were functioning with much improved director towers. By the end of 1918, all existing British capital ships were fitted with improved fire control, placed aloft as usual, but if possible the towers were repositioned on the control top rather than underneath it; if this were not possible, then additional rangefinders were fitted on top of the control top to give them an all-round vision. Small towers for the secondary armament were also being fitted on each side of the bridge, and there was also provision for director control to be worked from within one of the main turrets (usually 'X' turret). The towers themselves had been revamped and consisted of improved rangefinders, with many of the Barr and Stroud types having been replaced by different makes, and improved Dreyer or Argo electro-mechanical equipment. Personnel and their functions for the control was as follows.

1. Control officer: spotted the fall of shot to correct elevation and direction with direct fire, and maintained communications with the plotting and transmitting stations.

Left: Port quarter of *Ajax* in Devonport 1914. Note the director fire control in place.

Right: HM King George V, Sir George Callaghan and Prince Albert on the forecastle of *Neptune* watching competition rough weather firing trials to try out Sir Percy Scott's director system which was fitted to *Thunderer* against *Orion* without the system. *Thunderer* scored eight or nine hits compared with none for *Orion*.

2. Rate officer: worked the inclinometer and decided the rate of fire due to enemy movement in conjunction with the transmitter office and the station rate officer.
3. Direction layer: laid and fired, but also worked the gyro direction training lamp.
4. Direction trainer: trained the tower on to the target and worked the synchronized training transmitter (by power or hand) and corrected the vertical datum line.
5. Direction sight setter.
6. Telephone operator.
7. Rangefinder.
8. Voice pipe and human link operator.
9. Tower trainer (back up).
10. Inclinometer operator (back up).

The crews for the secondary directors were identical, except that numbers 8, 9 and 10 were not required. Further aids to control were seen at the end of 1917, when deflection scales and range clocks came into existence. The deflection scales were painted on turret sides and tops (usually 'B' and 'X') and told the leading or following ship the angle of fire. They were only used if the ship ahead or astern could not use her own rangefinders owing to smoke or other conditions affecting her vision. The range clocks told other ships what range the guns were firing at (in thousands of yards) so that all ships could fire their guns in a concentrated effort even if only one ship could see or had operable rangefinding equipment.

Armour and Protection

The subject of armour applied to British and German ships has long furnished fuel for heated debate. The main armour strakes fitted to both nation's ships were generally considered adequate to withstand heavy shell impact under normal battle ranges of the day. (It was envisaged that action would take place in about the 10,000-yard zone.) Although the German ships were given slightly thicker belts than their British opponents, there was very little to choose between them. War experience was to show, however, that as battle ranges frequently increased to over 10,000 yards, shells reached the target at a steeper trajectory, so that it was the deck armour that was threatened rather than the side of the ship. Here both British and German designs were deficient.

With regard to the oft-quoted superior strength and quality of German steel plates, it is interesting to note that when tests were carried out in the captured battleship *Baden* in 1919, only a slight difference was found between British and German steels; and when fired upon during the tests, her plates did not meet the strict standards required of British plates. *Baden*'s vitals were protected by Krupp armour, and it was very gratifying for the British to discover that the armour plates used in their later dreadnoughts were slightly superior to the Krupp process.

One feature in which many of the British battleships failed was the lack of adequate underwater protection against mine and torpedo attack. *Dreadnought* herself was fitted with protective screens covering the magazines and shell rooms, and this protection was seen as very innovatory at the time. It did not compare in any way with the first German dreadnought, however; *Nassau* was fitted with a continuous 1¼in anti-torpedo bulkhead protecting her vitals.

Some measure of rectification was seen in the *Bellerophon* class of 1907, in which particular attention was paid to suitable underwater protection. The screens were extended from 'A' to 'Y' barbettes and ran down to the double bottom, this forming a continuous anti-torpedo bulkhead that protected not only the magazines and shell rooms, but also the machinery and boilers. This was every bit as good as that fitted in the first two classes of German dreadnoughts (*Nassau* and *Helgoland* classes), but this great improvement over *Dreadnought* was not followed up in British designs, and a return to the small magazine screens was witnessed in the classes from *Colossus* to *Iron Duke* (1908–11 designs).

The last two British battleship classes to serve in the war (the *Queen Elizabeth* and *Royal Sovereign* classes) were provided with an anti-torpedo bulkhead protection system second to none and easily equal to anything produced for German ships throughout the entire war.

Shortly before the outbreak of war in 1914, work was undertaken to provide British battleships with adequate underwater protection. Experiments were hastily started at Portsmouth and Cambridge test centres. At Cambridge targets of 5⁄16in steel plating three feet square backed with angle iron ribs were constructed. The target formed the bottom of a floating tank, and a charge of 6–8oz of gun-cotton was detonated underwater a few inches away from it. Similar targets were prepared at Portsmouth, but scaled up to two and a half times the size, with proportionate charges under them. The targets at Portsmouth weighed about a ton. The distortion in both cases was compared and it was found that the smaller charge was relatively less effective than the larger one, but that the difference could be more than compensated by increasing its weight by 25 per cent. More tests of 1in plate with framing four feet apart, corresponding to a battleship's hull, were carried out using a 400lb charge. The results provided the Admiralty with excellent data for the protection of big ships as for example, was applied to *Ramillies*, while she was under construction in 1915.

The Admiralty was aware that the largest torpedo used by the German Navy contained as much as 400lb of high explosive, and a charge of this order was capable of blowing a hole in a steel plate 6in thick. The protection of a ship by underwater armour was, therefore, impracticable because of the weight of armour required. Moreover, it was accepted that at the mean point of impact the ship's structure would be destroyed over a very large area; with the ordinary plating then in use, it would work out at about 30 square feet. So protection would have to consist of either longitudinal bulkheads strong enough to remain intact and watertight after the explosion, or of an external hull fitting which would cause the torpedo to detonate outside the hull.

Of the two, the first method was the most widely used, and was fitted in its simplest form. The bulkheads were fitted approximately ten feet inboard from the outer hull, the space between being left empty to allow the gases from the explosion to expand and lose pressure and velocity. The problem, however, was that when the hull's skin plating shattered, the small fragments were projected against the inner bulkhead at a velocity as high as 3,000fps which was capable of piercing up to 2in of steel plate.

Experiments were carried out to full scale on the old pre-dreadnought *Hood*, which was fitted with various bulkheads and structures on the hull. One test showed that when the space between the outer hull and the inner bulkhead was filled with oil, the fragmentation problem was overcome to some extent. The oil caused the blast pressure to be dispersed in all directions, which pointed to the need to strengthen the transverse bulkheads within the inner compartments of the hull, but in general it was better to have these compartments full than empty.

In August 1915, a possible solution to the problem of underwater defence was seen in a design submitted by Vickers to the Board of Invention and Research for a first class battleship having a speed, armament and above-water armour equal to the latest Admiralty designs, but having in addition an entirely new form of underwater construction for defence against torpedo attack. The novel defensive arrangement in this Design 742 consisted of a strong structural defence in combination with the subdivision of the side compartments in such a way as to allow the expansion of the explosive gases into empty compartments with the minimum of damage. After the gas pressures had diminished they would, in theory, be resisted by strong, circular, outer explosion bulkheads, which were termed the main defence. The arrangement was designed to resist 220lb of gun-cotton detonated against the ship's side and, pending further investigations, could be made to resist a charge of 400lb. The system was made up of the following components:

1. The shell plating and frames of the ship, reinforced by horizontal timbers.
2. A perforated baffle screen of ¼in nickel steel, reinforced by a central, strong vertical steel stiffener and by horizontal timbers. The screen was approximately six feet from the ship's outer shell.

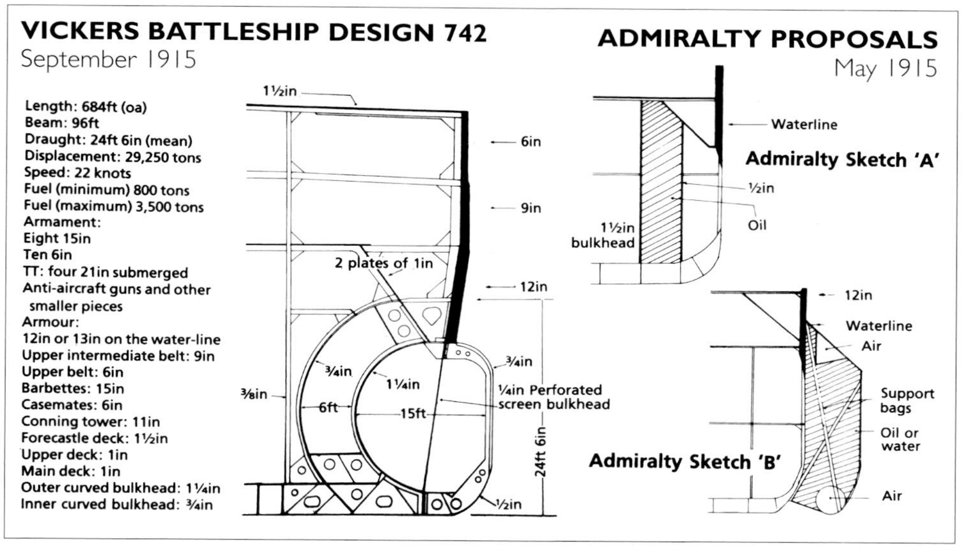

3. The interior of each explosion compartment was provided with the above baffle screen which was liberally perforated by 12in diameter holes for the penetration of gases, and arranged so that the screen would, under pressure, fracture gradually.
4. Small transverse oil fuel compartments were placed between the explosion compartments in the wings of the ship in order to add to the oil fuel stowage, with the transverse bulkheads in these compartments so shaped that no direct thrust would be transferred from the outside of the ship onto the main bulkheads.

The Board of Invention examined the design and reported to the Admiralty. The design, they reported, differed from existing Admiralty designs mainly in the provision of curved instead of flat bulkheads. The breakdown of inner transverse bulkheads under pressure after being struck was due primarily to the projectile action of fragments of the outer skin. These were sometimes projected with such velocity that bulkheads of up to 2in thick or more became riddled with holes and weakened to the extent that gas pressure could tear large holes in the structure. Vickers' design would be damaged in the same way. Both the baffle screen and the main defence would certainly be pierced or badly damaged by an explosion, and the system was not viewed as very promising. Concluding remarks from the Assistant DNC, W. J. Berry, summed up the general feeling about the revolutionary system:

> On the whole it is considered that the ship proposed would be slightly less vulnerable than the battleships now building, but this is entirely due to the feature of the underwater system being made the principal one. It is probable, however, that further investigations into the problem would result in a superior arrangement being arrived at; but not at the expense of modifying the machinery and armament from existing practice as seen necessary; the extra length, displacement and beam of this ship being accepted as part of the price paid.

Although this novel system of underwater protection was rejected, its submission shows that the problem was understood and a great deal of initiative was being used in an endeavour to come up with an adequate protective barrier against torpedo attack. At the beginning of the war, the need for this type of protection was not paramount in the design, but took second place to armour, armament and speed. Within a few short months, however, it was to become one of the most important features in ensuring a warship's survival. That the Germans did not feel obliged to enhance their ships' underwater protection reflects the obvious: their ships' bulkheads were quite adequate for the job.

Anti-Torpedo Nets

When the torpedo made its appearance in about 1873, consideration was given in warship design towards a suitable method of protection against the menace. Progress was slow, and the torpedo's menace seen as limited by its slowness and short range. By 1885, however, the torpedo-boat had arrived, capable of delivering a much-improved Whitehead torpedo reaching 30 knots and holding 200lb of gun cotton. When *Dreadnought* was completed in 1906, the Hardcastle torpedo then in use reached a speed of 33 knots, and had a range of approximately 7,000 yards. Countermeasures until then had been in the form of partially-armoured bulkheads within the ship's hull, and anti-torpedo nets. The former in its original form, which did not cover all of the important areas of the hull, was limited in value; the latter in practice was not that successful either.

The idea went back to approximately 1876. The method was to surround the ship with heavy wire netting, which would catch the torpedo in its path and render it harmless. The nets were suspended from long booms fitted along the ship's side; the depth of the nets when thrown out in to the water usually corresponded

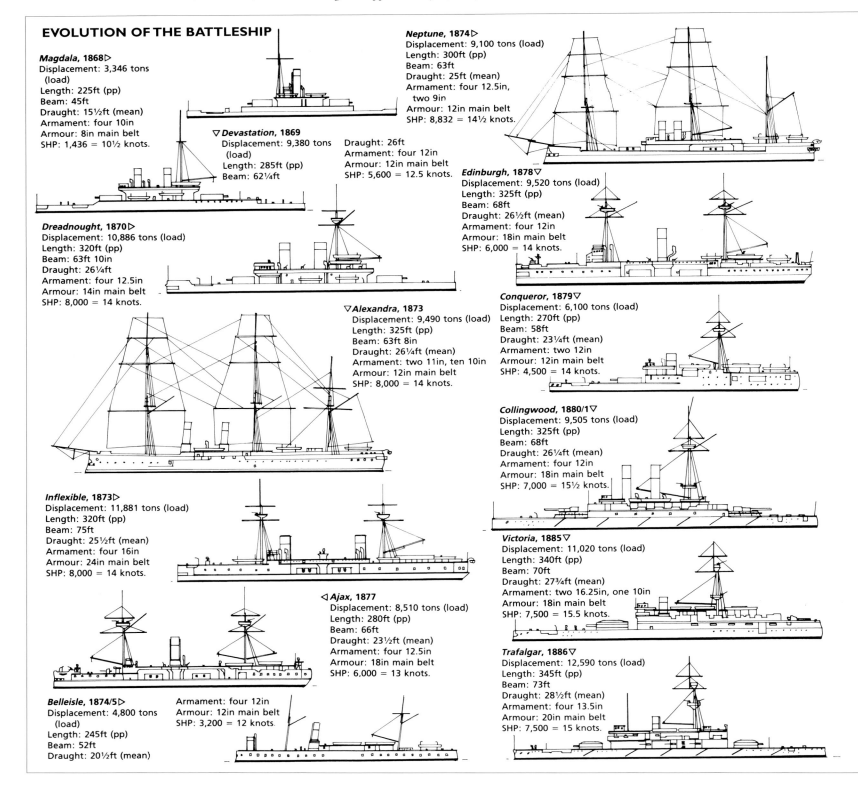

EVOLUTION OF THE BATTLESHIP

***Magdala*, 1868**▷
Displacement: 3,346 tons (load)
Length: 225ft (pp)
Beam: 45ft
Draught: 15½ft (mean)
Armament: four 10in
Armour: 8in main belt
SHP: 1,436 = 10½ knots.

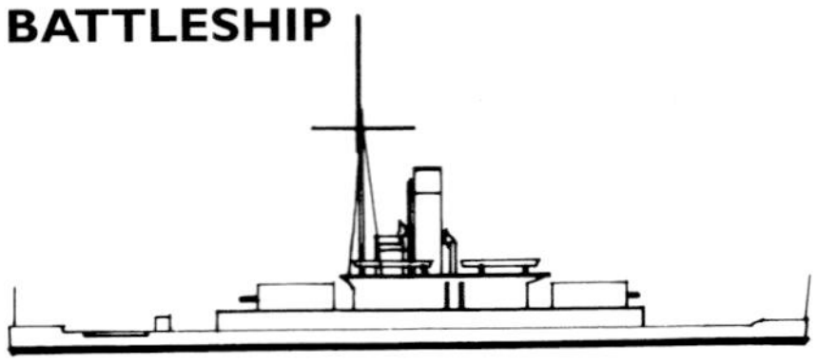

▽***Devastation*, 1869**
Displacement: 9,380 tons (load)
Length: 285ft (pp)
Beam: 62¼ft
Draught: 26ft
Armament: four 12in
Armour: 12in main belt
SHP: 5,600 = 12.5 knots.

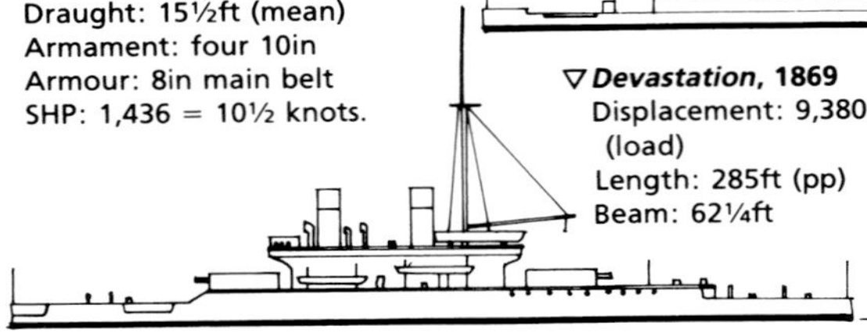

***Neptune*, 1874**▷
Displacement: 9,100 tons (load)
Length: 300ft (pp)
Beam: 63ft
Draught: 25ft (mean)
Armament: four 12.5in, two 9in
Armour: 12in main belt
SHP: 8,832 = 14½ knots.

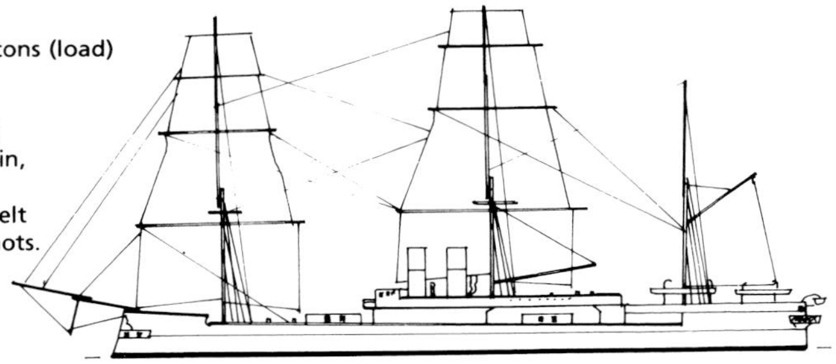

***Edinburgh*, 1878**▽
Displacement: 9,520 tons (load)
Length: 325ft (pp)
Beam: 68ft
Draught: 26½ft (mean)
Armament: four 12in
Armour: 18in main belt
SHP: 6,000 = 14 knots.

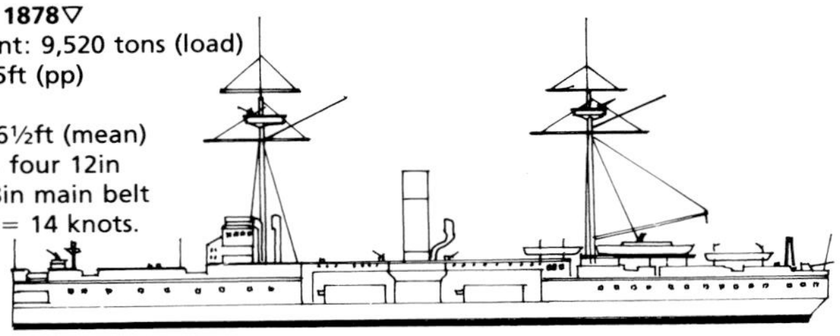

***Dreadnought*, 1870**▷
Displacement: 10,886 tons (load)
Length: 320ft (pp)
Beam: 63ft 10in
Draught: 26¼ft
Armament: four 12.5in
Armour: 14in main belt
SHP: 8,000 = 14 knots.

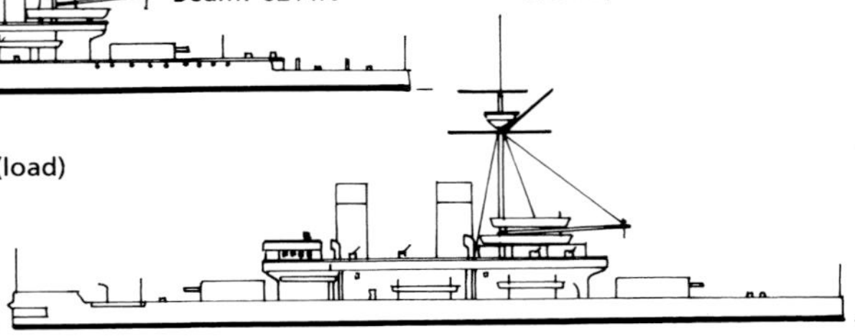

▽***Alexandra*, 1873**
Displacement: 9,490 tons (load)
Length: 325ft (pp)
Beam: 63ft 8in
Draught: 26¼ft (mean)
Armament: two 11in, ten 10in
Armour: 12in main belt
SHP: 8,000 = 14 knots.

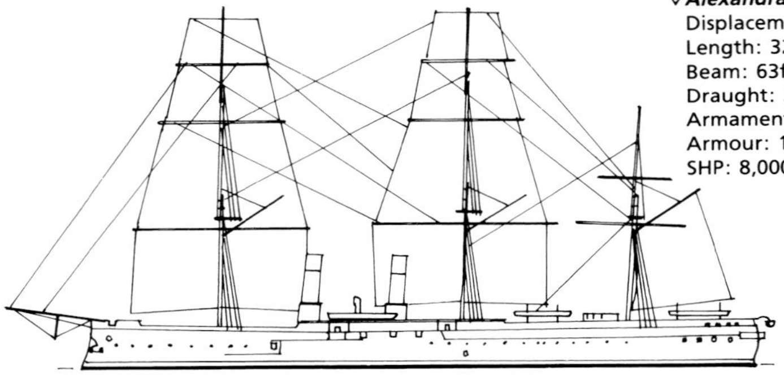

***Conqueror*, 1879**▽
Displacement: 6,100 tons (load)
Length: 270ft (pp)
Beam: 58ft
Draught: 23¼ft (mean)
Armament: two 12in
Armour: 12in main belt
SHP: 4,500 = 14 knots.

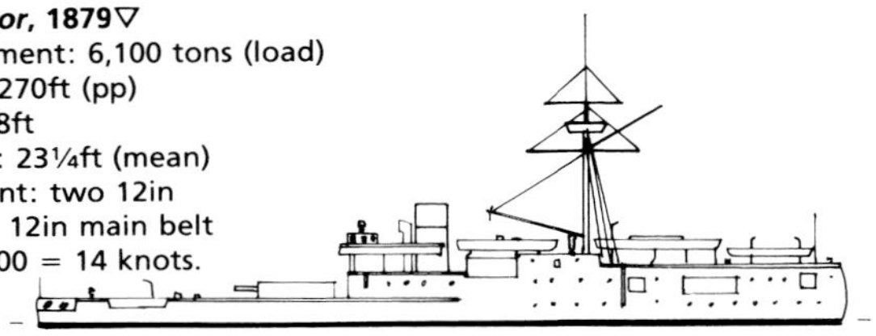

***Collingwood*, 1880/1**▽
Displacement: 9,505 tons (load)
Length: 325ft (pp)
Beam: 68ft
Draught: 26¼ft (mean)
Armament: four 12in
Armour: 18in main belt
SHP: 7,000 = 15½ knots.

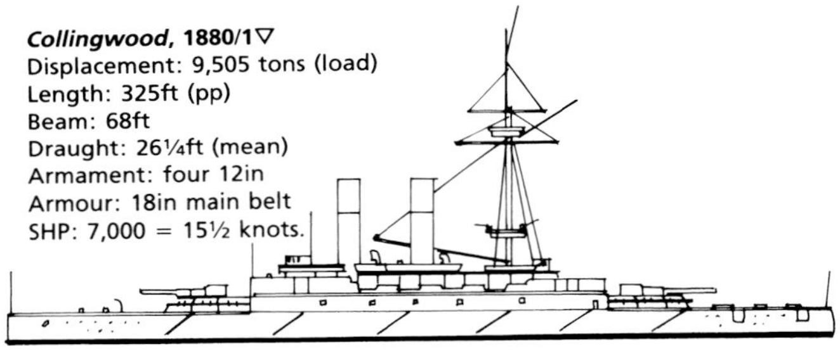

***Inflexible*, 1873**▷
Displacement: 11,881 tons (load)
Length: 320ft (pp)
Beam: 75ft
Draught: 25½ft (mean)
Armament: four 16in
Armour: 24in main belt
SHP: 8,000 = 14 knots.

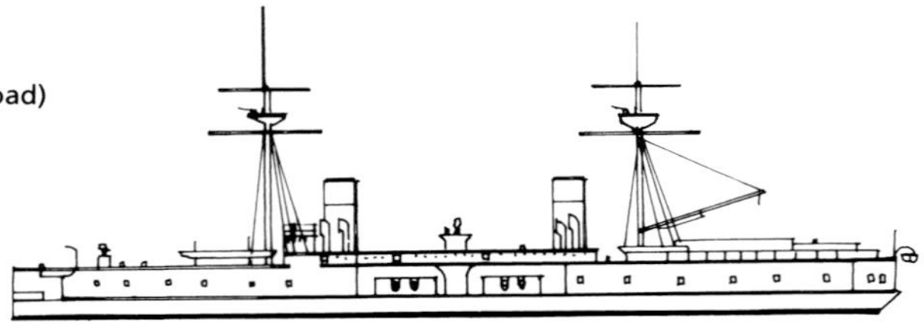

***Victoria*, 1885**▽
Displacement: 11,020 tons (load)
Length: 340ft (pp)
Beam: 70ft
Draught: 27¾ft (mean)
Armament: two 16.25in, one 10in
Armour: 18in main belt
SHP: 7,500 = 15.5 knots.

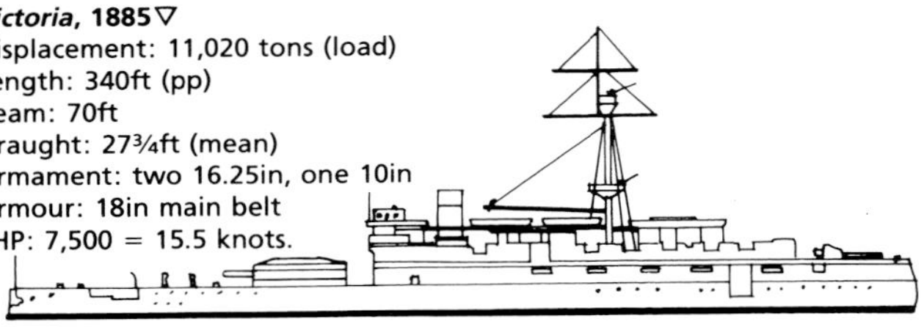

◁***Ajax*, 1877**
Displacement: 8,510 tons (load)
Length: 280ft (pp)
Beam: 66ft
Draught: 23½ft (mean)
Armament: four 12.5in
Armour: 18in main belt
SHP: 6,000 = 13 knots.

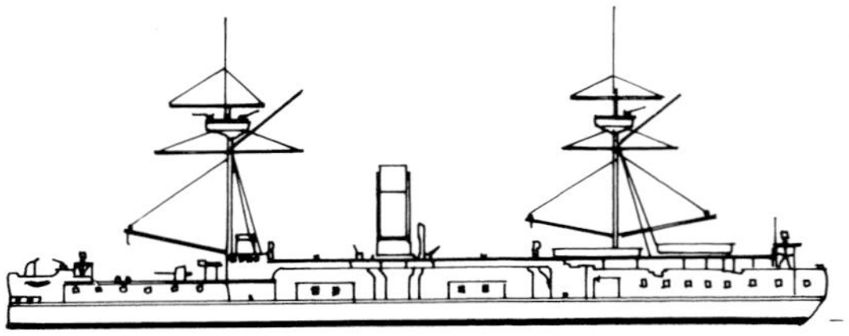

***Trafalgar*, 1886**▽
Displacement: 12,590 tons (load)
Length: 345ft (pp)
Beam: 73ft
Draught: 28½ft (mean)
Armament: four 13.5in
Armour: 20in main belt
SHP: 7,500 = 15 knots.

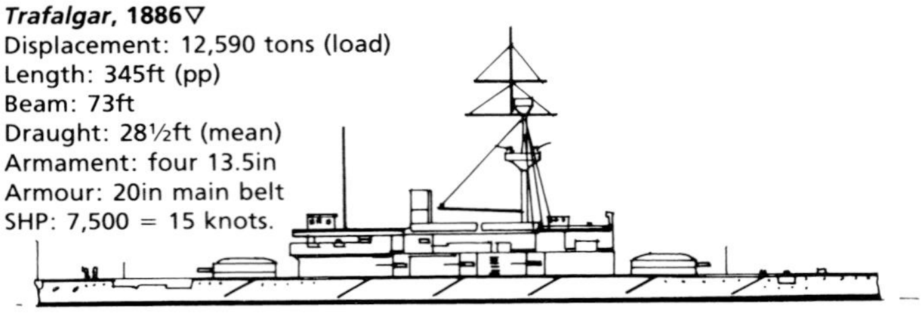

***Belleisle*, 1874/5**▷
Displacement: 4,800 tons (load)
Length: 245ft (pp)
Beam: 52ft
Draught: 20½ft (mean)
Armament: four 12in
Armour: 12in main belt
SHP: 3,200 = 12 knots.

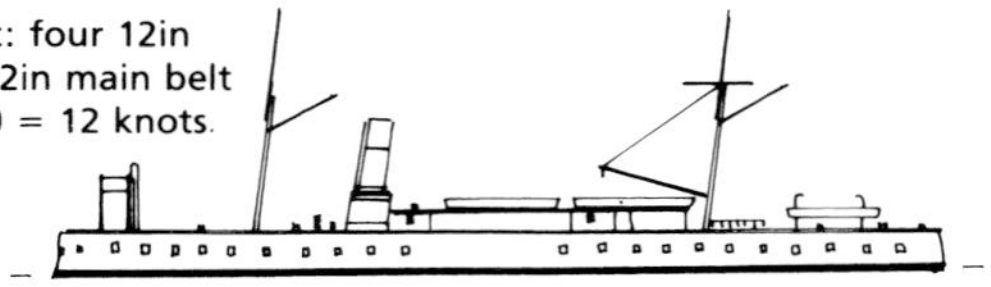

with the ship's keel, and the nets hung vertically while she was at rest. If the ship were moving, however, the nets tended to drag and sway, which reduced their effectiveness.

In the event, the nets proved useless even when the ship was stationary. The old battleship *Majestic* was torpedoed during the Dardanelles campaign in 1915, while stopped and with her nets out. She was sunk, nevertheless, simply because the torpedo in question had been fitted with wire cutters in its nose.

Provision for anti-torpedo nets within the Royal Navy's capital ship designs continued until 1911 (*Iron Duke* class), and was discarded in following designs. Those already fitted in ships were retained as late as 1916, even though it was accepted that they were of limited value.

Machinery

When *Dreadnought* was completed in October 1906, the Royal Navy was provided with the world's first turbine-driven battleship. The German Navy, however, although conducting experiments, were prepared to procrastinate so far as turbine installation was concerned, and fitted their first four dreadnoughts with stan-

***Royal Sovereign*, 1889▽**
Displacement: 14,240 tons (load)
Length: 380ft (pp)
Beam: 75ft
Draught: 27½ft (mean)
Armament: four 13.5in
Armour: 18in main belt
SHP: 9,000 = 16 knots.

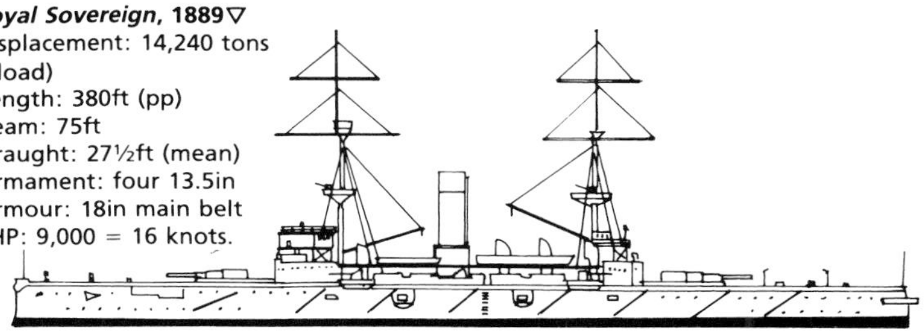

***Canopus*, 1897▽**
Displacement: 13,141 tons (load)
Length: 390ft (pp)
Beam: 74ft
Draught: 26ft (mean)
Armament: four 12in
Armour: 6in main belt
SHP: 13,763 = 18.5 knots.

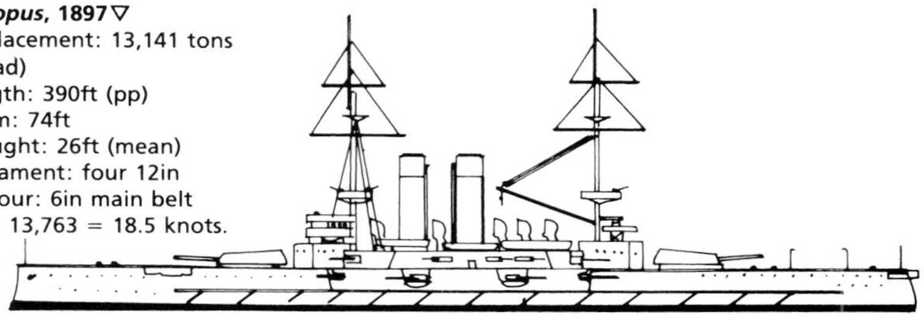

***Hood*, 1889▽**
Displacement: 14,200 tons (load)
Length: 380ft (pp)
Beam: 75ft
Draught: 27½ft (mean)
Armament: four 13.5in
Armour: 18in main belt
SHP: 9,000 = 16 knots.
(The last low freeboard battleship built for the Royal Navy.)

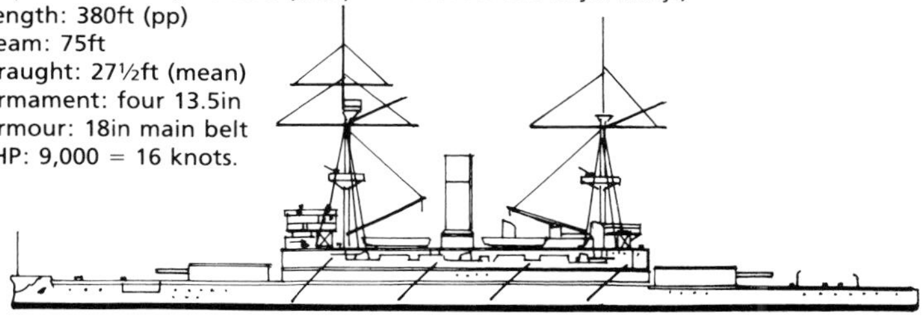

***Queen*, 1898▽**
Displacement: 14,140 tons (load)
Length: 400ft (pp)
Beam: 75ft
Draught: 25⅓ft (mean)
Armament: four 12in
Armour: 9in main belt
SHP: 15,564 = 18.4 knots.

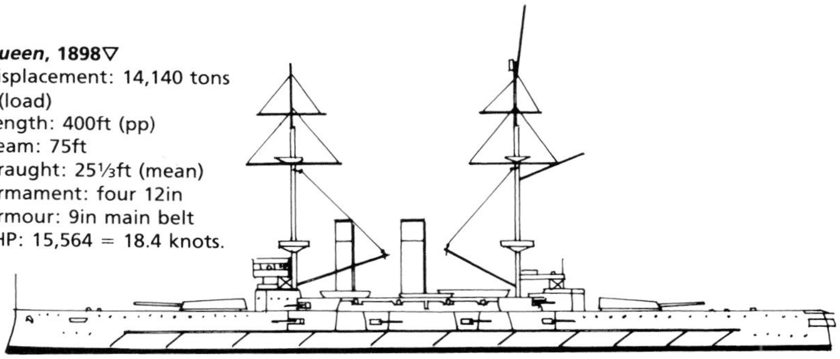

***Centurion*, 1889▽**
Displacement: 10,420 tons (load)
Length: 360ft (pp)
Beam: 70ft
Draught: 25½ft (mean)
Armament: four 10in
Armour: 12in main belt
SHP: 9,703 = 17.05 knots.

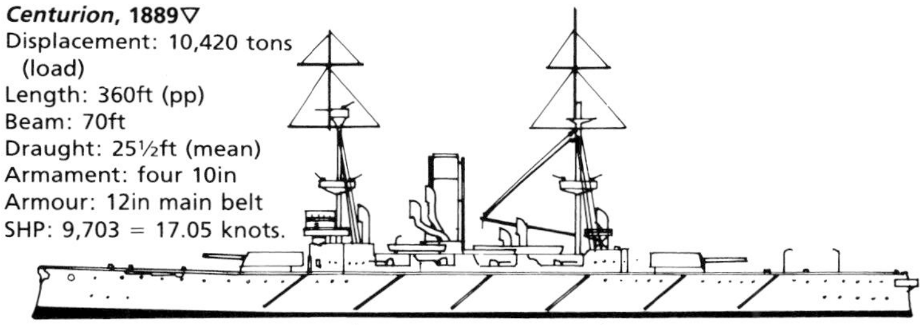

***Triumph*, 1901▽**
Displacement: 11,740 tons (load)
Length: 436ft (pp)
Beam: 71ft
Draught: 24½ft (mean)
Armament: four 10in, fourteen 7.5in
Armour: 7in main belt
SHP: 13,469 = 20.05 knots.

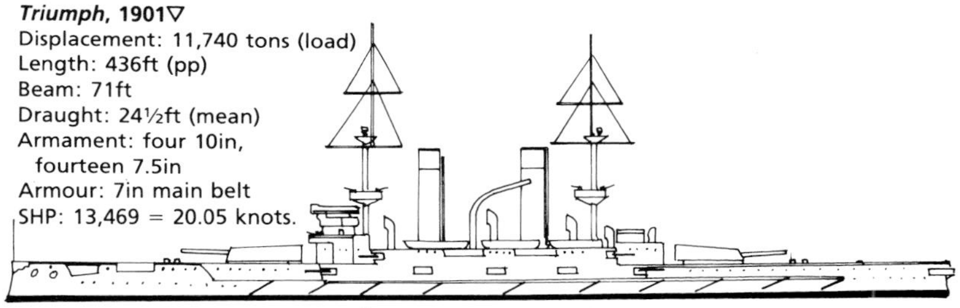

***Renown*, 1892▽**
Displacement: 11,690 tons (load)
Length: 380ft (pp)
Beam: 72ft
Draught: 25½ft (mean)
Armament: four 10in
Armour: 8in main belt
SHP: 10,708 = 17.9 knots.

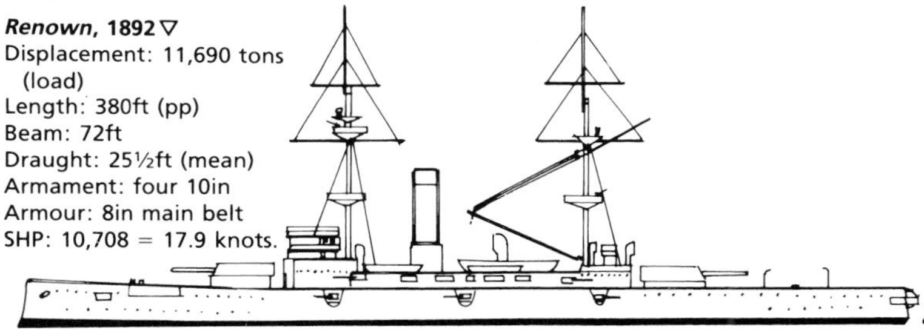

***King Edward VII*, 1901▽**
Displacement: 15,826 tons (load)
Length: 425ft (pp)
Beam: 78ft
Draught: 26ft (mean)
Armament: four 12in, four 9.2in
Armour: 9in main belt
SHP: 18,138 = 19.04 knots.

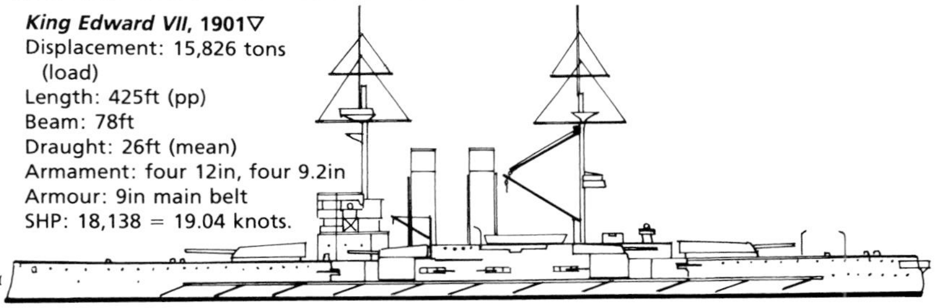

***Majestic*, 1893▽**
Displacement: 14,980 tons (load)
Length: 390ft (pp)
Beam: 75ft
Draught: 27ft (mean)
Armament: four 12in
Armour: 9in main belt
SHP: 12,554 = 17.8 knots.

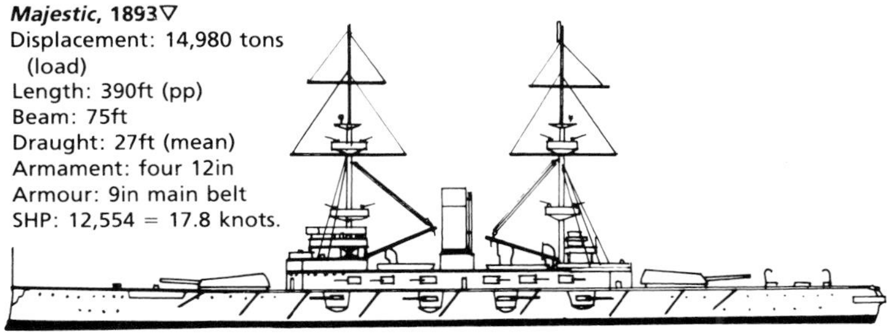

***Lord Nelson*, 1904▽**
Displacement: 16,090 tons (load)
Length: 410ft
Beam: 79½ft
Draught: 26½ft
Armament: four 12in, ten 9.2in
Armour: 12in main belt
SHP: 17,270 = 18.5 knots.

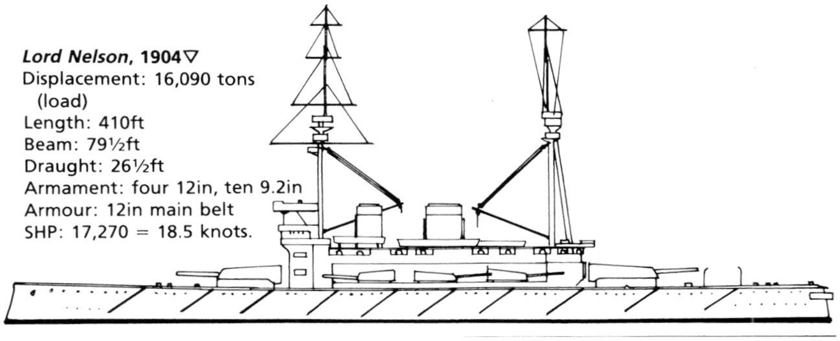

Above: *Ramillies*, November 1917. Port quarter.

Opposite: *Audacious* showing her 'one-off' camouflage which was painted during September and October 1914.

Below: Taken from *King George V* showing *Ajax* and *Centurion* 1917/18, cleared for action giving a good 'show' from their funnels. Probably during a routine sweep in the North Sea.

dard triple-expansion reciprocating engines. The *Nassau* class was provided with 20,000shp driving three screws, which gave them a designed speed of 19½knots. Their second group of four ships, the *Helgoland* class laid down in 1908, were also given reciprocating machinery, with a slight increase in power to 25,000shp, to provide a nominal speed of 21 knots – which gave them parity with British ships.

The German battlecruisers *Von der Tann* and the *Moltke* class, however, were fitted with Parsons turbines, which were much the same as those fitted in the *Invincible* class. *Von der Tann* was given a nominal 46,000shp for a speed of 24–25 knots, while *Moltke*'s was 52,000shp for 25–26 knots. On trials, however, the former reached 27½ knots at 79,000shp; the latter 28½ knots at 85,700shp. The boiler/machinery installation was pressed far beyond British safety limits, which reflects the great importance the Germans attached to having ships that could match or outstrip their British contemporaries.

One feature peculiar to the German ships was the weight saved in machinery and boiler rooms by using small-tube boilers and lighter materials than in British ships. The percentage of space and weight saved made the British designs look bulky in comparison. By Royal Navy standards, however, the German installations were decidedly cramped.

During the war there were frequent reports that the German dreadnoughts, both battleships and battlecruisers, suffered from machinery problems. *Von der Tann* had trouble with her turbine installation and both the *Nassau* and *Helgoland* classes were prone to engine-room trouble. Many of the difficulties were overcome in later ships. The British standard, well-proven turbine and large tube boiler installations were generally very reliable in all sea conditions throughout the war.

Camouflage

Although camouflage itself pre-dated the First World War, it was only in 1914 that protective colouring on warships began to make an appearance. The paucity of photographic evidence leaves some degree of uncertainty as to the patterns used, but it is certain that a high proportion of capital ships received such treatment at one time or another. During September 1914, in an experiment to ascertain what shades were most effective in making ships less visible, and in what lighting the shades would change, the battleships *Audacious* and *Orion* were treated to a 'leopard' pattern that featured large splashes of light grey, almost white tones, mixed on to a darker grey.

In some of the early schemes, black was the colour most frequently used, but it seems to have been confined to the smaller vessels (up to the size of destroyer), and soon became discredited in favour of a light-blue with greyish tints. Observations were carried out by Admiralty-appointed specialists with art experience, and G. Clark, who was one of these investigators, claimed that 'of all the colours used, light grey, in my opinion, is best; it reduced visibility under nearly all atmospheric conditions, and when other ships painted normally stood out quite sharply in the early grey morning, the light-grey definitely made for better hiding.' Such suggestions were passed on to the Admiralty, and the

result was the appearance of more experimental schemes during the winter of 1914/15. The battlecruisers *Princess Royal* and *Indomitable* were painted in very strange patterns during the last months of 1914, as the evidence of existing photographs shows. During the winter of 1915, *Superb* sported a scheme of light patches on a medium-grey background; the light patches were white – see layout of camouflage in the colour plates section.

Many of the ships deployed to the Dardanelles were camouflaged, the speciality of the time being a false bow wave intended to give a misleading impression of a ship's speed through a U-boat's periscope; it was soon discredited, however. If photographic evidence is anything to go by, most of the experiments were abandoned during the summer of 1915, especially in the big ships, but they reappeared in the spring of the following year, when various battlecruisers were to be seen with tiger-stripes around the funnels and long, dark-grey panels on their hulls to give the impression of a ship alongside. *St Vincent*, *Bellerophon*, *Superb*, *Collingwood*, *Conqueror*, *Monarch*, *Tiger*, *New Zealand*, *Indefatigable*, *Queen Mary* and *Repulse* were all photographically recorded with some type of experimental camouflage between 1915 and 1918, as the illustrations in the pages of this book show. How successful these unofficial experiments were is not certain because of the scarcity of official records on the subject. They can but have been of limited effectiveness, however.

A standard approach to camouflage did not appear until late 1917, when 'dazzle' was introduced by Lieutenant-Commander Norman Wilkinson, RNVR, who had submitted his ideas to the Admiralty in April of that year after being allowed to paint a test-piece, 'HMS Industry'. It was generally recognized that it was impossible to render warships totally invisible at sea, especially to a submarine, when the ship was seen in full silhouette against the sky. No matter how light the shade of paint used, parts of the ship would always be in deep shadow, providing an angular contrast to betray her. However, the principal factors required by an attacking submarine were an accurate estimate of the target's course and speed. The relative perspective position of masts and funnels provided the key to this. If invisibility were out of the question, at least it might be possible to mislead the enemy submariner: by painting a ship in such strongly contrasted colours and shapes, estimating her course or speed should be made considerably more difficult.

In June, experiments were carried out at the Royal Academy of Arts in Burlington House, London, where rooms were allotted for a 'camouflage school'. Officers, modellers and artists were recruited for the project, and the application of 'dazzle' began in July. The Admiralty decided to paint fifty transport ships along the lines of Wilkinson's first experiment and later, as a result of reports received, the entire mercantile fleet and a few selected warships were 'dazzle' painted. The 10th Cruiser Squadron, a few convoy cruisers and a number of sloops and gunboats joined the merchantmen in these strange patterns; so too did the battleships *Ramillies* and *Revenge* and the battlecruiser *Furious*. Unlike the merchant ships, however, the capital ships each received an individually-designed pattern. *Ramillies* was painted from November 1917 to March 1918; *Revenge*, although started in the same month as her sister, was only partially painted (hull only), and did not receive her full scheme extending over guns, masts, funnel and bridgework, etc., until January/February 1918. Both ships were repainted medium grey by April. *Furious* received her 'dazzle' during the Christmas period of 1917 and kept it until the spring of 1918.

Ordinary light and dark greys were deemed insufficiently contrasting, so the colours used were far stronger, ranging through greens, light and dark blues, blue-grey, four shades of grey, white, black, yellow and mauve. And it seemed to work: it was found that warships painted this way were more difficult to pick out at night than others painted entirely in dark grey. However – curiously enough – after the war, German U-boat officers denied that the dazzle painting of British warships ever confused them; yet German warships were seen with similar schemes during the Second World War!

Above: Starboard quarter view of *Repulse* in her one-off experimental camouflage in early 1918.

Dreadnought: 1905 ESTIMATES

Design

In order to understand how natural it was for Great Britain to complete the first seagoing 'all-big-gun' battleship in 1906, it is necessary to return to the origins of its concept, and to touch on some of the revolutionary ideas propounded during the previous eighteen years. The evolution of the battleship from the sail-powered line-of-battle ship took the form of a succession of more or less experimental warships, as designers responded to developments in weapons, armour and propulsive machinery. As guns became bigger, armour grew thicker; but the size of battleships did not grow in proportion, it being generally believed that investing in fewer, but larger ships (which would soon be rendered obsolete) made bad sense. With ever increasing weights of armour, armament and machinery, the designers were constrained to maintain stability by reducing freeboard, thus placing the armament near the water-line. In many battleships of this era, the guns were often partly submerged even in a moderate seaway.

In 1888, Sir William White, the Director of Naval Construction, submitted designs for a first class battleship substantially increased in both size and freeboard. The resulting battleships, the *Royal Sovereign* class, were authorized under the 1889 programme, itself the result of the realization of the growing threat from other navies. The seven ships of the class became the archetype of future battleship design, and were copied by navies throughout the world. Their greatly increased freeboard of 19ft 6in forward and 18ft aft compared very favourably with that of *Trafalgar* (completed 1890), 11ft 9in forward and aft. From this excellent high freeboard design, which was completed in 1892, slow but sure progress was made until by 1898 criticism was being voiced that the ultimate had been reached and that scope for future improvement was impossible if based on a design now ten years old. Since 1892, 29 British battleships had been built: *Majestic* class (nine ships); *Formidable* (three ships); *Canopus* (six); *London* and *Queen* (five); and the six *Duncans*. All these were along the lines of *Royal Sovereign*, and while new technology had been introduced into each successive class, improvements were confined to machinery and armament.

Towards the end of 1900, while White was absent because of illness, the Chief Constructor, Henry Deadman, put forward proposals for an extravagantly powerful battleship which would represent a marked advance on anything previously built. His proposals were not worked out in great detail and were rejected as impracticable, but the need for more powerful ships was clear, especially when the latest figures for foreign designs showed great advances over British counterparts. Details of the Italian *Benedetto Brin*, carrying four 12in, four 8in and twelve 6in on a displacement of 13,427 tons, and the American *New Jersey* class, sporting four 12in, eight 8in and twelve 6in on 14,948 tons, had become known during 1900 and, as the British *Queen* and *Duncan* classes of the current programme mounted only four 12in and twelve 6in on 15,000 tons, the Controller, Admiral Sir A. K. Wilson, called for a series of alternative designs embodying stronger secondary armaments. Constructor J. H. Narbeth prepared a series of sketches, based on *Queen*, with additional intermediate armaments of 9.2in or 7.5in guns. Dimensions varied according to length, stability and speed required. Work on this design, which was to emerge as the *King Edward VII* class, had not been completed by the time White returned to office early in 1901, and on his suggestion some modifications were made. White resigned on grounds of ill-health and left the Admiralty on 31 January 1902. The new design had been completed, however, and the drawings were approved by his successor, Philip Watts.

The first five ships of the *King Edward VII* class were laid down under the 1901–2 Programme. On a displacement of 16,350 tons normal load, they carried four 12in, four 9.2in and twelve 6in guns (and were, in fact, the last British battleships to carry 6in guns specifically for use against armoured ships). Although distinctly more powerful than the preceding classes, their actual

Right: *Dreadnought*, 'the cat amongst the pigeons' as she anchors at the head of the pre-dreadnought battle fleet during the 1907 Fleet Review.

DESIGNS FOR *DREADNOUGHT*

	'A1'	'A2'	'A3'	'A4'	'B'	'C'*	'D'
Displacement (tons)	17,500	16,000	15,750	16,500	15,750	15,000	18,000
Dimensions							
Length (pp)	450ft	460ft	460ft	460ft	425ft	410ft	500ft
Beam	79ft 6in	81ft 6in	81ft 6in	81ft 6in	82ft 6in	83ft	83ft
Draught	26ft 6in	25ft 9in	25ft 6in	25ft 6in	26ft 4½in	26ft 6in	27ft
SHP	25,000	23,000	23,000	23,000	19,000	15,000	23,000
Speed (knots)	20	21	21	21	20	19	21
Armament	eight 12in	eight 12in	eight 12in	eight 12in	eight 12in	eight 12in	twelve 12in
Armour	as *Lord Nelson* ———		12in belt	as *Lord Nelson* ———————			12in belt
Weights (tons)							
Hull							
Armour	4,650	4,650	4,650	4,275	4,085	3,925	4,700
Armament							
Machinery	2,450	1,700	1,700	2,150	1,800	1,420	1,700
General equipment	750	650	680	680	650	650	650

	'E' (vertical engines)	'E' (turbines)	'E4' (vertical engines)	'E5' (turbines)	'F' (vertical engines)	'F' (turbines)	'H1' (turbines)	'H2' (vertical engines)
Displacement (tons)	19,000	18,300	22,000	21,000	18,900	18,200	17,750	18,850
Dimensions								
Length (pp)	530ft	510ft	560ft	550ft	520ft	500ft	490ft	500ft
Beam	82ft	83ft	86ft	85ft	83ft	83ft	83ft	84ft
Draught	26ft	26ft	27ft	27ft	26ft	26ft	26ft 6in	27ft
SHP	25,000	25,000	28,000	27,500	25,000	25,000	23,000	23,500
Speed (knots)	21	21	21	21	21	21	21	21
Armament	ten 12in	ten 12in	twelve 12in	twelve 12in	twelve 12in	twelve 12in	ten 12in	ten 12in
–	–	sixteen 4in	twenty 4in	sixteen 4in	sixteen 4in	sixteen 4in	sixteen 4in	
Armour	**	**	12in belt	12in belt	as 'E'	as 'E'		
Weights (tons)								
Hull	6,100	5,900			6,000	5,750		
Armour	5,620	5,470	6,900	6,200	5,200	5,100	5,000	5,200
Armament	3,280	3,280	3,860	3,860	3,700	3,700		
Machinery	2,300	1,950	2,550	2,500	2,300	1,950	1,700	2,400
General equipment	600	600	630	600	600	600		

Notes:
*There were three 'C' designs, 'C2' and 'C3' being much larger than 'C1' with figures closely resembling those of 'D'. The displacement of 'C2' was 17,000 tons with a length of 555ft. 'C3' displaced 18,900 tons with a length of 520ft. In both 'C2' and 'C3', the main armoured belt was reduced to 10in on the waterline. Unfortunately full sets of figures are not available for these designs.
**Armour: 12in–9in–6in–4in; bulkheads 8in–6in; turrets 12in; barbettes 12in–3in; conning tower 12in; main deck 1½–1in; middle deck 4in-1in; lower deck 3in–1in.

'HMS UNTAKEABLE'

Displacement (tons)
17,000 (normal).

Dimensions
Length: 555ft pp
Beam: 80ft
Draught: 24ft 6in (mean).

Armament
Twelve 12in 45cal*
Sixteen 4in QF.

Armour
Main belt: 10in–9in
Bulkheads: 10in
Barbettes: 10in–8in
Conning tower: 12in
Communications tube: 6in
Turrets: 10in
Decks: main 1½in–1in, middle 2in–1in, lower 2½in.

SHP: 23,000 = 21 knots (normal).

Weights (tons)

Hull:	6,420
Armour:	6,390
Armament:	3,000
General equipment:	600

*BVIII mountings as in *Lord Nelson*.

fighting value on completion was rather less than had appeared on paper – the inherent disadvantages of the three mixed calibre armaments being accentuated by the developments in long-range firing that had occurred during their building period. Service opinion of the completed ships was critical; the multiplicity of calibres was disliked and it was considered that the ships were still undergunned for the displacement in comparison with foreign designs.

In 1902, after Watts had been appointed DNC, the question of battleship design came under complete reconsideration. The next set of designs were intended to meet the requirements of a new policy aimed at initiating battleship types having a definite superiority over foreign designs rather than merely matching developments abroad. A large number of drawings embodying many variations in armament, protection and speed were considered in an endeavour to combine all essentials on a minimum displacement and cost. In conjunction, the Controller, Admiral Sir William May, instigated exhaustive investigations into the relative efficiency of the armament and protection provided in various battleship types. These indicated:

1. The destructive effect of secondary guns was very small in relation to that of the main armament.
2. Damage caused by heavy projectiles was so extensive that the more lightly protected secondary armament was likely to be destroyed before it got within its effective range.
3. Heavier armour was required over a much larger area than had previously been customary.

The outcome of these findings was a design that should have been put in hand for the 1903 Programme, but the Board instead decided to build three more *King Edward VII*s and defer the new type until the following year. The 1904 ships were to have four 12in and twelve 9.2in, but by the time construction started the secondary armament had been reduced to ten as a result of constraints imposed by the docking facilities then available and the consequent limitation on beam. The two ships, *Lord Nelson* and *Agamemnon*, were to represent the end of the short-lived mixed calibre type in British battleship construction.

A major impetus to the evolution of the all-big-gun battleship came in 1904 with the appointment of Admiral Sir John Fisher

LORD NELSON

Outboard profile and plan, October 1908

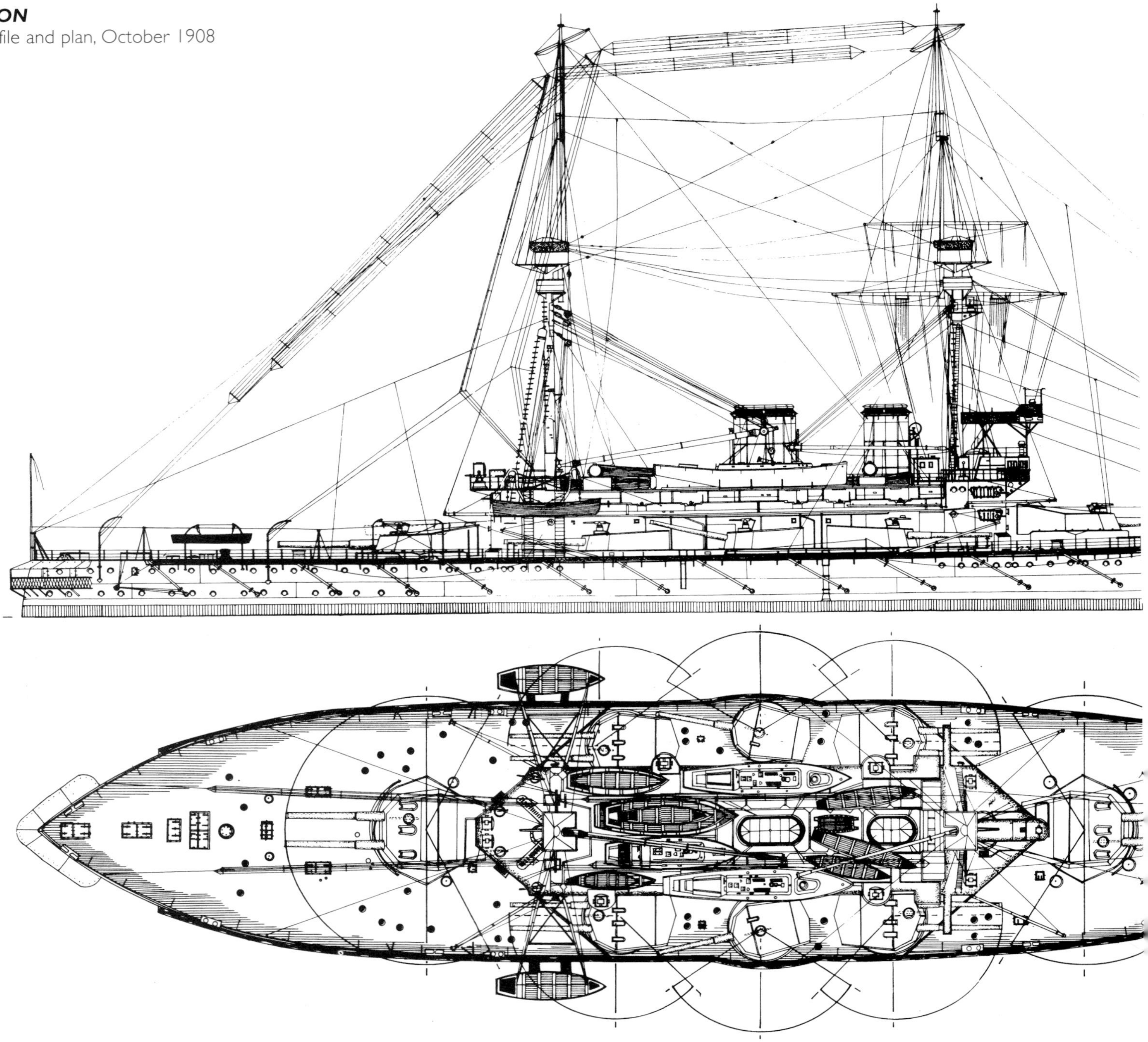

as First Sea Lord. While CinC Mediterranean Fleet, he had kept in close contact with developments in gunnery and torpedoes, and fully appreciated the necessity for armament changes to meet the requirements of increasing battle ranges. In conjunction with the Chief Constructor at Malta dockyard, W. H. Gard, he conceived the principles on which *Dreadnought* would eventually emerge – HMS 'Untakeable'. Subsequently, as CinC Portsmouth, with Gard as Chief Constructor there, he prepared a series of all-big-gun designs, aided by advice from Alexander Gracie (Managing Director of Fairfield shipyard) on machinery and boilers.

In the summer of 1902, Fisher had been considerably impressed by arguments put forward by Armstrong at Elswick in favour of the 10in gun; a new pattern of this calibre promised a very high rate of fire, and more of them could be carried on a given displacement than the standard battleship big gun, the 12in. Armstrong put forward a number of designs, the most interesting of which had been submitted in October 1902 and provided for eight 10in and twenty 6in, with a speed of 20 knots on a 17,000-ton displacement. These ideas coincided with Fisher's. Examining the sketches, he eliminated the 6in battery in favour of a design mounting sixteen 10in, so arranged that ten could fire ahead, astern or on either beam. Fisher circulated the design to three officers who were later to serve on the Design Committee for *Dreadnought*: Captain R. H. S. Bacon, Captain H. B. Jackson and Captain C. E. Madden. They expressed a preference for a lesser number of 12in guns: the larger calibre shell would be more destructive in effect, and fire control would be simpler with fewer turrets.

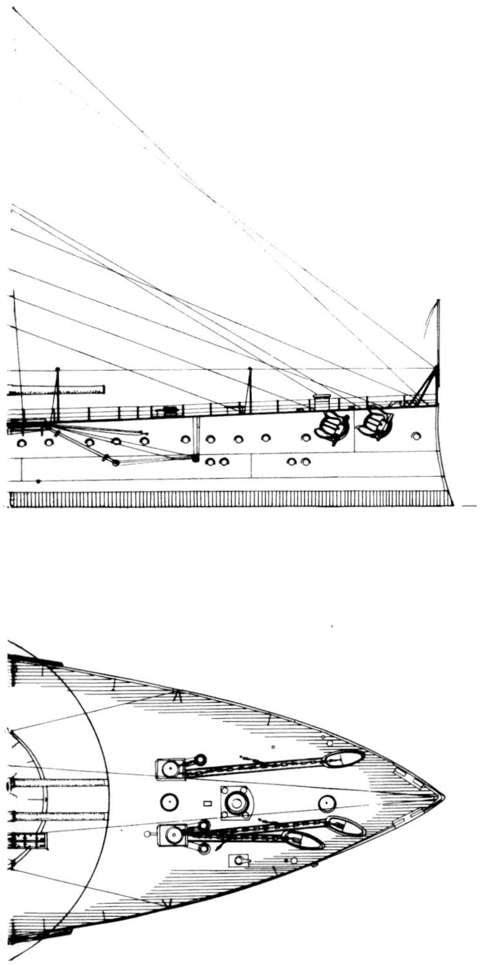

In parallel with these developments, a more public discussion centred upon an article in the 1903 edition of *Jane's Fighting Ships* by the celebrated Italian naval constructor, Vittorio Cuniberti. His proposal, 'An Ideal Battleship for the British Fleet', mounted a main armament of twelve 12in guns in four twin and four single turrets, on a displacement of 17,000 tons and with a speed of 24 knots. (The turret arrangement in Fisher's plan, of which no records have survived, is thought to have been similar.) And, on the other side of the Atlantic, views about the need for a one-calibre armament were being propounded by Lieutenant-Commander William Sims of the US Navy.

In the Admiralty itself, the design discussions for the *Lord Nelson* class in 1903–4 had produced two similar ideas. Philip Watts had revived a design concept dating back to 1882, when, in conjunction with Fisher, he had attempted to combine the best attributes of *Devastation* (1874) and *Inflexible* (1881). This proposed eight 12in guns in four twin turrets, one forward and one aft on the centreline, one on each beam amidships, echeloned. Meanwhile, the Assistant DNC, J. H. Narbeth, had put forward a plan that appears to have been similar to Fisher's ideas in 1900: twelve 12in guns mounted in six twin turrets, one forward and one aft on the centreline, with two on each beam amidships. In view of the radical increase in size and cost implicit in these proposals, they were not taken up; but the scene was now set for Fisher to bring the all-big-gun battleship into reality.

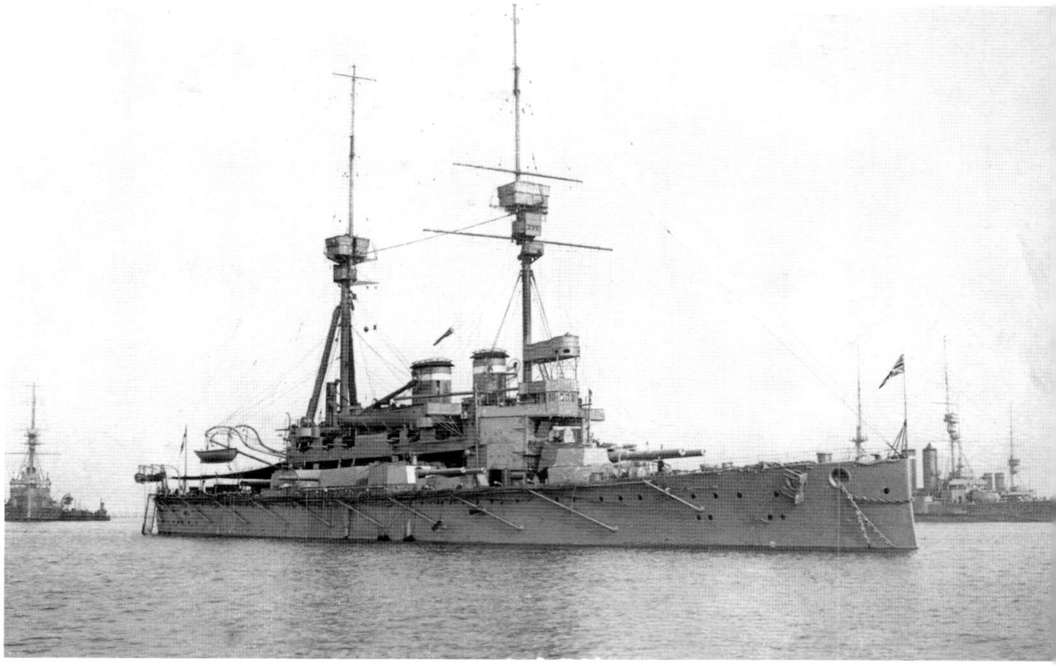

Above: *Lord Nelson*, 1911. Last of the British pre-dreadnoughts and the first British battleship for which Philip Watts, as DNC, was entirely responsible.

Specifically, the dreadnought type had its origins in these considerations:

1. The menace of the torpedo with its increasing range and accuracy made imperative longer battle ranges to over 3,000 yards.
2. Long-range hitting had become practicable with the introduction of satisfactory rangefinding instruments. Since 1899, shooting in the Mediterranean Fleet had indicated that, with efficient fire control, it might be possible to secure hits at 8,000 yards or over.
3. Effective fire control at ranges over 5,000 yards called for salvoes by eight or more guns of equal calibre, a large group of splashes being easy to observe. When the splashes straddled the target, the exact range could be determined.
4. The 12in gun combined destructive effect and accuracy to a degree that considerably outweighed the faster rate of fire of intermediate calibres, especially at long ranges. During the Russo-Japanese War, reports received by British Intelligence in May 1904 concerning actions fought by the Japanese off Port Arthur, Chemulpo (and, later, in the Gulf of Pechili) stressed the importance of long-range hitting and the substantially greater effect of 12in guns compared with 8in and under. Reports received after the Battle of Tsushima in May 1905 (after *Dreadnought*'s design had been approved) confirmed these findings.
5. A superior speed afforded important strategic and tactical advantages, especially when backed by superiority in armament. In the 1901 British fleet manoeuvres, Admiral Sir Arthur Wilson, a strong advocate of line-ahead formation and broadside firing, had utilized a speed advantage to envelope the head of the opposing line and concentrate the full weight of his

force's broadside to this. (In May 1905, similar tactics were used by Admiral Togo against a much slower Russian fleet at the Battle of Tsushima.)

6. The development of 'all-big-gun' ships abroad. Early in 1904, while CinC Portsmouth, Fisher had learned that designs had been worked out in the USA for a ship with a speed of 18.5 knots, carrying eight 12in guns on a displacement of 16,000 tons. The US Navy had tried unsuccessfully to increase these figures to ten 12in on 19,000 tons, but this had been thought too ambitious. (Construction of two ships to this design, *Michigan* and *South Carolina*, were to be authorized in 1905, at the same time as *Dreadnought*, but would not enter service until three years after the latter.) Late in 1904, information had been passed secretly to the Admiralty indicating that, as a result of their recent war experience, both the Japanese and the Russians intended to fit their future battleships with a uniform armament of eight or more 12in guns.

On becoming First Sea Lord in October 1904, therefore, Fisher took advantage of his position to press his views and, as a first step, submitted to the Cabinet a comparative evaluation of the 10in gunned design by Armstrong against his alternative design, HMS 'Untakeable', which now provided on the same displacement (17,000 tons) eight 12in guns, six of which would bear over the same end and broadside arcs as any ten of the sixteen 10in guns of the Armstrong design. It also embodied Captain Bacon's argument in support of the 12in gun, which Fisher regarded as conclusive, and stressed both their ideas in respect of armour, internal protection and speed (21 knots), the importance of the two latter items being strongly emphasized.

Admiralty approval for the essential features of the proposed design was secured by December 1904, and it was suggested that such a radical departure from conventional practice would probably encounter considerable opposition from the more conservative members of any committee. On 22 December 1904 a Design Committee was appointed for the purpose of examining these designs, and Fisher invited membership from those known to be in favour of the 'all-big-gun' school, naval experts and scientific officers alike. The Committee, chaired by Fisher, was required to act in an advisory capacity only, but its deliberations were to cover all points of design, including the arrangement of armament, fire control, protection, underwater integrity, torpedo net defence, machinery, fuel, communications, boat stowage and accommodation. The Committee members included: Rear-Admiral Prince Louis of Battenberg (Director of Naval Intelligence), Engineer Rear-Admiral Sir John Durston (Engineer-in-Chief of the Fleet), Rear-Admiral Sir Alfred Winsloe (Commander Submarine and Torpedo Flotillas), Captain H. B. Jackson (Controller), Captain J. R. Jellicoe (Director of Naval Ordnance), Captain C. E. Madden (Naval Assistant to Controller), Captain Reginald Bacon (Naval Assistant to First Sea Lord), Philip Watts (Director of Naval Construction), Professor J. H. Biles (Glasgow University), Lord Kelvin, Sir John Thornycroft, Alexander Gracie (Fairfield Shipbuilding), R. E. Froude (superintendent of Admiralty Experimental Works, Haslar) and W. H. Gard (Chief Constructor, Portsmouth Dockyard). J. H. Narbeth acted as Secretary to the DNC and was responsible for working out details of the various designs.

The Committee met for the first time on 3 January 1905 and was issued with instructions from the Admiralty stipulating that: the new vessel must be capable of docking at Portsmouth, Devonport, Malta and Gibraltar, but not at the smaller dock at Chatham. Armament was to consist of the maximum number of 12in guns practicable to any given design, all to be carried above main deck level and supplemented by an anti-torpedo battery heavy enough to counter destroyers. Under consideration were eight basic designs, all closely linked, differing only in armament layout and machinery. Some of the designs featured the latest turbine plant which had just come into service, in place of reciprocating machinery.

The procedure for design consideration was very complicated, but according to Professor Biles it went as follows: 'A' designs were progressively modified as far as 'F' and then reduced to 'G' which was thrown out because its low freeboard meant that elements of the main armament were too near the water-line. The final order of consideration was: 'A' reduced to 'B' to 'C' to 'D' to 'E' and then enlarged to 'F' and finally reduced to 'G'. Further modifications were called for and, as a result, it was one of the 'H' designs that went forward for final approval. The author has been unable to locate full sets of figures concerning all of the designs which were put before the Committee and it is doubtful if these are still in existence.

After long debate, the Committee recommended that the following elements be included in the design:

1. Retention of the 12pdr 18cwt gun as anti-torpedo armament.
2. Provision of armoured screens abreast magazines and shell rooms with all main watertight bulkheads solid (no doors).
3. Turbines instead of reciprocating machinery.

On an increase of 1,400 tons displacement, it was found that the basic comparisons of *Dreadnought* with *Lord Nelson* were:

1. Weight of broadside 28 per cent heavier (6,000lb against 5,300lb); greater destructive power with simpler fire control.
2. Vertical hull armour reduced in area and maximum thickness, but deck and internal protection stronger.
3. Nominal speed three knots higher.
4. Maximum fuel capacity slightly greater, but nominal extreme radius of action considerably less.

Innovations included such features as the raised forecastle deck, with strong flare, carried well aft; detachable mounts for some of the 12pdr guns; longitudinal armoured screens for magazines and shell rooms; location of the foremast abaft the forefunnel; detachable bridge wings; and a reversed accommodation plan, placing officers forward and ratings aft. The final design was criticized on the grounds that protection was sacrificed somewhat to armament and speed and, although it had been regarded as 'adequate' by the

DREADNOUGHT
Preliminary Layouts

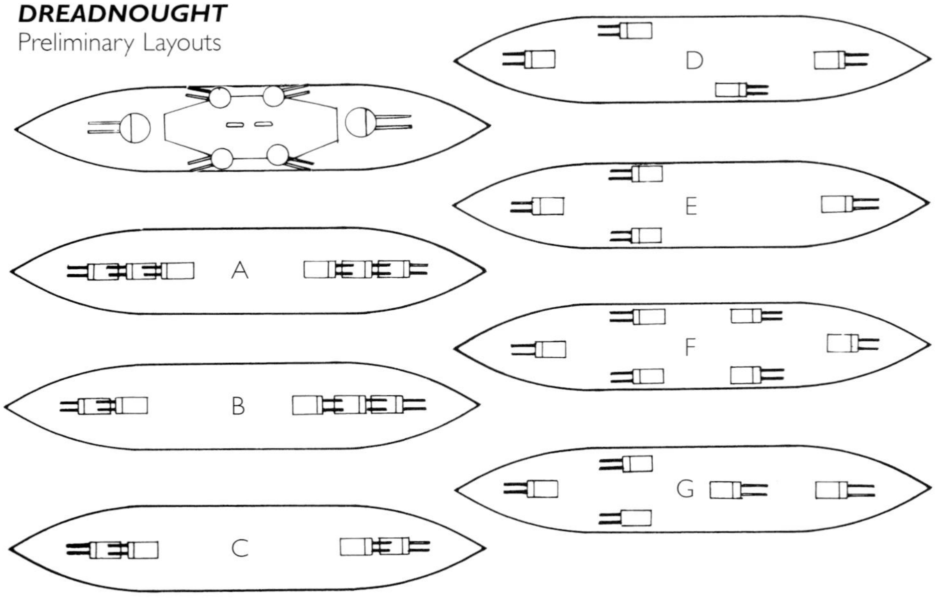

Committee, the reduction from the scale of armouring that had been considered essential when the *Lord Nelson* design was prepared (1902–3) was later admitted, officially, as a weak point, and was to be a common fault in all of the 12in-gunned dreadnoughts that served in the Royal Navy.

Exceptional measures were taken to ensure that *Dreadnought's* displacement and cost be kept to a minimum in order that the anticipated opposition to the type could not be based on these factors. After the Committee had delivered its deliberations on 22 February and reported their findings in March 1905, the ship was laid down on 2 October 1905, but as the design was experimental it was decided that further building would be deferred until after her trials. Secrecy and speed of construction were considered essential in order to gain a lead over foreign Powers. To this end, there was no official intimation that the design was in any way different from usual constructions, but the building slip was screened off from prying eyes. The whole of Portsmouth Dockyard's resources were mustered in the interests of speedy construction, with every possible time-saving procedure being employed. The 12in guns being made for the *Lord Nelson* class were allocated to the new ship. This greatly delayed the *Nelsons*, but they were considered to be of less importance. An excellent rate of construction was achieved, and the ship was ready for sea one year and a day after being laid down.

Armament

The Committee was well aware of the need to give the new ship a suitable main armament, their instructions having been to procure the maximum practicable number of guns on the given displacement. A number of alternative plans and sketches were considered, including proposals for superfiring and triple turrets, the primary objective being to secure a high percentage of 'all round' as well as broadside fire together with freedom from blast between individual turrets. The problem of blast, which restricted the total number of guns that could be effectively carried, featured prominently in all of the plans discussed. The use of triple turrets was discussed by the Committee, but there is no record of any actual design embodying these having been prepared and considered. Captain Bacon recorded that neither triple nor superfiring turrets were thought practicable by the Admiralty at that time. Their future adoption was by no means ruled out, but at this juncture there was insufficient time for the trials such fittings would entail.

At the first two meetings Philip Watts suggested two alternative sketches based on the *Lord Nelson* layout, but with increased numbers of 9.2in guns. Their distribution was: Sketch 1, four 12in main armament and eighteen 9.2in, three in casemates; Sketch 2, four 12in main armament and sixteen 9.2in in eight twin turrets mounted amidships. The sketches were quickly discarded.

Some of the most promising designs are listed here for comparison:

1. Twelve 12in in six twin centreline turrets, three forward and three aft, the inner turrets in each group superfiring over the outer. This design, which embodied Fisher's ideas in respect of heavy end-on fire, was actually put forward to the Committee as having been prepared in accordance with the strong recommendations of Admiral Sir Arthur Wilson, whose opinion had been requested by the Board. Wilson, who had a high reputation as a strategist and tactician, emphasized that all recent experience stressed the predominating importance of broadside fire in fleet actions. The proposed arrangement was intended to satisfy both theories, and it made a strong impression, being well liked by the Committee. However, it was rejected because of potential blast effect from the upper turrets on the lower ones; general lack of experience with superfiring turrets, and time required for the design and manufacture of these – the rapid construction stipulated by Fisher necessitating the use of turrets and mountings already in hand. The final point of rejection for the design was that the grouping of the turrets, both forward and aft, entailed great risk of complete disablement of an entire group, especially as no armoured bulkhead had been provided between the barbette bases. There was also some mention of prohibitive size and cost of the design.
2. Ten 12in guns in five centreline twin turrets, two forward and three aft, arranged as in the first design, but the upper turret in the forward group was suppressed and the after turret was lowered one deck level. This too was rejected for similar reasons, and for being even less economical than the first design (needing more armour in the turret areas).
3. Twelve 12in guns in six twin turrets, three forward and three aft. Two turrets in each group were disposed abeam, with the third on the centreline above and between them. This was a modification of the first design although reduced in size and cost, yet providing a compromise of broadside and end-on fire. This design was rejected because of the distinct disadvantages of the beam turrets in respect of blast and seaworthiness; there was also the possibility of total disablement of a group of turrets because of their close proximity.
4. The Design 'D' series proved very interesting, calling for displacements ranging from 19,000 to 21,000 tons. The first sketch sported twelve 12in guns in six twin turrets, all on one (upper deck) level. Two turrets were centreline, one forward and one aft. The other four were abeam, two on each side and well spaced. This design, thought to coincide with Fisher's original plan begun at Malta in 1900 and completed at Portsmouth in 1904, was similar to a proposal put forward by the Assistant DNC, J. H. Narbeth, during 1903–4 as an alternative to the *Lord Nelson*. The design was rejected because of its low freeboard and restricted arcs of fire caused by blast interference between turrets.
5. Twelve 12in guns arranged as in Design 4, but with the forward turret on a raised forecastle deck and the beam turrets placed closer together (Design 'D1'). This was rejected on grounds of blast interference and turrets too closely spaced.
6. Design 'D2' was similar, with twelve 12in guns, although the beam turrets were even more widely spaced than before. This again was rejected because of the restricted arcs of beam and after turrets, relatively low percentage of broadside fire, and excessive size and cost.

A graph showing blast curves indicated that the only arrangement giving better results than 'D2' would be the substitution of a single centreline turret for the after pair of beam turrets, and this plan, which reduced displacement to 17,850 tons, had been approved by Rear-Admiral Prince Louis of Battenberg and was finally accepted on 13 January 1905. The final design was 'H1', mounting ten 12in guns in five twin turrets: three on the centreline (one forward on a raised forecastle, one amidships and one aft, all on upper deck level). The other two were disposed one on each beam amidships on the upper deck. This arrangement allowed a nominal ahead and astern fire of six guns with a broadside of eight and, although inferior to all of the centreline superfiring plans, provided a high percentage of all-round fire, and was generally conceded to represent the best compromise of the various wing and centreline proposals. With one turret less, the broadside was the same as in the 12-gun designs while, next to four, eight guns were considered the best workable unit for fire-control purposes.

After the 1914–18 war Sir Philip Watts implied, in a paper written for the Institute of Naval Architects, that the final armament plan for *Dreadnought* was developed along different lines, and that only four stages were needed to arrive at the final layout. He said that the six-turret, all centreline superfiring design was the

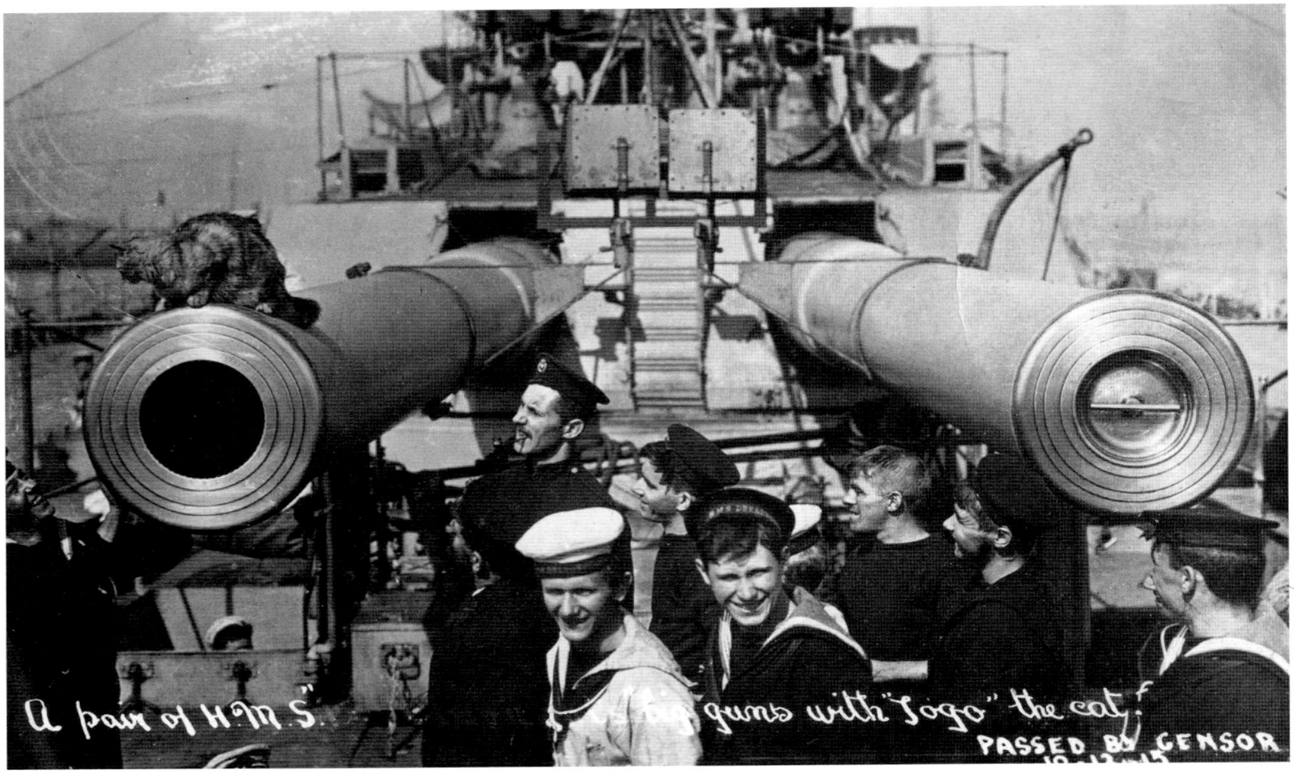

Right: The main feature of *Dreadnought* was her all-big gun armament (12in) with nothing smaller as all battleships built before her (9.2in and 7.5in etc to support a usual 4 x 12in). The two views here show some of her crew posing for a photograph (note the ship's cat on the gun) and across her deck looking aft whilst at battle practice (cleared for action) 1907.

first and then, reducing the upper turrets in each group produced the second layout. A further modification of the turrets resulted in the third stage, with the final layout showing the superfiring turrets brought down to the upper deck amidships, one on each beam and one amidships aft on the centreline. However, the majority of accounts (including the Ship's Covers and *Dreadnought*'s Book) refer to a considerably greater number of alternatives discussed by the Committee, with eight basic designs and many variations considered (see Tables).

The completed ship was fitted with the same mountings (BVIII) as those in the *Lord Nelson* class and allowed ahead fire for the beam turrets, the forecastle sides being well recessed for this purpose. In practice, however, they could not be fired within approximately 10° of the axial line for fear of blast damage to the superstructure. Direct astern fire from these amidships turrets was precluded for the same reason. The fore turret was set farther back than usual and, as a result of the high forecastle, had a considerably higher command than in preceding classes, the guns being carried approximately 6ft 6in and 4ft 6in higher than in the *King Edward* and *Lord Nelson* classes respectively.

Left: When *Dreadnought* arrived in Portsmouth harbour after her acceptance trials in 1906 there was a huge rush of local press and commercial photographers taking to small boats in a bid to capture her image and show the public the new addition to their fleet. This over-exposure continued right up until the appearance of the *Bellerophon* class. A close-up of *Dreadnought* showing her bridge and forward 12in guns taken by Mr Ernest Hopkins, 1908.

The secondary armament consisted of twenty-eight 18cwt 12pdrs, an increase of four over *Lord Nelson*, the guns being much more widely spread than in that ship so as to reduce the risk of simultaneous disablement and to ensure, as far as possible, that some would remain operable during the closing stages of an action when a torpedo attack was considered to be especially probable. At the time it was believed that the unprotected quick-firing guns, widely dispersed in the open, stood a better chance of survival than if closely grouped together in a battery, even if light armour protection was allocated. The detachable mounts on the forecastle and quarterdeck, which enabled the guns to be lowered below deck when not in use, was a novel feature adopted after experiments had shown that they suffered badly from blast from the main armament.

Because of the ever-increasing size of destroyers, the 3pdrs were abandoned, and retention of the 12pdr, which had been the Royal Navy's principal anti-torpedo gun for the last ten years, was subjected to severe criticism. All reports from British Naval observers with the Japanese fleet during the Russo-Japanese War had emphasized the ineffectiveness of the 12pdr and recommended that nothing smaller than 4.7in could be considered adequate. The provision for nothing heavier than the 12pdr in *Dreadnought* appears to have been largely due to a current report that it was not actually essential to sink attacking destroyers, provided they could be stopped or put out of action before coming into range.

The Committee considered that the new 18cwt 12pdr was quite sufficient for this purpose, and that twenty of them would be more effective than fourteen 4in quick-firing pieces which represented an equivalent weight. However, a substantial body of opinion, which included the former DNC, Sir William White, stated that the 12pdr had become quite inadequate and that a heavier calibre was required. Without the benefit of foresight the Admiralty were unable to see that this was, in fact, quite true, although they did later admit to this fault and some rectification was seen in the *Bellerophon* and *St Vincent* classes, which sported a 4in QF secondary battery. *Dreadnought* was actually completed with twenty-eight 12pdrs, although this was increased to thirty-one afterwards by the addition of an extra gun fitted on each of the centreline 12in turrets.

Armour

Admiralty instructions to the Committee called for 'adequate protection' which had to be interpreted in terms of what was possible on an acceptable displacement and cost after priority requirements for armament and speed had been satisfied. The final armour protection of *Dreadnought* showed no advance over the immediately preceding *Lord Nelson* class, although the percentage of displacement vis-à-vis protection had increased. *Dreadnought's* vertical hull armour was actually inferior, though maximum thickness of deck and internal protection was much stronger. The principal modifications over *Lord Nelson* were:

1. Maximum thickness of main belt was reduced by 1in, the upper level of 8in being omitted.
2. Lower side armour from fore barbettes to stem was 6in uniform against the 6in and 4in of *Lord Nelson*.
3. The ¾in upper deck armour amidships was omitted.
4. Middle deck armour between end barbettes increased by ¾in on slope and flat.
5. Lower deck armour forward increased by ½in.
6. Maximum thickness of turrets reduced by 1in at rears.
7. Conning tower thickness reduced by 1in.
8. 4in and 2in magazine screens added longitudinally.

The reduced thickness of the belt, barbettes, turrets and conning tower was accepted to allow for the addition of the magazine screens which were considered essential protection against torpedo attack or mines, especially the wing magazines which could only be placed approximately fifteen feet inboard of the hull. The actions fought during the Russo-Japanese War indicated that most battleships stood a good chance of survival after being hit by a torpedo provided that an internal explosion did not occur; the screens were fitted in *Dreadnought* specifically for this reason. Upper side armour above the main deck was abandoned mainly because there was no secondary battery in this location. Another factor that influenced the reduction in thickness of the main belt, from 12in to 11in, was that *Dreadnought* required a longer strake for her hull, and a 12in belt's tonnage (which would have added 850 tons to that in *Lord Nelson*) was not acceptable for the design.

Top left: *Dreadnought* in October 1905, just one week after being laid down.

Above left: The completed hull 3 February 1906, seven days before launch (the armour plates are not yet in place).

Top right: 7 April 1906; the armour plates have just been positioned.

Above right: At the fitting-out stage, 11 August 1906.

DREADNOUGHT: FINAL LEGEND

Displacement (tons)
17,850.

Dimensions
Length: 490ft pp
Beam: 83ft
Draught: 26ft 6in
Freeboard: 28ft forward, 16ft 6in amidships, 18ft aft
Gun heights: 30ft forward, 22ft amidships, 22ft aft.

Armament
Ten 12in
Eighteen 12pdr
Five 18in torpedo tubes.

Armour
Main belt: 11in tapering to 4in
Bulkheads: 11in–3in
Turrets: 11in–3in
Barbettes: 11in–3in
Conning tower: 11in
Signal tower: 8in
Communications tube: 5in–4in
Magazines: 2½in–2in
Decks: main ¾in, middle ¾in–1¾in, inclines 4in, lower 2½in–1½in.

Weight breakdown (tons)

Hull:	6,100
Armour and backing:	5,000
Armament:	3,100
Machinery:	2,000
General equipment:	650

Fuel
900 tons coal minimum; 2,400 tons maximum plus 900 tons oil.

SHP
23,000.

Complement
700.

It was anticipated that the upper shell plating would act as a 'burster' for striking shells, with the armoured inclines on the deck providing the principal protection for the vital parts of the ship below. The Assistant DNC, J. H. Narbeth, recorded that Philip Watts would probably have preferred to have maintained, or even increased, the *Lord Nelson* standard of protection for *Dreadnought*, but as the considerably increased displacement involved would have mitigated against the *Dreadnought* design's acceptance as a relatively economical type, a lower but admittedly weaker standard was accepted at the time.

Watts had paid particular attention to the underwater protection and subdivision and stated that *Dreadnought* should be able to sustain hits from one or two 18in torpedoes yet remain afloat. In addition to the six main transverse bulkheads which were unpierced below the main deck level, sufficient stability had been provided to ensure against possible capsizing if some of the compartments became flooded below the middle deck level. Independent pumping, draining and ventilating systems were provided for each compartment; the usual drainage, running the full length of the ship, of previous designs being finally abolished.

Dreadnought's main armoured belt consisted of an 11in strake which ran from the outer face of the forward barbette to abeam the after barbette. The upper edge was at middle deck level while reaching approximately five feet below the water-line at normal displacement. The 11in thickness tapered at the lower edge of the complete run to 7in.

The 6in forward strake ran from the 11in belt, at the same height, to the stem of the ship; the after strake reduced to 4in and was placed higher than the main belt, but lower than the 8in run. This 4in run was approximately three feet above the 11in belt. The 8in upper main belt sat above the 11in run with the top edge being 8ft 6in above the water-line at normal displacement. The

DREADNOUGHT: LAUNCH FIGURES, 10 FEBRUARY 1906

Displacement: 6,088 tons
Length: 490ft pp
Beam: 82ft 1in
Beam as moulded: 81ft 11¼in
Depth of keel from upper deck: 43ft 2¼in
Length of boiler rooms: 132ft 0½in (144ft 0⅜in incl. cross bunkers)
Length of engine rooms: 68ft 0¼in
Weight of hull: 5,446.6 tons
Breakage at launch:
longitudinal in a distance of 407ft = 1¼in hog
transverse in a distance of 77ft 3in = nil.

DREADNOUGHT: PARTICULARS, AS COMPLETED

Construction
Portsmouth DY; laid down 2 Oct 1905; launched 10 Feb 1906; completed for trials early Oct 1906.

Displacement (tons)
18,120 (normal), 20,730 (deep), 21,765 (extra deep).

Dimensions
Length: 490ft pp, 520ft wl, 527ft oa
Beam: 82ft 1in
Draught: 26ft 6in (normal), 29ft 7½in (deep), 31ft 1½in (extra deep)
Freeboard: 28ft forward, 16ft 6in amidships, 18ft aft
Height of 12in guns above lower wl: 31ft 6in forward, 22ft 6in amidships, 23ft aft (normal); 29ft forward, 20ft 6in amidships, 20ft aft (deep).

Armament
Ten 12in 45cal Mk X; BVIII mountings; shell stowage 80rpg
Twenty-eight 12pdr 18cwt; PIV mountings; 300rpg
One 12pdr 8cwt field gun
Five MG
Five 18in torpedo tubes; twenty-three torpedoes plus six 14in.

Fire control
None fitted as completed. Director control gear fitted in tower over control top in 1914/15.

Armour*
Main belt: 11in tapering to 7in
Upper tier: 8in
Ends: 6in forward, 4in aft
After bulkhead: 8in
Barbettes: 11in–8in–4in
Turrets: 12in–11in–3in
Conning tower: 11in sides
Communications tube: 8in
Decks: middle ¾in, main 1¾in, inclines 2¾in, lower 1½in (forward), 3in–2in aft.

Breakdown of armour weights (tons)

6in side belt forward:	427
11in side:	641
8in side:	510
4in side aft:	184
11 in screen:	47
8in screen	63
12in barbettes:	
'A' (excluding fittings)	358
'B' and 'X'	429
'Y'	188
Conning tower:	52
Signal tower:	46

Machinery
Parsons direct-drive turbines working four propellers
Eighteen Babcock & Wilcox boilers in three groups; normal working pressure 250psi reducing to 185psi at the turbines. Each boiler was fitted with six oil sprayers giving a total output of 960lb per boiler/hour at 150psi.
Total heating surface: 55,400sq ft
Grate area: 1,599sq ft
Engines: Vickers with designed SHP of 23,000 for 21 knots
Fuel: 900 tons coal normal; 2,900 tons maximum plus 1,120 tons oil
Radius: 6,620nm at 10 knots (with oil fuel); 4,340nm at 10 knots (without).
Using 2,220shp, consumption was 127 tons of coal per 24 hours. Continuous seagoing speed was 18.4 knots, giving radius of 4,910nm (520nm more than that of *Lord Nelson*).

Ship's boats
Steam pinnaces: two 45ft, one 36ft
Launches: one 42ft
Cutters: three 32ft
Whalers: four 27ft
Gigs: one 32ft, one 30ft
Skiff dinghies: one 16ft.

Searchlights
Twelve 36in: two bridge, four forward superstructure, four amidships structure, two after superstructure; one 24in signalling lamp on platform below control top.

Anchors
Three 125cwt stockless (bower and sheet), one 42cwt stream (close stowing), one 15cwt kedge. 475 fathoms 2 11/16 cable.

Wireless
Mk I type plus short-radius set.

Complement
685–692 (1905 Estimate); 700 (1907); 732 (1909); 798 (1910); 810 (1916).

Cost of vessel
£1,672,483 (guns: £113,200).

Notes:
*All KC except decks which were non-cemented. Decks of less than 3in and the communications tube were of mild steel.

belt terminated at the same point as that of the 11in strake. The main bulkhead, which was fitted aft only, was 8in thick and ran obliquely inwards from the after extremities of the lower side armour to the outer face of the after barbette. It did not drop below the middle deck level. The ¾in-thick main deck ran from the stem of the vessel through to the lip of the 8in bulkhead aft.

The middle deck was protected by a total of 1¾in made up of two plates, one of 1in the other of ¾in. The inclines of that deck consisted of three plates, one of ¾in and two of 1in thickness (2¾in total). Towards the extremities of this middle deck, just before dropping to the lower deck, was an increase to 3in in the areas of the forward and after barbettes. The lower deck forward ran from the extremities of the fore barbette, sloping steeply downwards with a thickness of 4in; on the flat at lower deck level it reduced to 1½in, running to the stem of the ship. Aft, this lower deck, having left the middle deck at a steep fall, of 4in thickness, ran toward the stern at 2in for approximately 28 feet then rose slightly, increasing to 3in, and dropped again to 2in for another 25 feet or so, after which it again dropped at a thickness of 3in.

The forward barbette was 11in on the outer face above main deck level; below, it thinned to 8in. The inner face was 8in above the main deck level and then thinned to 4in below. Beam barbettes were given 11in uniform on the faces, with the inner faces 8in above the main deck and 4in below.

The after barbette's face was 11in uniform, with the inner face 8in above main deck and 4in below. Turrets were reduced from that of *Lord Nelson* by reducing the back plates from 13in to 12in and the faces and sides to 11in from 12in. Roof plates ranged from

DREADNOUGHT
Outboard and inboard profiles, 1906

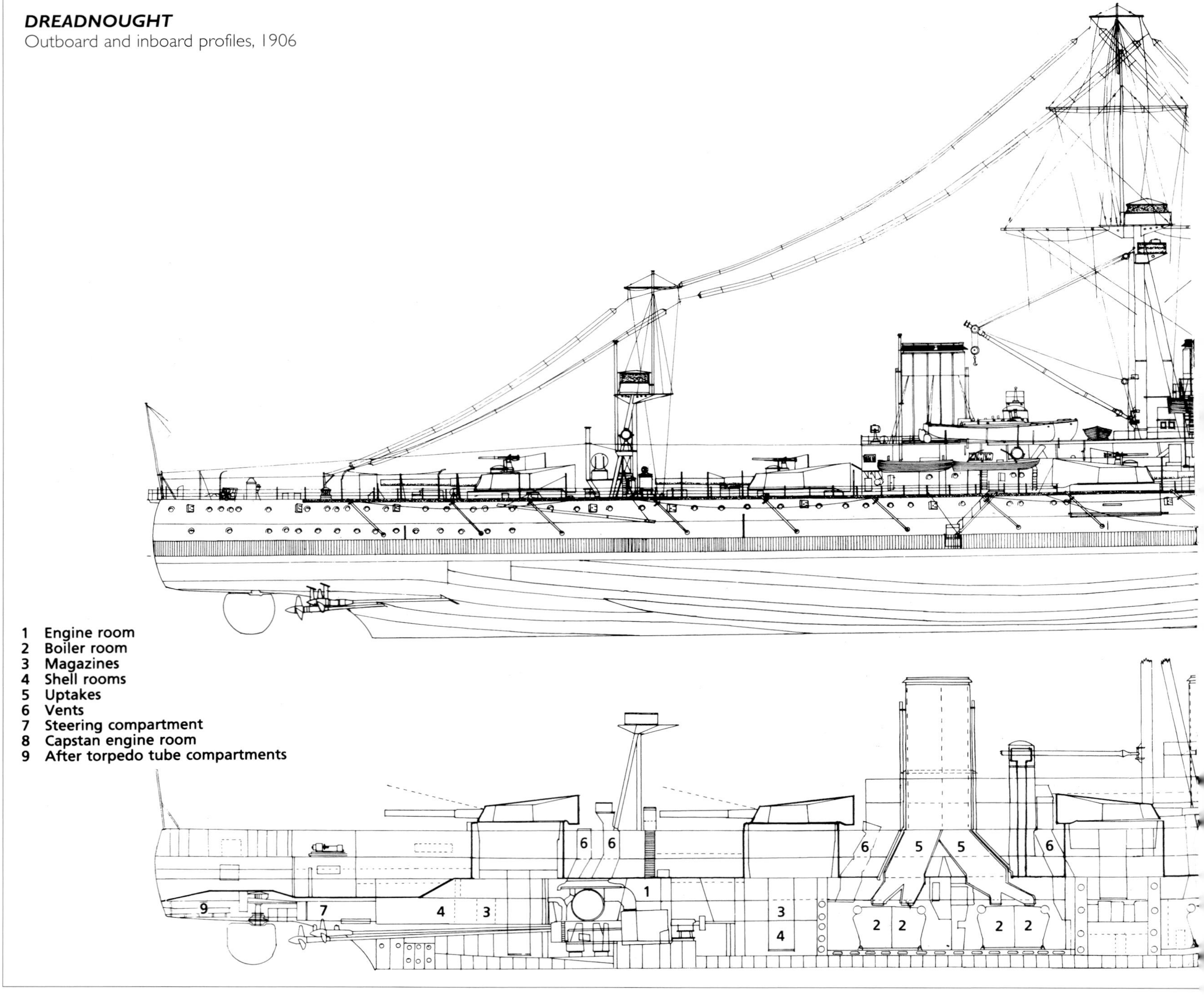

4in on the forward part to 3in on the crown. The forward conning tower had 11in sides and a 3in roof; the floor was 4in thick. The communications tube was 5in and ran down to behind the main belt at main deck level. The after conning tower, which was located behind the second funnel, had 8in sides, a 3in roof and 4in floor; the communications tube for this was also 4in. The underwater magazine screens varied in thickness according to location: 2in thickness on the forward screen, 4in on the beam fittings, and 2in on both of the after screens. These screens were fitted to port and starboard of the magazines, but were not continuous. The oil and coal bunkers, placed behind the armour belts between the main and middle decks abreast the boiler rooms, afforded a little extra protection for the internal parts of the ship.

A note concerning the reduction of the armour protection on the turrets is worthy of mention. Captain Jellicoe told the Committee that, although a thickness of 11in or 12in was quite sufficient to keep shells out, it had never been tested to see whether or not the actual turret mechanism could withstand the shock of a direct hit; he felt there was little need to increase the thicknesses, but suggested that an all-round reduction could be made.

The torpedo net defence was devised by Captain Bacon, and was the most elaborate and complete system fitted to a warship to that date, yet needed only two or three minutes to drop the nets from a stowed position. The net defence ran for three-quarters of the length of the ship along the upper deck level.

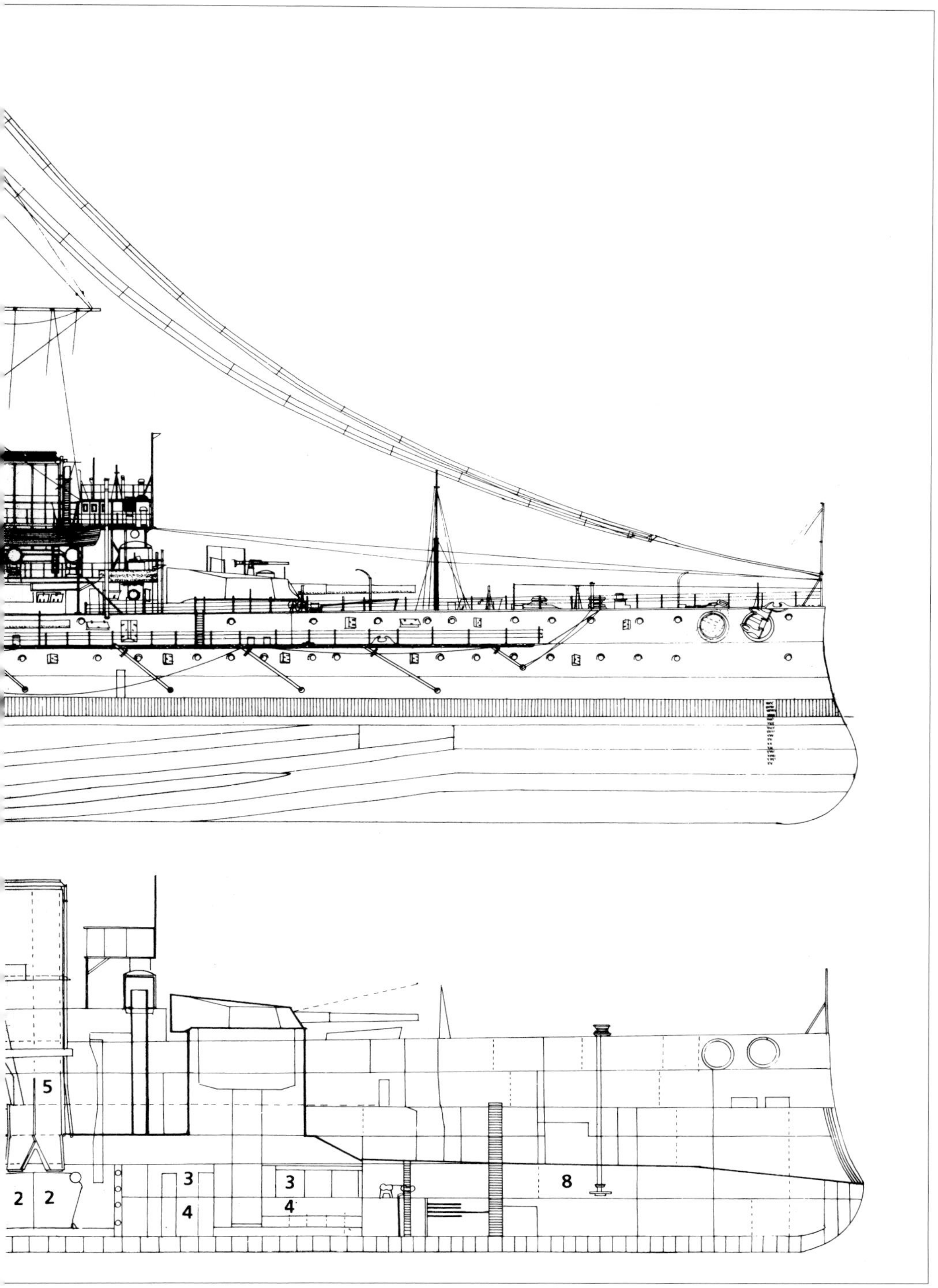

Machinery

The original proposals for the new ship was that she be fitted with reciprocating engines, although the obvious advantages in efficiency and economy of turbines were well known, but whether or not it was practicable to fit them to such a large vessel was debatable. It was estimated that with reciprocating engines and earlier hull forms of equal fullness, about 20,000 tons displacement and 30,000 SHP would have been required for the 21 knots asked for in the initial design. The first four designs all had reciprocating engines, turbines appearing in designs after this, with comparisons of both turbines and reciprocating machinery in the same basic layouts. The main difficulty in fitting turbines to the new vessel was her size, and it was debated whether or not she would have adequate stopping, turning and astern power for rapid manoeuvring under all conditions.

In January and February 1905, comparative trials were carried out between the *Gem*-class cruisers *Amethyst* (turbines) and *Sapphire* (reciprocating), and the *River*-class destroyers *Eden* (turbines) and *Waveney* (reciprocating). Throughout the trials it was seen that the most satisfactory results came from the ships with turbine propulsion, and it was found that to secure the requisite stopping and astern power one turbine needed to be fitted to each shaft, which afforded greater astern power than in any previous machinery.

The principal advantages of having turbines fitted in *Dreadnought* were:

1. Substantial saving in weight, space and cost compared with reciprocating plant.
2. Smoother running, easier operation and reduced engine room complement.
3. Economy in fuel at high powers.
4. Reduced risk of damage in action because of machinery being fitted lower in the hull.

DREADNOUGHT: STEAM TRIALS 1906

Preliminary steam speed trials were held off the Isle of Wight 1–9 October 1906. Winds of Force 3–4 and Strength 2 seas prevailed throughout. The ship had left dock after hull inspection on 28 September, so her bottom was clean.

Draught: 25ft 6in forward, 27ft 1½in aft
Steam pressure: 241 psi boilers, 221psi engine room
Shaft revolutions: 321 starboard outer, 337 starboard inner, 321 port outer, 333 port inner
Mean revolutions: 328.4 on all shafts
Pitch of propellers: 8ft 4½in
During the 8-hour full power trials, 12,225shp was developed by starboard engines, 12,487shp by port. A total of 24,712shp gave a mean speed of 21.05 knots
A total of 134 tons of best, handpicked Welsh coal was used throughout
Feedwater temperature: 70°F starboard, 66°F port
Various speeds were achieved on the measured mile runs, the following figures being logged: 21.78; 21.45; 21.78; 21.39 knots.

Dreadnought coaling on a Saturday afternoon late in 1906, just outside Portsmouth Harbour.

5. Increase in ship's handiness because of using four propellers instead of two; the wing shafts being farther off the centreline.

The installation in *Dreadnought* was: the high pressure (HP) turbines were fitted on the wing shafts, the low pressure (LP) on the inner shafts. These inner shafts were also fitted with cruising turbines. There was one HP ahead and one HP astern on each wing shaft, plus one LP ahead and one LP astern on the inner shaft. The steam for low power was passed from the boiler into the cruising turbines and thence to the HP wing turbines, before returning to the LP turbines and finally into the condensers.

On trials of the completed ship it was seen that the continuous seagoing speed was greater than that of *Lord Nelson*, but at low speeds *Dreadnought*'s radius was less. This was because at speeds of 10–12 knots, *Dreadnought* was using her cruising turbines which proved troublesome, a feature which could not have been foreseen; fuel consumption of the cruising turbines was extremely high and after *Dreadnought* they were not fitted. In all other respects, the turbines fulfilled expectations; there was much less vibration in the ship and noise was considerably reduced. As the first turbine-driven battleship completed for any navy (the Japanese *Aki*, begun seven months before *Dreadnought*, was the first turbine-engined battleship laid down, but was not completed until 1911), *Dreadnought* proved a successful innovation in design and, together with improved hull lines, gave a speed of more than three knots higher than preceding classes without excessive rise of displacement or cost.

Other Features

The rig details, fire control and boat arrangements were worked out by Captains Bacon, Jackson and Jellicoe. The problem of reducing vibration to a minimum for fire-control purposes received particular attention. Nine alternative proposals for cranes or gallows for boats were submitted, one of which embodied a mast, of light girder construction, which did not require stays. The final proposal, which was accepted, was for a tripod mast, this being considered safe, strong and easy to construct. The tripod mast had first appeared in the Royal Navy in the 1860s in the rigged turret ships *Wyvern* and *Captain*, as a means of eliminating shrouds which had always considerably restricted arcs of fire. It was reintroduced in *Lord Nelson* in 1904, although only on the mainmast which needed adequate support for the main derrick. The position for the tripod mast in *Dreadnought*, close abaft the fore funnel, was selected in the belief that smoke and fumes would be carried away from the control top, but this did not prove to be the case and was one of the design's weak points.

The reversed forward rake of the tripod legs was so designed to enable the boat derrick to swing well outboard without hindrance. The alternative possibility of a tripod mainmast with derrick does not seem to have been considered at that date. No mainmast was originally proposed for *Dreadnought*, although subsequently it was considered necessary to have some kind of after control top which could also be used as a spreader for the wireless aerials. The small baby tripod, finally fitted in *Dreadnought*, was greatly criticized in service as being too low and of little use for anything except perhaps the W/T lines. It was never repeated after *Dreadnought*.

The design of the superstructure, which was broken up by the amidships turret, was entrusted to the same three Captains. Boat stowage was located between the funnels, and the main derrick handled the heavy steam launches and larger pinnaces. There was also a pair of long topping davits fitted on each side of the forward superstructure for the smaller seaboats (gigs and cutters, etc.). The wings of the bridge on the forward superstructure were detachable, this being a concession to Captain Bacon who had recommended a narrow, more compact bridge structure without the usual long wings. The Admiralty had at first been opposed to this,

but the wings were detachable and could be removed if necessary (they were removed later during the war).

Much praise was lavished on *Dreadnought*, and after her successful sea trials she underwent a lengthy special test cruise to the Mediterranean and Trinidad from January to March 1907. During this cruise a report was written on the capabilities of the vessel in general. Close inspection of the hull revealed that while her framework was ideally suitable for a ship of such proportions, some of the framing in the area of the forecastle had buckled slightly while she was in a swell. No real damage had been done, but it was noted that extra supports were needed in future vessels of similar size.

The accommodation of the crew and officers constituted a direct change from previous battleships; with the officers now quartered forward and the ratings aft. This reversal had been instigated by Admiral Fisher with a view to having the officers' quarters nearer their normal action stations on the bridge and in the conning towers, bearing in mind the greater length of the vessel over previous designs. In hot weather, awnings could be erected on the quarterdeck for the men, and the officers, who had their own compartments, would not suffer. Another advantage of having the crew aft was that they could get to and from their quarters easily, without having to negotiate long passageways cluttered with coalbags which was the normal practice. The men had better ventilation from the long rows of scuttles abaft the armoured belts; this would lead to fewer cases of TB, which had been prevalent throughout the Navy in previous years. The system proved unsatisfactory, however, and was very unpopular with the officers. They felt that their accommodation was insufficiently segregated, their cabins were situated on the main deck level and were very small, distributed haphazardly wherever space could be found. The Admiral's quarters were in the forward superstructure so, of course, there was no traditional sternwalk.

Dreadnought averaged 17 knots from Gibraltar to Trinidad (3,430 miles) and 19 knots from Trinidad to Portsmouth (3,980 miles) which was considered an unprecedented performance in high speed. En route she conducted manoeuvring and turning trials (see tables) and could not be faulted, especially in view of the

Opposite, top: *Dreadnought*, late 1906.

Opposite, bottom: Starboard quarter view of *Dreadnought* in 1907.

Above: Superb view of *Dreadnought* fully dressed for inspection during the Imperial Press Conference Review of 1909. Note the rangefinder drum on top of the foretop rather than on the face.

DREADNOUGHT: GM AND STABILITY

Based on inclining experiments, 8 September 1906

	Draught	GM	Maximum stability	Stability vanishes at
'A' Condition (= load)*	26ft 6in	5ft	33°	63°
'B' Condition (= deep)**	29ft 7½in	5.6ft	32°	65°

*Fully equipped plus 360 tons coal upper, 540 tons lower bunkers.
**Fully equipped plus 2,900 tons coal.

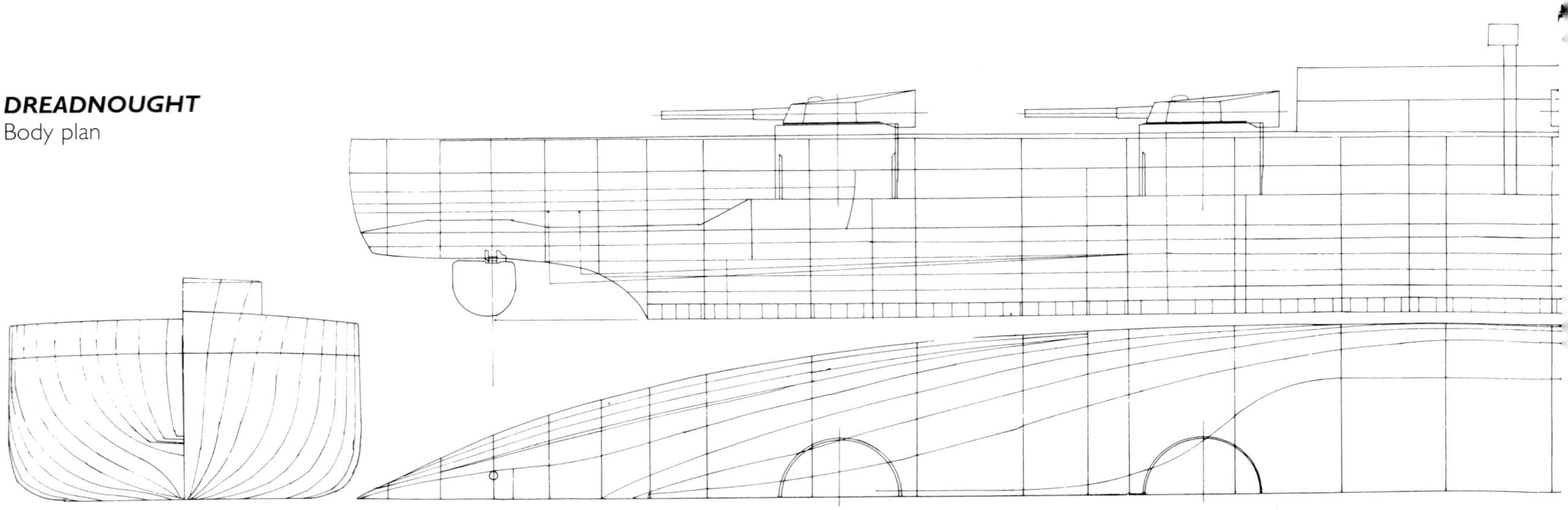
DREADNOUGHT
Body plan

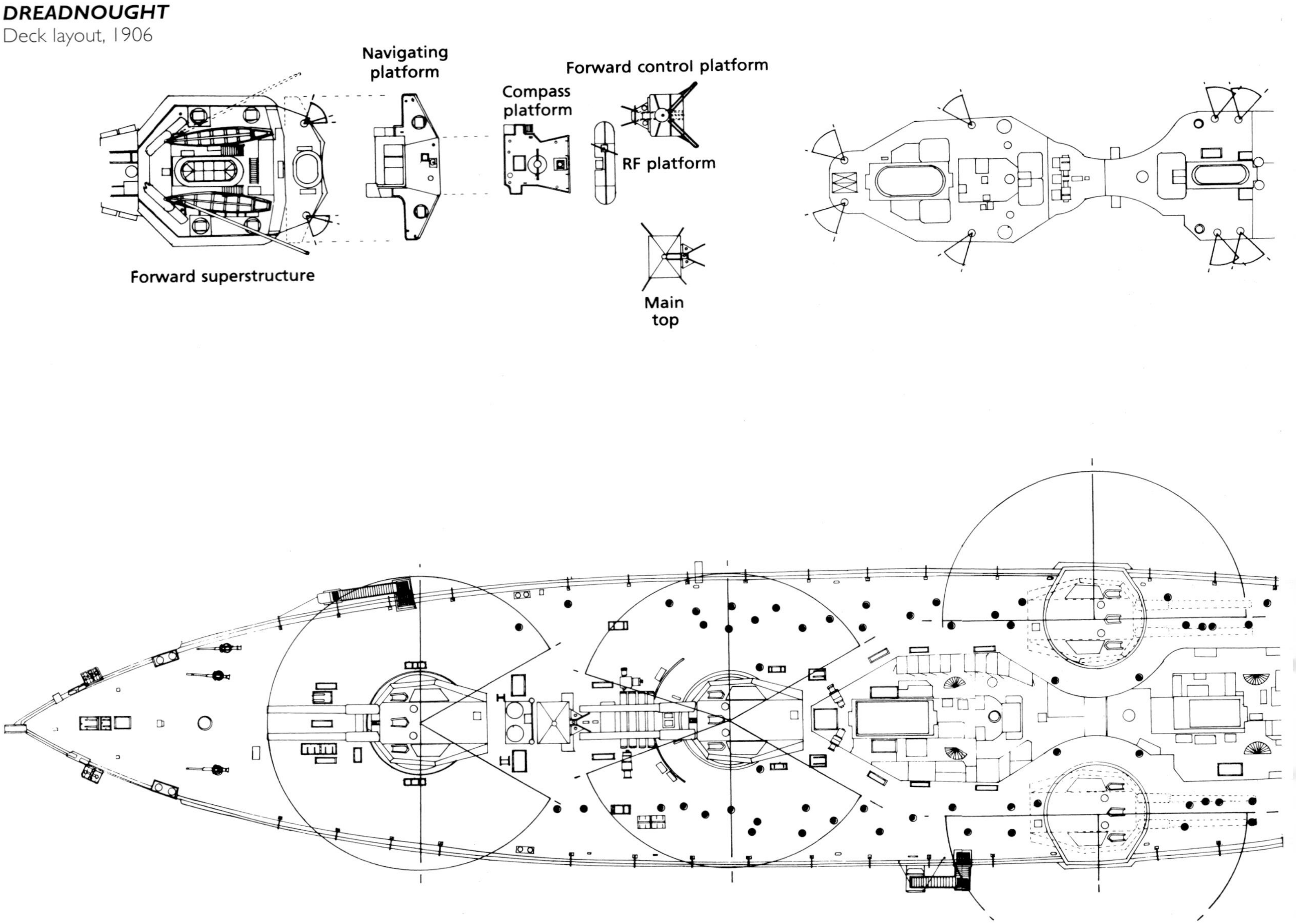
DREADNOUGHT
Deck layout, 1906
Navigating platform
Forward control platform
Compass platform
RF platform
Forward superstructure
Main top

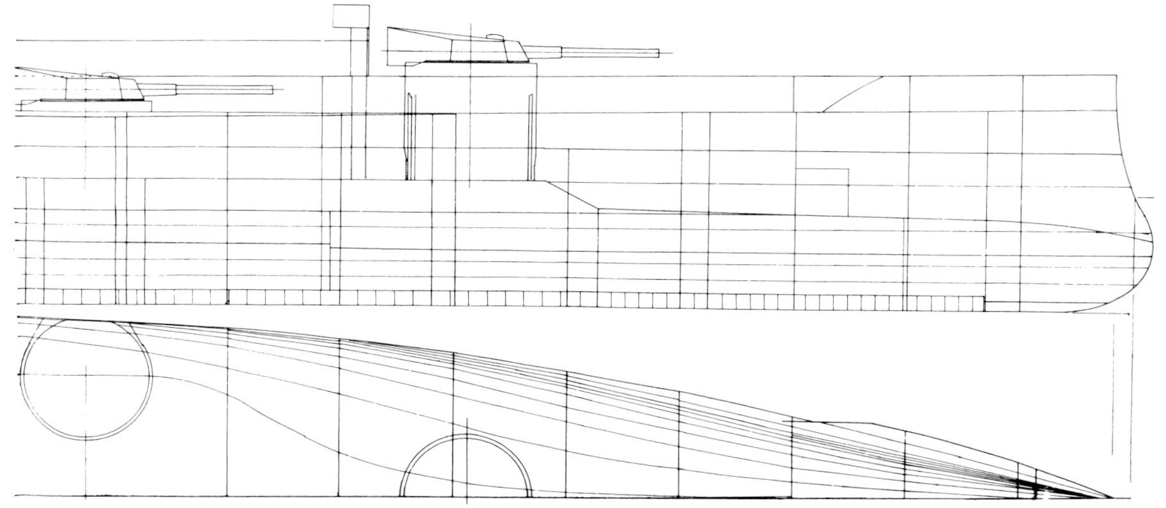

DREADNOUGHT

Sections

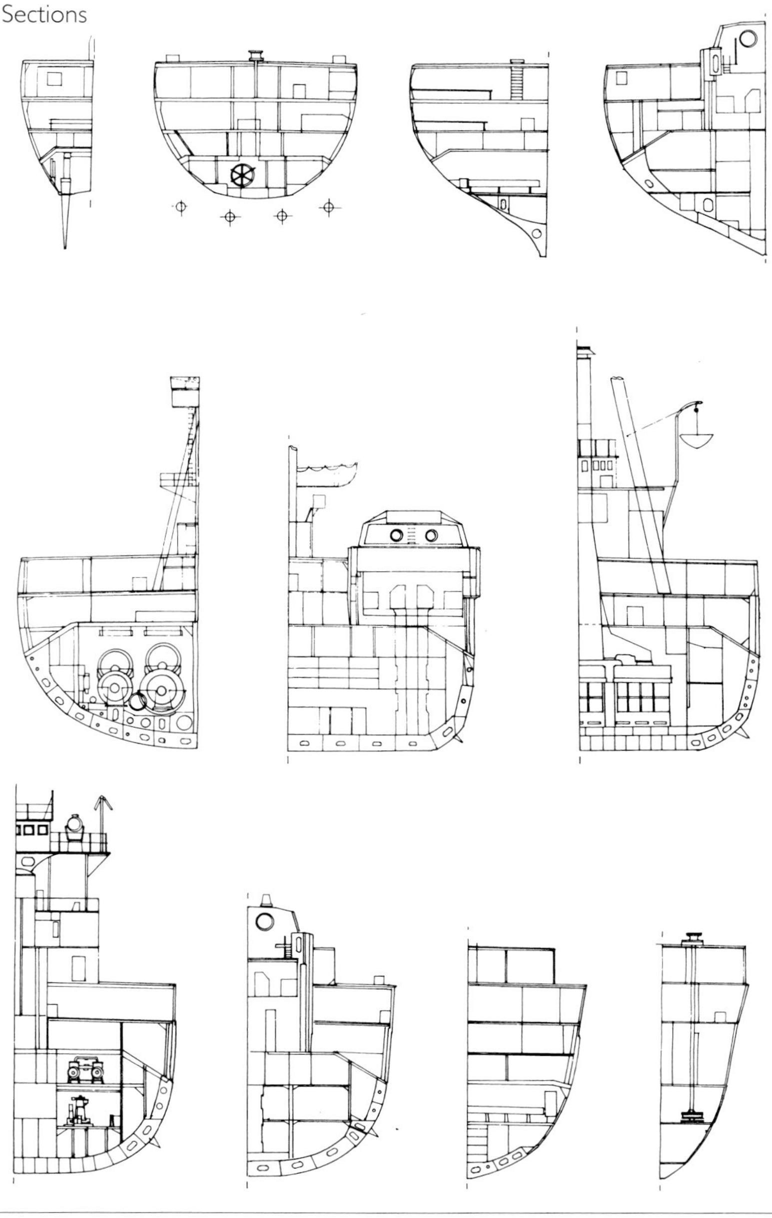

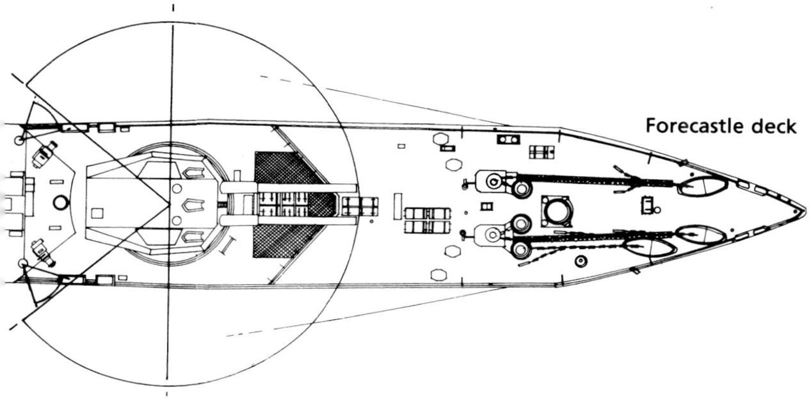

Forecastle deck

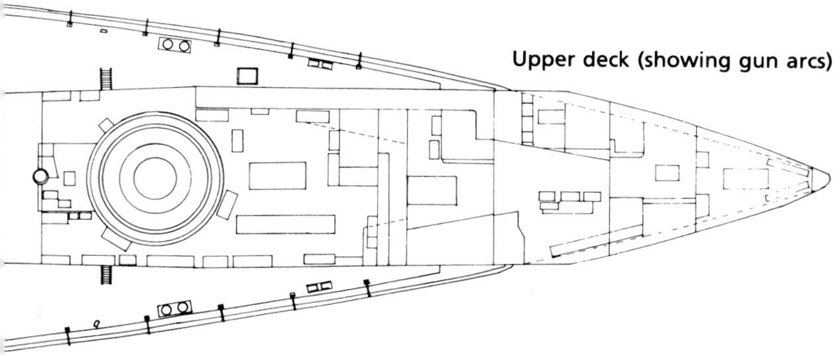

Upper deck (showing gun arcs)

DREADNOUGHT: TURNING TRIALS

All held in English Channel

Run:	1	2	3	4	5	6
First 4 points turned in (seconds)	36	25	27½	32 7/10	34⅘	39
Distance in turning (yards)	359	268	156	165	175	169
Speed (knots)	17.72	14.8	10.9	9.02	8.9	7.71

DREADNOUGHT: STEAM TRIALS JUNE/JULY 1914

The relatively poor performance throughout these trials stemmed from the fact that the ship had not been docked since March 1913 and her bottom was foul. Wind Force 3–4 NE, sea swell 3–4.

Draught: 29ft forward, 30ft 2in aft

Steam pressure: 206psi boilers, 191psi engines

Shaft revolutions: 228.4 starboard outer, 330.7 starboard inner, 324.8 port outer, 287.2 port inner

Mean revolutions: 306.2 on all shafts

11,240shp developed by starboard engines, 11,410shp by port; total SHP 22,641 gave a recorded speed of 18 knots

A total of 158 tons of best Welsh coal was used.

fact that she was of considerably greater length than previous battleships. She was able to keep a straight line while steaming astern, and could be brought extremely quickly to rest from moderate speeds by using the propellers in reverse. The anchor gear was stated to be perfection for the day, but the machinery for the boat booms was inadequate and would have to be of a more powerful type in future. The winches used for coaling the ship were too weak for the job; larger engines were required, as was the case for the working of the ventilation fans.

The lifeboat equipment was noted as being perhaps the best yet installed in a battleship. The arrangements for control of the vessel were considered to be impressive; the entire ship could be viewed from the charthouse and bridge and it was claimed that *Dreadnought* was as easy to handle as a destroyer. The searchlight location was also praised.

Gunnery trials were carried out, and thought to be most satisfactory, although the size of the secondary armament was disliked, it being considered too small to combat attacking vessels. Throughout these trials, careful notes and observations were made

by a Lieutenant Dreyer who, in collaboration with Captain P. Scott, was to change fire control within the Royal Navy with the introduction of the 'director control system' a few years before the First World War.

Appearance Changes

Dreadnought conveyed an immediate impression of exceptional power and fighting efficiency. She was always easily distinguishable by her large, heavy tripod foremast, its legs raked forward close abaft the fore funnel, but in any case her appearance was radically different from preceding ships or, in fact, from any battleship then afloat. Prominent features included: a raised forecastle with cutaway sides; a heavy turret on each beam and on the centreline amidships; flat-sided funnels, the fore noticeably smaller than the after funnel; stump tripod mainmast, its legs raked aft, carrying the after control top; tall derrick topped up vertically each side of the mainmast. Changes in appearance during the course of her life included:

1906–7 Rangefinder added over after conning tower behind second funnel. Prominent flaps (collapsible) fitted at each side of rangefinder platform (probably blast screens). Extra 12pdr guns added on each of the centreline turrets.

1909–10 Experimental range indicator fitted over fore control top; relocated on face of top during 1910–11 and removed in 1912. Fitted with short-radius W/T set. Forward pair of searchlights removed from superstructure amidships.

1912–13 Blast screens added abaft 12pdrs on fore turret.

1913 24in searchlight and platform below control top removed. Main topmast removed. Long signal struts fitted forward, below fore control top.

1914–16 Director control for main armament fitted, the director tower being located over fore control top. Rangefinder removed from after conning tower. Small rangefinder added on bridge. 12pdrs removed from fore turret and superstructures with the exception of the upper pair in the forward superstructure which were decked in. There is some uncertainty as to whether the forecastle and quarterdeck 12pdrs were removed (detachable mounts?), the official lists showing a figure of

Left: *Dreadnought* in 1909, with civilians aboard. Looking aft from the forecastle. Note twin 12in guns, twin 12pdr on top, one 36in SL on each bridge wing, two pairs of 36in on conning tower level, and single 24in on lower foretop position.

Centre: *Dreadnought*. View forward over the forecastle deck from the foretop. Note the simple and uncluttered bridge with compass positioned centrally in front.

Right: *Dreadnought*. View aft over the stern and after funnel from the foretop. Note spaciousness of the decks, and the streamlined superstructure and fittings.

Right: *Dreadnought*, 1913/14, showing a few changes in the rig. Blast screens have been fitted around 12pdrs on top of 12in gun turrets, and long signal struts have been fitted forward below fore control top. The 24in SL has been removed from the lower foretop.

twenty 12pdrs for the beginning of 1917. Four 12pdr AA are reported to have been added, two right aft on the quarterdeck, but the location for the other pair is uncertain, though probably near the after tripod. The bridge searchlights were remounted on platforms, low down on the fore tripod legs. Anti-torpedo nets removed. In order to give the conning tower a clear view ahead, the wings were removed from the bridge and the navigating platform was extended forward.

1916–17 Stern torpedo tube removed. After control top removed, its searchlight remounted on a platform on the mainmast. Special anti-flash protection fitted to magazines and ammunition hoists after Jutland. Some extra deck protection fitted in areas of magazines, but very slight because by now she was the oldest of the dreadnoughts.

1917 Deflection scales painted on sides of forward and after turrets. Quarterdeck 12pdr AA guns replaced by two 3in AA guns. Foretopmast was reduced in height.

Below: *Dreadnought* sails out of Malta in November 1913 after manoeuvres with the Mediterranean Fleet. Note the very dark grey paintwork.

History: *Dreadnought*

Built under the 1905–6 Naval Estimates after the design had been approved in March 1905. The order to commence was issued on 8 July 1905.

1906 *1 Sept* Commissioned in Reserve Fleet at Portsmouth for trials.
3 Oct Began trials.
3 Dec Completed official acceptance trials.
11 Dec Commissioned to full complement at Portsmouth for prolonged trial cruise.
1907 *5 Jan* Left Portsmouth. Called at Arosa Bay, Gibraltar and Golfo d'Aranci (Sardinia) before proceeding to Trinidad.
23 March Returned to Portsmouth.
27 March Commissioned for service as flagship of Nore Division of Home Fleet on its formation (formerly Channel Fleet).
Summer Further trials of different types of propeller.
7–14 May First practice cruise of Home Fleet (Nore Division).
18 June With Nore Division cruised to Norway and throughout parts of Scotland.
22 July Mobilization of Home Fleet and cruise to Torbay and Cowes.
3 August Home Fleet reviewed off Cowes by HM King Edward VII, followed by fleet manoeuvres (4–8 August).
1908 *12 July* Home Fleet assembled off Deal and anchored in the Downs.
16–21 July Annual exercises in North Sea with Nore Division and Atlantic Fleet.
1909 *23 March* Paid off at Portsmouth and recommissioned the following day for service as flagship of CinC Home Fleet.
4 May Combined exercises north of Scotland with Nore Division and Atlantic Fleet.
12 June Imperial Press Conference Review at Spithead, delegates aboard *Dreadnought*.
6 July Annual combined manoeuvres in Atlantic with Nore Division, Atlantic and Mediterranean Fleets.
17–24 July Visited Southend with other units of Home and Atlantic Fleets.
31 July Review of Home Fleet at Cowes, Isle of Wight. Inspection

by HM King Edward VII during visit of HIM the Tsar of Russia.
Aug On reorganization of fleets, Nore Division became 1st Division Home Fleet.
1910 *April* Exercises in Scottish waters with 1st and 2nd Divisions of Home and Atlantic Fleets.
July Combined manoeuvres off west coast with Atlantic and Mediterranean Fleets. 1st and 2nd Divisions, with part of the 3rd and 4th Divisions taking part also.
26–29 July With Home Fleet in Torbay for visit by HM King George V.
1911 *Jan* Combined exercises off north-west coast of Spain with Mediterranean Fleet.
March Relieved as flagship of 1st Division Home Fleet by *Neptune* and paid off for refit.
28 March Recommissioned with nucleus crew after refit at Portsmouth.
6 June Completed to full complement at Portsmouth for service as private ship in 1st Division Home Fleet.
24 June Present at Coronation Fleet Review by HM King George V.
6 July Combined exercises with 1st Division Home Fleet, Atlantic Fleet and 4th CS off south-west coast of England and Ireland.
July Exercises with combined fleets in North Sea.
1912 *1 May* 1st Division became 1st BS of 1st (Home) Fleet on introduction of 3rd Fleet reorganization scheme.
7–11 May Royal inspection of 1st and 2nd (Home) Fleets at Weymouth, followed by four days of exercises at sea.
9 July Present at Parliamentary Review of Home Fleets at Spithead, followed immediately by annual manoeuvres with 1st and 2nd Fleets and parts of 3rd and Mediterranean Fleets.
Oct Tactical exercises with 1st Home Fleet.
Dec Transferred to 4th BS (late Mediterranean Fleet) of 1st Home Fleet, the squadron being based on Gibraltar rather than the usual Malta harbour.
1913 *1 July* Recommissioned as flagship of 4th BS with 1st Home Fleet at Portsmouth.
Nov Manoeuvres in the Mediterranean with Mediterranean Squadron, 4th BS, 1st BS, 3rd CS and the light cruiser squadrons.
1914 *15 July* Left Portland for Spithead with 1st (Home) Fleet.
16 July Arrived at Portsmouth.
17–21 July Present at Test Mobilization and Royal Review of the Fleet by HM King George V. This review was probably the largest gathering of dreadnought types ever.
25 July Returned to Portland with 1st Fleet.
29 July Left Portland for Scapa Flow.
Aug On the outbreak of war 1st Home Fleet became the Grand Fleet without change in the organization of the battle squadrons.
20 Oct With 4th BS which consisted of the battleships *Erin*, *Temeraire*, *Bellerophon*, *Agincourt* and *Iron Duke*. All were patrolling between Rockall Bank and the Hebrides. During the evening the squadron just missed intercepting the German minelaying vessel *Berlin* which was bound for Stanton Banks from Iceland.
22 Oct–3 Nov With 4th BS which was temporarily based in Lough Swilly pending completion of anti-submarine defences at Scapa Flow.
Dec Relieved as flagship of 4th BS by *Benbow* and reverted to role of private ship in that squadron.
1915 *18 Feb* At 12.30 *Dreadnought* was returning from tactical exercises with the fleet, ESE of the Pentland Firth, – 4th BS having just parted company with the main fleet to return to Cromarty – when she sighted *U29* which had broken the surface immediately ahead after firing a torpedo unsuccessfully at *Neptune*. After a brief chase *Dreadnought* rammed and cut *U29* in two, almost colliding with *Temeraire* which was also trying to ram the submarine. There were no survivors from *U29*.
Aug With 4th BS based at Cromarty.
1916 *April* Refit at Portsmouth.
May Temporarily transferred to 3rd BS to strengthen that squadron on its relocation from Rosyth to Sheerness, as a precaution against further raids on the east coast by German High Seas Fleet. Later relieved by *Royal Oak*.
31 May 3rd BS moved out in readiness to join Grand Fleet in action at Jutland.
June Rejoined the Grand Fleet.
14 June Sighted and attempted to ram a U-boat off Dunnet Head while exercising with the fleet.
Late June Returned to Sheerness as flagship.
1918 *March* Rejoined 4th BS at Scapa Flow.
12 April Grand Fleet main base transferred from Scapa Flow to Rosyth.
7 Aug Paid off into Reserve at Devonport.
1919 *25 Feb* Transferred to Reserve at Rosyth and recommissioned as the tender *Hercules*, and as a parent ship in Reserve.
1920 *31 March* Ordered to be paid off onto the sale list and crew was reduced to prepare vessel for sale.
1921 *9 May* Sold at Rosyth to Messrs T. W. Ward Shipbreakers Ltd for approximately £44,750.
1923 *2 Jan* Reached Inverkeithing in Scotland where she was broken up.

Above: *Dreadnought* at war, 1916/17. By this time, *Dreadnought* was, in fact, obsolete compared to the super-dreadnoughts then in existence. Note control top is being completely smoked out while the ship is at speed.

Below: *Dreadnought*, showing her final wartime changes: turret scales, director control on foretop, SL on platform on top of baby tripod, no main foretopmast, and reduction in number of 12pdrs.

Invincible Class: 1905 ESTIMATES

Design

The *Dreadnought* Design Committee of 1905 had been asked also to examine designs for an advanced type of armoured cruiser that embodied Fisher's ideas with regard to heavy armament and high speed. The vessel was intended primarily for independent cruiser operations, but had to be able to act as a fast wing of the battlefleet if required.

Early in 1902, when Fisher and Gard had collaborated on designs for an 'all big gun' battleship (HMS 'Untakeable'), drawings had also been prepared for a cruiser version (HMS 'Unapproachable') which embraced all the features of the battleship except armour and speed. At that time, however, there were no plans for an 'all big gun' cruiser and the armament was intended to be a mix of 10in and 7.5in, as was planned for *Constitucion* and *Libertad* which were being built for Chile by the British firms Vickers and Armstrong Whitworth. Early requirements for the British cruiser were:

1. Main armament 10in, secondary armament 7.5in, all to be so arranged as to secure maximum arcs of fire.
2. Magazine and shell rooms were to be located below the guns so as to eliminate ammunition passages and personnel required to pass ammunition along these.
3. Protection to armament to be proof against 8in shell fire.
4. Possibility of turbine machinery.
5. Speeds far superior to that of any existing foreign armoured cruiser.
6. Oil fuel.
7. Bridgework to be reduced to a minimum.
8. Telescopic funnels.
9. Motor-operated gantries instead of derricks.
10. No wooden fittings.

Later, Fisher and Gard also provided figures for a design having these particulars: length 500 feet, beam 70 feet; displacement 14,000 tons normal; SHP minimum 35,000 for 25 knots; four 9.2in, twelve 7.5in; armoured belt 6in; decks 1½in–2in–3in (middle). The 10in guns were rejected because their ballistic increase over the 9.2in was considered insufficient to justify the increase in weight.

The Committee considered seven basic designs: one by Fisher and Gard, the remainder provided by Philip Watts and J. H. Narbeth. The members were reminded that the role of the cruiser had not yet been clearly defined but that, theoretically, it was considered to include:

1. Reconnaissance in force.
2. Support of smaller scouting cruisers.
3. Independent commerce protection duties.
4. Rapid concentration, and to envelope any fleet actions.
5. Pursuit of an enemy battlefleet, picking up stragglers if possible.

At this juncture the most modern cruisers in the fleet were the *Minotaurs* and their predecessors, the *Warrior* and *Duke of Edinburgh* classes, none of which were adequately armed either for battlefleet work or for dealing decisively with contemporary foreign cruisers, nor were they fast enough to overhaul the large German armed liners, intended for use as commerce raiders in wartime. Another item for consideration was foreign construction: towards the end of 1904 it had become known to the Admiralty that a design for a powerful cruiser had been proposed and accepted by Japan. *Tsukuba* and *Ikoma* were to be armed with four 12in and twelve 6in guns on a displacement of 13,750 tons, and as both these ships had been laid down at the same time as *Minotaur*, it was obvious that the latter was completely outclassed.

Philip Watts was an advocate of mixed calibre armament and particularly favoured the 9.2in gun. He had always opposed the 'all big gun' concept and was still of that mind at the time when the Committee was deliberating its efficacy. Not long after his appointment as DNC he had watched battleships of the fleet firing salvoes at an old *Orion*-class battleship in Polperro Bay, Cornwall. Strangely, all their 12in shells straddled the target without scoring a hit. Then a *Drake*-class cruiser fired while passing astern of the target. One of her 9.2in shells hit abaft the after turret and penetrated the armour deck. It then deflected horizontally, passed through all the machinery compartments and deflected upwards forward of the 13.5in barbette where it exploded against a heavy steel riding bitt, causing very considerable damage. Watts was tremendously impressed by the extraordinary and eccentric path of this single shell and its 'smashing' effect. The 9.2in gun and mounting were immensely popular in service; officers and men delighted in the working of it and regarded it as an excellent weapon from the point of view of aiming.

A further slight to the notion of an 'all big gun' ship came when Narbeth submitted sketch designs for such a vessel to Watts. The designs represented the logical expression of definite conclu-

MINOTAUR CLASS: PARTICULARS, FOR COMPARISON WITH *INVINCIBLE* CLASS

Construction

	Dockyard	Laid Down	Launched	Completed
Minotaur:	Devonport DY	2 Jan 1905	6 June 1906	1 April 1908
Shannon:	Chatham DY	2 Jan 1905	20 Sept 1906	Nov 1907
Defence:	Pembroke DY	22 Feb 1905	24 April 1907	Nov 1908.

Displacement (tons)
14,600 (load), 17,410 (extra deep).

Dimensions
Length: 490ft pp, 519ft oa
Beam: 74ft 6in
Draught: 25–26ft (mean).

Armament
Four 9.2in 50cal Mk XI
Ten 7.5in 50cal Mk II
Sixteen 12pdr (20cwt)
Five 18in torpedo tubes.

Armour
Main belt: 6in–4in–3in
Barbettes: 7in
Decks: lower 2in–1in, slopes 2in, flat amidships 1½in, ends 2in flat
Conning tower: 10in
9.2in turrets: 8in
7.5in turrets: 7in.

Machinery
Two sets 4-cyl triple expansion engines, four propellers
Twenty-three watertube boilers
Designed SHP: 27,000 for 23 knots
Fuel: 950/1,000 tons coal min., 2,060 tons coal plus 750 tons oil max.
Radius of action: 8,150nm at 10 knots; 2,920nm at 20.6 knots.

The design can be considered as a cruiser version of the contemporary *Lord Nelson*-class battleships and marked the end of the cycle of pre-dreadnought era armoured cruisers specifically intended for operations with the battlefleet.

sions reached by serving officers of the fleet, but the step was too drastic and was repugnant to Watts. On impolite insistence by Narbeth, Watts submitted the scheme to the Controller, Sir William May. He was rather amused at the idea, but pleased that some enterprise was being exhibited. He discussed the matter with Narbeth very kindly and very courteously but, Narbeth was later to recall: 'I remember well how he stood at his desk and, placing his right hand on my shoulder, with a very beneficient smile said he thought we could hardly go in for that at present, and I could almost hear the man at the back of his head saying, "Fancy poor old Narbeth come to that."' It can be seen that Sir William May and Philip Watts were in hearty agreement about a 9.2in armament.

The Committee tried to determine the best way to dispose guns in pairs if 12in guns were to be carried, and many rough sketches were made by the Members as they groped their way towards a satisfactory solution. In fact, no satisfaction could be found, either for the battleship or for the armoured cruiser, though it was generally held that the 12in should be adopted for both ships. Watts was rather disgruntled that his pet scheme for a mixed armament of 12in and 9.2in evoked little response.

All the time the Committee was sitting, Narbeth had been doing Watts's work in the department, but at the same time he prepared a series of designs for ships carrying 12in guns, with speeds ranging from 21 to 25 knots. He made several attempts to persuade Watts to show these to the Committee, but Watts was firmly of the opinion that the Members should find their own way out of their difficulties. One morning, however, when Narbeth was more than usually persistent and Watts less than adamant, he agreed to take the bundle of sketches to the meeting, although assuring Narbeth that he was wasting his time. At the meeting the agenda was called for; the Secretary had to report that there was no agenda. The observations of Fisher on such a situation can be well be imagined. At this point Watts produced Narbeth's drawings and Fisher clutched the straw. The following details and notes led to one of Narbeth's sketches being accepted as the basis for a battleship and another for the armoured cruiser. The main features of the accepted design as compared to the *Minotaur* class were:

DESIGNS FOR *INVINCIBLE*

Design	'1'	'2'	'3'	'4'	'5'	'6'
Displacement (tons)	17,000	17,200	15,600	16,950	17,250	17,750
Length	540ft	540ft	520ft	520ft	540ft	550ft
Beam	77ft	77.6ft	76ft	76ft	78ft	79ft
Draught	26ft	26ft	26ft	26ft	26ft	27ft
Armament	eight 12in	eight 12in	six 12in	eight 12in	eight 12in	eight 12in
Speed (knots)	25	25	25	25	25	25

All to be fitted with reciprocating machinery.

Below: *Inflexible* fitting-out at John Brown's shipyard, 1908. 'A' turret, fore tripod and bridgework seen from forecastle. Blast shields are being built around the 4in secondary guns on top of 12in turret. Also, note detachable wings to bridge.

INVINCIBLE CLASS: FINAL ARMAMENT LAYOUTS

Fisher-Gard Design
Guns: Eight 12in in four twin turrets.
Disposition: Two forecastle; two upper deck aft, all centreline; second and third superimposed over first and fourth.
Provided: Eight-gun broadside, four ahead and astern.
Rejected: Lack of experience with superimposed mountings and anticipated blast effect.

Design '1'
Guns: Eight 12in in four twin turrets.
Disposition: Forecastle, two port, two starboard; two centreline aft; one on main deck; third turret superimposed over fourth.
Provided: Six-gun broadside, four ahead and astern.
Rejected: Beam turrets too far ahead for good seagoing.

Design '2'
Guns: Eight 12in in four twin turrets.
Disposition: Forecastle, two port, two starboard; two port and starboard upper deck aft.
Provided: Four-gun broadside, four ahead and astern.
Rejected: Weak broadside and turrets too far ahead.

Design '3'
Guns: Six 12in in three twin turrets.
Disposition: Forecastle, two port, two starboard, but well aft; one centreline upper deck aft.
Provided: Four-gun broadside, four ahead, two astern.
Rejected: Weak broadside and astern.

Design '4'
Guns: Eight 12in in four turrets.
Disposition: One forecastle centreline; one upper deck aft centreline; two upper deck amidships, port and starboard.
Provided: Six-gun broadside, ahead and astern.

Design '5'
Guns: Eight 12in in four twin turrets. Identical with Design '4', but midships turrets echeloned, allowing offside turret to bear on a limited arc on opposite beam.

Design '6'
Guns: Eight 12in in four twin turrets.
Disposition: As in Design '5', but forecastle deck extended aft to give midships turrets higher command.
Accepted.

INVINCIBLE CLASS: FINAL LEGEND, SUMMARY OF WEIGHTS, 10 AUGUST 1905

Load condition	tons
Hull:	6,200
Armour:	3,460
Machinery:	3,300
Armament:	2,440
Coal:	1,000
General equipment:	660
Engineers' stores:	90
Board margin:	100
Total:	**17,250**

Deep condition	
Hull:	6,200
Armour:	3,460
Machinery:	3,300
Coal:	3,000
Armament:	2,480
General equipment:	740
Oil:	700
Reserve feedwater:	350
Engineers' stores:	90
Board margin:	100
Total:	**20,420**

1. A nominal displacement increase of 2,650 tons. Length increase was 48ft, with beam and draught increases of 4ft and 6in respectively.
2. Eight 12in and sixteen 4in against four 9.2in and ten 7.5in.
3. Turbine machinery of 41,000shp against 27,000shp with reciprocating machinery.

Construction of the vessels was carried out in great secrecy and, at Fisher's instigation, erroneous reports were circulated implying that the design was merely a development of the *Minotaur* class. This misled the German Admiralty into starting their own construction of *Blücher*, a distinctly inferior type in respect of speed and armament. True particulars of the British ships were not made public until the summer of 1906 when it was too late for the Germans to revise their designs.

Right: *Invincible*, mid 1909, showing painted funnel bands for identification: one white third funnel *Indomitable*; one white first funnel *Inflexible*; one white on each *Invincible*.

Armament

One of the very early alternative layouts showed ten 9.2in in five twin turrets, arranged as in *Dreadnought*, but as the Committee had discarded the 9.2in gun, only the designs with 12in armament were considered. The 12in guns were finally adopted on the grounds that the ships were required to run down and destroy any other cruiser then extant. This was the primary role, but they should also be capable of forming a fast division to supplement the battlefleet, and perhaps attack the van of an enemy fleet.

The uniform heavy-calibre armament adopted for these new ships provided maximum destructive effect, together with the greatest possible accuracy and efficiency in long-range fire control. On the basis of the Admiralty requirements, the main armament of eight 12in guns was the maximum commensurate with a speed of 25 knots, protection similar to that of *Minotaur* and dimensions conforming to existing docks. A primary requirement was the capability for maximum fire ahead unhindered by blast interference from individual turrets. The value of powerful ahead fire for engaging a retreating enemy had been particularly stressed by Lord Fisher and was in contrast to the requirements for *Dreadnought* where a heavy weight in broadside was the primary objective.

The plans of the cruiser type were very distinctive and the final arrangement was not, in any way, a discarded design for the battleship. The final plan, with the midships turret arrangement in close echelon, and allowing a nominal all-round fire of six guns with a good command for three of the four turrets, was considered the best that could be produced on the available length and beam, these in turn being dependent on the internal capacity of the hull form with proper arrangement of magazines, machinery and boilers. Because of anticipated blast effect, there was never any intention of providing an eight-gun broadside by placing the midships guns *en echelon*, and the most that was expected was to maintain a six-gun broadside over a limited arc of fire if the other turret became inoperable.

During the spring of 1905 consideration was given to fitting electrically-operated turrets in one of the new cruisers of the following year's Estimates; this would be on an experimental basis, but it had long been accepted that electrical machinery might have advantages over the hydraulic equipment in use. *Invincible* was selected for the experiment; her centreline turrets were to be manufactured by Vickers, those on the beam by Armstrong-Whitworth; all were to be electrically-operated. The centreline mountings were Mk B1X, the beam mountings Mk BX.

After completion of the ship, a lengthy series of gun trials revealed that the fittings were something of a failure; training was a little slower than usual and the system was unpopular with turret crews. The machinery showed no marked superiority over the hydraulic equipment, and it was decided to reinstate the standard hydraulic gear during her next refit (it was not refitted until 1914).

Originally it had been intended that these vessels carry 12pdrs as in *Dreadnought*, but this was abandoned in favour of a new 4in gun introduced early in 1907.

Armour

In accordance with the Admiralty's instructions to the Committee, protection, which was largely subordinated to arma-

Below, left: *Inflexible* at Chatham in October 1908. Note boat stowage arrangements, and 12pdrs located below flying deck level.

Below, right: *Inflexible*, as completed and commissioned, Chatham DY in October 1908.

INVINCIBLE
Outboard profile and plan, 1909

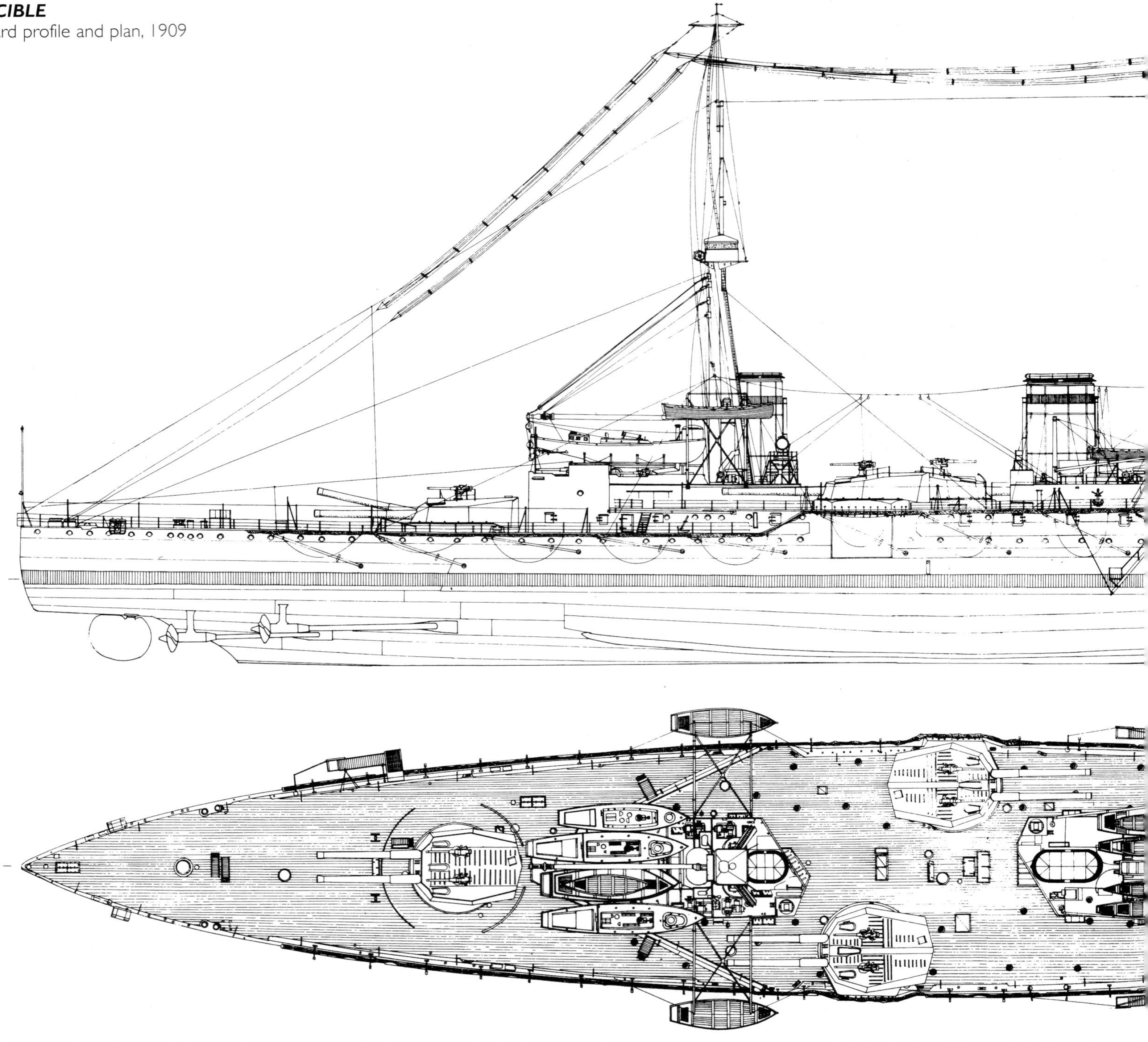

ment and speed, was only to the same scale as the immediately preceding *Minotaur*-class armoured cruisers. Although adequate against attack by medium-calibre, long-range shellfire, such as might be anticipated in the cruiser role for which the ships were primarily intended, it was quite incapable of withstanding the heavy-calibre projectiles to which they would be exposed in their alternative role as part of the battlefleet.

The horizontal armouring was especially meagre, in which connection Philip Watts recorded that 'Admiralty requirements called for protection only against "flat trajectory" fire at about 9,000 yards and that, with a displacement limit of approximately 17,000 tons, no weight was available to increase the thickness of deck armour, although realizing the danger of plunging shellfire from heavy-calibre shells at 15,000 yards and over.' The probability of future fleet actions being fought at ranges greater than 15,000 yards, with heavy shells falling at steep angles, was not fully appreciated in official circles at that date, although it had been pointed out by, among others, Captain Mark Kerr, when he was in command of *Invincible* during her first commission in 1909.

The main armoured belt of the class was 6in thick amidships and extended from just outside 'A' barbette to abreast of the centre of 'Y'. The upper edge was at main deck level, some 7ft 5in above the load waterline. The lower edge was 3ft 10in below the waterline in the same load. The belt forward was 4in thick and ran

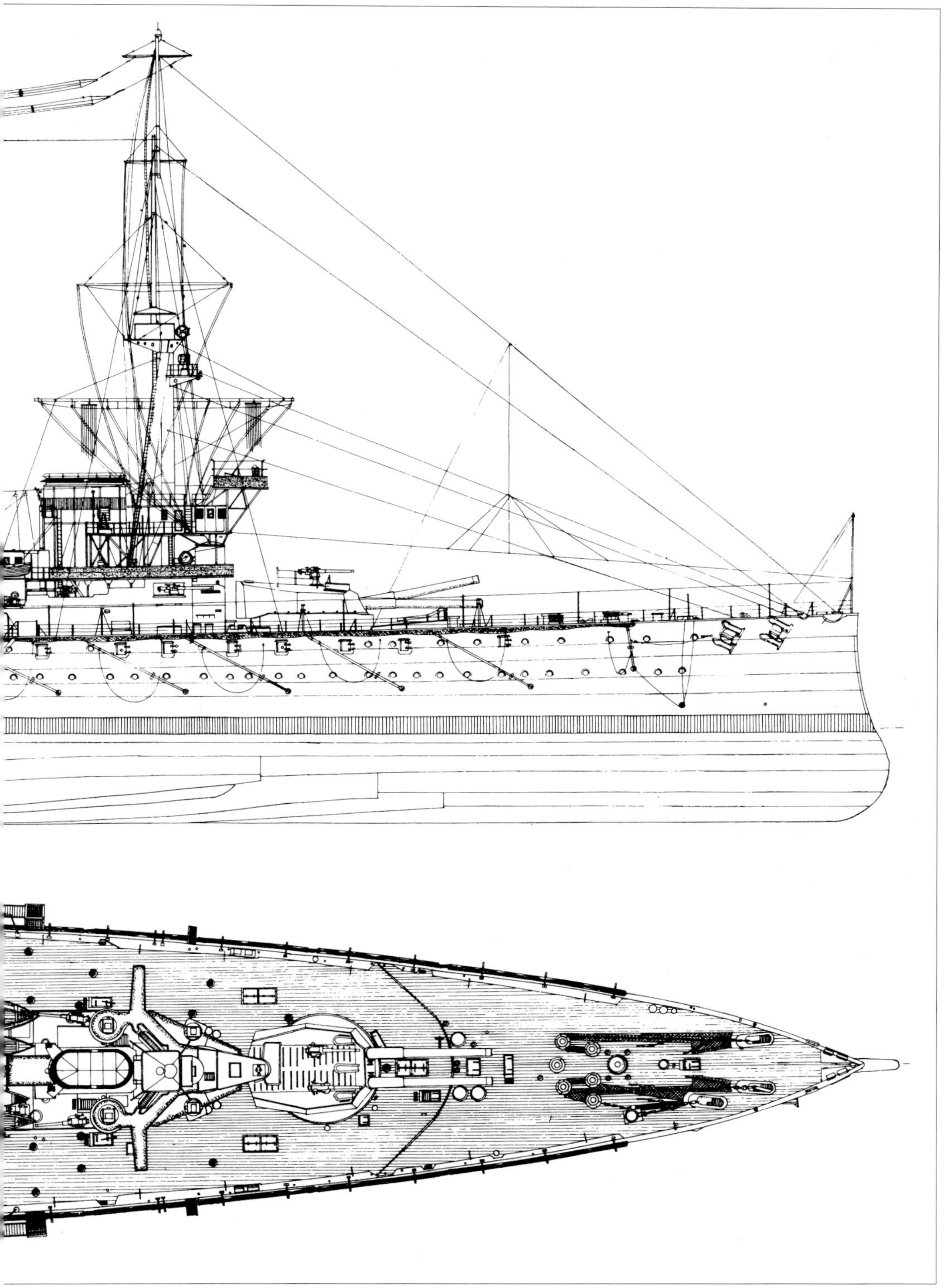

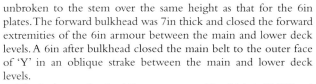

unbroken to the stem over the same height as that for the 6in plates. The forward bulkhead was 7in thick and closed the forward extremities of the 6in armour between the main and lower deck levels. A 6in after bulkhead closed the main belt to the outer face of 'Y' in an oblique strake between the main and lower deck levels.

The barbettes for the 12in turrets were 7in thick in 'A' 'P' and 'Q' mountings, and ran down to the protective deck at this thickness. Below deck they were enclosed by 2in rectangular bulkheads extending out to the vessel's side below 'P' and 'Q'. The outer face of 'Y' was 7in to the lower deck and then, as before, reduced to 2in once below.

Right: *Indomitable*. Extreme port bow and starboard quarter views, showing the high freeboard afforded to the ships. Note height of after superstructure which housed most of the ship's boats, all easily handled by the main and two stump derricks, (P+S) between the first and second funnels.

2. CRIBB.

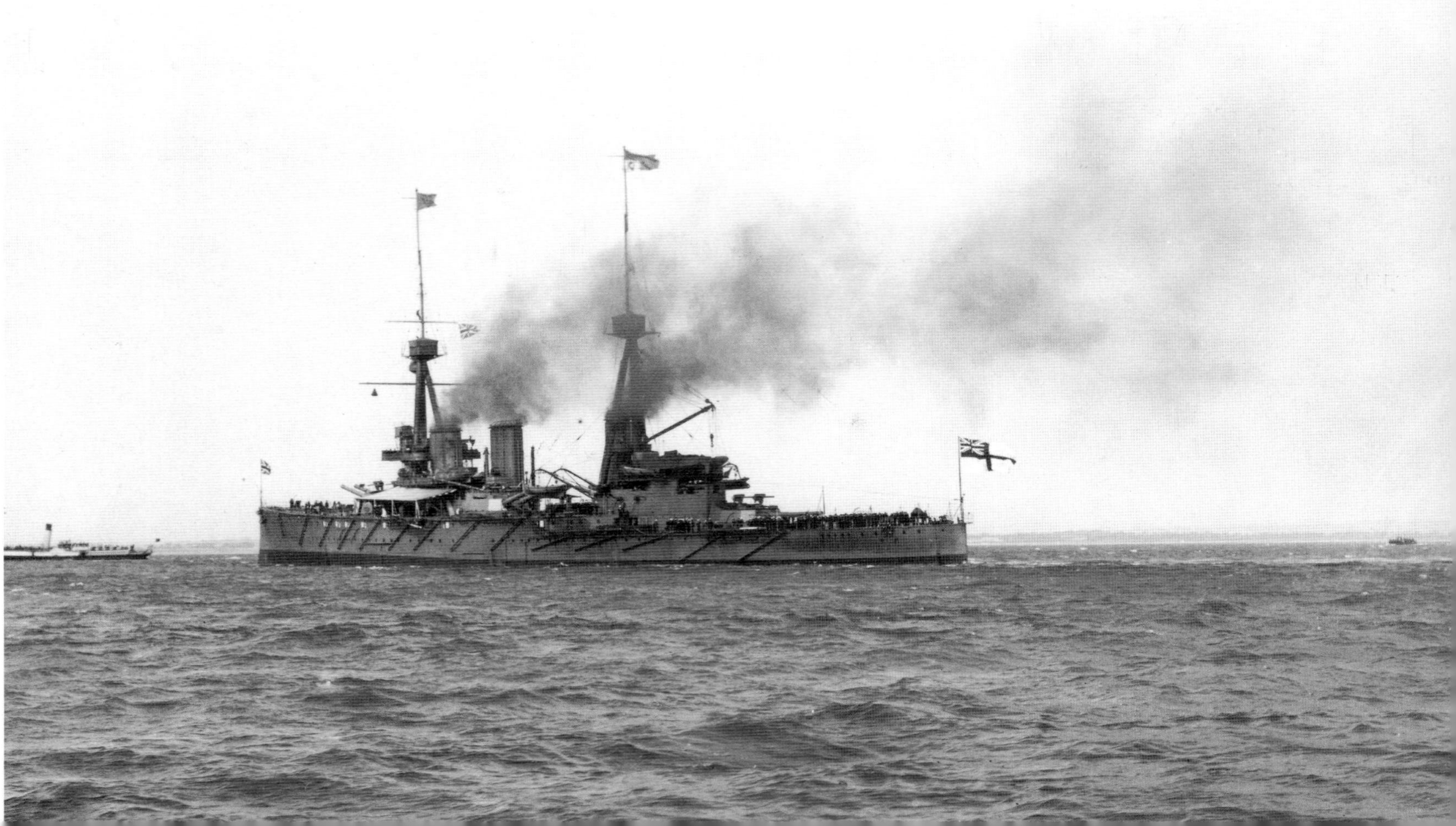

Turrets were given 2½in–3in on the roofs and sides, faces and backs were 7in. The main deck was ¾in from the stem to the forward belt bulkhead after which it increased to 1in. Lower deck thickness ranged from 1½in to 2½in, the crown being at waterline level and the lower edge being at the lower edge of the armoured belt, 3ft 10in below water. The 2½in ran on the slopes with 1½in on the flat between the belt bulkheads. Outside these bulkheads it was 1½in forward and 2½in aft.

The forward conning tower had a 10in face and a 7in rear which was located below the bridge level. The spotting and signal tower at the rear of the conning tower was 3in on the sides with a 2in roof and floor. The communications tube had 4in plates. The torpedo conning tower on the after superstructure was 6in on the sides with a 2in roof and floor; the tube was 3in. There was a lower conning tower aft, below the main deck, which was given 2in protection. The magazine screens for limited torpedo protection were 2½in thick, and were fitted longitudinally port and starboard abreast the forward, amidships and after magazines.

Machinery

The early designs all provided reciprocating machinery, although some Members of the Board were optimistic about the fitting of turbine machinery in the cruiser type. Fisher had stressed that the importance of maintaining superiority over enemy cruisers in speed as well as armament was paramount, and as it was anticipated that new foreign cruisers might be designed with speeds of up to 24 knots, it was considered necessary to exceed this figure. The completed vessels were all fitted with Parsons direct drive turbines and four screws. The high pressure turbines were fitted on the wing shafts and the low pressure on the inner shafts. There was

Opposite, top: The quarterdeck of *Indomitable c.* 1911, shortly after a coaling session and a welcome rest for the stokers no doubt.

INVINCIBLE CLASS: PARTICULARS, AS COMPLETED

Construction

	Dockyard	Laid Down	Launched	Completed
Inflexible:	John Brown	5 Feb 1906	26 June 1907	20 Oct 1908
Indomitable:	Fairfield	1 March 1906	16 March 1907	25 June 1908
Invincible:	Armstrong	2 April 1906	13 April 1907	20 March 1908.

Displacement (tons), 1909 figures
Inflexible: 17,290 (load), 19,975 (full load)
Indomitable: 17,410 (load), 20,125 (full load)
Invincible: 17,420 (load), 20,135 (full load).

Dimensions
Length: 530ft pp, 560ft wl, 567ft oa
Beam: 78ft 8½in
Draught: 25ft 1in (load), 26ft 8in (full load)
Freeboard: 30ft forward, 21ft amidships, 17ft aft.

Armament
Eight 12in 45cal Mk X; Mk VIII mounting (*Indomitable* and *Inflexible* only, see Gunnery Notes)
Sixteen 4in 45cal Mk III (one 3in AA added in *Invincible* 1914)
Seven MG
Five 18in torpedo tubes (four beam, one stern); twenty-three torpedoes plus six 14in for the boats.

Director control
None fitted as completed.

Armour
Main belt: 6in amidships; extending 7ft 5in above water-line, 3ft 10in below (at normal condition)
Bulkheads: 7in forward, 6in aft
Forward belt: 4in
Turrets: 7in face and sides, 3in roof
Barbettes: 7in through to armoured deck where they reduced to 2in
Decks: main 1in–¾in, lower 2½in–2in–1½in
Conning tower: 10in face, 7in rear, 2in roof and floor
Communications tube: 4in
Spotting and signal tower: 3in sides, 2in roof and floor
Torpedo conning tower: 6in sides, 2in roof and floor
Communications tube: 3in
Magazine screens: 2½in.

Machinery
Four sets Parsons direct-drive turbines, four propellers
Thirty-one Yarrow large-tube boilers, 250psi (normal), each fitted with five (*Indomitable* four, *Inflexible* three) single-orifice oil sprayers (180psi per hour per burner, *Invincible*; 300psi per hour per burner, *Inflexible*)
Total heating surface: 103,880sq ft
Grate area: 1,750sq ft
Length of boiler rooms: (1) 51ft 11in, (2) 34ft 1in, (3) 33ft 11¾in, (4) 33ft 10¾in
Length of engine rooms: 76ft
Fuel: 1,000 tons coal min., 3,084 tons max. (*Inflexible*); approx. 725 tons oil (each ship varied)
Coal consumption: 660 tons per day at full power
Radius of action: 6,210nm at 10 knots (oil added); 3,050nm at seagoing speed of 22.3 knots.

Ship's boats	Capacity
Pinnaces (steam): two 50ft	140
Pinnaces (sail): one 36ft	86
Launches (sail): one 42ft	140
Life cutters: two 32ft	118
Cutters: one 32ft	59
Gigs: one 30ft	26
Whalers: three 27ft	72
Dinghies: one 16ft	10
Balsa rafts: one 13ft 6in	8
Total	**659**

Searchlights
Eight 36in, two forward superstructure abeam conning tower, two on platforms abeam fore funnel, one high on platform abeam second funnel (port), one high on platform abeam third funnel (starboard), two low down on platform on main tripod legs, one 24in signalling lamp on platform below foretop.

Anchors
Three 125cwt Wasteney Smith stockless
Two 42cwt stream and kedge (close stowing)
Two 5cwt Admiralty type.

Wireless
Mk II W/T set on completion; later changed to Types 1 and 9.

Complement
Inflexible: 779 (1910); 808 as flagship (1912)
Indomitable: 781 (1914)
Invincible: 755 (1906 Estimate); 729 (11 Feb 1909); 799 (1914); 1,032 as flagship (1916).

Cost
Estimate: £1,621,015
Revised Navy estimate: £1,634,316
Final estimate: £1,625,120
Actual cost: *Inflexible* £1,630,739; *Indomitable* £1,662,337; *Invincible* £1,677,515, guns £90,000.

Opposite, bottom: *Indomitable* at sea 15 July 1908, bound for Quebec, taking HRH the Prince of Wales to Canada for tercentenary celebrations. The Royal Standard flies from the topgallant mast.

INVINCIBLE

Body plan, inboard profile and sections, as fitted, 1908-9

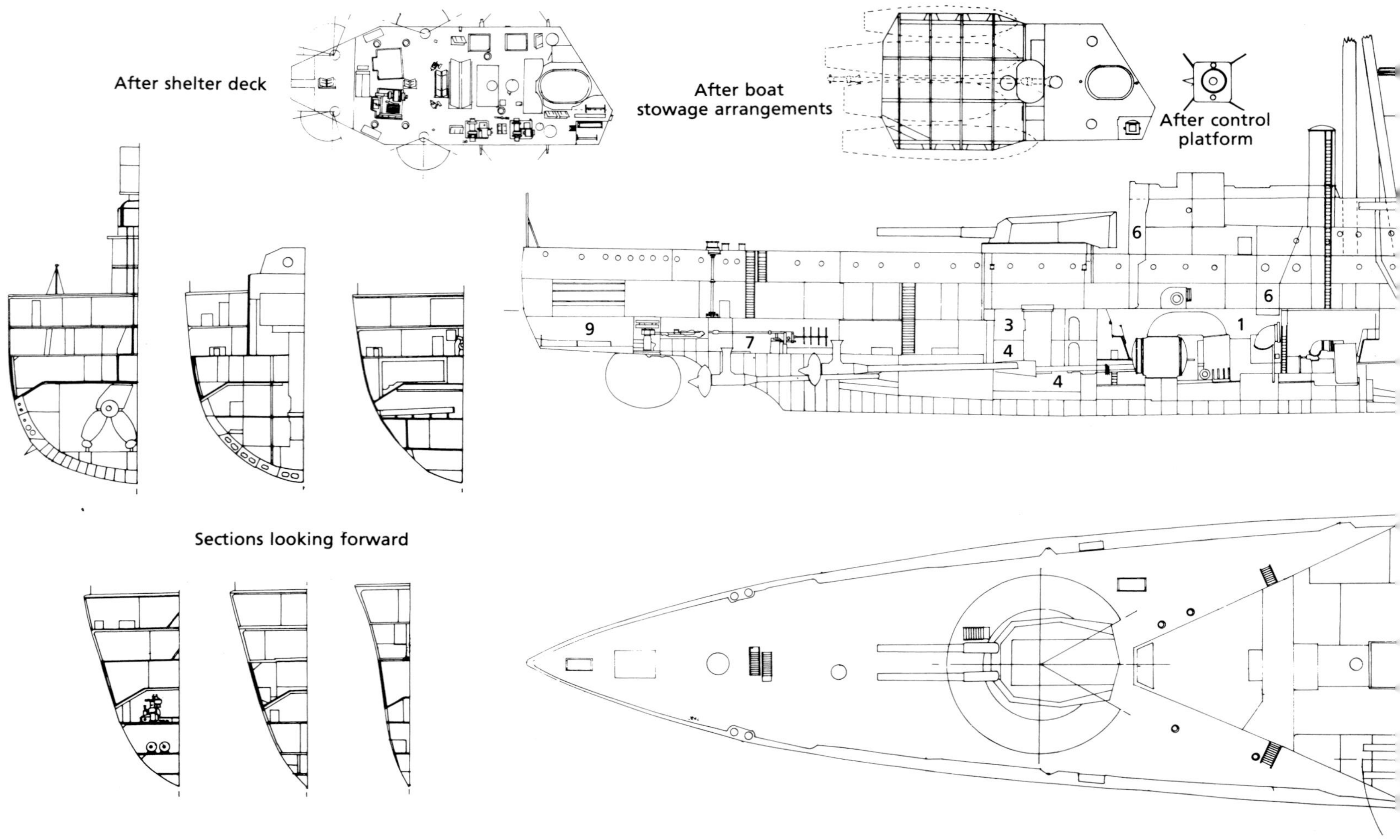

INVINCIBLE

Outboard profile, as fitted February 1915

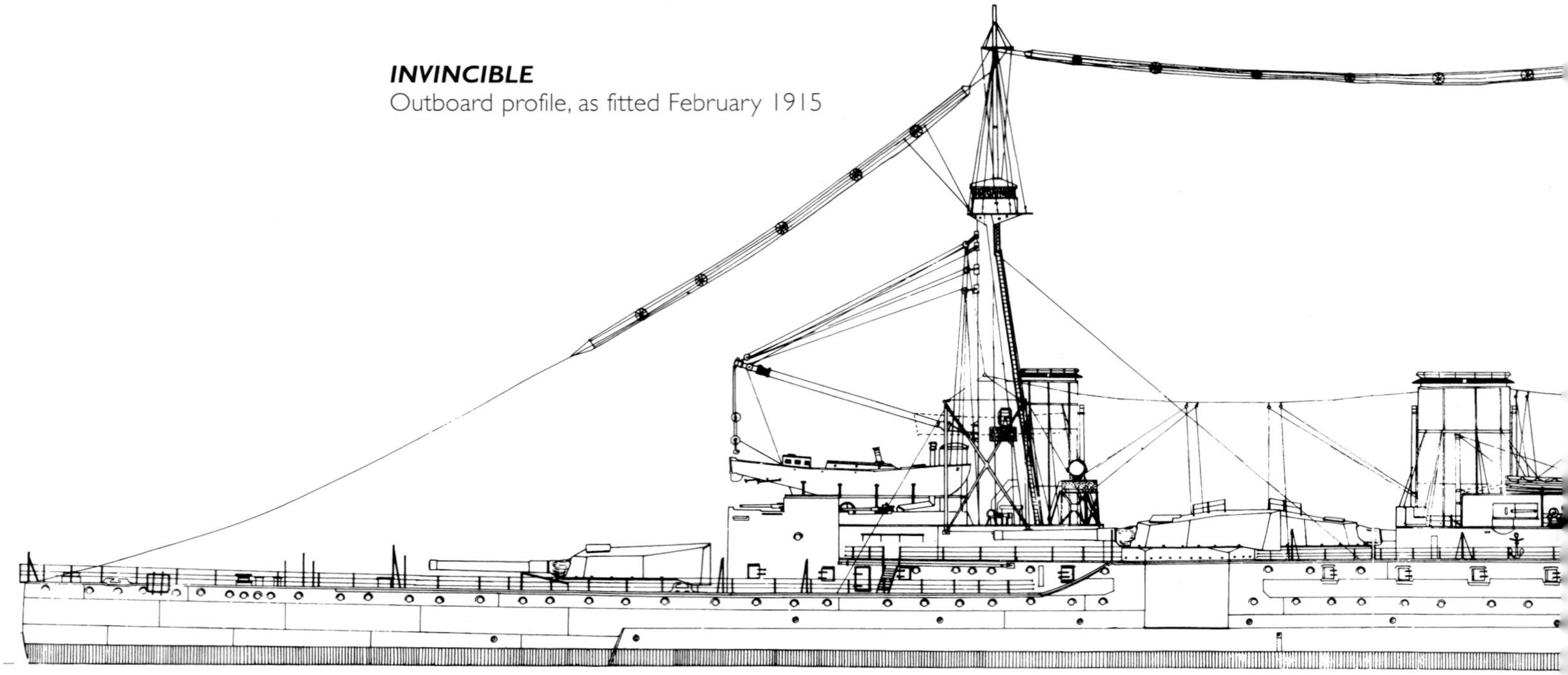

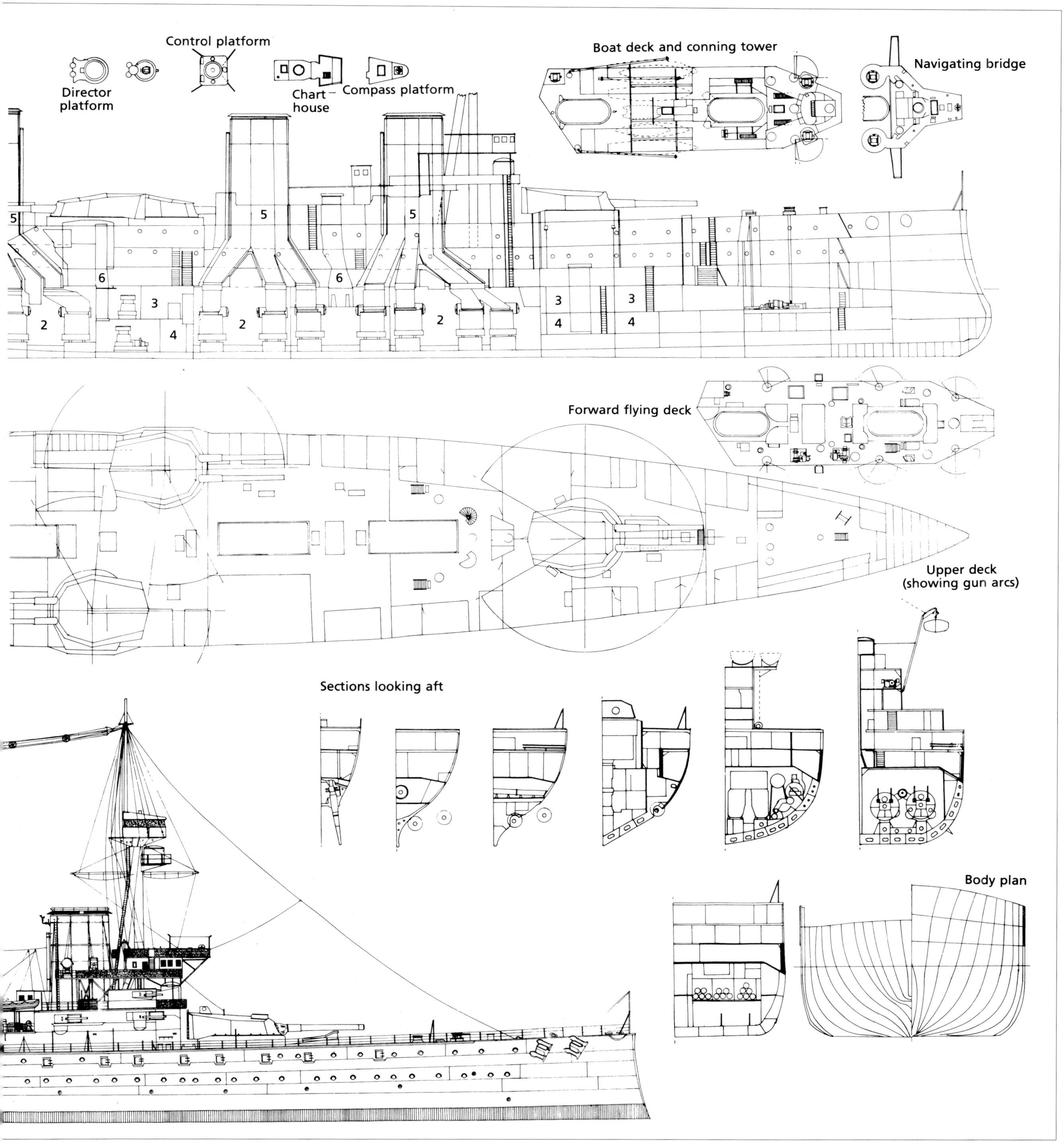
Control platform
Director platform
Chart house
Compass platform
Boat deck and conning tower
Navigating bridge
Forward flying deck
Upper deck (showing gun arcs)
Sections looking aft
Body plan

one HP ahead and astern turbine on each shaft, also, one LP ahead and astern turbine fitted to each inner shaft. The cruising turbines were also fitted to the inner shafts. On completion these ships had the most powerful turbine installation of any warship afloat, and were easily the fastest heavy cruisers in the world.

Funnel arrangements had varied greatly throughout the designs, and although no record is available of the Fisher-Gard layout, the second, third and fourth designs provided for four tall, thin, evenly spaced and slightly raked funnels. The fifth and sixth were much the same except that the after funnel was placed well back so as to clear the echeloned turret amidships. This spacing was retained in the final layout, but the first three funnels were combined into two larger funnels, and were not raked.

General Notes

As in *Dreadnought*, the traditional accommodation plan of officers aft and ratings forward was reversed. Although proving unsatisfactory and very unpopular, it was not rectified until the building of

INDOMITABLE: LAUNCH FIGURES, 16 MARCH 1907

	tons
Displacement:	7,461
Armour:	1,097½
Men and ballast:	460
Machinery:	170
Recorded weight of hull:	5,744

Length: 530ft 1¾in pp
Beam: 78ft 7¾in
Beam as moulded: 78ft 4¼in
Depth of keel from flying deck: 48ft 2¾in
Length of boiler rooms: 153ft 10½in
Length of engine rooms: 75ft 11⅝in
Draught at launch: 11ft 5in forward, 15ft 8in aft
Breakage at launch:
longitudinal in a distance of 406ft = 1½in hog
transverse in a distance of 73ft 8in = nil
Invincible **launch weight:** 7,889 tons (hull: 6,022 tons)
Inflexible **launch weight:** 7,592 tons (hull: 5,810 tons).

Opposite: *Indomitable* at Weymouth 1911/12.

Below: *Invincible*. Port bow view showing her general layout in 1909. Seen here shortly after her trials period when her funnels bands were painted up.

INFLEXIBLE: GM AND STABILITY

Based on inclining experiments, 4 September 1908

	Displacement (tons)	Draught	GM	Maximum stability	Stability vanishes at
'A' Condition (= load)*	17,426	25ft 10¼in	3.8ft	–	–
'B' Condition(=deep)**	19,975	29ft2in	4.22ft	–	–

*Fully equipped plus 400 tons coal upper, 600 tons lower bunkers.
**Fully equipped plus 3,084 tons coal, 725 tons oil fuel.

the battlecruiser *Queen Mary* and the battleships of the *King George V* class.

Appearance Changes

General appearance of the class was unlike that of any preceding class of armoured cruisers. Outstanding features were:

1. Long forecastle.
2. Three short, flat-sided funnels of equal height, unevenly spaced and without rake. Third funnel placed well abaft second and close to mainmast.
3. Navigating platform raised high over bridge and extended prominently forward.
4. High superstructure aft.
5. Full tripod masts main legs raked forward.

As completed, they were rated the best-looking warships in the navy. They were very hard to tell apart being practically identical except for the following.

Invincible: Second yard on foremast well above control top. Solid siren brackets abaft fore funnel.

Inflexible: Straight slope to edges of starfish on mainmast. Open brackets for sirens.

Indomitable: Angled slope to lower edge of starfish on mainmast. Solid brackets for sirens.

1909 Range indicators fitted to faces of control tops in *Indomitable* and *Inflexible*, but only to forward control top in *Invincible*. Standard funnel bands painted: *Invincible* 1 white on each funnel; *Indomitable* 1 white on 3rd funnel; *Inflexible* 1 white on fore funnel.

1911 Range indicator fitted to face of after control top in *Invincible*. 24in signalling searchlights removed from foremast in all. Remounted on superstructure abaft forward funnel in *Inflexible* and *Invincible*. Extra yard fitted to head of foretopmast in all.

1912–13 Forward control top in *Indomitable* and *Inflexible* modified with narrow faces. Range indicators removed in all. Blast screens fitted abaft 4in guns on 'A' and 'Y' turrets. Extra 36in searchlight added at end corner of forward superstructure in *Invincible*.

1913–14 Blast screens removed from 4in guns as vessels were refitted. Forward superstructure searchlight remounted on bridge in *Indomitable*, 24in SL removed in *Inflexible*. Torpedo nets removed in all.

1914 *Indomitable*: 4in guns removed from 'A' and 'Y' turrets. Two remounted (P+S) over forward pair in forward superstructure and two on same level abaft (see 1915 drawing).

Forward guns plated in, affording some protection for crews. *Invincible*: As refitted in 1914. Director control top fitted for main armament, this being placed on new platform just below foretop. The 24in SL and its platform were removed. Fore control top modified with narrow face. Turret electrical gear replaced by hydraulic (see notes). 4in guns removed from 'A'

Below: *Inflexible* at Weymouth, c.1911. The fore funnel has been heightened to clear the bridge in an endeavour to alleviate smoke and fumes.

INDOMITABLE: SPEED TRIALS, 1908

Polperro and Skelmorlie courses

26 April, 7/10th-power
Draught: 25ft forward, 26ft 10in aft
Displacement: 17,620 tons
Port outer: 260rpm; 7,035shp; inner: 229rpm; 5,427shp
Starboard outer: 271 rpm; 8,501shp; inner: 232rpm; 5,771shp
Speed: 22.488 knots (mean figures of six runs).

27 April, 30-hour 1/5th-power
Draught: 25ft 1in forward, 26ft 3in aft
Displacement: 17,120 tons
Port outer: 185rpm; 3,323shp; inner: 173rpm; 2,339shp
Starboard outer: 187rpm; 2,734shp; inner: 167rpm; 1,908shp
Speed: 16.05 knots (mean figures of four runs).

28 April, 7/10th-power
Draught: 25ft 1in forward, 26ft 3in aft
Displacement: 17,120 tons
Port outer: 272rpm; 7,954shp; inner: 243rpm; 6,791shp
Starboard outer: 277rpm; 8,680shp; inner: 250rpm; 7,553shp
Speed: 23.665 knots (mean figures of six runs).

29 April, full power
Draught: 25ft forward, 27ft aft
Displacement: 17,435 tons
Port outer: 316rpm; 12,967shp; inner: 285rpm; 11,705shp
Starboard outer: 307rpm; 12,429shp; inner: 277rpm; 10,681shp
Speed: 26,106 knots (mean figures of four runs).

INVINCIBLE: SPEED TRIALS, 1908

Invincible began her preliminary sea trials off Chesil Beach on Thursday, 22 October
Type of trial: 30-hour, 1/5 power
Sea condition: smooth
Draught (before leaving the Tyne)**:** 26ft 11in forward, 27ft 2in aft
Revolutions: 174.3rpm
SHP: 9,695
Speed: 16.24 knots (mean figures of six runs)

Polperro course, 3 November
Type of trial: 13-hour, 7/10th power
Revolutions: 269.5rpm
SHP: 34,124
Speed: 24.26 knots (mean figures of six runs)

Polperro course, 7 November
Type of trial: full power
Sea condition: rough; wind ESE, Force 9
Revolutions: 295.2rpm
SHP: 46,500
Speed: 26.64 knots (mean figures of six runs)

Type of trial: cruising
Low power: 122.45rpm; 3,854shp; 11.55 knots
Intermediate power: 196.25rpm; 13,291shp; 18.2 knots
High power: 225.62rpm; 21,266shp; 20.812 knots (mean figures of six runs).

and 'Y' turrets and fitted as in *Indomitable*. New SL platform added to forward superstructure, 36in lamps placed in position.

On outbreak of war anti-torpedo nets replaced while in home waters, although not carried in Mediterranean, and removed from *Inflexible* and *Invincible* before they left for South Atlantic in December 1914 shortly before the Battle of Falkland Islands. Topgallants removed in *Inflexible*, *Invincible* and *Indomitable* with anti-rangefinder spirals fitted to *Invincible*'s masts during the Falkland battle period. Funnel bands painted out. *Indomitable* painted in experimental two-tone camouflage while serving in the eastern Mediterranean in late 1914; painted out after her return in December 1914.

1915–16 Director control for main armament fitted in *Inflexible* and *Indomitable* (1915). 4in guns removed from turrets of *Inflexible* during her refit in Malta, March 1915. Remounted in forward superstructure as in other two. No 4in guns remaining on any of the turrets from this date. 3in AA gun added on platform on aft superstructure during mid-1915. AA armament later altered to 2 x 3in AA on platforms abeam second funnel. Uncertain if this modification was ever made to *Invincible*. Torpedo nets no longer carried.

Fore funnel of *Invincible* raised while under refit at Gibraltar in February 1915. (*Inflexible* 1911, *Indomitable* 1910). Extra upper wing added to bridge in *Indomitable*. Both topgallants and yards removed from foremast in *Inflexible*. Short signal struts fitted to starfish below fore control top in *Inflexible*.

Various types of camouflage used throughout this period: in the Dardanelles *Inflexible* had irregular white patches on hull sides with dark patches on funnels except for the second which was painted a very light colour. All three ships sported a dark rectangular panel along the hull while serving in North Sea during 1915, as did all the battlecruisers patrolling those waters. Panel was painted out during the early months of 1916.

1916–17 3in AA gun fitted abeam third funnel on small platform was removed and a 4in AA was substituted in its place, although not on old platform, a new platform being erected abeam the fore funnel on the centreline. After Jutland extra armour plating was worked into the surviving pair in the areas of the magazines and turret roofs, ammunition hoists also received some sort of addition, although not to a very grand scale and it is doubtful whether more than 100 tons were added.

1917–18 Fore control top enlarged. Range clock fitted to face of control top and at extremity of after superstructure. Deflection scales painted on 'A' and 'Y' turrets. Stern torpedo tube removed after April 1917. Six searchlights were removed from abeam fore funnel and from main tripod legs. Two were remounted on lower bridge and the other four were placed in new 'coffee-box' control towers abeam third funnel. An extra 36in lamp was fitted on platform low down at extremity of after superstructure. Two 24in signalling lamps added, one on each corner of fore funnel platform.

1917–18 Flying-off platforms for aircraft fitted over 'P' and 'Q' turrets. Splinter shields fitted to remaining 4in guns in both

Below: *Invincible* moves through the long line of warships assembled for the Fleet Review at Spithead July 1909.

Below: *Invincible* arrived in Gibraltar on 15 January 1915 and stayed for about five weeks, receiving a minor refit and the addition of her fore funnel extension (shown here being lifted into place).

Bottom: 'Invincible' (ex-*Patrician*) leaving Harland & Wolff's yard, Belfast on 17 February 1915. In an endeavour to mislead the enemy as to strength and positions of the Grand Fleet, squadrons of merchantmen were disguised as capital ships. Apart from the cutaway hull, this conversion of *Patrician* was remarkably convincing.

groups. Large platform added low on fore tripod legs, close above bridge in *Inflexible*. Topping davits removed. Fore topmast removed. Signal struts fitted to starfish below fore control top in *Indomitable*, and earlier struts fitted to *Inflexible* were considerably lengthened.

1918 High-angle rangefinder added to fore control top.

History: *Invincible*

Built under 1905–06 Estimates. Left builder's yard for finishing touches at Pelaw prior to trials in September 1908. Completion of trials in March 1909. Placed in Nore Reserve during trials at end of 1908, and commissioned at Portsmouth 20 March 1909 for service with 1st CS in 1st Division Home Fleet. Present for delegates of the Imperial Press Conference Review at Spithead in June 1909. Took part in the annual manoeuvres in June and July of that year.

1909 *17–24 July* Present at visit to Southend by Home and Atlantic Fleets.

31 July Present at Royal Review of Home and Atlantic Fleets at Spithead.

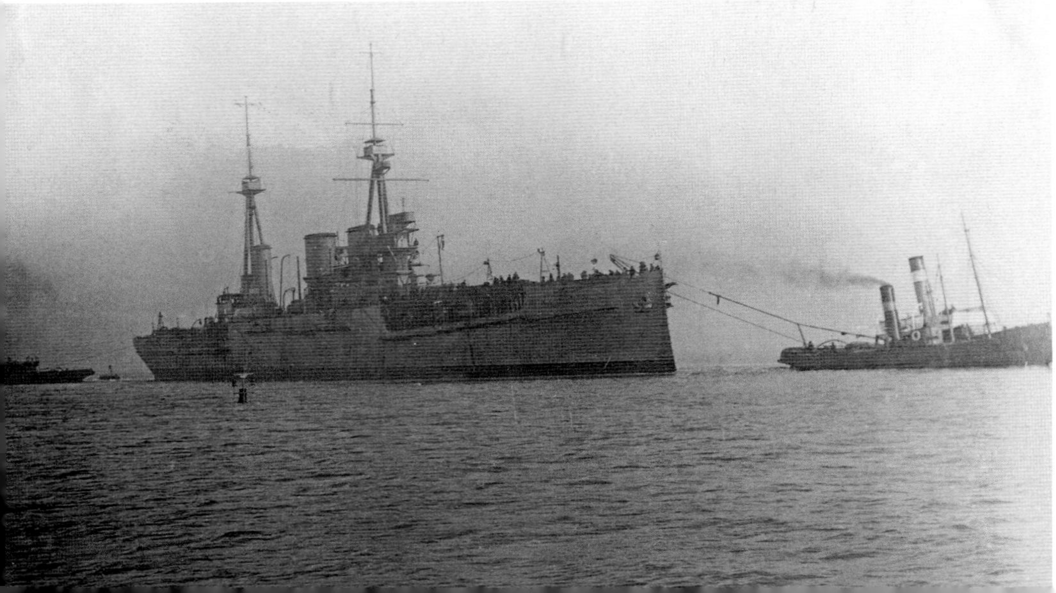

1910 *April* Took part in exercises with Home and Atlantic Fleets in Scottish waters.

July Annual manoeuvres including a visit to Torbay with Home and Atlantic Fleets, and part of Mediterranean Fleet.

1911 *Jan* Combined exercises off the NW coast of Spain with all three fleets.

16 May Recommissioned for service in 1st CS. Visited Dublin with 1st and 2nd Divisions of Home Fleet.

24 June Present at Coronation of King George V Review at Spithead.

June–July Annual manoeuvres in the Channel and North Sea.

1912 *9 July* Took part in Parliamentary Review at Spithead.

July Annual manoeuvres and visited Torbay.

Autumn Cruise to Norway and Denmark.

1913 *July* Annual manoeuvres.

Aug Transferred to Mediterranean Squadron on conclusion of manoeuvres. 2nd BCS formed (Mediterranean).

Nov Combined exercises with part of Home Fleet.

1914 *March* Paid off at Portsmouth for extensive refit and changes to her gun mountings involving removal of electrical gear and substitution of hydraulic equipment.

6 Aug Completed refit and sailed for Queenstown on commerce protection duties.

19 Aug Ordered from Queenstown to the Humber as flagship of newly formed 2nd BCS (with *New Zealand*).

28 Aug Battle of Heligoland Bight. With *New Zealand* she was supporting the Harwich Light Forces when the battlecruisers were ordered in from the west to cover a withdrawal. At 11.30 they were unsuccessfully attacked by a U-boat which passed astern. At 12.10 the British destroyers and *Fearless* were sighted retiring westwards hotly engaged with enemy light cruisers. *Invincible* engaged the German cruiser *Köln* and eventually sunk her at 13.25. A general retirement to the west was ordered and action was closed.

31 Aug *New Zealand* and *Invincible* ordered to the Forth.

2 Sept At 22.30 general alarm caused by *U21* penetrating the harbour defences. No action evident.

10–11 Sept With the Grand Fleet in a sweep into Heligoland Bight, after which she was sent into Scapa to coal.

Mid Sept Transferred to 1st BCS Grand Fleet and based at Rosyth.

14–17 Sept With *Inflexible* and 3rd BS supporting cruiser sweeps in North Sea.

End Sept With *Inflexible* patrolled North Sea and in particular the Faroe Islands. Rejoined 1st BCS at sea on 29 September.

Start Oct Transferred to 2nd BCS Grand Fleet on its reorganization.

3–10 Oct Patrolling off Shetland Islands during the crossing of the First Canadian Contingent.

4 Nov Detached with *Inflexible* as a special squadron for operations against Count Von Spee. *Invincible* was to be flagship and they were both ordered to Devonport to prepare for this service. This move was made only six hours after receiving news of the Royal Navy's disaster at the Coronel Islands on 1 November.

5 Nov Hauled down flag of 2nd BCS at midday, being relieved by *New Zealand*. Left Cromarty at midnight and proceeded to Devonport via west coast of Ireland.

8 Nov Reached Devonport and was found to require docking and repairs which could not be completed before 13 November. The Admiralty gave orders that the ships must sail by 11 November and workmen would have to remain aboard if necessary.

11 Nov Work completed and both ships left for Falkland Islands at 16.45.

18–19 Nov Coaled at St Vincent, Cape Verde Islands.

26 Nov Reached Abrolhos Rocks base and joined the squadron already concentrated there under Admiral Stoddart.

28 Nov In company with cruisers *Cornwall*, *Kent*, *Carvarvon*,

Bristol and *Glasgow*, the two battlecruisers left Abrolhos Rocks for the Falklands.
1 Dec Squadron diverted on receipt of distress call from merchantman which eventually proved groundless.
7 Dec At 10.30 reached Port William in the Falkland Islands.
8 Dec Battle of the Falkland Islands. At 04.00 *Invincible* commenced coaling. At 07.50 enemy ships were reported in sight by the signal station on the Islands. General chase ordered at 10.20.

At 10.50 ordered to ease speed to 24 knots so as to reduce smoke. Speed reduced again at 11.10 to allow cruisers to catch up with battlecruisers. At 12.20 speed again increased and at 12.58 *Invincible* opened fire on the German cruiser *Leipzig* at a distance of 16,000 yards. At 13.20 enemy light cruisers broke away to SW, followed immediately by *Kent*, *Cornwall* and *Glasgow*. At 13.02 *Invincible* opened fire on German flagship *Scharnhorst*. At 13.25 *Scharnhorst* and *Gneisenau* opened fire on British battlecruisers. 13.45 *Invincible* struck by 8.2in shells whereupon she turned two points to starboard to increase the range. *Scharnhorst*'s fire broken off at 14.10 as range increased. At 14.48 *Invincible* reopened fire on *Scharnhorst*, altering fire to *Gneisenau* at 15.15 for approximately five minutes. At 16.10 *Scharnhorst* rolled over and sank seven minutes later. *Gneisenau*, her fore funnel shot away and her general condition bad, suddenly turned towards the British ships and stopped, with a heavy list to starboard, although not before she had hit *Invincible* once more. At 18.02 *Gneisenau* turned turtle and sank. *Invincible* picked up seven officers and 24 men. Throughout the action, *Invincible* had drawn most of the enemy's fire and had received 22 hits, including two below the waterline, but sustained no casualties and no serious damage.
8–10 Dec In company with *Inflexible*, searched for the escaped cruisers *Nürnburg* and *Dresden* in the Cape Horn area.
11 Dec Returned to Port William.
16 Dec Left Falkland Islands for home, returning independently.
20 Dec Visited Montevideo.
26–31 Dec Called at Pernambuco.
1915 *Jan* Coaled at St Vincent. On arriving in Gibraltar *Invincible* hauled down flag of Admiral Sturdee and began a five-week refit, during which her fore funnel was lengthened, the last in the class to have this feature. In the latter part of Feb 1915, *Invincible* arrived at Scapa Flow and commenced gunnery trials and practice. Transferred to 3rd BCS as flagship.
1916 *Early March* Based at Rosyth having joined 3rd BCS.
April Under refit on River Tyne, having some of her 12in guns replaced.
26 May Hoisted Flag of Rear-Admiral the Hon. Horace Hood, GB.
May 3rd BCS, temporarily transferred to Scapa Flow for gunnery practice.
30 May Left Scapa with Grand Fleet for a sweep into the Skaggerak. 'Battle of Jutland'.
31 May At 14.30 3rd BCS increased speed, screened by *Chester*, *Canterbury*, *Shark*, *Acasta*, *Ophelia* and *Christopher* all of which were scouting some 21 miles ahead of the main battlefleet. At 15.30 again increased speed to reinforce Sir David Beatty in *Lion* of 1st BCS. The weather had now become misty. At 17.40, having steered a slightly too easterly course, heard firing to the NW and altered course to investigate. At 17.46 sighted the *Chester* which was retiring on the 3rd BCS and hotly engaged with the enemy light cruisers believed to be *Frankfurt*, *Weisbaden*, *Pillau* and *Elbing*. At 17.50 *Invincible* with *Inflexible* opened fire on *Weisbaden* and *Pillau*, badly damaging both. At 18.10 enemy launched a torpedo attack to cover retreat and *Invincible* was forced to turn to starboard to avoid it. At 18.20 she sighted 1st and 2nd BCS to port steering north. *Invincible* swung into line ahead of them on an ESE course. At 18.30 she engaged the German battlecruisers *Derfflinger* and *Lützow* inflicting serious damage on both of them. At approximately 18.33 she was hit in 'Q' turret but apparently not badly damaged. She was hitting the enemy vessels very hard, but had now come under the fire of more than one ship, some of which were the van of the German High Seas Fleet. The strikes on and around 'Q' turret reached her propellant charges which in turn reached her amidships magazines. The ship blew up with a tremendous explosion, flames rising about 400 feet, and when the smoke had cleared about twenty minutes later, both bow and stern were visibly projecting bottom up from the water, the smashed amidships section apparently resting on the bottom. She vanished during the night, time uncertain. 61 officers and 965 men (including five civilians) were lost, only six survivors being picked up by *Badger*.

History: *Inflexible*

Built under the 1905–6 Estimates. Began steam trials 20 June 1908. Completed trials in October of that year.

1908 *20 Oct* Commissioned at Chatham to relieve *Jupiter* in Nore Division of Home Fleet. At end of 1908 cruised in Mediterranean.
1909 *March* Transferred to 1st CS (later 5th CS) Home Fleet on its transformation.
June Took part in Imperial Press Conference Review.
6–7 July Annual manoeuvres with the combined fleets.
17–24 July Visited Southend with units of Home and Atlantic Fleets.
31 July Present at Royal Review of Home and Atlantic Fleets at Spithead.
Sept With Special Squadron which represented Great Britain at the Hudson-Fulton celebrations at New York, she flew the flag of Admiral of the Fleet, Sir Edward Seymour.
16 Sept Left for New York.
24 Sept Reached Sandy Hook.
9 Oct Left New York for return voyage.
19 Oct Returned to Portsmouth.
1910 *April* Exercises in Scottish waters with Home and Atlantic Fleets.
July Annual manoeuvres with Atlantic, Home and Mediterranean Fleets, and visited Torbay.
1911 *Jan* Combined exercises off the NW coast of Spain with the above fleets.
Spring With 2nd Division Home Fleet in Dublin Bay for State Visit of the King and Queen.

Below: *Inflexible* in the Dardanelles early 1915, wearing a one-off three-tone camouflage scheme.

Above: Bow-on view of *Inflexible* after running into a mine in Eren Keui Bay on 18 March 1915. Listing to port and receiving assistance from auxiliary vessels. She was later taken in tow by *Canopus* (see History: *Inflexible*).

Right: *Inflexible* showing damage received during the Dardanelles campaign whilst bombarding Hamidieh (fort 16) and Namazieh (fort 17) on 18 March 1915.

26 May Collided with *Bellerophon* at Portland, sustained slight damage to bows.
24 June Present at Coronation Review at Spithead.
June–July Annual manoeuvres off SW coast and in North Sea.
18 Nov Temporarily relieved *Indomitable* as flagship 1st CS Home Fleet during latter's refit.
1912 *8 May* Relieved as flagship and became a private ship again.
9 July Took part in Parliamentary Review followed by more manoeuvres and visit to Torbay.
Autumn Cruising, and visited Norway and Denmark.
Nov Transferred to Mediterranean Squadron as flagship of the C in C, replacing *Good Hope*.
5 Nov Commissioned for this service at Chatham.
1913 2nd BCS Mediterranean Squadron was formed.
19 July Visited Piraeus.
Nov Combined exercises in Mediterranean with part of Home Fleet.
1914 *July* Visited Constantinople.
27 July At Alexandria with *Indefatigable*, *Warrior*, *Black Prince*, *Chatham*, *Dublin*, *Weymouth*, *Gloucester* and fourteen destroyers.
3 Aug Left Malta.
5 Aug Concentrated off Pantellaria with *Indomitable* and *Indefatigable*.
6 Aug Patrolling off Pantellaria with *Indomitable* and *Indefatigable*.
7 Aug Reached Malta at 12.00 to coal.
8 Aug With *Indomitable*, *Indefatigable* and *Weymouth*, left Malta at 00.30 to search for the German *Goeben* and *Breslau*.
10 Aug At 04.00 the Squadron rounded Cape Malea.
10–11 Aug Searching the Aegean Islands.
18 Aug Left Malta for home.
Late Aug Joined 2nd BCS Grand Fleet at Rosyth.
10–11 Sept With Grand Fleet in a sweep to the Heligoland Bight, then, with *Invincible*, to the North.
14–17 Sept With 3rd BS and *Invincible*, covering cruiser sweeps in North Sea.
Late Sept With *Invincible* cruising north of Faroe Islands, rejoined 1st BCS at sea on 29th.
2 Oct Left Scapa Flow.
2–10 Oct With *Invincible*, *Sappho* and three minelayers on patrol between Shetlands and Faroes during the crossing of the Canadian Contingent.
18–25 Oct With *Invincible* covering unsuccessful air raid on Zeppelin sheds at Cuxhaven.
5–6 Nov With *Invincible*, left Cromarty for Devonport at midnight and proceeded west around Ireland.
8–11 Nov At Devonport fitting out for detached service.
11 Nov Sailed for Falkland Islands. At Battle of the Falklands 8 December 1914 (see *Invincible*). Sustained no damage during the battle and was able to pick up 10 officers and 52 men from *Gneisenau* after that vessel sank. *Inflexible* had one man killed and two slightly wounded.
13 Dec With *Glasgow*, left Port Stanley at 08.30 to investigate rumours that *Dresden* was at Punta Arenas.
17 Dec Passed into Pacific and met *Bristol* and *Glasgow* in Gulf of Penas where she received orders to return home immediately. Left for Port Stanley.
Late Dec/Jan 1915 Refitting at Gibraltar.
1915 *24 Jan* Reached Dardanelles to replace *Indefatigable* as flagship of British Dardanelles Squadron, intending to engage *Goeben* should she come out. The flag was transferred at Skyros.
Feb At Mudros. She was to have returned home when *Agamemnon* had arrived, but accident to *Queen Elizabeth* prevented this.
19 Feb First bombardment of Dardanelles outer forts. The pre-dreadnoughts *Albion*, *Cornwallis* (flag) and *Triumph*, plus the cruiser *Amethyst* and the French battleships *Bouvet*, *Suffren* and *Gaulois* began their bombardment at 09.51. *Inflexible* bombarded Fort Sedd el Bahr and closed to short range at 15.00. At 17.50 she engaged Fort Orkanieh and assisted *Vengeance*. At 17.50 ceasefire was called.
20–24 Feb At Tenados during a gale.
25 Feb Second bombardment of outer forts. She was stationed about 11,000 yards NW of Cape Helles and spotting for *Queen Elizabeth* whose 15in guns did considerable damage to the forts. *Agamemnon* also in this action.
4 March Supported bombardment of Forts Dardance and Messaudieh and covered Marines landed to destroy the forts at Helles and Orkanieh.

Left: *Inflexible* showing final wartime additions and alterations: new and heavy bridgework, enlarged foretop and director control, 4in guns in casemates, 'coffee-box SL towers around base of mainmast tripod, AA gun behind first funnel, runways on midships 12in turrets with an aircraft on each.

5 March With *Prince George* supported *Queen Elizabeth* in bombarding Rumili Medjidieh and Namazgieh at long range, from the Gulf of Saros. At 14.40 with *Prince George* silenced a battery of field guns which were hitting *Queen Elizabeth.*

11 March Left for Malta to change her two 'A' turret guns which had become worn.

17 March Back to Dardanelles.

18 March Left for Tenados at 08.30. At 11.30 joined by *Queen Elizabeth, Agamemnon* and *Lord Nelson,* to bombard Hamidieh (Fort 16) and Namazieh (Fort 17) from range of 14,000 yards. *Inflexible* came under heavy fire from Eren Keui, but knocked out two of the Hamidieh heavy guns. At 12.20 hit on foremast and bridge and set on fire, being hit seven times by 12.23. At 13.25 withdrew from line to extinguish fire and attend to wounded. At 14.36 she was again in action and became heavily engaged with the gunfire from the forts. At 15.45 she was hit again, but not seriously. At about 16.10 struck a mine on the starboard bow while turning in Eren Keui Bay. Forward torpedo flat was flooded and 39 men drowned. At 18.00 reached Tenados and beached in shallows, having shipped approx 2,000 tons of seawater. A cofferdam was quickly fitted over the hole which measured some 30 feet by 26 feet.

6 April Left Mudros for Malta, escorted by the old pre-dreadnought *Canopus* and the cruiser *Talbot.*

10 April Reached Malta, having nearly foundered in heavy weather when the cofferdam worked loose. Towed stern first for six hours by *Canopus,* until Malta was finally reached.

9 June At Gibraltar.

19 June Returned home and joined 3rd BCS Grand Fleet.

1916 *May* 3rd BCS transferred to Scapa Flow for gunnery practice.

30 May Left Scapa with Grand Fleet for a sweep to the Skaggerak.

31 May Battle of Jutland. See *Invincible.* After *Invincible* sank, *Inflexible* led the battlecruiser line until 18.54 when, during a lull 3rd BCS was ordered to reduce speed to 18 knots and take up line astern of *New Zealand.* At 19.14, the battlecruisers were again in action at a distance of 15,000 yards. A torpedo attack to cover enemy withdrawal was repelled at 19.25. *Inflexible* was heavily engaged throughout action but sustained neither damage nor casualties.

5 June 3rd BCS dissolved and *Inflexible* transferred to 2nd BCS on fleet reorganization.

19 Aug At 19.50 off Blythe passage, two torpedoes fired by *U65* passed astern and caused no damage.

1918 *31 Jan* At about 18.00 while leaving the Forth with the fleet, collided with *K 14,* striking her a glancing blow, after that submarine had collided with *K 22.* ('Battle of May Island' disaster to 13th Submarine Squadron.)

22 April 2nd BCS and 7th LCS covered passage of Scandinavia convoy from Methil. 2nd CS and battle ships *Hercules* and *Agincourt* were ordered from Scapa to reinforce the escort, as strong enemy forces were reported in the area.

21 Nov With 2nd BCS present at surrender of German High Seas Fleet off the Forth.

1919 *March* Became flagship of Nore Reserve Fleet after abolition of Grand Fleet.

July Earmarked for disposal.

1920 *31 March* Paid off into the disposal list from Nore Reserve. From April 1921 she was prepared for sale at Chatham, and then laid up at Sheerness.

1921 *End June* Taken from Sheerness to Devonport, having been selected for part of the training establishment '*Impregnable*', but because of the high cost of converting her, the project was abandoned and she reverted to the Disposal list at Devonport.

1 Dec Sold to Stanlee Shipbreaking Co. of Dover.

1922 *8 April* Left Devonport for Dover in tow of Dutch tugs *Zwartzee* and *Wittezee.*

April Resold and towed to Germany where she was broken up.

History: *Indomitable*

Built under the 1905–6 Programme, being ordered on 21 November 1905.

1908 *8 April* Began sea trials.

20 June Commissioned at Portsmouth for special detached service to convey HRH Prince George to Canada.

15 July Left Portsmouth for Quebec, escorted by *Minotaur.*

29 July Left Quebec.

3 Aug Reached Cowes, Isle of Wight, having broken *Drake*'s speed record of three years ago.

Autumn Joined Nore Reserve.

1909 *March* Transferred to 1st CS Home Fleet on its organization.

June Present at Imperial Press Conference Review at Spithead.

Below: *Indomitable* leading *Inflexible* during sweeps in the North Sea, 1918.

June–July Took part in combined manoeuvres.
17–24 July Visited Southend with units of Home and Atlantic Fleets.
26 July Relieved *Drake* as flagship 1st CS Home Fleet.
31 July Took part in Royal Review Home and Atlantic Fleets at Spithead.
1910 *April* Exercises off the coast of Scotland with Home and Atlantic Fleets.
July Combined manoeuvres with Atlantic, Home and Mediterranean Fleets, and visited Torbay.
9 Aug Recommissioned at Chatham for service as flagship of 1st CS Home Fleet.
1911 *Jan* Combined exercises with Atlantic and Mediterranean Fleets off NW coast of Spain.
Spring State Visit to Dublin with 1st and 2nd Divisions. Further visits included Aberystwyth, for the investiture of HRH the Prince of Wales at Caernarvon.
24 June Coronation Review of King George V at Spithead.
June–July Annual manoeuvres off SW coast and in North Sea.
Nov Reduced to nucleus crew for refit.
Nov–Feb 1912 Under refit, being relieved of flag by *Inflexible*.
1912 *21 Feb* Recommissioned for service as flagship 2nd CS Home Fleet, relieving *Shannon*.
9 July Parliamentary Review of Home Fleet at Spithead.
Autumn Cruising in Baltic.
11 Dec Temporarily transferred to 1st BCS Home Fleet, having been relieved by *Shannon* as flagship of 2nd CS.
1913 *17 March* In collision with minelayer *C4*, in Stokes Bay, sustaining slight damage to bows.
During 1912/13, it was decided to withdraw all battleships from the Mediterranean, replacing them with a powerful cruiser squadron consisting of: *Indomitable*, *Inflexible*, *Invincible*, *Indefatigable*, *Defence*, *Black Prince*, *Warrior* and *Duke of Edinburgh*. There was to be a light cruiser squadron, and a flotilla of destroyers also.
July Annual manoeuvres.
27 Aug Transferred to 2nd BCS Mediterranean Squadron; her position in 1st BCS was taken by *New Zealand*.
Nov Annual manoeuvres in Mediterranean with units of Home Fleet and 3rd CS.
1914 *10 Feb* Recommissioned at Sheerness for service with 2nd BCS Mediterranean Squadron.
24 July Docked in Malta for annual refit which was cancelled abruptly on 30th.
2 Aug Ordered to sea. Sailed at 21.00 with *Indefatigable*, *Defence*, *Duke of Edinburgh*, *Warrior*, *Gloucester* and eight destroyers to patrol entrance to the Adriatic.
3 Aug At 15.15 detached, with *Indefatigable*, to search for *Goeben* and *Breslau* between Cape Bon and Cape Spartivento. At 20.00 they were ordered to proceed immediately to Straits of Gibraltar to prevent enemy breaking out of the Mediterranean.
4 Aug At 10.35, 50 miles west of Galita Island, *Breslau* was spotted first, then *Goeben*, both returning from bombardment of Phillipville and Bona. *Indomitable* and *Indefatigable* turned and followed at a distance. From 14.30 to 19.00 shadowed enemy vessels, later joined by *Dublin*. Just after 19.00, the British force lost contact with the enemy, and were later ordered to turn west.
5 Aug Concentrated off Pantellaria with *Inflexible* and *Indefatigable*, and afterwards detached to Bizerta to coal.
6 Aug At 19.00 left Bizerta to rendezvous with flagship west of Milazzo.
7 Aug Reached Malta at 14.00.
8 Aug At 00.30 left Malta with *Inflexible*, *Indefatigable* and *Weymouth* for Cape Matapan, having stayed at Malta while the other ships coaled.
10 Aug With Squadron, rounded Cape Malea, Greece.
10–11 Aug Searching for *Goeben* and *Breslau*.
11–19 Aug Searching Aegean Islands for German ships and watching entrance to Dardanelles.
19 Aug Ordered to Gibraltar.
20 Sept In Dardanelles blocking squadron.
3 Nov Preliminary bombardment of Dardanelles outer forts at dawn to ascertain range of Turkish heavy guns. With *Indefatigable*, bombarded Fort Sedd el Bahr, while French battleships *Suffren* and *Vérité* engaged Kum Kale and Fort Orkameh. The magazines at Sedd el Bahr were seen to blow up.
Nov Returned home.
23 Dec Ordered to rendezvous with Grand Fleet between Scotland and Norway.
26 Dec Joined 1st BCS at sea in a gale, and was nearly fired upon by *New Zealand*, who failed to recognize *Indomitable*'s 'dazzle' camouflage and topmasts still in position. Until 14 January 1915, undergoing refit.
1915 Joined 2nd BCS which had been reformed. *New Zealand* was flagship.
24 Jan Battle of Dogger Bank.
Enemy sighted at 07.30, steering SE, 14 miles off port bow. General chase ordered, *Indomitable* worked up to her maximum speed. At approximately 10.45, *Indomitable* came into action with Panzerschiffe *Blücher* which was later sunk. At 15.38 ordered to take *Lion* in tow, underway by 17.00. Towed *Lion* to the Forth escorted by sixty destroyers. Dropped anchor just below the bridge, at 02.45 on 26th, and took *Lion* up to her moorings at midday.
Jan–Feb Repairing and refitting after a fire caused by a defective electrical circuit.
11 March Unsuccessfully attacked by U-boat en route from Scapa Flow to Rosyth.
1916 *May* 3rd BCS transferred to Scapa for gunnery practice.
31 May Battle of Jutland (see other two ships for details). No damage to ship, although heavily engaged with enemy.
1 June Left the area with units of 3rd LCS, and en route engaged a Zeppelin which had been following part of the fleet.
5 June Transferred to 2nd BCS on cruiser reorganization.
Aug Under refit.
1918 *22 April* With 2nd BCS and 7th LCS covering the Scandinavia Convoy of 39 vessels.
23 April Covering outward bound convoy from Methil.
21 Nov With 2nd BCS, was present at surrender of German High Seas Fleet.
1919 *March* Placed in Nore Reserve.
July Earmarked for disposal.
1920 *31 March* Paid off onto disposal list.
7 April Placed on sale list.
1921 *1 Dec* Sold to Stanlee Shipbreaking Co., Dover.
1922 *30 Aug* Towed to Dover to be broken up.
1923 *April* Under cutter's torch.

Below: *Inflexible* enters her home port after the war.

Bellerophon Class: 1906 ESTIMATES

Design

The construction Programme for the 1906 Estimates had initially been for four new dreadnought-type battleships, but reluctance on the part of the Board of Control reduced it to three. This state of affairs had been reached after much debate on the subject of naval armament limitation, and the decision to build only three ships stemmed from the policy of 'treading softly' by politically conscious Members of the Admiralty. It was generally held that, although the appearance of *Dreadnought* would probably provoke an arms race by the major Powers, it would not necessarily begin immediately. News of the cutback was most unwelcome, both in the private and public sectors, but the ensuing outcry failed to evoke any suitable explanation from the DNC, at least not to any satisfactory degree.

Although *Dreadnought* was now nearing completion, it was still a period of great anxiety among those responsible for her design and construction who felt that no further capital-ship construction should proceed until *Dreadnought*'s trials results were available, although it was considered safe to put forward sketch designs for the next building programme, towards the end of 1905. One point upon which all agreed was that *Dreadnought* would undoubtedly place Great Britain in the lead with regard to this kind of construction and there seemed little reason why that lead should not be maintained.

On 2 December 1905 a sketch design was proposed, showing details of a 'super' dreadnought type whose immense proportions greatly surpassed those of *Dreadnought* herself. Designated 'X4', the design carried the same main armament as *Dreadnought* and was much better protected yet considerably faster. A return to an adequate secondary armament was proposed, this to be in addition to the same number of 12pdrs as fitted in *Dreadnought* in her legend design. Examination of 'X4' shows it to be a remarkably advanced design, closely resembling the *Colossus* class of the 1909 Programme. Sadly, Their Lordships could not see this and the design was shelved as being far too ambitious.

BELLEROPHON: LAUNCH FIGURES, 27 JULY 1907

	tons
Displacement:	6,284
Equipment:	150
Recorded weight of hull:	6,132

Actual beam: 82ft 4¾in

Breakage at launch:

longitudinal in a distance of 415ft = 1¼in hog

transverse in a distance of 77ft 6in = 0⅛in sag

Temeraire displacement 7,420 tons; recorded beam 82ft 4⅜in

Superb displacement 8,808 tons; recorded beam 82ft 5⅞in.

Above: *Bellerophon.* The first of the dreadnought programmes takes shape with the launching of *Bellerophon* on 27 July 1907.

Left: *Temeraire* fitting out during 1908 (Devonport) Note that 'A' and midships 12in guns and turrets are not yet in place.

Opposite, top: *Bellerophon* on manoeuvres with the Home and Atlantic Fleets in 1910 (*Majestic*-class pre-dreadnoughts in background).

Opposite, bottom: *Temeraire* shortly after completion.

Further calculations were made during the last weeks of 1905 and the early days of 1906, and further drawings were submitted. The basic requirements called for an 'improved *Dreadnought*', and took into account the fact that the results of *Dreadnought*'s trials might result in minor modifications to the new ships. After a great degree of manipulation, the DNC, Philip Watts, managed to provide a suitable design. Displacement was 700 tons greater than that of *Dreadnought*, but the machinery installation was to remain the same; this, as was expected, would mean a fall off in speed, but with the great improvements then taking place in marine engineering, it was not expected to be large. An innovation in the final design was that it sported a very powerful secondary armament, probably as a result of seeing the figures for the 'X4' layout, and although this feature was one upon which Lord Fisher frowned, he was outvoted; foreign vessels were being armed with similar, powerful secondary batteries (see armament notes). The new ships were planned at a legend displacement of 19,018 tons, 17,902 tons light, and 22,270 tons in the deep condition.

Armament

Twenty-five alternative sketches were submitted for the armament layout, all of which showed considerable variation in number and location of guns. They had been prepared while *Dreadnought* was under construction, but on that ship's completion of a series of successful trials, it was decided to retain the basic armament layout as before. Fire-control arrangements had to be modified to some extent, partly because of the placement of the foremast before instead of abaft the fore funnel, but also because of the provision

BELLEROPHON CLASS: PARTICULARS, AS COMPLETED

Construction

	Dockyard	Laid Down	Launched	Completed
Bellerophon:	Portsmouth DY	3 Dec 1906	27 July 1907	20 Feb 1909
Temeraire:	Devonport DY	1 Jan 1907	24 Aug 1907	15 May 1909
Superb:	Armstrong	6 Feb 1907	7 Nov 1907	9 June 1909.

Displacement (tons)
Bellerophon: 18,596 (load), 22,540 (deep)
Temeraire: 18,596 (load), 22,359 (deep)
Superb: 18,596 (load), 22,211 (deep).

Dimensions
Length: 490ft pp, 522ft wl, 526ft oa
Beam: 82ft 6in (deck: 77ft)
Draught: *Bellerophon* 31ft 4⅜in (deep); *Temeraire* 31ft 1⅞in (deep); *Superb* 30ft 11⅞in (deep)
Freeboard (load): 28ft forward, 17ft 3½in amidships, 18ft aft
Height of 12in guns above water-line (load): 'A' turret 31ft 6in; 'Q' and 'X' 22ft 6in; 'Y' 23ft
Height of CT vision slits above lower wl: 42ft 9in
Height of fore funnel above lower wl: 67ft
Height of lower masthead above lower wl: 100ft
Depth of keel from upper deck: 52ft.

Armament
Ten 12in 45cal Mk X; Mk VIII mountings; 80rpg*
Sixteen 4in 45cal Mk III; 200rpg**
Four 3pdr
Two MG
Three 18in torpedo tubes (two beam, one stern); fourteen torpedoes.

Director control
None fitted on completion.

Armour***
Main belt: 10in–9in–8in–7in–5in
Bulkheads: 8in–4in
Barbettes: 10in–9in–5in
Turrets: 11in face, 12in rear, 3in roof
Conning tower: 11in side, 3in roof
After CT: 8in side, 3in roof
Decks: main 3in–1¼in–¾in, armoured 3in–2in–1½in–1½in, aft behind 'Y' barbette 4in–3in–1½in
Continuous bulkheads from 'A' to 'Y' barbettes (magazine screens) 3in–2in–1in

Machinery
Four sets Parsons direct-drive turbines, four propellers
Eighteen Babcock & Wilcox (*Temeraire* Yarrow) boilers, 235psi (working), each fitted with four single-orifice oil sprayers (960lb per boiler/hour)
Heating surface: 55,530sq ft
Length of boiler rooms: (1) 37ft 11⅝in, (2) 38ft 0½in, (3) 38ft
Length of engine rooms: 68ft 0⅞in
Fuel: 900 tons coal min., 2,648 tons max.; 840 tons oil
Coal consumption: 324 tons per 24 hours at 17–18 knots
SHP: 23,000 for 20–21 knots
Radius of action: 2,930nm at 18 knots (coal only); 3,970nm at 10 knots (129 tons coal per 24 hours); 4,230nm at 18 knots (oil fuel added); 5,720nm at 10 knots (oil fuel added).

Ship's boats
Pinnaces (steam): two 50ft
Pinnaces (sail): one 36ft
Launches: one 42ft
Cutters: two 32ft
Gigs: one 30ft
Whalers: three 37ft
Skiff dinghies: one 16ft
Balsa rafts: one 13ft 6in.

Searchlights
Ten 36in: two on bridge forward, four close together on forward superstructure, two on midships superstructure, two on after superstructure, one 24in signalling lamp below fore control top (not in *Superb*).

Rangefinder positions
One in each 12in turret
One each side of after boat deck.

Battle signal stations
One immediately abaft upper forward conning tower.

Anchors
Three 125cwt (bower and sheet) stockless, one 42cwt on boat deck.

Wireless
Mk II and Type 1 W/T; Type 9 short-radius W/T fitted in 1910.

Complement
Bellerophon: 680 (1909); 720 (1910)
Temeraire: 681 (1909); 729 (1911)
Superb: 840 (1914).

Cost

Machinery and armour:	£444,046
Hull:	£425,000
12in guns:	£12,586
Steam boats:	£6,460
Bellerophon:	£1,647,191 plus £116,300 guns
Temeraire:	£1,627,987 plus £116,300 guns
Superb:	£1,524,814 plus £116,300 guns.

*240 AP, 400 common, 160 Lyddite.
**One 4in AA and one 3in AA added later, see Appearance Changes.
***KC Decks over 3in non-cemented; under 3in, mild steel.

BELLEROPHON CLASS: TURNING TRIALS, 1908–9

Tactical diameter (at full speed):
Bellerophon: 445 yards; rudder put over in 8 seconds
Temeraire: 412 yards; rudder put over in 11¾ seconds
Superb: 405 yards; rudder put over in 10 seconds

Comparison with earlier battleships:
Agamemnon: 386 yards (17 knots)
King Edward VII: 438 yards (18 knots)
Duncan: 530 yards (18 knots)
Dreadnought: 408 yards (18.12 knots).

TEMERAIRE: GM AND STABILITY

Based on inclining experiments, 30 January 1909

	Displacement (tons)	Draught	GM	Maximum stability	Stability vanishes at
'A' Condition (= load)*	19,018	27ft 2in	4.8ft	35°	60°
'B' Condition (= deep)**	22,270	31ft 2¼in	6.45ft	–	–

*Fully equipped plus 360 tons coal upper, 540 tons lower bunkers, feedwater tanks empty.
**Fully equipped plus 2,648 tons coal, 840 tons oil, feedwater tanks full.

BELLEROPHON CLASS: SPEED TRIALS, 1908–9

Full sets of figures have not survived. The following figures are taken from available Ships' Covers. Seven months after completion, *Bellerophon 19 knots, Temeraire* 19.46 knots

Temeraire
Draught: 29ft 10in (mean)
Revolutions: 251rpm
SHP: 11,483
Speed: 16.3 knots
Temeraire, Oct 1909
Wind Force 3–6, Sea 4–5
Draught: 27ft
SHP: 24,558
Speed (max.): 21.005 knots

Measured mile figures (collective)
Bellerophon
2 Nov 1908
Revolutions: 327.9rpm; 335.6rpm
SHP: 25,061; 26,836
Speed (knots): 21.25; 21.64
Temeraire, 5 March 1909
Revolutions: 322rpm; 331rpm
SHP: 24,919; 26,966
Speed (knots): 21.05; 21.55
Superb, 2 April 1909
Revolutions: 324.8rpm; 332.9rpm
SHP: 25,373; 27,407
Speed (knots): 21.06; 21.56.

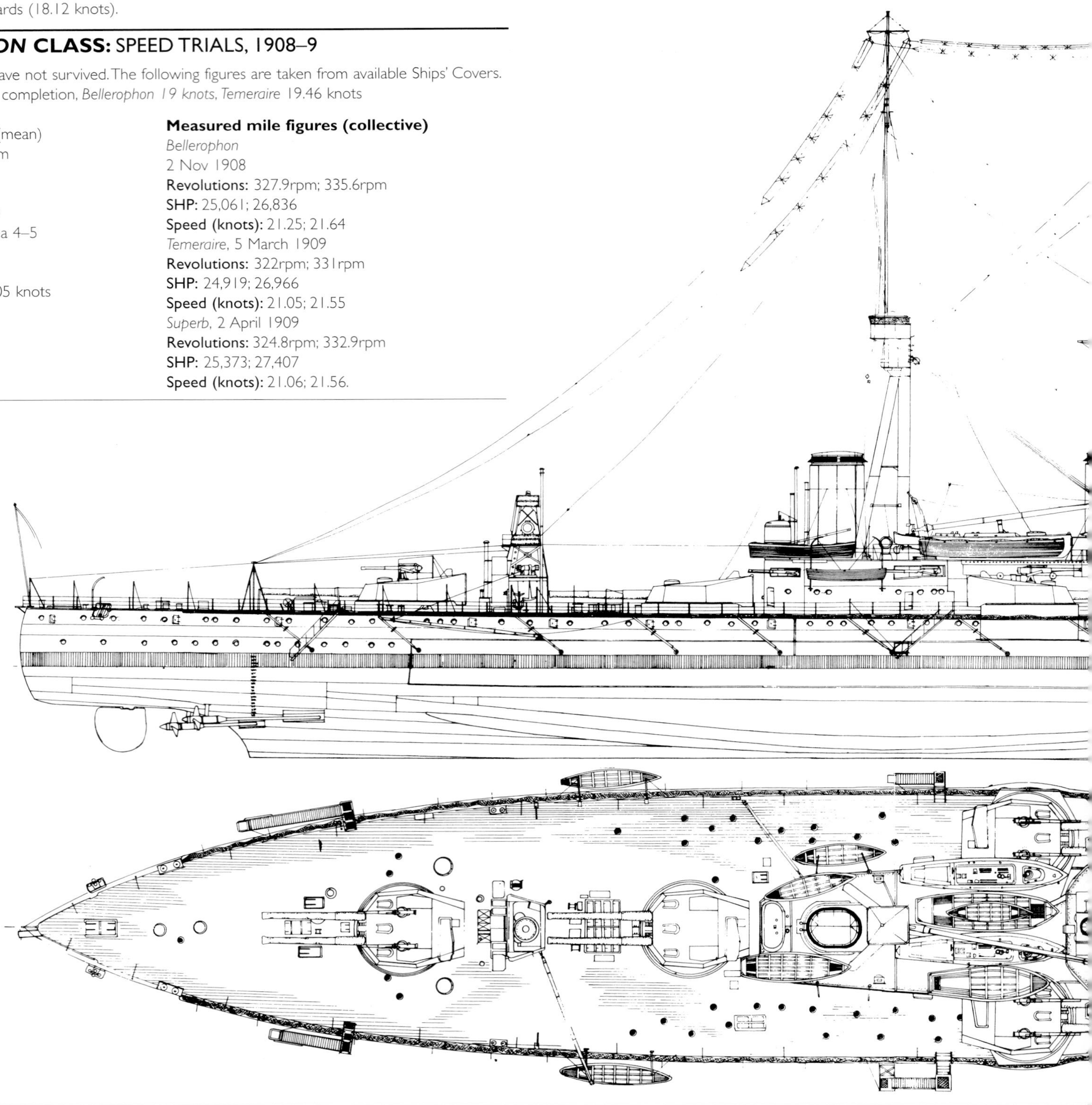

Right: On board *Superb* looking forward to 'X' 12in turret. Summer 1909.

Below, right: *Superb*, bow view as completed, 1909. Note the height from the forecastle to main deck level, rangefinder drums in lower foretop, crew washing out anchor hawsepipes, extremely tall tripods, 101 feet above the lower water-line.

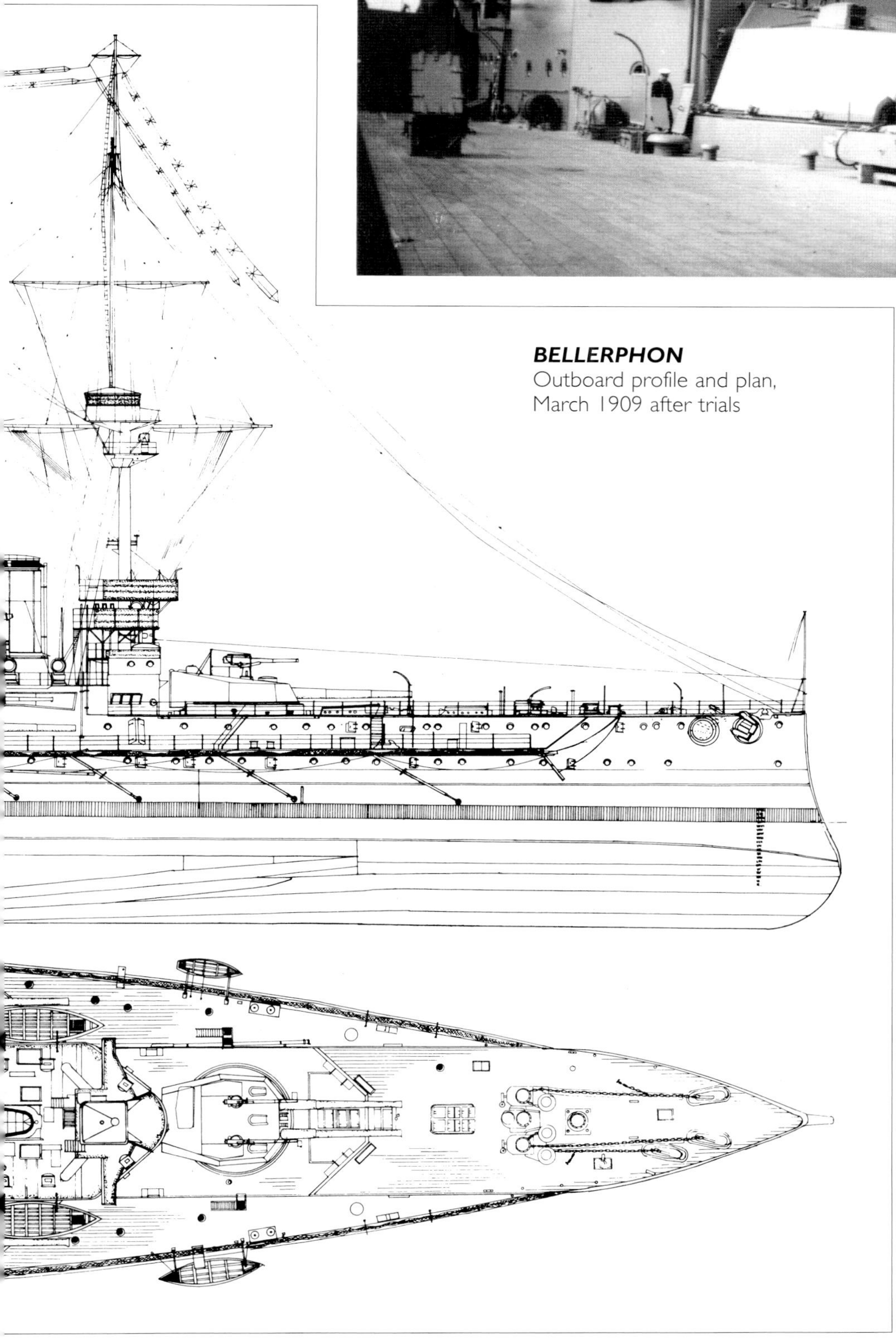

BELLERPHON
Outboard profile and plan, March 1909 after trials

Superb as commissioned for trials, early in 1909. A much more pleasing profile was presented by these ships than by *Dreadnought*. The twin tripods closely spaced, equal-sized and short funnels made for a symmetrical appearance.

of a full-height mainmast with the after control top being carried at the same height as that of the foremast. In the original design, *Bellerophon* was to have been fitted with the same rig as *Dreadnought*, but in order to eliminate smoke from the fore control top, it was decided to reverse the funnel-tripod arrangement, and make the tripod legs rake aft instead of forward as in *Dreadnought*. On completion, the fitting of the two tripods proved of limited value; the foremast and fore funnel arrangement was a distinct improvement, but the high after control top received fumes from the fore funnel to such an extent that at times the top was untenable.

The secondary armament was markedly superior to *Dreadnought*'s, a powerful battery of 4in guns being fitted in addition to the 12pdrs as fitted in *Dreadnought*, although the latter were numerically reduced. The new ships were the last to be designed with 12pdrs as anti-torpedo armament. After *Dreadnought* had been fitted with her 12pdrs, it was decided to conduct experiments to ascertain the power and capabilities of the weapon. It was realized that the small torpedo-boats were getting ever larger and that their potential threat to the big ship was most serious. Early in February 1906, shortly after *Dreadnought*'s launch, trials were held using a small vessel, HMS *Skate*, as the target. She was fired at from various distances by 4in guns and by 8cwt and 12cwt 12pdrs. The results were inevitable. As expected, the 4in was able to pierce the attacking vessel at all angles of shell descent, but the 12pdr failed for the most part, even though its rate of fire was much greater. The experiments were carried out fastidiously by a staff whose report showed definitely that the 12pdr was valueless. The 4in, on the other hand, would almost always destroy the attacker, whether from a direct or an indirect hit, and its effectiveness was increased when firing high-explosive shells. The 4in could also open fire long before the 12pdr, and before the craft could launch its torpedo.

A deciding factor in the fitting of a 4in battery in the new ships was that the French Navy was building torpedo-destroyers with at least 1in protective plating which would keep out a 12pdr shell at certain ranges. Furthermore, reports had reached the DNC that Germany also was preparing designs for such ships.

Further trials had been carried out in the old pre-dreadnoughts *Queen* and *Duncan* while they were serving in the Mediterranean, and the results were basically the same as those carried out with HMS *Skate*; it was generally agreed that although the 12pdr saturated the target, the effect was less than devastating. The 4in was said to be just as easy to train, and was definitely the better weapon for night shooting.

The 4in guns fitted in the *Bellerophon*s were so distributed as to give maximum arcs of fire, and special arrangements were made to secure better co-operation between guns and searchlights, including a control system of circuits connecting guns, rangefinders and searchlights. The torpedo armament was reduced in the new ships, the after pair of beam tubes being suppressed.

Armour

Several alternative armour schemes were considered and the one finally selected was considered adequate even though thickness had been reduced in some areas. For the first time consideration was given to the fitting of a complete underwater bulkhead specifically against torpedo attack, and the system was much more complete than that fitted in *Dreadnought*. The value of a continuous longitudinal bulkhead had been demonstrated during the Russo-Japanese War when units of the *Borodino* class showed remarkable resilience against torpedo damage.

The main protective belt was 10in thick and 7ft 6in deep. It extended from just ahead of the fore barbette to abeam the after barbette. The lower edge of the belt was 5ft 2in below the waterline at normal condition, but reduced in thickness to 8in. Abeam the forward barbette it reduced to 9in.

Forward of the main belt was a strake of 7in–6in. This was complete to the stem of the vessel, with 7in thickness for approximately 50 per cent of the run, then reduced to 6in. Aft, this run was 5in thick back to the stern, the upper edge being carried 3ft above the midships section. Above the 10in strake was a thickness of 8in (upper belt) which ran along the same length as the 10in plates; the top edge was 8ft 6in above the waterline at normal condition.

The main bulkhead (aft) was 8in and ran obliquely inwards from the after extremities of the lower side armour to the outer face of the after barbette. The barbettes were 9in–5in on the centreline; 9in above and 5in below the main deck, except for the outer face in the aft fitting which was 9in uniform thickness. The barbettes on the beam were 10in on the outer faces, 9in on the inner faces running down to the main deck; below the thickness reduced to 5in.

The turrets had 11in faces and sides, 12in on the rear and 3in roofs. That for the main deck was 1¼in between the 4th and 5th

Opposite, top: *Bellerophon* under way in Scapa Flow early 1916 (*Royal Oak* in background).

Opposite, bottom: *Temeraire* showing funnel bands and general appearance in August 1910.

Below: From the forecastle looking aft showing the compass platform and bridgework around the fore tripod of *Bellerophon*. 1909.

turrets, but reduced to ¾in elsewhere. The middle deck was 1¾in on the slope and flat, but increased to 3in at the after extremity around the after barbettes thus increasing protection for the magazines. The lower level, which was underwater, ranged from 2in–4in. Forward, it ran from the forward end of the middle deck to the stem; the inner extremity sloped steeply upwards from before the forward barbettes to meet the middle deck. There was a thickness of 4in on the slope; elsewhere the thickness was 1½in. Aft, the inner ends sloped steeply upwards from abaft the after barbette to meet the middle deck. The slope was 4in with 2in–3in plates on the rest of the runs.

The forward conning tower had 11in faces, 8in rear, 3in roof and a 2in floor. The communications tube was 5in. The signal tower, located abaft the forward conning tower, was 3in on the sides, 2in on the roof and 2in on the floors. The after conning tower, located close abaft the after funnel, had 8in faces and rear.

The anti-torpedo bulkheads, which ran longitudinally port and starboard, extended completely between the forward and after magazines, and brought in close to the centreline abreast the end magazines. The thickness ranged from 1in to 3in to 2in respectively abreast forward, beam and after magazines; 2in abreast midships centreline magazine and engine rooms, 1½in abreast boiler rooms.

Machinery

The machinery was a repeat of that installed in *Dreadnought*, but the ships were expected to be approximately half a knot slower because of increased beam and displacement. On entering service, however, they all proved to be excellent seaboats and easily equalled *Dreadnought*'s speed. The installation consisted of twin HP turbines and twin LP turbines. Each ship had four shafts. The two LP turbines had cruising turbines coupled to them, and the astern turbine consisted of a separate HP casing on the HP ahead shaft.

As in *Dreadnought*, the ships were fitted with a separate HP cruising turbine, but it proved less effective than had been expected; consumption was high and the machinery was troublesome. On 6 November 1907, while cruising, *Dreadnought*'s port cruising turbine was opened up and the blades of the second and third expansions were found to be badly stripped as a result of a slight distortion of the cylinder. Furthermore, after completion both *Dreadnought* and *Bellerophon* had trouble with cracked case covers on their cruising turbines. This led to their being disconnected, but the Admiralty did not abandon the idea of cruising turbines, and they were fitted in battleships up until the design of *Neptune* (1908).

Appearance Changes

The outstanding characteristic of these ships and the succeeding *St Vincent* class, was the unusual arrangement of the main mast close before the second funnel; the masts were more closely spaced than usual, with the mainmast exactly amidships. The raised searchlight platform over the after superstructure, with the high compass platform above this, and the long derricks, placed vertically at each side, were prominent features. The siren brackets fitted to the fore tripod legs instead of on the funnels was an arrangement that was retained in all later classes of battleships, right up to the *Nelson* class of 1925.

It was not easy to distinguish the *Bellerophons* from the *St Vincent* class, although there were some differences:

1. Shorter, equal sized funnels in *Bellerophon*.
2. Longer topmasts and shorter topgallants in *Bellerophon*.
3. Both topmasts stepped abaft and topgallants before.

Individual differences in the three ships of the class were as follows.

BELLEROPHON
Inboard profile and deck plans, 1909

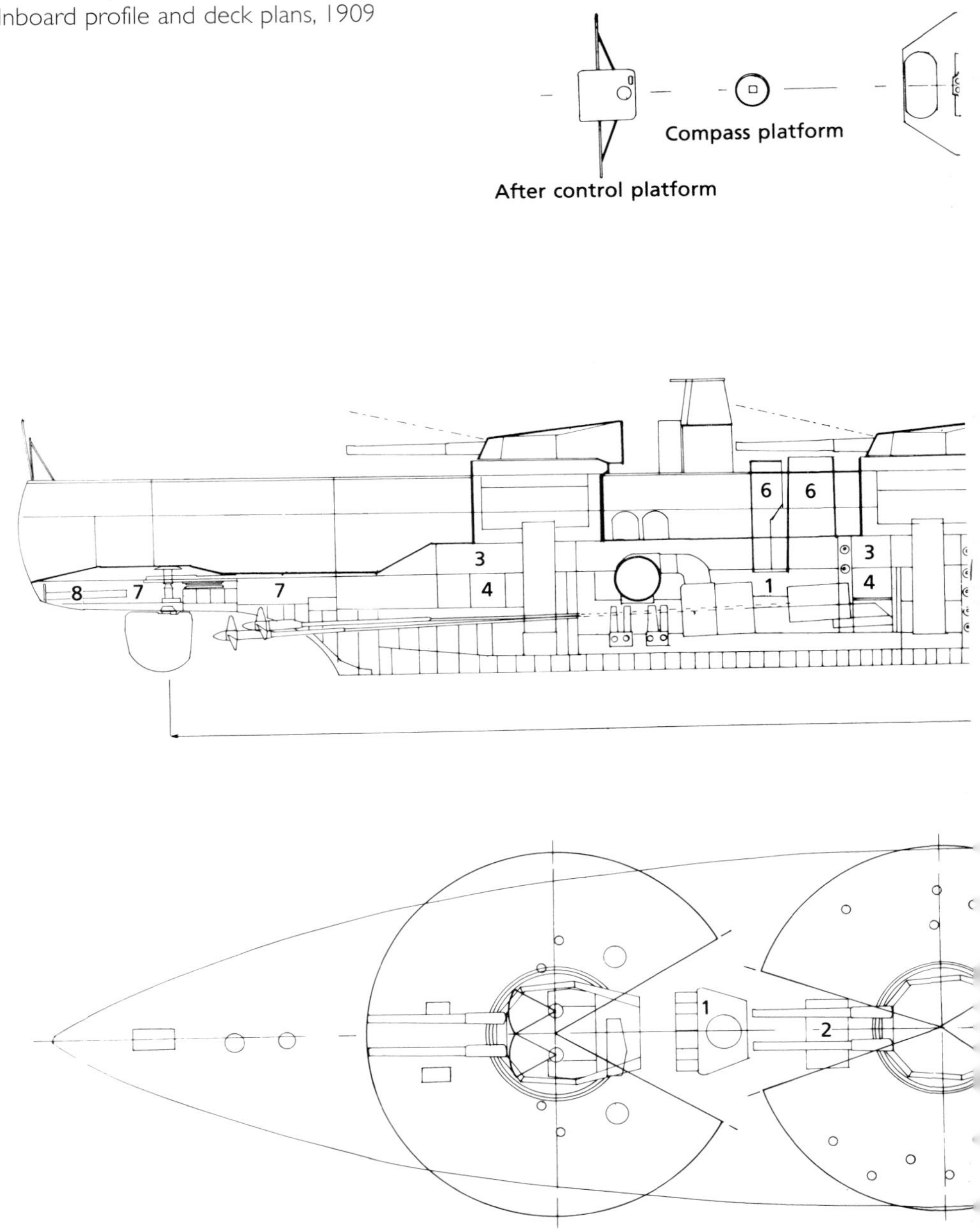

Bellerophon: Flat caging on both funnels. Prominent crest on face of bridge (sometimes removed). No funnel bands.

Temeraire: Funnel caging as in *Bellerophon*. Two white bands on each funnel.

Superb: Prominent caging to second funnel. Two white bands on fore funnel.

There were also some minor differences in the forecastle scuttles in all three.

1909–10 *Bellerophon* reported to have been fitted with director control equipment as experimental measure. The range indicators, fitted in all three ships on completion, replaced by modified pattern, itself removed from the class by 1911–12. They, like the original type, were experimental and had been discarded by 1914.

1911–12 Forward control top rebuilt with narrow face in

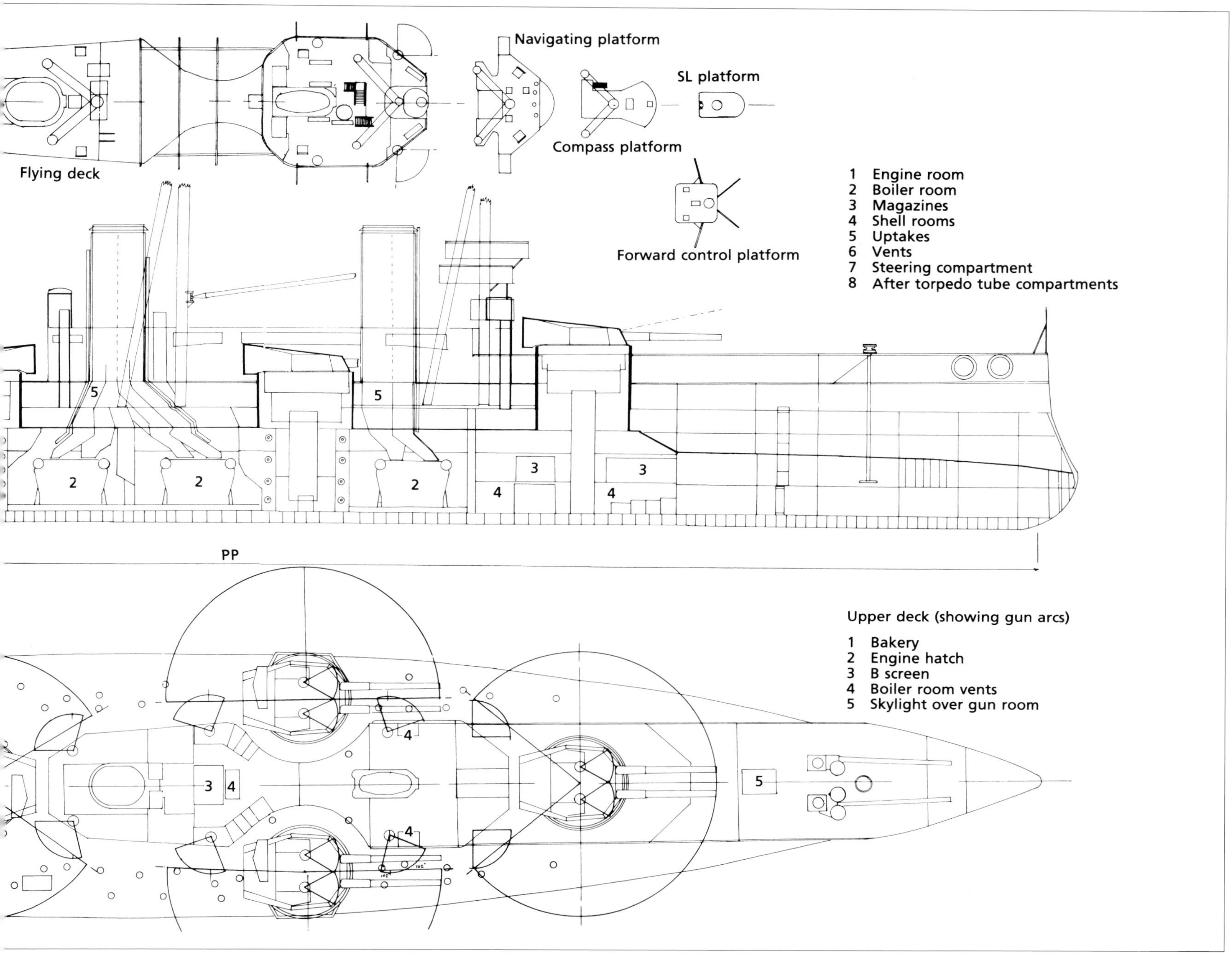

Temeraire. Range indicators below control tops in *Superb* replaced by high, curved screens. 24in searchlight removed from lower top in *Bellerophon*.

1912–13 Fore control top in *Bellerophon* and *Superb*, rebuilt as in *Temeraire*. Blast screen fitted behind 4in guns on fore turret in *Superb*, and beam face turrets in *Temeraire*. 24in searchlights removed from *Temeraire*.

Large platform added low on foremast in *Bellerophon* (by March 1913). Removed sometime in 1913.

1913–14 *Bellerophon*: 4in guns removed from fore turret and remounted over forward pair in superstructure. Blast screens added behind 4in guns on beam turrets. Searchlights redistributed as experimental measure; they were raised as high as practicable and were more concentrated in an endeavour to conceal the length and course of the ship. Four were remounted on a platform low on the foremast and fore tripod legs, two, port and starboard, on high platforms abeam fore funnel. Four on

Bellerophon entering Valletta, 1913/14. Many improvements to bridgework since completion in 1909. SL towers on both fore and main tripods, extended bridgework, 4in guns in casemates, no SL on lower spotting top, shields to 4in guns on midships turrets only, no 4in on 'A' turret.

platform, low on main tripod legs. The original simple bridgework over the conning tower was replaced by enlarged and modified structure, being built back around the tripod legs, leaving the conning tower well clear ahead. The navigating platform was extended well ahead.

Superb: Fore control top again modified with a curved face. Blast screens removed from the fore turret.

1914 4in guns removed from fore turret in *Superb* and *Temeraire*, and remounted as in *Bellerophon*. Searchlights in *Superb* were redistributed much the same as in *Bellerophon*, with the exception of the bridge SL, which were not remounted abeam the fore funnel. Work not complete by August 1914. Although the platforms had been placed, the SL were not relocated in this position. Topgallants were removed and topmasts were reduced in *Bellerophon*. This rig, which became practicable as a result of improved W/T arrangements, first appeared in *Bellerophon* and *Collingwood* in 1914; it became general practice throughout the Grand Fleet by 1915–16.

Bellerophon had the heaviest appearance in the class at this time. Funnel bands painted out at the beginning of hostilities.

1914–15 Director control for main armament fitted, the platform for this being located below fore control top which was enlarged. Four 4in guns removed from beam turrets and remounted on superstructure over after pair in each group. Except for two guns retained for a short period on after turrets, secondary armament was massed in two groups, greatly facilitating control and concentration of fire. One 3in AA gun added on former SL platform between 4th and 5th 12in turrets. Searchlights in *Temeraire* redistributed as in *Superb*. Topgallants removed from *Superb* and *Temeraire*, although original height of topmasts retained. Forward pair of 4in guns removed from midships structure and remaining upper superstructure 4in guns plated in, affording some protection for crews.

1916 Kite balloon equipment fitted in *Bellerophon*. Anti-torpedo nets removed from all ships. Modifications in *Temeraire* were not so as extensive as in her sisters, the bridgework not built back clear of conning tower. *Bellerophon* and *Superb* however both had bridgework enlarged and modified. Topmasts reduced in height in *Superb* and *Temeraire* (after May 1916 in *Superb*).

1916–17 3in AA gun on after turret replaced by 4in (by April 1917). Improvements in armour protection fitted after Jutland. Middle and main decks given ¾in–1in plates over magazines (23 tons total). Rangefinder baffles fitted to both masts in all ships, although this varied from ship to ship. Experimental camouflage painted on bows of *Bellerophon* (1917). Others may have been painted same, but lack of photographic evidence. Baffles and camouflage removed by end 1917/early 1918 (camouflage in *Bellerophon* removed by August 1917).

1917–18 Range clocks fitted to fore control top in *Bellerophon* and *Superb*, and to face of bridge in *Temeraire*. Deflection scales painted on forward and after 12in turrets (1917). Starboard lower 4in gun in each after group removed from *Superb*. Extra control positions added on SL platforms on fore tripod legs, replacing searchlights. Stern torpedo tube removed by April 1917. Searchlights again redistributed and 'coffee-box' towers fitted around the second funnel, each carrying one 36in lamp. The towers were variable in each ship; they were stepped down from forward to aft. SL were removed from main tripod platform in all three ships and from abeam fore funnel in *Bellerophon*, and from bridge in *Superb*. Those on fore tripod leg platforms removed from *Superb* and *Temeraire*. Clinker screen (or cap) fitted to fore funnel in all ships (by August 1917 in *Temeraire* and *Bellerophon*).

1918 4in AA gun removed from after turret and relocated right aft on quarterdeck, in all three ships. High-angle rangefinders fitted in fore control top. Flying-off platforms fitted to fore and

Left: A portrait view of *Bellerophon* shortly after commissioning, 1910.

Above: *Bellerophon* after the cessation of hostilities (1919/20), at Devonport after a short refit.

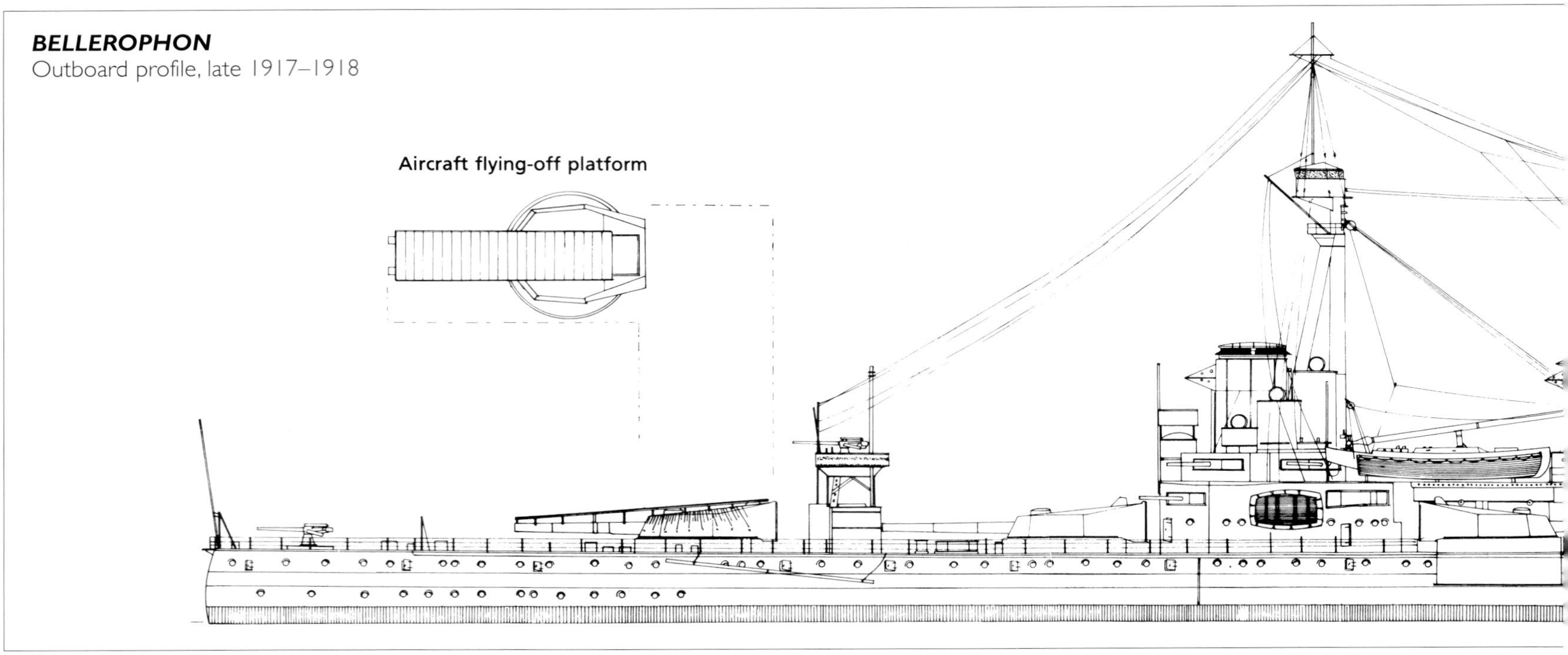

Below: *Temeraire* anchored at Rosyth, 25 August 1917. Note the enlarged control top, very unusual range clock on face of bridge (square rather than round), 4in guns all enclosed, deflection scales on 'A' turret, and AA guns on aft structure and 'X' turret.

aft turrets in *Bellerophon*. Foretopmast removed to accommodate masthead rangefinder. Mechanical semaphore fitted to fore control top in *Bellerophon*.

By November 1918 Searchlights: *Bellerophon* and *Temeraire*, ten 36in; *Superb*, nine 36in. Secondary armament: *Bellerophon* and *Temeraire*, twelve 4in; *Superb* eleven 4in. All: one 3in, one 4in AA.

1919–20 Deflection scales on turrets painted out in all ships. Upper pair of 4in guns in after group, and lower pair in forward group removed from *Temeraire* to provide extra accommodation while serving as training ship. AA guns removed from *Superb* and *Temeraire*.

History: *Bellerophon*

Built under the 1906–7 Estimates. Ordered 30 October 1906. Began her trials in October 1908.

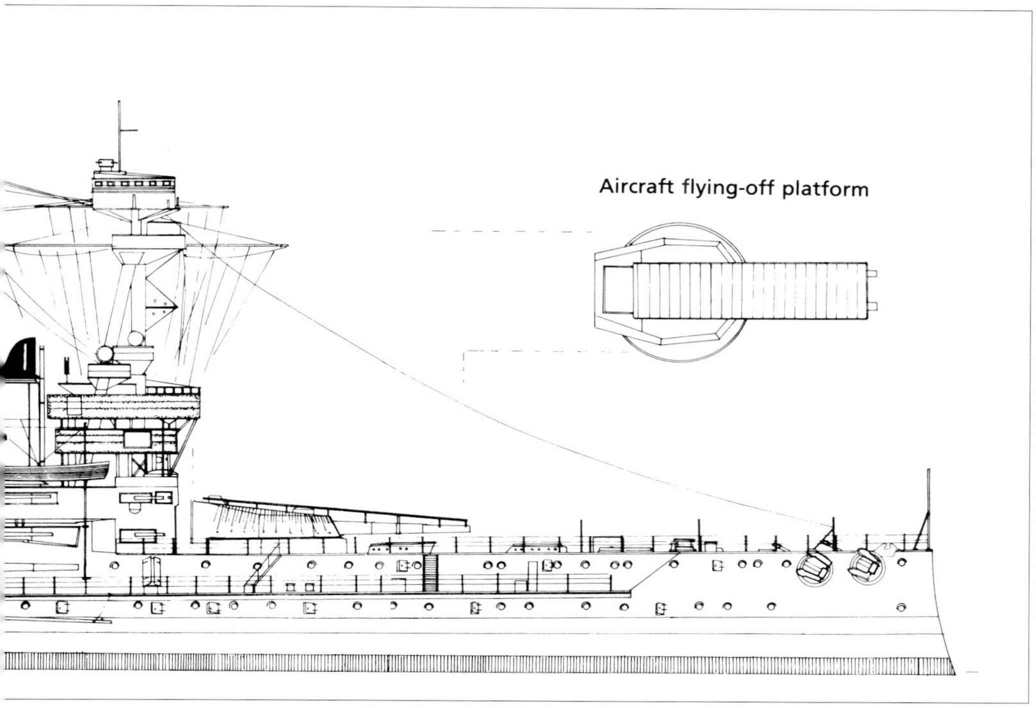

1909 *20 Feb* Commissioned at Portsmouth for service in Nore Division Home Fleet, relieving *Victorious*.
March The Nore Division became the 1st Division.
4 May Combined exercises with Atlantic Fleet off Scottish coast.
12 June Present at Imperial Press Conference Review at Spithead.
June–July Annual combined manoeuvres in Atlantic with Mediterranean and Atlantic Fleets and all Divisions of Home Fleet.
17–24 July Visited Southend with units of Home and Atlantic Fleets.
31 July Present at King Edward VII's Review at Cowes, in honour of visit by HIM the Tsar of Russia.
1910 *April* Exercises off Scottish coast with Home and Atlantic Fleets.
26–29 July Visit by King George V to combined Home Fleets at Torbay.
1910/11 Under refit at Portsmouth.
1911 *Jan* Combined exercises off NW Spain with Mediterranean and Atlantic Fleets, and part of Home Fleet.
1 Feb Recommissioned at Portsmouth for service in 1st Fleet.
26 May Collided with *Inflexible* while entering Portland, but sustained no serious damage.
24 June Coronation Fleet Review at Spithead.
June–July Tactical exercises with Atlantic Fleet and 4th CS off SW coasts of England and Ireland.
July Exercises with Atlantic Fleet in North Sea.
1911/12 Under refit at Devonport.
1912 *1 May* The 1st Division Home Fleet became 1st BS of 1st Fleet.
7–11 May Royal visit to 1st and 2nd Home Fleets at Weymouth, followed by four days' exercises.
9 July Parliamentary Review of Home Fleet at Spithead followed by annual manoeuvres.
Oct Tactical exercises.
1913 *1 April* Recommissioned at Devonport for service in 1st BS.
Nov On manoeuvres with Mediterranean Fleet, part of 4th BS and 1st BS. Units of 3rd CS and LCS also took part.
Nov Visited Athens.
1914 *10 March* Relieved from 1st BS Home Fleet by *Neptune* and transferred to 4th BS relieving *Cornwallis*.
15 July Left Portland with 1st Fleet.
16 July Reached Spithead.
17–20 July Test mobilization and Royal Review of combined fleets at Spithead.
26 July En route to Gibraltar for annual refit, but recalled.
30–31 July Joined Home Fleet at Scapa Flow.
Aug On outbreak of hostilities 1st Home Fleet became Grand Fleet, composition of battle squadrons remained unchanged.
27 Aug At 21.30 collided with SS *St Clair* off the Orkneys while latter was passing through Grand Fleet, no important damage sustained.
22 Oct–3 Nov With 4th BS temporarily based at Lough Swilly pending completion of submarine defences at Scapa Flow.
1915 *May* Under refit at Devonport.
Aug With 4th BS based at Cromarty.
1916 *31 May* Battle of Jutland. In 4th Division battlefleet with *Benbow*, *Temeraire* and *Vanguard* and was 14th ship in battle line after the deployment. She was the oldest British battleship present at the action.
1917 *June–Sept* Served temporarily as 2nd flagship of 4th BS, relieving *Colossus* during latter's refit.
1918 *12 April* Grand Fleet base transferred from Scapa Flow to Rosyth.
21 Nov Present (southern line) at German High Seas Fleet surrender.
1919 *March* On abolition of Grand Fleet *Bellerophon* was attached to Nore establishment as turret drill ship.

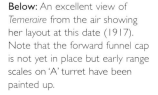

Below: An excellent view of *Temeraire* from the air showing her layout at this date (1917). Note that the forward funnel cap is not yet in place but early range scales on 'A' turret have been painted up.

Above: *Bellerophon* in summer 1917, showing camouflage on her bows.

25 Sept Relieved by *Superb* and paid off into the Reserve at Devonport.
Sept–early Jan 1920 Under refit at Devonport.
1920 *Jan* Earmarked for early disposal.
1921 *March* Placed on Disposal list at Devonport.
14 Aug Placed on Sale list.
8 Nov Sold to Slough Trading Co. for £44,000.
1922 *Sept* Resold to German firm of shipbreakers.
14 Sept Left Plymouth, under tow, for breaking in Germany.

History: *Superb*

Ordered on 26 December 1906. Began her trials at the end of March 1909. Labour disputes delayed her construction considerably.

1909 *29 May* Commissioned at Portsmouth for service with 1st Division Home Fleet, relieving *Formidable*.
12 June Present at Imperial Press Conference Review at Spithead.
17–24 July Visited Southend with units of Home and Atlantic Fleets.
31 July Present at Review by King Edward VII for HIM the Tsar of Russia.
1910 *April* Tactical exercises off Scottish coast with Home and Atlantic Fleets.
July Annual manoeuvres with Mediterranean, Atlantic and Home Fleets.
26–29 July Present when HM King George V visited Fleet at Torbay.
Under refit at Portsmouth.
1911 *Jan* Combined exercises with Mediterranean, Atlantic and Home Fleets, off NW coast of Spain.
30 May Recommissioned at Portsmouth for service with 1st Division Home Fleet.
24 June Coronation Fleet Review.
June–July Combined exercises off SW coast of England and Ireland, with Atlantic Fleet and 4th CS.
July Exercises with Home Fleet in North Sea.
1912 *1 May* The 1st Division Home Fleet became 1st BS of 1st Fleet.
7–11 May Royal visit to 1st and 2nd Fleets at Weymouth followed by four days' exercises.
9 July Parliamentary Review of Home Fleet at Spithead followed by annual manoeuvres with 1st and 2nd Fleets and part of 3rd Fleet plus Mediterranean Fleet).
Oct Tactical exercises with 1st (Home) Fleet.
1913 *6 May* Recommissioned at Portsmouth for service in 1st BS.
July Visited Cherbourg with part of 1st BS.
1914 *15 July* Left Portland with 1st Fleet.
16 July Reached Spithead.
17–20 July Test mobilization and Royal Review at Spithead.
20–25 July Fleet exercises at sea.
25 July Fleet returned to Portland.
29 July Left Portland for war base at Scapa Flow.
22 Oct Based at Lough Swilly pending completion of defences at Scapa Flow.
1915 *18 Jan* Left Scapa Flow for repairs to turbines at Portsmouth.
11 March Rejoined Grand Fleet.
2–5 Sept Cruising at sea with Grand Fleet and sighted a U-boat.
10 Nov Relieved from 1st BS by *Agincourt* and transferred to 4th BS.
1916 *May* Served temporarily as 2nd flagship 4th BS in place of *Emperor of India* during latter's refit.
31 May Battle of Jutland. Flagship of 3rd Division battlefleet with *Iron Duke* (flagship), *Royal Oak* and *Canada*. *Superb* was 11th ship in line after the deployment.
1918 *12 April* With Grand Fleet when it was transferred from Scapa to Rosyth.
June Recommissioned at Portsmouth.
Oct Detached with *Temeraire* to reinforce British Eastern Mediterranean Squadron. The squadron was strengthened so as to enable Vice-Admiral Gough-Calthorpe, then senior flag officer at Mudros, to assume command of the entire Allied force in those waters, and to take charge of any major operations should the Russian Black Sea Fleet try to make a sortie. Prior to this reinforcement the French 2nd BS was stronger than the combined Allied forces.
31 Oct Reached Mudros and relieved *Foresight* as flagship of

Below: *Superb* as flagship of the Allied Squadron, anchored off Sebastopol, November 1918.

Vice-Admiral Sir Somerset Calthorpe, CinC British Eastern Mediterranean.
12 Nov Led combined Allied squadrons (as flagship) through Dardanelles to Constantinople after signing of Armistice with Turkey.
13 Nov Reached Constantinople.
Nov–April 1919 Flagship of British Naval Forces in Turkish waters and Black Sea.
1919 *April* Relieved as flagship by *Iron Duke* and returned home to pay off.
26 April Paid off into the Nore Reserve at Sheerness and was reduced to Third Fleet complement.
Sept Relieved *Bellerophon* as turret drill ship at the Nore.
Dec Relieved from these duties by *Erin*.
1920 *26 March* Paid off into the Disposal list at the Nore.
Dec Detailed for gunnery experiments.
1922 *May* Used as target ship at Portsmouth in connection with 'anti-flash' protection to magazines.
Autumn Used as target for various forms of aerial attack at Portsmouth.
Dec Sold to Stanlee Shipbreaking Co. of Dover.
1923 *7 April* Left Portsmouth under tow bound for Dover where she was broken up.

History: *Temeraire*

1906 *30 Oct* Ordered.
1909 *15 May* Commissioned at Devonport for service in 1st Division Home Fleet, relieving *Implacable*.
12 June Present at Imperial Press Conference Review.
June–July Annual Combined manoeuvres in Atlantic with other units of Mediterranean, Atlantic and Home Fleets.
17–24 July Visited Southend and the Thames.
31 July Review at Cowes by King Edward VII for Tsar of Russia.
1911 Under refit at Devonport.
16 May Recommissioned at Devonport for service with Home Fleet.
24 June Coronation Fleet Review.
June–July Combined exercises off SW coasts of England and Ireland with Atlantic Fleet and 4th CS.
July Exercises in Atlantic.
1912 *1 May* The 1st Division became 1st BS Home Fleet.
7–11 May Royal Visit to 1st and 2nd Fleet at Weymouth.
9 July Took part in Parliamentary Review of Home Fleets.
Oct Tactical exercises.
1913 *July* Visited Cherbourg with part of 1st BS.
30 Sept Recommissioned at Devonport for service with 1st BS.
1914 *15 July* Transferred to 4th BS and left Portland with the fleet.
16 July Reached Spithead.
17–20 July Test mobilization and Fleet Review.
20–25 July Exercises with combined Fleets.
25 July Returned to Portland.
29 July Left Portland for Scapa Flow.
8 Aug Outbreak of war, Home Fleet became Grand Fleet.
22 Oct–3 Nov At Lough Swilly until Scapa had been made secure against U-boats.
1915 *18 March* Endeavoured unsuccessfully to ram *U29*

Above: *Temeraire* off Sebastopol, February 1919.

Right: *Superb* 1918/19 as flagship of the British Naval Forces in Turkish waters. Note the wartime additions to her foremast and the large range clock on the face of the searchlight platform.

Above: *Temeraire.* The only remaining unit of the class in service by 1921, *Temeraire* was refitted and used as a training ship for a short period before being relieved by *Thunderer* in April 1921. (Note the lower 4in guns have been removed for extra crew accommodation.)

Below: *Temeraire* at anchor in Devonport, November 1919.

(Weddigen) after she tried to torpedo *Neptune*, and only just avoided collision with *Dreadnought* which cut the U-boat in half.

1915 *Summer* Refit at Devonport.

Aug Recommissioned and joined 4th BS at Cromarty.

1916 *31 May* Battle of Jutland. In 4th Division of battlefleet with *Benbow*, *Vanguard* and *Bellerophon*, and was fifteenth ship in line after the deployment.

1918 *12 April* Left Rosyth with *Superb* to reinforce British Eastern Mediterranean Squadron.

12 Nov With Allied Squadron passed through Dardanelles to Constantinople after the signing of armistice with Turkey, being second ship in line as her predecessor of the same name had been in 1878. Remained in Turkish waters and Black Sea until April 1919, visiting Gulf of Ismid, Sebastopol and later Haifa.

1919 *3 April* Relieved by *Marlborough* and returned home to pay off.

23 April Paid off into the Reserve at Devonport.

23 Sept Paid off from the Reserve at Devonport and recommissioned the same day for service as seagoing cadet training ship, replacing *Cornwall* and *Cumberland*.

8 Oct Left Devonport on first training cruise.

13 Nov Reached Palma, Majorca.

1921 *11 April* Reached Portsmouth on termination of last training cruise and relieved by *Thunderer.*

15 April Left Portsmouth for Rosyth, and placed on Disposal list.

Late 1921 Sold to Stanlee Shipbreaking Co.

1922 *Feb* Towed to Dover and broken up.

***IRON DUKE* OCTOBER 1914.**

Dark slate grey with white guns and turrets ('A', 'B', 'X'), white on tripod legs and after conning tower structure. At some point in time another vessel of the class was painted with white dashes on guns and funnels but lack of photographic evidence of the whole layout makes it impossible to make a plan.

***TIGER* JANUARY 1915.**

Dark grey panel on hull over medium grey upper works with white slashes on funnels and masts etc.

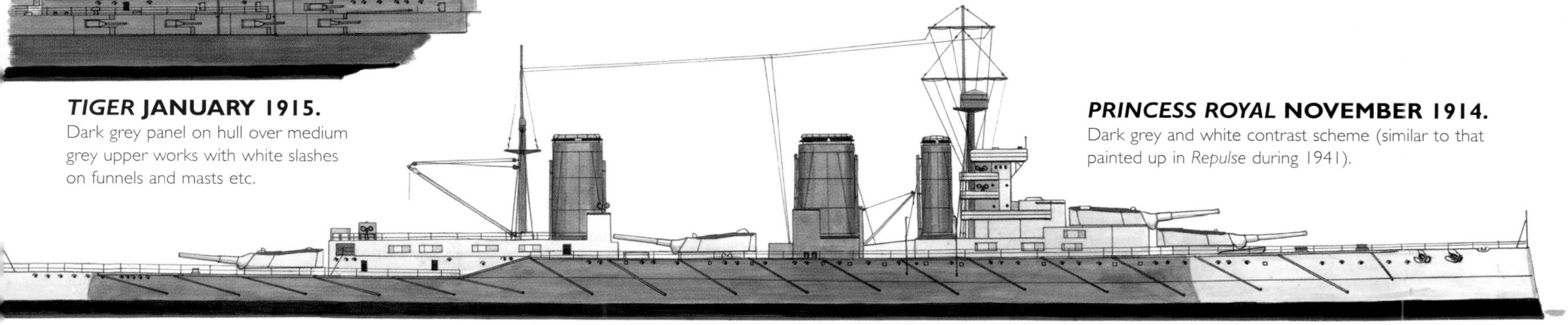

***PRINCESS ROYAL* NOVEMBER 1914.**

Dark grey and white contrast scheme (similar to that painted up in *Repulse* during 1941).

More so than the battleships, the Royal Navy cruisers took advantage of the message to experiment with camouflage following Professor Kerr's principles of confusion (see overleaf). This did however result in some rather bizarre schemes of paintwork.

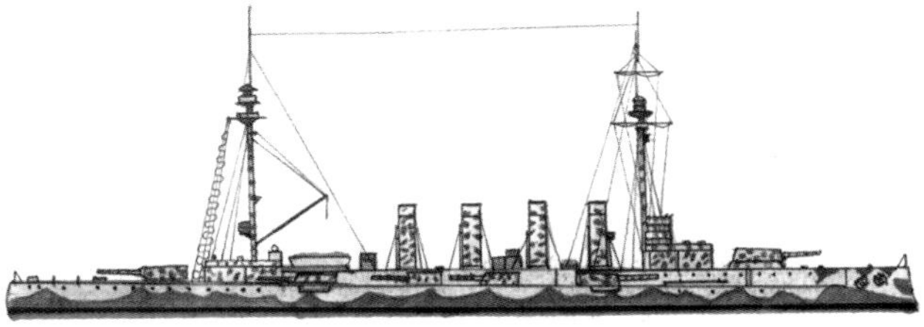

***COCHRANE* (CRUISER) LATE 1914.**

Medium grey with dark grey mottled hull and splashes of dark grey on upper works and turrets etc.

***LEVIATHAN* (CRUISER) NOVEMBER 1914.**

Medium grey with very dark grey splashes on funnels and large bow wave type white dash at the bows. The port side was very different from the starboard side.

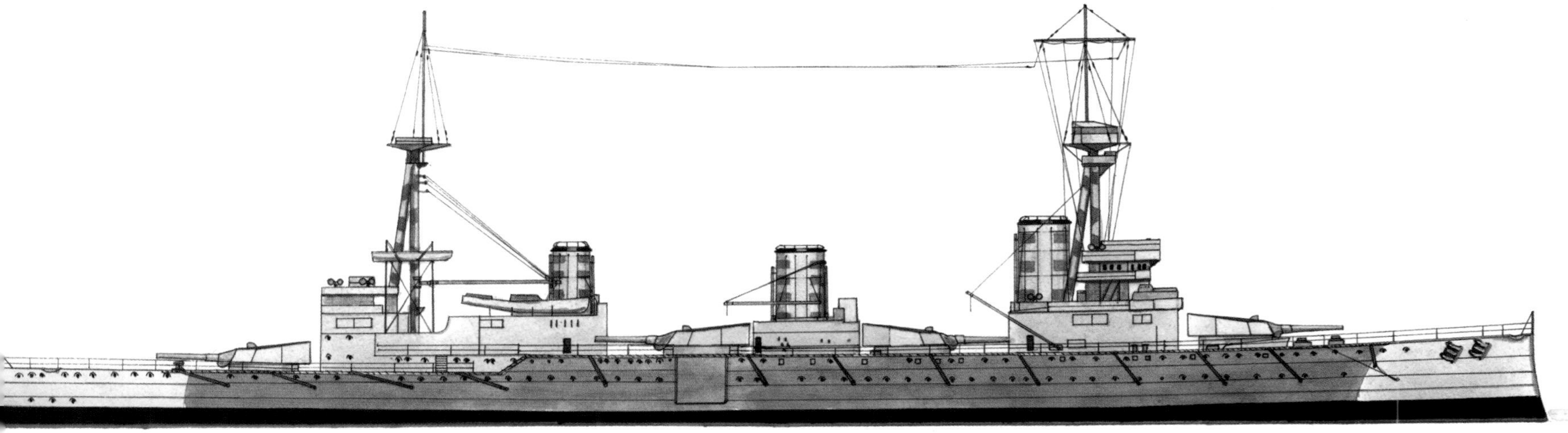

***NEW ZEALAND* LATE 1914 – EARLY 1915.**

Medium grey with dark grey dashes on funnels and long dark grey panel along hull.

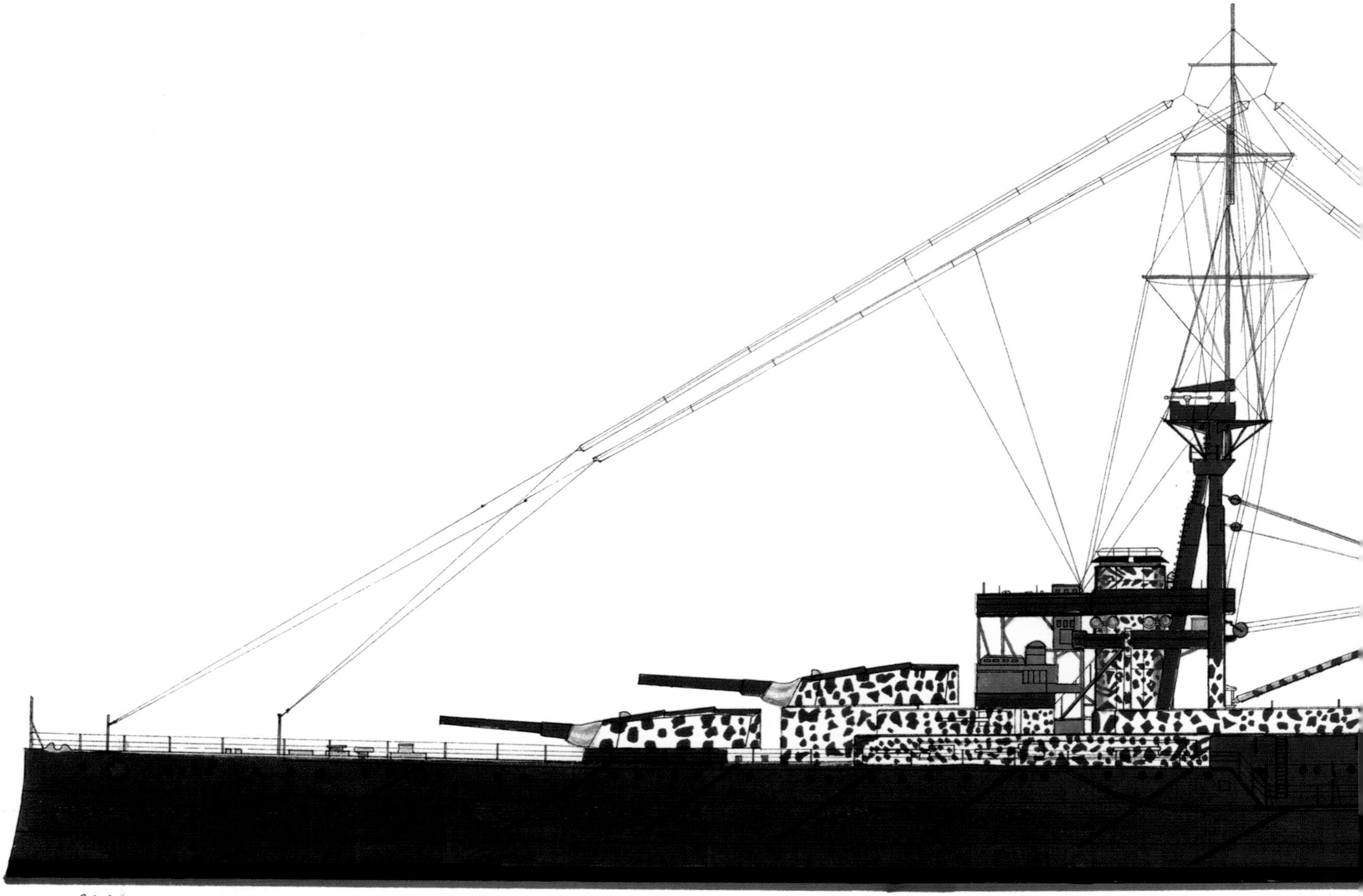

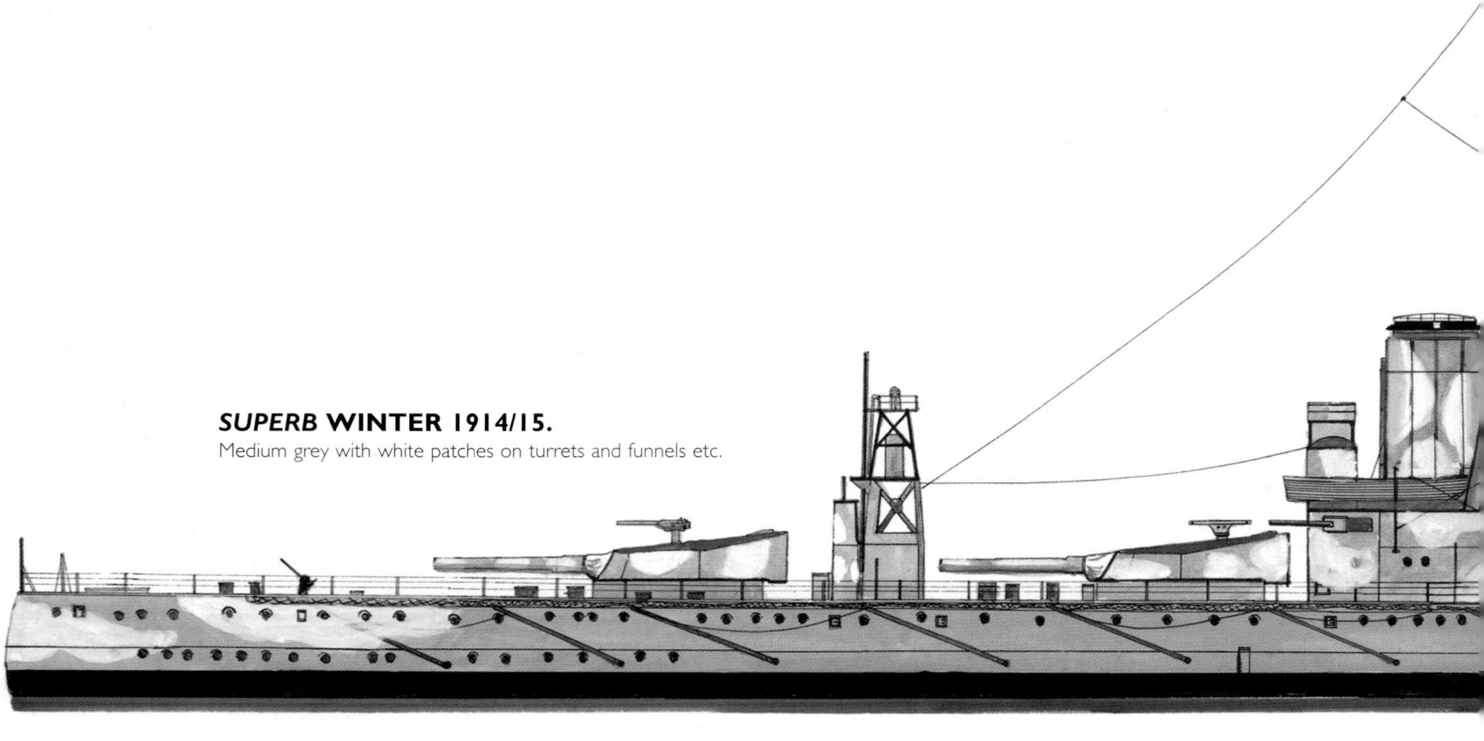

***SUPERB* WINTER 1914/15.**

Medium grey with white patches on turrets and funnels etc.

During the early weeks of war camouflage had made an appearance in HM ships with all early schemes based on an idea and experiment of Professor Graham Kerr who was an expert on natural history at Glasgow University. The records show he suggested in a letter to the Admiralty that warships might well be able to make themselves inconspicuous to the enemy by painting strong violent contrasting lines and patches all over and thus breaking up the image of the vessel.

Referring to natural animal colouration with their odd shapes and patterns which indeed rendered them inconspicuous in certain conditions there was a strong case for a trial. These early schemes were not dazzle paintwork but confusion of the eye experiments.

Kerr had made a long study of the subject and later stated that the words 'dazzle', as so often used during World War One (later adopted by the Admiralty and Norman Wilkinson in 1917), and 'confusion of image' was first used in Abbott Handerson Thayer's book on animal colouration (published in 1909). An Admiralty message was issued to all HM ships in September 1914 resulting in many vessels painted in this way suggested by Professor Kerr.

Surviving records and photographic evidence of many of these layouts during the early months of the war are extremely scarce (especially when there was a restriction on photography) but it is a fact that colours circulated around shades of dull grey white and black (see plans). There was little control over the way patches and lines were applied or even to what part of the ship should be painted to give the best effect. As a result many of the paintwork schemes were rather dramatic but futile in their application toward rendering the ships less conspicuous. The whole scheme as proposed by Professor Kerr seems to have been stopped after about six months although modifications along the same lines were seen during the Dardanelles campaign in March 1915.

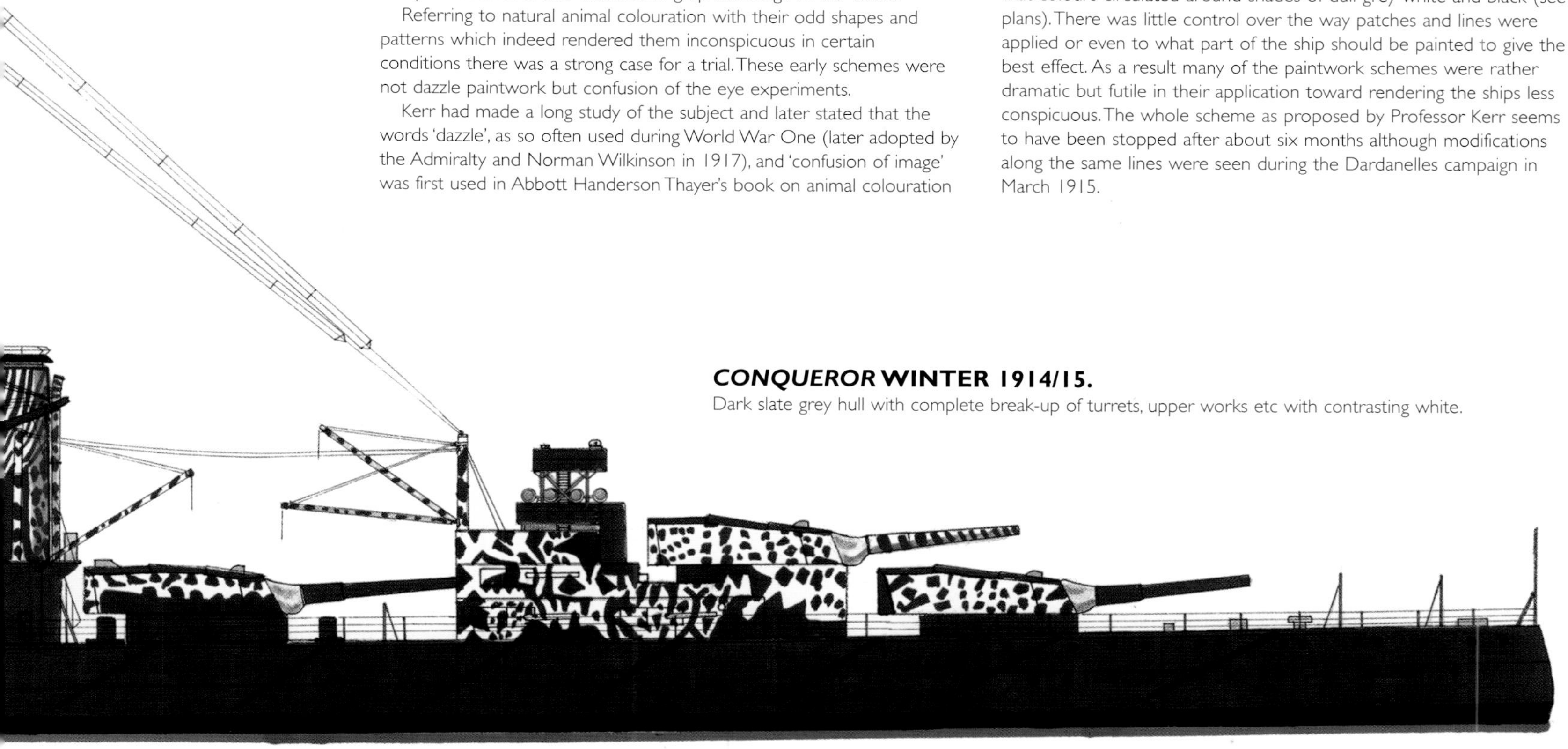

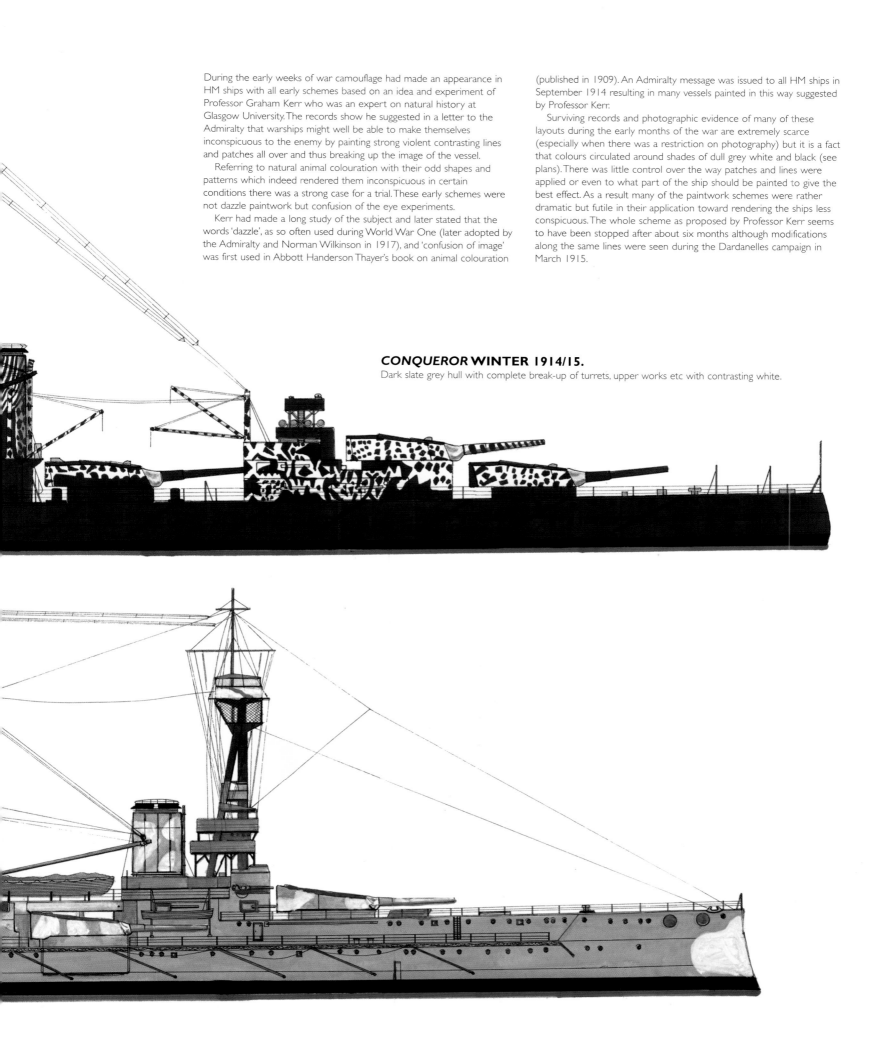

***CONQUEROR* WINTER 1914/15.**

Dark slate grey hull with complete break-up of turrets, upper works etc with contrasting white.

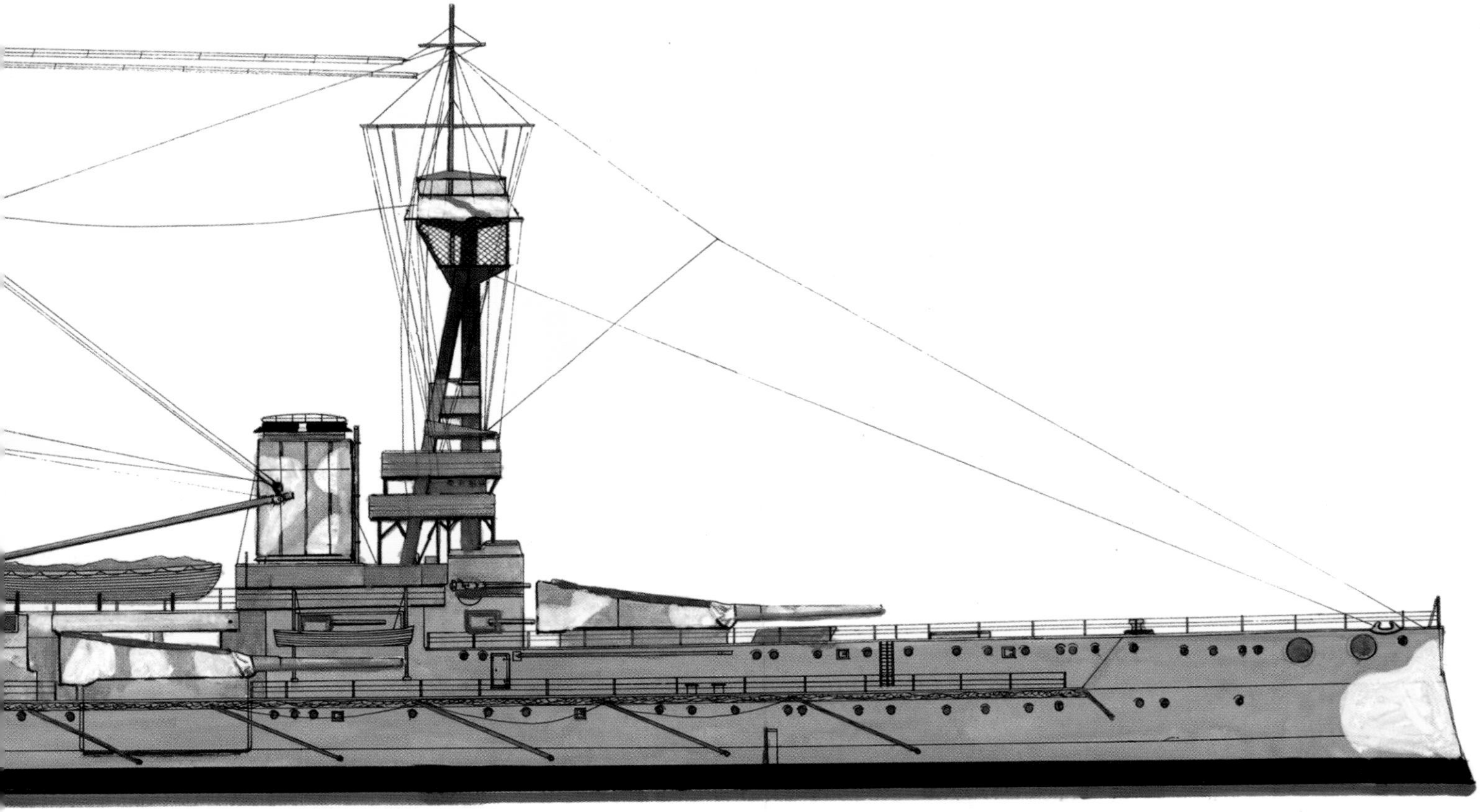

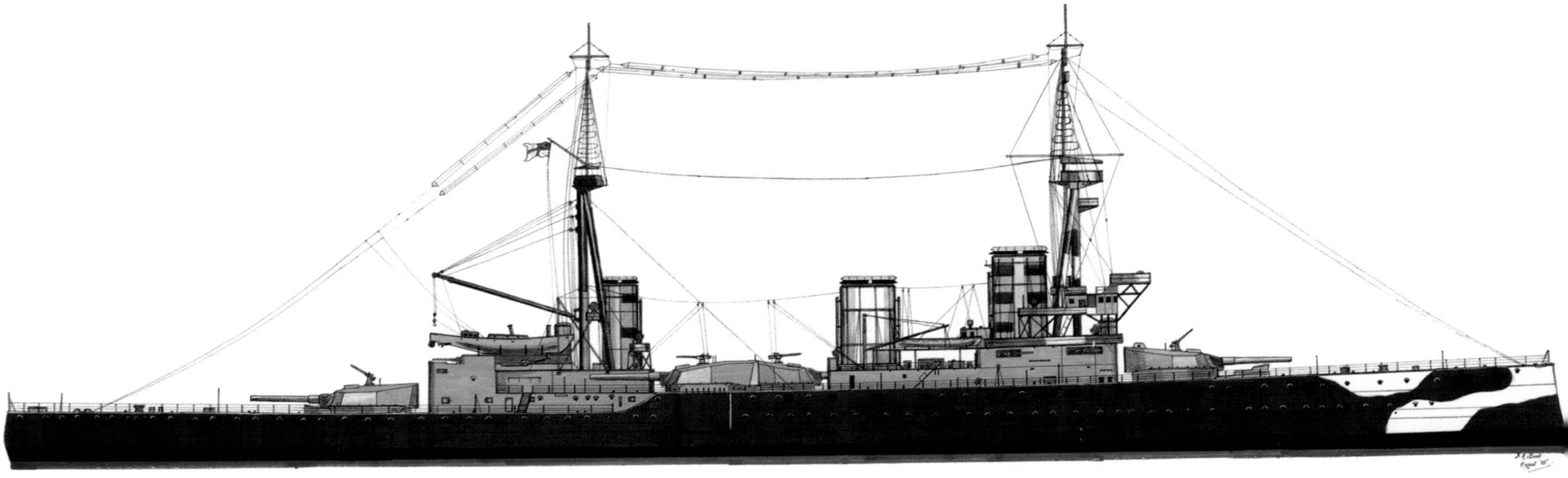

***INFLEXIBLE* DARDANELLES CAMPAIGN, MARCH 1915.**
Dark grey hull, medium grey upper works with white splashes at bows and masts, and white centre funnel. Dark grey lines on funnels.

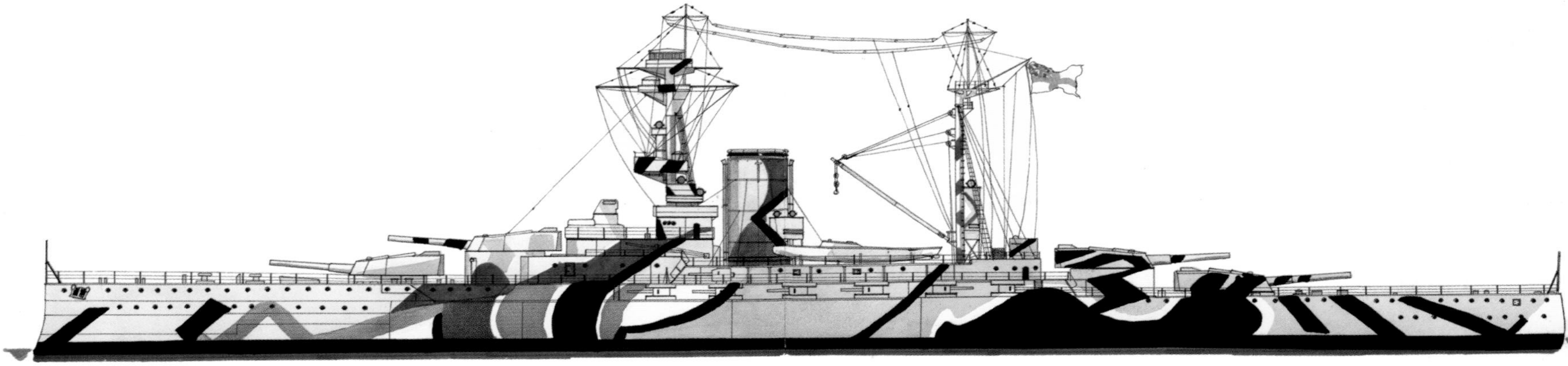

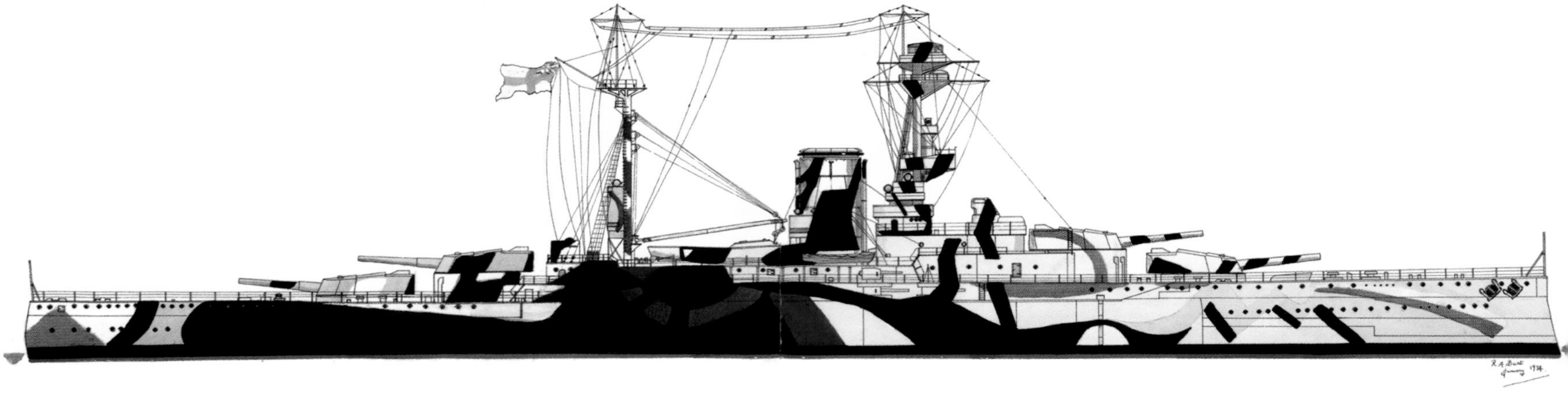

***RAMILLIES* LATE 1917 TO EARLY 1918 DAZZLE LAYOUT.**
Unfortunately there are no colour swatches for any of the dazzle schemes. The colours actually used on the ships for dazzle layout although carefully following guidelines would be slightly different when made up (mixed). Therefore one ship with number one olive green may well have looked slightly lighter or darker than another painted the same colour (the same can be said of World War Two layouts).

St Vincent Class: 1907 ESTIMATES

Design

Towards the end of 1906 the necessity for building a large number of dreadnoughts was being questioned. The Government asserted that, as Germany was claiming only a moderate dreadnought programme for the year, the three ships laid down for the Royal Navy need not be repeated, especially in view of their enormous cost. The Admiralty Board countered by stressing the potential threat if Germany increased its programme; the United States had laid down two ships, *South Carolina* and *Michigan*; and Great Britain should follow suit and lay down at least three. Matters were finally settled towards the end of 1907 when sufficient funds were allocated to allow the building of three capital ships.

The design would perpetuate that of the *Bellerophon* class, although some small modifications were called for. On completion of the programme Great Britain would have eight dreadnoughts which, if required, could form a homogeneous squadron. The three *Bellerophons* and *Dreadnought* would form one powerful group; the three *St Vincents* plus a fourth unit would form the second. This fourth unit, which was to have been named *Foudroyant*, was cancelled, but later it was redesigned and became the *Neptune* of the 1908 Programme.

At the end of 1907 the Admiralty invited Vickers and Armstrong-Whitworth to tender for the construction of one unit each, the third would be built at the Royal Dockyard, Portsmouth. Vickers quoted £384,891 for the hull and a total figure of £1,900,000. Armstrongs quoted £488,000 for hull and £1,890,000 total. The Admiralty accepted Vickers' figure and instructed them to prepare their drawings. It was decided that the third ship would be built at the Royal Dockyard at Devonport. The ships were designated 'Battleships F' and did not receive their names of *Vanguard*, *Collingwood* and *St Vincent* until 13 August 1907. The new ships were the last to be constructed along the lines of *Dreadnought*. Slightly enlarged and modified versions of *Bellerophon*, their essential features were:

1. Displacement was increased by 650 tons nominal, with an increase in length and beam of 10ft and 1ft 6in respectively.
2. A more powerful 12in gun replaced the Mk X as fitted in the previous four dreadnought types.
3. Hull armouring was slightly modified.
4. Designed speed was raised by approximately ¼ knot (although in service *Bellerophon* turned out to be equally as fast).
5. Fuel capacity was slightly increased

Armament

Throughout the construction period of the *Bellerophon* class, tests were being conducted at Vickers, Elswick, Coventry and Woolwich Ordnance departments, to produce a greater range and penetration capability for the existing 12in 45cal Mk X gun. The Mk X on the B VIII mounting had been fitted in all battleships since *Lord Nelson* (1904), and there was no question of its being inferior to any foreign contemporary. The Board was seeking further improvement without resorting to a heavier calibre, which would necessitate greatly increased displacement and therefore further design and experimental work – and cost. Procedure centred around modification of breech, hoops and collar, after which the new gun, Mk XI, was presented by Vickers, although further modifications were made at a later stage. The new gun, which was to be fitted in the three *St Vincents*, had a muzzle velocity of 2,852ft/sec as opposed to the 2,725ft/sec of the Mk X. It did not live up to expectations. The increased length (from 45cal to 50cal) produced a disconcerting muzzle droop; the increased muzzle velocity caused considerable erosion and the enhanced accuracy fell off after a relatively small number of rounds. These defects made it clear that the 12in piece had been developed to its limits and this, coupled with the demand for a greater burster charger than could be carried in the 12in shell, led to the adoption of the 13.5in gun. The latter did not enter service until 1912 (*Orion* class), however, and not before three more battleships had been armed with the 12in 50cal Mk XI. (While the *St Vincents* were under construction in 1908, proposals were put forward for arming them with the 13.5in, but the idea was vetoed by the First

COLLINGWOOD: LAUNCH FIGURES, 7 NOVEMBER 1908

	tons
Displacement:	7,893
Anchors:	25
Armament:	3.5
Armour:	766
Men and ballast:	364.5
Recorded weight of hull:	6,770

Draught: 9ft 5in forward, 16ft aft
Breakage at launch:
longitudinal in a distance of 393ft = 0⅞in hog
transverse in a distance of 79ft 9in = 0 1/32in sag
St Vincent displacement 6,580 tons
Vanguard displacement 9,662 tons.

Left: *St Vincent* launched at Portsmouth DY by Lady Beauchamp, 10 September 1908.

Right: Beam 12in turret and guns of *St Vincent* 1917 showing the weight and pressure on the extremities of the ship's hull.

Below: *Vanguard* being towed from the builder's yard on completion to undergo trials. Early 1910.

Sea Lord, Lord Fisher, despite the fact that practically the entire Board voted heartily for the change: procuring the new guns and modifying the turrets would take too long.)

The layout remained almost identical with that of the *Bellerophon* class, but 'X' and 'Y' turrets were located ten feet farther apart to accommodate the slight increase in length of the new gun. The anti-torpedo armament was 25 per cent larger than that of *Bellerophon* and was not equalled in any of the later classes equipped with 4in guns, all of which reverted to sixteen guns as in *Bellerophon*. Distribution was identical with that of *Bellerophon*, but an extra pair of guns was added to each superstructure group; the additional guns to the forward group were mounted in a slightly higher position, and the after mountings were provided with better arcs of fire by cutting away part of the embrasure sides. This class were the last British battleships to carry any anti-torpedo armament on the turret tops.

Armour

The armoured scheme retained the same features as those in the *Bellerophon* class. Exceptions were:

1. The 10in strake was carried to the outer faces of the forward and after barbettes instead of terminating at the inner face of the former and abreast the centre of the latter.
2. The 7in strake forward terminated after only a very short run, being met by a 4in–5in bulkhead running from lower to upper deck level. The extension after the 7in thickness reduced to 2in as opposed to the 6in and 7in in *Bellerophon*. Aft, the thickness was again reduced to 2in from a uniform 5in fitted in *Bellerophon*.
3. The forward sloped armoured deck, which usually ran from the middle to lower decks, was omitted and in its place a 4in–5in bulkhead terminated the 10in main belt strake. Aft, the bulkhead was 8in thick as in *Bellerophon*.
4. The maximum thickness of the main deck armour was increased from 1¼in to 1½in and was applied outside the fore barbette instead of between the 4th and 5th barbettes. The middle deck around the outer face of the after barbette was reduced in thickness from 3in to 1½in.

ST VINCENT CLASS: PARTICULARS, AS COMPLETED

Construction

	Dockyard	Laid Down	Launched	Completed
St Vincent:	Portsmouth DY	30 Dec 1907	10 Sept 1908	May 1909
Collingwood:	Devonport DY	3 Feb 1908	7 Nov 1908	April 1910
Vanguard:	Vickers	2 April 1908	22 April 1909	1 March 1910.

Displacement (tons)
19,400, 19,700 (load), 22,800 (deep).

Dimensions
Length: *St Vincent* 500ft 3in pp, 531ft wl, 536ft oa
Collingwood 500ft 0½in pp, 531ft wl, 536ft oa
Vanguard 500ft 0¼in pp, 531 ft wl, 536ft oa
Beam: *St Vincent* 84ft 0¾in
Collingwood 84ft 2in
Vanguard 84ft 3in
Draught: 27ft–31ft (mean); see inclining experiments
Height of CT vision slits above lower wl: 44ft
Height of fore funnel above lower wl: 65ft
Height of fore lower mast above lower wl: 100ft
Depth of keel from upper deck: 52ft 6in.

Armament
Ten 12in 50cal Mk XI; 80–100rpg
Eighteen 4in Mk III; 150rpg (wartime 200)
One 12pdr
Four 3pdr (saluting)
Seven MG
Three 18in torpedo tubes (two beam, one stern); nine torpedoes.

Director control
None fitted on completion.

Armour*
Main belt: 10in–8in
End belts: 7in–2in forward, 2in aft
Upper belt: 8in
Main bulkheads: 5in forward, 8in aft
Extra forward bulkhead: 4in
Decks: main 1½in–¾in, middle 1¾in slope and flat, lower 1½in forward, 3in aft
Barbettes: 9in–5in, wing faces 10in
Turrets: 11in face, 8in rear, 3in crown, 2in floor
Conning tower: 11in side, 8in rear; tube 5in
After CT: 8in side, 3in crown, 4in floor; tube 4in
Anti-torpedo bulkheads: 3in–2in–1½in.

Machinery
Parsons direct-drive turbines, four propellers
Boilers: eighteen Babcock & Wilcox large-tube (*Collingwood* 18 Yarrow)
Working pressure: 235psi
Total heating surface: 63,414sq ft
Length of boiler rooms: *St Vincent* 124ft 1in (incl. cross bunkers); *Collingwood* 114ft; *Vanguard* 113ft 9⅜in
Length of engine rooms: 68ft 0½in
Fuel: 900 tons coal min., 2,700 tons max.; 850 tons oil
Designed SHP: 24,500 for 21 knots
Radius of action: 4,690nm at 10 knots (111 tons coal per 24 hours); 6,900nm at 10 knots (plus oil spray).

Ship's boats
Pinnaces (steam): two 45ft
Pinnaces (sail): one 36ft
Launches (steam): one 42ft
Cutters: three 32ft
Whalers: three 27ft
Gigs: one 30ft
Skiff dinghies: one 16ft
Balsa raft: one 13ft 6in.

Searchlights
Seven 36in: two foremast, two mainmast, two after superstructure.

Rangefinder positions
One each spotting top, one each turret, one each side after boat deck.

Battle signal stations
One immediately abaft forward upper conning tower.

Anchors
Three 127cwt Admiralty type (bower and sheet), one 42cwt, one 15cwt, one 5cwt.
475 fathoms 2¹¹⁄₁₆th cable.

Wireless
Mk I W/T, Type II W/T, Type 9 W/T (short-radius).

Complement
St Vincent: 756 (1909); 823 (1915)
Collingwood: 758 (1911)
Vanguard: 753 (1910).

Cost
Official estimate *St Vincent*

Hull and labour:	£235,000
Armour:	£440,000
Contract work:	£110,000
Steamboats:	£18,000
Incidental charges:	£112,000

St Vincent: £1,579,970 (plus £142,000 guns)
Collingwood: £1,538,888 (plus £142,000 guns)
Vanguard: £1,464,030 (plus £142,000 guns).

*All KC. Decks Nickel Chrome; anti-torpedo bulkheads non-cemented; conning tower KC with 'Era steel' on tubes.

This reduction in thickness of the ends of the ship was seen as detrimental to an otherwise well-balanced armour layout and provided controversy with respect to this and succeeding designs for many years to come. The *St Vincent* class can be characterized as a reversion from the complete water-line armour belt to the 'all or nothing' practice of thirty years before. (See *Neptune*, armour.)

The 10in strake amidships extended between the outer faces of the end barbettes, the upper edge at middle deck level, and the lower edge 4ft 11in below the water-line where it reduced in thickness to 8in. Above the 10in thickness was another run of 8in which lay over the top and was 8ft 7in above the water-line at normal displacement. The 7in strake forward ran for a short

ST VINCENT: GM AND STABILITY

Based on inclining experiments, 19 February 1910

	Displacement (tons)	Draught	GM	Maximum stability	Stability vanishes at
'A' Condition (= load)*	19,488	28ft 11 in	5ft	33°	65°
'B' Condition (= deep)**	22,016	30ft 10in	5.6ft	34°	71°
'B' Condition plus 860 tons oil	22,876	31ft	6.55ft	–	–
'C' Condition (= light)	18,364	–	4,75ft	–	–

*Fully equipped plus 900 tons coal. **Fully equipped plus 2,700 tons coal.

distance, then reduced to 2in and ran to the bows at this thickness. Forward this 2in run was raised to nearly upper deck level, but aft, the strake was lowered to slightly below main deck level and retained the same thickness throughout.

The main 5in bulkhead forward closed the extremities of the 10in main belt and the 8in side armour between the lower and main decks. The main bulkhead aft closed the same extremities, but was 8in thick. The extra bulkhead forward closed the extremities of the 7th run forward and ran from the lower deck through to upper deck level.

The barbettes on the centreline were given 9in thick plates above the armoured deck; below this they reduced to 5in. On the beam barbettes it was still 9in above the armoured deck, but a 10in maximum was fitted over the exposed outer faces. Below the armoured deck it reduced to 5in as in the centreline barbettes. The turrets were the same as those in the *Bellerophon* class.

The forward conning tower had 11in on the faces, an 8in rear, 3in crown and 2in floor. The communications tube was 5in. The aft CT, close abaft the second funnel, had 8in plates on the faces, 3in crowns and a 4in floor. The signal tower, immediately abaft the forward CT, had 3in faces, 2in crowns and a 2in floor.

The main deck, which ran from the forward bulkhead to the after main bulkhead, was 1½in thick outside the forward barbette

Below: *St Vincent* nearing completion at Portsmouth DY in 1910. Note compass platform, twin SL and pair of 4in guns on top of 'Y' turret.

and ¾in elsewhere. The middle deck extended between the main bulkheads with the lower edge at the ship's side, along the lower edge of the belt. The thickness was 1¾in throughout on both flat and inclines. The ends of the lower deck were underwater outside the forward and after barbettes. Thicknesses were 1½in forward and 3in aft.

The two main longitudinal anti-torpedo bulkheads varied in thickness from 1in–1½in–3in, and extended from the forward end of 'A' barbette to the after end of 'Y' magazine. The depth was from the outer bottom of the vessel, rising to the main armoured deck. The bulkheads were pierced in the way of the boiler rooms for coaling. At the level of the lower deck there were passages for electrical wiring and hydraulic piping. Air space bulkheads were built into the shell and magazine rooms near the boiler and engine spaces.

Machinery

The machinery layout was almost identical with that of the *Bellerophon* class, but the SHP was increased from *Bellerophon*'s 23,000 to 24,500 giving a marginal speed increase of approximately ½ knot. Separate cruising turbines were fitted despite the difficulties being experienced with these, although one should say that this class did not suffer from the inherent defects of previous ships, and the machinery was generally found to be

Below: Bow view of *St Vincent*, 1910.

ST VINCENT

St Vincent during trials in May 1910.

Left: *St Vincent* anchored at Portland, c. 1912.

satisfactory. Each boiler was fitted with four burners of the single-orifice, pressure-sprayer type. Total output of oil sprayed per boiler at 150psi was 900 pounds. The Devonport-built *Collingwood* was fitted with only three sprayers, as was *Temeraire* of the *Bellerophon* class. It is not known why these Devonport ships were given only three sprayers, but it certainly did not impair their performance when steaming with the battlefleet. The output from these oil sprayers differed from ship to ship: *Vanguard*, *Bellerophon* and *Superb* having 960 pounds, *Temeraire*, *St Vincent* and *Collingwood* 900 pounds, the slight variation stemming from experiments to achieve maximum efficiency from each burner/boiler.

Appearance Changes

The *St Vincents* differed from the *Bellerophon* class only in minor

ST VINCENT CLASS: SPEED TRIALS, 1909–10

St Vincent
Measured mile, off Chesil Beach, 17 Dec 1909
Full power
Revolutions: 321.6rpm; 333.4rpm
SHP: 25,875; 28,218
Speed (knots): 21.275; 21.665

Collingwood
Polperro, 17 Jan 1910
1/5th-power
SHP: 2,310; 4,900
Speed (knots): 10; 13

3/5th-power
SHP: 9,100
Speed (knots): 16.4

4/5th-power
SHP: 19,600
Speed (knots): 19.8

8-hour, full power
Revolutions: 326.2rpm
SHP: 26,789
Speed (knots): 20.62.

Vanguard is reported to have made 22.3 knots with 25,780shp while on trials. This is an unofficial figure and she was probably in the light condition if this speed was logged.

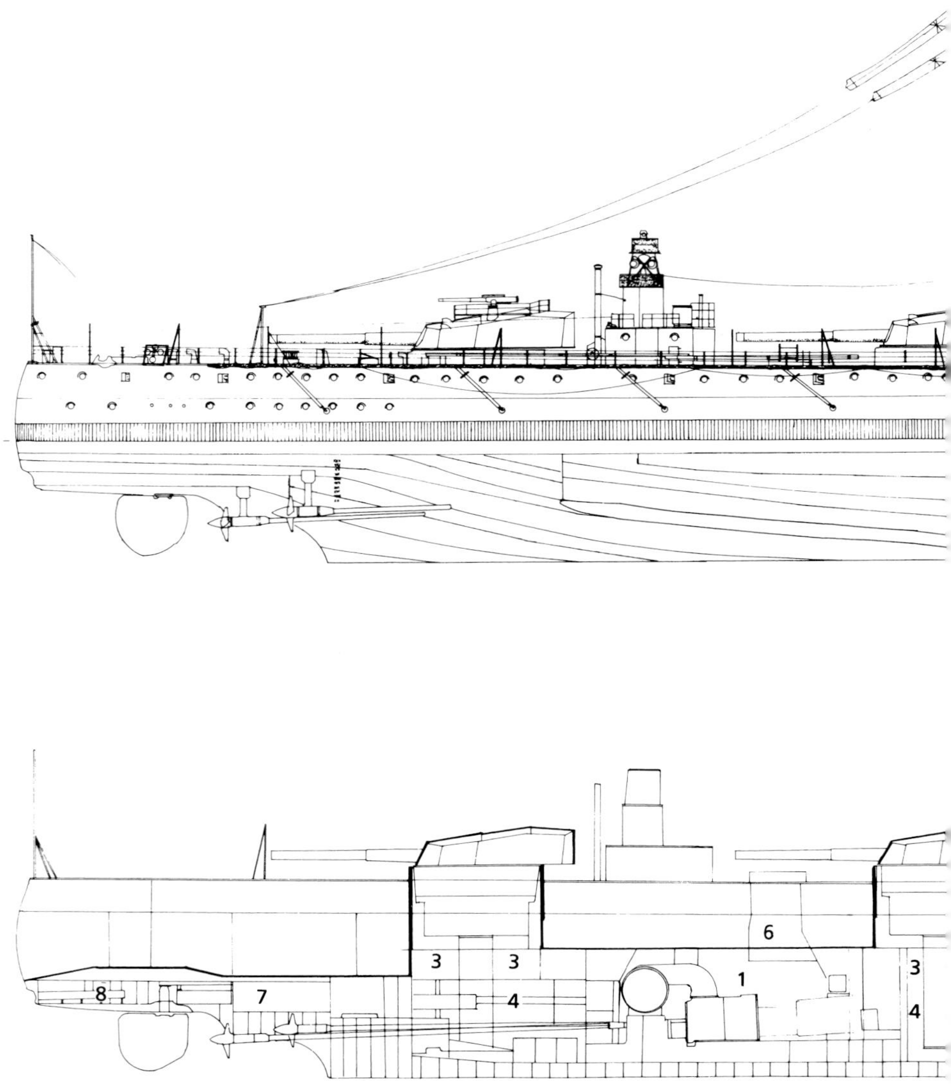

details, and from certain angles it was very difficult to distinguish them. The main differences were:

1. Unequal and taller funnels than the *Bellerophons*, the after funnel being distinctly larger than the fore.
2. Shorter topmasts and longer topgallants.

All three vessels looked alike with the following exceptions.

St Vincent: Large steampipe abaft fore funnel. Flagpole to fore topgallant mast. Two white bands on second funnel.
Vanguard: Slightly more prominent caging to funnels. One red band on each funnel.
Collingwood: Low, obscure caging to funnels. One white band on second funnel.

1910–11 4in guns removed from fore turret in *Vanguard*. Small rangefinder later mounted on turret. Blast screen fitted at rear of fore turret in all. Two pairs of searchlights transferred from bridge to forward superstructure, abeam fore funnel, in *Collingwood*.
1911–12 R/F and screen removed from fore turret in *Vanguard*. 4in guns and screens removed from fore turret in other two.
1912–13 Fore control top rebuilt with a narrower face. Searchlights redistributed in *Collingwood* (same as in *Bellerophon*).

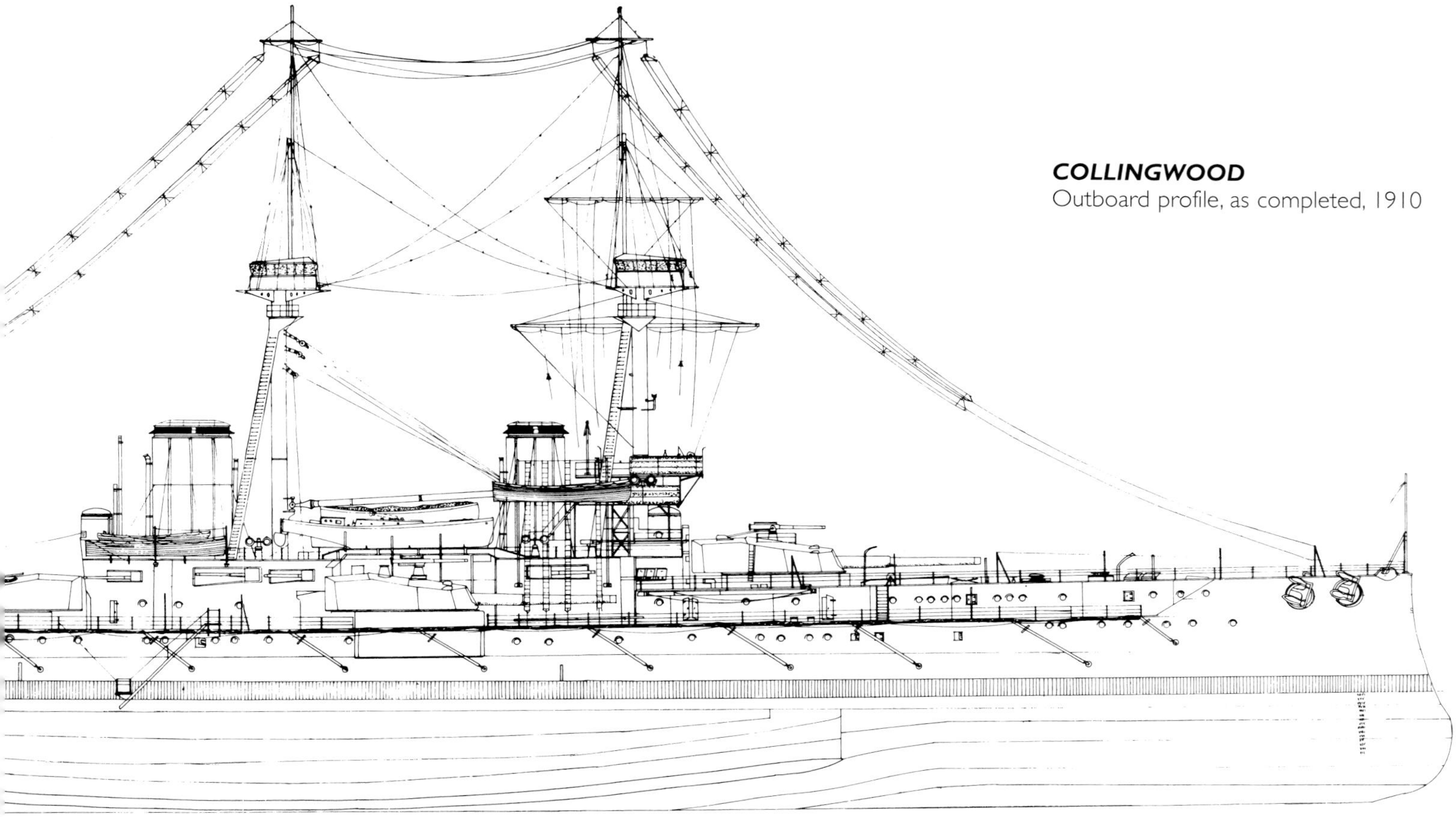

COLLINGWOOD
Outboard profile, as completed, 1910

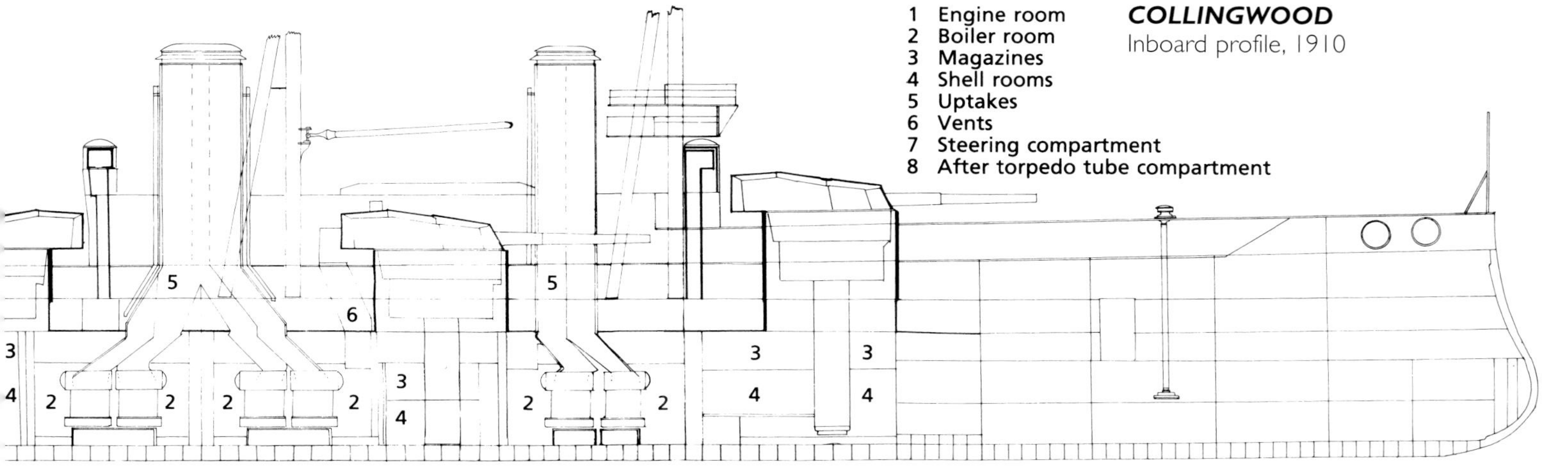

COLLINGWOOD
Inboard profile, 1910

Collingwood July 1912. 4in guns have been removed from turret tops, four instead of three yards on fore masts, extra SL near bridge positions.

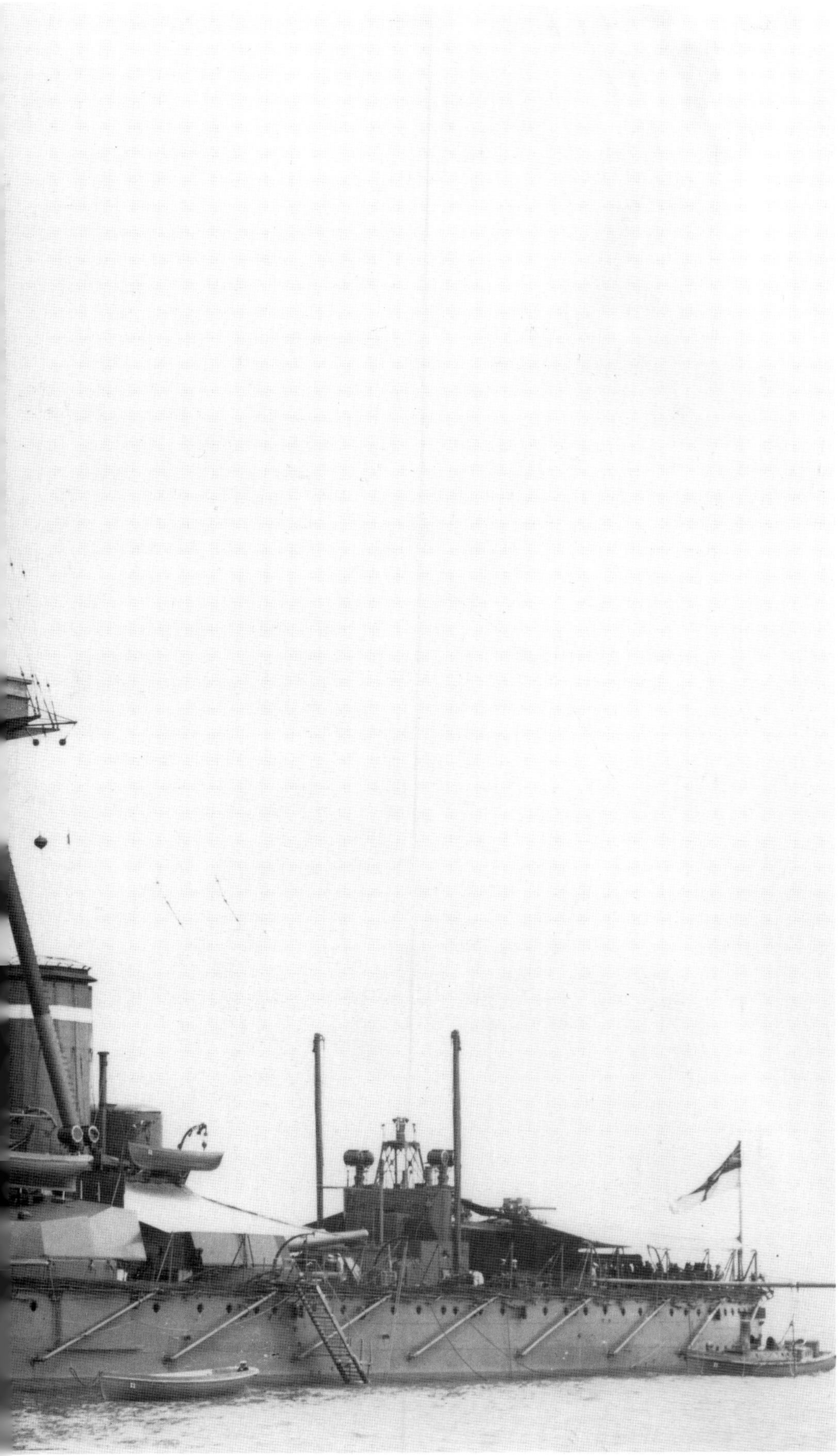

1913–14 *Collingwood* and *Vanguard*: Upper pair of 4in guns in forward group were plated in. Two pairs of searchlights were transferred from forward superstructure, and repositioned in bridge wings. One 24in added, port and starboard on forward superstructure, in *Vanguard*. SL was modified as in *Collingwood*. Splinter shields fitted to superstructure 4in guns, the exception being the two forward pairs in midships group in *Vanguard*. Original simple bridgework, over conning tower, replaced by an enlarged and modified structure, built back around the tripod legs, leaving conning tower well clear of obstruction. Navigating platform now extended well forward.

1913–14 Topgallants and topmasts removed from *Collingwood*.

1913–14 *St Vincent*: upper pair of 4in guns in forward group plated in. Two pairs of bridgework SL remounted in superstructure abeam bridge. Splinter shields fitted to forward group of 4in guns. Bridge modifications as in *Collingwood* and *Vanguard*.

1914 Funnel bands deleted on outbreak of hostilities.

1914–15 Director control fitted for main armament, the director tower being located beneath foretop. Fore control top enlarged. 4in anti-torpedo guns reduced in number and relocated in two central positions in forward and aft superstructures. Two 3in AA added. SLs in *St Vincent* redistributed as in the other two. Topgallants removed from *St Vincent* and *Vanguard*, but original height of topmasts retained.

1915–16 Anti-torpedo guns further reduced in number. Torpedo nets removed. Topmasts reduced in height in *Vanguard* and *St Vincent*.

1916–17 Anti-torpedo guns reduced to thirteen by April 1917. AA armament again modified to carry one 4in and one 3in by April 1917. Extra deck protection added around areas of shell rooms and magazines after Jutland (approximately 50 tons). Kite balloon equipment fitted in *St Vincent*. Rangefinder baffles fitted to both masts, and camouflage painted on bows of *St Vincent*. Both features removed by end of 1917 to early 1918.

1917–18 Rangefinder clocks fitted to face of fore control tops, and to rear of centre SL tower on after superstructure in *Collingwood*. AA guns removed from platform between 4th and 5th turrets and remounted right aft on quarterdeck in *Collingwood*, but for some reason this is not evident in *St Vincent*. Stern TT removed.

1917–18 SL redistributed and 'coffee-box' towers fitted abeam mainmast and funnel. One pair of 24in lamps fitted on each at first, these eventually being replaced by 36in lamps. SLs removed from forward superstructure, mainmast and central platform on foremast. Clinker screen (or cap) fitted to forward funnel in *St Vincent* and *Vanguard*. Like the others, *Collingwood* had her screen fitted on fore funnel at first, but by August 1917 she had a screen on after funnel as well. 1917 *Vanguard* lost.

1918 High-angle rangefinder fitted on fore control top in *St Vincent* and *Collingwood*. Fore control tops further enlarged in both surviving ships, with extensions at rear for *St Vincent*, and in front for *Collingwood*. After control top removed in *Collingwood*, being found of little value, because of smoke interference, although retained in *St Vincent*. Aircraft flying-off platforms fitted over tops of forward and after turrets in *Collingwood*. Forward topmast removed from both ships to accommodate masthead rangefinder. Mechanical semaphore fitted over fore control top in *St Vincent*.

1919–22 36in SL on fore tripod platforms in *Collingwood* replaced by 24in signalling lamps which had been removed from forward superstructure previously. Clinker screens removed from both funnels in *Collingwood*. Foretopmast replaced in *Collingwood*. Mechanical semaphore replaced by small flagpole in *St Vincent*. By 1922 the class was now very easy to distinguish from *Bellerophon* class. Bridgework in all vessels was different and after island structure was very different in *St Vincent* class.

The Loss of *Vanguard*

On the evening of 9 July 1917, the battleship *Vanguard* suddenly blew up and disappeared within a matter of minutes. A Board of Inquiry was appointed to ascertain the cause. Such incidents had happened before – the pre-dreadnought *Bulwark* and the armoured cruiser *Natal* had both blown up as a result of spontaneous combustion in the areas of the magazines. Great Britain was now very much at war and it was vital to establish clearly whether the ship's destruction was caused by enemy penetration of the anchorage, or by a cordite mishap. The lengthy proceedings were very interesting and threw much light on practices concerning the disposition and use of cordite in battleships at that time.

During the afternoon of the 9th, *Vanguard* had been practising the 'Abandon ship!' routine and had dropped anchor near the north shore of Scapa Flow at about 18.30, having finished her exercises at approximately 17.00. Most of the ship's boilers were in use: 'A' boiler room had numbers 2, 3, 4, 5 and 6 firing, while 'B' boiler room had all boilers in use. Numbers 4, 5 and 6 of 'B' were kept alight for auxiliary purposes, and 'A' had kept numbers 2 and 3 alight only. At this time the 'Red' and 'Sea-Doors' were open. Although it was wartime and these doors should have been closed, this was not thought necessary because the ship was in the safe waters of a home port. Relative to this, an order was given at 20.30 for all of these doors to be closed for the night. All seemed well with the ship, which had now come to rest. The explosion occurred at 23.20.

From the many varying accounts given by witnesses aboard nearby ships, it would seem that smoke was seen to issue from the area just below the foremast. After a short interval a heavy explosion was accompanied by an enormous sheet of flame, after which the ship became enveloped in dense smoke. A second explosion followed the first and greatly increased the flame area, but the precise location of this eruption was never determined because of the dense smoke. Some eyewitnesses claimed that there was a third explosion, but this was considered to have been rumblings within the moving hull. One witness said that he had noticed some alteration in *Vanguard*'s trim, but as he was the only one to claim positively that he had seen the ship explode, his evidence was received with a certain amount of scepticism. No one actually witnessed the sinking of the ship.

A general opinion was that the explosions had occurred in the area of 'P' and 'Q' 12in turrets, probably in the magazines beneath. An enormous amount of debris was thrown up and the nearby *Bellerophon* was showed with particles of steel, including a large chunk of plate measuring 5ft by 6ft. These fragments were seen to come from the area of 'P' and 'Q' turrets. The large chunk that landed on *Bellerophon* was matched on a sister ship and was found to have come from the central dynamo room, which proved that the explosion originated in the central part of the ship and not near 'A' magazine as had been supposed at one point. If, as was thought, one of the magazines had exploded, the gases would have had a large venting area through the uptakes in that vicinity so that plating in the passageway would not have been subjected

Above: A poor but shocking photograph of the remains of *Vanguard* after she exploded whilst at anchor in harbour, July 1917 (*Erin* in background).

Opposite, top: An excellent starboard close up of *St Vincent* as she begins her preliminary sea trials in February 1910.

Opposite, bottom: *Vanguard* July 1914, anchored in Spithead Roads and preparing for what was probably the largest Fleet Review of dreadnoughts ever held. Note SL distribution around bridgework forward and around main tripod legs.

Left: *Collingwood* in dry dock at Rosyth 1918. In for a hull inspection and clean. Note the freshly-painted black waterline and funnel caps on both funnels.

Vanguard c.1912. Rangefinder on 'A' turret roof.

to great heat, but would have received extreme blast effects.

The only two survivors had been at the end of the ship and were unable to give any useful evidence as to the condition of the ammunition passageways. At the Inquiry it was made abundantly clear that at no time was there any indication of anything abnormal in the conditions aboard the ship. The cause of the disaster was initially ascribed to one or more of three possible alternatives:

1. Negligence on the part of officers in charge of cordite stowage.
2. Ashes from boilers being placed against adjacent bulkheads of either 'P' or 'Q' magazines.
3. Enemy action, either by U-boat or saboteur placing a slow-fuzed bomb aboard.

The cases of the battleship *Bulwark* and the cruiser *Natal*, which had both been lost in similar circumstances, were re-investigated. Although probably a coincidence, it was noted that all three ships were Chatham based.

When the Board asked all ships in the vicinity to furnish figures showing magazine temperatures as at dusk on the day of the disaster, a startling fact emerged. There was no statutory system for

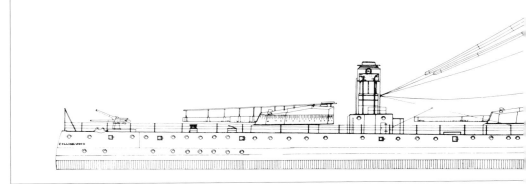

COLLINGWOOD
Outboard profile, 1918/19, showing wartime modifications

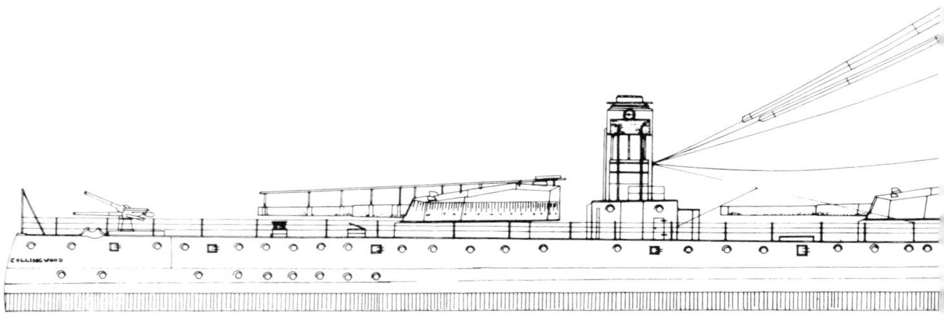

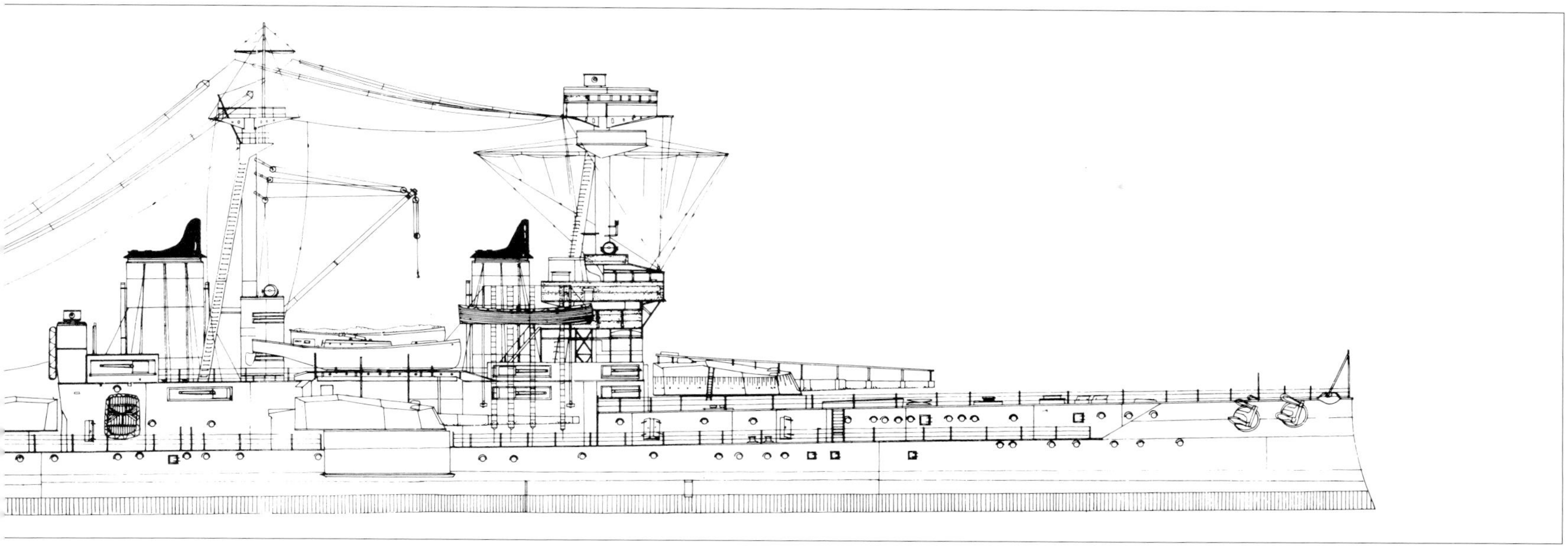

Above: *St Vincent*, late 1917, showing wartime alterations and additions. Heavy bridgework anti-rangefinder baffles on masts and funnel, deflection scales on turrets, SL towers around main tripod legs and strange paintwork around bows.

Left: *Collingwood* as completed and during her trials period. On the night of 9 September 1909, while she was completing for sea, a small fire broke out in one of her bunkers. The bunker was flooded and the fire extinguished before any significant damage could be caused.

logging temperatures; the job was sometimes left to the chief stoker and his squad, who made spasmodic random checks. In fact, no abnormal temperatures had been logged, in any of the ships for some time because as the war progressed, with a general order of alert permanently in being, it had become normal practice to maintain shell and magazine rooms to a high degree of safety. But no 'standard procedure' had been laid down.

The preliminary finding was that sacks of coal had been stowed in the patent fuel spaces adjoining 'P' and 'Q' handing rooms, and when the hatches were closed there was little or no ventilation in the vicinity. One of the bulkheads to these spaces formed a wall of the 4in magazines. The temperature rose beyond the normal and cordite ignited spontaneously. It was noted that there had been a fire in one of *Vanguard*'s coal bunkers in 1914, and the bunker had had to be flooded. The cause of the fire was never ascertained. Similar incidents had occurred aboard *St Vincent* some two years previously.

Evidence had shown that *Vanguard*'s 4in gun deck had been completely closed in by protective mattresses shortly before her loss, and this certainly would have prevented circulation of cool air to the magazine and shell spaces. Another discovery was that the funnel uptakes and ventilation trunking were hardly ever inspected and could – and frequently did – become clogged by foreign bodies.

The Board of Inquiry had to reach a conclusion concerning the loss of one of His Majesty's ships, and its final deliberations were that: the loss of the vessel was caused by a fire starting in a 4in magazine, which quickly spread to either 'P' or 'Q' magazine rooms, set off the cordite charges therein, and destroyed the ship. Other suggestions as to cause of the explosion were ruled out after thorough investigation. These were:

1. That an explosive device was triggered from the shore.
2. That the cordite was old or inferior.
3. That two ordnance fitters who had left the ship shortly before its destruction had planted an explosive device.
4. That an enemy agent had got aboard.

It was not ruled out, however, that an explosive device could have been placed among canteen supplies, which had been newly brought aboard. The canteen supplies room was in the area of the magazines, and stowage in this area would certainly be avoided in the future. No blame was attached to any of the 804 men who were lost with the ship.

History: *St Vincent*

Ordered on 26 October 1907. Began trials in February 1910.

1910 *3 May* Commissioned at Portsmouth for service with 1st Division Home Fleet as 2nd flagship.
July Annual manoeuvres with Atlantic and Mediterranean Fleets.
26–29 July With the combined Home Fleet assembled in Torbay for the visit by HM King George V.
1911 *Jan* Combined exercises off NW coast of Spain with Mediterranean and Atlantic Fleets and 4th CS.
24 June Present at Coronation Fleet Review at Spithead.
June–July Combined exercises off SW coasts of England and Ireland.
July Exercises in North Sea.
1912 *1 May* Fleet reorganization, 1st Division became 1st BS.
7–11 May Royal visit to 1st and 2nd Fleets at Weymouth, followed by four days' exercises at sea.
28 May Recommissioned at Portsmouth for service as Second-in-Command, 1st BS Home Fleet.
9 July Present at Parliamentary Review at Spithead.
Oct Tactical exercises with Home Fleet.
1912–13 Extensive refit (£17,818).
1914 *21 April* Recommissioned at Portsmouth for service in 1st BS as flagship of Second-in-Command.
15 July Left Portland.
16 July Arrived Spithead.
17–20 July Test mobilization and Fleet Review. This was the greatest of all reviews, the dreadnoughts present exceeding the number at any subsequent review.
20–25 July Exercises at sea with combined fleets.

Above: *St Vincent*, starboard profile, during listing trials, hence the extremely low freeboard. Note peculiar anti-rangefinder baffles behind second funnel.

Right: *St Vincent*, at Rosyth with kite balloon, late 1917/18.

25 July Returned to Portland.
29 July Sailed for Scapa Flow.
22 Oct–3 Nov Based at Lough Swilly (see *Bellerophon*).
1915 *8 July* Visit by HM King George V to Scapa; all personnel of 2nd Division of 1st BS were assembled for inspection on board *St Vincent*.
Nov Relieved as flagship of Second-in-Command by *Colossus* and became private ship in same squadron.
1916 *31 May* Battle of Jutland; In 5th Division of Battle Fleet with *Colossus*, *Neptune* and *Collingwood*, and was 20th ship in the line alter the deployment. From 18.54 to 19.26 engaged enemy battleship believed to be of the *König* class. Her fire was effective at a range of 9,500–10,000 yards and scored hits on that vessel.
June Transferred to 4th BS.
1918 *17 April* With Grand Fleet based at Scapa when they were transferred to Rosyth.
24 April With *Hercules* ordered from Invergordon where she was undergoing repairs, to support *Agincourt* and 2nd CS, isolated in the Orkneys during the last sortie of the German High Seas Fleet, but was unable to leave port.
21 Nov Present in the line (Southern) at the surrender of the High Seas Fleet.
1919 *March* On abolition of Grand Fleet, reduced to Reserve, and became gunnery training ship at Portsmouth.
June Serving as flagship Reserve Fleet at Portsmouth.
4 Dec Recommissioned in Reserve at Portsmouth.
Dec Relieved as gunnery training ship at Portsmouth by *Courageous* and transferred to the Reserve in Rosyth as tender to *Hercules*.
1921 *March* Placed on Disposal list at Rosyth.
1 Dec Sold to Stanlee Shipbreaking Co.
1922 *March* Towed to Dover for breaking.

History: *Vanguard*

Ordered 6 February 1908. Began trials in November 1909.

1910 *1 March* Commissioned at Devonport for service with 1st Division Home Fleet.
April Exercises off Scotland with 1st and 2nd Fleets.
July Annual manoeuvres with combined fleets.
26–29 July Visit by HM King George V to Torbay.
1911 *Jan* Exercises off NW coast of Spain with Mediterranean and Atlantic Fleets.
24 June Present at Coronation Fleet Review.
June–July Combined exercises with Atlantic Fleet off SW coasts of Scotland and Ireland.
July Exercises in North Sea with Atlantic Fleet.
1911–12 Refit at Devonport (£17,551).
1912 *28 March* Recommissioned at Devonport.
7–11 May Royal visit to Weymouth, followed by four days' exercises at sea.
Oct Tactical exercises with 1st Fleet.
1914 *31 March* Recommissioned at Sheerness for service in 1st BS.
15 July Left Portland.
16 July Arrived Spithead.
17–20 July Test mobilization and fleet review.
20–25 July Exercises at sea.
25 July Returned to Portland.
29 July Left Portland for Scapa.
1 Sept At approximately 18.00 she opened fire during a submarine false alarm, after which the entire fleet put to sea for the night.
1916 *April* Transferred to 4th BS.
31 May Battle of Jutland. In 4th Division with *Benbow*, *Bellerophon* and *Temeraire*, 16th ship in line after deployment.
1917 *9 July* While lying at anchor in Scapa Flow, blew up at approximately 23.20 (see narrative of incident, 'loss of *Vanguard*').

Above: *St Vincent*, late 1918. Paint work on bows, and rangefinder baffles now removed.

History: *Collingwood*

Ordered 26 October 1907. Commenced trials in February 1910.

1910 *19 April* Commissioned at Devonport for service in 1st Division Home Fleet.
July Annual manoeuvres with Mediterranean and Atlantic Fleets, and 1st, 2nd, 3rd and part of 4th Division Home Fleet.
26–29 July Present when the King visited Fleet at Torbay.
1911 Jan Combined exercises off NW coast of Spain with Mediterranean and Atlantic Fleets.
11 Feb Touched an uncharted rock in Ferrol harbour sustaining some damage to her bottom plates.
24 June Present at Coronation Fleet Review.
June–July Combined exercises off SW coasts of Scotland and Ireland with Atlantic Fleet and 4th CS.
July Exercises in North Sea.
1912 *26 March* Recommissioned at Devonport for service in 1st Division Home Fleet.
1 May Fleet reorganization, 1st Fleet becoming 1st BS.
11 May Royal visit to 1st and 2nd Fleets at Weymouth.
22 June Became flagship of 1st BS Home Fleet.
9 July Present at Parliamentary Review at Spithead.
Oct Took part in tactical exercises.
1912–13 Under refit (£19,097).
1913 *March* Visited Cherbourg with 1st BS.
1914 *18 April* Left Devonport on a short cruise with HRH the Prince of Wales on board.
22 June Relieved as flagship of 1st BS by *Marlborough* and became private ship in same squadron.
15 July Left Portland.
16 July Arrived Spithead.
17–20 July Test mobilization and Fleet Review.
20–25 July Exercises at sea with combined fleets.
25 July Returned to Portland.
29 July Left Portland for Scapa Flow.
22 Oct Temporarily based at Lough Swilly while anti-U-boat preparations were underway at Scapa Flow.

Below: *Collingwood* approaches her anchorage at Rosyth, 25 August 1917.

1916 *31 May* Battle of Jutland. In 5th Division of Battle Fleet with *Colossus*, *Neptune* and *St Vincent*. She was 18th ship in line after the deployment. At approximately 19.12, with *Colossus*, she concentrated accurate fire on an enemy battlecruiser believed to be *Lützow*. Hits were observed and the ship was reported to be on fire. At 19.23 *Collingwood* turned sharply to avoid two torpedoes.

June Transferred to 4th BS.

1918 *12 April* Sailed with Grand Fleet from Scapa Flow after the base was transferred to Rosyth.

1919 *Jan* Reached Devonport from Grand Fleet, and with *Colossus* and the old pre-dreadnought *London* formed temporary Reserve Fleet with *Colossus* as flagship.

18 March On breaking up of Grand Fleet, 3rd Fleet was formed,

and *Collingwood* relieved *Colossus* as flagship.
Sept Selected for service as turret drill ship and wireless telegraphy school at Devonport.
1 Oct Commissioned for this service.
Dec Relieved by *Glorious* and became tender to the Gunnery School and port W/T ship at Devonport.
1920 *1 June* Relieved by *Glorious* and placed in the Reserve.
1921 *20 July* Paid off on Disposal list, but reassigned as overflow ship attached to HMS *Impregnable* training establishment.
11 Oct Reached Portland to take up these duties.
1922 *March* Paid off.
Dec Sold to Messrs. J. Cashmore of Newport.
1923 *3 March* Towed to Newport from Portsmouth for scrapping.

Collingwood 1919/20. Amidships port side showing detail of her bridgework. Both funnel caps have been removed.

Indefatigable Class: 1908 ESTIMATES

Design

During the long summer months of 1908 fierce controversy raged over the capital ship programme for the following year. Naval Intelligence reported that Germany had stepped-up its 1908 Programme to four capital ships and everything pointed to a another four in the next year's estimates. Furthermore, Germany was beginning to stockpile war materiel. In Britain, the new Liberal Government led by Mr Asquith proposed amendments to reduce naval expenditure, however. The Sea Lords and the DNC were unable to muster convincing arguments for a full and unreduced programme, so funds for only two ships were allocated. There was wild reaction from the Press; Fred Jane put the message clearly and bluntly:

> Mr Asquith is still hammering at the wheeze about the mysterious new German Dreadnoughts of the 1908 programme as

> an excuse for not building further British Dreadnoughts. The exact cost of obtaining that information for the latest edition of *Jane's Fighting Ships is* £4 7s 2¾d., and the Government, the Naval Intelligence Department, or anyone else, could have got it for the same figure. As a matter of fact, they have got it. They are perfectly aware of the new German Dreadnoughts.

He concluded: 'Either we have to be absolutely supreme at sea or not; there is no middle way', and asked whether Mr Asquith begrudged paying £4 7s 2¾d. for the country. 'We should', he said, 'sleep more quietly in our beds if some other Party were at the helm.'

Agitation continued throughout the summer of 1908 and into

INDEFATIGABLE CLASS: LEGEND, SUMMARY OF WEIGHTS (TONS)

Hull:	7,000
Armour:	3,735
Machinery:	3,591
Fuel:	3,170
Armament:	2,628
General equipment:	872
Engineers' stores:	100
Reserve feedwater:	45
Board margin:	100
Total:	**21,241**

Below, left and right: *Australia* under construction at John Brown's shipyard shows deck layout and second and third funnels during 1912.

the winter, when public outcry forcefully demanded that an emergency programme be put in hand immediately; Asquith's cutback policies were defeated. The 1908 Estimates had provided for one battleship and one battlecruiser, the latter closely to follow the design of the preceding *Invincible* class, which had been accepted and proven. Throughout the controversy concerning the concept of this single unit, Admiral Fisher had been unusually quiet. Later, he was to state that he never quite forgave those who were responsible for the near-disastrous reduction in naval construction in 1908. (Certain aspects of his criticism were levelled at Winston Churchill, who was seen to be sailing with those on the 'cutback' campaign.)

The new battlecruiser (actually called armoured cruiser at the time; the term battlecruiser did not come into effect until 1912–13) was an enlarged and slightly modified *Invincible*, with wider spacing of the midships turrets to secure increased cross-deck arcs of fire. Compared with *Invincible*, essential features were:

1. Nominal displacement increased by 1,500 tons on a length

increase of 23 feet oa, 18in beam and 6in on the designed draught.
2. Midships turrets more widely spaced.
3. Armouring similar, but distributed rather differently.
4. Designed speed unchanged, although in service *Indefatigable* was found to be the faster of the ships.
5. Fuel capacity and radius of action increased by approximately 388 tons fuel and 380 miles at 10 knots.
6. Other modifications included relocation of the conning tower and some superstructure rearrangement.

INDEFATIGABLE : GM AND STABILITY

Based on inclining experiments, 17 May 1913

	Displacement (tons)	Draught	GM	Maximum stability	Stability vanishes at
'A' Condition (load)*	–	26ft 3in	3.5ft	43°	74°
'A' Condition**	–	30ft	4.8ft	–	–

*Fully equipped plus 1,000 tons coal, reserve feedwater tanks empty.
**Fully equipped plus 1,000 tons coal, 840 tons oil.

The public queue up to get on board *Australia*, 1913.

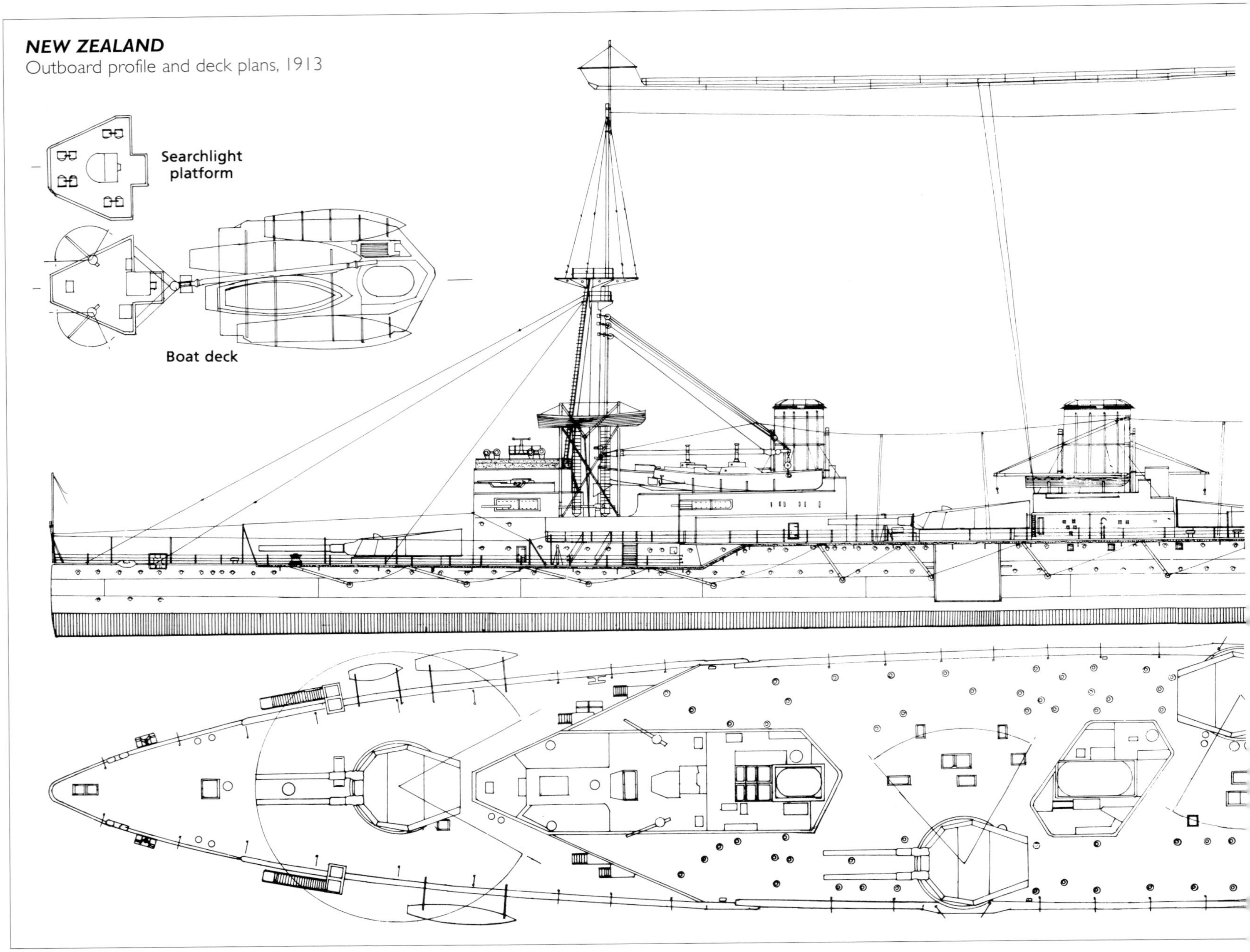

The inclusion of a battlecruiser in the 1908 Estimates suited Admiral Fisher very well; after all, the ship was his brain-child. But instead of developing the design, he ordered an enlarged version of *Invincible*. This put the new ship on a worse basis than the preceding trio – already known as the 'flying haystacks' because of their large funnels, which made large targets; and because the design did not incorporate extra protection, they were no better than the armoured cruiser types built some ten years previously. During construction, Fisher had stressed the need for secrecy, and no indication of *Indefatigable*'s armour, armament or speed had been divulged. It was stated, however, that she would be an improved *Indomitable*, and the following passage from the *Naval and Military Record* in 1909 shows that the secrecy was maintained.

> 'The *Indefatigable* will indeed be a very much improved *Indomitable*, so much so that she will be unlike any other warship that has ever yet been put upon the water for the British Navy. We are not in a position to disclose the full extent of her original features, but when internal combustion engines are hinted at, it will be manifest that at least one striking new step is in contemplation. Another point which may be predicted with a certain degree of confidence is the advent of the much talked about 13.5in guns, alike in the *Indefatigable* and *Neptune*, now building at Devonport and Portsmouth.'

The misconceived notions of the Liberal Government were partly offset by a welcome stroke of patriotism from the Dominions. New Zealand and Australia each offered adequate funds for the building of one dreadnought type, and made no bones about their feelings regarding the ridiculous reduction of the battleship programme, especially in view of Germany's increased programme. The offer was accepted and Fisher was quick to divert the funds to the building of two more battlecruisers of the *Indefatigable* type. New Zealand's contribution was an outright gift to Britain, no stipulation being made as to how the ship was to be employed. Australia's ship would join the RAN on completion, and would be 'on offer' to the Royal Navy if needed.

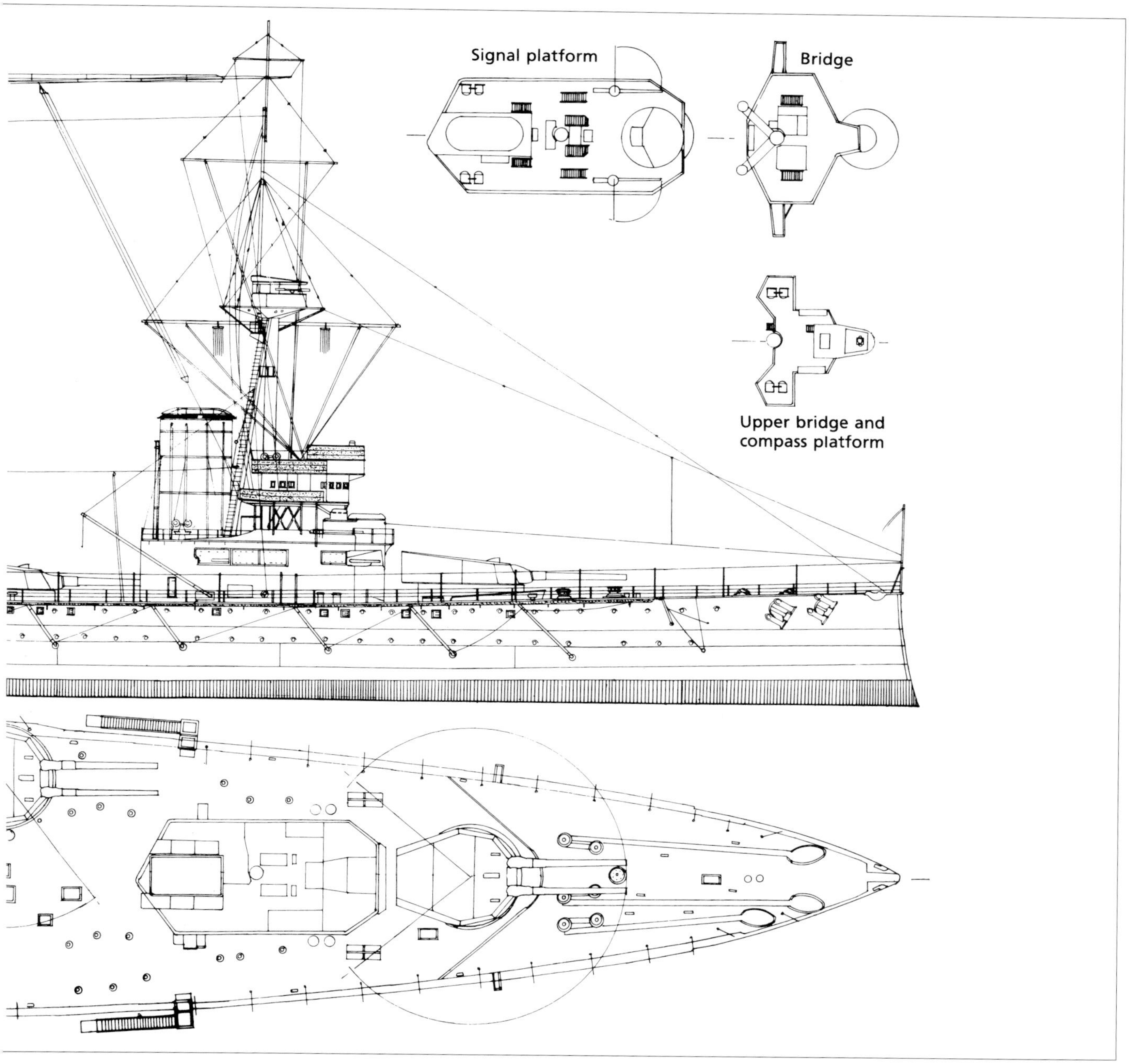

Left: *Indefatigable* as completed.

H.M.S. New Zealand

Armament

The wing and centreline armament disposition, as in *Invincible*, was repeated, but the midships turrets were spaced farther apart in order to achieve wider arcs of fire. Even so, the arcs had to be restricted because of blast effect, particularly to the deck. The end-on arcs of fire were restricted to 5° within the axial line forward and aft for the same reason, but this was considered acceptable because, it was stated, heavy end-on or astern fire would not be necessary in action; an adequate broadside was far more important. The wider turret spacing (the essential feature that distinguished the class from the *Invincible*) necessitated separating the midships magazines into two groups, and the interpositioning of these and the boiler rooms required special cooling arrangements. The length of the ship had to be increased by some 23 feet, and the end turrets had to be placed nearer the extremities of the ship, which made her less of a good seaboat than *Invincible*. This was seen as a weak spot in the design, but was accepted in view of the enhanced positions of the turrets.

The *Indefatigables* were the last British battlecruisers to have 12in turrets mounted en echelon. Amid erroneous Press speculation about 13.5in armament, it was established that the ships would receive the 12in; naturally, it was assumed that this would be the new 50cal Mk XI, but because of availability they received the Mk X. Anti-torpedo armament was a modified arrangement of *Invincible*'s layout. The 12in turret top location was abandoned, and the guns were mounted in two groups in the superstructure, six forward, and ten aft; four guns in each group were fitted in ports while the others were left in the open. The torpedo armament was reduced from that of *Invincible*, the stern tube and forward pair on the beam being suppressed.

Armour

Admiral Fisher's dictum 'speed is armour' was never better exemplified than in this class. Their extremely poor protection made

Opposite, top: *New Zealand*. Forward 12in guns, turret and bridgework are clearly shown. Note crest on bridge face and gun tampions.

Opposite, bottom: *New Zealand* as completed. After commissioning, she made the long trip to her name country to honour the government for the gift of the ship.

INDEFATIGABLE CLASS: PARTICULARS, AS COMPLETED

Construction

	Dockyard	Laid Down	Launched	Completed
Indefatigable:	Devonport DY	23 Feb 190	28 Oct 1909	April 1911
New Zealand:	Fairfield	20 June 1910	1 July 1911	Nov 1912
Australia:	John Brown	23 June 1910	25 Oct 1911	June 1913.

Displacement (tons)
18,750 (load), 21,240 (deep; coal only), 22,080 (deep; plus oil).

Dimensions
Length: 555ft pp, 588ft wl, 590ft oa
Beam as moulded: 79ft 10¼in
Draught: 26ft 3in to 30ft
Freeboard: 30ft forward, 22ft 3in amidships, 17ft 3in aft
Height of CT vision slits above lower wl: 44ft 3in.

Armament
Eight 12in 45cal Mk X
Sixteen 4in 50cal Mk VII
Four 3pdr
Five MG
Two 18in torpedo tubes (one each beam, submerged).

Director control
None fitted on completion.

Armour*
Main belt (298ft): 6in
Ends: 4in–2½in forward, 4in–2½in aft
Bulkheads: 4in–3in forward, 4½in aft
Barbettes: 'A', 'B', 'Q' 7in, 'Y' 7in–4in–3in
Turrets: 7in face, 7in side, 3in roof
Ammunition hoists: 2in
Decks: main 2in–1in, lower 2½in–2in–1½in
Conning tower: 10in side, 3in roof, 3in floor
Communications tube: 4in
Spotting and signal tower: 4in side, 3in roof, 3in floor
After conning tower: 1½in–1in
Uptakes: 1½in–1in
Magazine screens: 2½in.

Machinery
Parsons direct-drive turbines, four propellers
Boilers: thirty-one Babcock & Wilcox, working pressure 250psi
Twenty-eight boilers had three oil burners; the remaining three had two
Each burner had a single-orifice oil sprayer, capacity 3001b per hour per burner
Length of boiler rooms: 172ft 0¾in
Length of engine rooms: 83ft 11¾in
Designed SHP: 43,000 (*New Zealand* 44,000) = 25.8 knots
Fuel: 1,000 tons coal (*Indefatigable* 3,340 plus 870 tons oil); (*New Zealand* 3,170 plus 840 tons oil)
Coal consumption per day (tons): 192 at 14 knots (economical speed); 530 at ⅗th power; 790 at full power
Radius of action (coal and oil): 3,360nm at 23.5 knots; 6,690nm at 10 knots.

Ship's boats
Pinnaces (steam): two 50ft
Pinnaces (sail): one 36ft
Launches (sail): one 42ft
Life cutters: three 32ft
Gigs: two 30ft
Whalers: three 27ft
Skiff dinghies: two 16ft
Balsa rafts: one 13ft 6in.

Searchlights
Sixteen twin 24in: two bridge forward, two forward superstructure (abeam fore funnel), four on large platform on after superstructure abaft mainmast (two port, two starboard).

Anchors
Three 125cwt Wasteney Smith stockless, one 42cwt, two 5cwt.

Wireless
Mk I W/T, W/T 9 short-radius.

Complement
Indefatigable: 790 (1913)
New Zealand: 806 (1913); 853 (1919); 1,070 (1921)
Australia: 818 (1913); 840 (1919).

Cost
Estimate: machinery £366,690; 12in armament (turntables, turrets, etc.), £120,255
Totals:
Indefatigable: £1,430,091 plus £98,500 guns
New Zealand: £1,684,990 plus £98,200 guns
Australia: £1,684,990 plus £98,200 guns.

*Main belts, bulkheads, barbettes, turrets, CT all KC; decks, magazine screens, uptakes nickel steel; CT tubes 'Era' steel. Data refers to *Indefatigable* only; other two slightly different.

Above: *Australia* during her trials period.

Below: *Australia* in heavy weather at the beginning of the war.

them very vulnerable as capital ships. The scale of armouring was little more than a modification of the preceding class of battle-cruisers, although from the secrecy that surrounded their design the impression had been given that they would be fitted with a 9in main belt. The principal differences were:

1. The belt abreast 'A' and 'Y' turrets was reduced from 6in to 4in.
2. Right forward the belt was reduced from 4in to 2½in, but the after extremities were carried to the stern, with a thickness of 2½in, instead of terminating at 'Y' barbette.
3. The main deck armour of ¾in outside the forward bulkhead was suppressed.
4. The main deck thickness over the magazines was increased from 1in to 2in.
5. The lower deck was increased from 1½in to 2in in the forward section, but reduced from 2½in to 2in aft.

Indefatigable's main belt was 6in thick and extended over machinery and boiler spaces before terminating inside the end barbettes. The upper edge at main deck level was approximately 8ft above the load waterline, the lower edge being 3ft below. Forward of this thickness was another strake of 4in which ran to just beyond 'A' barbette at the same height as the midships section; it was met by 2½in plates which then ran through to the stem of the ship at a higher level, almost reaching the upper deck. Aft of the main belt a 4in strake ran to the outer face of 'Y' barbette where it was met by a thickness of 2¼in which ran through to the stern at a height between lower and main decks. The bulkheads were 4in to 3in forward, and closed the forward extremities of the 4in side armour. They rose from lower deck to upper deck level. The 4½in after bulkhead closed the extremities of the 4in side armour and was fitted immediately behind 'Y' barbette; it rose from lower to main deck level.

The poor deck protection consisted of a 1in–2in thickness for the main deck. The 2in thickness was placed around the barbette, otherwise it was generally 1in. The lower deck consisted of plates ranging from 1½in to 2in. It ran from end to end of the ship, the crown being slightly above waterline level and the lower edge, which ran along the bottom of the 6in side armour, being 3ft below water. The 1½in thickness was generally on the flat and ran between the belt bulkheads; outside of these, at the ends, it

increased to 2in and ran to the extremities of the ship. The inclines of this deck throughout the midship section were 2in thick.

'A', 'B' and 'Q' barbettes were 7in thick, but this only ran down to the main deck where it then reduced to a 2in trunk. The aft barbette ('Y') was 7in uniform down to the main deck and then reduced to 3in on the inner face uniform down to the main deck and then reduced to 3in on the inner face and 4in on the outer face; below this were the usual 2in trunks. The turrets were 7in on the faces and sides with 3in crowns.

The forward conning tower had a 10in face and a 3in floor and roof. This was sited well clear of the bridge structure. Behind this was the spotting and signal tower, which was given plates of 4in on the sides and 3in on the roof and floor. The after conning tower for torpedo control had 1in plates and was situated in the rear face of the after superstructure. Plates of 1in–1½in were fitted in the uptakes which ran from the main deck through to the forecastle level. The machinery hatches were given the same protection of 1in–1½in, but terminated just above the main deck. Protection to the magazine and shell rooms consisted of close-fitting screens of a uniform 2½in thickness, varying in width according to location.

This inadequate protection was somewhat modified in the following colonial pair (*New Zealand* and *Australia*) and differed from *Indefatigable* in the following particulars:

1. Belt armour terminated 60ft short of the stem and 55ft from the stern, the extremities being closed by bulkheads.
2. The belt was increased from 4in to 5in abreast 'A' and 'Y' barbettes and from 2½in to 4in abaft 'Y' barbette.
3. Upper section of the belt bulkhead was reduced from 3in to 1½in forward, and from 4½in to 4in aft, but the after bulkhead was situated much farther aft than in *Indefatigable*.
4. Main deck armour extended to within 55ft of the stern instead of terminating at 'Y' barbette. The lower deck forward and aft was increased from 2in to 2½in.
5. Spotting and signal tower was sited over instead of behind the conning position, and thickness of plating was increased from 4in and 3in to 6in and 3in.

The inability of this poor protection to resist heavy calibre projectiles at normal battle ranges was to be well illustrated at Jutland when *Indefatigable* was sunk by direct hits from the German battlecruiser *Von der Tann* at approximately 14,000–15,000 yards. The first three shells fell in the vicinity of 'Y' turret, followed by two more in close proximity. The magazines exploded and she sank by the stern.

A special Board of Inquiry to investigate the loss of the British battlecruisers at Jutland was appointed immediately after the action. The most generally accepted theory was the one advanced by the DNC, Eustace Tennyson D'Eyncourt, that the losses stemmed from inadequate protection to magazines and ammunition hoists rather than from penetration of turret or barbette armour, which would not be necessarily fatal in itself. It was noted that penetration of several turrets in German ships had not proved fatal because their magazines and shell rooms were more completely segregated. Also, the German procedures for packing and handling cordite were safer and none of their magazines exploded. Later, however, it was contended that only in the case of *Invincible* could D'Eyncourt's theory be definitely established. Evidence relating to *Indefatigable* indicated that shells penetrated her magazines through side, deck or barbette armour; it was known that German 11in guns were more than capable of achieving this.

Machinery

As enlarged *Invincibles*, the class naturally received the same basic layout of boiler and engine rooms. A higher proportion of astern power was provided and no cruising turbines were installed. The boilers were arranged in three separate groups instead of two as before, this being necessitated by the wider spacing of the midships turrets; this in turn caused considerable problems in the internal running of the ship because of restricted size of individual boiler rooms.

While building, they were dubbed 'wonder ships' by the Press and speeds quoted were often far in excess of their true capability. A typical paragraph read:

> The Australian and New Zealand *Dreadnought* cruisers have now been laid down. Little of what type they are has been heard, but from all accounts they are sisters of the *Indefatigable* – an *Invincible* in which the cardinal error of that design has been done away with [Reference to the poor armour protection]. It is hoped that the *Indefatigable* will have better nautical

Below: *Australia* in dry dock – hull freshly painted, 1913.

Right: *Australia*, 1913.

INDEFATIGABLE CLASS: SPEED TRIALS, 1913

Collective results

	Revs	SHP (average)	Speed (knots)
Full power trial			
Indefatigable	308.6	55,880	26.89
New Zealand	299.7	49,050	26.38
Australia	315.3	55,140	26.79

8-hour trial; average SHP: *Indefatigable* 48,420, New Zealand 46,900, *Australia* 44,596.

Australia
18-hour speed trial, 8 March 1913
Boiler pressure: 220psi
Engine pressure: 210psi
Turbine pressure: 115psi starboard high, 115psi port
Air pressure at stockholds: 0.78atm
Vacuum: 28.5atm
Coal consumption per hour: 1.4 tons
Total water loss (all hours): 36.3 tons
Port outer: 261.1rpm; 6,751shp; inner: 262.3rpm; 8,956shp
Starboard outer: 260.2rpm; 6,965shp; inner: 257.7rpm; 8,839shp
Mean SHP per hour: 32,383
Collective SHP: 31,511.

qualities than the *Invincibles*, which leaves something to be desired in this respect, but it is expected that the new ships should reach speeds well over 27 knots.

In fact, the ships were capable of short spurts up to and over 27 knots, which reflects great credit on the turbine design fitted in these dreadnought types. Shaft horsepower was raised only slightly over that of *Invincible*, but if forced *Indefatigable* could boast 48,420shp to give a speed of 26.89 knots. This was partly because the class had been given much finer lines than *Invincible*. Fuel capacity was increased by 170 tons of coal with a maximum of 340 tons. Oil stowage was increased by 132 tons. Both classes were heavy consumers of fuel, but stowage was adequate for North Sea and most fleet operations, with no danger of an embarrassing shortage.

Appearance Changes

Their very large, well-spread tripod masts and abnormally long midships section made the *Indefatigables* appear much larger than the *Invincible* class. The short forecastle and quarterdeck presented a rather awkward profile, and the ships were not as pleasing to the eye as the *Invincibles*. They could be easily distinguished by:

1. Wider spacing of masts, first and second funnels and midships turrets.
2. Third funnel farther away from mainmast.
3. Conning tower well clear of bridgework and not under it as before.
4. Navigating platform not extended forward.
5. Main tripod legs raked aft instead of forward.

Individual differences were distinct (although from certain angles *New Zealand* looked very much like *Indefatigable*).
Indefatigable: Single wings to lower bridge. No rangefinder on after superstructure. Control top on each of the masts. Yard on fore topmast low. Ensign gaff fitted on mainmast.
New Zealand: Extra upper wing to bridge forward.
Australia: Small rangefinder on after superstructure. No after control top. Yard on fore topmast high. No gaff.
1914–15 *Indefatigable*'s 4in guns decked in. Small AA gun (probably 3pdr) mounted on after superstructure in *Indefatigable* and

RALIA
AUSTRALIA

Right: *Australia* at war, late 1915/16. Note enlarged top and additional bridgework.

Opposite, top: *Indefatigable* as completed, 1911 (*Invincible* ahead). Commissioned at Devonport in February 1911 just in time to take part in the Coronation Fleet Review of that year. Shown here a few days before that review.

Right: *Indefatigable* anchored at Devonport, *c.* 1913/14.

Opposite, bottom: *Indefatigable c.* 1913.

Opposite, top: *Indefatigable* and *Inflexible* on a visit to Genoa on 5 March 1914. Note that her anti-torpedo nets have been removed.

on 'P', 'Q' and 'Y' turrets in other two ships. Two 24in signalling lamps added on low platform on foremast in *Indefatigable*. One pair 24in remounted in centre of superstructure, other lamps suppressed. Splinter shields fitted to all *Indefatigable*'s 4in guns. Bridge in *New Zealand* and *Australia* modified, navigating platform being closed in. After superstructure built up in *Indefatigable*; cut away around mainmast in other two. Topgallants removed from all. Main topmast reduced to stump in *Indefatigable*. Yard removed from fore topmast and from below fore control top in all ships. Signal struts fitted to starfish on each mast. These struts were extra long in *New Zealand*. Camouflage painted in all by early 1915. In *Indefatigable* and *Australia* it consisted of long, dark-grey panels which ran along the hull amidships. In *New Zealand*, however, the scheme was more elaborate, consisting of irregular vertical patches which were continued on and around the funnels, superstructure and 12in guns.

1915–16 Director control fitted for main armament located, as usual, on platform under forward control top. AA guns (3pdr) removed from turret tops in *New Zealand*. Anti-torpedo nets removed from *New Zealand* during spring of 1916; *Australia* retained hers for a longer period (they were out by late 1916–17). Camouflage painted out in all vessels.

1916–17 4in AA added to extremity of after superstructure in *New Zealand* and *Australia*, one 3in AA added on 'P' turret. Armour protection of surviving two ships improved in area of magazines and shell rooms after Jutland (approximately 80 tons).

1917 Control top enlarged and modified. Range clocks fitted to face of control top. Deflection scales painted on 'A' and 'Y' turrets. 12in guns painted very light-grey, almost white in *Australia*. Fore topmast removed from both and HA RF fitted on top of fore control top.

1917–18 Rangefinder at end of control top removed from both. Searchlights redistributed with improved control facilities. All 24in lamps removed and replaced by eight single 36in lamps. Searchlight control tower with two 36in SL added each side of second funnel. Towers placed well away from funnel and arranged en echelon, forward tower to port, after to starboard. Two 36in SL mounted on upper bridge and two on centreline platform on after superstructure before AA platform. Two 24in signalling lamps added on lower bridge, and one on a sponson at extremity of after superstructure. Some modifications evident in the bridgework of both ships during this period. Flying-off platforms added to both 'P' and 'Q' turrets.

1919 *New Zealand* refitted for tour of the Dominions. Lord Jellicoe sailed in her. Refit was from December 1918 to February 1919 when the following changes were made: Range clocks removed and deflection scales on turrets painted out. Lower 4in guns in forward group removed. Flying-off platforms removed from wing turrets. Forward superstructure enlarged and modified to provide extra accommodation. Fore topmast and both topgallants replaced.

1923–24 *Australia* stripped of all small fittings, searchlights, masts, and parts of superstructure before being scuttled with honours, outside Sydney Harbour.

History: *Indefatigable*

Laid down 23 February 1909. Began trials October 1910.

1911 *24 Feb* Commissioned at Devonport for service with 1st CS Home Fleet, where she remained until Dec 1913.

24 June Coronation Review at Spithead.

1913 *1 Jan* 1st CS Home Fleet (*Lion* [flag], *Princess Royal*, *Indefatigable*, *Indomitable*, *Invincible*) became 1st BCS and a new 1st CS was formed (*Defence* [flag], *Warrior*, *Black Prince*, *Duke of Edinburgh*).

1912–13 In Nov 1912 because of public agitation over a proposed discontinuance of any battleship squadron in the Mediterranean, it was decided to deploy a squadron of four battlecruisers (*Indefatigable*, *Invincible*, *Indomitable*, *Inflexible*) to replace the battleships withdrawn. The squadron was designated 2nd BCS from Jan 1913. *Inflexible* transferred (as flagship) in Nov 1912; *Indomitable* and *Invincible* joined in Aug 1913.

1913 *Dec Indefatigable* joined 2nd BCS Mediterranean Fleet.

1914 *2 Aug* Dispatched with *Indomitable* to Adriatic approaches to reinforce 1st CS in search for German battlecruiser *Goeben* and light cruiser *Breslau*, sighted off Galatea Island; contact lost by 4 Aug when hostilities commenced.

Below: *Australia*, c. 1915.

On 6 Aug overall responsibility in Mediterranean passed to the French. On 11 Aug British naval forces in Mediterranean reduced to a vice-admiral's command, the Vice-Admiral hoisting his flag in *Indefatigable* on 20 Sept. 2nd BCS broken up and reformed in home waters on reorganization of Grand Fleet. The French insisted that one battlecruiser be permanently available to intercept *Goeben* if she tried to break out. *Indefatigable* and *Indomitable* were assigned to Dardanelles Squadron for this purpose, but *Indomitable* left for home in Dec 1914.

18 Aug Vice-Admiral Carden transferred his flag from *Defence* and assumed command of Dardanelles Squadron.

3 Nov With *Indomitable* and French battleships bombarded forts at Kum Kale and Sedd el Bahr at entrance to Dardanelles.

1915 *24 Jan* Relieved by *Inflexible* and proceeded to Malta for refit.

14 Feb Left Malta for home. On 20 Feb the Grand Fleet established a separate battlecruiser force of three squadrons with *Lion* as flagship: 1st BCS *Princess Royal* (flag), *Queen Mary*, *Tiger*. 2nd BCS *Australia* (flag), *Indefatigable*, *New Zealand*. 3rd BCS *Invincible* (flag), *Indomitable*, *Inflexible*.

Feb–May 1916 At Rosyth with 2nd BCS Grand Fleet until lost.

1916 *April–May* Temporary flagship of 2nd BCS Grand Fleet while *Australia* underwent repairs after colliding with *New Zealand*.

31 May Battle of Jutland. *Indefatigable*, battered by *Von der Tann*, the last ship in the enemy line, exploded at approximately 16.02 and sank. Two survivors.

Above: *Indefatigable* about to open fire during the Battle of Jutland. The photograph was taken approximately half an hour before her destruction.

History: *New Zealand*

Presented to the Royal Navy as a gift from the Government of New Zealand. Laid down on 20 June 1910 and began trials in Oct 1912.

1912 *19 Nov* Commissioned with nucleus crew at Govan.

23 Nov Completed with full complement at Devonport for service with 1st CS Home Fleet.

Nov–Aug 1914 With Home Fleet.

1913 *20 Jan* Detached for world cruise.

6 Feb Left Portsmouth.

12 April Arrived Wellington via Capetown.

Above: *New Zealand*, c. 1915. tops, and hull camouflage.

28 June Left Auckland for home via Pacific Ocean and Panama Canal.

8 Dec Arrived Portsmouth. (It had been intended that she should stay in New Zealand waters, but she was released by that government for duties in British home waters.)

1914 *Feb* Visited Brest with 1st BCS.

June Visited Riga, Reval and Kronstadt.

19 Aug Transferred to 2nd BCS and stationed in River Humber with *Invincible* to support Southern Command's light forces in the event of enemy battlecruiser raids.

NEW ZEALAND
Outboard profile and deck plans, 1919, showing wartime modifications

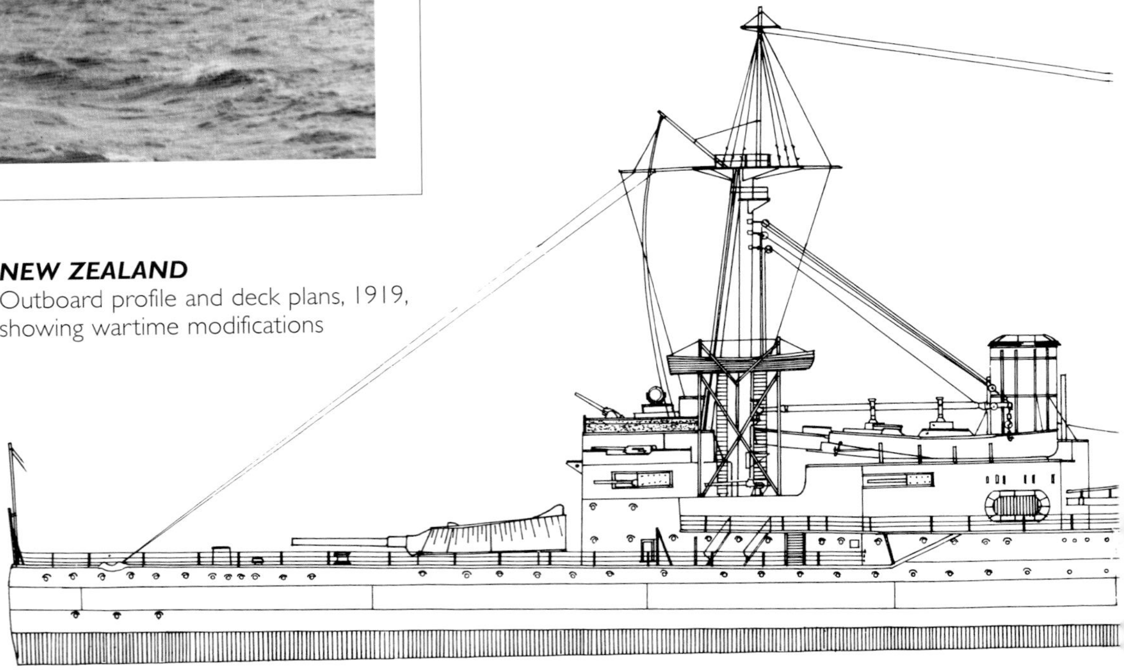

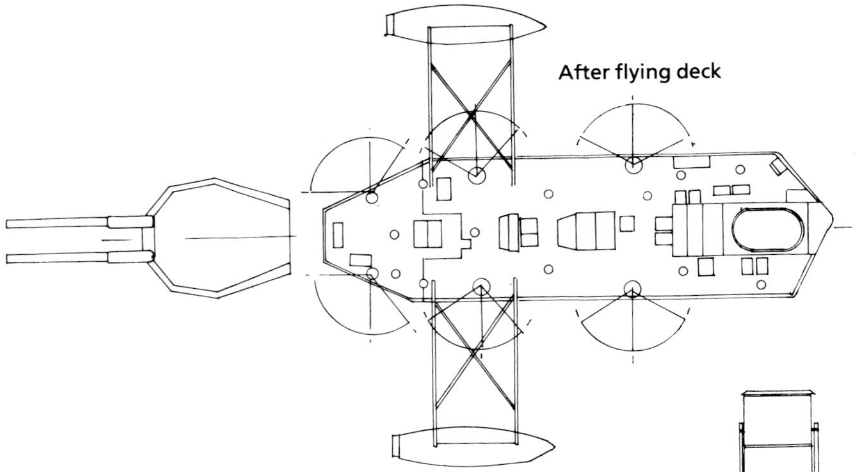

NEW ZEALAND
Inboard profile

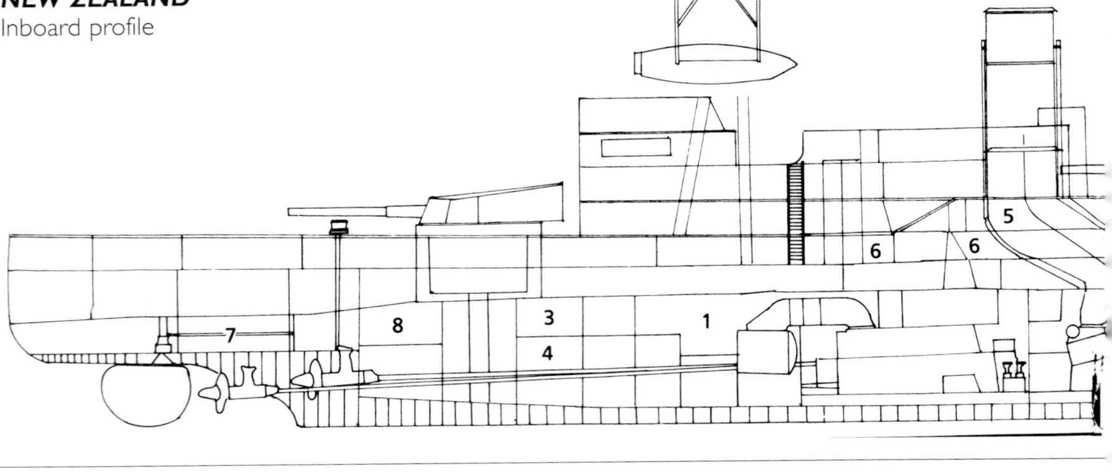

28 Aug With *Invincible* supported Harwich Force during Heligoland Bight action.

1 Sept Rejoined 1st BCS having been replaced in 2nd BCS by *Inflexible*.

Dec Flag of rear-admiral temporarily transferred to *New Zealand* when *Invincible* and *Inflexible* sailed for Falklands; flag transferred 2 Dec to *Leviathan* of 2nd CS at Cromarty.

1915 *15 Jan* Became flagship of the Rear-Admiral 2nd BCS as reconstituted on that date (*New Zealand*, *Indomitable* and *Invincible*).

24 Jan Present at Battle of Dogger Bank; engaged *Blücher* without sustaining damage.

1916 *22 April* Collided with *Australia* in fog 75 miles NW of Heligoland during Grand Fleet sweep in search of German High Seas Fleet.

April–May Under refit at Rosyth.

30 May Rejoined 2nd BCS Squadron relieving *Indefatigable* of flag while *Australia* was under repair.

31 May Battle of Jutland. Engaged battlecruiser *Moltke* during opening phase of battle; port side of 'Y' turret sustained minor

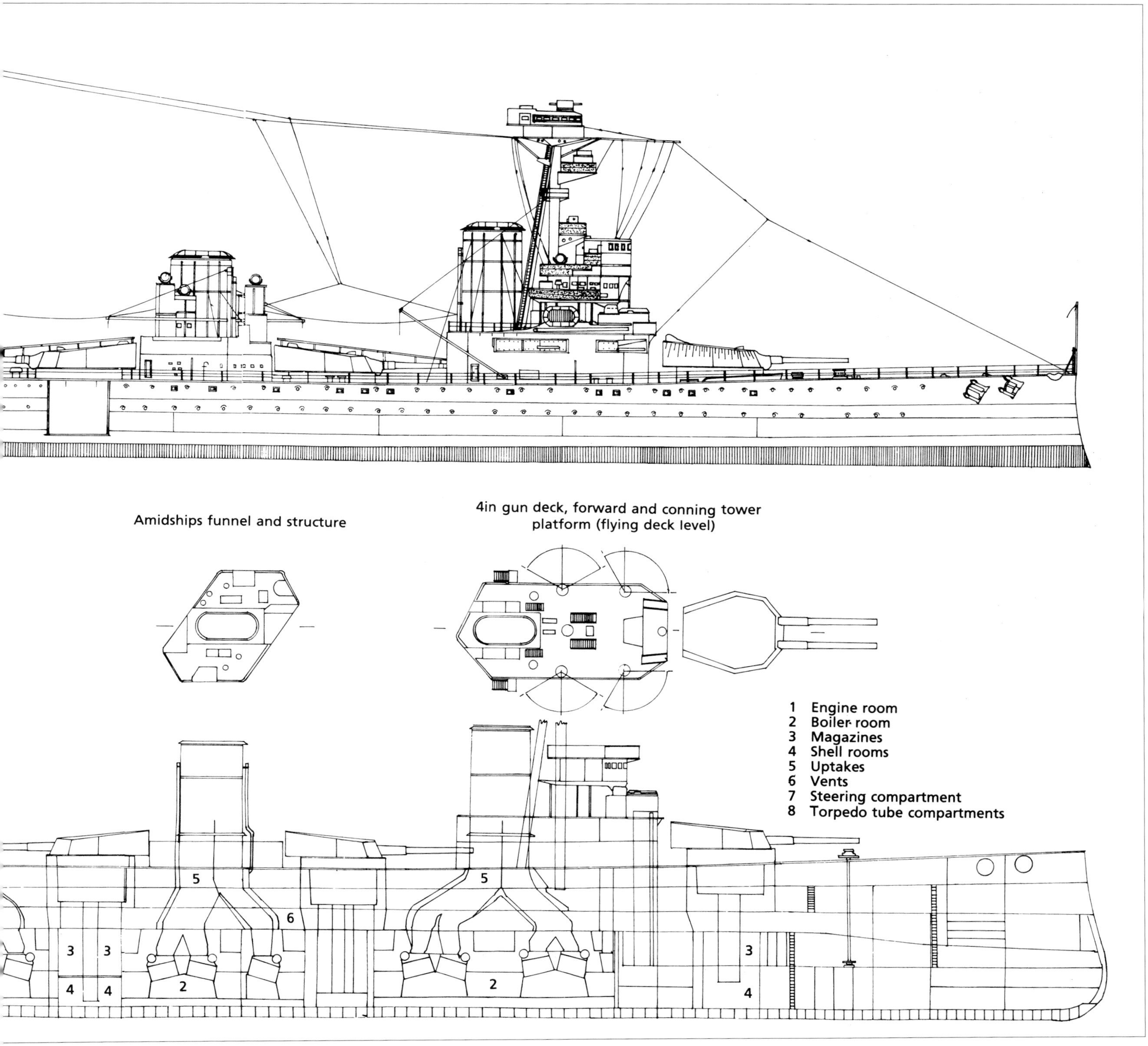

Above: *New Zealand*, 1918. Note wartime additions: heavy bridgework, enlarged control top with rangefinder on roof, SL towers around middle funnel, 4in guns in casemates.

damage from hit by 11in shell; turret remained operative, no casualties.

Nov Under refit at Rosyth.

17 Nov Took part in operations in Heligoland Bight while temporarily attached to 1st BCS.

29 Nov–7 Jan 1917 Replaced *Australia* as flagship 2nd BCS.

1918 *Dec–Feb 1919* Refitted for Admiral Sir John Jellicoe's tour to India and the Dominions.

21 Feb Left Portsmouth. Visited Gibraltar, Port Said, Suez, Bombay, Colombo, Cocos Islands, Australia, Tasmania, Pacific Islands, New Zealand, Vancouver, San Diego, Havana, Kingston, Port of Spain and many other places en route. Jellicoe left ship at Vancouver on 20 November 1919 to tour Canada and USA by rail. He rejoined at Key West on 8 January 1920.

1920 *3 Feb* Arrived Portsmouth. Total distance steamed 33,514 nautical miles.

15 March Paid off into Reserve at Rosyth.

1921 *July* Became flagship of Rosyth Reserve Fleet.

Oct Reduced to care and maintenance.

1922 *19 April* Paid off on to Disposal list under terms of Washington Treaty.

19 Dec Sold to Rosyth Shipbreaking Co. This company had been formed for the sole purpose of breaking up *Agincourt*, *Princess Royal* and *New Zealand* in accordance with the treaty.

1923 *13 Aug* Arrived at breakers.

History: *Australia*

Ordered by the Australian Government in 1909 as a result of the Imperial Conference of Defence of that year, it was originally intended that she should be the first unit of a new Australian Fleet of eight battlecruisers and ten light cruisers to cost approximately £20,000,000. *Australia* was laid down at the John Brown Shipyard on 22 June 1910 and was ready for her trials in March 1913.

1913 *21 June* Commissioned at Portsmouth for service as flagship of Rear-Admiral Patey, commanding the Australian Squadron, hoisting the flag on the following day.

30 June Visited in Portsmouth by HM King George V, who knighted Patey on the quarterdeck.

July Accompanied by HMAS *Sydney*, sailed from Portsmouth for Australia via South Africa.

4 Oct Reached Sydney where, on 13 October, the flag of the

Below: *New Zealand* amidships, and showing her bridgework in its final state. Taken as she came into Portsmouth Harbour on 3 February 1920 after her tour of the Dominions.

Left: A Sopwith Pup taking off from the beam turret of *New Zealand* in 1917 (*Australia* behind).

Australian Squadron was transferred to Australia from *Cambrian*.

1913 *Oct–Summer 1914* Cruises in Australian waters.

1914 *July* Annual winter cruise off the coast of Queensland.

30 July Admiralty requested that *Australia* search for the German Pacific Squadron in the Bismarck Archipelago.

1 Aug Coaling at Sydney.

12 Aug Patrolling in St George's Channel.

15 Sept Left Blanche Bay at 12.00 with *Sydney* and *Melbourne* en route to Albany to escort first contingent of Australian and New Zealand Army Corps.

17 Sept Urgently recalled to assist French cruiser *Montcalm* in covering expedition to German New Guinea, owing to appearance of *Scharnhorst* and *Gneisenau* in that area.

18 Dec At Caliao and later called at Felix Island.

26 Dec Reached Valparaiso, left the next day.

28 Dec Stopped engines at sea and held a short memorial service for those lost at the Battle of Coronel.

31 Dec Passed through the Straits of Magellan.

1915 *1 Jan* On entering straits she bent a propeller blade on a rock and was forced to alter course for the Falkland Islands and repairs, at only half speed.

2 Jan Reached Port Stanley, under repair until the 5th.

11 Jan Ordered to proceed to Plymouth, England.

28/29 Jan Arrived at Plymouth and paid off into short refit, having steamed some 59,514 miles in eighteen months.

17 Feb Joined 2nd BCS Grand Fleet.

22 Feb Flagship of 2nd BCS.

31 July Based at Rosyth.

1916 *27 Jan* Swept off Norwegian coast with 2nd BCS, 1st and 4th LCS.

26 Feb Combined exercises with Grand Fleet.

6 March At sea supporting the Harwich Force.

22 April In the afternoon collided with *New Zealand* in fog some 75 miles NW of Horns Reef. The fog was so dense that the destroyers *Garland*, *Ardent* and *Ambuscade* collided with one another, and the battleship *Neptune* was struck by a merchantman.

April Docked in Tyne for temporary repairs to serious damage to armoured belt. She left later for Devonport and full repairs.

1 June Recommissioned, too late to participate at Jutland.

3 June Reached Rosyth as flagship 2nd BCS.

27 Nov Vice-Admiral Packenham succeeded Admiral Sir David Beatty as Commander of the Battlecruiser Fleet and his flag was transferred to *Lion*.

1917 *May* While practising clearing ship for action, a 12in shell became lodged in the hoist. Lieutenant-Commander F. C. Darley climbed down the hoist, released the shell and defuzed it with a crowbar and spanner.

26 June Visited by HM King George V.

12 Dec Collided with *Repulse*.

1918 *18–21 Jan* Covering outward-bound Scandinavia convoy from Methil to Bergen.

23 April Supplied eleven volunteers, after two months' special training, for attack on Zeebrugge Mole and Ostend.

Sept–Oct With 2nd BCS covering US minelaying on Northern Barrage.

21 Nov At head of 2nd BCS, led Port Division Grand Fleet at surrender of German High Seas Fleet. On anchoring, each ship took a German ship under its custody; *Australia*'s was the German battlecruiser *Hindenburg*.

1919 *22 April* Farewell visit from HRH the Prince of Wales before sailing next day for home.

28 May Reached Freemantle, and spent six weeks visiting Australian ports.

1921 *12 Dec* Paid off into Reserve at Sydney.

1923 *Oct* In dockyard hands at Sydney being stripped of small fittings and preparing for disposal under terms of Washington Treaty.

1924 *12 April* Scuttled ceremoniously in 150 fathoms, 24 miles E of Sydney.

Neptune: 1908 ESTIMATES

Design

The single battleship provided under the 1908 Estimates was designated 'K2' after the name *Foudroyant* had been discarded (see *St Vincent*). Although on the same basic lines as *St Vincent*, the design was enlarged and modified and, for the first time, marked a radical departure from the basic dreadnought layout. The principal difference was in the siting of the turrets, in the endeavour to secure a full broadside of ten guns on each beam. While in the preparatory stage, the DNC, Philip Watts, had been able to re-locate the fourth turret over the fifth – at last, the superimposed mounting had appeared in the Royal Navy. True, 'X' turret's guns could not fire astern because of the blast effect on the lower turret, but this space-saving change had given the guns much wider arcs of fire on each broadside. In practice, however, the system proved generally unsatisfactory, and the superiority of broadside fire over *St Vincent* was little more than nominal.

NEPTUNE: FINAL LEGEND, SUMMARY OF WEIGHTS
(tons)

	Load	**Deep**
Hull:	6,750	6,750
Armour:	5,706	5,706
Armament:	3,569	3,624
Machinery:	2,131	2,370
Coal:	900	2,090
General equipment:	690	831
Oil:	–	792
Engineers' stores:	60	60
Board margin:	100	100
Totals:	**19,906**	**22,323**

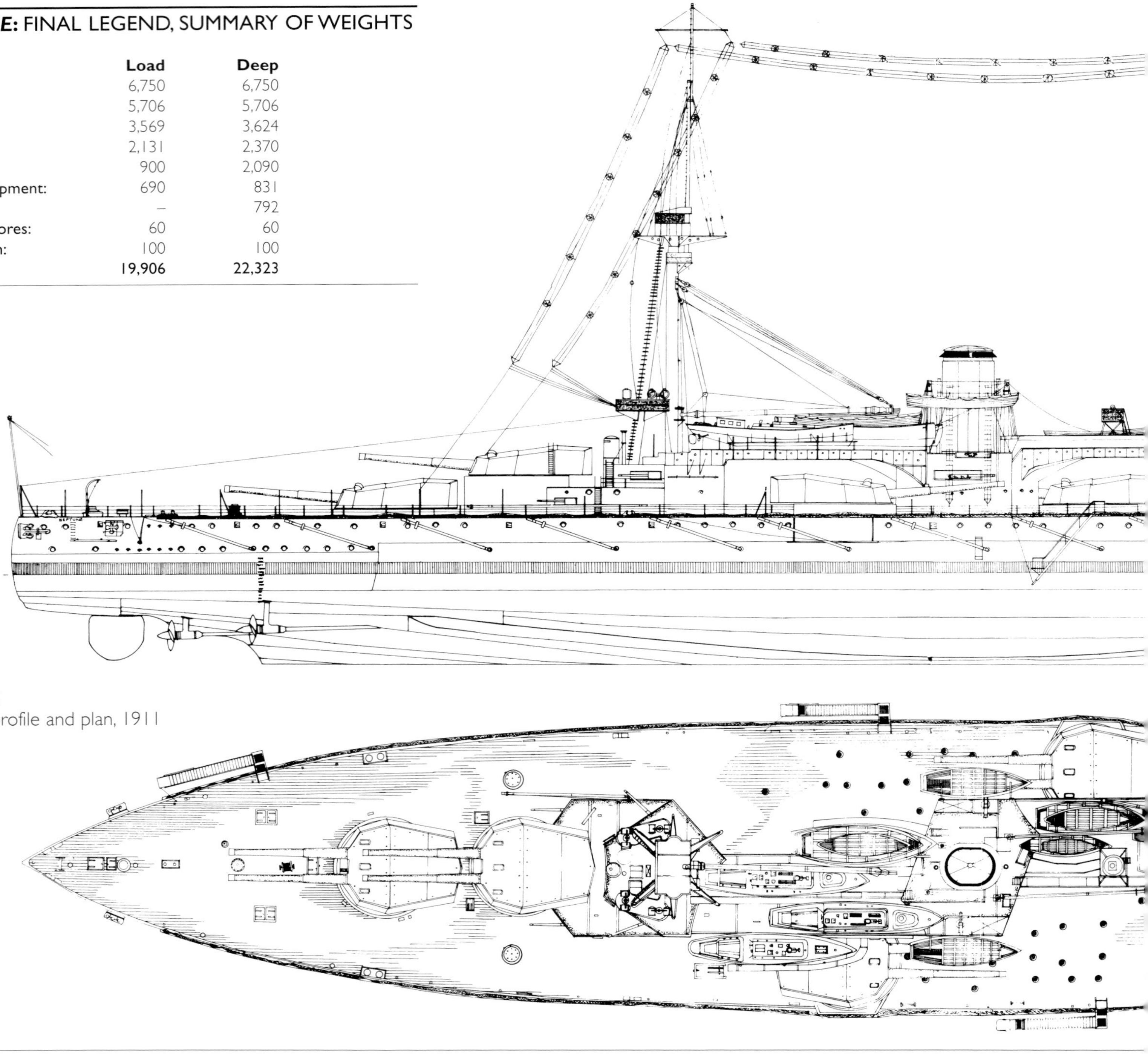

NEPTUNE
Outboard profile and plan, 1911

Right: *Neptune* takes the water at Portsmouth on a displacement of 7,134 tons. Main armour strakes are not yet in position.

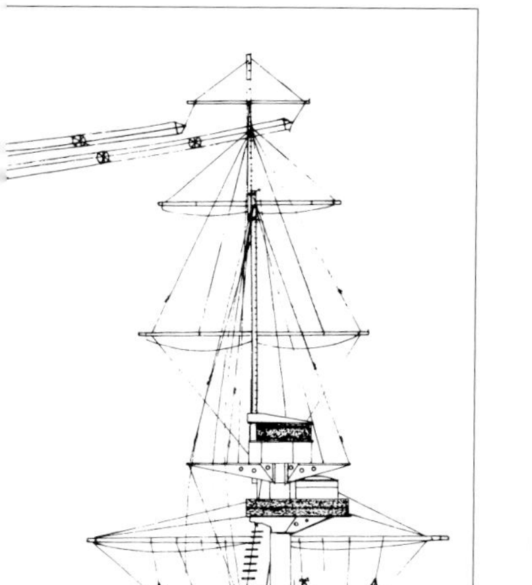

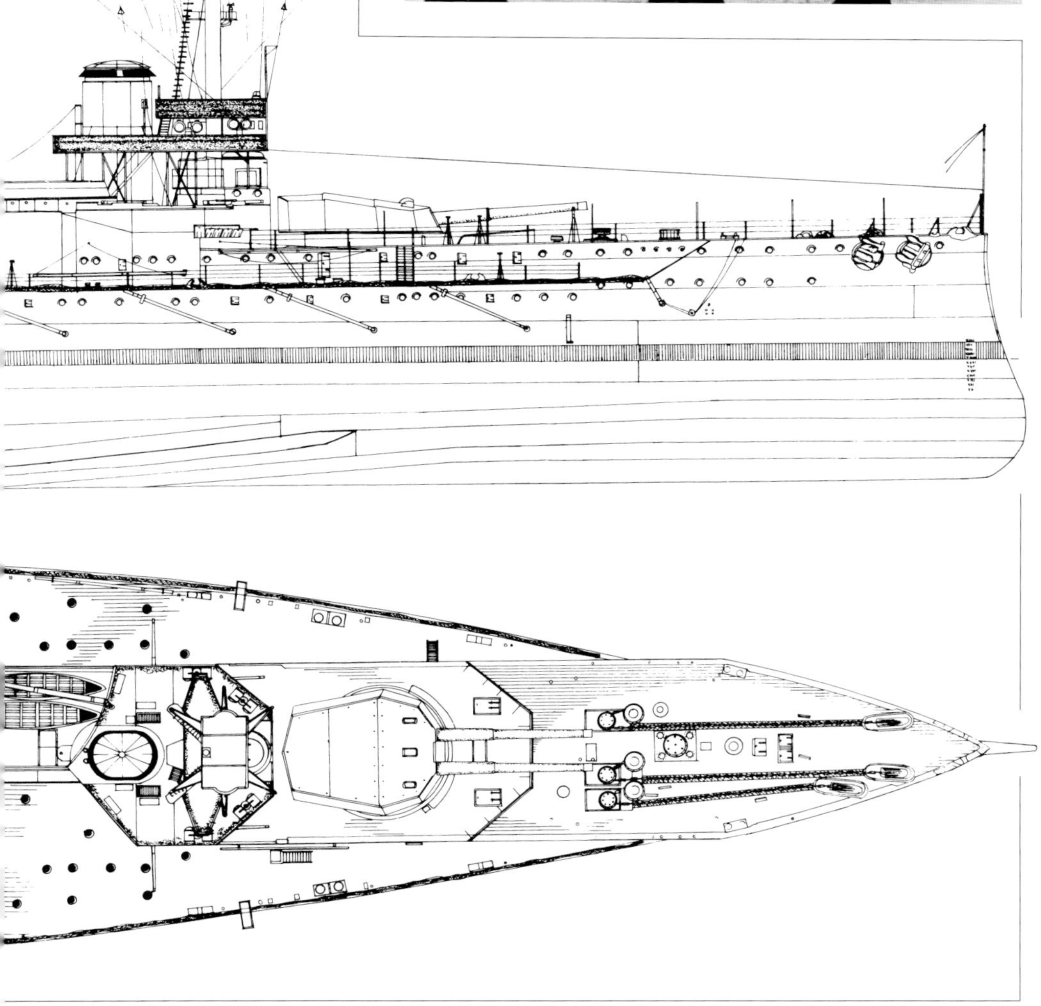

Basic design differences from the *St Vincent* class were:

1. Displacement increased by 650 tons on an increased length of 10 feet, and 1ft beam, although staying at the same nominal draught.
2. Anti-torpedo armament reduced and rearranged.
3. Vertical hull armour belts were given thicker plates at the extremities and the funnel uptakes were given consideration with regard to protection.
4. Fuel capacity slightly reduced.
5. Superstructure rearranged, and flying deck fitted amidships. Mainmast relocated abaft instead of before the second funnel.

As with *Indefatigable*, Admiral Fisher had insisted on total secrecy during *Neptune*'s construction, and frequent reports such as the following paragraph appeared in local and national newspapers:

> The raised amidships turret, which report gave to the *Bellerophons*, and later the *St Vincents*, has now been given to the *Neptune*. It is extremely doubtful whether she will be so fitted, for one thing because there is no British naval tactic requiring a heavy fire astern; for another because unless the aftermost turret were very differently placed, it would be quite impossible safely to fire the amidships turret guns over it.

And early in 1909 the *Daily Telegraph* produced some magnificent flights of fancy:

> For some time it has been rumoured that the Admiralty intend to introduce two important and novel features in this battleship which belongs to this year's programme.
>
> One of these is a new type of gun. Since the breechloading principle was adopted in the Navy, with the system of winding the weapons with wire ribbon under pressure, the fleet has had no bigger than the 12inch. Now it is stated that the new battleship will mount guns of a new 13.5in type.
>
> The other departure may be, that the new ship will make no smoke, and will therefore require no funnels. Because of the idea of a man-o-war without funnels appears novel, it is no reason to dismiss the suggestion that this great battleship will be fitted with gas powered engines, and will thus throw against the sky no smoke pennant to disclose her presence to an enemy before she is on the enemy's horizon.

Armament

The provision of a ten-gun broadside in the US *Delaware* class, and the Brazilian *Minas Geraes* pair laid down in 1907 necessitated a modification of the *Dreadnought* arrangement of turrets to equal these foreign designs. The Board had considered a number of alternatives and decided that excessive length could only be avoided by adopting the superfiring system. The concomitant problem of blast was accepted in the interests of keeping length within bounds, and a compromise was reached wherein the after turrets would be superimposed and the midships structure would be cut away so as to allow the echelon turrets some degree of cross-deck firing. This arrangement would save up to 50 feet on the length of the new design. The superfiring turret was placed aft instead of forward because the concentrated weight forward would have made for a bad seaboat. It was never intended that the superimposed guns would fire over the lower ones, and stops were fitted to prevent this. Moreover, it was never intended that the echelon turrets should fire over each other in peacetime, but in war a full ten-gun broadside was possible, and made *Neptune* the first British dreadnought with a full broadside of the entire main armament. In British battleships, the turret sighting ports were located in hoods in the turret roof, which meant that the observers were in danger of severe concussion if the top turret

Right: *Neptune* steaming out of Portsmouth after completion of trials, February/March 1911.

Opposite, top left: *Neptune*. Taken from the forecastle looking at the forward 12in turret ('A') and superstructure around the foremast. Note large conning tower below compass and bridge platforms.

Opposite, top right: *Neptune*. The superimposed 12in twin turrets made their first appearance with this ship. The mainmast tripod behind shows SL platform which houses eight lamps. Note gun tampions.

Opposite, bottom: *Neptune*, c. 1913. Battle practice for main armament.

Below: *Neptune* late 1910. Fitting out and preparing for builder's preliminary sea trials.

guns were fired directly, overhead or even near the axial line.

The modified turret distribution in *Neptune* represented the first departure from the original *Dreadnought* plan and an initial step towards the adoption of the all centreline superfiring system in the British Navy. The disadvantages inherent in the echelon system, which represented a time-honoured means of securing nominal all-round fire at the expense of a general dislocation of internal economy and actual efficiency, represented the best compromise at that time. In practice, however, the system proved something of a failure. The cross-deck arcs of fire were restricted and, after trials, it was found that the deck amidships was sagging badly as a result of blast; extra pillars and 'Z' bars had to be fitted to strengthen the area. The forecastle sides were well strengthened to permit nominal ahead fire for the beam turrets, but direct end-on fire, either ahead or astern, was precluded by the effect of blast on the superstructures, and a bearing limit of 5° within the axial line was imposed both forward and aft.

The anti-torpedo armament was reduced (from the *St Vincents*' twenty) to sixteen guns, and their disposition was changed: the turret roof location of preceding classes was abandoned and all the 4in guns were re-located in three groups in the superstructures. The anti-torpedo guns had first been mounted on turret tops in

the *King Edward VII* class of 1902 so that the guns should have an armoured base and be widely dispersed to avoid simultaneous disablement. Abandonment of the scheme in *Neptune* was mainly because of:

1. The exposed nature of the position and the difficulty in fighting the guns when the main armament was in action.
2. The advantages of close grouping in control and concentration of fire, plus easy supply of ammunition.

On completion, *Neptune* was fitted with the first director control system ever installed in a British battleship (see page 13). Lengthy trials were carried out with this innovatory feature, which had been developed by Sir Percy Scott, but it did not live up to expectations and further development led, in 1912, to a modification being installed in the battleship *Thunderer* (1909). Made by Vickers, it was gradually fitted in most of the Grand Fleet's capital ships during the war.

Armour

The armouring was very similar to that of *St Vincent* with the following exceptions:

1. The 10in section of the belt terminated just short of the outer faces of the end barbettes instead of being carried right past these.
2. The forward extremities of the belt were increased from 2in to 2½in.
3. The after conning tower was abandoned and a lightly armoured signal tower was fitted instead.
4. For the first time in a British battleship, 1in armoured plates were added on the funnel uptakes between the middle and upper decks, to reduce splinter damage and the possibility of the lower decks being smoked out. In previous classes, where no armour was fitted on the uptakes, instructions were issued that if the uptakes were pierced during an action, the holes should be stuffed with silicate of cotton in the form of pillow-shaped bags which were readily available from the storerooms nearest to the uptakes.

The main belt was 10in thick and was 2ft 6in above the water-line at normal load condition. The upper edge was at middle deck level and the lower edge 4ft 4in below the water-line. The strake was 10in uniform, but reduced to 8in at the lower edge. Forward, this belt reduced to 7in for approximately 33 feet and then reduced to 2½in running right through to the stem. Aft, the strake was 2½in thick and at the same height as that of the midships section; the strake ran through to the stern of the vessel. Above the 10in main belt was a thickness of 8in and this ran along the same length as the 10in strake.

The main bulkheads ran obliquely inwards from the forward and after extremities of the 10in and 8in armoured belts to the outer faces of the end barbettes between lower and main decks. The forward bulkhead was 5in thick; the after bulkhead was 8in. The forward bulkhead, which closed the extremities of the 7in forward side armour, was 5in to 4in, the 4in being above the main deck level and the 5in below.

The main deck was 1¼in thick and ran between the forward bulkhead and the after bulkhead. The middle deck was 1¾in on the inclines and flat strake, running between the outer face of the end barbettes. The crown of the middle deck was approximately 2ft 9in above the water-line, the lower edge at the ship's side at the same height as the lower edge of the main belt. The lower deck ranged from 1½in forward, running from the forward barbette, and 3in aft, again from the outer face of the aft barbette.

Turret thicknesses were identical with those in previous classes (*Bellerophon*, etc.). The barbettes on the centreline were 9in above the main deck and then reduced to 5in when below this level.

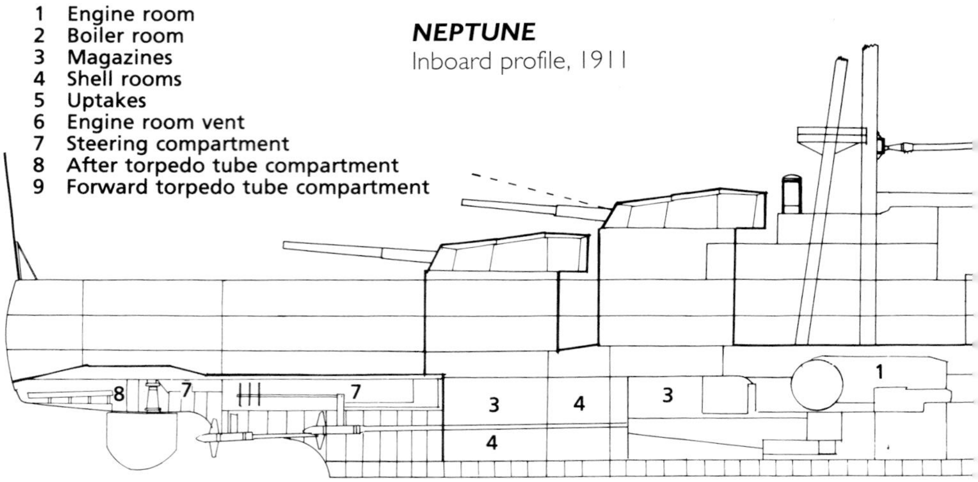

NEPTUNE
Inboard profile, 1911

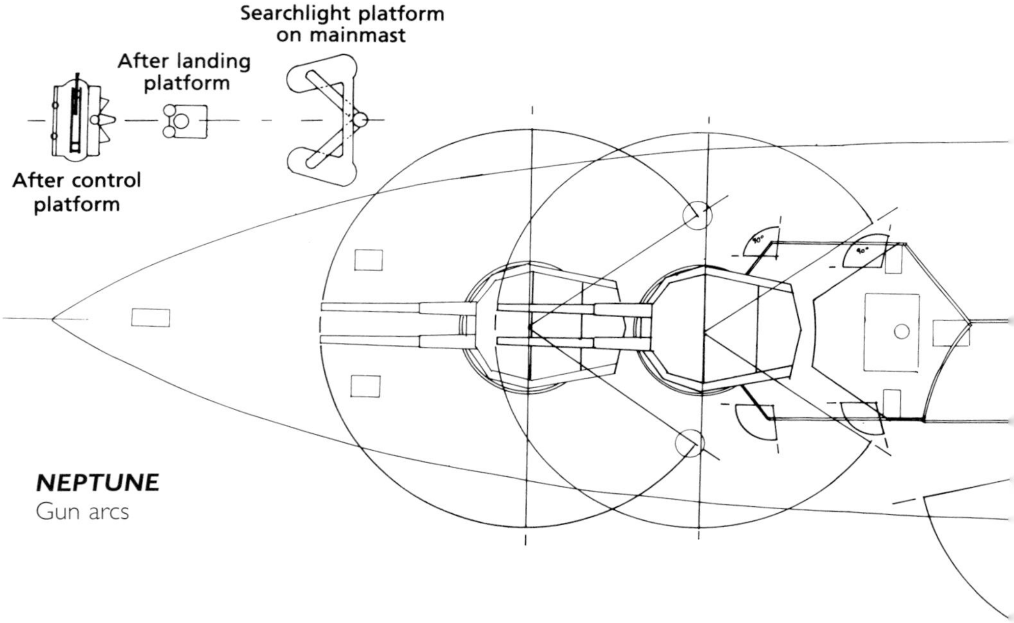

NEPTUNE
Gun arcs

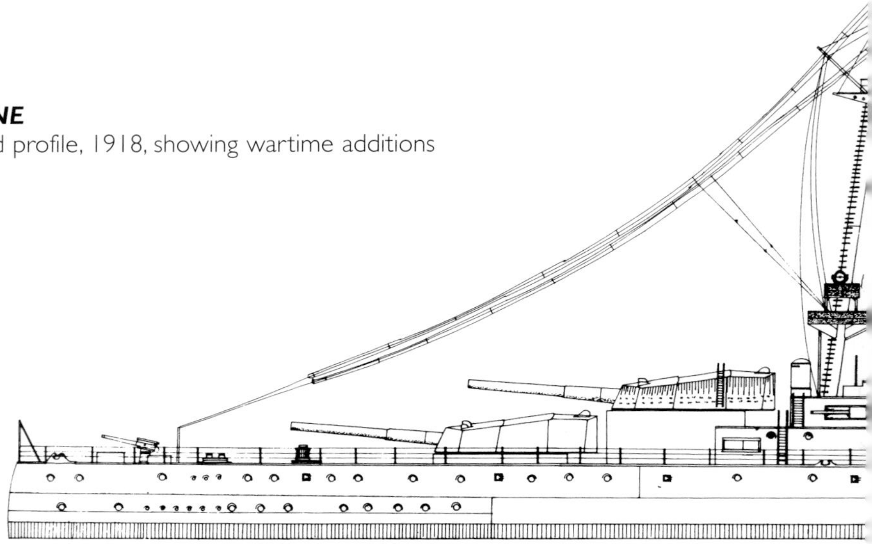

NEPTUNE
Outboard profile, 1918, showing wartime additions

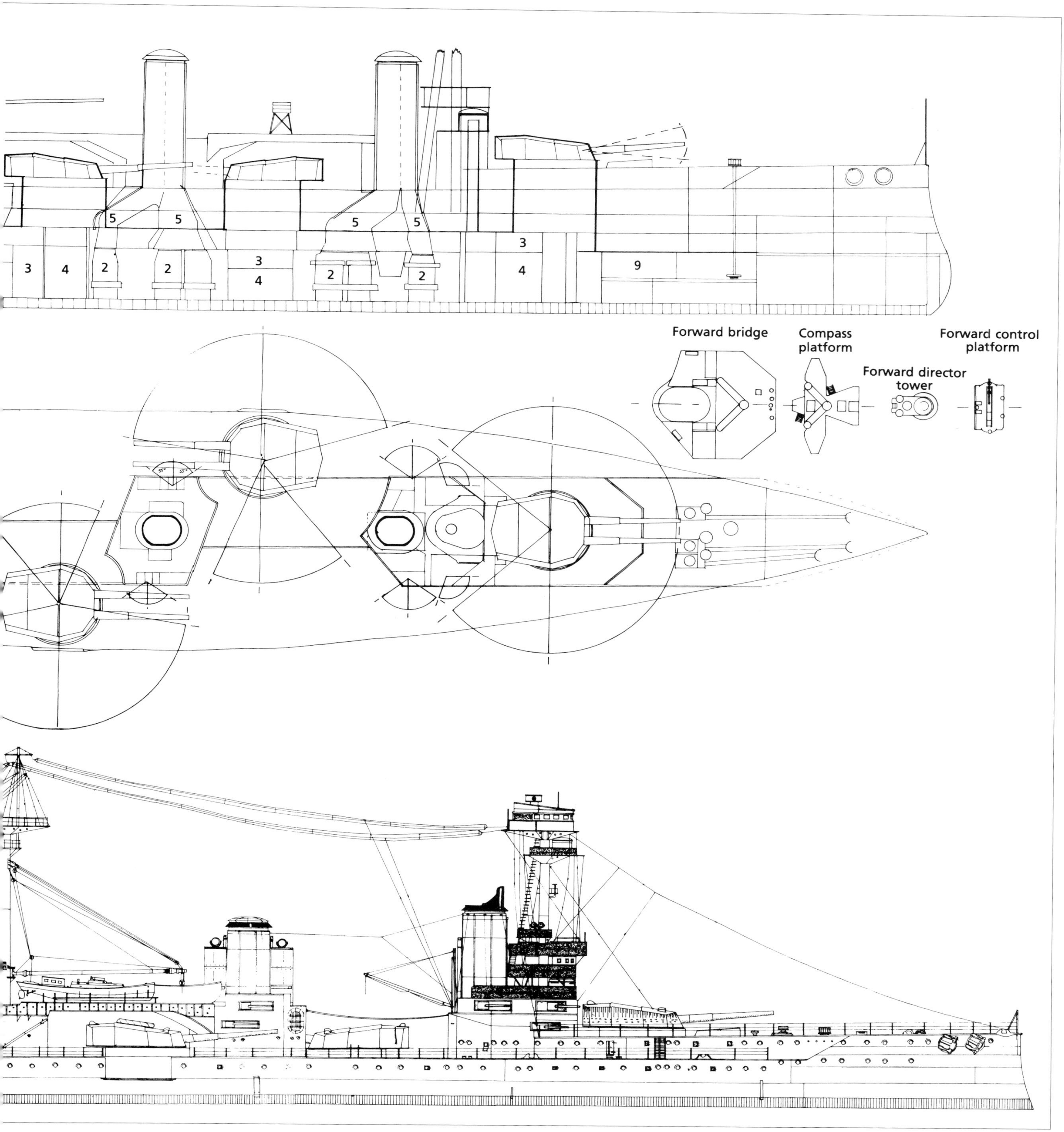
5
5
5
5
3
3
4
2
2
3
4
2
2
4
9
Forward bridge
Compass platform
Forward director tower
Forward control platform

NEPTUNE: PARTICULARS, AS COMPLETED

Construction
Portsmouth DY; laid down 19 Jan 1909; launched 30 Sept 1909; completed Jan 1911.

Displacement (tons)
19,680 (load), 23,123 (deep).

Dimensions
Length: 510ft 1in pp, 541ft 1½in wl, 546ft aft
Beam: 85ft 0½in
Draught: 24ft forward, 28ft 6in aft
Freeboard: 28ft forward, 16ft 6in amidships, 17ft 6in aft
Height of 12in guns above wl: 'A' turret 31ft 6in; 'P', 'Q' 23ft, 'X' 31ft 6in, 'Y' 22ft.

Armament*
Ten 12in 50cal Mk XI; Mk XI mountings; 100rpg
Twelve 4in Mk V11; Mk II mountings; 150rpg
One 12pdr 8cwt
Four 3pdr (saluting)
Five Maxim MG
Three 18in torpedo tubes; eighteen torpedoes.

Ship's boats
Pinnaces (steam): two 50ft
Pinnaces (sail): one 36ft
Launches (steam): one 42ft
Cutters: three 32ft
Gigs: one 30ft
Whalers: three 27ft
Skiff dinghies: one 16ft
Balsa rafts: one 13ft 6in.

Searchlights
Seven 36in: two foremast, three around after funnel, two mainmast.

Rangefinder positions
One spotting top, one each turret.

Battle signal stations
One in signal tower.***

Director control
A new type, developed by Sir Percy Scott, was fitted on a platform beneath the foretop shortly after ship's completion.

Armour**
Main belt: 10in–8in
Ends: 7in–2½in
Lower side: 8in–7in–2½in
Main bulkheads: 8in–5in
Fore bulkhead: 5in–4in
Decks: main 1¼in, middle, flat and slopes 1¾in, lower 3in–1½in
Barbettes: 10in–9in–5in
Turrets: 11in–8in
Conning tower: 11in side, 8in rear, 3in roof, 2in floor
CT tube: 5in–3in
Signal tower: 3in–2in
Uptakes: 1in
Anti-torpedo bulkheads: 3in–2in–1½in–1¼in.

Anchors
Three 130cwt Admiralty type stockless (bower and sheet), one 42cwt stern.

Wireless
Mk I, Mk II and Type 9 W/T short-radius.

Complement
756 (as commissioned); 759 (1913); 813 (1914).

Cost
£1,527,916 (plus £141,000 guns).

Machinery
Parsons direct-drive turbines, four propellers
Rotor diameter: HP 82in; LP 109in
Eighteen Yarrow boilers in three groups, working pressure 235psi; each boiler fitted with three oil sprayers; total output of oil per boiler per hour at 150psi: 900lb
Total heating surface: 63,630sq ft
Length of boiler rooms: 52ft forward, 51ft 11½in aft
Length of engine room: 64ft
Designed SHP: 25,000 for 21 knots
Fuel: 900 tons coal normal, 2,710 tons max.; 790 tons oil
Coal consumption (tons):
102 = 4,260nm at 12.8 knots (5,000shp)
280 = 3,100nm at 16 knots (10,000shp)
335 = 2,900nm at 18 knots (15,000shp)
Radius of action: 4,500nm at 10 knots (coal only); 6,620nm at 10 knots (oil added).

*Two 3in AA added later, see Appearance Changes.
**KC except decks, CT tube, etc.
***Fitted immediately abaft upper CT; 3in roof plates pierced for signal halyards.

NEPTUNE: SPEED TRIALS, 1910

Preliminary steam trials, 23 September 1910
Revs: 324.9rpm; SHP: 26,333; speed: 20.939 knots

A further six runs produced mean figures:
Revs: 352.9rpm; SHP: 31,041; speed: 21.786 knots
Some disappointingly low figures produced throughout these trials were blamed on inferior coal; usually best handpicked Welsh coal was used

Acceptance trial, 17 November 1910
Six runs: 323.3rpm; 24,431shp; 21.04 knots (mean)
Six runs: 328.8rpm; 25,531shp; 21.294 knots (mean).

Beam barbettes were identical except for the exposed outer face which increased to 10in.

The conning tower had face plates of 11in, an 8in rear, 3in crown and 2in floor. The communications tube was 5in and 3in. The signal tower, immediately abaft the CT, had 3in sides and a 2in roof. The signal and torpedo control tower abaft the mainmast was 1½in thick.

The funnel uptakes were 1in between middle and upper deck levels. The anti-torpedo bulkheads (or screens) varied in thickness: 1in–3in abreast forward and midships magazines respectively; 1¼in–2in abreast after magazines; 2in–1½in abreast engine and boiler rooms respectively. These port and starboard longitudinal screens extended between the forward and after magazines and

NEPTUNE: TURNING TRIALS, 1910

23 September. Sea smooth, wind moderate

Angle of rudder:	35° port	35° starboard
Time taken to apply rudder:	12 seconds	8½ seconds
First four points turned in:	38½ seconds	35 seconds
Advance (yards):	502	440
Speed (knots):	21	21

NEPTUNE: GM AND STABILITY

Based on inclining experiments, 20 December 1910

	Displacement (tons)	Draught (mean)	GM	Maximum stability	Stability vanishes at
'A' Condition (= load)*	19,680	26ft 9in	5.3ft	33°	61°
'B' Condition (= deep)**	22,720	30ft 1in	6.5ft	30°	65°
'C' Condition (= light)***	18,560	25ft 6in	4.9ft	31°	60°

*Fully equipped plus 320 tons coal upper, 540 tons lower bunkers, reserve and feedwater tanks empty.
**Fully equipped plus 2,710 tons coal, 790 tons oil, reserve and feed water tanks full.
***Brought to light condition but boilers still full.

were brought in close to the centreline abreast the end magazines.

As in preceding dreadnoughts, the belt armour was almost completely submerged at deep load condition, and this feature was the subject of much criticism. The main belt thickness of only 10 inches, which was still less than that in *Dreadnought*, was not considered adequate against 11in and 12in guns at ranges of 11,000 yards and closer, though it was thought that the range would have to close to less than 8,000 yards before *Neptune*'s 10 inches could be pierced. The solid internal bulkheads, fitted in preceding battleships, were abandoned as inconvenient in *Neptune*.

Machinery

The installation was identical with that of the *St Vincent* class, but with an extra 500shp. *Neptune* was the first dreadnought-type battleship not to be equipped with separate cruising turbines (because of previous unfavourable experience), but the proportion of astern power was increased over that of earlier ships. Like *Indefatigable*'s, the internal layout was complicated and the magazines and shell rooms were in dangerously close proximity to the engine and boiler spaces. To alleviate the danger of heat near explosives, special magazine cooling arrangements were installed in *Neptune*'s and *Indefatigable*'s separation spaces. (Since *Dreadnought*'s completion, it had become ever more obvious that the echelon turret arrangement placed cordite charges and shells too close to the propulsion unit, so she and all later battleships were given some sort of cooling system. However, it was soon seen that temperatures rose so steeply when the ships were under way that the cooling systems obviously needed to be improved. On 16 January 1907, *Bellerophon* logged figures of 52°F in 'A' magazine and 84°F in 'X', and these temperatures were too high.)

Above: Stokers stop for a quick photograph in *Neptune*'s engine room. Note the extremely cramped conditions.

Left: Coaling sheet covers on *Neptune*, 1911. Coaling was the most arduous of tasks for the crew and preparations were no less stressful. Important areas of the ship would be covered up with canvas sheets to stop the copious amounts of coal dust from entering vital areas.

Documents relevant to the 'special' cooling equipment given to *Neptune* show that it merely took the form of extra ventilation, but it seems to have proved satisfactory.

Neptune was fitted with Parsons direct-drive turbines, which connected to four propellers; the high pressure rotors were 82in in diameter, the low pressure 109in. Although having a slightly increased shaft horsepower, *Neptune*'s radius of action was smaller: 6,330 nautical miles at 10 knots as against *St Vincent*'s 6,900 at the same speed. Coal consumption was 113 tons per hour using 2,350shp against *St Vincent*'s 111 tons using 2,310shp.

Appearance Changes

As completed in 1911, *Neptune* was a handsome, well-proportioned ship, but her rig was rather spoilt by the removal of the forward flying bridge. Some felt that this gave her a spacious profile, but it seemed to detract from her balanced appearance. Principal features were:

1. Large flying deck amidships.
2. Echeloned turrets amidships, superimposed turret aft.
3. Forward bridge extending around the funnel.
4. Prominent compass platform on flying deck between funnels.
5. Tall tripod mainmast, well abaft the funnel.

1911–12 Fore control top rebuilt, narrow face forward. Single white band painted on each funnel.

1912–13 Navigating platform extended forward, fore funnel raised to clear bridgework.

1913–14 (After September 1913) Upper 4in guns in forward superstructure plated in. Searchlights redistributed for experimental purposes; two pairs on mainmast as a reserve. Remainder removed from bridge, and the two forward pairs from main tripod platform. Three SL platforms added immediately above bridge, one pair of SL on each. Two pairs added high on platforms abreast fore funnel. Splinter shields fitted to forward 4in guns.

1914 Funnel bands painted out at start of hostilities.

1914–15 Upper 4in guns in midships group decked in. 3in AA gun added right aft on quarterdeck. Main tripod SL raised on individual platforms. Forward section of flying deck removed to avoid damage to 12in guns below if flying deck collapsed in action. Both topgallants and main topmast removed.

1915–16 Anti-torpedo nets removed and camouflage painted out.

1916–17 Centre and lower group of 4in guns removed by April 1917. Official list gives one 4in and one 3in AA guns added, but these are not evident in photographs.

Armour additions (50 tons) fitted after Jutland. Fore topmast reduced to stump, and mainmast had very short W/T

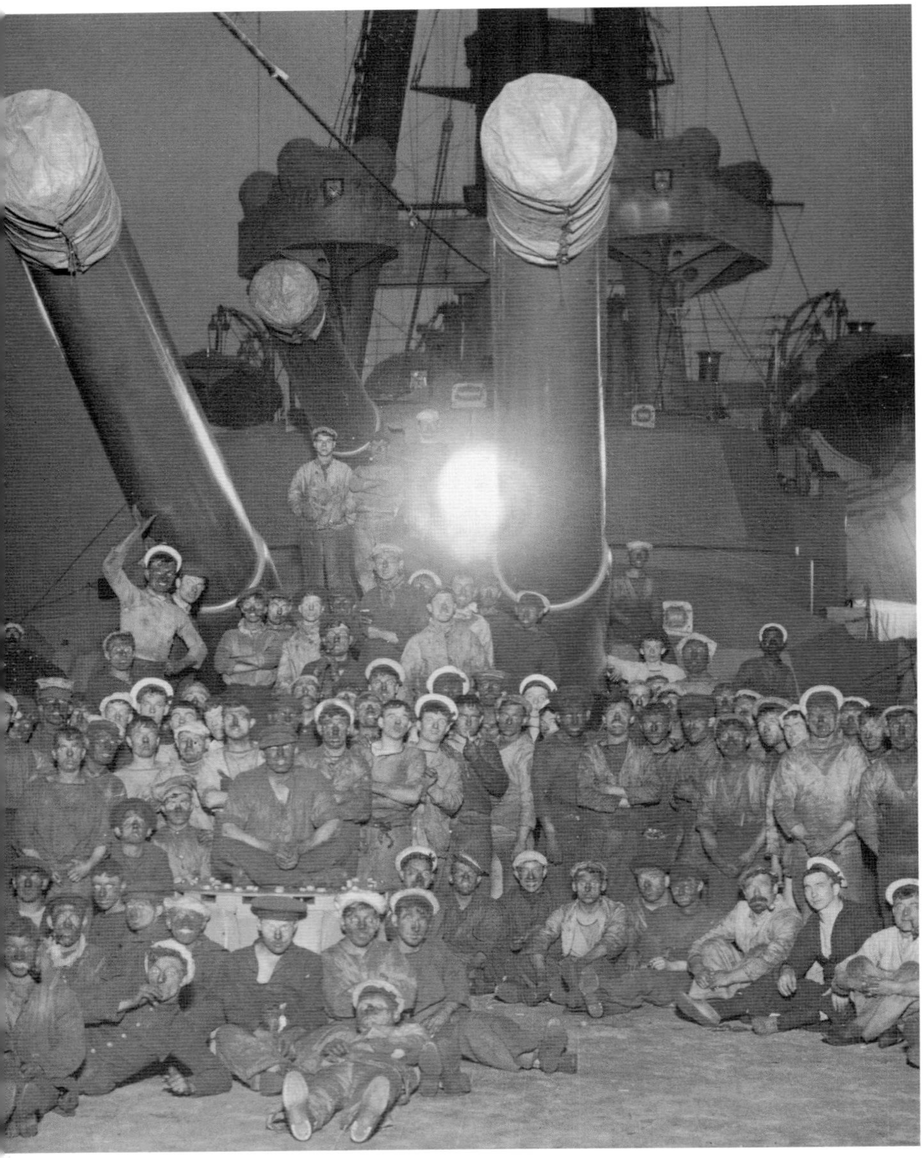

Below, left: Hours and hours of hard work started in the daylight would often finish in the dark as shown. Stokers lie exhausted under the 12in guns of *Neptune* glad that the job is over ... until the next time. 1911.

Below, right: Looking back over the bridge and forward 12in guns of *Neptune* whilst anchored in Scapa Flow in 1917. Note the net around the starfish.

pole fitted. Lower yard on foremast replaced by short signal struts at starfish level with long, very prominent forward struts.

1917–18 Forward control top enlarged. Aft control top removed because of smoke problems. Deflection scales painted on 'A' and 'Y' turrets. Stern torpedo tube removed. Searchlights modified with improved control facilities. Most of the twin 24in lamps were removed and replaced by single 36in. Three 'coffee-box' towers added abeam second funnel in a staggered arrangement (see plan). Clinker screen (or cap) added to fore funnel in 1917.

1918 High-angle rangefinder added to foremast control top. 36in SL and platform abeam fore funnel removed. SL platform on main tripod legs replaced by towers. Aircraft flying-off platform fitted over 'A' turret only. Fore topmast removed to make way for masthead RF. W/T mast on mainmast replaced by short topmast. Derrick stumps abreast second funnel removed.

1919 Clinker screen removed from fore funnel. *Neptune* was said to have looked rather unsightly during her latter years.

History: *Neptune*

Ordered on 14 December 1908, having been withheld while original design was modified from that of the fourth unit of *St Vincent* class. Built under 1908–09 Estimates. Began trials on 7 Sept and completed them on 9 Nov 1910.

1911 *19 Jan* Commissioned at Portsmouth to carry out trials of 'director control' equipment, which were carried out in the Mediterranean.

11 March Final trials off Gibraltar.

25 March Commissioned as flagship of CinC Home Fleet, and as flagship 1st Division, relieving *Dreadnought*.

24 June Present at Coronation Fleet Review. Although *Neptune* was flagship CinC Home Fleet, the pre-dreadnought *Lord Nelson* was flagship CinC the Grand Fleet and not just the Home Fleet.

June–July Combined exercises off SW coasts of England and Ireland with Atlantic and Home Fleets, and 4th CS.

Above: *Neptune*, February/March 1911.

Below: *Neptune* amidships, showing flying decks and boat arrangements.

Right: *Neptune c.* 1914. Note SL disposition around forward bridgework, and four yards on forward topmasts.

Opposite, top left: Whether it was wartime or not traditional values were still carried out and morning prayers were one of them. Amidships on HMS *Neptune* as a sermon takes place, 1911.

Below: Superb wartime port bow view of *Neptune* showing her additions since the start of hostilities. Note the bridge build up with the many blast mats which hide the fore funnel at certain angles. She has no net defence and numerous SL platforms, 1917.

July Exercises in North Sea with Atlantic Fleet.
1912 *7 Nov* Royal visit to 1st and 2nd Home Fleets at Weymouth followed by four days' exercises at sea.
9 July Parliamentary Review at Spithead followed by annual manoeuvres.
22 June Relieved as flagship 1st BS.
Oct Tactical exercises with 1st Home Fleet.
1913 *28 Jan* Recommissioned as flagship of CinC Home Fleet.
1914 *10 March* Relieved as flagship by *Iron Duke* and joined 1st BS as a private ship, relieving *Bellerophon*.

15 July Left Portland with the fleet for Spithead where the Fleet review was about to take place from the 17th–20th.
20–25 July Fleet exercises at sea.
25 July Fleet returned to Portland.
29 July Left for Scapa Flow.
11 Dec Under refit.
1915 *18 March* At 12.18, just after fleet had parted company with 4th BS to return to Scapa Flow after tactical exercises, unsuccessfully attacked by *U29* ESE of Pentland Firth.
14 April Battle cruising exercises, after which a U-boat was reported in the area, east of the Orkneys, no attack made.
1916 *22/23 April* Run into at night by SS *Needvaal* in thick fog in North Sea while on a sweep with Grand Fleet to Horns Reef. Some damage sustained by both ships but that of *Neptune* superficial.
31 May Battle of Jutland. In 5th Division Battle Fleet with *Colossus*, *Collingwood* and *St Vincent*, and was 19th ship in line after the deployment. At approximately 18.15 she engaged battlecruiser of the *Lützow* class at 14,000–9,000 yards and secured hits on that vessel. Between 19.08 and 19.38 she avoided three torpedoes that were fired at her.
June Transferred to 4th BS.
1918 *12 April* Transferred to Rosyth with rest of Fleet.
21 Nov With fleet (southern line) at surrender of German High Seas Fleet.
1919 *1 Feb* Reduced to Reserve at Rosyth, and became tender to *Hercules*.
1920 *20 May* Recommissioned in Reserve at Rosyth.
1921 *March* Placed on Disposal list at Rosyth. Until end of October 1921 was tender to *New Zealand*.
1922 *Sept* Sold to Hughes, Boickow & Co.
22 Sept Left Rosyth in tow for Blyth to be broken up, arriving same day.

Below, left: *Neptune*, mid 1918. Compared with previous photograph, only minor alterations: no topmast on fore, slightly increased topmast to main, SL (36in) previously around fore funnel now fitted in towers around second funnel. The only other alteration made to *Neptune* before the end of her career was the removal of her funnel cap.

Below, right: *Neptune* entering Rosyth 25 August 1917. Note alterations: short topmasts, single 36in SL around main tripod legs and fore funnel, enlarged control top, forward flying deck removed, clinker screen to fore funnel, deflection scales on 'A' and 'X' turrets, anti-torpedo nets removed.

Bottom: *Neptune* at the end of hostilities. Note that her funnel cap has been removed. Late 1918/19.

Colossus Class: 1909 ESTIMATES

Design

Agitation during the naval armament crisis of 1908 was exacerbated by continual reports that Germany, far from reducing its construction programme was, in fact, increasing it. Three battleships and one battlecruiser were being laid down in Germany against a meagre two in Britain. A paragraph in *The Standard* illustrated the uneasy situation all too clearly:

> The German ships are being built, and being built fast; moreover, unless reports are wholly at fault, they will be quite equal, if not superior, to anything yet begun in England. It is to be hoped that the Admiralty will not wait too long, because the progress Germany is making is most serious and it can no longer be contended that the German programmes are failing to materialize.

COLOSSUS: LAUNCH FIGURES, 9 APRIL 1910

	tons
Displacement:	7,325
Machinery:	129
Armour:	441
Men, ballast, launch gear:	247
Recorded weight of hull:	6,539

Draught: 7ft 9in forward, 15ft 6in aft
Beam as moulded: 84ft 10in
Breakage at launch:
longitudinal in a distance of 391ft = 1⅛in hog
transverse in a distance of 84ft = 0⅛in sag
Hercules weight at launch, 7,833 tons (hull 6,934 tons).

Although this message projected a gloomy outlook for Britain as the supreme maritime power, the Government would not yield in its determination to decrease expenditure for the following year (1909). Mr Churchill, at that time a member of the Cabinet, stated that: 'The British battlefleet has a great number of pre-dreadnoughts which mount a total of 152 12in guns against forty 11in guns for the German battlefleet.' He paraded the old warships as the ultimate answer to the problem and deplored the 'Dreadnought-fear-all school who hold that naval predominance in the future will depend on Dreadnoughts and Dreadnoughts alone.'

The argument was taken further by the eminent naval correspondent, H. W. Wilson, who wrote:

> Some fifteen of these pre-dreadnoughts will have disappeared from the front line by 1912. The position will have radically changed supposing that Great Britain has sixteen dreadnoughts ready for sea to thirteen German.
>
> If eight dreadnoughts are laid down this year, there will be no great margin of superiority, as strategy demands, on the British side, and the figures would be as follows:
>
> British 12in guns: 284. German: 256.

Below: *Hercules* fitting out at Palmers shipyard, 1910. She was second of the class to be laid down and the second to be launched but the first to be commissioned (4 July 1911).

Bottom: *Hercules* on sea trials, March 1911.

Above: *Hercules* as completed, showing the return to one tripod. Although retaining the improved feature of the superimposed 'X' and 'Y' main gun positions, the class reverted to the bridge–funnel–mast arrangement and brought with it the concomitant problems of such a layout.

Left: *Colossus*. Bow and stern views during trials period.

Left: *Colossus.* 'A' turret guns and forward superstructure. Taken during her trials period in about March 1911. Note 4in guns are completely unprotected.

HERCULES

Outboard profile and plan, 1913, after raising of forward funnel

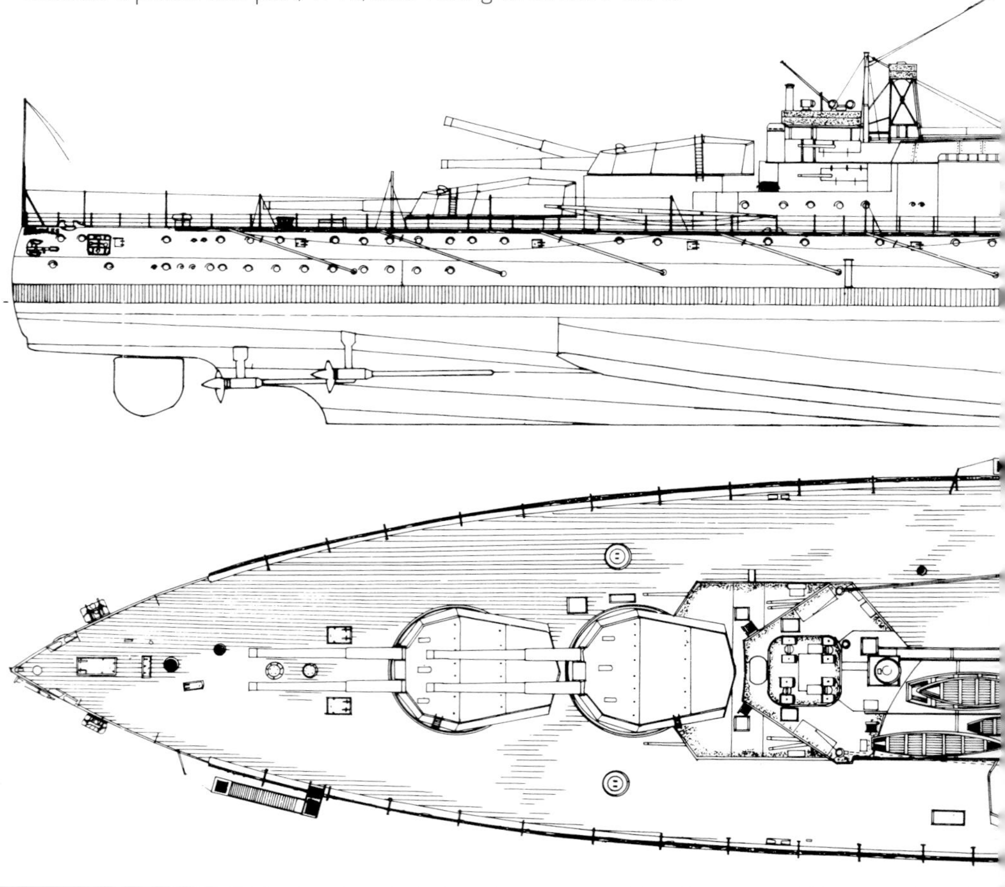

This advantage was much too small, especially if two or three ships were lost to mine or torpedo. The danger was actually even greater because Churchill, when stating that Britain could build ships faster than Germany, forgot to mention that the limiting factor in dreadnought construction, both in Britain and Germany, was the output of guns and mountings, which took considerable time to procure. In 1908 the British average annual output was approximately 35 sets of mountings, whereas the German output was known to be more than 50. Five or six sets were needed for each dreadnought which meant that while Britain could adequately arm six or seven vessels, Germany could prepare and arm eight to ten in the same time. It was considered that Germany would greatly increase its advantage by stepping up its programme, and that if Britain were to wait any longer for a suitable construction programme, British naval supremacy, on which the very existence of the country depended, would pass for ever. After much debate and the expression of strong public feelings, it was accepted that eight new capital ships would be provided for the 1909 programme, which would more than compensate any foreign competition envisaged. The eight ships that formed the agitated public's 'We want eight and we won't wait' programme were the battleships *Colossus* and *Hercules*, the four *Orion*-class battleships, and the battlecruisers *Lion* and *Princess Royal*.

The first two vessels laid down under the 1909 Programme were designated 'K5' and were to be modified versions of *Neptune*. Philip Watts and his constructors were able to improve the lines of the new ships over those of *Neptune*, but although the increased water-line belt and main armament armour thickness corrected some of *Neptune*'s deficiencies, there was a reversion to the 'dreadnought' arrangement of mast and fore funnel, which was a distinctly retrograde step. A further weakness, common to all preceding battleships, was the fitting of a light anti-torpedo armament coupled with the absence of any side armour above the main deck. The principal modifications of the 'K5' pair over *Neptune* were:

1. Rearrangement of anti-torpedo armament into two groups

instead of three, the main concentration being located forward.
2. Thicker armour on the main belt and barbettes, but the side armour was not carried right through to the extremities and the internal protection was less complete.
3. The machinery was arranged into three compartments instead of two, the main concentration of boilers being served by the forward uptake.
4. The mainmast was suppressed and the foremast was relocated abaft instead of before the funnel.

The flying deck amidships followed that of *Neptune* except that the heavy boats were stowed on the forward instead of the after structure because of the location of the main derrick on the fore.

The mainmast was done away with as a result of years of consideration which led to the conclusion that the mast was:

1. Limited in value because of smoke interference.
2. Not really needed for aerial spreading; a short stump would suffice.
3. Wasting some 50 tons weight.

Armament

The main armament and turret distribution was identical with that of *Neptune* except for the beam turrets which were brought closer together. This permitted the midships structure to be shortened and gave some measure of deck economy. The class

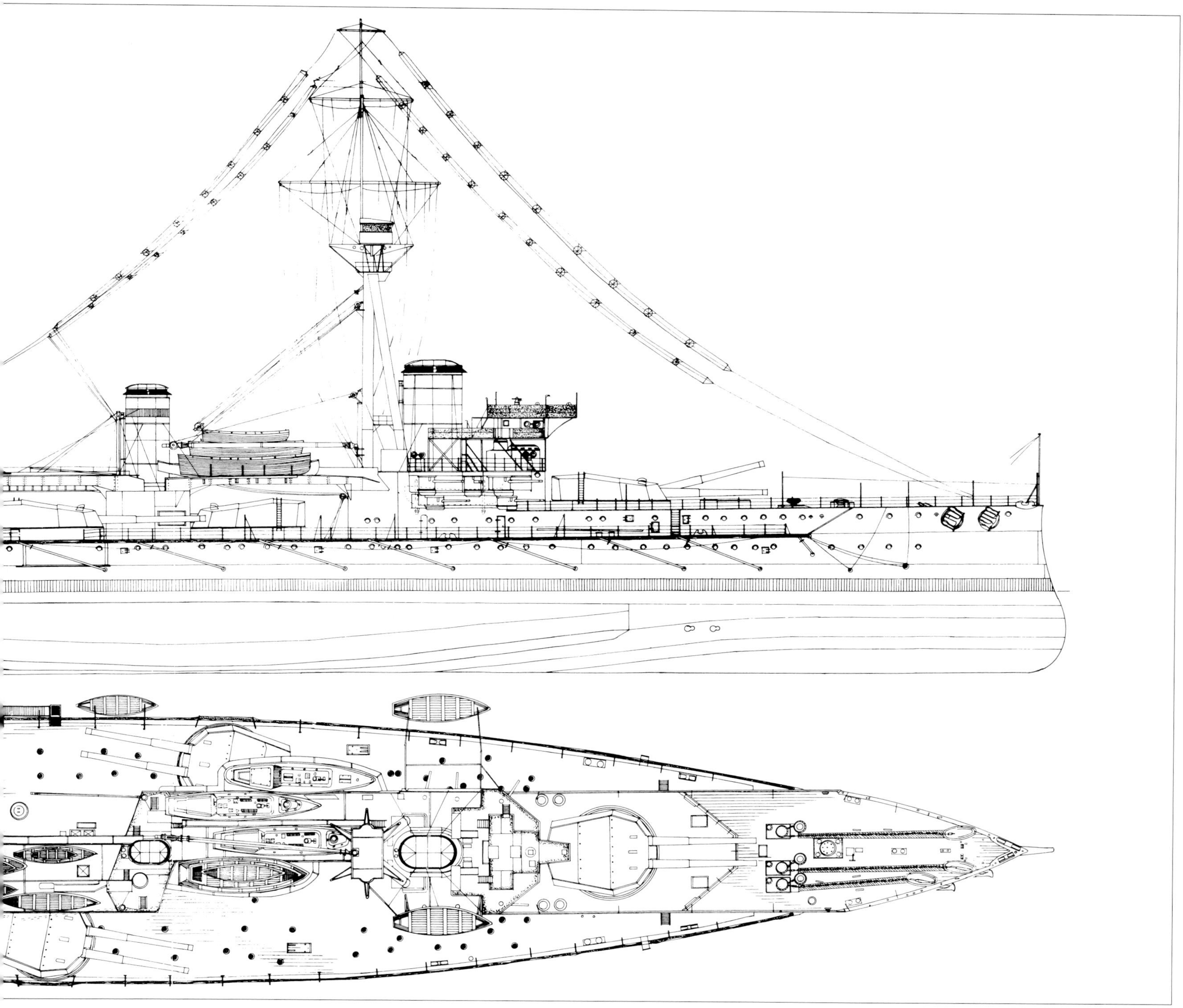

Above: Bow-on view of *Hercules* during gunnery practice in 1912.

were the last British battleships to carry the 12in armament and the last to have the echelon arrangement. But the same blast effects were experienced as in *Neptune*; when, at Jutland in 1916, *Colossus* fired her 12in guns over the deck amidships, the framing and deck supports were badly strained, especially after full charges had been used.

A feature peculiar to the class was that the standard magnetic compass position, usually in the forebridge, was moved to the after superstructure because of magnetism from the oblique layout of the two close-fitted 12in turrets. *Neptune*, because of her greater space amidships, did not suffer in this way.

The anti-torpedo armament was the same as in *Neptune*, but the guns were arranged in two groups instead of three, the four midships guns being transferred to the forward group on the assumption that any torpedo attack would come from ahead. To accommodate this redistribution of the secondary battery, the midships structure was made shorter than in *Neptune*, but the forward structure was made longer to accommodate the extra guns.

While in the construction stage, experiments with the new 21in torpedoes were completed, and it was decided to fit them. Nothing was altered in the torpedo flats to accommodate the increased size, so the flats became even more cramped than usual. The class were the first British battleships to receive 21in tubes.

Armour

Increase in protection to the waterline belt and barbette areas was a primary concern when this class were at the design stage, but while extra thicknesses were provided for these, the internal arrangements suffered some reductions. Differences from *Neptune* were:

1. The main belt was 1in thicker amidships, between the end barbettes, but the belt and upper strake were not carried to the extremities of the ships, so that for the first time since 1893, a British battleship was not given complete water-line protection.
2. The main deck protection was ¼in thicker.
3. The maximum barbette armour was increased by 1in, with 1in–2in reductions in less exposed areas; several different thicknesses were used throughout the barbettes.
4. Internal protection was less complete in order to offset the increased side and barbette armour. The longitudinal screens were fitted abreast shell and magazine spaces only and not from end to end, which was a distinctly retrograde feature of the design.

The main belt was 11in thick and extended from just inside the fore barbette to abreast the centre of the after turrets. The upper edge was at middle deck level approximately 2ft 9in above the waterline, and the lower edge 5ft 6in below. At the very lower edge of the belt, the 11in thickness was reduced to 8in. The extension of the belt forward was at the same height and was 7in thick; it ran for approximately 20 feet and was then met by a thickness of 2½in which terminated some 40 feet from the bows. Aft, the belt was 2½in uniform and extended to about 50 feet from the extreme stern. Above the 11in strake was a thickness of 8in which ran over the same length as the 11in belt, but at middle and main deck level. This upper belt reduced before the fore and after the aft barbettes.

The main bulkhead forward was 4in and ran obliquely inwards from the side armour to the outer faces of the barbette between the lower and main decks. The after main bulkhead, which was

COLOSSUS : GM AND STABILITY

Based on inclining experiments, 2 July 1911

	Displacement (tons)	Draught (mean)	GM	Maximum stability	Stability vanishes at
'A' Condition (= load)*	–	27ft	5.6ft	32°	61°
'B' Condition (= deep)**	–	29ft 5in	5.8ft	31½°	61½°
'C' Condition (= light)***	–	25ft 3in	5.2ft	32°	59½°

*Fully equipped plus 360 tons coal upper, 540 tons lower bunkers.
**Fully equipped plus 2,900 tons coal, tanks and boilers full.
***Made light but boilers and feed tanks full.

8in thick, closed the side belts and then ran into the barbette face. There was a forward 5in inner bulkhead which closed the upper 7in side armour strake, and an outer bulkhead of 1½in–2in which closed the ends of the 2½in side armour on the bows. The outer bulkhead aft was 2in thick and closed the ends of the 2½in side armour.

The barbettes varied in thickness according to need, that is to say, outer faces were thicker than inner faces and so on. 'A' barbette had 10in on the outer face above the upper deck and this reduced to 7in below it, and to 5in once below main deck. The inner faces were 9in above the upper deck and 7in from upper to main deck, then reduced to 4th below this. 'P' and 'Q' barbettes were given 11in faces, but elsewhere were 9in uniform above the main deck, reducing to 6in and 4in once below. 'X' barbette was 10in on the exposed face and 9in on the rear and front above the main deck level, below this it reduced to 4in. 'Y' had 10in uniform on the sides and faces down to the main deck, where it reduced to 4in.

The decks were as follows: middle deck ran from the outer faces of the end barbettes and was 1¾in thick. The main deck of 1½in ran from the outer fore bulkhead through to the after main bulkhead. The lower deck forward ran from the outer base of the fore barbette, through to the stem of the ship. The thickness was 1¾in below the 7in side armour, and 2½in for the rest of the run. Aft, the lower deck ran from the base of the after barbette and was 3in thick inside the after bulkhead. Once outside this it increased in thickness to 4in, and covered the steering gear.

The turrets were the same as in *Neptune*.

The conning tower had 11in sides, 3in roof and 2in floor; the communication tube was 5in. The spotting tower over the rear of the conning tower was 6in on the sides and had a 3in roof, the floor being the base of the conning tower. The torpedo control tower on the after superstructure was 3in on the sides and roof, its tube being of 3in armour also.

The funnel uptakes were armoured, 1in plates being fitted between the middle and upper deck levels. The screens protecting magazine spaces varied: 1in–1¼in abreast forward magazine; 3in and 1½in abreast beam magazines, 3in on the exposed sides and 1½in on the inboard side; 1¼in to 1¾in abreast after magazines. All screens were longitudinal and fitted close to the magazines

Machinery

Internal sub-division of machinery spaces was increased over all preceding classes of capital ships, the engine rooms being arranged for the first time in three groups instead of two. The ships are stated to have been able to maintain considerable speed using the central engine room only, leaving the wing engine rooms on standby in case full speed was needed. As a result, fuel consumption at seagoing speeds was reduced, enabling 6,680 nautical miles at 10 knots to be achieved. This, using both coal and oil, was an

Below: *Hercules*, summer of 1911. Note the four pairs of SL mounted on the platform behind the torpedo control tower.

Hercules, 1912. Showing old funnel bands (2 red).

increase of 350nm over *Neptune*. Admittedly, they had an extra 200 tons of fuel in their bunkers, but a substantial advantage had been gained.

Because of the closer spacing of the midships turrets, the after boiler room was separated from the forward rooms which necessitated a larger smoke uptake forward. This served twelve boilers and gave the fore control top many problems with heat and fumes, far worse than in *Neptune* or preceding classes. The machinery installation was the same as that fitted in *Neptune*, with identical shaft horsepower and turbine arrangements.

Appearance Changes

The class looked very much like *Neptune*, but their profile was marred by the lack of an after tripod, which made them look rather 'unbalanced'. They differed from *Neptune* in that:

1. The fore was considerably larger than the second funnel.
2. The forward superstructure was longer and the midships structure was correspondingly shorter.
3. The bridgework was not carried around the fore funnel.

As completed the pair were almost identical except for the following. *Colossus*: very prominent funnel caging; *Hercules*: low to normal funnel caging.

1911 Very prominent compass platform fitted over after superstructure in both ships.

1912–13 Control top forward rebuilt in *Colossus* only, that of *Hercules* remained unchanged (wide face). Small rangefinder added to roof of 'X' turret in *Hercules*. Searchlights redistributed: two pairs left on after superstructure as a reserve.

Colossus: two pairs removed from bridge and two pairs from after superstructure. These were remounted on new platform over forward superstructure spaced well apart.

Hercules: two pairs from after superstructure plus two more pairs mounted on new platform over forward superstructure, as in *Colossus*.

Navigating platform extended forward and fore funnel raised approximately 10 feet to clear bridge. Funnel bands painted in 1912. *Colossus*: one red band low on each funnel; *Hercules*: two red on each.

1913–14 Small control position added on forward superstructure at base of each tripod leg in *Colossus*. Forward superstructure searchlights in *Colossus* remounted on bridge and platforms, low down on tripod legs: two pairs on bridge, one pair on each tripod platform. Splinter shields fitted to forward 4in guns in *Hercules* only.

1914 Funnel bands painted out on outbreak of hostilities.

1914–15 Director control for main armament fitted on its own

Below: *Hercules*, 1914. Fore funnel raised (1912), extension to bridge, pair of SL mounted over forward 4in battery, and lower yard out.

COLOSSUS CLASS: STEAM TRIALS, 1911

Hercules undocked 18 February
2–3 March
Wind Force 3–4 increasing to 6–8, sea moderate
Draught: 26ft 10¾in forward, 27ft 5¼in aft
Propeller diameter: 8ft 11in
Propeller pitch: 8ft 0¼in

7/10th-power
300rpm; 19,218shp; 19.653 knots max.
Full power
335.8rpm; 28,922shp; 21,585 knots max.
Astern power: 253rpm; 11,374shp

10-hour (open exhaust) trial
First run
Port: outer 291rpm; 4,149shp; inner 293rpm; 4,602shp
Starboard: outer 288rpm; 3,930shp; inner 292rpm; 4,589shp
Total 17,270shp; 18.9 knots
Second run
Port: outer 286rpm; 3,824shp; inner 306rpm; 5,321shp
Starboard: outer 285rpm; 3,737shp; inner 300rpm; 5,131shp
Total 18,063shp; 19.5 knots

Colossus undocked 24 March
Wind Force 4-5, sea slight swell
Propeller diameter: 8ft 11in
Propeller pitch: 8ft 0¼in
7/10th-power
289.6rpm; 17,558shp; 18.716 knots

10-hour trial
First run
Port: outer 295rpm; 4,647shp; inner 282rpm; 3,895shp
Starboard: outer 290rpm; 4,332shp; inner 292rpm; 4,839shp
Total 17,713shp; 18.8 knots
Second run
Port: outer 284rpm; 3,870shp; inner 310rpm; 5,786shp
Starboard: outer 285rpm; 3,862shp; inner 303rpm; 5,691shp
Total 19,209shp; 19.57 knots
Full power
337rpm; 29,296shp; 21.569 knots

30 March
8-hour full power
First run
Port: outer 329rpm; 6,628shp; inner 322rpm; 6,187shp
Starboard: outer 318rpm; 5,715shp; inner 321rpm; 6,915shp
Total 24,445shp; 20.774 knots
Second run
Port: outer 5,996shp; inner 327rpm; 355rpm; 8,886shp
Starboard: outer 319rpm; 5,801shp; inner 347rpm; 8,958shp
Total 29,317shp; 21.569 knots
Third run
Port: outer 322rpm; 5,766shp; inner 347rpm; 8,373shp
Starboard: outer 315rpm; 5,196shp; inner 315rpm; 8,627shp
Total 27,963shp; 21.268 knots.

Below: Close-up of *Colossus* as completed. Port side amidships 1911. Known in service by a variety of nicknames such as 'Goloshes', Slasher' and 'Costly'.

COLOSSUS CLASS: PARTICULARS, AS COMPLETED

Construction

	Dockyard	Laid Down	Launched	Completed
Colossus:	Scott	8 July 1909	9 April 1910	July 1911
Hercules:	Palmer	30 July 1909	10 May 1910	Aug 1911

Displacement (tons)
20,030 (load), 23,266 (deep).

Dimensions
Length: 510ft pp, 541ft 6in wl, 545ft 9in oa
Beam: *Colossus* 86ft 8in; *Hercules* 85ft 2in
Draught (mean): 27ft (load), 29ft 5in (deep)
Height of 12in guns above lower wl: 'A' turret 31ft 6in; 'P', 'Q' 23ft; 'X' 31ft 6in; 'Y' 22ft
Height of CT vision slit above lower wl: 45ft 6in
Height of fore funnel above lower wl: *Colossus* 75ft; *Hercules* 72ft (before raising)
Height of lower foremast above lower wl: 100ft
Depth of keel from upper deck: 52ft.

Armament
Ten 12in 50cal Mk XI; Mk XI mountings; 100rpg
Sixteen 4in 50cal Mk VII; Mk II mountings; 150rpg
One 12pdr (8cwt)
Four 3pdr (saluting)
Seven MG
Three 21in torpedo tubes (one each beam, one stern) submerged.

Director control
None on completion.

Armour*
Main belt: 11in–8in amidships
Forward belt: 7in–2½in
After belt: 2½in
Barbettes: 11in–10in–9in–7in–4in
Turrets: 11in–4in–3in
Conning tower: 11in side, 8in rear, 3in roof, 2in floor
Spotting tower: 6in side, 3in roof
Communications tube: 5in
Torpedo control tower: 3in side, 3in roof
Tube: 3in
Uptakes: 1in
Magazine screens: 3in–1½in–1¼in.

Armour weight breakdown (tons)	
11in side belt:	1,026
8in belt:	434
7in belt:	150
'A' barbette:	352
'P', 'Q' barbettes:	451
'X' barbette:	341
'Y' barbette:	200
No. 29 bulkhead:	68
No. 42 bulkhead:	26
After screen bulkhead:	147
Bolts:	32
Main deck:	675
Middle deck:	805
Lower deck forward:	110
Lower deck aft:	180
Torpedo protection:	210
Uptakes:	57
Forward CT and tube:	125
After director tower:	12
Lower CT:	8
Backing:	65
Total armour protection:	**5,474**

Machinery
Parsons direct-drive turbines, four propellers
Boilers: *Colossus* eighteen Babcock & Wilcox; *Hercules* eighteen Yarrow; working pressure: 235-240psi. Each boiler fitted with three Admiralty-type single-orifice burners, 300lb per hour per burner
Length of boiler rooms (*Hercules*): (1) 37ft 11¼in; (2) 39ft 11¾in; (3) 37ft 11½in
Length of engine rooms: 67ft 11¼in
Fuel: 900 tons coal min., 2,900 tons max.; 800 tons oil
Coal consumption (tons): 335 per day = 3,100nm at 18 knots; 430 tons per day for 20,000shp (⅘th power) = 19.75 knots
Radius of action: 4,810nm at 10 knots (coal only); 6,680nm at 10 knots (oil added).

Ship's boats
Pinnaces (steam): two 50ft
Pinnaces (sail): one 36ft
Launches (steam): one 42ft
Life cutters: two 32ft
Cutters: one 32ft
Gigs: one 30ft
Whalers: three 27ft
Skiff dinghies: one 16ft
Balsa rafts: one 13ft 6in.

Searchlights
Eight 36in: two bridge forward, four around funnel, one after superstructure.

Rangefinder positions
One each spotting top, one each 12in turret, one after superstructure.

Anchors
Three 133cwt Admiralty (bowers and sheet), one 44cwt stern.

Wireless
Mk I, Mk II, Type 9 W/T short-radius.

Complement
Colossus: 751 (as commissioned)
Hercules: 778 (as commissioned); 791 (July 1916)

Cost

	Colossus	*Hercules*
Hull, gun-carriages, fittings:	£887,873	£893,276
Armour:	£355,924	£354,288
Machinery:	£257,185	£241,667
Total cost:	£1,540,403	£1,529,540
Plus guns:	£131,700	£131,700

*KC except CT, decks, etc.

platform just beneath fore control top. Two 3in AA added: one on platform over after superstructure, one right aft on quarterdeck. After section of flying deck and compass platform removed for same reason as in *Neptune*.

Topmast reduced in height and topgallant mast removed. W/T poles fitted to after pair of stump derricks. Derrick stumps abeam funnels removed.

1915–16 Two pairs of bridgework SL remounted in after superstructure in *Colossus*.

Bridge searchlights redistributed in *Hercules*: two pairs remounted on platform low on tripod legs and two on after superstructure. The remaining two were suppressed. *Hercules* fitted with equipment for kite balloons (August 1916). First trials with a kite balloon were carried out in *Hercules* on 19 August 1916, during a sweep by the Grand Fleet against the August sortie of German High Seas Fleet.

HERCULES
Outboard profile, 1918

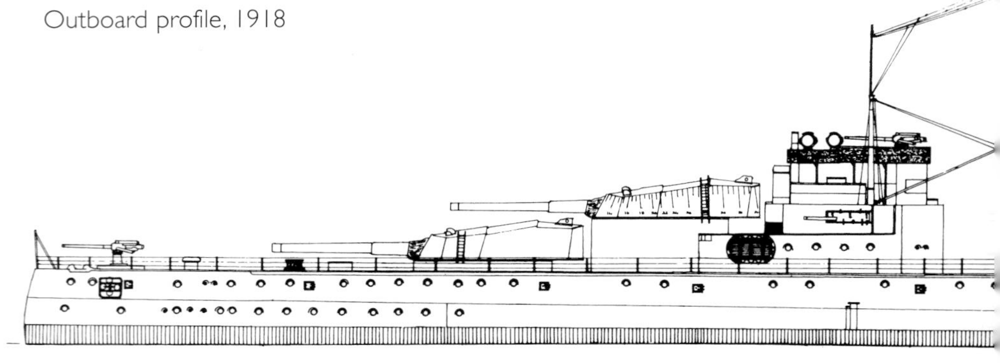

Above: *Hercules*, c. 1916/17. Close-up showing bridgework. Note director control for main battery, SL arrangement on bridge and mast and 4in guns in casemates.

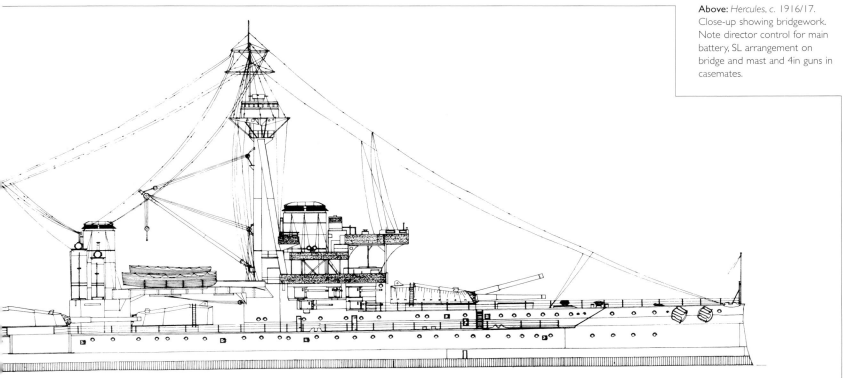

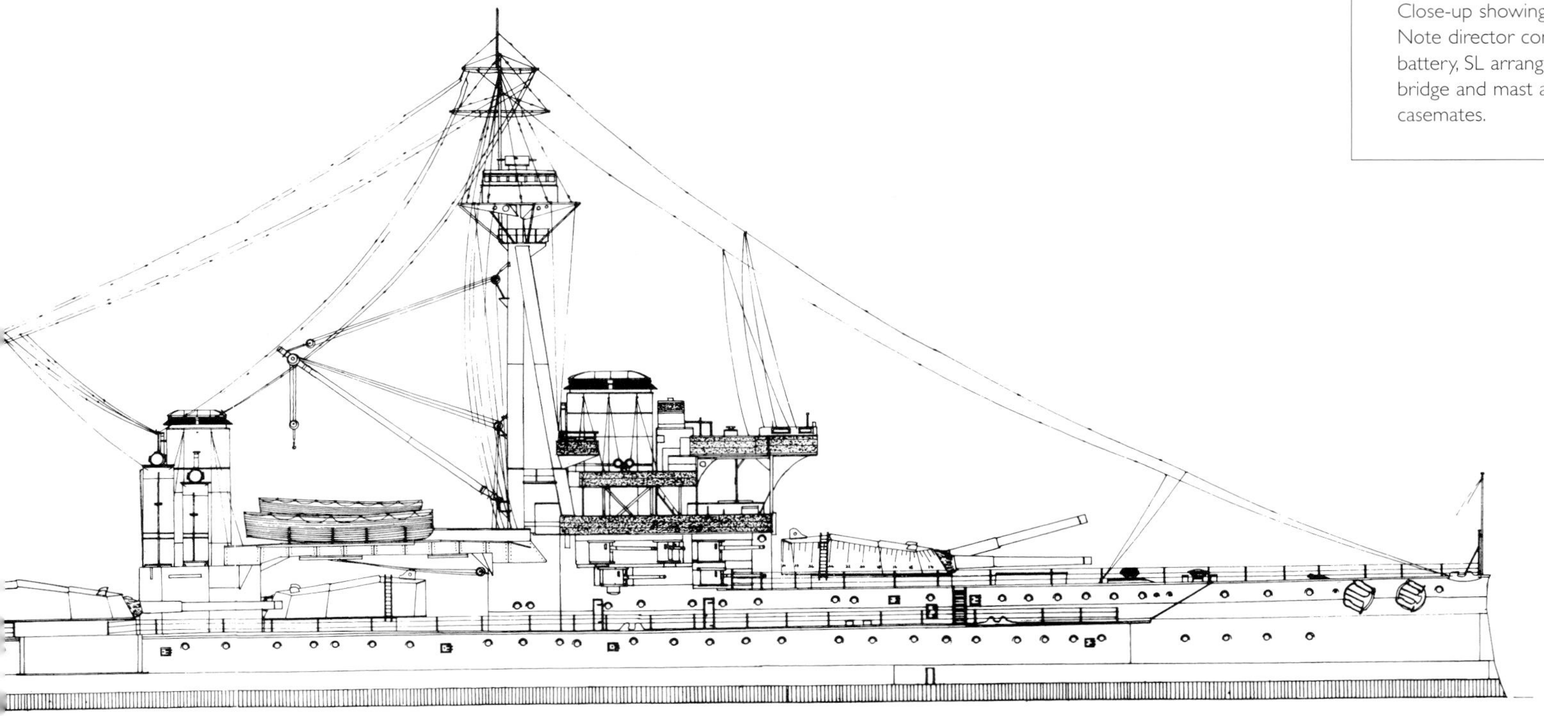

Torpedo nets were removed from both ships.

In *Hercules* navigating tower extended well above conning tower.

1916–17 Upper and lower pairs of 4in guns in the after group removed. Official Navy List states ships were fitted with one 4in AA and one 3in AA by April 1917.

Protection improvements after Jutland added approximately 50 tons.

1917–18 Control top enlarged in both ships. Rangefinder clocks fitted at rear of after superstructure in *Colossus*. Deflection scales painted on 'A' and 'X' turrets. Stern torpedo tube removed. Searchlights redistributed: twin 24in replaced by single 36in with exception of two pairs on bridge in *Colossus*. 'Coffee-box' towers fitted abeam second funnel in both ships; one pair of 24in lamps were a first fitted to these, then replaced by single 36in lamps. Twin 24in lamps removed from tripod platforms; replaced by single 36in lamps on small towers in *Colossus* only. Twin 24in lamps on alter superstructure replaced by 36in in both ships.

1918 HA RF added on control top in both vessels, topmast was retained.

1919–20 *Colossus* only (*Hercules* on sale list). AA armament removed. Under refit from September to October 1921 for service as Training Ship at Devonport. Some 4in and searchlights removed. At one time during this period she was painted in the old Victorian 'Livery buff', having a black hull with white lines on the water-line. Upperworks were light-grey. Some machinery removed so as to render her non-effective (Washington Treaty).

History: *Colossus*

Built under the 1909 Estimates and ordered on 1 June 1909. Began trials on 28 Feb 1911 which continued until July of that year.

1911 *31 July* Completed with full complement at Portsmouth.

8 Aug Commissioned at Devonport for service with 2nd Division of Home Fleet, relieving one of the *King Edward VII* class.

1912 *1 May* Fleet reorganization in which 2nd Division became 2nd BS 1st Fleet (Home).

7–11 May Royal visit to 1st and 2nd Fleets at Weymouth, followed by four days' exercises at sea.

9 July Parliamentary Fleet Review.

Autumn Temporary flagship 2nd BS, and of 2nd-in-Command 1st Fleet while *Hercules* was under refit.

Oct Exercises with 1st Fleet.

Nov Flag transferred to her sister. Long-range battle practice off Portland with shootings of up to 14,000 yards, the greatest attempted to that date. Previously, average range was 9,500 yards.

Late 1912 Transferred to 1st BS Home Fleet.

1913 *March* Visited Cherbourg with part of fleet.

25 Nov Recommissioned at Devonport for service in 1st BS.

1914 *May* Gunnery practice off Lamlesh.

15 July Left Portland for Spithead with 1st Fleet.

17–20 July Fleet Review.

20–25 July Manoeuvres at sea with combined fleets.

25 July Fleets returned to Portland.

29 July Sailed for Scapa Flow.

8 Aug With *Iron Duke* and *Monarch* during battle practice off Fair Isle.

22 Oct–3 Nov Based at Lough Swilly.

7 Nov Returned to Scapa Flow.

1915 *Nov* Became flagship of Second-in-Command of 1st BS relieving *St Vincent*.

1916 *31 May* Battle of Jutland. Lead 5th Division of Battle Fleet with *Neptune*, *Collingwood* and *St Vincent*. *Colossus* was 17th ship in line after deployment. At 17.51 sighted head of enemy line. At 18.30 fired three salvoes and at 19.00 opened fire on a three-funnelled cruiser believed to be *Wiesbaden*. At a range of 9,700 yards it is almost certain that this vessel was badly damaged by the fire. At 19.05 opened fire on a destroyer and

Below: Good starboard broadside of *Colossus* after her forward funnel was raised, 1912.

stopped it in its tracks. From 19.00–19.20 with *Collingwood* in action against German battlecruiser squadron at 8,400–10,000 yards. This was during the so-called *Kehrtwendung* (about turn) when the German ships fell under the guns of the British battlefleet. *Colossus* fired five or six salvoes at *Derfflinger* and scored several hits. The light being most favourable to the British, the German ships were unable to reply.

At 19.16 *Colossus* was hit by heavy shells on the forward superstructure; no serious damage, six men injured. She was the only British battleship to be hit by gunfire during the action. Evaded three torpedoes

At 23.30 she scraped her bottom, slightly damaging port and starboard propellers.

1 June Evasive action during the sighting of a Zeppelin.
1917 *June–Sept* Under refit.
1918 *12 April* Moved with Grand Fleet when Scapa Flow base transferred to Rosyth.
21 Nov Present in the Southern line at the surrender of the German High Seas Fleet off Firth of Forth.
1919 *Jan* Reached Devonport with *Collingwood* and *London* and became flagship of the temporary Reserve Fleet then formed.
Feb Joined regular Reserve Fleet at Devonport as flagship.
4 March On dispersal of Grand Fleet, *Colossus* became flagship of Vice-Admiral Reserve Fleet at Devonport and joined 3rd Home Fleet on its formation (3rd BS).
18 March Flag of 3rd BS Home Fleet transferred to *Collingwood*.
1921 *30 June* Relieved by *Glorious* and paid off onto Disposal list.
Sept Taken from Disposal list for selected service as Boys' Training Ship at Portland. Refitted at Devonport (partially dismantled) reduced to a non-effective status.
22 Sept Commissioned at Devonport as Boys' Training Ship.
11 Oct Arrived at Portland.
1922 *May* Portland Training Establishment closed down.
11 May Returned to Devonport.
25 May Paid off into Suspense section of Disposal list at Devonport.

Above: *Hercules* at Rosyth, July 1917. Additional bridgework, SL towers around second funnel, after flying deck removed, additional superstructure to aft island, AA gun mounted on top of this, and greatly enlarged control top.

1923 *July* Withdrawn from Disposal list for employment as hulk attached to HMS *Impregnable* training establishment.
1923 *July* At Devonport as above.
1927 *Aug* Withdrawn from training establishment.
1928 *23 Feb* Paid off into Dockyard control.
Aug Sold to Charlestown Shipbreaking Industries, later resold to Metal Industries.
25 Aug Left Devonport in tow for Charlestown (Rosyth).
5 Sept Arrived at Charlestown to be broken up.

History: *Hercules*

Ordered on 1 June 1909 and began trials after completion on 8 March 1911.

1911 *4 July* Commissioned at Portsmouth with nucleus crew.
31 July Completed to full complement at Portsmouth for service as flagship 2nd Division Home Fleet.

Below: *Colossus* (2nd Flag) leads *Neptune*, *St Vincent* etc past Inchcolm Island toward Scapa Flow in 1918.

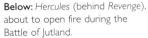

Above: *Hercules* at the end of the war. She joined the Reserve Fleet at Rosyth as Flagship on the breaking up of the Grand Fleet in 1919.

Below: *Hercules* (behind *Revenge*), about to open fire during the Battle of Jutland.

19 Dec Vice-Admiral Sir John Jellicoe appointed Commander 2nd Fleet.
1912 *7–11 May* Royal visit to 1st and 2nd Fleets at Weymouth.
9 July Parliamentary Fleet Review at Spithead.
Nov–Dec Under refit at Portsmouth.
1913 *7 March* Relieved as flagship 2nd BS and of 2nd-in-Command 1st Fleet by *King George V.* Became private ship in 2nd BS.
22 March During a gale collided in Portland Harbour with SS *Mary Parkes* of Glasgow, booms carried away. Not extensively damaged, but damage to steamer much worse.
May Transferred to 1st BS.
1914 *15 July* Left Portland for Spithead with 1st Fleet.
17–20 July Fleet Review.
20 July Manoeuvres at sea with combined fleets.
25 July Returned to Portland.
29 July Sailed for Scapa Flow.
22 Oct Based at Lough Swilly.
1916 *Feb* Refitted (turbine trouble) at Scapa Flow.
19 March Rejoined 1st BS.
31 May Battle of Jutland. In 6th Division of battle fleet with *Marlborough*, *Revenge* and *Agincourt*, a mixed bag if ever there was one. *Hercules* was 23rd ship in line after deployment. At 19.00–19.15 engaged enemy battlecruisers, sustaining hits with her fifth and sixth salvoes.

Although straddled, and hit by splinters, sustained no damage or casualties. Avoided several torpedoes, one of which passed right alongside after she had turned. By 23.20, because of torpedo hit received by *Marlborough* 6th Division had fallen well astern of battlefleet.
1 June Division sighted and opened fire on a Zeppelin.
June Transferred to 4th BS as flagship.
19 Aug At sea with Grand Fleet to intercept German High Seas Fleet's abortive raid on Sunderland. During this advance, *Hercules* carried out the first experiments with a towed kite balloon which was sent up without observers to test towing apparatus.
1918 *12 April* Based at Rosyth with the fleet.
24 April With *St Vincent* ordered to Orkneys to support *Agincourt* and 2nd CS during High Seas Fleet's last sortie.
21 Nov Present in Southern line at surrender of German Fleet.
3 Dec Detached from Grand Fleet to carry Allied Armistice Commission to Kiel.
20 Dec Returned to Rosyth.
1919 *30 Jan* Reduced to Reserve Fleet at Rosyth.
1921 *Oct* Placed on the Disposal list.
8 Nov Sold to Slough Trading Co.
1922 *Sept* Resold to German shipbreaking firm.
Oct Left Rosyth in tow for Kiel to be broken up.

Orion Class: 1909 ESTIMATES

Design

The early designs for the *Orion* class called for an improved *Colossus* type with all big guns on the centreline. Early sketches showed layouts for ten 12in 'A' guns (see below), a secondary armament of sixteen 4in and a speed of 21 knots; one scheme made provision for speeds of up to 23 knots.

The first of the class (*Orion*) was provided under the normal 1909 Programme, but the other three were authorized under the 'contingency programme' (see also *Lion* class), greatly against the wishes of the Prime Minister, Mr Asquith, who was still insisting that these extra ships were just not needed. Sheer weight of opinion forced the Liberal Government to concede to an accelerated capital ship construction programme (see design notes in other classes). Report after report was coming in about the huge building programme taking place in Germany, and it is difficult to understand how the Government could have been in any doubt as to Germany's real intentions. The naval correspondent of *The Daily Graphic* wrote:

> The news that six German Dreadnoughts are now building, and some of them well advanced, draws attention to the mystery which prevails with regard to these ships. Though secrecy was nominally preserved by the British Admiralty as to the designs of the British Dreadnought, all the important facts about her became common property within six months of her commencement. But of the German Dreadnoughts it is correct to say that little or nothing is known in this country even now, and it may be doubted whether the British Intelligence Department is in possession of their details. The first of the German Dreadnoughts building is the large armoured cruiser 'E' originally laid down in 1906, then her construction was suspended, and changes were made to her, to enable her to meet the newest of British ships in her class. Her construction was the second begun last year. In the summer of 1907 four large battleships were laid down, and in the November, another large armoured cruiser was drawn up, which is said to be the largest of its type ever laid down. There are also reports that Germany has in fact laid down four more very large battleships this year.

DESIGNS FOR *ORION* CLASS

	Design K5*	23-knot Design	Design 'L'
Displacement (tons):	20,000	24,250	22,500
Length:	510ft pp	575ft pp	540ft pp
Beam:	85ft	88ft	82ft
Draught (deep):	31ft	31ft 6in	31ft 6in
Freeboard:	28ft	26ft	25ft
Sinkage (tons):	76	86	82
Armament			
12in 'A':	10	10	10
4in:	16	16	16
21in TT:	3	3	3
Armour (inches):	11–10–9–7–6–5–4	10–9–7–6–5–4	10–9–6–2
Fuel (tons)			
Coal:	3,000	3,100	3,000
Oil:	800	900	850
SHP:	25,000	35,000	27,000
Speed (knots):	21	23	21

*Actual design for *Colossus*.

THUNDERER: LAUNCH FIGURES, 1 FEBRUARY 1911

	tons
Displacement:	9,184
Equipment on board:	1,430
Recorded weight of hull:	7,820
Total displacement:	**10,614**

Draught: 9ft 5in forward, 10ft 3½in aft
Length: 545ft 2in pp
Beam as moulded: 88ft 5in
Total length of boiler rooms: 114ft
Total length of engine rooms: 67ft 11¾in.

In the early designs the 23-knot ship was to have a length of 575 feet, a substantial increase (65 feet) over that of *Colossus*, and a beam increase to 88 feet (3 feet wider). Displacement was roughly worked on a legend of 24,250 tons at a cost of £2,500,000. The 21-knot ship was 540 feet by 88 feet, but had 6 inches less draught at 27ft 6in, on a corresponding displacement of 22,750 tons, and was costed at £500,000 less than the 23-knot ship. The Board met in June 1909 to study the preliminary layouts, but although at least half the members favoured the faster ship, it was the design for the 21-knot ship that was finally approved. In a letter to the First Sea Lord dated 17 June 1909, the DNC, Philip Watts, explained:

> The new ships should most definitely be the 23-knot vessel, owing to the latest reports of similar speeds from some of the German battleships. I know the Board favour the slower ship for some strange reason, and I cannot understand this at all.
>
> I for one do not agree with the slower ship, because I believe that the Royal Navy should not be outclassed by any type of ship: extra money which would be needed for the faster units would indeed be money well spent.

The Board, however, seemed to turn a deaf ear to such reports, and in November of that year approved the layout for the slower ship, which was designated 'L', and sent the sketches off to the constructors for final confirmation. The 'L' design was a

Below: A large crowd turn out for the launch of *Thunderer*, the last battleship to be launched on the River Thames and the last ship constructed by the Thames Ironworks at Blackwall before the company went into liquidation, 1 February 1911.

ORION CLASS: FINAL LEGEND AND WEIGHT BREAKDOWN

Design 'L'

Displacement (tons): 22,500.

Dimensions

Length: 545ft pp
Beam: 88ft 6in
Freeboard: 26ft forward, 16ft 6in amidships, 17ft 6in aft
Draught: 27ft 6in (mean), 31ft 4in (deep)
Main gun heights above normal draught wl: 'A' 30ft 6in; 'B' 40ft; 'Q' 24ft; 'X' 32ft 6in; 'Y' 23ft
Height of armour belt top above lower wl: 16ft 6in; 4ft below
Depth of keel from upper deck: 44ft.

Armament

Ten 12in 45cal 'A' type
Sixteen 4in 50cal
Three 21in torpedo tubes; twenty torpedoes.

Armour

Main belt: 12in
Uppers: 9in–8in
Bulkheads: 10in–6in
Barbettes: 10in–9in–6in–3in–2in
Turrets: 11in–8in
Conning tower: 11in
Director control tower: 3in
Communications tubes: 5in forward, 3in aft
Magazine and shell room plating: 1in–2in
Uptakes: 1½in
Decks: upper 1¾in–1½in, main 1½in, middle 1in, lower 2½in–1in forward, 4in–3in aft.

Weight breakdown (tons)

Load	
Hull:	7,950
Armour:	6,460
Armament:	4,000
Machinery:	2,420
Coal:	900
General equipment:	670
Board margin:	100
Total:	**22,500**
Deep	
Hull:	7,950
Armour:	6,460
Armament:	4,065
Coal:	3,275
Machinery:	2,680
General equipment:	812
Board margin:	100
Oil:	860
Total:	**26,202**

Below: *Orion* fitting out. Port amidships. Note roof plates to 'B' turret have not yet been positioned, incomplete conning tower, simple bridgework, splinter protected space (between funnels) for lifeboats, and no sign of 'Q' turret at this date (early 1911).

Left: *Orion* fitting out, early 1911. Taken from the forecastle, looking aft, and showing 'A' and 'B' 13.5in guns and turrets.

considerable improvement over that of 'K5' (*Colossus* and *Hercules*). Outstanding features were:

1. Unprecedented rise in displacement over preceding classes.
2. Adoption of the 13.5in gun with all centreline superimposed firing arrangements.
3. Provision for side armour above the main deck (for the first time in any British dreadnought).

The great rise in displacement was necessitated by the adoption of the 13.5in gun, all centreline disposition of turrets, and increased protection: the rise was greater than in any previous class to class increase in the British Navy, and almost double that from *Lord Nelson* to *Dreadnought*.

The hull lines were modified from the preceding class and resulted in a much better prismatic coefficient with maximum beam carried farther abaft rather than before the midships section. Moreover, owing to the absence of beam turrets, the forecastle retained a full width reaching almost amidships where it was angled sharply into the centreline abaft this, which in turn allowed for a greater arc of fire for the midship gun turret ('Q').

The extra weight of the superimposed turrets, plus the upper

Below: *Monarch* nears completion at Elswick, October 1911. She left her builders for preliminary trials on 6 November 1911 then left for Devonport for official trials on 12 November. She returned to the builders for completion on 17 December 1911, having constituted a record in rapid construction.

side armour, raised the CG considerably by comparison with the *Colossus* type, resulting in provision for additional beam to ensure adequate metacentric height (GM) and provide suitable stability. Despite an increase of 35 feet in length, the additional beam was only 3ft 6in, and gave a length/beam ratio of 6.56:1. Constructors A. M. Worthington and E. N. Mooney, who were responsible for the design, had at one time considered an increase in beam to over 88ft 6in providing additional stability and extra anti-torpedo protection, but they rejected such a move in favour of the lower figure which was seen as sufficient to ensure the requisite initial stability, with a GM of 5.5 feet in the legend condition.

On completion, it was reported that although the class were good seaboats, they were prone to heavy rolling. This caused considerable alarm in construction circles and at first it was denied. Then a report appeared in *The Standard and St James's Gazette* commenting that:

> The new super dreadnought *Orion*, in the voyage across the Bay of Biscay has proved to be a tremendous roller. Reports were somewhat as to whether she rolled enough to cause any serious anxiety. According to some alarmist versions she nearly turned turtle. But there is no question whatever about her having more than lived up to the old navy legend about ships with 13.5inch guns rolling terribly. Though in neither case had the 13.5inch anything whatever to do with it, both the 'Admirals' and '*Royal Sovereigns*' (1890) rolled abominably in the old days – the latter so badly that bilge keels had to be fitted.

There was no reason to fear that *Orion* might follow the example of the old *Captain* of 1870 and turn turtle, but the problem was serious and had to be rectified. On inspection, and after a few calculations, it proved to be a simple matter of enlarging the existing bilge keels. But then another problem arose: with the largest bilge keels applicable to the class, the ships would not fit into existing docks. The result was a compromise – the fitting of enlarged bilge keels, but not of the size the constructors deemed necessary. All vessels of the class were fitted, and the problem of rolling greatly diminished; *Orion*'s degree of inclination (20°) while on passage in the Bay of Biscay was not experienced again.

Armament

These were the first battleships of the dreadnought era to carry a calibre heavier than 12in; as completed, the main armament was the most powerful yet fitted in any warship. The greatly increased weight of broadside – 12,500lb against *Dreadnought*'s 6,800lb and *Neptune*'s 8,500lb – was unequalled until the US *Texas*-class battleships entered service early in 1914.

The 13.5in gun was adopted because of the increasing ranges at which ships could engage and the concomitant need for greater accuracy, penetration and destructive effect. The 12in gun, the standard battleship weapon for the past fifteen years, had reached its peak with the 50cal model fitted in the *St Vincent*, and it was found to be impossible to improve performance without increasing the size of bore. The 13.5in, at first officially designated 12in 'A' to conceal the increase, had been under test for some time before it was decided to fit it into the new ships. The estimated total weight of five twin turrets (excluding guns) was 2,344 tons which, though substantial, was thought to be acceptable in the interest of fighting efficiency.

The decision to fit all turrets on the centreline resulted from careful investigation of foreign designs. The arrangement had first appeared in the US *Michigan* class of 1905, and it had been under consideration for some of *Dreadnought*'s layouts, but was not deemed feasible at that particular time because of weight, size and

Right: *Conqueror.* A striking view down the muzzles of her 13.5in guns, while fitting out at Beardmore in 1912.

cost. The construction department quickly found that the fitting of 13.5in guns on the beam was impracticable because of the increased weight; furthermore, the arcs of fire were greatly restricted and, as Watts said, 'What on earth is the good of guns that cannot fire in an all-round position?' The solution was borrowed from *Neptune*: the beam turrets were brought into the centreline, one superfiring over the forward turret and the other amidships abaft the second funnel, which necessitated 35 feet extra deck length at the design stage.

Although director control for the main armament was not included in the original design, provision was made for such a fitting in *Thunderer* late in 1911 and trials took place in the spring of 1912. This director, which had proved successful so far, was mainly a Vickers design, rather superior to the Scotts-type in *Neptune*, which it superseded.

Special trials were arranged with *Orion* and *Thunderer* during October/November 1912, the latter using director control, the former none. An article in *The Times* left little doubt as to the best method:

> A further report on the fitting of a new method of director controlled firing was in evidence this afternoon. The battleships *Orion* and *Thunderer* were ordered to fire at a selected target from different ranges and angles at the same time. The trial was held in rough squally weather, with the ships rolling and pitching up to at least 5 or 6 degrees. Under these conditions, it was witnessed that the *Thunderer* scored at least five times as many hits as the *Orion*, and that of the *Thunderer* seemed to rain in a more concentrated area than that of the latter's shell splashes. At this rate of improvement, our ships should be able to hit an enemy vessel when in action, with the opening salvoes.

The retention of the 4in secondary armament was again seen as the ships' main disadvantage, although the guns were distributed differently from the layout in *Colossus*: the guns were fitted equally between the forward and after superstructures instead of being concentrated forward as before. While the reason for this is not totally clear, it was obvious that an evenly distributed battery was much better than the closely bunched group fitted in many previous designs.

These ships were the first British battleships to be fitted with 21in torpedo tubes at the design stage. (The *Colossus* class was designed to receive 18in tubes, but later, while they were still under construction, modifications were made to give them the 21in.)

Armour

In anticipation of likely increases of calibre beyond 12 inches in foreign naval guns, protection of the new class was substantially improved over earlier dreadnought types, with much increased vertical hull armouring, but, strangely, deck thicknesses and internal protection were on a lesser scale than that of *Neptune*. While the *Orions* were under construction the question of the 'soft ends' had been examined, and the Sea Lords decided that it would give them much pleasure if more armour could be worked into these areas.

Modifications were made whereby the 6in armoured belt forward was taken further to terminate at frame 29; it then reduced to 4in as far as frame 15. This extra belt rose from lower deck level to the main deck where it was met by a 4in bulkhead which reduced at lower deck level to 1½in. Aft, the 2in belt now extended as far as frame 236 where it was met by a 2in bulkhead. This modification increased protection at the ends by 25 per cent.

The scale of armouring compared to that of *Colossus* was:

1. The belt and lower side armour was 1in thicker amidships, and 6in and 4in forward against 7in and 2½in; the lower edge of the belt was not reduced.
2. Upper side armour: 8in was added from main to upper deck levels between 'A' and 'Y' turrets.
3. Deck protection was spread over four decks instead of three by transferring the main deck armour to the upper deck level, between 'A' and 'Y' barbettes.
4. Main deck armour extended abaft 'Y' turret instead of terminating at this point.
5. Lower deck forward was reduced from 2½in–1¾in to 2½in–1in.
6. Maximum armour on barbettes and turrets remained the same, but the bases once below main deck level were reduced from 4in to 3in.

The main protective belt extended almost to the outer face of the

Left: *Monarch* leaves Armstrong's for her first sea trials in November 1911. Note slightly reducing thickness of the tops to the tripod which could be lowered when passing under the bridges of the River Tyne to and from her builders.

Left: *Orion* amidships 1915. Bleak conditions but work and duty carry on as one of her steam pinnaces is lowered into the water.

end barbettes, with the upper edge at middle deck level and the lower edge at 3ft 4in below the water-line. Total belt height was 20ft 6in.

The 6in–4in forward extended to within approximately 42 feet of the stem, at the same height as the midships section, and was 6in for about 55 feet beyond 'A' barbette before being met by a 4in thickness. Aft, this extension reached to within 45 feet of the stern, at the same height as the midships section.

The lower edge belt of 9in–6in–4in–2½in was fitted over the same length as the main belt, but was between middle and main deck level. The 8in upper side extended to just beyond the inner faces of the end barbettes between the main and upper decks.

The main bulkheads (6in forward, 10in aft) ran obliquely inwards from the forward and aft extremities of the 12in belt and 9in lower side armour to the outer faces of the end barbettes between the main and upper decks. The upper side 8in bulkhead ran inwards from the forward and after ends of the upper side armour to the sides of the end barbettes between the main and upper decks. The forward 4in–1½in bulkhead closed the forward 4in strake at the same thickness between main and lower deck, but reduced to 1½in from main to upper levels. The after 2½in bulkhead closed the after 2½in strake between the lower and main decks.

The 1½in upper deck ran from the end barbettes, while the 1½in main deck ran from the ends of the forward upper side bulkhead to the forward bulkhead, and from the after upper side bulkhead to the after bulkhead. The middle deck was 1in on the slope and flat between the outer faces of the end barbettes. The 2½in–1in lower deck forward was below water from the outer base of the forward barbette to the stem of the ship. Aft, the 4in–3in lower deck was also below water and ran from the outer base of the after barbette to the stern. It was 3in inside the after bulkhead and 4in outside.

Turrets had 11in on the face, 8in on the sides and 3in–4in crowns. The barbettes were of a variety of thicknesses: 'A' was 10in–9in–7in–6in–3in: the outer face being 10in above and 6in below the main deck, the inner face being 9in above and 7in reducing to 3in below the main deck. 'B' barbette was identical

ORION
Outboard profile and plan, late 1912, as completed

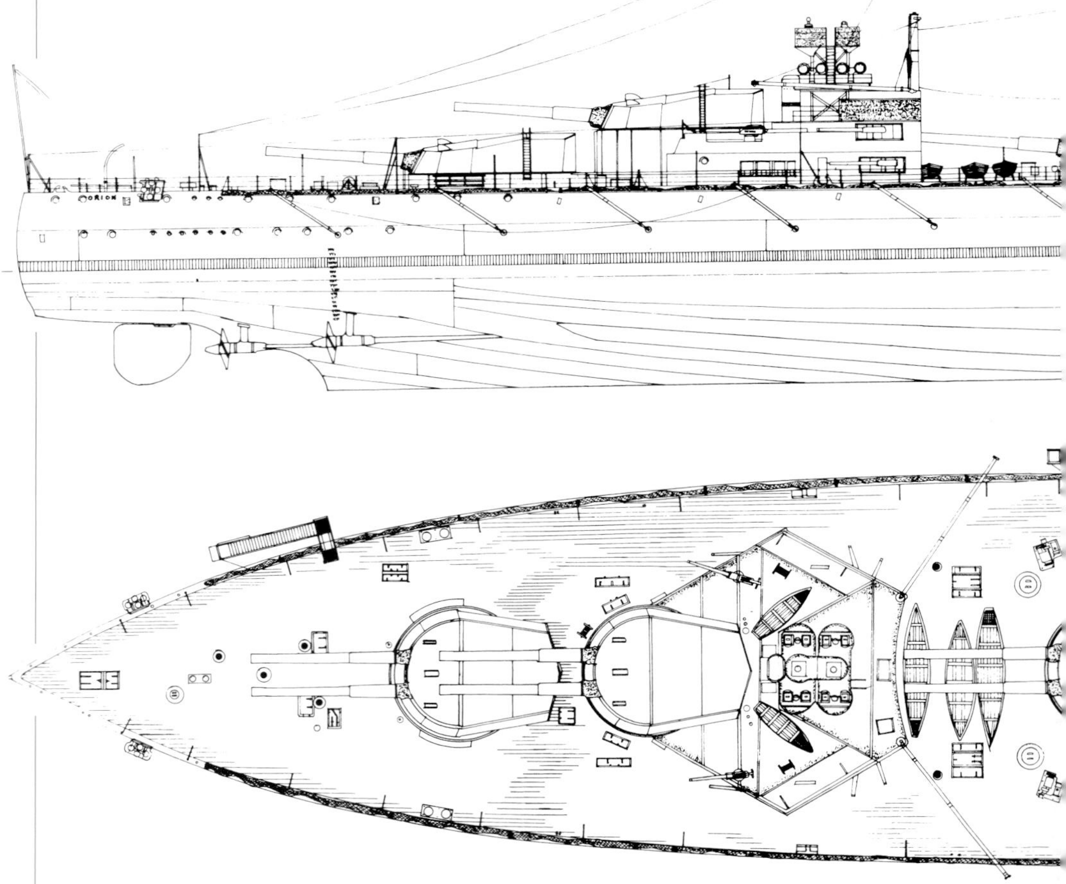

with 'A'. 'Q' and 'X' had 10in sides, with 9in and 7in faces, again reducing to 3in below main deck level. 'Y' had 10in outer face and sides and an inner face of 9in and 7in reducing to 3in below the main deck.

The conning tower had 11in sides, a 3in roof and 4in floor. The communications tube was 5in, and the spotting tower was given 6in sides and a 3in roof. The torpedo control tower was 3in as was its tube. Funnel uptakes were 1in–1½in between middle and forecastle decks.

Machinery

Main machinery consisted of Parsons direct-drive turbines driving four propellers. The high pressure turbines were located on the wing shafts, the low pressure turbines on the inner shafts. The arrangement consisted of one high pressure ahead and astern on each wing shaft, and one low pressure ahead and astern on each inner shaft.

Orion, *Conqueror* and *Thunderer* had eighteen Babcock and Wilcox boilers, while *Monarch* was fitted with Yarrow-type

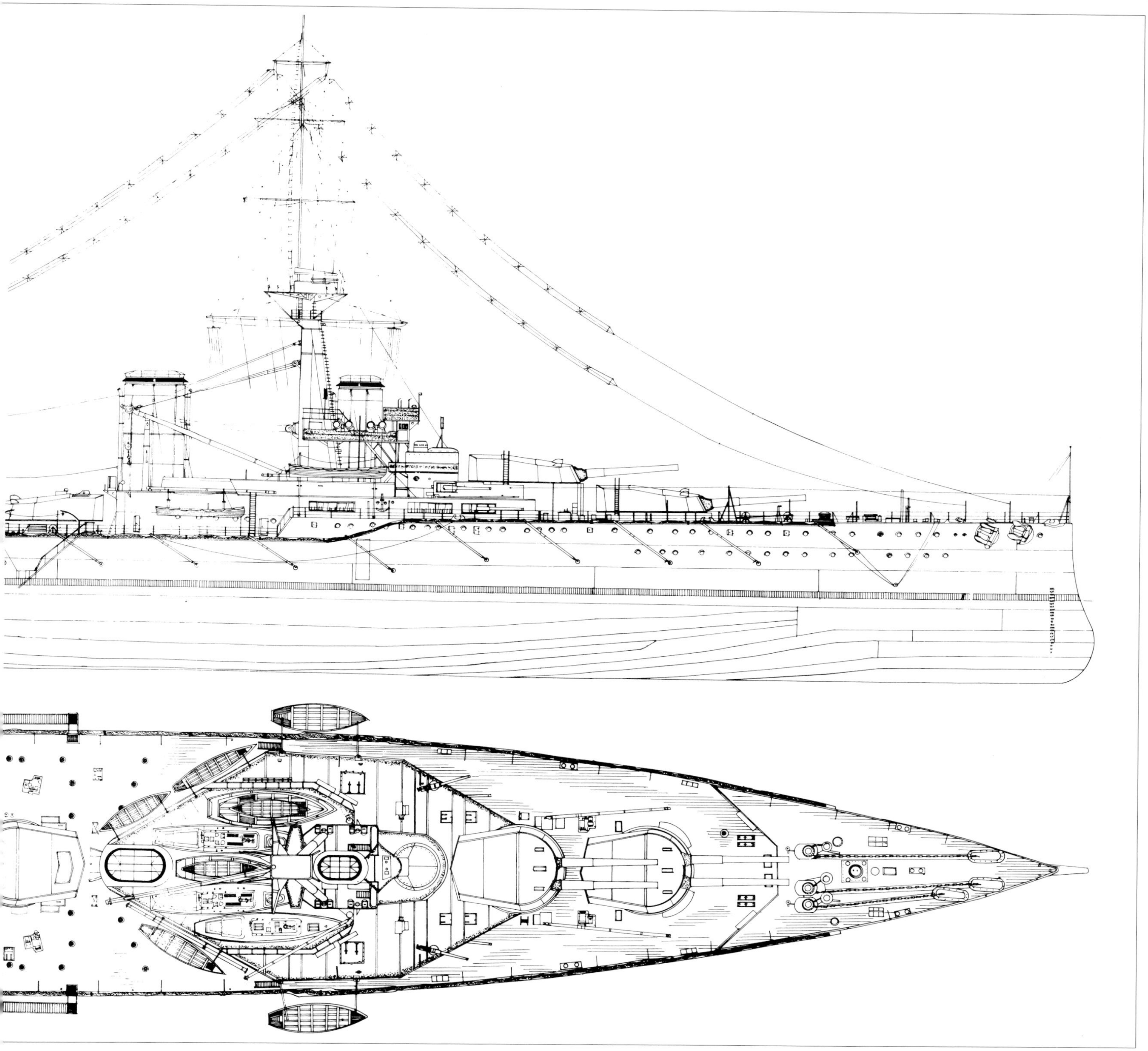

ORION CLASS: STEAM TRIALS

Contractors' trials (collective results)

	Date	Revolutions	SHP	Speed (knots)
Orion:	19 Nov 1911	358.3rpm	30,112	21.045
Monarch:	9 Dec 1911	334.3rpm	32,277	21.883
Conqueror:	7 June 1912	339.2rpm	33,198	22.126
Thunderer:*	5 March 1912	300rpm	27,427	20.799

***Orion*, September 1911** Measured mile, Polperro

Open exhaust

	Outer		Inner		Total SHP	Speed (knots)
First run						
Port:	280rpm	3,516shp	313.3rpm	5,984shp	18,470	18.985
Starboard:	286.7rpm	3,562shp	303.3rpm	5,408shp		
Sixth run						
Port:	300rpm	4,429shp	283.3rpm	5,178shp	18,967	19.072
Starboard:	303.3rpm	4,295shp	286.7rpm	5,064shp		
Closed exhaust						
First run						
Port:	326rpm	5,213shp	300rpm	4,872shp	19,714	10.341
Starboard:	310rpm	4,742shp	295rpm	4,897shp		
Fourth run						
Port:	310rpm	4,957shp	293.3rpm	4,763shp	19,361	19.560
Starboard:	313.3rpm	4,758shp	296.7rpm	4,883shp		
Full power						
First run						
Port:	345rpm	6,189shp	360rpm	8,596shp	28,762	21.180
Starboard:	345rpm	5,773shp	360rpm	8,204shp		
Third run						
Port:	353.3rpm	6,353shp	376.7rpm	9,477shp	30,532	21.268
Starboard:	345rpm	5,843shp	370rpm	8,939shp		
Fourth run						
Port:	350rpm	6,310shp	370rpm	9,471shp	30,563	20.925
Starboard:	345rpm	5,843shp	370rpm	8,939shp		

Mean revs.: 358.3rpm; 29,896shp; 21.045 knots.

**Thunderer* results were inferior because of boiler malfunction.

boilers. The boilers were arranged in two compartments, six forward and twelve aft. Each boiler was fitted with three Admiralty-type oil burners with a capacity of 300 pounds per hour. In order to reduce heat and excessive smoke interference in the control top, arrangement of the boilers was reversed from that of the *Colossus* class, the forward funnel serving only six boilers, while the after funnel served twelve.

The designed shaft horsepower of 27,000 was adequate to achieve a speed of 21 knots and, on trials, all units of the class reached this figure with ease except *Orion*; she had been fitted with experimental four-bladed propellers, which were not as successful as had been hoped. On inspection after the trials, however, it was found that the framing around the shafting in *Orion* had buckled slightly and it was a combination of this and the propellers that gave *Orion* poor figures in her primary sea trials.

Auxiliary machinery was supplied by three hydraulic engines on the lower deck level, one steam dynamo on the same level, two turbo-generators on the platform deck and four air compressors. Maximum fuel capacity was 400 tons greater than in the *Colossus* class with the same oil arrangements.

Appearance Changes

As completed, the *Orions* were fine, powerful-looking ships with an exceptionally impressive profile. It was very difficult to distinguish one from another because they differed only in minor detail, as follows.

Orion: prominent funnel caging; two white bands on each funnel.
Conqueror: plain-top galley funnels on forecastle; splinter shields to 4in guns.
Monarch: high-top galley funnels on forecastle; two white bands on fore funnel.
Thunderer: director tower below control top; three white bands on each funnel.

1914 Funnel bands deleted in September.
1914–15 Director control for main armament fitted in *Conqueror* and *Orion* (April 1915 in *Orion*). All director towers located on

platforms below control top. Splinter shields fitted to 4in guns in *Thunderer* during late 1914. Topgallant masts removed in all. Short poles fitted to after pair of derrick stumps for improved W/T reception.

1915–16 Torpedo nets removed. Navigating platform extended aft in *Monarch*, *Thunderer* and *Orion*. This extension was abreast fore funnel in *Thunderer*, and right round tripod legs in the other two (*Conqueror's* was fitted shortly before the war). Topmast further reduced.

1916–17 Various searchlight modifications during this period as well as reduction of 4in guns, but although reported to be down to fourteen guns in *Thunderer*, and thirteen in the other three, the guns were not removed in uniform, but taken out from various positions in the different ships, and from either or both groups. The guns were not always taken out in corresponding pairs of port and starboard. *Monarch* and *Orion* were fitted with equipment for towing kite balloons and special crews for these were drafted in. One 4in and one 3in AA guns added in *Conqueror* late 1917, but other three ships only one gun, well aft, at certain times. Extra 'flame cut' armour plating fitted around deck areas of magazines, as a result of Jutland experience, but efforts to trace official details proved fruitless. Special anti-flash precautions fitted, and improved flooding arrangements in evidence. Rangefinder baffles fitted to topmasts, and *Monarch* had camouflage on her bows during this period. There is little or no evidence that others of the class were so painted.

1917–18 Control tops enlarged. Range clocks fitted on or over control tops and at rear of after superstructure. Deflection scales painted on 'A' and 'X' or 'B' and 'Y' turrets. Searchlights

ORION: GM AND STABILITY

Based on inclining experiments, 9 December 1911

	Displacement (tons)	Draught	GM	Maximum stability	Stability vanishes at
'A' Condition (= load)*	–	26ft (mean)	5.4ft	33¾°	62¼°
'B' Condition (= deep)**	–	29ft 10in	5.9ft	34°	65½°

*Fully equipped plus 360 tons coal upper, 540 tons lower bunkers.
**Fully equipped plus 3,300 tons coal, reserves and all tanks full.

Opposite, left: *Orion* completed, leaving Portsmouth to begin her preliminary sea trials in September 1911.

Opposite, right: *Conqueror* c. October/November 1914. (See colour plates)

ORION CLASS: PARTICULARS, AS COMPLETED

Construction

	Dockyard	Laid Down	Launched	Completed
Orion:	Portsmouth DY	29 Nov 1909	20 Aug 1910	Jan 1912
Monarch:	Armstrong	1 April 1910	30 March 1911	Feb 1912
Conqueror:	Beardmore	5 April 1910	1 May 1911	Nov 1912
Thunderer:	Thames	13 April 1910	1 Feb 1911	May 1912.

Displacement (tons) (1912)
21,922 (legend), 20,797 (light), 25,596 (deep)
Displacement (tons) deep (1918):
Orion 29,108; *Monarch* 28,556; *Conqueror* 28,430; *Thunderer* 27,416.

Dimensions
Length: 545ft pp, 576ft wl, 581ft oa
Beam: 88ft 6in
Draught: 27ft 6in (mean normal), 31ft 3in (mean deep)
Height of CT vision slits above lower wl: 46ft 6in
Height of fore funnel: 70ft
Depth of keel from forecastle deck: 51ft 6in.

Armament*
Ten 13.5in 45cal Mk V; 80–100rpg
Sixteen 4in 50cal; 150rpg
One 12pdr (8cwt)
Five Maxim MG; 5,000rpg
Three 21in torpedo tubes; twenty torpedoes.

Armour
Main belt: 12in amidships
Forward belt: 6in–4in
Lower side: 2½in
Upper belt: 8in
Main bulkheads: 6in forward, 10in aft
Upper side bulkheads: 8in
Forward bulkhead: 4in–½in
After bulkhead: 2½in
Decks: upper 1½in, main 1½in, middle 1in slope and flat, lower 2½in–1in forward, 4in–3in aft
Barbettes: 10in–9in–7in–6in–3in
Turrets: 11in–4in–3in
Conning tower: 11in–4in–3in
Tube: 5in
Spotting tower: 6in–3in
Torpedo control tower: 3in
Uptakes: 1½in–1in
Magazine screens: 1¾in–1½in–1¼in–1in.

Machinery
Parsons marine turbines, four propellers
Boilers: eighteen Yarrow (Babcock & Wilcox *Monarch*)
Length of boiler rooms: 114ft
Length of engine rooms: 67ft 11¾in
Designed SHP: 27,000 = 21 knots
Fuel: 900 tons coal min., 3,300 tons max.; 800 tons oil
Coal consumption per 24 hours: 122 tons (at 10 knots)
Radius of action: 4,110nm at seagoing speed (17–18 knots); 4,660nm at ⅗th-power; 6,730nm at 10 knots (oil added)
Auxiliary machinery: three hydraulic engines on lower deck, one steam dynamo on lower deck, two turbo-generators on platform deck.

Ship's boats (average)
Pinnaces (steam): two 50ft
Pinnaces (sail): one 36ft
Launches (steam): one 42ft
Cutters: three 32ft
Whalers: three 27ft
Gigs: one 30ft
Skiff dinghies: one 16ft
Balsa rafts: one 13ft 6in.

Searchlights (1918)
Seven 36in: two bridge, three around after funnel, two superstructure.

Rangefinder positions
One on spotting top, one each 13.5in turret, one over after shelter deck.

Battle signal stations
One in rear of conning tower (11in walls, 3in floor).

Anchors
Two 140cwt Byers stockless (bower), one 140cwt Wasteney Smith stockless (sheet), one 42cwt stern.

Wireless
Mk 1-34 main office (1918); Type 3 short-radius set second office.

Complement
Orion: 754 (1911); 754 (1914)
Monarch: 738 (1911); 750 (1914)
Thunderer: 738 (1912); 1,107 (1917).

Cost
Orion: £1,711,617 (plus £144,300 guns)
Monarch: £1,741,836 (plus £146,900 guns)
Conqueror: £1,744,264 (plus £146,900 guns)
Thunderer: £1,745,923 (plus £146,900 guns).

*One 4in QF AA; 75rpg, one 3in QF AA; 150rpg added later; see Appearance Changes.

Conqueror during the summer of 1914. Note extension to compass platform forward, and addition of chart house on this level; also lookout position on topmast.

Right: *Orion* fitting-out at Portsmouth DY in 1911. Just how close the control top was to the fore funnel can easily be seen.

Far right: *Orion*, September/November 1914, looking forward from amidships at the second funnel and tripod. She is being painted in an experimental leopard-type camouflage which was applied to a few ships in the class during the early months of the war.

Below: *Monarch* showing her 'A' and 'B' turrets, bridge and tripod arrangements. Note SL layout around the funnel.

redistributed, all except two pairs of 24in being replaced by 36in lamps. Three 'coffee-box' towers fitted around after funnel, one 36in lamp in each. Rangefinder baffles removed.

Aircraft runways fitted over 'B' and 'Q' in *Orion*, 'B' and 'X' in *Conqueror* and *Thunderer*, and 'B' only in *Monarch*.

1919–20 Deflection scales painted out.

1921 *Thunderer* refitted from February to May 1921 as seagoing cadet training ship. Secondary armament reduced to eight 4in to provide additional accommodation.

Official lists give AA armament as two 3in, but photographic evidence shows only one gun mounted well aft on the quarterdeck. Aircraft platforms removed from turret tops. Extra cabin accommodation added on after superstructure replacing former rangefinding position.

1922–3 Range clocks removed.

Monarch Bomb/Shell Tests

In August 1922 an order was put through for the sale of *Monarch*, but at a later date she was withdrawn from the sales list and attached to the training establishment, HMS *Vernon*. It had been decided to use her for extensive experiments to gain information pertaining to the armour and structural strength of the Royal Navy's battleships, and during October 1923 she was prepared as a target. In particular the Board of Admiralty was most anxious to see if the British ships' alleged weakness of deck armour and magazine deficiencies were as grave as frequent reports reaching Whitehall during the war had claimed.

After all small fittings had been removed, *Monarch* left Portsmouth on 6 January 1925 and arrived at Plymouth next day. She left Plymouth on 20 January and met the Atlantic Fleet off the Scilly Isles during the morning. Having been positioned and prepared, she was attacked for nine hours: by cruisers' 6in gunfire in the morning, by aircraft from HMS *Argus* in the afternoon and, finally, by battleships' main armament in the early evening and into the night.

The tests were also used to compile data on the newly introduced armour-piercing shells, which had come into service just before the end of the war, but had never been used against a 'live' target. The shells were a new type of APC with an extra-hard cap and a delayed-action fuze. The Lyddite explosive in the older shells had been replaced by Shellite which was proving much more effective. Throughout the tests, ordinary shells were also used; these were of the CPC type, but with Trotyl being used as a burster for the first time.

Throughout the 'shoot' officers from HMS *Excellent*, the gunnery training school and establishment, were compiling lengthy reports for the Board of Admiralty, and the following data is extracted from the official report submitted on 14 August 1925, showing just how well *Monarch* had withstood her ordeal.

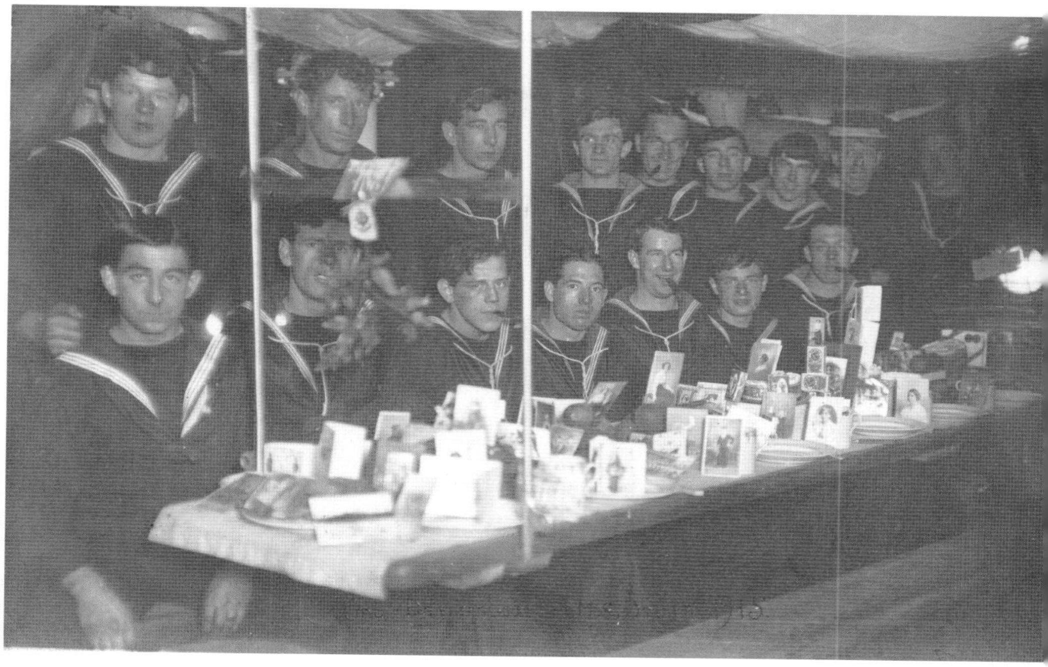

Above: Away from family and close friends, the crew of *Orion* do the best they can to enjoy Christmas on board. Note the cards and family photographs on the table.

Left: *Monarch.* 'A' and 'B' 13.5in turrets after she was used as a target. The 13.5in guns in 'A' are being forced up by the deck plating after a direct hit in the area (see notes on tests).

Above: Aboard *Thunderer* in a swell, showing the conditions 'Jack' had to endure even in such a big ship as this.

Left: Amidships around 'Q' turret.

Right: The forecastle and 'A' and 'B' turrets.

Below: *Conqueror* as completed during the summer of 1912. Note shields not yet fitted to 4in guns (during trials period).

Above: *Conqueror* patrolling with her sisters in May 1917 (either *Monarch* or *Thunderer* in background).

Opposite: *Monarch* after completion of her sea trials in April 1912.

Test I
APC. Shellite–16D (13.5inch).
Target: Between upper and main decks at station 137.
Structure: 8in armour and with 3in teak backing supported by 10in 'Z' bars.
The shell struck 2ft 3in above the main deck level, making a hole 18in by 16in. The disc punched out was 3ft 6in in diameter, and the frame at station 137 was carried away completely between the upper and main decks and 136 was cut badly by the flying disc.

A hole was made in the main deck immediately in front of the entry and extended 4ft 6in from the ship's side about 18in across. Three other small holes were made 6ft from the ship's side. Four fragments went into the ship and reached the other side. The shell path was a descending one, and touched the deck just before reaching the funnel casing, the end of the

1 Engine room
2 Boiler room
3 Magazines
4 Shell rooms
5 Uptakes
6 Vents
7 Steering compartment
8 After torpedo tube compartment
9 Forward torpedo tube compartment
10 Capstan engine room

Upper deck
1 Torpedo hatch
2 Skylight to sick bay
3 Vent supply to engine room
4 Exhaust from engine room
5 Midships study
6 Boiler room vents
7 Chief of Staff's quarters
8 Captain's day cabin
9 Admiral's sleeping cabin
10 Admiral's bathroom
11 Ship's office
12 Accountant's office
13 Engineer commander
14 Medical officers
15–18 Cabins
19 Ward- and ante-rooms
20 Gun room
21 Warrant officers' cabin
22 Wardroom galley
23 Warrant officers' cabin
24 Officers' stores and heads

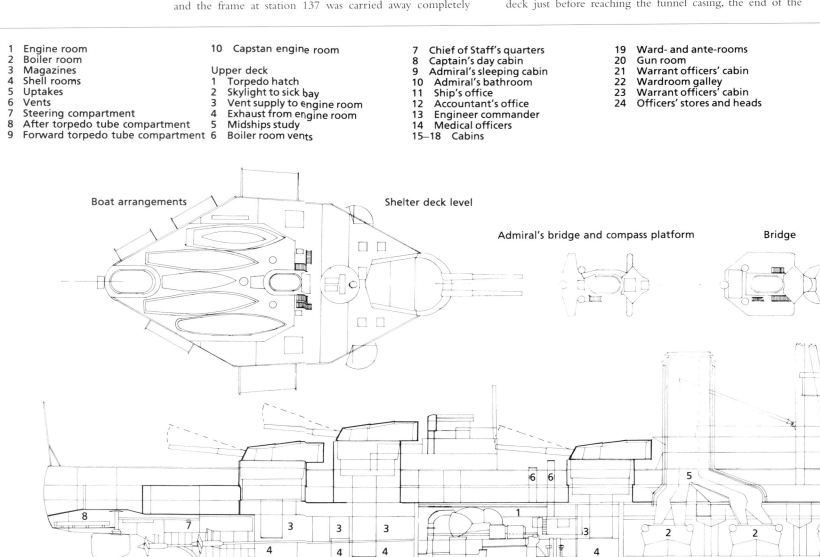

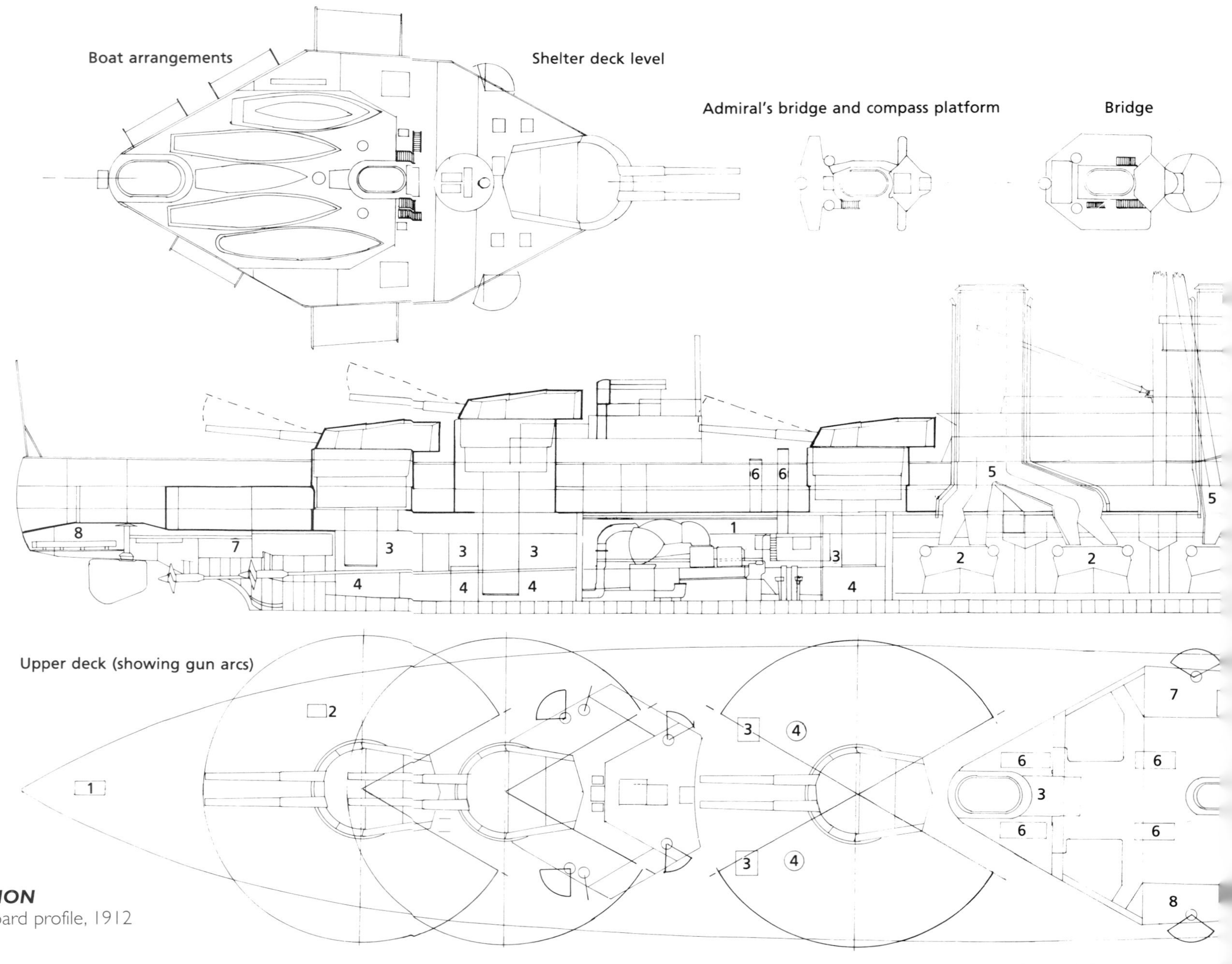

ORION
Inboard profile, 1912

beam on 134 station under the main deck was carried away. On impact, the deck was blown down for 6ft outboard of the funnel casing. Two large fragments of armour followed the path of the shell, and were brought up against the funnel casing. A 10in pillar at 138, which was some 14ft away from the ship's side, was cut completely through and carried away. The shell itself touched the top of the funnel casing bulkhead and turned slightly upwards and burst on the centreline of 133 station at

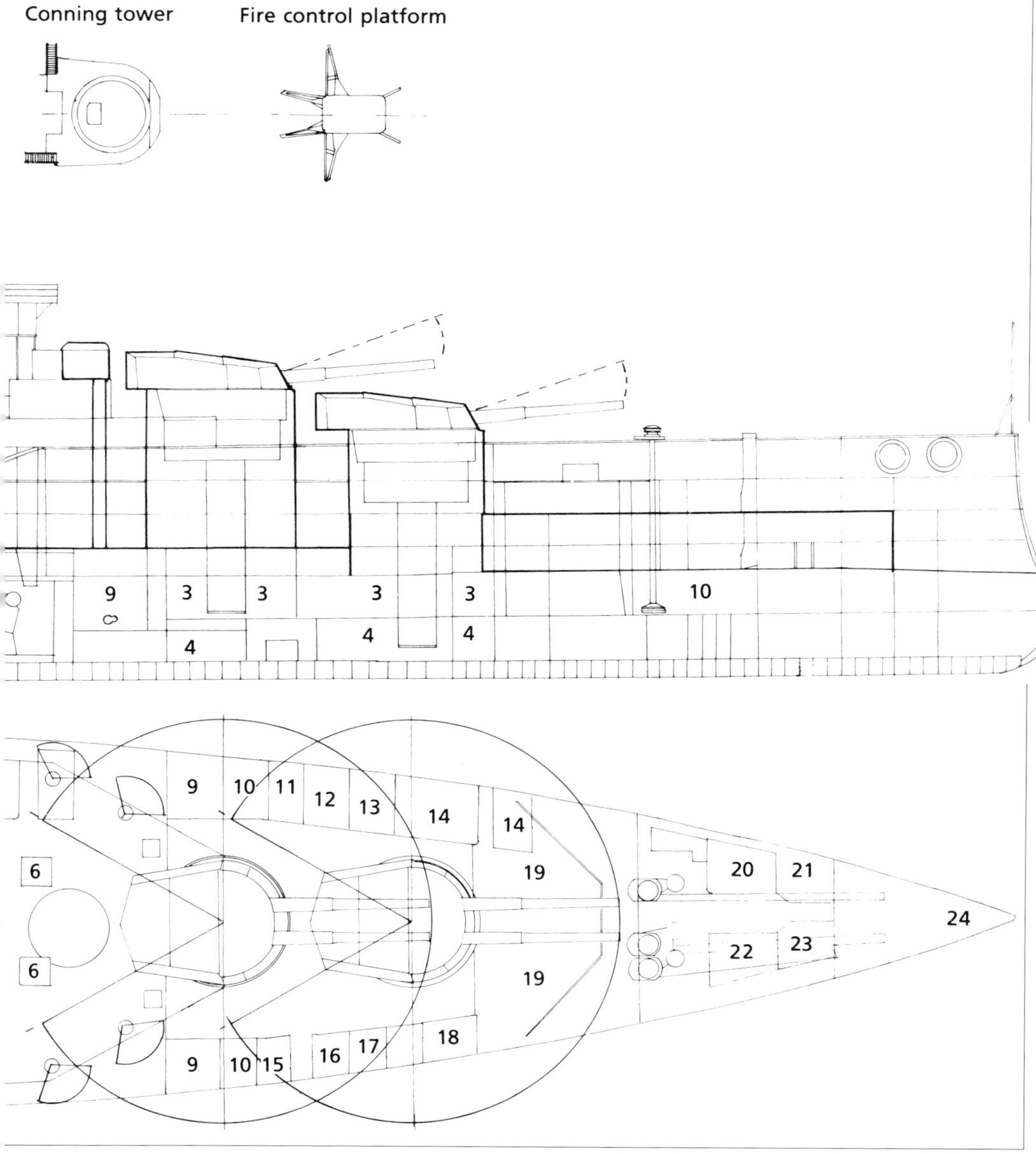

44 feet from entry and 44 feet from the opposite side of the ship, being then in the after funnel.

The funnel casing in front of the burst was wrecked and the funnel stack collapsed. On the middle deck, the bulkhead at 137, which had already been damaged by bombs from the aircraft, was torn away, and there was a split along the middle seam.

This shell had a very large vent up the funnel and therefore comparatively little blast effect, and was probably, from its fragmentation, of only mid explosion.

Test 6

APC. Shellite–16D (13.5inch).
Target: 'B' turret barbette armour (11 inches).

The shell struck the armour at about 90° at the level of the roller path, 3ft from the junction of two plates. The shell penetrated making a hole of 18in by 18in, with very little of the plate flaking off behind the strike. The shell passed between the upper and lower roller paths, carrying away the live roller ring for about 6ft and taking a roller with it. It then cut the training shaft and carried away a portion between the training pinion and the floor of the training engine socket.

The path of the shell was slightly before the athwartships line of the turret, and after passing through one fore and aft and two cross girders of the turntable and carrying away one of the gun loading hoist presses, it reached the left front side of the working chamber about 8 feet from the centreline of the turret, still at the level of the roller path. Here the shell burst, probably just before striking the armour and between the two roller paths. There were slight traces of filling left around the position of the burst.

A hole of about 5 feet across was blown in the working chamber wall and both roller paths were wrecked, the lower being carried away for 6 feet from its support; the live roller ring was also carried away for over 6 feet. A hole of 2 feet by 15 inches was blown in the turntable floor immediately over the burst.

The structure at the position of burst was very strong and accounted in some measure for the apparently small effect of the burst. The armour on the far side of the barbette was not affected. There were several heavy strikes to the ship's side between frames 76 and 82 with various degrees of damage ranging from torn plate to severe disruption of internal fittings. The decks fared no better and as a result of one burst, the main deck immediately in front of the burst was bulged down to a

Above: *Orion* in line at the surrender of the German High Seas Fleet, 21 November 1918. Note the crew gathered on the deck to catch a good look at the German ships.

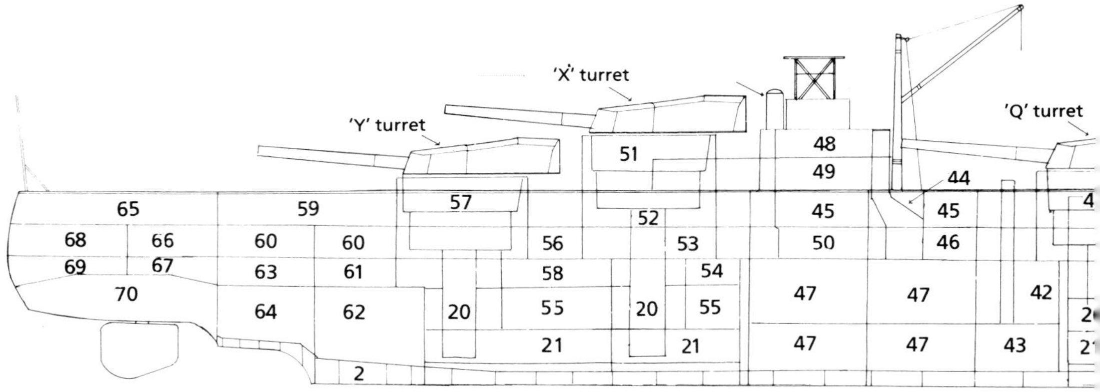

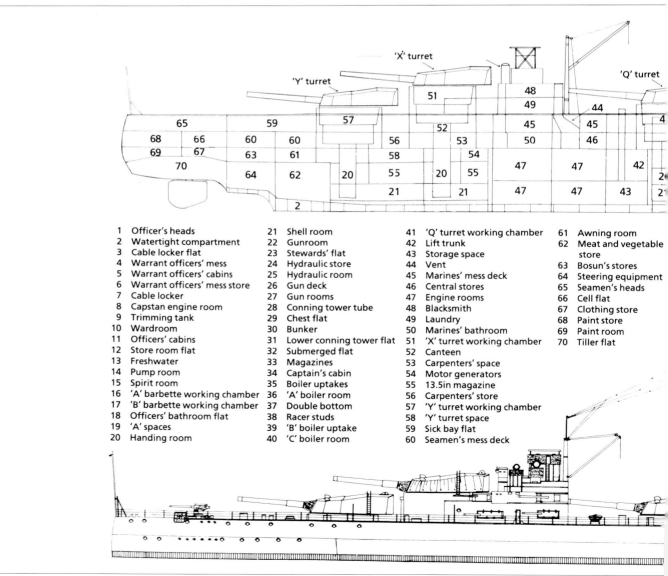

1 Officer's heads
2 Watertight compartment
3 Cable locker flat
4 Warrant officers' mess
5 Warrant officers' cabins
6 Warrant officers' mess store
7 Cable locker
8 Capstan engine room
9 Trimming tank
10 Wardroom
11 Officers' cabins
12 Store room flat
13 Freshwater
14 Pump room
15 Spirit room
16 'A' barbette working chamber
17 'B' barbette working chamber
18 Officers' bathroom flat
19 'A' spaces
20 Handing room
21 Shell room
22 Gunroom
23 Stewards' flat
24 Hydraulic store
25 Hydraulic room
26 Gun deck
27 Gun rooms
28 Conning tower tube
29 Chest flat
30 Bunker
31 Lower conning tower flat
32 Submerged flat
33 Magazines
34 Captain's cabin
35 Boiler uptakes
36 'A' boiler room
37 Double bottom
38 Racer studs
39 'B' boiler uptake
40 'C' boiler room
41 'Q' turret working chamber
42 Lift trunk
43 Storage space
44 Vent
45 Marines' mess deck
46 Central stores
47 Engine rooms
48 Blacksmith
49 Laundry
50 Marines' bathroom
51 'X' turret working chamber
52 Canteen
53 Carpenters' space
54 Motor generators
55 13.5in magazine
56 Carpenters' store
57 'Y' turret working chamber
58 'Y' turret space
59 Sick bay flat
60 Seamen's mess deck
61 Awning room
62 Meat and vegetable store
63 Bosun's stores
64 Steering equipment
65 Seamen's heads
66 Cell flat
67 Clothing store
68 Paint store
69 Paint room
70 Tiller flat

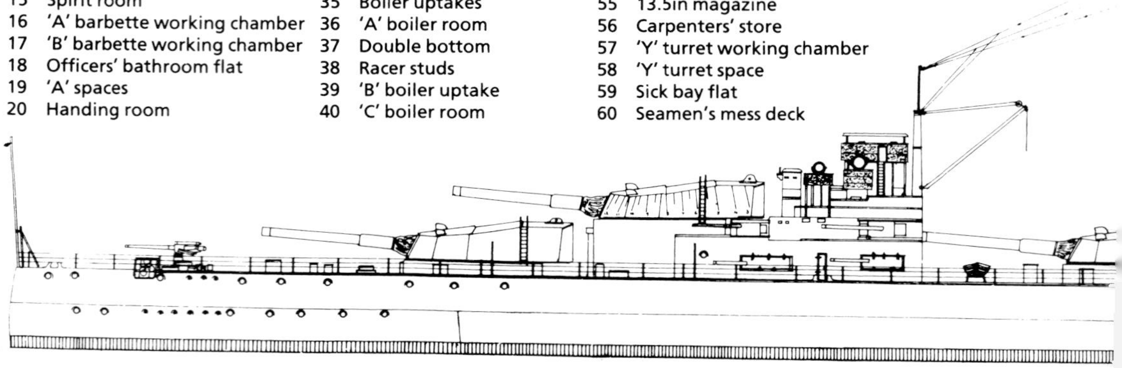

maximum of 1 foot, and holed in sixteen places. There was one hole just before station 80, two feet abaft the burst.

The damage below the main deck at frames 78 to 80 showed that the electrical store was completely wrecked and at least 70lb of the striking shell was recovered in this position.

A burst near the upper deck (1½in armour) blew a hole 5 feet square at frame 82, and also cut away the beam. About one half of the deck plating near the hole was detached, with the remainder being folded back. A hole 6 feet long by 2 feet wide was made in the forecastle deck immediately over the burst, and damage extended from frames 81 to 84, with several further holes being made in various parts of that location.

Two holes were made in the signal deck, one over two feet wide, and another smaller hole apparently by a flying fragment from a lower deck. Some further bursts from APC shells with TNT and gaine made for very effective blast damage and did much internal disruption to important parts of the ship (the engine room, machinery and boiler uptakes, etc.).

The conclusion of these tests showed that the armour thickness and distribution needed some improvement; the framing and securing of armour was demonstrated to be inadequate to give proper support for the strakes of long runs. All thicknesses of armour fired upon were penetrated by the 13.5in APC shell, and this also did extensive damage once inside the ship upon bursting. The deck protection was quite useless, and when fired on by 8in

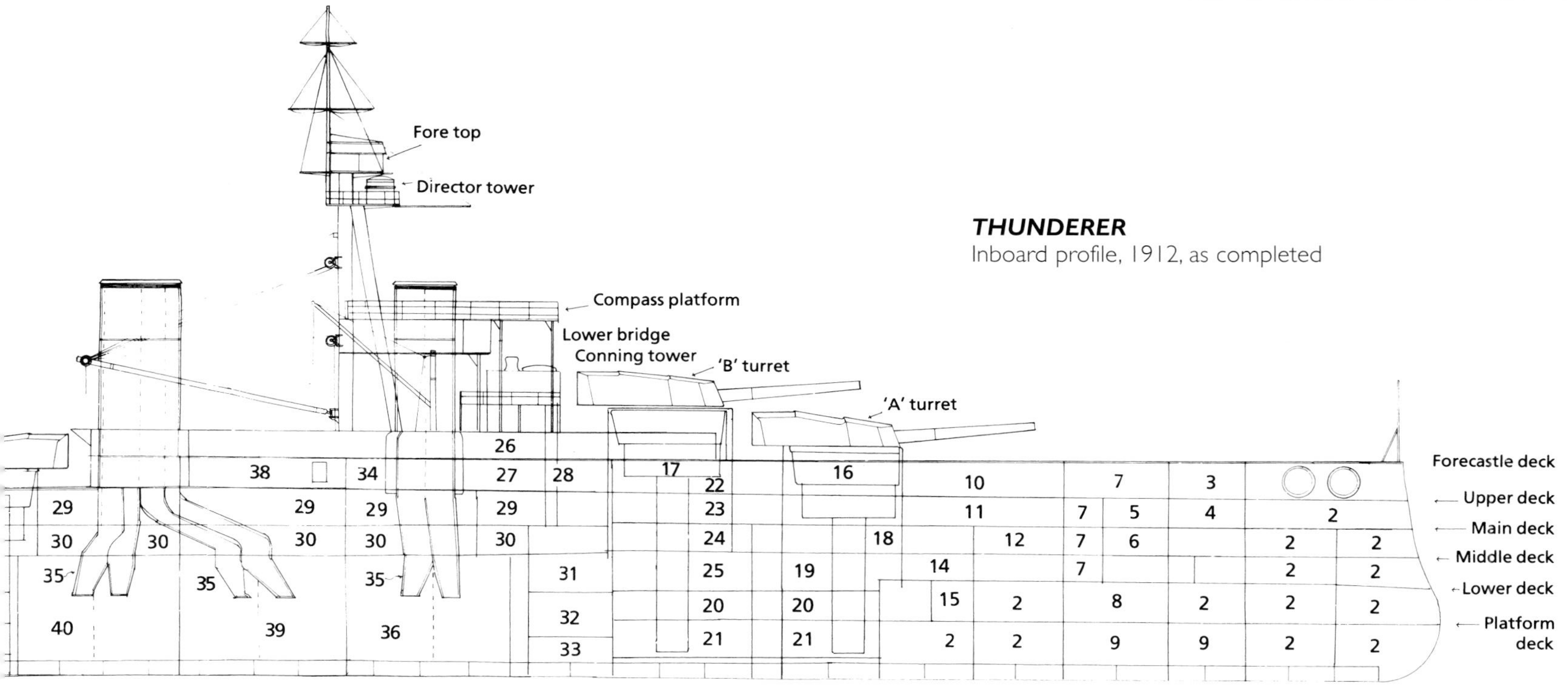

THUNDERER
Inboard profile, 1912, as completed

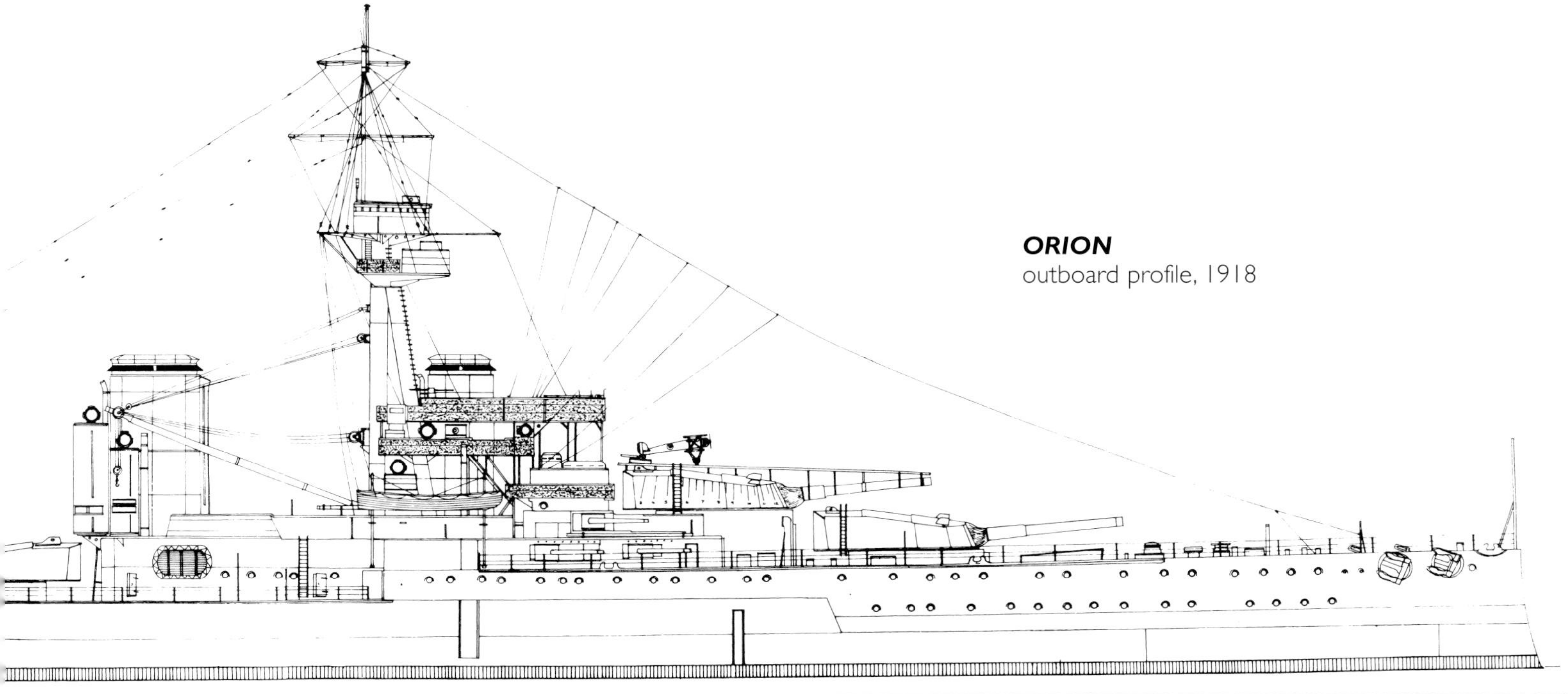

ORION
outboard profile, 1918

Opposite, top: *Monarch* passes under the low bridge on the River Tyne showing her tops lowered and some very careful manoeuvring no doubt, 6 November 1911.

Opposite, bottom: *Orion* coming into Portsmouth DY (seen here passing Southsea) while flagship, Portsmouth Reserve, 1920/21.

Below: *Orion* leads *Monarch*, *Conqueror* and *Thunderer* in the North Sea during 1918.

shells from cruisers was seen to receive damage from fragments rather than from the actual shell itself.

The thinner armour of the vessel was tested by the cruisers with 6in guns; this too was pierced, and shown to be of little use.

Tests also showed that the shells used could now penetrate armour thicknesses at oblique angles, a performance that was not available at the time of the Battle of Jutland in 1916.

The results of these extensive tests were obviously well received by the Board who forwarded them to the construction department. Later, when it came to determining the armour protection to be given to the battleships *Nelson* and *Rodney* (in 1925), the 'all or nothing' policy was applied, and no thought was given to the thin strakes used in all previous battleship designs.

History: *Orion*

1911 *Sept* Began sea trials.

1912 *2 Jan* Commissioned at Portsmouth and relieved the battleship *Hibernia* as 2nd flagship 2nd Division Home Fleet. Remained with Home Fleet until August 1914.

7 Jan Collided with the old pre-dreadnought *Revenge* when the latter broke loose from her moorings at Portsmouth and drifted across *Orion*'s bows, striking her near her 13.5in turret on the port side. Slight damage to both. 2nd flagship 2nd BS Grand Fleet until March 1919.

1916 *31 May* Battle of Jutland. In action with the battlecruiser squadron, and claimed at least four heavy hits on *Lützow*.

1919 *March–Oct* 3rd BS Home Fleet. Placed in Reserve at Portsmouth and then Portland. Flagship of the Reserve while at Portsmouth, after relieving *King George V.*

1921 *June–March 1922* Relieved of flag by *Conqueror* and commissioned as seagoing gunnery training ship at Portland.

1922 *12 April* Paid off onto the Disposal list at Devonport under Washington-London naval treaty.

19 Dec Sold to Cox & Danks, Queensborough.

1923 *Feb* Arrived at Upnor for scrapping.

History: *Monarch*

Began sea trials on 6 November 1911 and left Tyne for Devonport on 12 November.

1912 *31 March* Handed over to Royal Navy on completion.

16 April Commissioned at Portsmouth with nucleus crew.

27 April Completed with full complement and joined 2nd BS Home Fleet. Until Aug 1914, as *Thunderer*.

1914 *8 Aug* With *Orion*, *Ajax* and destroyer force in target practice SE of Fair Isle unsuccessfully attacked by *U15* at 21.30 – the first attack against a warship by a submarine.

22 Oct Based at Loch-na-Keal.

26 Oct With 2nd BS in target practice on 27th was with *Audacious* when she hit a mine and later sank.

15 Dec With 2nd BS (less *Thunderer*) left Scapa Flow to meet 1st and 2nd BCS and the Harwich Force 25 miles SE of Dogger

Right: *Conqueror* after the war, showing her final appearance *c.* 1921. Note flying-off runways on 'A' turret guns, superstructure almost hiding the forward funnel, rangefinder on 'A' turret top, and control top, and short topmast with three yards.

Below: Final appearance of *Conqueror* seen here as part of the Home Fleet (3rd BS) on the break-up of the Grand Fleet in 1919.

Bank to intercept anticipated enemy raid on east coast.
27 Dec Returning to Scapa Flow with fleet, was struck from behind by *Conqueror* (see that ship) and sustained damage to stern.
29 Dec Received temporary repairs at Scapa and left for Devonport on 4 Jan 1915.
1915 *4 Jan* Arrived Devonport.
20 Jan Rejoined Grand Fleet. Until 18 Aug 1916, as *Thunderer.*
1916 *18 Aug* Lying at Invergordon. Joined Grand Fleet at sea and remained with the fleet until war's end.
1918 *12 April* Based at Rosyth with Grand Fleet.
21 Nov Present at surrender.
1919 *March* Transferred to Home Fleet with her sisters.
24 July With *King George V*, *Conqueror*, *Orion* and *Thunderer* at Portland.
1 Oct Home Fleet reduced to status of Reserve.
1920 *Summer* Commissioned for trooping reliefs to Mediterranean, after which reduced to Reserve.
1921 *Summer* Commissioned again for same service.
1922 *5 May* Paid off to Disposal list at Portsmouth under naval treaty terms.
Aug Put up for sale, but later withdrawn and attached to the training establishment, HMS *Vernon*. Later used as gunnery target and, sunk at sea by 15in guns from British battleships (see test notes on *Monarch* as target).

History: *Thunderer*

Began trials March 1912.

1912 *15 June* Commissioned at Devonport in time to take part in the manoeuvres of that year. Soon afterwards joined 2nd BS relieving the older battleship *Zealandia*.
9 July Parliamentary Review at Spithead and then took part in the exercises with Prince Louis of Battenburg, commanding 'Blue Fleet', on board.
Dec Tactical exercises with the Fleet.
1913 *24 June* Assembled with 2nd BS, 1st LCS and 4th Flotilla to receive President of France at Spithead.
Aug Annual manoeuvres, flagship of Sir John Jellicoe commanding 'Red Fleet'.
1914 *15 July* Left Portland for Spithead.
17–20 July Grand Fleet Review and test mobilization.
25 July Fleets dispersed and returned to their respective bases. At the outbreak of war, the Grand Fleet came into being and *Thunderer* was temporarily based at Loch-na-Keal (Isle of Mull) pending completion of anti-submarine defences at Scapa Flow.
6 Oct Left Loch-na-Keal for target practice off Tory Island.
27 Oct Present when *Audacious* struck a mine and later sank.
8 Dec To Devonport for short refit, and some attention to her condensers.
1915 Fleet patrols.
1916 *May* With 2nd BS based at Invergordon.
31 May Battle of Jutland. With *Orion*, *Conqueror* and *Monarch*, formed a truly homogeneous squadron. Eighth ship in line after deployment. At 18.50 had to alter course 4 points to the south to close the range by divisions, which involved some blanketing, and at one time involved *Thunderer* firing across the bows of the Fleet flagship. At 22.30 challenged by enemy cruiser, but did not open fire on that ship being unwilling to reveal presence of Battle Fleet. General Fleet patrols during the rest of this year and 1917.
1918 *12 April* Moved from Scapa Flow to the base at Rosyth.
21 Nov Present in the Northern line at German High Seas Fleet surrender.
1919 *March* Grand Fleet broken up. *Thunderer* transferred with rest of her class to 3rd BS Home Fleet.
24 June With *Orion* and *Conqueror* at Rosyth.
1 Oct Home Fleet reduced to Reserve status.
14 Nov At Portland.
1920 *1 April* Transferred to Reserve Fleet at Portland.
Summer Temporarily commissioned for trooping service with relief crews to the Mediterranean.
12 Aug Rejoined Reserve Fleet at Portland.
1921 *Feb* Selected as cadets' seagoing training ship, to replace *Temeraire* and the cruiser *Carnarvon*. Extensively refitted at Rosyth including new bathrooms and extra laundry equipment.
5 May Commissioned at Rosyth.
24 June Left Portland on her first training cruise. In Nov 1921, although earmarked for disposal, her place on the Disposal list was taken by *Erin* which, although a newer ship, had been designed for foreign service and did not conform to the usual British layout. *Thunderer* served as a training ship until 31 Aug 1926 when she was relieved by the monitor *Erebus*, and paid off into the charge of care and maintenance parties at Portsmouth.
1926 *6 Nov* Paid off into Disposal list. Sold to Hughes, Boickow & Co. for £66,150.
17 Dec Left Portsmouth in tow for Blyth.
24 Dec Ran aground at Blyth and became stranded.
31 Dec Refloated, but Harbour Master refused permission to enter port and she was towed back to Rosyth.
1927 *12 April* Left Rosyth in tow for Blyth once more, and finally reached the scrapyard there on 14 April.

History: *Conqueror*

Began sea trials in July 1912.

1912 *23 Nov* Commissioned at Devonport with nucleus crew.
1913 *March* Completed with full complement and joined 2nd BS Home Fleet, remaining until August 1914. She was with Grand Fleet from August 1914 until March 1919.
1914 *27 Dec* Collided with *Monarch* off Hoxa entrance near Scapa Flow when both ships received substantial damage. The Grand Fleet was returning to Scapa after exercises. The weather was foul and visibility poor. *Monarch* had slowed down and altered course to avoid a patrol trawler, and *Conqueror*, which was astern, was unable to keep clear and struck *Monarch* a glancing blow aft. *Conqueror's* stem was badly damaged, and her hull buckled for approximately 150 feet. Temporary repairs were effected at Scapa and Invergordon, and the final repair work at Devonport.
1915 *March* Rejoined Fleet.
May Present at Jutland. With 3rd BS Home Fleet until October 1919.
1921 *June* Relieved *Orion* as flagship Reserve Fleet at Portsmouth.
1922 *June* Placed on Disposal list at Portsmouth.
19 Dec Sold to Upnor Shipbreaking Co.
1923 *30 Jan* Arrived at Upnor for scrapping.

Lion Class: 1909 ESTIMATES

Design

The normal 1909 Programme included three battleships (*Colossus*, *Hercules* and *Orion*) and one battlecruiser (*Lion*), but special provision was made for laying down four more capital ships (three *Orion*s and *Princess Royal*) known as 'contingency dreadnoughts' and which were approved on 28 August of that year.

This greatly increased construction programme anticipated the acceleration of new building in Germany. As a result of the uneasy political situation and intense naval rivalry with Germany, designs for British capital ships were virtually freed from the parsimony which had exerted such a cramping influence on most of the earlier battleship designs. The DNC, Philip Watts, stated that 'It is now possible for advanced fighting qualities to be embodied in the new designs.'

The general design for the new battlecruiser was designated 'CV'. It represented a cruiser version of *Orion*, although originally it had been planned early in 1909 to duplicate *Indefatigable*'s layout with some modification where necessary.

Uncertainty surrounding the German programme was clarified to a certain extent by information from a private source which reached the Admiralty before any of the British designs were approved. The projected *Moltke*-class battlecruisers would be considerably larger than had been anticipated, and any design to counter them would have to be much more powerful than the *Indefatigable* type. A free hand and the perspicacity of constructors E. L. Attwood, W. T. Davis and Philip Watts, produced the *Lion* class as a reply to the new German construction, and gave Britain the largest warships in the world. As had been the case with *Orion*, the new ships embodied increases in armament and protection over the preceding classes:

1. 13.5in guns in an all-centreline arrangement.
2. Provision of side armour above main deck.

Essentially the design differed from *Indefatigable* as follows:

1. Displacement increased by 7,600 tons with an increase of 110ft length (oa) 8ft 6in beam and 1ft 6in designed mean draught.
2. Calibre of main armament increased from 12in to 13.5in with an all-centreline arrangement of turrets.
3. Maximum thickness of armoured belt increased from 6in to 9in, with 4in to 6in between upper decks (not fitted in the *Indefatigables*). Maximum armour on barbettes was increased from 7in to 9in.
4. Designed speed raised from 25 to 27 knots.
5. Nominal radius reduced by 1,080 miles.

As completed, *Lion* was 3,710 tons heavier than the German *Moltke* and sported a more powerful armament. However, a 9in armoured belt, a 1¼in deck and 9in barbettes, did not compare favourably with *Moltke*'s 11in, 3in and 10¼in respectively. The German *Seydlitz*, laid down in 1911, was an enlarged version of *Moltke*, and much comparison was made with *Lion* by the Board of Admiralty. *Lion* was 42 feet longer, 5 feet less in beam, 6 feet greater in freeboard and 1,420 tons heavier than *Seydlitz*: the propulsive power of *Lion* was 15 per cent greater, but boiler spaces were 25 per cent, and engine room spaces 60 per cent greater. The reduction in space allotted to machinery in *Seydlitz* enabled her to be considerably reduced in length and displacement, with the weight saved being worked into the design as extra armour.

	Lion	*Seydlitz*
Power:	70,000shp	61,000shp
Length of machinery space:	112ft	69ft
Breadth:	62ft	63ft
Length of boiler room space:	170ft	152ft 6in
Breadth:	66ft	65ft

The original rig for *Lion* provided a heavy tripod foremast. Looking down from the control top on the foremast it was just 39ft 6in to the funnel mouth, and so repeated the defects of *Colossus* and the new *Orion*-class battleships. The ordnance expert, Sir Percy Scott, sent recommendations for a modified arrangement of foremast and funnel in view of the probability of heat and smoke interference to the top. This was rejected by the Board which, although agreeing in principle with his views, preferred the arrangement of funnel before mast – apparently solely because it enabled the main boat derrick to be worked from the foremast. *Lion* was therefore completed in this condition, but on her preliminary sea trials in January 1912 heat and smoke from the

Right: *Lion, Queen Mary, Princess Royal* and *New Zealand* pass HM King George V on the Royal Yacht off the Nore after the Fleet Review on 20 July 1914.

funnel rendered the control top untenable and affected delicate bridge instruments. When the ship was at full speed the tripod legs became so hot that passage through them was impossible. Remarks made by Captain A. A. M. Duffy of *Lion* summed up the situation very well:

> Arrangements for control from the top, and spotting from the signal tower would be of little or no use in war. Presumably no ship would go into action without having fires in all boilers, and these conditions would suffocate the operator in the top as well as burn him. As a result of seeing *Lion* on trials, I feel it would be worse than useless to trust the control top. With the wind aft, it would be impossible to stay there and steam at any speed, and with the wind originally in any direction a necessary turn of the helm would produce the same effect. The next place one would naturally look would be the spotting tower (rear of conning tower) but with a roll of 5 degrees, and we have never had less at sea, the bridge compass obscures the view from this: so at present that is impossible.

As a result of this, and other factual advice, the battleships *Orion* and *Monarch* were considered for alteration of the funnel/mast arrangements; but in the end no action was deemed necessary. *Lion* was refitted, funnel and mast altered to mast and funnel. The total cost of this refit for *Lion* and *Princess Royal* was £68,170 which did not include the new conning tower arrangements or fittings, etc. The refit was chiefly instigated by the First Lord (Winston Churchill), who had gained much information about the ship's condition in her original rig from Jellicoe and members of *Lion*'s staff, and it was he who made sure the funds were allocated for the alteration. Modifications carried out during refit (also to *Princess Royal* while still under construction) were:

1. Forward funnel removed from its position, and replaced farther aft near the position where the foremast tripod had been.
2. Original pole mainmast removed and repositioned as foremast (2ft 6in in diameter) in front of fore funnel.
3. Legs of original tripod dispensed with.
4. Changes in stowage positions of all boats.
5. Modifications to original foremast to make stump mainmast.
6. Centre and after funnels raised to same height as fore funnel, bringing them all up to 81 feet above the water-line.
7. Spotting top removed and conning tower enlarged.
8. Revolving rangefinder hood fitted.
9. Casemates to port and starboard 4in guns fitted.
10. Officers' lookout position in 'B' and 'X' turrets fitted.
11. Rangefinder hoods to turrets fitted.
12. Short range W/T added.
13. Bulkheads to steering gear strengthened (in *Lion* only).

PRINCESS ROYAL: LAUNCH FIGURES, 29 APRIL 1911

	tons
Displacement:	10,500
Machinery:	280
Armour:	972
Men, ballast, equipment:	420
Recorded weight of hull:	8,828

Draught: 13ft 4in forward, 14ft 1in aft
Length: 660ft 0$\frac{13}{16}$in pp
Beam: 88ft 6$\frac{7}{16}$in
Length of boiler rooms: 'A' 33ft 11¾in; 'B' 51ft 11⅜in; 'C' 51ft 11⅜in; 'D' and 'E' 52ft 0⅛in
Length of engine rooms: 62ft 0⅛in forward; 50ft 0⅛in aft
Breakage at launch:
longitudinal in a distance of 550ft = 3$\frac{3}{16}$in hog
transverse in a distance of 80ft = nil
Lion launch weight 8,535 tons (hull 7,845 tons).

Armament

Adoption of the 13.5in gun with superimposed firing arrangements, as in the contemporary *Orion*-class battleships, constituted

Below: *Lion* as completed, with funnel before mast arrangement. Note the short second and third funnels.

Left: Another early view of *Lion* as completed showing mast abaft funnel arrangement.

Right: *Lion*, broadside view, late 1912/early 1913.

LION

Outboard profile and plan, 1914, as fitted

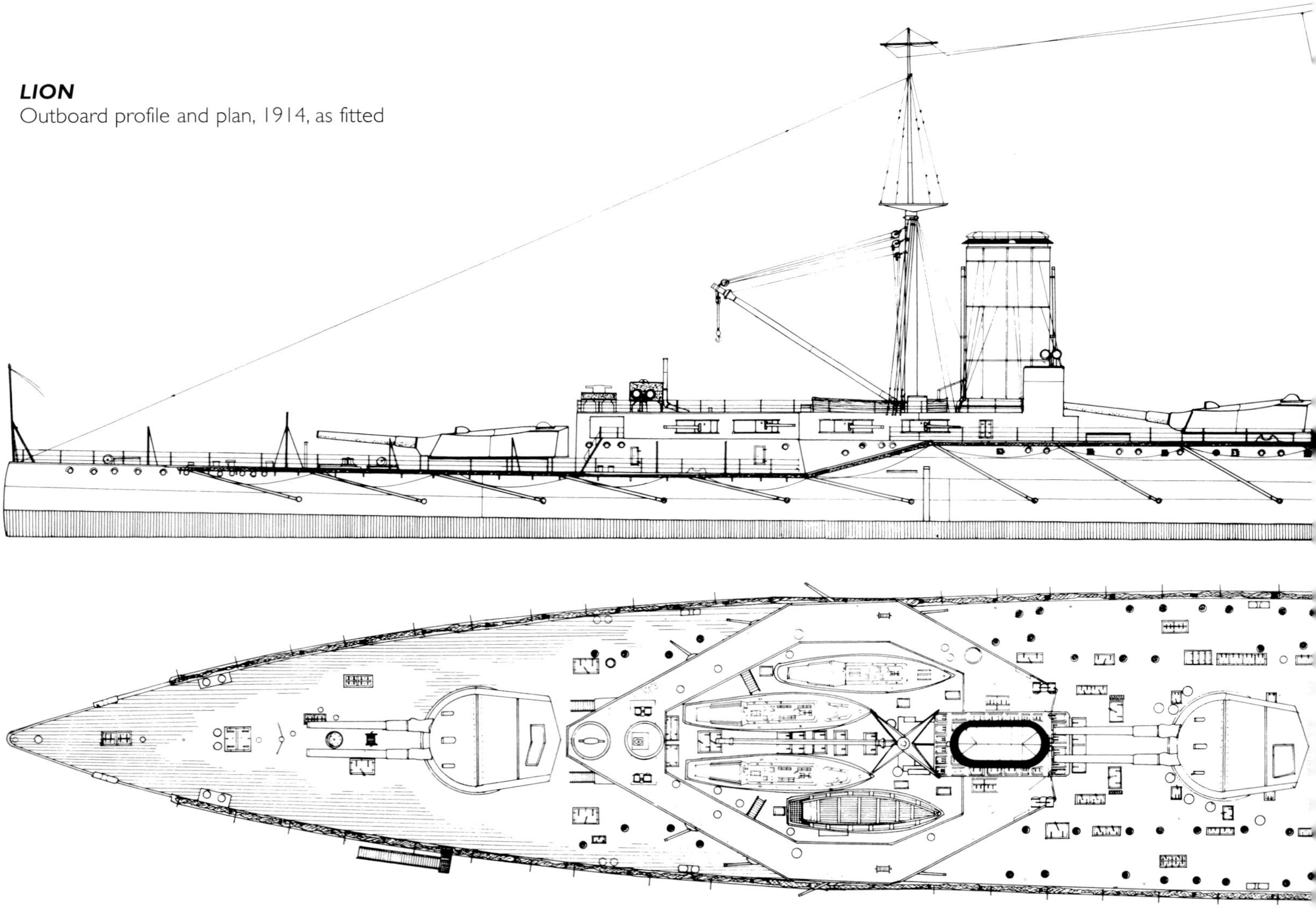

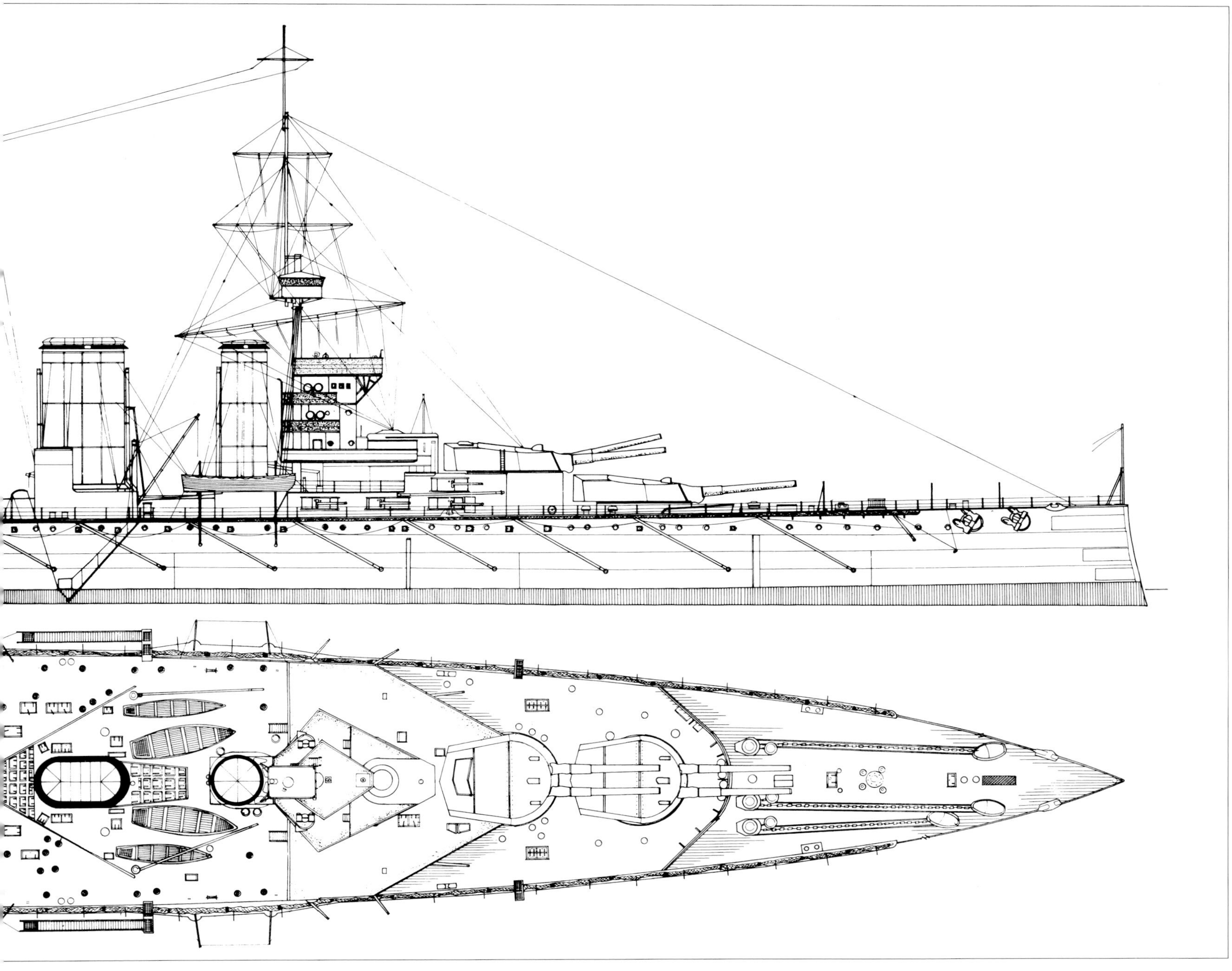

the outstanding advances in design over preceding classes of the *Invincible* and *Indefatigable* type. The weight of broadside almost doubled against the practicable broadside of those ships (10,000lb against 5,200lb) and the substantial increase in penetrative power and destructive effect was unsurpassed at this time. The increase in calibre from 12in was mainly due to ever-increasing battle ranges, and the demand for a higher degree of penetrative power. The new 13.5in gun was more accurate and had greater destructive effects at long ranges than the 45cal and 50cal 12in guns as mounted in *Invincible* and *Indefatigable*, and in all earlier dreadnoughts.

One of the major factors influencing the siting of the 13.5in guns on the centreline was that their extra weight and additional armour rendered beam turrets quite impracticable. The constructors had been able to develop the turret arrangement from that of *Indefatigable* by simply bringing both beam turrets into the centreline, and at one stage it was seriously considered giving the ships five turrets instead of four. Watts had implied that by increasing the ship's length by three frames amidships (9ft), it would be possible to place a superimposed layout in the space, much the same as in the *Colossus* class. Not all the constructors agreed that this would be practicable and a four-turret arrangement was finally approved. The two forward ('A' and 'B') turrets were superimposed, while the third ('Q') was located between the second and third funnels, which was later seen as a weakness because of its limited arcs of fire (60° before and abaft the beam). Moreover, this layout embodied the disadvantage of interspersing magazine and boiler spaces: the midships magazine was located between two groups of boiler rooms! The fourth turret was placed well aft, and had excellent arcs of fire.

The 4in Mk VII secondary armament was well arranged, and had a good high command with a well-planned concentration of fire of eight guns ahead, four astern and eight abeam on each side. The forward pair in the after group were mounted in the angles of the superstructure, which provided a considerable degree of fire ahead. Even though the layout of these guns was carefully planned, their retention in the design was sharply criticized as being totally inadequate for dealing with torpedo-boats or modern destroyers with any degree of efficiency.

Armour

Vertical armouring was materially stronger than in the preceding classes, but the original design's overall protection scheme was considered inadequate and it was decided to enhance the vertical armour from stations 18 to 138 (the forward extension of the armoured belt) and position the forward armoured bulkhead farther forward. The lower and upper deck thicknesses in this area were also improved. Approval for this modification was given by the First Sea Lord on 3 January 1910. The class now had a total vertical armour weight of 3,878 tons, but this was still a lesser percentage than was given to the German counterpart, *Seydlitz*. Protection in *Lion* and *Princess Royal* compared to the *Indefatigable* class generally as:

LION CLASS: PARTICULARS, AS COMPLETED

Construction

	Dockyard	Laid Down	Launched	Completed
Lion:	Devonport DY	29 Nov 1909	6 Aug 1910	May 1912
Princess Royal:	Vickers	2 May 1910	29 April 1911	Nov 1912.

Displacement (tons)
26,350 (designed legend), 30,084 (designed deep load),
26,400 (normal load, Sept 1917), 30,186 (deep load, Sept 1917).

Dimensions
Length: 660ft pp, 675ft wl, 700ft oa
Beam: 88ft 6¾in (*Lion*)
Draught: 28ft (normal), 31ft 4in (deep).

Armament
Eight 13.5in 45cal Mk V
Sixteen 4in 50cal Mk VII
One 12pdr (boat and field)
Four 3pdr (saluting)
Five MG
Two 21in torpedo tubes; fourteen torpedoes.

Ammunition stowage
13.5in: 80rpg peace, 110rpg war
4in: 150rpg peace, 200rpg war.

Director control
None on completion.

Armour (KC)
Main belt: 9in amidships
Forward belt: 6in–5in–4in
After belt: 5in–4in
Upper belt: 6in amidships, 5in–4in forward, 5in–4in aft
Bulkheads: 4in forward and aft
Screen bulkheads: ¾in
Decks: forecastle 1½in–1¼in amidships, upper 1in, lower 2in–1¼in–1in
Barbettes: 9in–8in–3in
Turrets: 9in face, 9in side, 8in rear, 3¼in–2½in roof
Conning tower: 10in side, 3in roof
Conning tower tube: 4in
Uptakes: 1½in–1in–¾in–½in
Magazine screens: 2½in–1½in–1in.

Machinery
Parsons direct-drive turbines, four propellers
Boilers: forty-two large-tube Yarrow, working pressure 230psi, arranged in 5 compartments (3 before, 2 abaft 'Q' turret magazine), fitted with three single-orifice oil burners, 300lb per burner per hour
Length of boiler rooms: 189ft 11¼in
Length of engine rooms: 112ft 0⅜in
Fuel: 1,000 tons coal normal, 3,520 tons max.; 1,135 tons oil
Coal consumption per day (tons): 336 at 14 knots (economical speed); 1,410 at full speed
Radius of action: 2,420nm at 24.6 knots continuous seagoing speed; 3,345nm at 20.5 knots; 5,610nm at 10 knots.

Ship's boats
Pinnaces (steam): one 50ft
Pinnaces (sail): one 36ft
Launches (steam): one 42ft
Cutters: four 34ft, one 30ft
Gigs: one 30ft
Whalers: three 27ft
Dinghies: one 16ft.

Searchlights
Sixteen twin 24in.

Rangefinder positions
One spotting top, one each 13.5in turret, one after superstructure.

Anchors
Three 150cwt Admiralty stockless, one 42cwt stockless, four 5cwt kedge.

Wireless
Mk I, Mk II, Type 9 W/T short-radius.

Complement
Lion: 907 (as designed); 984 (final legend, 1910); 1,000 (1912); 1,092 (1915)
Princess Royal: 985 (1912).

Cost
Lion: £1,965,699 (plus £118,300 guns)
Princess Royal: £1,955,922 (plus £120,300 guns).

1. The main armoured strake was 3in thicker over the midships magazines, boiler and engine rooms, of the same thickness for the forward magazine, and 1in thinner over the after magazine.
2. Armour (6in and 5in) was fitted between main and upper deck areas, protecting magazine, boiler and machinery spaces; there was none in *Indefatigable*.
3. Total deck armour was 2in less over magazines and ½in less over machinery spaces.
4. Maximum thickness of barbette armour increased by 2in.
5. Longitudinal screens were 2½in–2in–1½in as against 2in uniform thickness in *Indefatigable*.

The paucity of protection for these ships showed only too well when *Lion* went into action at Dogger Bank on 24 January 1915; she was hit twice below the water-line and seven times above. The first two hits caused considerable damage, driving the armoured belt well into the ship's side and wrecking the supports in the area. As a result, the submerged flat, body room, capstan flat, chain locker, engineers' workshops, 'A', 'D' and 'E' bunkers on the port side, and the exhaust bend to the port engine were completely flooded. The latter item was almost shot through, which put the port engine out of action. The ship took a list of 10°, but was later righted to 5° although water was still creeping in through the torpedo hatch, which had also been shot away.

The main 9in armoured belt extended from abreast the conning tower to just inside 'Y' barbette, its upper edge at main deck level, about 8ft 6in above the water-line. The lower edge was 3ft below the water-line at normal load. The 6in–5in–4in strakes forward extended to within 50 feet of the stem over the same area as the midships section, the 6in to just inside 'A' barbette and the 5in to just beyond this barbette, where it reduced to 4in.

A 5in–4in belt aft extended to within 73 feet of the stern, again at the same height as the midships section. The 6in strake on the side amidships ran over the same length as that for the 9in armour and was located between the main and upper deck levels.

The 4in bulkheads forward and aft closed the extremities of the

LION CLASS: FINAL LEGEND, 1 OCTOBER 1909

Dimensions
Draught (normal): 27ft forward, 29ft aft, 28ft mean
Sinkage: 98.2 tons.

Estimated GM
5.83ft (see GM and stability table).

Weights (tons)	Load	Deep load
Hull:	9,710	9,710
Machinery:	5,190	5,428
Armour:	5,140	5,140
Armament:	3,260	3,260
Coal:	1,000	3,700
General equipment:	800	800
Engineers' stores:	150	150
Board margin:	100	100
Oil:		1,130
Water (overflow):		140
Reserve feedwater:		590
Totals:	25,350	30,148

Below: *Princess Royal* fitting out at Vickers. Japanese *Kongo* (battlecruiser) alongside.

Above: *Lion* early 1913, after conversion of original foremast and fore funnel arrangements.

Opposite:: *Princess Royal* on a visit to Halifax and showing early confusion painting (see colour plates) based on Kerr's principles. Note that the anti-torpedo net defence is out in position. There is evidence that the forward funnel was white then repainted grey the same as the other two.

4in belt and side armour between the lower and upper decks. ¾in screen bulkheads ran longitudinally between forecastle and upper decks amidships, and were set well inboard from abreast the second funnel to abaft the third.

The upper deck was given a thickness of ¾in–1in, and this ran over the complete length of the armoured belt. The lower decks, which sloped from end to end, had their crowns at water-line level and the lower edge at the bottom of the belt armour strake, approximately 3ft below the waterline. There was 1in on the slope and flat from the forward bulkhead to the outer face of 'Y' barbette, 1¼in from the outer faces of 'Y' barbette to the after bulkhead, and 2½in at the extremities outside the after and forward bulkheads.

'A', 'B' and 'Q' barbettes were given 9in on the sides above the armoured deck, and 3in below. The rears were 8in, reducing to 3in below the armoured deck. 'Y' barbette had 9in on the sides above the armoured deck and 4in below. Rears were the same as in the others. Turrets had 9in faces and sides, 3½in–4¼in roofs and 2in floor.

The conning tower was 10in on the sides, with a 3in roof, 4in floor and 4in communications tube. The sighting hood over the conning tower was 3in, and the torpedo control tower, inside the extremity of the after superstructure, was 1in uniform thickness.

The forward funnel's uptakes were 1in–1½in, the second's ½in–1in–1½in and the third's ½in–1¾in.

Funnel screens, 2in thick, were provided around the bases of the second and third funnels at forecastle deck level.

The port and starboard magazine screens, which ran longitudinally, were 1½in–2½in for the forward magazine, while those for the port side screen abreast the midships magazine were 1½in thick and placed well inboard of the ship's side. The starboard screen was 2½in thick but placed close to the ship's side.

Machinery

The machinery consisted of Parsons direct-drive turbines with four propellers. The high pressure turbines were located on the wing shafts, and the low pressure on the inner shafts, one ahead HP and one astern HP on each wing shaft, and one LP ahead and one LP astern on each inner shaft. A cruising stage was fitted at the forward end of each HP ahead turbine. All four shafts were capable of ahead or astern power. The boiler installation consisted of 42 large tube Yarrow with an average working pressure of 235psi. On completion, the ships were the fastest cruiser type in existence, their nominal speed being some two knots faster than in the *Invincible* and *Indefatigable* classes.

As can be seen from the ships' steam trial data, they both came up to expectations as far as the DNC's department was concerned, but strangely enough the Board of Admiralty made it known that all was not well so far as they were concerned; they

Below: *Lion* 1913.

had expected the ships to do much better, with 'at least 29 knots' being made.

On 8 July 1913 further trials were held to see if *Princess Royal* could exceed 29 knots if her boilers and machinery were pushed to maximum. On her first runs she attained a speed of 27.965 knots with 76,700shp, and a maximum of 28.5 knots as her best, with 78,803shp. The arguments as to whether she might have been able to make higher figures if the weather had been better, or if she ran on a course other than Polperro, where depth was only 24 fathoms, could not detract from the fact that she was capable of very high speeds.

As usual there were frequent reports in the Press and all kinds of speculation as to the new ship's speeds. None were more incorrect than a paragraph in *The Army and Navy Gazette* which read:

> Speeds for the *Princess Royal* have reached 34.7 knots which ensures that the next German battlecruisers will have to reach a speed of 35 knots to counter that of the British ship.

Appearance Changes

As modified, the ships were typically British in appearance, and were a considerable improvement over the original design in which the fore funnel was in front of the tripod mast. Nicknamed the 'splendid cats', they were exceptionally handsome and were generally regarded as the finest-looking warships to date. There were no major changes during the pre-war years except for the following.

1912–13 Splinter shields fitted to lower forward 4in guns in *Lion*.

1913–14 Splinter shields fitted to remaining upper 4in guns. Long forward signal struts added on fore starfish in *Princess Royal*.

1914 Individual differences in *Lion* and *Princess Royal* were quite difficult to spot, but the main feature was that the starfish of *Lion*'s mainmast was higher than her sister's, and her siren brackets were low on the second funnel, and high in *Princess Royal*. 13pdr AA added on platform on after superstructure and on former SL platform in *Princess Royal*. After superstructure SL in *Princess Royal* were remounted on each side of the superstructure as in *Lion*. Forward struts from the fore starfish were removed in *Princess Royal*.

1915 Director control for main armament fitted early, after the Dogger Bank action in January; added in *Lion* during repairs and refit from January to March. Camouflage painted in both during these months.

1915–16 Torpedo nets removed. Signal yard removed in *Lion*. Signal yard removed from foretopmast in *Princess Royal*, and wide yard added low down at the base of director platform. W/T yard used for signalling (flag) in both ships. Camouflage painted out.

1916–17 AA guns increased to one 4in and one 3in which were mounted port and starboard abreast second funnel on forecastle deck level. 13pdr AA removed. Single 24in SL temporarily fitted port and starboard on after superstructure in *Lion*.

Rangefinder baffles fitted to both topmasts in *Princess Royal* and to foretopmast and first and second funnels in *Lion*.

Funnel baffles in *Lion* painted black-and-white chequered. Identification letters 'PR' painted on side and on quarterdeck of *Princess Royal* for identification by aircraft.

1917–18 Control tops enlarged. Range clocks fitted over or on face of control top and on after superstructure. These were later relocated at rear of SL tower abaft third funnel in *Princess Royal* only. Deflection scales painted on 'B' and 'Y' turrets. Starboard forward group of 4in guns removed in *Lion*, and starboard after gun in *Princess Royal* after April 1917. Searchlights redistributed. SL control tower with two 36in lamps fitted on each side and well away from third funnel. SL on towers carried at different levels (upper light before lower). Third SL tower with two 36in

LION: STEAM TRIALS

Contractors' trials, 11 January 1912. Measured mile, Polperro, 24 fathoms

	Time mins.	secs.	Outer		Inner		Total SHP	Speed (knots)
Closed exhaust, closed bypass								
First run								
Port:	2	38	269rpm	15,750shp	261 rpm	17,620shp	65,470	26.195
Starboard:			266rpm	14,450shp	260rpm	17,650shp		
Second run								
Port:	2	34.4	271rpm	15,870shp	263rpm	17,810shp	66,420	26.806
Starboard:			268rpm	14,510shp	264rpm	18,250shp		
Third run								
Port:	2	40.2	268rpm	15,680shp	264rpm	17,850shp	66,200	25.837
Starboard:			266rpm	14,260shp	262rpm	18,410shp		
Fourth run								
Port:	2	35	272rpm	15,910shp	265rpm	17,910shp	66,220	26.702
Starboard:			264rpm	14,180shp	264rpm	18,220shp	(true mean 26.345)	
Closed exhaust, open bypass								
First run								
Port:	2	32	284rpm	17,700shp	279rpm	21,100shp	76,520	27.230
Starboard:			280rpm	16,620shp	282rpm	21,100shp		
Second run								
Port:	2	28	280rpm	17,780shp	279rpm	21,250shp	75,890	27.966
Starboard:			278rpm	15,960shp	276rpm	20,900shp	(true mean 27.623)	
Closed exhaust, at 16,000shp								
First run								
Port:	4	16	170rpm	4,025shp	165rpm	4,260shp	15,935	17.131
Starboard:			167rpm	3,840shp	164rpm	3,810shp		
Second run								
Port:	3	58	170rpm	4,130shp	165rpm	4,330shp	15,860	17.390
Starboard:			162rpm	3,720shp	158rpm	3,680shp	(true mean 17.177)	

LION : GM AND STABILITY

Based on inclining experiments, 1 June 1912

	Displacement (tons)	Draught	GM	Maximum stability	Stability vanishes at
'A' Condition (= load)*	-	27ft 9in	5ft	43°	76°
'B' Condition (= deep)**	-	30ft 9in	5ft	42°	78°

*Fully equipped plus 200 tons coal upper, 800 tons lower bunkers.

**Fully equipped plus 3,520 tons coal.

lamps fitted close before mainmast. Single 36in lamps (port and starboard) added on after superstructure in *Princess Royal*.

Flying-off platforms added over 'Q' and 'Y' turrets during the early part of 1918. 'Y' platform was fitted before 'Q' and was an early experimental type raised well clear of turret – almost like a ski-jump. Large screen to protect aircraft evident. Wide yard fitted at rear of tripod legs below funnel height in *Lion* only (removed sometime in 1918). Rangefinder baffles removed.

1918–19 High-angle rangefinder fitted over control top in both ships. Torpedo control tower added at extremities of after superstructure in *Lion* only. Distinct funnel cap fitted to fore funnel in *Lion*.

History: *Lion*

Began sea trials in January 1912. Modified at Devonport from January to May 1912, because of constant interference of funnel smoke and heat in control top.

1912 *4 June* Commissioned at Devonport as flagship 1st CS.

1913 *1 Jan* CS became the BCS, with *Lion* as flagship 1st BCS.

1 March Rear-Admiral Beatty hoisted his flag in *Lion*.

1914 *Feb* Squadron visited Brest.

June Squadron visited Riga, Reval and Kronstadt.

3 Aug Beatty became acting Vice-Admiral, remaining in command of 1st BCS. *Lion* with Grand Fleet from Aug 1914 until April 1919.

28 Aug Heligoland Bight action. Sank German cruiser *Ariadne* and assisted in sinking of *Köln*.

16 Dec Squadron took part in operations against the enemy battle-cruisers which were raiding Hartlepool and Scarborough, but did not make contact.

20 Dec The BCF was moved to Scapa Flow from Cromarty.

1915 *24 Jan* Dogger Bank action. Engaged *Blücher*, *Seydlitz* and *Derfflinger*, hitting *Blücher* and *Seydlitz* heavily. One hit on *Seydlitz* from 17,500 yards penetrated the after barbette and put

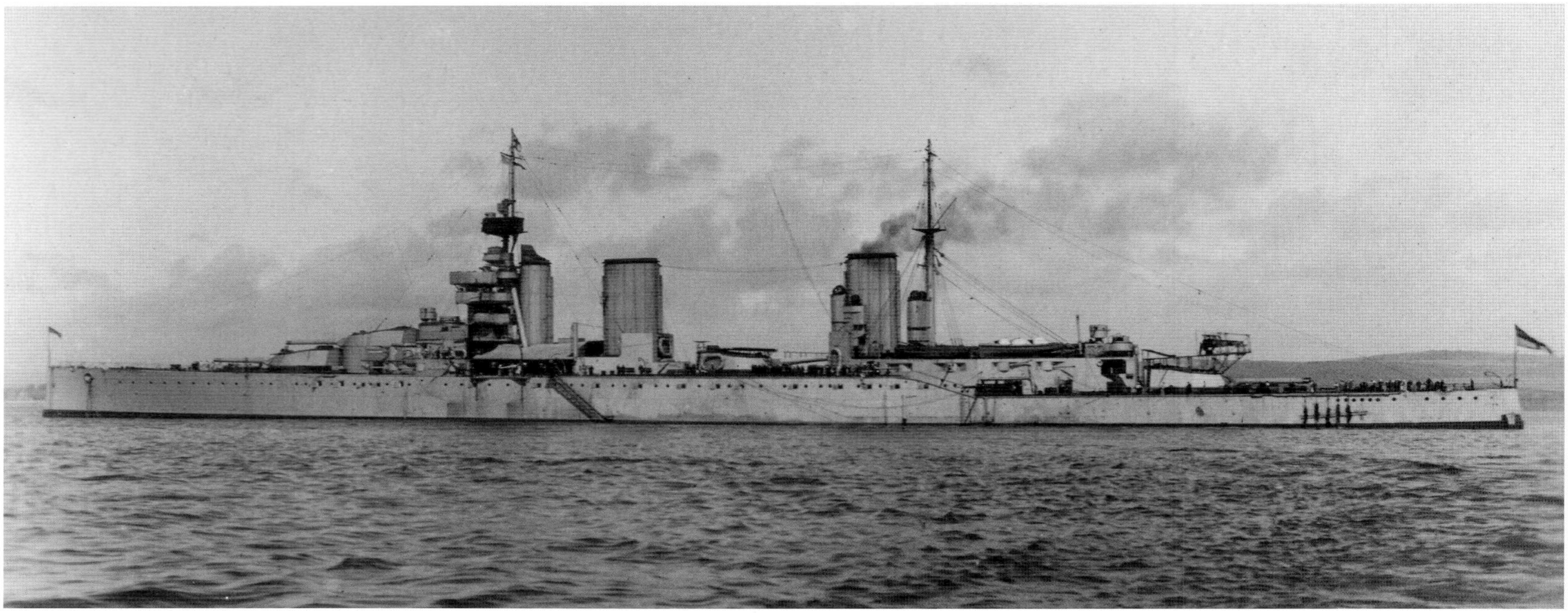

Below: *Lion* shortly after the cessation of hostilities. She was the only ship of the class to be fitted with a funnel cap, and in fact the only British battlecruiser to have one.

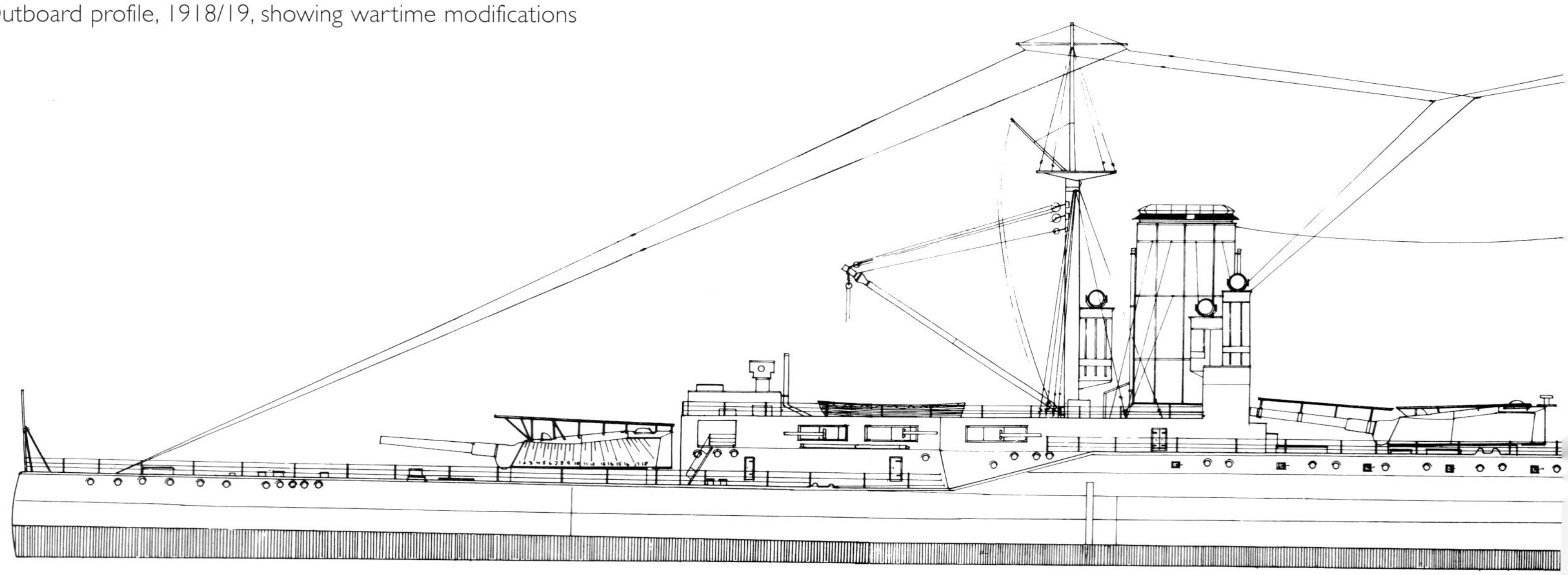

LION
Outboard profile, 1918/19, showing wartime modifications

both turrets out of action. *Lion* subjected to concentrated fire from *Moltke*, *Seydlitz* and *Derfflinger*, and hit about twelve times. First hit on water-line penetrated bunkers, second damaged roof of 'A' turret, putting one gun temporarily out of action, subsequent hits mainly on or below water-line. Flooding in engineers' workshop, after fire control station disabled, anti-torpedo armaments circuits damaged. A fire started in the forward magazines and flooding took place in many forward compartments causing a list to port. A heavy hit on the armour at the water-line abreast one of the boiler rooms damaged the feed tank in the port engine room and stopped the port engine. Light and power failed, the list increased to 10°, and speed was reduced to 15 knots, forcing her to leave the line. Later, her speed was reduced to 8 knots, and she was taken in tow by *Indomitable*.

26 Jan Reached Rosyth, temporarily repaired and taken to the Tyne where she was properly repaired by Armstrong.

7 April Rejoined BCF at Rosyth.

1916 *31 May* Battle of Jutland. With *Princess Royal* engaged in the opening stages of the action. *Lion* received twelve hits, but apart from the loss of 'Q' turret, overall damage was not serious and she reported ready for action on the following day. 99 killed and 44 wounded during the action.

The damage to 'Q' turret was caused by a 12in shell from *Lützow*, which penetrated the roof of the turret and burst inside, killing almost the entire crew: ammunition in hoists caught fire, and the rush of flame rose as high as 200 feet. But for swift action by the turret officer in flooding the magazine, the ship would have probably blown up.

2 June Taken in hand at Rosyth for repairs.

19 July Rejoined BCS, but without 'Q' turret.

1917 *17 Nov* Took part in the Heligoland Bight operations. *Repulse* only unit to make contact with enemy.

1919 *April* Atlantic Fleet.

Below, left: *Lion*, June 1916. Part of the damage received at Jutland. Taken from inside the reserve bunker looking aft, at bulkhead 94. The passage bulkhead has been removed, and damaged plating and framing behind the armour is showing.

Below: *Lion* showing her 'A' and 'B' turrets and forward superstructure. She is listing to starboard because of the damage received at Dogger Bank, January 1915.

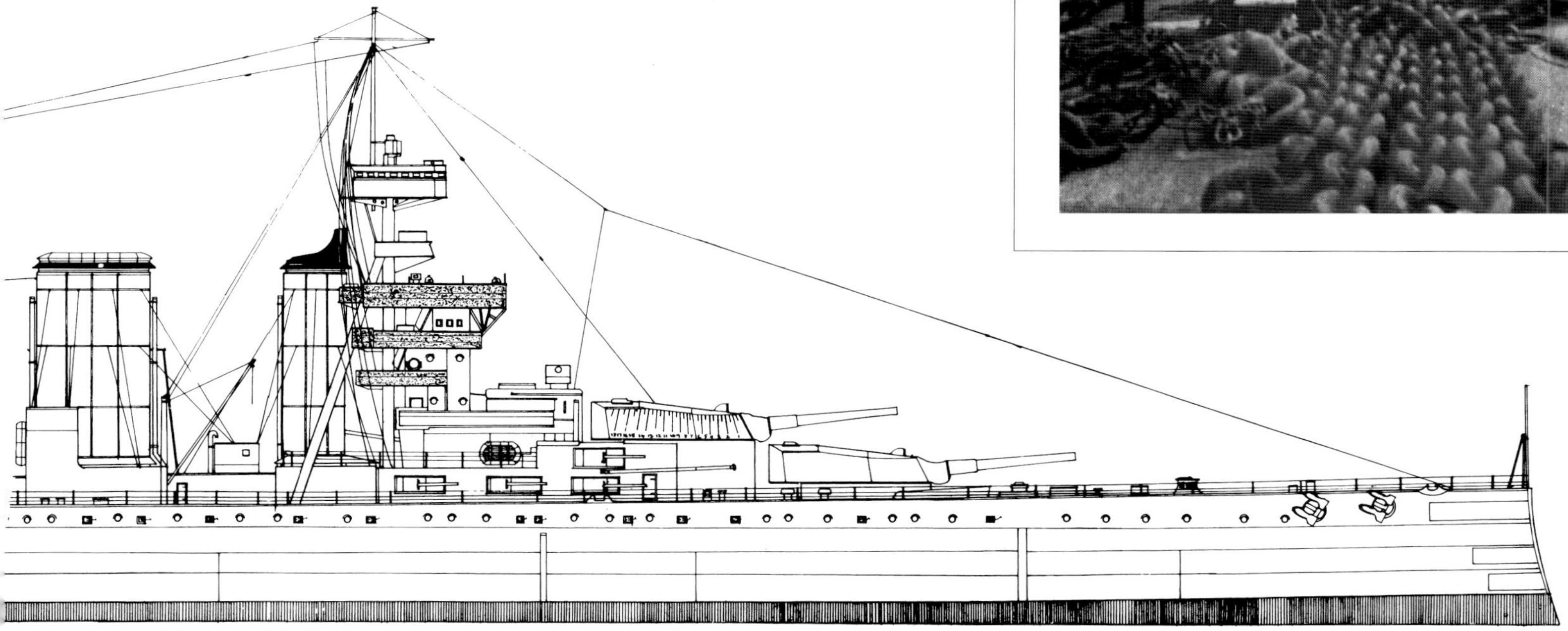

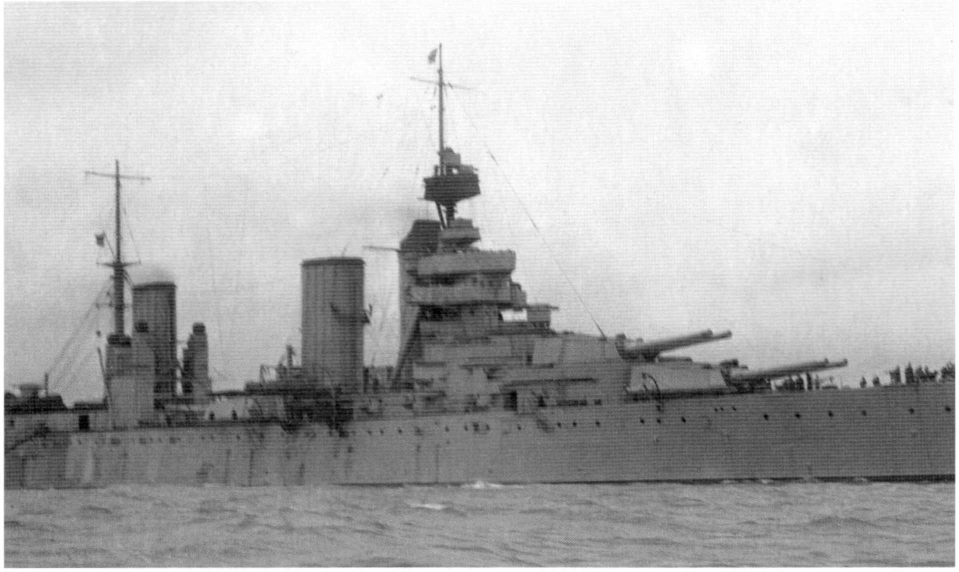

Above, left: *Lion*, 1 June 1916, on her way home after the Battle of Jutland.

Above: Damage to *Lion* received at Jutland. Sections 194 to 214 on the port side looking aft. Damage to port feed tank and wing abreast the port engine room. A portion of the damaged plate has been cut away by acetylene equipment.

Left: *Lion*, starboard midships, 1919.

Below: *Lion* anchored in Weymouth Bay in 1919. Note the additions: SL towers, aircraft runways, funnel cap, increased bridgework, etc.

Above: *Princess Royal* and *Furious* at Scapa Flow in 1918.

1920 *March* In reserve at Rosyth.
1922 *30 May* Paid off onto Disposal list at Rosyth.
1924 *31 Jan* Sold for £77,000 and cut in two before scrapping.

History: *Princess Royal*

Began sea trials in September 1912.

1912 *14 Nov* Commissioned at Devonport. With Grand Fleet from August 1914 to April 1919.
1914 *28 Aug* Heligoland Bight action.
Sept Detached from BCF to meet and escort a Canadian contingent to Britain.
28 Sept Left Cromarty and met convoy in North Atlantic on 10 October.
26 Oct Rejoined 1st BCS.
Again detached to reinforce North Atlantic and West Indies Squadrons against possibility of Von Spee's squadron showing up in that area.
21 Nov Arrived at Halifax.
29 Nov Stationed in New York area.
Transferred to West Indies and based on Jamaica as SNO Caribbean. Operated mainly in the Panama Canal area.
19 Dec Left Kingston for home having been recalled following destruction of Von Spee's ships at Battle of the Falkland Islands on 8 Dec.
1915 *24 Jan* Dogger Bank action. Engaged *Blücher* and *Derfflinger*. No damage or casualties.
31 May Battle of Jutland. With *Lion*, engaged *Lützow* and came under fire from *Derfflinger*. Hit six times by 11in and 12in shells; 22 killed, 78 wounded. Damage to ship included: training gear of 'A' turret put out of action for short while; holed on port side near upper deck causing casualties among 4in gun crews; 'Y' turret disabled; port reserve bunkers penetrated, fires raged in that area and lighting and fire mains failed.
June–July Refitted at Portsmouth.
15 July Rejoined Fleet.
17 Nov Heligoland Bight operations.
1919 *April–Oct* With Atlantic Fleet.
1920 *Summer* With Reserve Fleet at Rosyth. Offered to sale in Chile during summer of 1920, but proposal rejected.
1922 *28 Feb* Became flag CinC Scottish Coast.
March Placed on Disposal list at Rosyth under terms of naval treaties. Sold to Rosyth Shipbreaking Co. specially formed for the purpose of breaking up *Agincourt*, *Princess Royal* and *New Zealand*.
1923 *13 Aug* Arrived at breaker's yard.

Below: *Princess Royal* in Rosyth dockyard, 1917/18. Note the wartime additions including SL towers, range scales, built-up bridge and large 'PR' painted on 'A' turret for identification.

Queen Mary: 1910 ESTIMATES

Design

The 1910 Programme provided for four battleships and one battlecruiser, the latter being named *Queen Mary* on 14 March 1911. Laid down ten months after *Lion* and *Princess Royal*, she was in most respects an improved version of those ships, differing as follows:

1. Beam and displacement increase of 6 inches and 650 tons respectively.
2. Arrangement of 4in guns slightly modified, with light protection for these.
3. Horizontal armouring slightly increased, with variations in distribution.

Right and below: *Queen Mary* as completed, and leaving for preliminary sea trials in June 1913.

4. Accommodation of officers forward and men aft reversed.

Lion and *Princess Royal* retained the unsatisfactory plan of officers forward and ratings aft, as did all battleships and battlecruisers from *Dreadnought* (1906) onwards. This particular alteration had been instigated by Admiral Fisher in *Dreadnought* and *Invincible* with a view to quartering the officers nearer their normal action stations on bridge and conning towers, given the great length of the ships. This accommodation proved very unpopular with officers and ratings alike, and brought all sorts of unfavourable comments, one

QUEEN MARY: PARTICULARS, AS COMPLETED

Construction
Palmer; laid down 6 March 1911; launched 20 March 1912; completed for trials May 1913; handed over Aug 1913.

Displacement (tons)
26,780 tons (normal), 31,486 (deep).

Dimensions
Length: 660ft pp, 698ft wl, 703ft 6in over sternwalk
Beam: 89ft
Draught (mean): 28ft (normal), 31ft 11in (deep).

Armament
Eight 13.5in 45cal Mk V
Sixteen 4in 50cal Mk VII
One 12pdr (boat and field)
Four 3pdr (saluting)
Five MG
Two 21in torpedo tubes; fourteen torpedoes.

Armour*
Main belt: 9in
Torpedo control tower: 6in side, 4in floor, 3in roof
Main CT floor: 3in
Rear bulkhead: 3in
Secondary battery: 3in side, 1in roof
Decks: main 1in, upper between 'A' and 'B' turrets thickness to 2in, forecastle 1½in–1¼in
Uptakes: ¾in–½in.

Machinery
Forty-two Yarrow large-tube boilers (as *Lion*)
Designed SHP: 75,000 = 27.5 knots.

Boats
Similar to *Lion*.

Searchlights
Sixteen 24in: two pairs middle bridges, two pairs lower bridges, four pairs on blast screens before 3rd funnel.

Anchors
As *Lion*.

Wireless
Type IX main office (decoding office fitted), Mk I, II and 9 short-radius.

Complement
999 (as designed); 1,275 (1916).

Cost
£2,078,491.

* General armour thicknesses as in *Lion*.

Below: *Queen Mary* shortly after completion (1913), coming into Portsmouth.

QUEEN MARY: STEAM TRIALS

2 June 1913. Polperro

Full power, open exhausts

Runs	Revs	SHP	Speed (knots)
First:	284.5rpm	77,180	27.630
Second:	283.5rpm	76,500	27.410
Third:	285rpm	77,370	27.471
Fourth:	284rpm	77,220	27.582

Full power, closed exhausts

First:	288.5rpm	82,650	28.348
Second:	287.75rpm	82,640	27.852
Third:	290.5rpm	83,350	28.465
Fourth:	288.5rpm	83,450	27.582

Steam pressure: 203psi
Ship steamed for 24 hours with 57,467shp at 25,08 knots.

in particular from Admiral Schofield, who served in *Indomitable* for more than two years:

> The Captain was under the bridge in a rather cramped office, and the wardroom was situated on the starboard side amidships, with the gunroom placed in the after superstructure where the sailors on the quarterdeck could look straight in, and on guest-nights, they often did!

Apart from personal dislike, the scheme proved impracticable; the ratings' amenities and living quarters being scattered as a result of the disposition of turrets, funnel uptakes, and machinery spaces.

Below: *Queen Mary* as completed and approaching Portsmouth harbour (*Victory* in background), 1913.

Accommodation in *Queen Mary* and the *King George V* battleships reverted to the traditional plan of officers aft and men forward, and the sternwalk once more made an appearance.

In *Queen Mary*, the machinery provided a nominal increase of 5,000shp, but on average the speed was identical with her half-sisters.

Armour

Except for the 5in forward upper belt extending past 'B' barbette (further than in *Lion*), and the extremity of the 4in upper belt aft

QUEEN MARY: GM AND STABILITY

Based on inclining experiments, 20 September 1913

	Displacement (tons)	Draught	GM	Maximum stability	Stability vanishes at
'A' Condition (= load)*	26,670	28ft (mean)	4.97ft	–	–
'B' Condition (= deep)**	31,486	32ft 1in	5.7ft	–	–

*Fully equipped plus 1,000 tons coal.
**Fully equipped plus 3,700 tons coal, 1,130 tons oil.

Left: Fallen-in on the forecastle for a photograph aboard *Queen Mary* whilst anchored in Portsmouth dockyard, late 1913.

Above, left: *Queen Mary*, *Lion*, and the battleship *Iron Duke* anchored in Spithead Roads, preparing for the Fleet Review in July 1914.

Above: *Queen Mary* coaling in the Firth of Forth in January 1915, just after the Dogger Bank action. Note the strange camouflage.

Left: *Queen Mary* c. 1914. Anti-torpedo net defence drill while anchored at Portsmouth.

Right: Superb portrait view of *Queen Mary* in Weymouth Bay during the summer of 1914.

QUEEN MARY

Outboard profile, 1913, as fitted

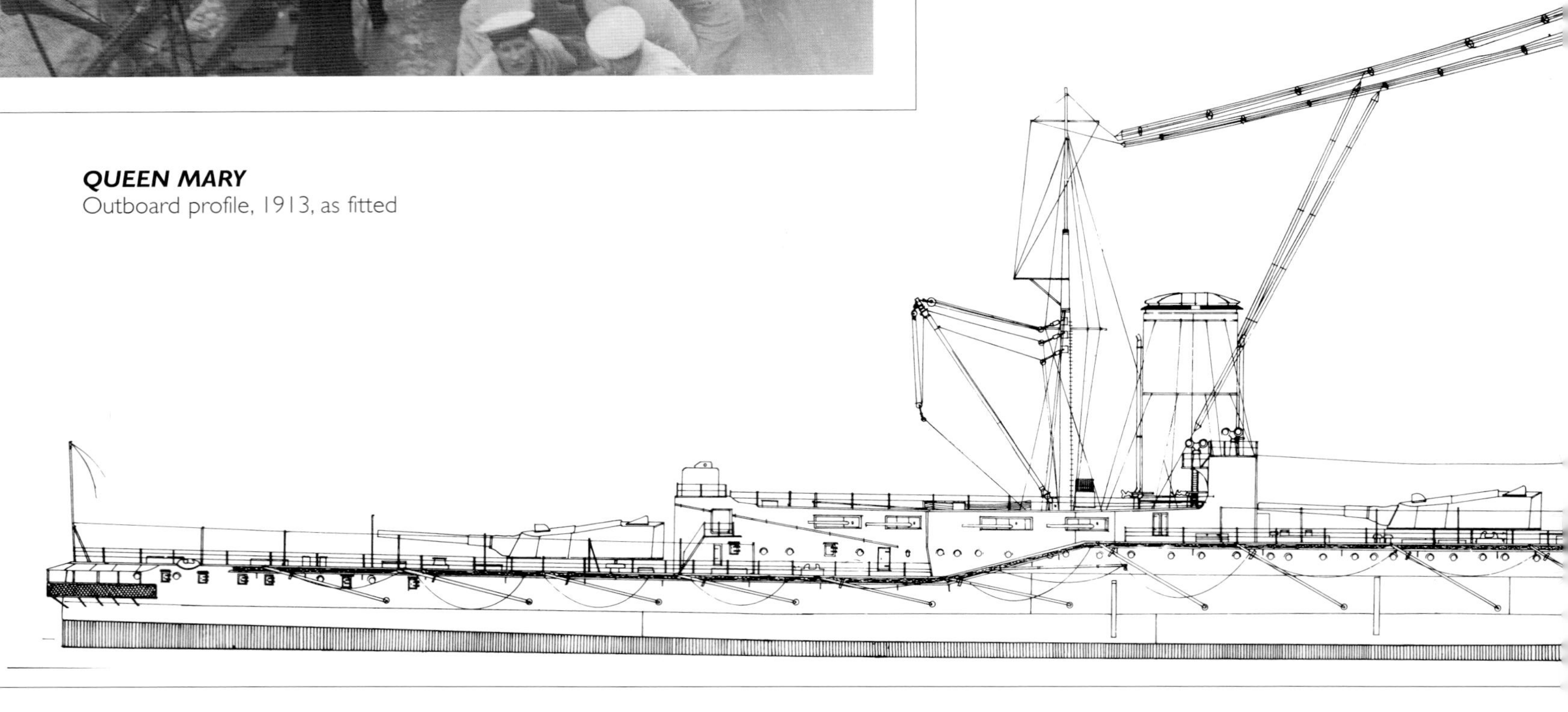

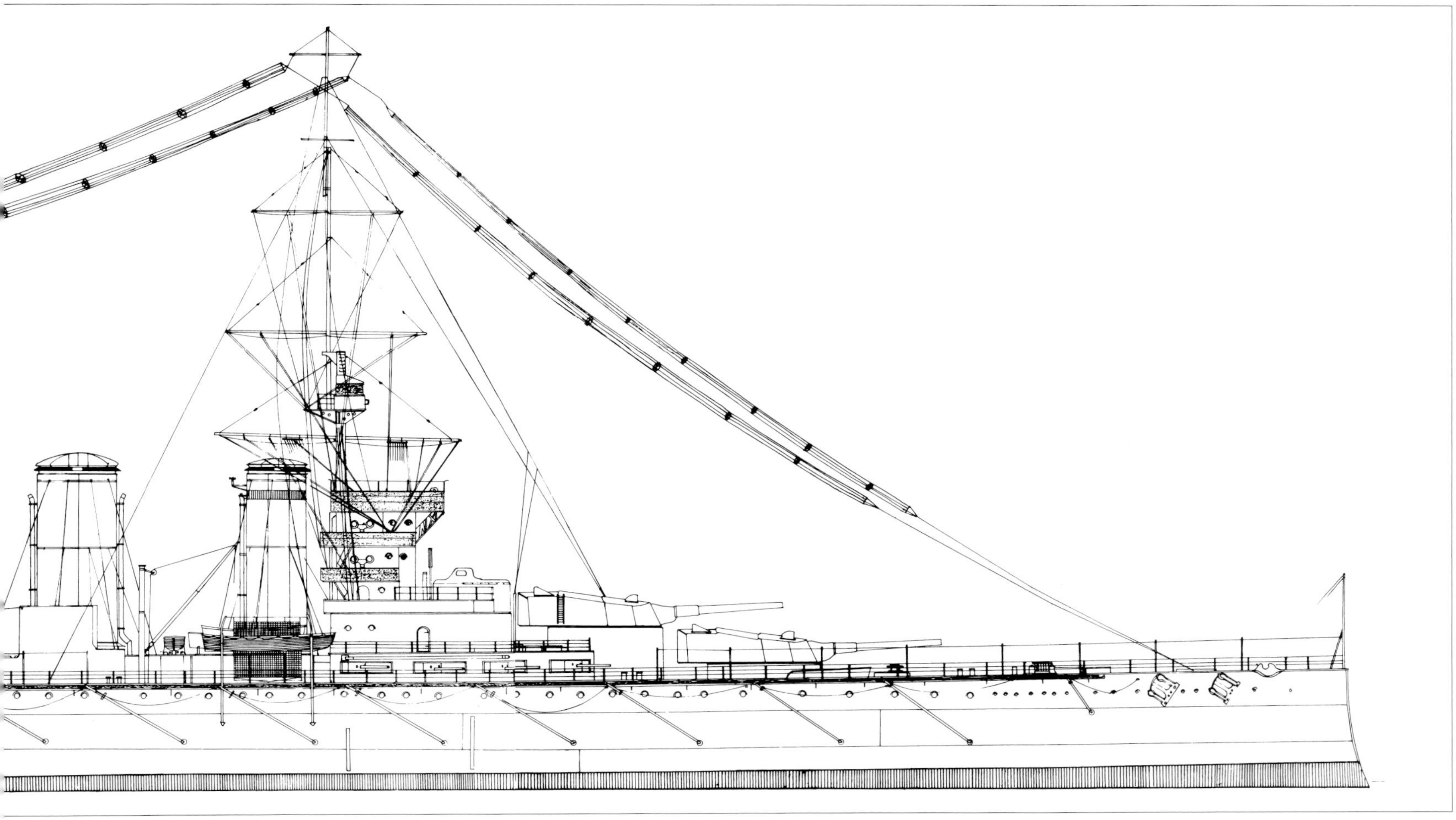

Right: In July 1914 the largest fleet review to date was in preparation. *Queen Mary* is shown here photographed from *Lord Nelson* preparing for the event.

stopping about 10 feet shorter than in *Lion*, the vertical protection was identical. Funnel uptakes were reduced to ¾in compared to ½in–1¼in in *Lion*. The secondary battery was protected with 3in plates on the sides, a 1in roof and a 3in rear bulkhead which was not continuous across the ship. This protection was not given to the after group of secondary guns. The after torpedo control tower was given 6m sides, a 3in roof and a 4in floor, compared to *Lion*'s 1in uniform thickness.

History: *Queen Mary*

Began trials in May 1913.

1913 *4 Sept* Commissioned at Portsmouth.
Sept 1st BCS Home Fleet.
1914 *Aug* 1st BCS Grand Fleet.
28 Aug Heligoland Bight action.
1915 *Jan–Feb* Refit at Portsmouth; not present at Dogger Bank action on 24 Jan.
1916 *31 May* Battle of Jutland.

Soon after coming into action she hit *Seydlitz* and disabled one of her turrets. Later engaged *Derfflinger*. Hit once, which disabled one gun in 'Q' turret. In action against *Seydlitz* and *Derfflinger*, between 16.24 and 16.26, three or more 11in or 12in shells struck her forward at a range of 14,500 to 15,800 yards. A dazzling flash followed immediately afterwards, and then she was hit by a salvo amidships near 'Q' turret. Another heavy explosion occurred and she appeared to go down by the bows.

In the final explosion, masses of steel, quantities of documents, and a picket boat (upside down) were blown into the air. Turret roofs were blown to a height of 100 feet, and a mushroom-shaped cloud rose to more than 1,000 feet. As the smoke cleared, the stern was still visible, the propellers still turning, and men were seen climbing out of the after turret. 57 officers, 1,209 ratings were lost. Two officers and five ratings, all wounded, were picked up. One officer and one rating were later picked up by a German destroyer.

Below: *Queen Mary* heavily engaged at Jutland on 31 May 1916 shortly before her destruction. Her devastated wreck was found and inspected in 1991 and lays upside down in three close sections indicating that there was more than one explosion from her magazines. Flashtight doors were also found open and cordite charges in passages where they should not have been.

Right: *Queen Mary*. The end of the giant battlecruiser, Battle of Jutland, at 16.26 on 31 May 1916.

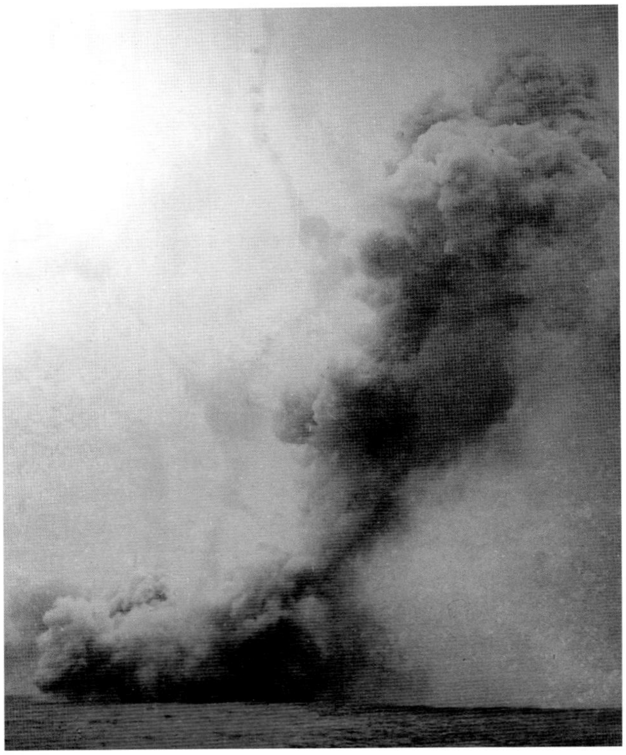

King George V Class: 1910 ESTIMATES

Design

These four ships were essentially a development of the *Orion* class, in which the faults built into the *Orions* were rectified. During the latter part of 1909, the DNC had submitted several sketches that showed a modified and slightly enlarged *Orion* to which they compared essentially as:

1. Nominal displacement increase of 500 tons, with an increase of 13ft 4in in length, and 6in in beam.
2. Anti-torpedo armament rearranged to give increased fire ahead, with light splinter protection for guns.
3. Internal protection more complete.
4. Maximum designed speed raised by almost 1 knot.
5. Adoption of a modified and improved type of bridgework.
6. Modified rig, with a light pole mast stepped before the funnel instead of heavy tripod close abaft.

A rearrangement of mast and funnel, reducing smoke and heat interference in the control top, eliminated one of the principal defects of *Orion*, but the retention of the 4in gun for torpedo-boat defence, despite the ever-increasing size of torpedo-boat destroyers, and the provision of nothing heavier than splinter shields for these guns, were considered weak points in an otherwise well-balanced design. While a measure of consideration towards the lobby that held dreadnoughts were becoming too large and too expensive may have played some part in limiting the secondary armament to 4in, it is more than likely that Admiral Fisher strongly influenced the decision. He was firmly opposed to any increase in the secondary calibre, and pointed out that a 6in battery would cost about £150,000–£170,000 per ship.

When the class (designated 'L1') was building during the summer of 1912, Admiral Sir Percy Scott pointed out that the single-pole mast to be fitted to the ships would be quite inadequate to support the director tower and the large control top for the director control system which he was then strongly urging. In view of the difficulties which had emerged in 1911, during the Scott director trials in *Neptune*, the Admiralty were opposed to its adoption and declined to make any provision for it in the new ships. *King George V* entered service as originally designed, with a single pole mast.

This decision was subsequently reversed, however, following further successful trials with a mainly Vickers-type director in the battleship *Thunderer* in October/November 1912 (see page 153). With this better system in mind, provision was made for the *King George V* class (L1) to refit for director firing, and the original small spotting top was replaced by a much larger circular control top. In an endeavour to secure the necessary rigidity to support this top without resorting to a heavy tripod, as in earlier ships, short (and lighter) tripod legs were fitted to the masts in one of the ships (*Centurion*). These proved quite successful, and the other two units (*Ajax* and *Audacious*) were fitted in a similar way. *King George V*, however, ran through a series of experiments, and was at first fitted with large flange-type girders to support the pole mast although, finally, she was given full-length tripod legs in 1917 when the control top was enlarged and a rigid support was vital. *Centurion* and *Ajax* ran their trials in the original rig, but were altered prior to entering service. The director tower itself was not fitted to any of the class until 1914.

Although designed to be 500 tons heavier than the *Orions*, they came out more than 800 tons heavier, with draught increased by 3½ inches. On the whole, the completed ships were a very well-balanced and pleasing design, but because many had been led to expect a strong 6in secondary armament to counter the German 5.9in guns, they were received into service with little or no enthusiasm. It is not surprising that so much was expected of the class if one bears in mind the fact that inflated reports about them were constantly appearing in the Press. For example, *The Daily Telegraph*'s correspondent, H. C. Bywater, wrote:

> Under such circumstances, the 'Telegraph' sees no impropriety in letting the people of England know what foreign Admiralties are now discussing. The new ships will be as superior to the *Dreadnought* and her sisters as the *Dreadnought* was to the vessels which preceded her. The new vessels will make a further notable effort by the naval authorities to ensure their complete supremacy for the British Fleet, not only in aggregate, but unit for unit. The four ships in offensive and defensive power and speed, will be without rivals – unless of course the foreign powers can benefit by information received from their sources and lay down similar ships.
>
> The new ships will carry an improved 13.5in gun which will throw a heavier shell than before, and instead of the 4in secondary battery, they will now mount at least 16 x 6in pieces. The vessels are to have better protection against the explosion of mine or torpedo, this end being achieved by better subdivision of the hull, and it is believed that owing to this precautionary measure, these men-of-war will be practically unsinkable.

AUDACIOUS: LAUNCH FIGURES, 14 SEPTEMBER 1912

Displacement: 9,095 tons
Draught: 9ft forward, 16ft 4½in aft
Length: 555ft 0½in pp
Beam as moulded: 88ft 10¼in
Breakage at launch:
longitudinal in a distance of 354ft 6in = 0⅝in hog
transverse in a distance of 83ft 9in nil.

Armament

Apart from the fact that 'Q' turret's arc was wider than in *Orion*, the main armament was identical with that of the preceding four

Below: *Ajax* leaves her builders (Scotts) for sea trials and voyage to Portsmouth, May 1913. Note the incomplete state of the vessel (revolving hood not yet fitted on conning tower). Also note topmast on derrick stump, and shallow triangular struts below.

Left: *Audacious* on preliminary sea trials. Note the civilians on board (probably her builders), absence of anti-torpedo nets, and four yards on main tripod.

Below: *Ajax* port broadside during her trial period, May 1913.

ships. The wire-wound Mark V gun was the same as in *Orion*, but by improving the shell it was possible to increase the weight by another 150lb to 1,400lb. Elevation was identical at 20°and gave a range of 23,820 yards with a charge of 297lb.

The new Dreyer system of fire control was introduced in these ships, with a separate rangefinder for each turret, and an armoured fire control and rangefinding position over the conning tower. This eliminated the necessity for the large control top of the earlier vessels and the large tripod to support it. The original design for *King George V* was a single pole foremast.

The secondary armament was the same as in *Orion*, but distributed somewhat differently to secure an increased ahead fire. Experience in service had shown that more torpedo attacks could be expected from the bows than from any other angle, and during torpedo attack on manoeuvres it was found that the forward guns did twice as much work as those fitted aft. Furthermore it was found that on a given ammunition supply, a number of rounds had to be transferred from the after guns to replenish those in the forward group. The after group was reduced from eight to four guns, the remaining four being relocated in a short forecastle battery abeam the forward 13.5in turrets. Although these forward guns had quite a good bearing abaft the beam, only the after group could fire directly astern.

This modification gave an ahead and astern fire of twelve and four guns respectively, against eight and eight in *Orion*. (A concentration of the majority of secondary guns forward had been adopted in the *Colossus* type.) These four ships were the last British battleships to mount the 4in.

Above: *Audacious*, 1914, showing director control on foretop, and upper deck 4in gun doors open.

Centurion was completed with an experimental fire control system for working the 4in guns alongside the searchlights during night actions, but little progress was made in developing and extending the system until at least 1917.

Armour

Although protection was more complete than in the *Orion* class, it did not match that of the *Neptune*, in which the longitudinal anti-torpedo bulkheads were continuous between the end barbettes, a feature which made itself apparent in 1914 when

KING GEORGE V CLASS: FINAL LEGEND, WEIGHTS (TONS)

Design 'L1'

Displacement (tons)

22,960 (load), 26,708 (deep).

Main armament

Revolving weight (excluding guns)

'A' 595	'Q' 592	'X' 596
'B' 600		'Y' 592

Total weight 13.5in turrets:	3,770
plus max. shell stowage	76
Hydraulic machinery:	50
Water in hydraulic tanks:	30
Spare gear:	16
Training racks:	27
Lower roller paths:	26
Shell room machinery:	28
Brackets and pipes:	38
'A' and 'B' turrets:	
Cordite cases	75
Shells	158
'Q' turret	
Cordite cases	37
Shells	79
'X' and 'Y' turrets:	
Cordite cases	74
Shells	158

Armour

12in strake:	1,150
9in strake:	469
8in strake:	698
6in forward:	190
4in forward:	63
2in aft:	60
Conning tower and tube:	124
Director:	12
Secondary director:	3
4in gun protection:	190
Upper deck:	771
Main deck:	110
Middle deck:	560
Lower deck forward:	74
Lower deck aft:	207
Bulkhead at 'A' barbette:	183
Bulkhead at 'Y' barbette:	230
Barbettes:	
'A'	236
'B'	401
'Q'	193
'X'	286
'Y'	192
Torpedo protection:	316
Funnel:	26
Backing:	100
Total armour protection:	**6,960**

Left: *King George V*, 1913, showing original supports to pole foremast.

Below, left: *Audacious*, showing a 'one-off' camouflage which was painted up during the months of September/October 1914.

AUDACIOUS
Outboard profile and plan, 1914

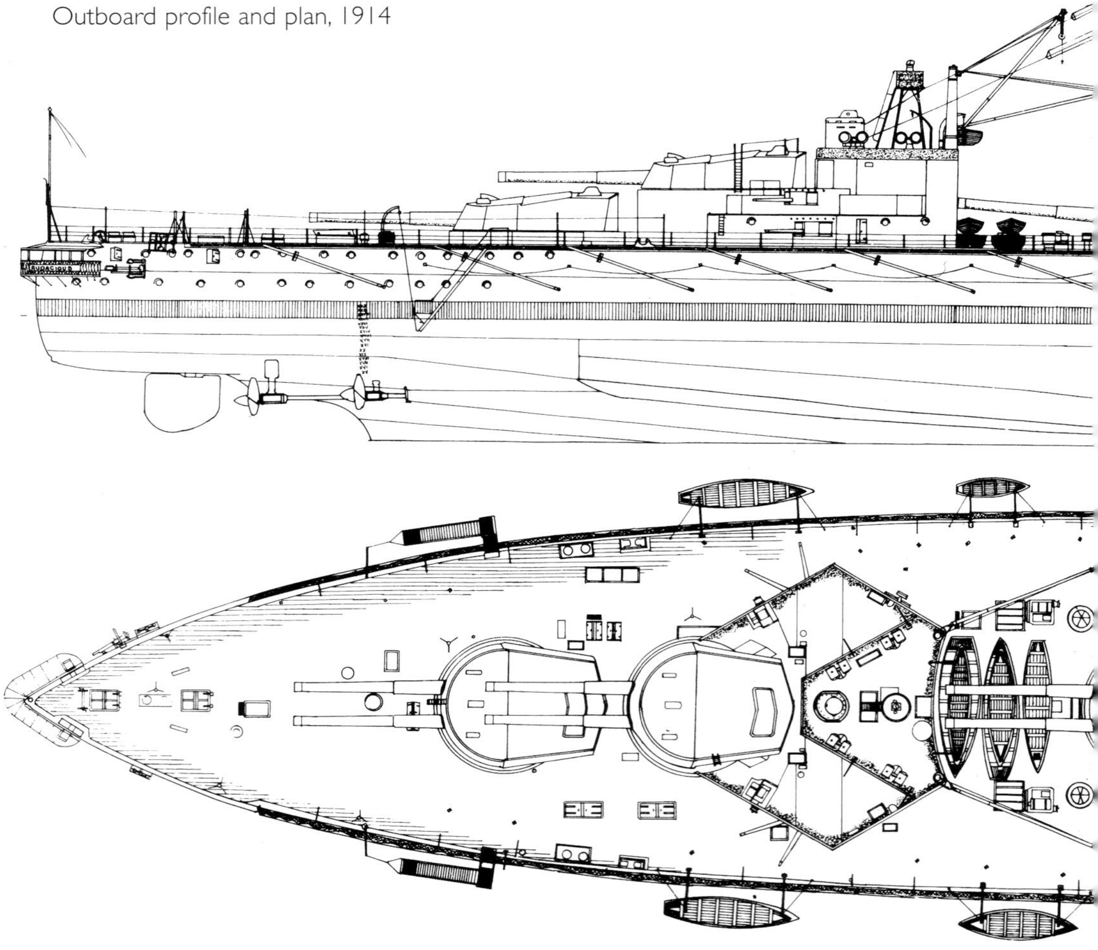

Audacious hit a mine and sank after thirteen hours (see pages 199–202). General protection was somewhat improved over the *Orions*, the principal modifications being:

1. Forward main bulkhead was increased from 6in to 10in between middle and main decks.
2. Upper side bulkhead forward was increased from 8in to 10in.
3. After bulkhead reduced from 2½in to 2in.
4. Upper deck around 'Q' barbette increased from 1½in to 1¾in.
5. 3in–3½in protective plating given to forward group of 4in guns, whereas the *Orions* had only splinter shields.
6. 1in longitudinal screens provided abreast engine rooms (only abreast magazines in *Orion*).

Item 5, concerning the 3½in protective plating of the 4in secondary armament, was a first in British battleships. In the *Orion*-class *Conqueror*, splinter shields had been fitted as an experiment during her trials, but these were not a feature of the original design of the class and were not provided for the rest of the class as completed.

The *King George V* class were the last to enter service with anti-torpedo nets, and although these were provided for the succeeding class of *Iron Dukes*, they were only fitted to *Iron Duke* during her trials period and were removed before she commissioned.

The main armoured strake amidships was 16ft 10½in above and 3ft 7½in below the load water-line in the normal condition. It extended from the inner face of the forward barbette to a little short of the outer face of the after barbette. The upper edge was located at middle deck level. The 6in–4in forward run extended

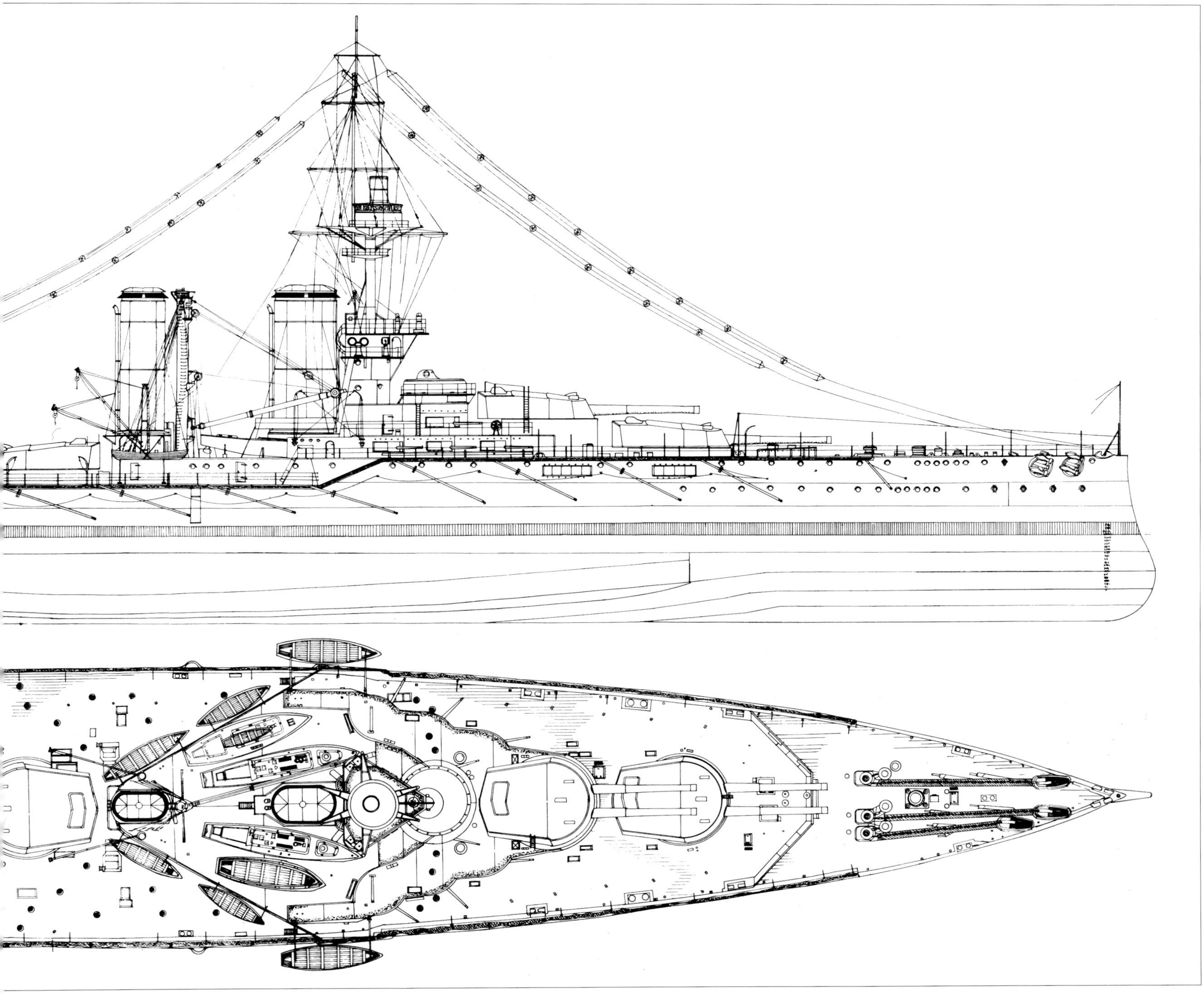

KING GEORGE V CLASS: PARTICULARS, AS COMPLETED

Construction

	Dockyard	Laid Down	Launched	Completed
King George V:	Portsmouth DY	16 Jan 1911	9 Oct 1911	Oct 1912
Centurion:	Devonport DY	16 Jan 1911	18 Nov 1911	Feb 1913
Ajax:	Scott	27 Feb 1911	21 March 1912	May 1913
Audacious:	Cammell Laird	23 March 1911	14 Sept 1912	Aug 1913.

Displacement (tons)
25,420 (load), 27,120 (deep) (28,422 (deep) *King George V*. 1918).

Dimensions
Length: 555ft 3¼in pp, 589ft 6in lwl, 597ft 9in oa (594ft 4in *King George V*)
Beam: 89ft 0¾in
Draught (load): 25ft 7in forward, 28ft 8in aft (*King George V*)
Height of main guns above lower wl: 'A' 30ft 6in; 'B' 40ft; 'Q' 24ft; 'X' 32ft 6in; 'Y' 23ft
Height of CT vision slits above lower wl: 48ft 3in
Height of fore funnel above lower wl: 78ft
Height of lower foremasthead above lower wl: 100ft
Depth of keel from battery deck: 52ft.

Armament*
Ten 13.5in 45cal Mk V; 100rpg
Twelve 4in 50cal Mk VII; 150rpg
One 12pdr (8cwt)
Four 3pdr (saluting)
Five Maxim MG; 5,000rpg
Ten Lewis guns; 5,000rpg
Three 21in torpedo tubes (two beam, one stern); fourteen torpedoes.

Director control
A gun director was fitted shortly after completion.**

Armour
Main belt: 12in
Upper belt: 9in–8in
Ends: 6in-4in forward, 2½in–2in aft
Bulkheads: 10in–6in forward, 10in upper side, 8in aft
After bulkhead: 2in
Barbettes: 10in–9in–7in–6in–3in
Turrets: 11in–4in–3in
Conning tower: 11in–3in
Communications tube: 5in
Decks: forecastle 1in, upper 1¾in–1½in, middle 1in, lower 2in–1in forward, 4in–3in aft
Uptakes: 1½in–1in
Magazine screens: 1¾in–1½in–1¼in–1in
Engine room screens: 1in.

Machinery
Parsons direct-drive turbines, four propellers, two parallel rudders
Boilers: eighteen Babcock & Wilcox *King George V* and *Ajax*; eighteen Yarrow *Audacious* and *Centurion*: three compartments, six boilers in each
Heating surface: 60,780sq ft
Grate area: 1,746sq ft
Length of boiler rooms: (1) 37ft 11in, (2) 38ft 0½in, (3) 38ft
Length of engine rooms: 68ft 0⅜in
Designed SHP: 27,000 = 20–21 knots
Fuel: 900 tons coal min., 3,100 tons max.; 840 tons oil
Coal consumption per day (tons): 128 at 10 knots
Radius of action: 3,805nm at seagoing speed; 5,910nm (6,310nm *Ajax*, *Centurion*) at 10 knots (oil added).

Ship's boats
Pinnaces (steam): two 50ft
Pinnaces (sail): one 36ft
Launches (sail): one 42ft
Cutters: three 32ft
Whalers: three 27ft
Gigs: one 30ft
Skiff dinghies: one 16ft
Balsa rafts: one 13ft 6in.

Searchlights (1918)***
Eight 36in: two SL platform forward, four around after funnel, two after superstructure.

Rangefinder positions****
Two 18ft, two 15ft, five 9ft, one 6ft 6in.

Battle signal stations
Two built-in at main deck level (port and starboard) at station 104, under protective deck.

Anchors
Three 140cwt stockless (two bower, one sheet), one 42cwt stern.

Wireless (1918)
Main office Types 1–34 (plus Types 1–16 *Ajax*, *Centurion*); Third office Type 3 (*Ajax*, *King George V*); Type 76–86 (*Centurion*); Fire control Type 31.

Complement
King George V: 869 (1913); 1,114 (1916)
Centurion: 862 (1913)
Ajax: 869 (1914)
Audacious: 860 (1914).

Cost
King George V: £1,961,096
Centurion: £1,950,671
Ajax: £1,889,387
Audacious: £1,918,813.

*Two 3in AA; 150rpg added later, see Appearance Changes.
**This was fitted in a tower aloft for use with the main armament. There were also provisions for a directing turret ('X'), and 'follow the pointer' gear in all turrets. Flexible voice pipes were fitted for night action.
***Sixteen 24in in *King George V*, *Audacious*, *Ajax* as completed; twenty 24in in *Centurion* as completed.
****18ft in two of the main turrets; one 15ft on top of gun control tower; one 15ft on torpedo control tower; 9ft in other three main turrets and in gun control tower and fore bridge; 6ft 6in fitted for high angle.

KING GEORGE V: GM AND STABILITY

Based on inclining experiments, 10 March 1913

	Displacement (tons)	Draught	GM	Maximum stability	Stability vanishes at
'A' Condition (= load)*	25,420	27ft 4in	4.56ft	32½°	58°
'B' Condition (= deep)**	27,680	29ft 3½in	5.17ft	33°	60°

*Fully, equipped plus 900 tons coal lower and wing bunkers.
**Fully equipped plus 3,100 tons coal.

to within approximately 45ft of the stem at the same height as the midships section. It was 6in thick until about 50ft beyond the fore barbette and then reduced to 4in. The 2½in strake aft extended to 50ft short of the stern, again at the same height as the midships section. The lower side armour ran over the same length as the main belt armour between main and middle deck levels, with its maximum of 9in running the same length as the 12in run and then reducing. The 8in upper side extended to just beyond the inner face of the forward barbette, and then to abeam the inner face of the after barbette at main and upper deck levels.

The main bulkheads ran obliquely inwards from the forward and after extremities of the 12in and 9in armoured strakes to the outer faces of the end barbettes at lower and main deck levels: the forward bulkhead was 6in from the lower to middle deck, and 10in from the middle to the main level. The after bulkhead was 10in uniform from lower to main deck level. The upper side bulkheads ran obliquely inwards from the forward and after extremities of the upper side armour to the outer face of the forward barbette and centre of the after barbette, between the main and upper decks. The 1½in–4in forward bulkhead closed the extremities of the 4in belt and lower side armour between lower and main deck levels, and carried this to above the upper deck. The 2in after bulkhead closed the extremities of the lower side armour between lower and main decks.

The 1in forecastle deck ran below the superstructure along the 4in secondary battery. The upper deck was 1½in–1¾in running between the end barbettes, and the 1½in main deck was located at the ends from the forward upper side bulkhead to the forward bulkhead, and from the after upper side bulkhead to the after bulkhead. The middle deck, which was 1in on the inclines and on the flat, ran from the end bulkheads. The lower deck was 1in inside the forward bulkhead, increasing to 2½in outside this, and ran from the outer base of the forward barbette to the stem of the vessel. Aft, this deck ran from the after barbette to the stern of the ship, and was 3in inside the after bulkhead and 4in outside this, over the steering gear.

'A' barbette had a 10in outer face above the main deck, reducing to 3in once below. The inner face was 7in above the main deck, and then reduced to the same 3in below this level. 'B' and 'X' barbettes were given 9in faces above forecastle level, then reduced to 7in from forecastle to upper deck levels. The rear was 9in and the sides 10in above the upper deck. The sides were 6in from main to upper and then reduced to 3in below the main deck. 'Q' had 10in sides above the main deck and 9in elsewhere, all reducing to a uniform 3in once below the main deck. 'Y' barbette was almost identical with 'A'.

The turrets had 11in faces, 4in roof plates at the front, 3in at the rear, a 3in floor, 8in rear and 11in sides.

The forward superstructure, housing the 4in secondary armament, was 3in–3½in with 3in sides and 3½in on the gunports. The battery was given a 1in floor and roof. The after superstructure had splinter shields only. The conning tower had 11in sides, a 3in roof, a 1in–3in base, a 4in hood, and 5in tube. The torpedo control tower on the after superstructure had 6in and 3in. Funnel uptakes were provided with 1in–1½in above the middle deck which was carried up to shelter deck level.

The magazine screens ran longitudinally abreast the magazines, and were continuous between midships and after magazines. Thicknesses were 1¼in–1½in–1¾in abreast forward magazines, 1½in abreast the midships magazine and 1in–1½in abreast the after magazine. Screens of 1in were given to the engine rooms and formed a continuation of the midships and after magazine screens.

Machinery

During her preliminary sea trials, *Ajax* ran with new experimental, four-bladed propellers, but these did little to increase the speed of the ship; in fact, quite the opposite was the case, if sea trial figures are compared with those of her sisters. The four-bladed type were removed and she was fitted with the usual three-bladed type as in the rest of the class.

Excellent speeds were achieved by *King George V*, with a figure of just over 22 knots realized, and this was exceeded by *Centurion* which recorded a figure of 22.866 knots at full power over the measured mile. The main machinery consisted of two sets of Parsons marine turbines located in three watertight compartments divided by two longitudinal bulkheads.

Two main and two auxiliary condensers were fitted in all the ships, the main condenser and main machinery in the middle compartment, the auxiliary machinery and condensers being located in the wing compartments. Each ship had four shafts, with the HP ahead and astern located on the outer shafts in each wing

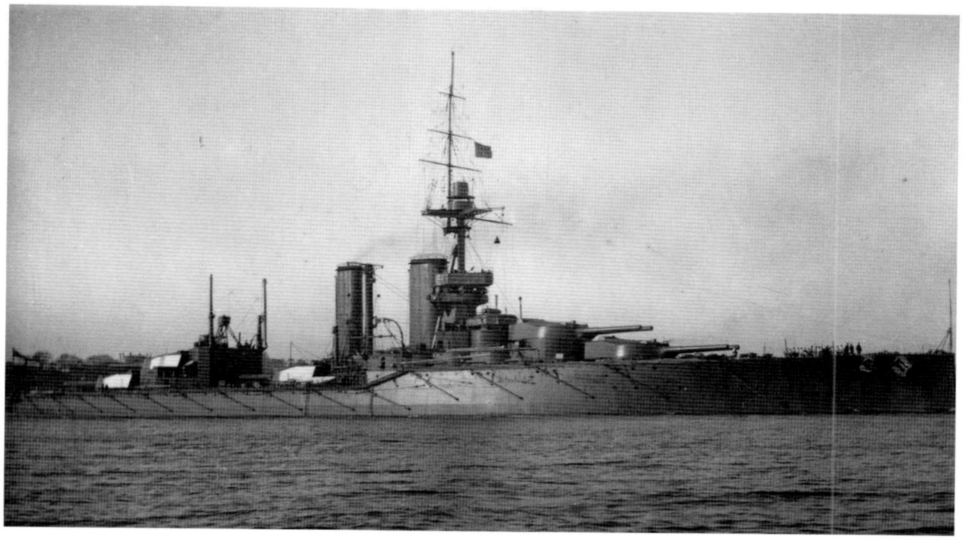

Top: *Centurion*, early 1914. Note the very dark-grey paintwork.

Above: *Ajax*, as above. Note very prominent caging to funnels.

KING GEORGE V: SPEED TRIALS, 1912

4 November. Full power

	Outer		Inner		Mean revs	Total SHP	Speed (knots)
First run							
Port:	338rpm	6,852shp	340rpm	9,537shp	339rpm	32,762	22.134
Starboard:	334rpm	6,646shp	344rpm	9,727shp			
Second run							
Port:	336rpm	6,848shp	338rpm	9,404shp	336.5rpm	32,400	21.923
Starboard:	334rpm	6,725shp	336rpm	9,423shp			
Third run							
Port:	338rpm	6,928shp	340rpm	9,576shp	339rpm	33,022	22.373
Starboard:	340rpm	6,884shp	338rpm	9,634shp			
Fourth run							
Port:	338rpm	6,704shp	340rpm	9,614shp	339.5rpm	33,100	21.922
Starboard:	–	–	–	–	–	–	–

CENTURION: SPEED TRIALS, 1913

19-20 February, 09.15 to 13.15, Plymouth
Wind NEbyE, Force 5–6; sea rough
Draught: 26ft 9in forward, 27ft 10in aft
Three-bladed propellers

Outer diameter: 9ft
Inner diameter: 9ft 6in
Outer pitch: 8ft 7in
Inner pitch: 8ft 7in

Developed area of outer: 33sq ft
Developed area of inner: 42sq ft
Bypass valves open 1¼–1¾
Propulsive coefficient: 0.411

	Outer		Inner		Mean revs	Total SHP	Speed (knots)
First run							
Port:	340rpm	6,900shp	346rpm	10,450shp	345.5rpm	34,530	22.866
Starboard:	344rpm	7,110shp	352rpm	10,070shp			
Second run							
Port:	340rpm	6,800shp	352rpm	10,610shp	342rpm	34,440	20.924
Starboard:	340rpm	6,850shp	350rpm	10,100shp			
Third run							
Port:	340rpm	6,920shp	352rpm	10,700shp	345.5rpm	35,120	22.742
Starboard:	340rpm	7,140shp	350rpm	1 0,360shp			
Fourth run							
Port:	340rpm	6,980shp	344rpm	10,380shp	341 rpm	34,660	21.224
Starboard:	332rpm	7,010shp	348rpm	10,290shp			

AJAX: SPEED TRIALS, 1913

12–13 May, Polperro

	Outer		Inner		Mean revs	Total SHP	Speed (knots)
First run							
Port:	347rpm	6,860shp	332rpm	8,200shp	337.25rpm	29,210	21.095
Starboard:	340rpm	6,650shp	330rpm	7,500shp			
Second run							
Port:	340rpm	6,720shp	328rpm	7,840shp	334rpm	28,600	20.967
Starboard:	338rpm	6,610shp	330rpm	7,430shp			
Third run							
Port:	347rpm	6,780shp	334rpm	8,210shp	337.75rpm	29,250	21.225
Starboard:	340rpm	6,650shp	330rpm	7,610shp			
Fourth run							
Port:	342rpm	6,760shp	336rpm	8,700shp	336.5rpm	29,420	20.756
Starboard:	336rpm	6,640shp	332rpm	7,770shp			

compartment, and the LP ahead and astern fitted to the inner shafts in the middle compartment. The boilers for *King George V* and *Ajax* were Babcock and Wilcox, the other two ships being fitted with Yarrow type. *Ajax* was engined by her builders (Scotts), *Audacious* by her builders (Lairds), *Centurion* by Hawthorn Leslie and *King George V* by Parsons.

Appearance Changes

A modified and improved type of bridge was introduced consisting of a high, narrow, central structure, set back well clear of the conning tower, as in the *Orion*s. It contained charthouse, sea-cabins, etc., and had a large navigating platform encircling the top and lower bridges. The navigating platform extended well forward, and all bridgework was entirely clear of the fore funnel. This type of structure proved very successful and was retained, with minor improvements and variations for the next three classes of battleships (*Iron Dukes*, *Queen Elizabeths* and *Royal Sovereigns*).

They were fine-looking ships, with a somewhat lighter appearance than the *Orion* class, chiefly because of the modified rig and rearrangement of mast and fore funnel. On completion they were quite difficult to tell apart. Individual differences were:

King George V: Plain pole mast, smaller control top, with topmast through this; no struts below yard at head of main derrick stump.
Others: Short tripod legs to mast; larger control top, with striking topmast stepped well abaft of it.
Ajax: Very prominent caging to funnels. Topmast to main derrick stump; shallow triangular struts to derrick stump mast.
Audacious: No topmast to derrick stump.
Centurion: Small platform low on mast; topmast to stump; deep struts to yard; SL platforms low down around second funnel (only ship completed with this).

1914 All funnel bands painted out where applicable. Elaborate camouflage painted in *Audacious* during September, but was painted out by time of loss in October.
1915 3in AA added on quarterdeck right aft.
1915–16 Torpedo nets removed from all. Two pairs SL ex bridge, and two pairs ex after superstructure remounted around second funnel on low platform, very similar to *Centurion*'s. Topmast reduced and flagpole removed.
1916–19 Medium-based rangefinder added over conning tower. 4in guns removed from ports by April 1917 having been found of little use because of their liability to be washed out in head seas. Ports plated up, and some of the gun rooms used for accommodation. Extra 3in AA added on quarterdeck right aft. Original 3in AA in *Centurion* replaced by 4in AA. Official list of April 1917 states that *Centurion* was fitted with two 4in AA, but it would appear, although two guns provisionally approved, only one actually fitted. *King George V* was fitted for towing kite balloons. As with all British battleships and battlecruisers, this class were given improved anti-flash protection after Jutland in May 1916. There were also improvements in armouring certain parts of decks over magazines, but it has proved difficult to obtain any detailed official data. In general, flame-cut armour was used, and a greater devotion was given to the newer ships than to the older dreadnoughts (*Bellerophon* received a little over 23 tons; *King George V* approximately 80 tons). Lower yard on foremast replaced by signal struts on starfish. W/T poles fitted to after pair of derrick stumps in *Centurion* only. Rangefinder baffles fitted to topmast in *Centurion* and *King George V* and to topmast and funnels in *Ajax*.
1917–18 Original circular control top replaced by a much larger rectangular fitting. Deflection scales painted on 'A' and 'Y' or 'B' and 'X' turrets. Range clocks fitted to foremast below control top in all ships, and on after superstructure in *Centurion* and *King George V*. Stern torpedo tube removed from all. Twin (24in) SL replaced by 36in single lamps with improved control facilities. SL platform around second funnel replaced by 'coffee-box' control towers, one tall and one short, on each side of the funnel. Taller towers in after position in *Ajax* and *Centurion*, but forward in *King George V*. One pair 24in lamps mounted in each at first, later replaced by single 36in lamps. The twin 24in lamps on bridge and after structure replaced by 36in lamps: two on bridge, two on after superstructure. Flanges to foremast in *King George V* replaced by full-length tripod legs. W/T poles fitted to after pair of derrick stumps as in others. Rangefinder baffles removed during this period.
1918 Torpedo control and concentration top added low down on foremast in *King George V* and *Centurion*.
Aircraft platforms fitted on 'B' turret in *Ajax*, 'B' and 'X' in *Centurion*, 'B' and 'Q' in *King George V*.
1919 Aircraft not in evidence and only embarked when on exercises. Runways not normally carried during this period. The appearance of the remaining three ships had changed considerably, and they had a heavier look than in 1914 as a result of the many war modifications. It was now easier to tell them apart because of the full-length tripod legs in *King George V* and the short legs in the other two. *Centurion* had the extra top low on the mast, whereas *Ajax* had none.
1926–27 (*Centurion* only) Converted by Chatham Royal Dockyard at a cost of £359,000, from April 1926 to June 1927, for service as radio-controlled fleet target ship for guns up to

8in. Stripped of all small fittings and rig and top weight reduced. Turrets were not reduced at first, but later they were thought unnecessary after all relevant data on their strength and quality had been recorded. To compensate their weight, certain underwater compartments, such as the wings which had been used as fuel bunkers, were now filled with shingle. The corresponding draught increased to 31ft 3in mean, which in turn brought the lower edge of the armoured belt to 7ft 6in below water which minimized the risk of her being holed below the waterline by steeply diving shells fired from maximum distance.

Her machinery remained intact, but was modified by altering the burners to fire a light type of diesel oil instead of coal: this was done to simplify steaming abilities under remote control, as had been fitted in the destroyer *Shikari*.

Centurion was fitted with many whip aerials for this service, which gave her an odd and distinctive appearance. She was capable of making 16 knots for periods of up to three hours, completely unmanned. Her rig was later reduced even more by the removal of the control top and the after pair of derrick stumps. She had a complement of 242 who maintained the ship and navigated her to the firing range and were then taken off. In 1933 her bridge and superstructure was reduced, and her funnels considerably reduced.

In June 1940 she was rearmed with a miscellaneous collection of guns for the anti-invasion forces, and was later fitted as a maintenance and repair ship for the local defence vessels at Devonport.

From April to May 1941 she was refitted at Devonport as a blockship for the proposed blocking of Tripoli harbour; this operation was subsequently abandoned and she was then refitted to look like a dummy *Anson* (*King George V* class, 1936 Estimates). Her AA armament consisted of two 2pdrs (singles) and eight 20mm. In June 1942 she was rearmed at Suez with four 2pdrs and seventeen 20mm and used as an escort on the Malta convoys. From May to June 1944 she was stripped at Portsmouth for use as a breakwater.

The Loss of *Audacious*

On 27 October 1914 the 2nd Battle Squadron was ordered to carry out firing practice near Tory Island off the coast of Donegal. The battlefleet consisted of:

Firing line	Target line
Centurion (flag)	*Orion*
Ajax	*Monarch*
Audacious	*Thunderer*
King George V	

When the explosion occurred, *Audacious* was steering SS E in 55° 34' N, 8° 12 ½' W. Wind Force 4 to 5, heavy sea swell.

Firing was to take place from 09.00 and 'exercise stations' was sounded as soon as the signal for the firing line to turn to the firing course was hoisted. The official time for this move was logged at 08.40, and the course had been previously indicated as SW. There was an allowance for the target line to get into position which was judged to be 15 to 20 minutes.

At approximately 08.45 a dull thud was felt in *Audacious* and an officer on the bridge thought that she had accidentally fired her after 13.5in guns, although there was no signs of smoke. He then thought it might have been *King George V*. It was also thought that *Audacious* might have been hit by a torpedo, but there had been no usual column of water, or for that matter, no explosion. Port helm was taken off, but the ship did not right herself properly. Orders were given to close all watertight doors and hatches and to place the ship in a state of emergency.

By 09.00 all doors and hatches had been closed, and the ship's company were at action stations. At about this time the ship took a slight list to port, and it was then realized that she might be mortally stricken. All bulkheads and doors in the vicinity of the explosion were checked to see whether any shoring-up was needed and to determine whether the starboard wing compartments could be flooded to compensate the weight of water in the port side and get the ship back on an even keel.

Audacious was brought out of the line away from *Ajax* and *Centurion*, and was put into the wind to keep her steady. She was now heeling at approximately 10°–15°, and although the starboard compartments had been flooded, she did not appear to be righting herself. At first it was thought that the port wing engine room was the only section to have been flooded as a result of the damage, but later reports confirmed that although the central bulkhead was holding up, water, which was thought to be coming through the joint, was slowly seeping into the central compartments. *Audacious* set course for Lough Swilly, and full speed ahead on the starboard engines was ordered: the ship began to steer quite badly, but even though the seas were heavy, she was able to make a little over 9 knots. She continued at this speed for the next twenty minutes or so, and then all her electrical circuits failed, though she was still able to maintain a steady 9 knots.

On examination it was found that the explosion had taken place approximately five to ten feet forward of the after engine

Below: *Audacious*. Two familiar, but none the less arresting views of her loss. Taken at about 14.00 on 27 October 1914, all derricks are in operation and a general 'abandon ship!' is in progress.

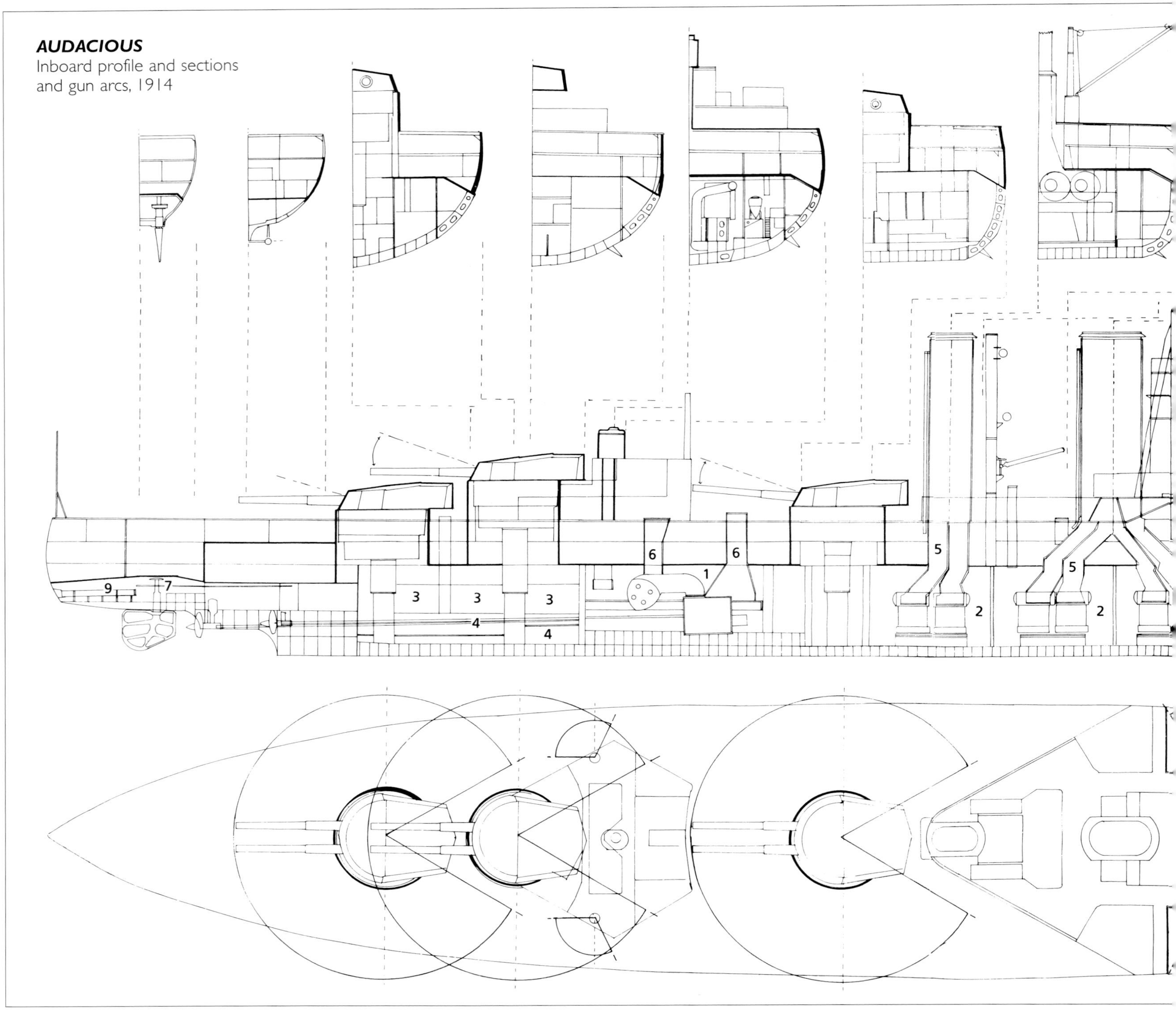

room bulkhead, and that there had, in fact, been a small splash of water in that area some sixteen feet above the main deck level; furthermore, eye-witnesses stated that the condenser in the port wing engine room lifted slightly and then dropped again when the explosion occurred. As a direct result of the explosion, the following compartments were flooded: port wing engine room; port after hydraulic engine room; dynamo room. The following areas filled up from seepage: 'X' shell room; watertight compartments near port wing engine room; bunkers on starboard side; central engine room; junior officers' bathrooms; 'X' turret cooler spaces; after medical distribution spaces; bathroom flat; main deck abaft 'X' 13.5in turret; middle deck in the area.

When trying to right the ship, the crew had great difficulty in closing many of the valves, and water could not be prevented from entering the central engine room; by 10.00 it was five feet deep. There was no evidence of the longitudinal bulkheads having cracked. The port engines were out of action, but the starboard engines were running at full power and it seemed that the ship might be saved. But water continued to creep into the starboard compartments and they had to be abandoned shortly after 10.00, leaving the ship dead in the sea. The boats had been readied except those aft where the quarterdeck was nearly awash. By 11.00 all steam power had been lost, which made it very difficult to operate any of the boat-handling gear.

On the scene were the cruiser *Liverpool* and several destroyers, which had answered distress calls from *Audacious*, and it was

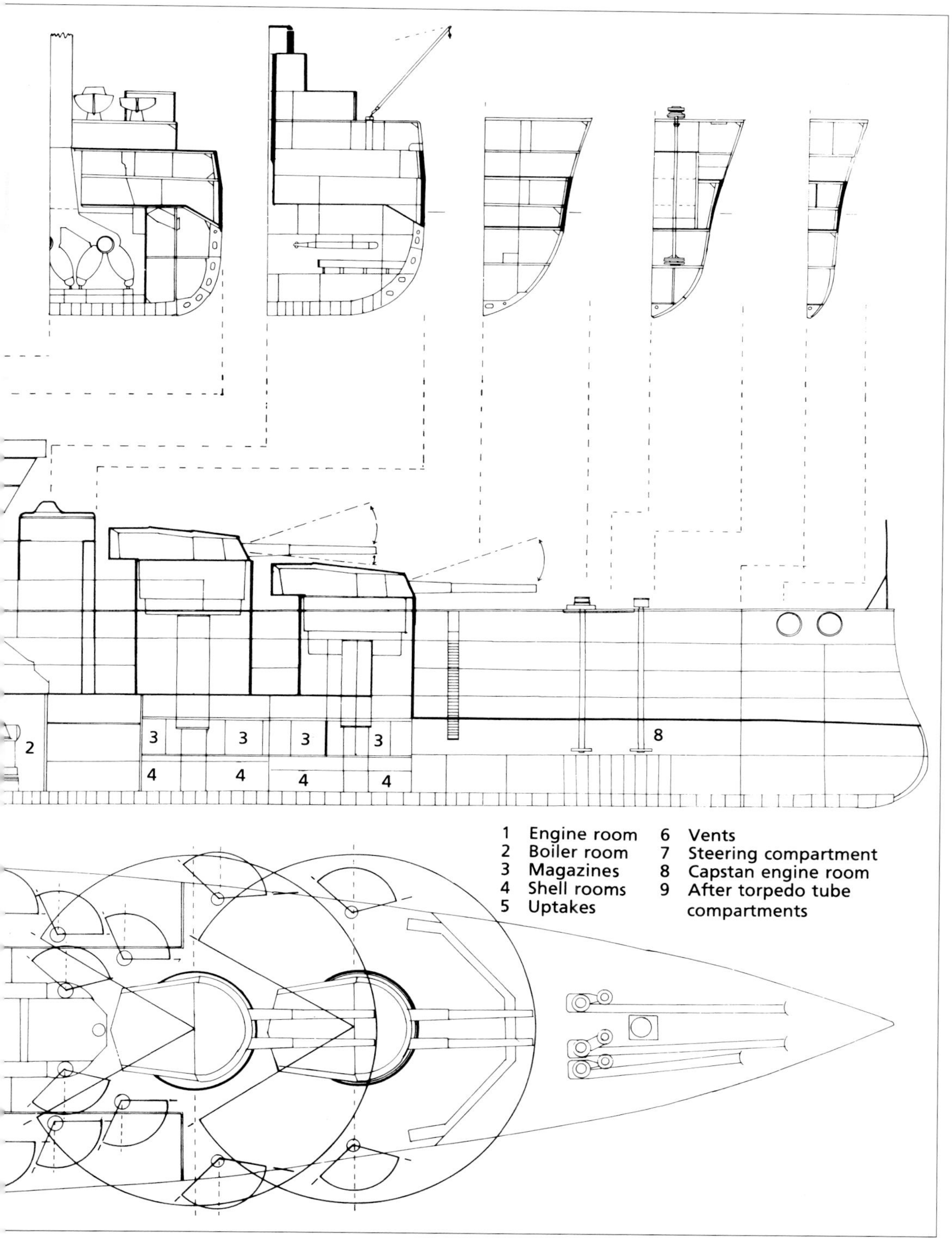

Above: *Ajax* during battle practice, 1917/18.

Below: *Centurion* towards the end of the war.

quickly decided to take her in tow. All non-essential personnel were disembarked into the other vessels and by 14.00 there were not many more than 250 men aboard. Although the quarterdeck was awash, the towing operation was pursued and the newly arrived SS *Olympic* took a line from *Audacious*. As the battleship could not answer her helm, the operation was extremely difficult; she was drifting west and *Olympic* was trying to pull her south. Inevitably the tow parted. A little later a second attempt was made by *Liverpool*, it being thought a lighter ship might have more luck because of her greater manoeuvrability. The line was cast, but became entangled in *Liverpool*'s propellers and parted. A final attempt was made by the collier *Thornhill*, but once again the line parted and with much regret it was decided to abandon the idea.

Above: *King George V.* The big guns of 'Q', 'X' and 'Y' turrets trained to starboard during gunnery practice, *c.*1917/18. *Ajax* and *Centurion* follow.

It was now 17.00 and getting dark. The quarterdeck was completely awash, the mushroom vents had been smashed off by the sea and so much water was getting below that the ship was becoming very unsteady. Shortly after 17.00 it was decided to take off all hands except for 50 volunteers. The ship was now in a very sorry condition, very sluggish and rolling heavily. At 18.15 it was decided to abandon her. Officers observing the scene from the destroyers and *Liverpool* stated that the ship had not inclined any farther throughout the day, seeming to hang poised without movement. By 18.50 the angle had reached 30°, but she still gave no sign of turning over. However, at 20.45, with her maximum stability vanished, she was seen to raise by the bows with her stern submerged, and turn turtle – some twelve hours after the explosion.

Audacious lay upside down until approximately 21.00, when there was a terrific explosion and flames and debris shot to a height of at least 300 feet. Two lesser explosions in the air were reported, and these were thought to have been 4in shells exploding. It would seem that either 'A' or 'B' magazine had exploded, the theory being that the high-explosive shells had been displaced by the ship's list and had detonated on hitting the floor; this would have ignited the cordite and produced the spectacular explosion and the large sheet of flame. It was recorded that the magazines contained 1,120 13.5in and 2,400 4in shells with their charges. Eye-witnesses claimed that the ship's bows were at an angle of at least 45° during the explosion. Almost immediately afterwards, *Audacious* disappeared beneath the surface.

The cause was never officially confirmed, but it was thought that she had struck a floating mine displaced by *Centurion* or *Ajax*, which were steaming ahead of her; the possibility that she had been torpedoed was never ruled out. The Inquiry into the loss of a practically new battleship found that the strength of the longitudinal bulkheads was inadequate to stop water from reaching the central part of the ship – the major factor contributing to her loss. Bulkheads buckled, doors could not be closed, and valves stuck, all of which made it extremely difficult to prevent the ship from filling rapidly.

History: *King George V*

Began sea trials in October 1912. In November she was fitted with experimental anti-rolling tanks which did not prove as successful as had been hoped. These tanks were later used for additional oil fuel stowage.

1912 *16 Nov* Commissioned at Portsmouth with 2nd BS Home Fleet.

1914 *June* Flagship during visit to Kiel Canal celebrations, and received the Kaiser in his first visit aboard a British dreadnought.

Aug With Grand Fleet.

Oct Under refit until Feb 1915.

Left: *King George V* as completed and showing her girder supports to the foremast. She was Flagship of the British squadron representing the British Navy during the celebrations at Kiel, 23 to 30 June 1914. On 25 June the Kaiser went on board, his first visit to a British dreadnought. His Flag, as an Admiral in the British Navy, being temporarily hoisted and that of Sir G Warrender, commanding the squadron was temporarily transferred to *Centurion*.

Below: *King George V*. Looking back from the forecastle on the superstructure and 'A' and 'B' 13.5in gun turrets. Taken when HM King George V visited her at the end of the war.

Right: *King George V*, c. 1920. Note the difference of the SL towers around second funnel when compared with other two ships of the class.

1916 *31 May* Battle of Jutland.
At approximately 19.07 she opened fire on what was probably the leading German vessel, at a distance of 12,000 yards, and was one of the first British battleships in the line to open fire.
19 Aug At sea with the Fleet to intercept the German High Seas Fleet in their unsuccessful raid on Sunderland.
1918 *12 April* Based at Rosyth with Grand Fleet.
21 Nov Present in the Northern line at the German surrender.
1919 *March* Joined Home fleet (flagship 3rd BS) after Grand Fleet was broken up.
Oct Transferred to Reserve at Portsmouth.
31 Oct Home Fleet abolished and she became flagship of Vice-Admiral Reserve Fleet at Portsmouth.
1920 *July* Ten-day mobilization of Reserve Fleet.
Sept Relieved as flagship by *Orion*, and paid off for refit.
31 Oct Commissioned at Portsmouth to relieve *Marlborough* in 4th BS Mediterranean Fleet.
Served with that Fleet until Jan 1923.
1922 *31 July* Left Constantinople with Fleet during Greek crisis and threat to city.
2/3 Sept Struck an uncharted rock in the Moselim Channel, and flooded one of her boiler rooms. She later put into Smyrna for repairs.
1923 *Jan* Relieved by *Emperor of India*. Paid off and returned to

Below: *Ajax*, 1917/18. 'X' and 'Y' turrets viewed from the quarterdeck.

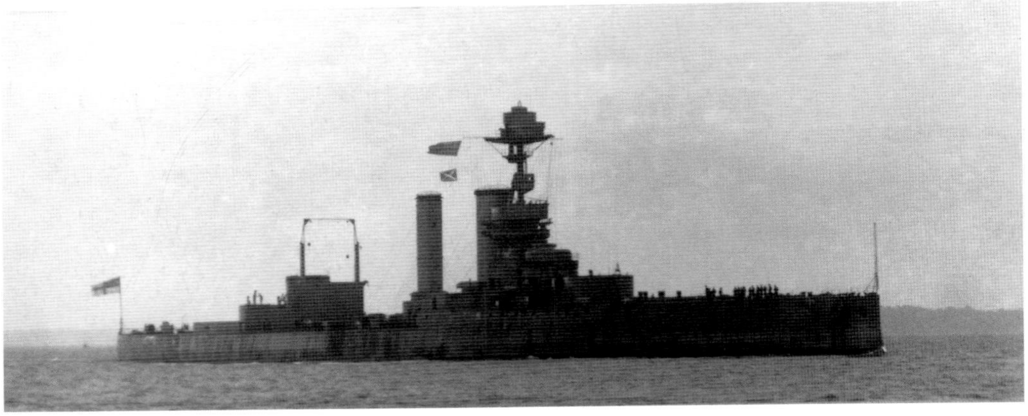

Below, right: *Centurion* as completed for service as target ship, summer 1927. To compensate the loss in weight after her turrets, etc., had been removed, the wing fuel bunkers were filled with shingle.

KING GEORGE V
Outboard profile, 1918, showing wartime modifications

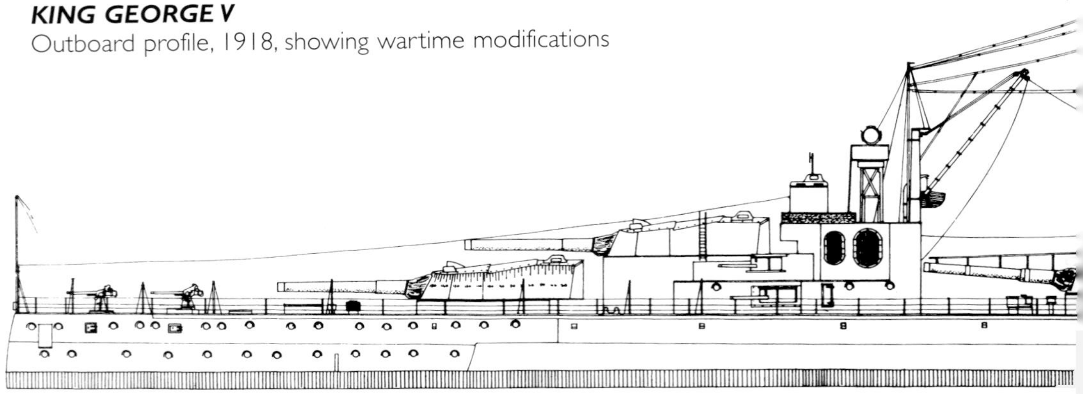

Devonport, where she was commissioned as gunnery training ship, relieving *Tiger* which was due for refit.
Feb–Nov Gunnery training ship at Portsmouth. Relieved by the monitor *Marshall Soult*, and then attached to the training establishment, HMS *Impregnable*. Based at Devonport in Reserve.
1926 *28 Sept* Paid off to Care and Maintenance.
1 Dec Placed on Disposal list.
Dec Sold to the Alloa Shipbreaking Co.
1927 *19 Jan* Arrived at Rosyth for scrapping

History: *Audacious*

1913 *15 Oct* Commissioned for service with 2nd BS Home Fleet at Portsmouth, remaining in that duty until Aug 1914.
1914 *June* Present with her sisters when 2nd BS represented Royal Navy during Kiel Canal celebrations.
Aug 2nd BS Grand Fleet.
Sept Under refit at Devonport.
27 Oct Struck a mine and sank slowly off Tory Island. Only casualty was a rating on the cruiser *Liverpool* hit by flying debris when *Audacious* finally blew up (see report).
Considered to be the worst disaster (including Jutland) in the capital ship programme throughout the entire war.

History: *Ajax*

Began sea trials in April 1913.
1913 *31 Oct* Commissioned at Devonport in 2nd BS Home Fleet.
1914 *June* With her sisters at Kiel Canal celebrations.
2nd BS Grand Fleet from Aug 1914 until March 1919.
1916 *31 May* Present at Jutland. 2nd ship in line with *Erin*, *Centurion* and *King George V.* 3rd BS Home Fleet March to June 1919. 4th BS Mediterranean Fleet June 1919 until April 1924.
Present during operations against the Bolsheviks and Turkish nationalists in the Black sea, and Sea of Marmora during 1919/20. Conveyed the deposed Sultan of Turkey from Malta to Mecca in 1923.
1924 *April* Returned to Devonport. Reserve Fleet April 1924 until Aug 1926. Paid off on to the Disposal list as part of the reduction under the naval treaties.
1926 *Oct* On Disposal list.
10 Dec Sold to the Alloa Shipbreaking Co.
14 Dec Arrived at Rosyth to be scrapped

History: *Centurion*

Began sea trials in November 1912. On the night of 9/10 December 1912 she collided with the Italian SS *Derna* (during night trials) and the Italian ship sank with all hands. *Centurion's* stem was seriously fractured for about 40 feet, which also buckled some of her frames in that area. Under repair until March 1913, during which additional supports for the framing were fitted.

1913 *22 May* Commissioned at Devonport with 2nd BS Home Fleet.
24 June With 2nd BS and 1st LCS, visited by the President of France.
1914 *June* Present at Kiel Canal celebrations.
25 June Temporarily hoisted flag of Admiral Sir George Warrender, Commander of the squadron which visited Kiel.
15 July With 1st Home Fleet, left Portland for Spithead arriving next day.
17–21 July Test mobilization and Royal Review.
20–25 July Exercises with Combined Fleets.
25 July Returned to Portland.
1915 *25 Jan* With *Iron Duke* detached to Grand Fleet at sea and then proceeded to Cromarty for small refit.
22 Feb Under refit.
1916 *May* Based at Invergordon as measure against raiders. Small refit.
31 May Battle of Jutland with 1st Division; fired only four salvoes during entire action.
Aug Small refit.
1918 *21 Nov* In the Northern line at the German surrender.
1919 *March* Transferred to the newly organized Mediterranean Fleet (4th BS) on breaking up of Grand Fleet.
31 Dec Re-commissioned at Devonport for further service in Mediterranean.
1920 *March* Temporarily placed in Reserve at Malta.
8 Aug Completed to full complement for further service with Mediterranean Fleet.
1921 *April* Paid off into Reserve at Malta.

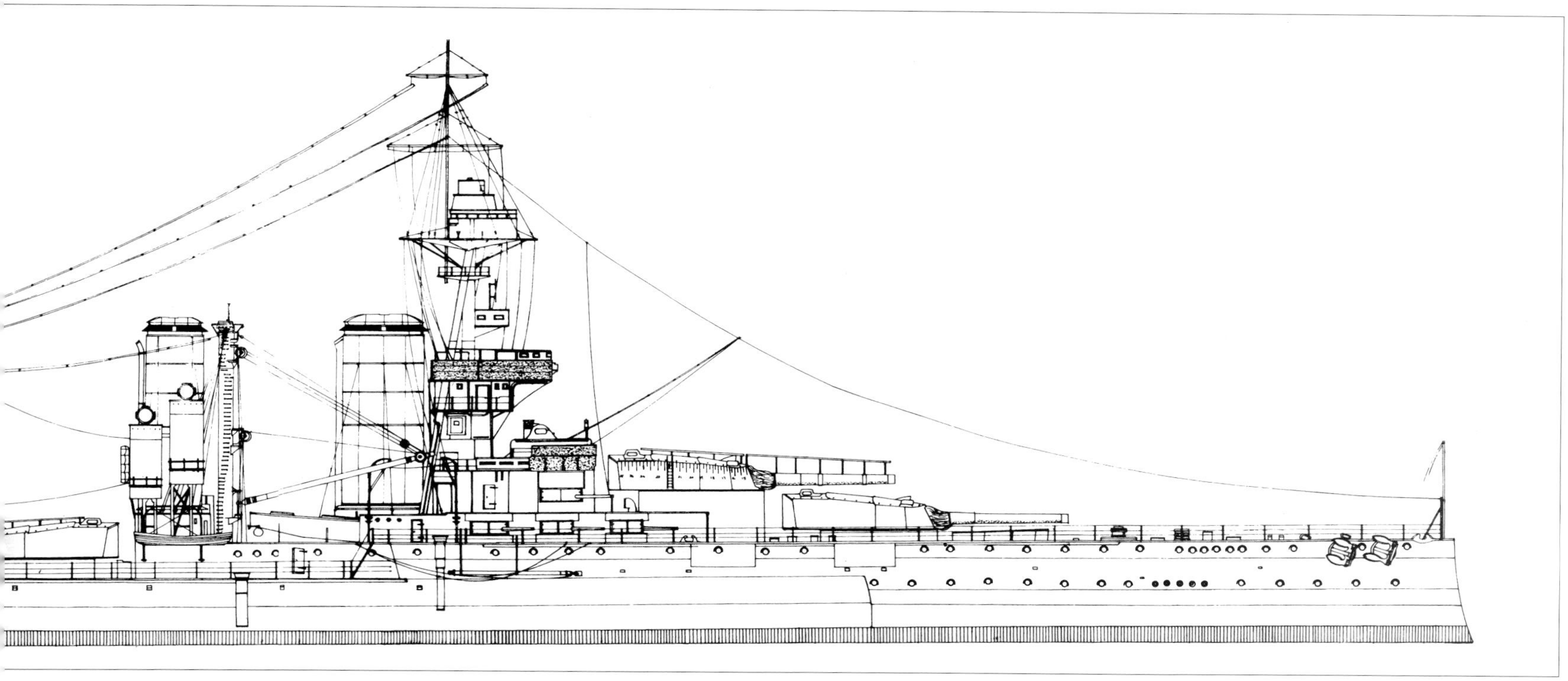

Above: *Centurion* and *Audacious* during battle practice during the summer of 1914.

1922 *1 Aug* Re-commissioned for further service with Mediterranean Fleet.
1924 *April* Paid off into Reserve at Portsmouth, relieving *Courageous* as flagship.
July Present with Reserve destroyers in Torbay for Review. From end of 1924 to 1925 transferred into Reserve based at Chatham.
1926 *April* Selected for radio-controlled target ship to replace the old battleship *Agamemnon*.
14 April Paid off into dockyard control for conversion. Until July 1927 under refit and conversion costing approximately £358,088.
1927 *20 July* Commissioned at Chatham for trials.
1928 *8 Nov* Left for spring cruise in Mediterranean.
1931 Laid up on the grounds of economy.
1932 *30 Jan* Paid off at Portsmouth.
1933 Refitted for further service after having been further dismantled for target.
1 June Target for Atlantic Fleet. Open to the public during Plymouth Navy Week.
1934 *Nov* Again under refit until Jan 1935 after her pounding as target.
17 July It was reported that she took a tremendous pounding during target practice by 8in guns of 1st CS.
1937 *20 April* Recommissioned at Devonport.
1939–40 Repair and maintenance ship. Rebuilt as dummy battleship *Anson*, of the new *King George V* class (1936 Estimates) and sailed 20,000 miles as such.
1942 Sent to Indian Ocean.
1944 *6 June* Sunk as blockship to help form breakwater for Mulberry prefabricated harbour at Verville in the American sector of Normandy beachhead.

Below: *Centurion* at Malta 1921/2. After the war *Centurion* served with the Mediterranean Fleet for a few years before being selected for use as a radio-controlled target ship. Shown here in her final state before that procedure

Iron Duke Class: 1911 ESTIMATES

Design

The programme for the 1911 Estimates was allocated sufficient funds to build four capital ships; the Board desiring a modified and slightly enlarged version of *King George V*. The legend design was to be 2,000 tons heavier than that class with an increase of 25–26 feet in length, 1 foot on the beam and 6 inches on the draught. The increase of approximately 2,000 tons was necessitated by the heavier and better-protected secondary armament, augmented torpedo armament and increased fuel capacity.

One or two of the earlier sketches proposed by Watts showed 4in guns, but other layouts featured a 6in secondary armament. These had been prepared as the result of a report in June 1909 by Admiral Mark Kerr who suggested the change, noting that most service personnel favoured the increase in calibre, both for anti-torpedo work and for close-quarters fighting. The 6in guns, although unable to pierce thick armour, would cause superficial damage to upperworks and make life very dangerous for personnel fighting the ship.

The ships' lines were rather finer than before, and freeboard was lower than in any British dreadnought with the exception of the later *Royal Sovereign* class. By careful planning the design was given a high degree of stability, the metacentric height being fixed at five feet in the load condition. When the ships completed, however, they showed even better figures; inclining experiments gave 4.9 feet and 6.6 feet in the load and deep conditions respectively. Additional length was provided for the forecastle and quarterdeck: the former would provide buoyancy against the additional weight of the secondary battery, while the latter accommodated the two main deck after 6in gun ports.

Essential differences from *King George V* were:

1. Nominal displacement increase of 2,000 tons, with an increase of 25–26 feet in length, and 6 inches on the designed mean draught.
2. Anti-torpedo armament increased from sixteen 4in to twelve 6in.
3. Torpedo tubes increased from 3 to 4.
4. Side and deck armour rearranged to some extent, and protection to secondary armament increased from 3½in (maximum) to 6in.
5. Maximum designed speed approximately a half-knot less.
6. Fuel capacity and radius increased.

Right: *Iron Duke* is launched at Portsmouth, 12 October 1912.

The four ships quickly proved their value and became highly regarded in service both at home and abroad, the design being generally conceded to have been among the most successful capital ships ever produced for the Royal Navy. Their principal weakness, of not being able efficiently to fight the 6in guns in a seaway (see below), did not seem to detract from their popularity.

BENBOW: LAUNCH FIGURES, 12 NOVEMBER 1913

Displacement: 10,640 tons
Recorded weight of hull: 8,909 tons
Draught 9ft 4in forward, 13ft 7¼in amidships, 18ft 1¼in aft
Length: 580ft 4in pp
Beam as moulded: 89ft 10¾in
Breakage at launch:
longitudinal in a distance of 386ft = 0 5/16in hog
transverse in a distance of 83ft 9in = 0 1/32in sag.

IRON DUKE: GM AND STABILITY

Based on inclining experiments, 28 February 1914

	Displacement (tons)	Draught	GM	Maximum stability	Stability vanishes at
'A' Condition (= load)*	–	28ft 8in (mean)	4.75ft	32°	60°
'B' Condition (= deep)**	–	32ft 9in	66ft	32°	70°

*Fully equipped plus 900 tons coal lower bunkers.
**Fully equipped plus 3,250 tons coal, 1,060 tons oil, reserve feed tanks full.

Armament

The main armament was practically identical with that of the *King George V* class, being mounted in five twin turrets. All the ships were completed with director control. Some of the early sketch designs provided a secondary armament of 4in guns, but alternative sketches showed a 6in battery. The final decision seems to have been taken after Admiral Fisher left the Admiralty in 1910. He had opposed anything larger than 4in for a battleship's secondary armament.

The guns were arranged so as to give concentration of fire ahead, as in *King George V*, but the superstructure positions were abandoned in favour of placing the battery in a somewhat cramped upper-deck position, behind 6in armour. The first four guns were stepped on each side to secure maximum ahead fire, the after pair bearing mainly abaft the beam. The remaining two were fitted in separate casemates on the main deck, right aft, where they would be sheltered from the blast of the after 13.5in guns.

The battery itself was positioned as far back as possible so as to reduce any risk of being 'washed out' in head seas, but as a result of space limitations in the design it could not be brought back far

Left: *Emperor of India*, looking forward from the quarterdeck and showing 'X' and 'Y' 13.5in turrets. Note the gun tampions which feature a swastika within the design.

Below: *Emperor of India* as completed, (late) 1914. This photograph was the first view of the class that the general public saw when it was published in Brassey's *Naval Annual* in 1915. Note main deck 6in guns.

enough to clear the broken water forward and, because of this and the way the guns were stepped, proved an extremely wet battery in all but a moderate seaway, which was a distinct weakness in an otherwise well-balanced design. The gun ports were fitted with shutter-type doors, but experiments showed that when the doors were dropped for action they caught the water from the ship's wash, and the crews found themselves manning the guns in several inches of water. After *Iron Duke*'s trials, however, these small doors were removed and the fitting of rubber joints and the erection of dwarf walls at the rear of the guns improved the situation somewhat.

During the early design stages it had been recognized that the battery would be undesirably congested, and was placed too far forward for practical purposes, but the retention of 'Q' main turret at upper deck level precluded any other satisfactory disposition, while to have raised this turret a deck, as in the Turkish *Erin*, would have involved a longer strake of 6in battery armour, and a slightly increased beam, necessitating a rise in displacement and cost, which was unacceptable to the Board at that date. The low position for the two main deck guns, aft, were selected in the belief that attacking destroyers would show up more clearly against the horizon from this level. These aft positions proved a failure in service, however, because they were found to be practically unfightable in anything other than a calm sea. They were later (1915) remounted on the forecastle deck amidships.

Armour

Less restricted financially, the construction department was able to offer a ratio of protection weight which at last lived up to the Board's expectations. The principal modifications compared with *King George V* were:

1. Main belt extended farther aft, but the 12in strake was less wide

EMPEROR OF INDIA: GM AND STABILITY

Based on inclining experiments, May 1926

	Displacement (tons)	Draught	GM	Maximum stability	Stability vanishes at
'A' Condition*	27,190	29ft 10in	4.65ft	30½°	58°
'B' Condition**	31,410	33ft	5.80ft	31°	65½°

*Fully equipped but with no oil fuel; 900 tons coal on board.
**Fully equipped with 1,603 tons oil plus 3,250 tons coal on board.

(8in) at the lower side. The after extension of the belt and lower side armour were increased from 2½in to 4in.
2. Maximum thickness of main bulkheads both forward and aft was reduced from 10in to 8in.
3. Extra bulkhead added aft closing after extremities of 6in and 4in lower side armour. After bulkhead was increased from 2in to 4in, but terminated at middle instead of main deck level.
4. Upper deck around 'Q' turret was increased from 1¾in to 2in.
5. Middle deck was extended beyond the forward and after barbettes.
6. Lower deck aft was increased from 2½in and 1in to 4in and 3in.
7. Maximum thickness of barbette armour remained unchanged, but was distributed differently.
8. Protection to secondary guns increased from 3in to 6in.
9. Maximum thickness of internal magazine screens reduced from 1¾in to 1½in.

The main 12in belt, which was 360 feet long, was narrower than in *King George V* and on completion it was found to be totally submerged in the deep condition, especially when the ship was trimmed one foot by the head. Total protection to the side of the ship was 16ft 1½in above the load water-line and 4ft 5½in below, in the normal condition. The 6in to 4in thicknesses extended, at the same height as the midships section, to within about 40 feet of the stem, the 6in being terminated about 60 feet before the fore barbette and continuing at 4in beyond this. The 6in and 4in aft, extended at the same height to about 20 feet from the stern, with a 6in thickness running to about 25ft abaft the after barbette and continuing at 4in after this. The 9in–6in–4in extended from the extremities of the 4in belt armour to the extremities of the 6in belt armour between middle and main decks. It was 9in over the same length as the 12in section of the belt, and 6in and 4in aft, over the same length, at corresponding thicknesses of the belt.

The upper side 8in bulkhead fitted forward was transverse and closed the extremities of the upper side armour between main and upper decks. It extended from the outer face of the forward barbette to abreast the centre of the after barbettes, between the main and middle deck levels. The main bulkheads of 6in and 4in ran obliquely inwards from the forward and after extremities of the 12in and 9in armour to the outer faces of the forward and after barbettes respectively, between lower and main decks. The 8in bulkhead aft ran obliquely inwards from abeam the inner face of the after barbette to the centre of this, between main and upper decks. The forward bulkhead closed the extremities of the belt and lower side armour between lower and main decks, and then carried above this to the upper deck; it was 4in from lower to main deck, reducing to 1½in from main to lower decks. The after inner 6in bulkhead closed the extremities of the 6in armour between lower and middle decks; the intermediate after 4in bulkhead closed the after extremities of the lower side armour between middle and main decks, while the outer aft bulkhead closed the 4in belt between lower and middle decks.

Below: *Iron Duke* completing in Portsmouth dockyard early in 1914.

The longitudinal wing bulkheads extended from the inner bottom up to the protective deck level and enclosed the boiler rooms, engine rooms and magazines. In the way of the latter compartments, the thickness increased and plates were not pierced except for boiler room passages for moving coal from adjacent bunkers, and for main electrical leads. Air space bulkheads were built into the shell and magazine rooms which were adjacent to the boiler and engine room spaces, except for the 6in magazine forward, which was separated from the forward boiler room by an athwartships coal bunker.

The forecastle deck over the secondary battery was 1in. The upper deck was 2in around 'Q' turret, 1¾in over engine rooms, 1¼in within the battery, and 1½in elsewhere. The main deck was 1½in at the ends, from the forward upper side bulkhead to the forward bulkhead, and from the after upper side bulkhead to the after intermediate bulkhead. The middle deck extended over the full length of the belt armour, with 1in on the flat and slope, 1in outside the forward barbette, 2½in aft inside the intermediate bulkhead, and 1½in outside this. The ends of the lower deck were below water from the outer bases of the forward and aft barbettes to the stem and stern respectively: 1in forward, inside the forward bulkhead, and 2½in outside this; 1in aft, inside the inner bulkhead and 2½in outside this, over the steering gear.

Turrets were 11in on the faces and sides with 4in and 3in crowns and a 2in floor. The barbettes were slightly different from one another: 'A' was given 10in on the outer face above the upper deck, with 10in to 8in from upper to main deck and 3in below this. Sides were 10in above and 4in below main deck level. The 9in inner faces above the main deck reduced to 3in once below. The outer faces were 9in above and 3in below main deck. 'B' outer face was 9in above and 3in below main deck.

Sides were 10in above and 3in below main, and inner faces reduced to 7in above and 3in below in 'Q' and 'X' turrets only. 'Y' was identical with 'A' except the inner face reduced from 9in to 7in.

The secondary battery had 6in on the sides, a 4in rear bulkhead, 2in centreline bulkhead, 2in transverse between guns, with 6in on the casemates. Sighting hoods had 3in on the sides and a 1in roof.

The conning tower was improved over *King George V*'s, and had

Below: Stern view of *Iron Duke* as opposite.

PROPELLER

Starboard quarter of *Emperor of India* on her preliminary trials for Vickers in November 1914.

a revolving hood carrying the rangefinder. Beneath this were two hexagonal compartments: the upper being the signal distributing station, and the lower an Intelligence office and auxiliary W/T room. The upper conning tower was given 11in sides and a 3in roof; the lower section had 6in sides and a 3in face and rear. The tube was 6in and 4in, and the conning tower hood was 4in on the sides and had a 3in roof. The torpedo control tower had 4in sides and a 3in roof; its tube was 4in. Funnel uptakes from middle to shelter deck were 1½in thick. Magazine screens (longitudinal) were 1in–1½in abreast forward and after magazines, 1½in abreast midships magazine and 1in abreast engine rooms, the latter forming an extension of the midships and after magazine screens.

Although the internal protective longitudinal screens were not as complete as those fitted in *Neptune*, they did at least prove adequate when *Marlborough* was hit at Jutland. She was struck amidships just abreast the forward bulkhead of the forward boiler room, about 20 feet below the water-line. The boiler room and all adjacent compartments such as the diesel, dynamo and hydraulic engine rooms were completely flooded, taking in as much as 1,000 tons. Damage to the hull side was quite extensive, about 70 feet longitudinally, and 20 feet vertically from keel to the upper edge of the middle deck. Despite this damage in what was an unfavourable position close to the main transverse bulkhead and where there was no proper anti-torpedo bulkhead, she was able by counter-flooding to right herself from a 7° list and proceed in line at a speed of 17 knots for several hours after being struck.

Right: *Iron Duke* during her trials period, end of November 1913. Note no director tower, incomplete bridgework, and no SL on second funnel.

Right: *Iron Duke* as commissioned, leaving Portsmouth early in 1914. The anti-torpedo nets have been removed.

Machinery

The main machinery consisted of two sets of Parsons turbines, which were located in three watertight compartments separated by two longitudinal bulkheads. Two main and two auxiliary condensers were fitted.

The main machinery and main condenser were fitted in the central compartments, and those for the auxiliary gear were placed in the wing compartments. Four shafts driving four propellers were provided, with the HP ahead and HP astern fitted to the outer shafts in each wing compartment; those for the LP ahead and astern were both in the same casing and were fitted to the inner shafts in the middle compartment. The turbines were of the reaction type, designed to give 300rpm at normal working conditions.

The auxiliary machinery all delivered into a common ring main which ran around the ship between screen bulkheads located below the waterline. The 13.5in turrets were served by four steam-driven, hydraulic pumping engines, the hydraulic mains being interconnected so that if one machine were put out of action, all turrets could be fed from the remaining machinery. The capstan machinery, steering gear, and minor auxiliary machinery were all interlinked. *Benbow* and *Emperor of India* were fitted with William Janney auxiliary steering gear in case of any failure in this department.

As can be seen from the steam trials, all ships proved up to expectations and delivered their designed speed of 21 knots, which was thought to be quite adequate for most service operations.

IRON DUKE CLASS: STEAM TRIALS

(only figures preserved)

25.11.1913	*Iron Duke*	MM. 8-hour full power.		
		30,040shp	305rpm	21.6kts
		32,784shp	314.1rpm	22.133kts
11.3.1914	*Marlborough*	MM 4-hour full power.		
		32,013shp	310.8rpm	21.7kts
12.3.1914	*Marlborough.*	32.342shp	312.8rpm	21.867kts
"		3,400shp		10.093kts
"		5,640shp		12.150kts
"		13,450shp	17.085kts	
22.10.1914.	*Emperor of India*	26,404shp	294.3rpm	21kts
9.10.1914.	*Benbow*	32,530shp	310.4rpm	21.5kts

Appearance Changes

Although not presenting such a handsome appearance as the *King George V* class, chiefly because of their small, narrow, round funnels, the *Iron Dukes* were nevertheless fine-looking vessels. As completed it was quite difficult to tell them apart, the only differences being: *Iron Duke* had a small rangefinder over the bridge, but *Marlborough* did not. *Benbow* had a small triangular strut to the derrick stump, but *Emperor of India* did not have this. *Emperor of India* was the only unit not to have a sternwalk as completed.

1914 Topgallant masts (where fitted) removed in August.

1915–16 After main deck 6in guns removed and remounted in port and starboard casemates on forecastle deck amidships, slightly abaft after pair of battery guns. Original casemates not plated over until later. Director control fitted for 6in guns, port and starboard lower bridge in *Iron Duke*, upper bridge in others of the class. Torpedo control and concentration post added close below control top. Topmast further reduced in height. Prominent nets fitted around lower control top in *Benbow* and *Emperor of India* for experiments in range-baffling.

1916–17 Control top was enlarged and modified. Medium-base rangefinder added over conning tower. Two pairs of SL (ex middle bridge) remounted on 'X' turret in *Benbow* late in 1916 for use with turret in night action experiments.

Emperor of India fitted with gear for towing a kite balloon during latter part of 1916, and a crew to serve this equipment were given a three-week course at Southampton. Total weight of just over 100 tons added to deck protection alter Jutland, mainly over magazine areas: *Marlborough* fitted July 1916, *Benbow* July to August, *Iron Duke* and *Emperor of India* October to December. Rangefinder baffles fitted to tripod legs, fore funnel and derrick stump, and in some cases to topmasts.

1917–18 Deflection scales painted on 'B' and 'X' or 'B' and 'Y' turrets. Range clocks fitted to faces of control tops and at rear of after superstructure. Twin 24in signalling lamps replaced by 36in lamps and improved control arrangements. SL platform on second funnel replaced by 'coffee-box' control towers: 2 port and starboard, with single 36in lamp in each. After tower on each side higher than forward fitting. Two 36in lamps mounted port and starboard on after superstructure. Clinker funnel cap

Below: *Marlborough* in the summer of 1918, practising with her kite balloon.

IRON DUKE CLASS: PARTICULARS, AS COMPLETED

Construction

	Dockyard	Laid Down	Launched	Began Trials	Completed
Iron Duke:	Portsmouth DY	15 Jan 1912	12 Oct 1912	25 Nov 1913	March 1914
Marlborough:	Devonport DY	25 Jan 1912	24 Oct 1912	10 March 1914	June 1914
Benbow:	Beardmore	30 May 1912	12 Nov 1913	11 Oct 1914	Oct 1914
Emperor of India:	Vickers	31 May 1912	27 Nov 1913	21 Oct 1914	Nov 1914.

Displacement (tons)
26,100 (load), 31,400 (deep).

Dimensions
Length: 580ft 4in pp, 614ft 3in wl, 623ft 9in oa (*Iron Duke, Benbow*); 623ft oa (*Marlborough*); 622ft 9in oa (*Emperor of India*)
Beam: 90ft 1in
Draught: 28ft 8in (load), 32ft 9in (deep)
Height of main guns above wl: 'A' 30ft 6in; 'B' 40ft; 'Q' 24ft; 'X' 32ft 6in; 'Y' 23ft.
Height of CT vision slits above wl: 48ft 3in
Height of fore funnel: 80ft

Armament*
Ten 13.5in 45cal Mk V; 100rpg
Twelve 6in Mk VII; 130rpg
One 12pdr (8cwt) field gun
Four 3pdr; 64rpg
Five Maxim MG
Ten Lewis guns
Four 21in torpedo tubes; twenty torpedoes Mk I, Mk II, later Mk IV.

Director control**
Three.

Armour
Main belt: 12in–9in–8in
Bulkheads: 6in–4in
Upper side bulkheads: 8in
Forward bulkheads: 4in–1½in
Barbettes: 10in–9in–8in–4in–3in
Turrets: 11in–4in–3in
Conning tower: 11in–6in–3in
Decks: forecastle 1in, upper 2in–1¼in, main 1½in, middle 2½in–1 in, lower 2½in–1in
Uptakes: 1½in
Magazine screens: 1½in–1 in
Estimated total weight: 7,700 tons.

Machinery
Parsons direct-drive turbines, four 3-bladed propellers
Boilers: eighteen Yarrow (eighteen Babcock & Wilcox *Iron Duke, Benbow*); three boiler rooms, six boilers in each
Heating surface: 63,756–69,840sq ft
Grate area: 1,180–1,819sq ft
Propeller diameter: 9ft 9in outer; 9ft 9in inner
Propeller pitch: 8ft 6in outer; 9ft inner
Developed area: outer 33sq ft; inner 42sq ft
Length of boiler rooms: 38ft forward, 38ft 0¼in amidships, 38ft aft
Length of engine rooms: 70ft 6in
Designed SHP: 29,000 = 21 knots
Fuel: 900 tons coal normal, 3,250 tons max.; 1,050 tons oil plus 550 tons emergency tanks
Coal consumption per day (tons): 135 tons at 12 knots; 325 tons at 16.4 knots
Radius of action (oil added): 3,800nm at full speed; 4,500nm at 20 knots; 5,700nm at 18 knots; 7,300nm at 15 knots; 8,100nm at 12 knots
Auxiliary machinery: one 150kw diesel, two 200kW steam diesels, one 200kW reciprocating diesel.

*Two 3in AA; 150rpg added later, see Appearance Changes.
**Replaced by eight 36in: two charthouse, four after funnel towers, two shelter deck aft.

Ship's boats
Pinnaces (steam): two 50ft
Pinnaces (sail): one 36ft
Launches (steam): one 42ft
Cutters: three 32ft
Whalers: three 27ft
Gigs: one 30ft
Skiff dinghies: one 16ft
Balsa rafts: one 13ft 6in.

Searchlights***
Sixteen 24in: two pairs bridge, one pair middle bridge, one pair lower bridge, two pairs lower platform rear second funnel, two pairs after superstructure.

Rangefinder positions (1918)
Two 25ft, one 18ft, one 15ft, one 9ft main turrets; one 15ft, one 9ft forward superstructure; one 15ft after torpedo control tower; two 9ft forebridge; two 6ft 6in HA.

Battle signal stations****
Two enclosed, port and starboard, at frame 108.

Anchors
Three 145cwt stockless (bower and sheet), one 60cwt stockless stern, one 16cwt Admiralty, one 12cwt Admiralty.

Wireless (1918)
Main office: *Iron Duke* Types 1–34, 35X; *Marlborough* Types 1–16, 32; *Benbow* Types 1–16; *Emperor of India* Types 1–35X
Second office: Type 2 (fitted later in *Benbow*)
Fire control office: Type 31
Additional office in *Iron Duke*: Type 9.

Complement
***Iron Duke*:** 1,102 (1914); 1,115–1,181 (1919)
***Marlborough*:** 925 (1914); 1,180 (1918)
***Benbow*:** 941 (1914); 1,099 (1918)
***Emperor of India*:** 1,012 (1914).

Cost
***Iron Duke*:** £1,945,824
***Marlborough*:** £2,043,437.

***The gun director was fitted aloft in the director tower with 'X' as directing turret. The 6in guns had two directors with 'follow the pointer' gear and flexible voice pipes for night firing.
****Each provided with lockers and equipment for working signals through W/T trunking between upper and forecastle deck levels. In peacetime signalling was conducted from the forward shelter deck in an office on the port side at frame 96.

Below: *Marlborough* at Devonport as completed, 6 June 1914. Note simple bridgework, twin 24in SL, director fire control on foretop, and small sea doors to faces of 6in casemates (later removed).

added in *Emperor of India* only. Long signal strut fitted to forward starfish below control top in *Emperor of India* and *Iron Duke*. W/T spreaders raised considerably in all except *Emperor of India*. Rangefinder baffles (where fitted) removed in all.

1918 Flying-off platforms fitted on 'B' and 'Q' turrets in all.

1919 Deflection scales on turrets painted out. Range clocks fitted over control top and on after superstructure in *Emperor of India*. Aircraft runways removed, although platforms remained. Clinker screen in *Emperor of India* removed early in 1919.

Other changes made during and after the war were:

1. Enlargement of transmitting station because of updating of W/T.
2. Extra working positions for flood valve controls in warhead magazine.
3. A portion of the ring bulkheads cut away in 'X' and 'B' turrets.
4. Various hatches enlarged (below deck only).
5. Ventilation improvements, with special attention to those serving boiler and engine rooms.
6. Galley extended by removing part of coal bunker in that area.
7. Anti-flash protection to 6in supply was modified.
8. Arrangements for protecting shells from damp improved.
9. Improvements for access to bridges, etc.

Above: *Emperor of India* 1918, during inclining experiments, which established the ship's metacentric height and stability.

Opposite: Late war appearance of *Iron Duke*, *Canada* and *Benbow* anchored in Scapa Flow 1918.

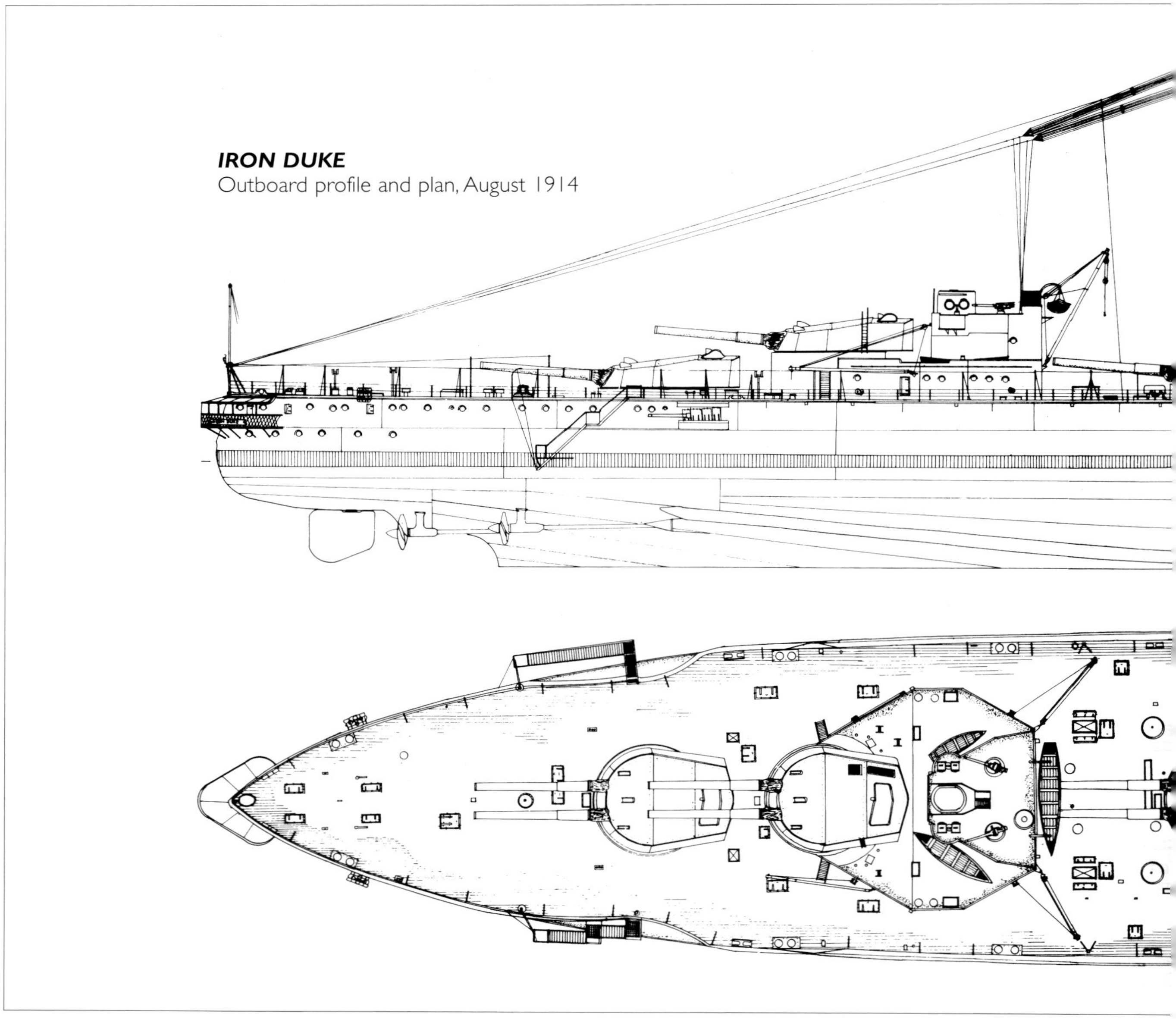

1920–1 12ft rangefinder added over torpedo control tower in after superstructure. Range clocks added in *Benbow* and *Marlborough* as in other two. SL taken from after superstructure and remounted on newly fitted mainmast. SL removed from bridges in all except *Iron Duke*. Aircraft platform removed from 'B' turret in *Marlborough*. Sternwalk fitted in *Emperor of India*. Fore topgallant mast fitted in all. Short mainmast added on after superstructure in all. W/T spreader removed in all. Topmast in *Benbow* and *Iron Duke* was taller than in the other two vessels. Long forward struts at fore starfish removed from *Iron Duke*.
1922–3 Long-base rangefinder fitted to rear of 'X' turret in all.
1924–6 Range clocks removed from over control top, but retained on after superstructure until 1929. 3in AA replaced by 4in.

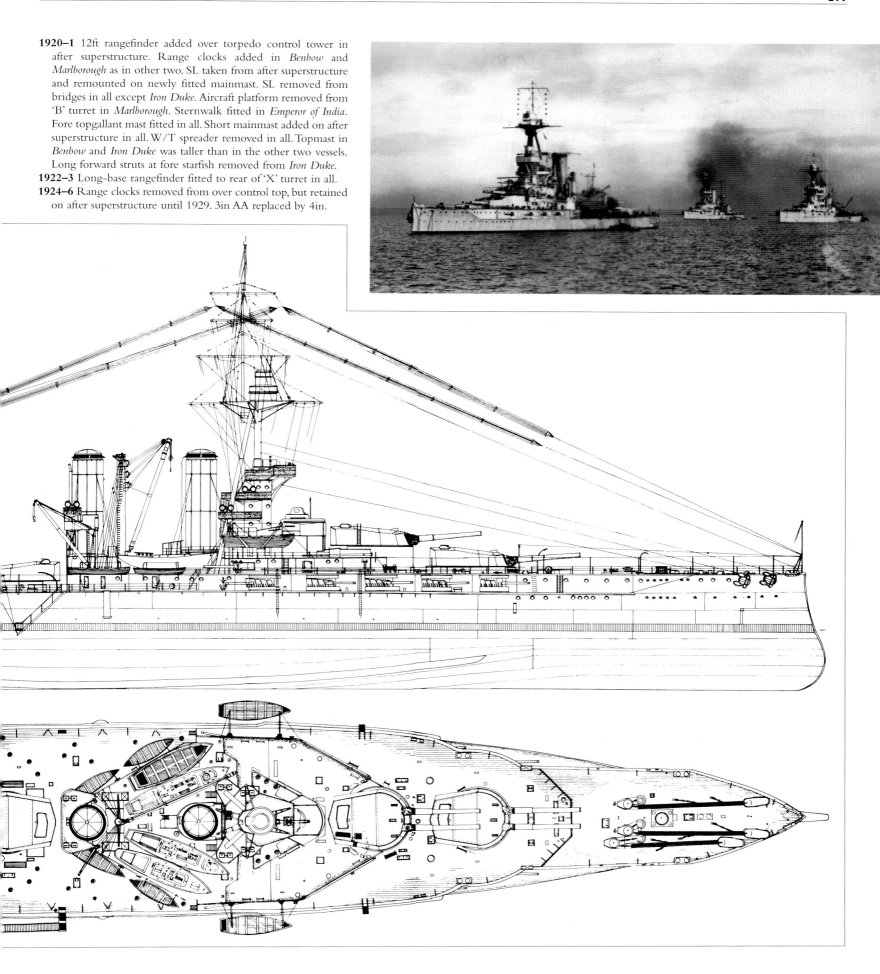

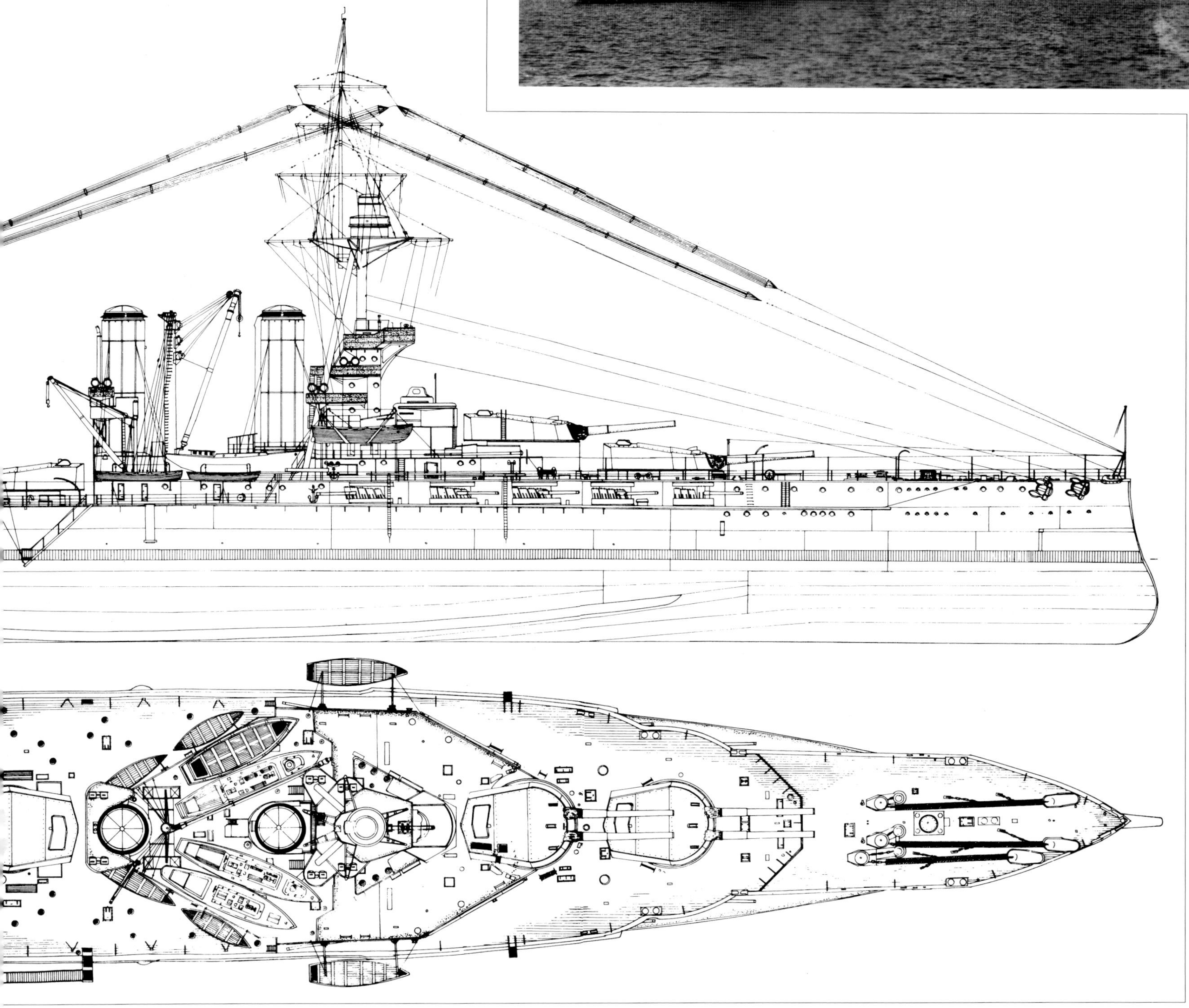

1927 Extra pair of 4in fitted to forward superstructure in *Marlborough*. Torpedo control tower on after superstructure removed from *Iron Duke* and *Marlborough*. SL removed from *Marlborough*'s mainmast, but platform retained. Aircraft platforms removed from 'B' turret in *Iron Duke*, 'Q' turret in *Marlborough*.

1928–9 *Iron Duke* refitted from May 1928 until May 1929. Small rangefinder added on high raised platform on after superstructure. Extra 4in AA added as in *Marlborough*. Searchlights removed from mainmast, but platform retained. Aircraft platform removed from roof of 'Q' turret.

1931 *Benbow* placed on Disposal list. *Emperor of India* and *Marlborough* from 1931.

1931–2 *Marlborough* used for experiments in magazines and shell

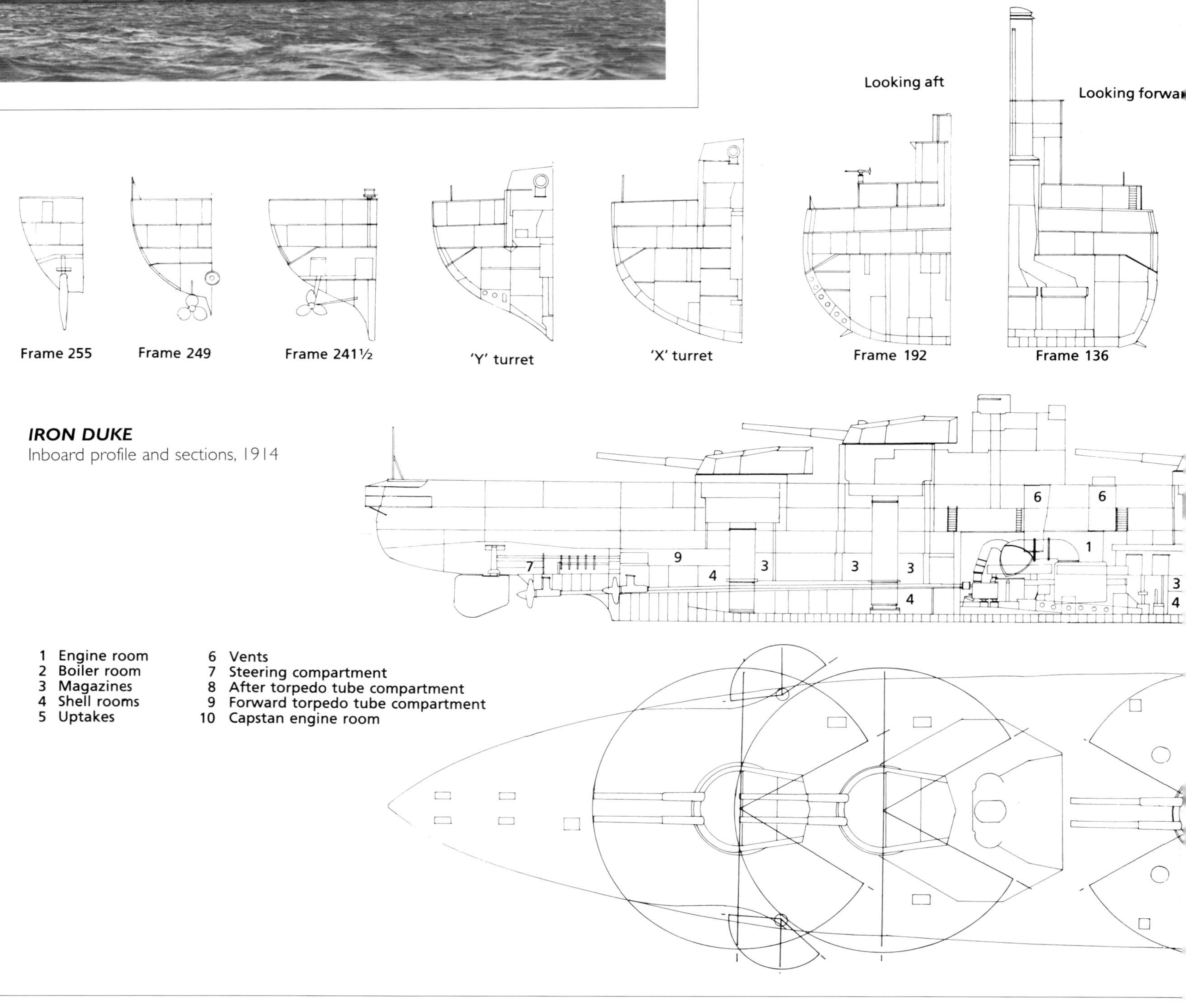

IRON DUKE
Inboard profile and sections, 1914

1 Engine room
2 Boiler room
3 Magazines
4 Shell rooms
5 Uptakes
6 Vents
7 Steering compartment
8 After torpedo tube compartment
9 Forward torpedo tube compartment
10 Capstan engine room

space ventilation. Reduced and full charges were exploded in these areas to determine how doors and bulkheads would take the strain. 'A' magazine main bulkhead was badly twisted, showing that improvements were necessary in order to secure safety within these areas. The data gathered enabled much improvement in the design of the five *King George V* class of the 1936 Estimates.

1932 *Iron Duke* only ship of class left. She was demilitarized (see notes) and used as training ship. 'B' and 'Y' main turrets were removed but barbettes were retained. Two 4.7in AA guns added on quarterdeck. Experiments with a range of small guns fitted on crown of 'B' barbette during this period (1932–1940). Rangefinder on after superstructure replaced by HA director. 4.7in guns on quarterdeck removed from August 1935.

1939 Twin 5.25in dual-purpose fitted abaft 'Y' turret.

1939–45 Used as depot ship and base AA ship at Scapa Flow. Additional AA guns added during the war. Attacked in October 1939 and hit by bombs near the engine room. She was flooded within that area and in great danger of sinking, but managed to move slowly away and beach herself where she remained for the rest of her life. She was still used as depot and base defence ship in this position

Proposed Bulging

In 1927 the DNC's department suggested that the class would benefit from the fitting of anti-torpedo bulges similar to those fitted in the *Royal Sovereigns* and *Queen Elizabeths*. *Emperor of India* was used as an example for basing calculations on displacements

Opposite: *Marlborough* in Scapa Flow during the last months of 1918. Note aircraft runways on 'B' and 'Q' turret tops (*Revenge* in background).

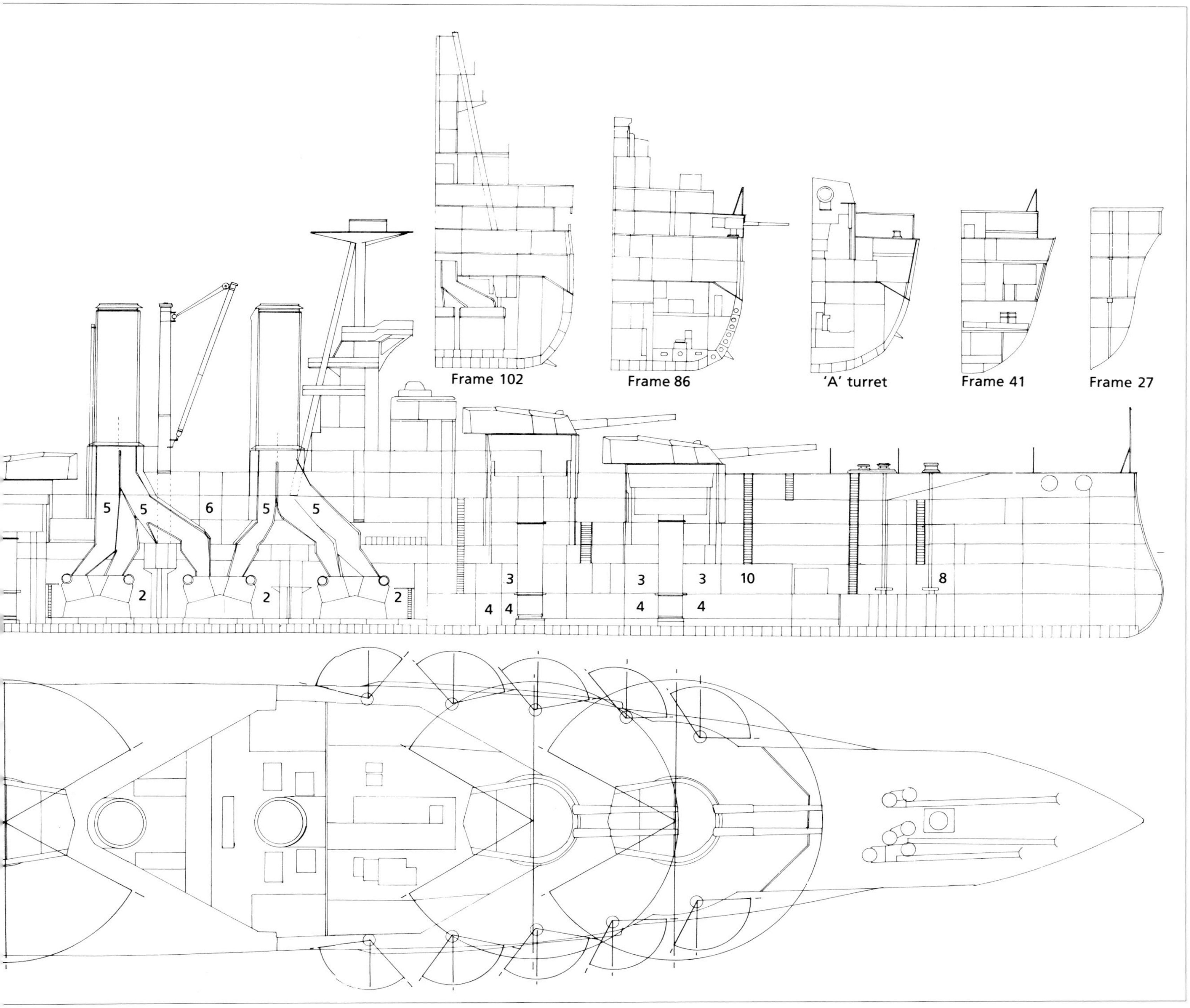

Above, left: *Marlborough* at Scapa Flow in the winter of 1916/17.

Above, right: *Benbow* leads *Marlborough* and *Iron Duke* (taken from *Emperor of India*) during a patrol in the winter of 1918. Note limited visibility which the gunlayers had to endure in these conditions while patrolling in the North Sea.

Right: *Marlborough* at sea in the early months of 1918. Note additional rangefinder on conning tower hood.

for any such addition, the figures being taken from inclining experiments carried out in May 1926.

It was calculated that the bulges would add 3,860 tons to the displacement, bringing the deep condition of the ship to approximately 35,000 tons, and an increase in beam of five feet (95ft) which was considered adequate, and in line with other ships that had been treated in a similar fashion.

Further experiments and calculations were demanded, but shortly after the proposals had been forwarded for approval to the Board, all plans were cancelled for three reasons:

1. The vessels were due for replacement by 1931/32 under the Washington Treaty.
2. Cost of the proposal.
3. Not economical, owing to the length of time the vessels would be out of service.

Demilitarization of *Iron Duke*

The class were placed on the Disposal list, with the exception of *Iron Duke* which was kept for use as seagoing gunnery training ship. She was demilitarized from November 1931 until being undocked on 21 September 1932. Basic deductions were:

Main belt 2,516 tons
Backing 72
Conning tower 117
'B' and 'Y' turrets 1,200
Ammunition for above 320
Torpedoes 13
Boilers (no figures available)

Total displacement loss was 4,258 tons, but 202 tons was reinstated by the fitting of pom-pom directors and a 6in gun on 'B' barbette crown. After this refit *Iron Duke* proved an excellent training ship, and she was used for many experiments to compare her with her condition before demilitarization. She was undocked in September 1932 and sent for sea steam trials.

Emperor of India as target

Early in 1931 when *Benbow*, *Marlborough* and *Emperor of India* were placed on the Disposal list, the latter was sanctioned for use as a fleet target ship. On Monday 8 June 1931, she was taken out of dock and proceeded under own steam from Portsmouth. Passing through the outer Owers Shoal, she scraped the seabed and stuck fast. Unsuccessful attempts were made to free her and it was decided to drop anchor, the ship being slightly inclined. Next day, stores, ammunition, extra fuel, spare valves, etc., were taken off in an endeavour to free her. Draught was 28ft 3in forward, 28ft 6in aft. The weather was detrimental to salvage operations and it was decided to leave her where she was and proceed with the firing tests.

On 10/11 June 1931 she was hit twelve times during the shoot, being holed twice below the water-line, which caused considerable damage and extensive flooding. After the shoot, she was examined and it was clear that salvage operations would be difficult because of her condition. One shell had struck the starboard side near station 123, and pierced the lower edge of the armour making a hole 2 feet long by 1ft 8in wide. Inside, the shell had pierced the inner bottom and sloping deck and torn away the bulkhead at station 122. After passing through the bunkers and piercing the longitudinal bulkhead, the shell entered 'B' boiler room and exploded near the forward boiler top. The explosion caused extensive damage, opening the boiler house and its bunker to the sea.

The other shell burst close to the ship's side, 15 feet below the water-line, and produced the same effect as a mine explosion. The outer plating and inner bottom were ripped open, the outer bulkhead and one of the engine rooms were holed and subsequently

IRON DUKE: COMPARISON OF PARTICULARS, 1926 AND 1932

	Deep	Legend	Light
1926			
Displacement (tons)	31,400	27,190	25,850
Draught	33ft 10in	29ft 10in	28ft 6in
Coal (tons)	3,250	900	–
Oil (tons)	1,600	–	–
Stability	31°	30½°	30°
1932			
Displacement (tons)	23,115	22,320	20,555
Draught	26ft 2in	25ft 5in	23ft 10in
Coal (tons)	275	275	–
Oil (tons)	1,596	800	–
Stability	37½°	36½°	36°

IRON DUKE: STEAM TRIALS, 1932

Displacement: 22,885 tons
Draught: 24ft 9¾in forward, 26ft 9⅛in aft
Wind: 1–2
Sea: Slight swell
Course: Measured mile at Tolland

First run	242rpm	14,563shp	17.062 knots
Second run	241.5rpm	14,469shp	18.127 knots
Third run	241.5rpm	14,548shp	16.925 knots
Fourth run	243rpm	14,749shp	18.237 knots

Tactical diameter: Helm put over at 15° which gave a circle of 700 yards, taking 5 minutes and 45 seconds to turn 180°.

Left: *Emperor of India* anchored in Scapa Flow during the spring of 1918. Her wartime additions can be seen: improved director fire control, enlarged foretop, increased superstructure, funnel cap (only unit of class to receive this), SL towers around second funnel and deflection scales on 'B' and 'X' turrets.

Left: *Benbow* anchored lazily in the Mediterranean, 1925.

Below: *Marlborough* enters Grand Harbour, Malta in January 1922 for four years further service with Mediterranean Fleet. Note the light paintwork (Mediterranean colours).

flooded. The tops of the lubricating tanks and gear near this were completely destroyed. A hole, 8 feet long by 7 feet high, was made, the seams and joints in the area opening up, as did those near the bilge keel. Much was learned about subdivision and under-water protective qualities as a result of these hits, and it was concluded that the armour belt in nearly all British battleships was not deep enough to keep out steeply diving shells.

Emperor of India was eventually raised, the operation providing valuable experience that was later called upon when the German

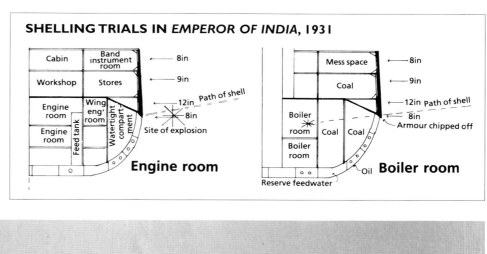

SHELLING TRIALS IN *EMPEROR OF INDIA*, 1931

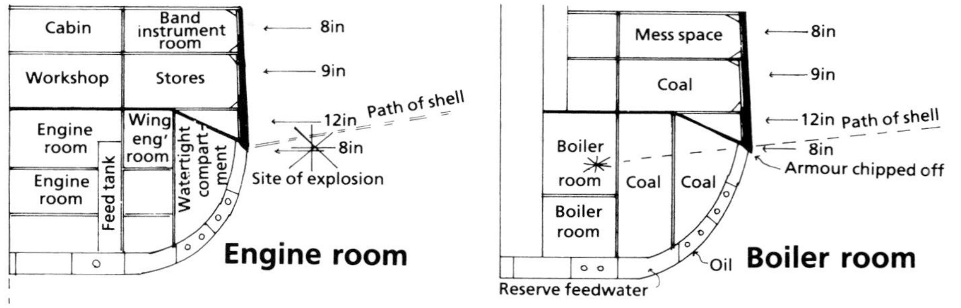

battlefleet was raised from the bottom of Scapa Flow during the 1930s.

History: *Emperor of India*

Originally was to have been named *Delhi* to commemorate the change of capital in India, and the King's visit in 1911–12. Renamed *Emperor of India* in Oct 1913. Began trials in Nov 1914.

1914 *Nov* Commissioned at Barrow-in-Furness as 2nd flagship 4th BS.

10 Dec Joined Grand Fleet at Scapa. With Grand Fleet until March 1919; 2nd flagship until June 1916, 2nd flag 1st BS from June 1916. Not present at Battle of Jutland, being under refit. March 1919 until March 1926 with the Mediterranean Fleet. 4th BS to Nov 1924 and 2nd flagship until Jan 1921. From Nov 1922

Above: *Benbow* at anchor in the Mediterranean, 1925.

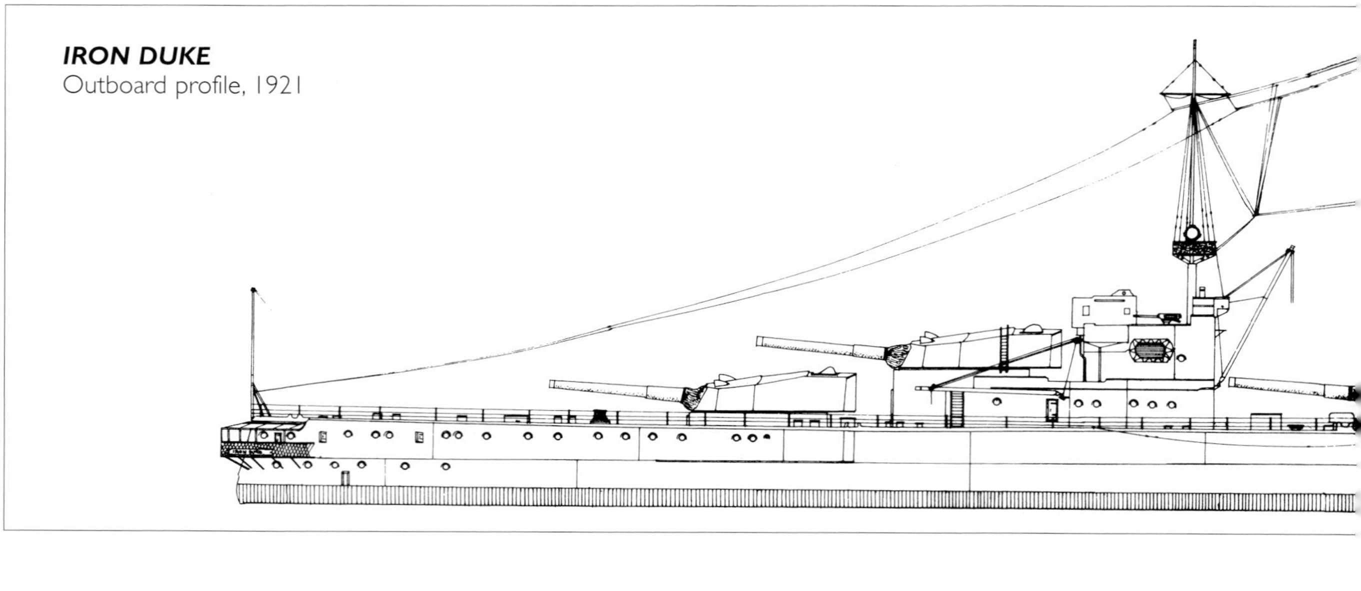

to Nov 1924 2nd flagship of 3rd BS. Operations against the Bolsheviks and Turkish rebels in the Black Sea.
1922 *Feb* Relieved by *Marlborough* and paid off at Devonport for extensive refit.
1923 *Feb* She was a unit of the squadron sent to Smyrna to demonstrate against the Turkish demands for evacuation of that port by all foreign warships.
1924 *Nov* 4th BS became 3rd BS; 3rd BS transferred to Atlantic Fleet.
1926 3rd BS Atlantic Fleet; Squadron flagship from June 1929.
1927 *July* Refit at Devonport (until Sept).
1929 *June* Relieved by *Benbow* as squadron flagship.
1931 *Jan* Relieved as flagship by *Marlborough*.
22 Jan Paid off into Disposal list. Used as gunnery target vessel (see notes). Placed on sale list.
1932 *Feb* Sold to the Alloa Shipbreaking Co.
16 Feb Arrived at Rosyth.

History: *Marlborough*

1914 *16 June* Commissioned at Devonport relieving *Collingwood* as flagship 1st BS, 2nd flag Home Fleet until August 1914.
1st BS Grand Fleet until March 1919, being Squadron flagship until Feb 1917 and then 2nd flag from that date.
1916 *31 May* Battle of Jutland. She was 21st ship in line of battle after the deployment and shortly after enemy battleships were sighted she opened fire.

At 18.00 sighted 5th BS (*Barham*, *Malaya*, *Valiant* and *Warspite*) and at 18.16–18.21 fired five salvoes at a *Kaiser*-class battleship from 9,000–11,000 yards scoring four hits with fifth salvo. At 18.24–18.29 she opened fire on a four-funnelled cruiser, and at 18.39 was again engaging a ship of the *Kaiser* class, firing only one salvo from 13,000 yards before thick smoke and mist obscured target.

At approximately 18.54 she was struck by a torpedo on the starboard side near the forward boiler house. Although taking a list of 7° she remained in the battle line at 17 knots for 7½ hours, avoiding three more torpedo attacks. At 19.03 she engaged a disabled four-funnelled cruiser firing four salvoes and securing hits with the third and fourth.

At 19.12–19.14 she fired fourteen rapid salvoes at a battleship of the *König* class from 10,750 yards, securing hits and forcing the German ship to turn out of line. At 19.12 she fired a torpedo at cruiser. 19.19 found her engaging a flotilla of destroyers with one full salvo and then using her big guns, hitting two of the ships.

At 19.33 she again turned away to avoid three torpedo attacks.

At approximately 20.00 she was forced to reduce speed because of the strain on her bulkheads after the torpedo damage.

At 02.45 Admiral Burney transferred his flag to *Revenge* (1 June). On the 2nd, because of the bad weather, and her pumps slowly becoming choked by the overload, there was great anxiety about ship's condition, but she finally reached the Humber and was towed in the rest of the way, to be repaired in floating dock at Tyne.
29 July Rejoined Grand Fleet.
1917 *Feb* Relieved as flagship by *Revenge* and became 2nd flagship.
May Relieved of this position by *Emperor of India*, she became private ship for a short spell.

Below: *Benbow* anchored off Rosyth in late 1918.

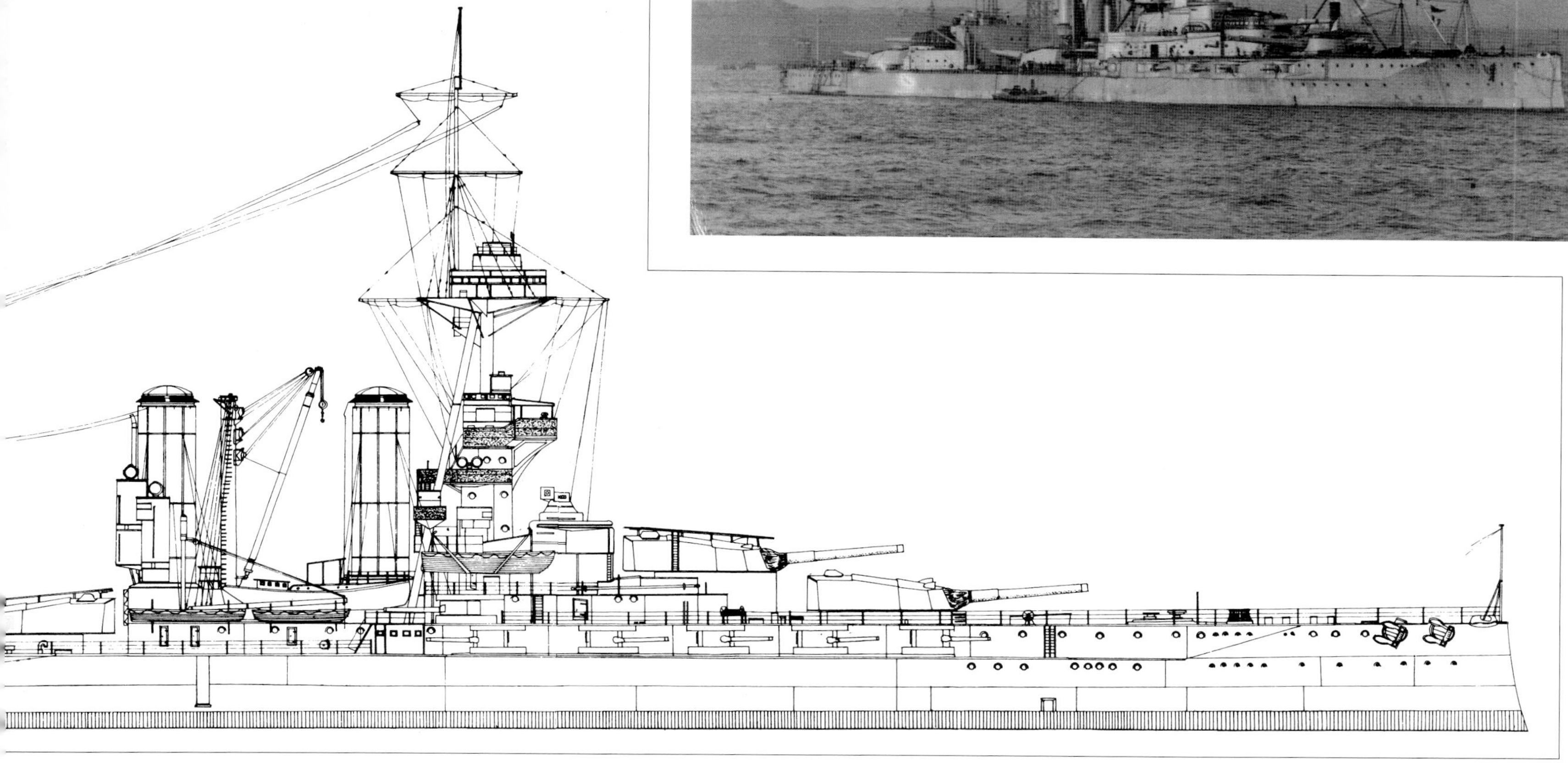

Opposite: *Benbow*'s 'Q' and 'Y' 13.5in turrets open fire on Panderma.

Below: *Iron Duke* enters Malta still showing her range scales on 'B' and 'X' turrets, 27 March 1919.

1919 *12 March* Commissioned at Devonport for 4th BS Mediterranean Fleet, remaining until October 1920. Black Sea operations against Bolsheviks and relieved *Temeraire* of her position.

1920 *Oct* Relieved by *King George V* and paid off at Devonport for refit. Placed in Reserve at Devonport until January 1922. Extensive refit from February 1921 until January 1922, the first major refit since completion.

1922 *Jan* Returned to Mediterranean Fleet relieving *Emperor of India* until March 1926; 4th BS until November 1925; 2nd flag until Oct 1922; 3rd BS from November 1924; 4th BS became 3rd BS on 1 November 1924. 3rd BS transferred to Atlantic Fleet as boys' training squadron March 1926. Atlantic Fleet March 1926 until June 1931; Squadron flagship January to June 1931.

Relieved *Emperor of India* as Squadron flagship and was thereafter the only unit in the Squadron. Of the original four ships in the squadron, *Iron Duke* was detached from May 1929 (see *Iron Duke*) while *Emperor of India* was used as target ship, and both *Benbow* and *Marlborough* were for the Disposal list although *Marlborough*'s disposal was postponed for short period.

1931 *5 June* Finally paid off for special experiments prior to

disposal. Experimental Service to May 1932. Used for internal explosion experiments July to August 1931 and then aerial bombing tests from spring of 1932. The internal tests were to determine the strength of the watertight compartments and hatches with full charges being placed in the vicinity of the magazines. On 21 April 1931 a full charge was exploded in 'B' magazine and twisted and buckled 'A' magazine's bulkhead beyond the safety margin.

1932 *May* Placed on Disposal list after tests and sold to Alloa Shipbreaking Co. almost immediately.

25 June Arrived at Rosyth for scrapping

History: *Benbow*

1914 *Nov* Commissioned at Dalmuir; relieved *Dreadnought* as flagship of 4th BS.

10 Dec Joined Grand Fleet at Scapa Flow; remained with fleet until March 1919. Flagship of 4th BS until 1 June 1916 and then private ship in 1st BS.

1916 *31 May* Present at Battle of Jutland.

1919 *March* On breaking up of Grand Fleet transferred to Mediterranean Fleet until March 1926; 4th BS until Nov 1924; temporary flag (2nd) 1921/22. 3rd BS from Nov 1924. Operations against Bolsheviks in the Black Sea April 1919 to June 1920, and against Turkish Nationalists in the Sea of Marmora.

1922 Refit at Malta.

Further operations against Turkish Nationalists, Sept to Oct 1922. It is reported that she landed some 6in guns at Kilid Bahr in Sept 1922 for the defence of the Dardanelles which was a neutral zone during these operations, but this cannot be verified.

1924 *1 Nov* 4th BS (*Iron Dukes*) became 3rd BS after transfer of *Queen Elizabeth* class as 1st BS to Mediterranean.

3rd BS Atlantic Fleet March 1926 until Sept 1930.

1928 *12 May* Relieved *Iron Duke* as Squadron flagship. Paid off into Devonport Dockyard for extensive refit which was postponed as a result of impending disposal.

1930 *Sept* Placed on sale list at Devonport.

1931 *March* Sold to Metal Industries (Alloa Shipbreaking Co., at the time).
5 April Arrived at Rosyth for scrapping

History: *Iron Duke*

Launched by Duchess of Wellington 12 October 1912. Began trials in November 1913.

1914 *10 March* Commissioned at Portsmouth to relieve *Neptune* as flagship CinC Home Fleet until Aug 1914. Aug 1914 until March 1919 Grand Fleet flagship until Jan 1917 then private ship from that date. Flagship of Admiral Sir John Jellicoe hoisted at Scapa Flow in Aug 1914.
1916 *12 Jan* Collided with oil tanker *Prudentia* which sank.
31 May Battle of Jutland. Engaged a *König*-class battleship at 12,000 yards and is stated to have obtained six hits. Later engaged a second ship of that class and a battlecruiser at 15,400 yards.
28 Nov Admiral Beatty relieved Jellicoe as CinC Grand Fleet and *Iron Duke* served as his flagship until Jan 1917 when his flag was hoisted in *Queen Elizabeth*.

Mediterranean Fleet March 1919 until March 1926; Fleet flagship until Nov 1924 then flagship 3rd BS later becoming 2nd flag (end of Nov). Black Sea operations April to June 1919.

Further operations against Turkish rebels in Asia Minor from Sept to Oct 1922. Flagship of British naval force evacuating refugees from Smyrna during Turkish occupation in Sept 1922. Conference between Allied forces and Turkish Nationalists to settle Greco-Turkish troubles held aboard *Iron Duke* at Mudania in Oct 1922.
1924 *Nov* Relieved as Fleet flagship by *Queen Elizabeth* and became flagship 3rd BS and 2nd BS.
1926 *March* 3rd BS transferred to Atlantic Fleet as boys' seagoing training squadron.
Flagship 3rd BS Atlantic Fleet March 1926 until May 1928.
1928 *30 May* Relieved as flagship by *Benbow* and paid off into Devonport Dockyard for refit until May 1929.
1929 *30 May* Recommissioned as seagoing gunnery training ship until Nov 1931. Demilitarized at Devonport Nov 1931 to Sept 1932 (see notes on demilitarization).
1932 *4 Oct* Recommissioned at Devonport for further service as gunnery training ship until Sept 1939.
1935 *16 July* Silver Jubilee Fleet Review at Spithead.
1937 *20 May* Coronation Fleet Review.
1939 *Sept* Became AA and Depot Ship at Scapa Flow on outbreak of war. Scapa Flow Defence Ship until March 1946.
17 Oct Badly damaged by bombs during raids on Scapa and beached off Lyness in six fathoms. Later refloated and taken to Long Hope where she was again beached and used as a Depot Ship as before. Sold as she lay to Metal Industries.
1946 *19 April* Refloated.
19 Aug Towed to Faslane for scrapping.
1948 *Sept* Towed to Clydebank to complete demolition.

Opposite, top: Looking aft from *Emperor of India* as *Benbow* and others follow, 1917.

Opposite, lower: *Benbow* opens fire with her starboard 6in secondary battery during the bombardment of Panderma in 1920.

Below: *Iron Duke*: as demilitarized, 14 July 1935, and showing herself at the Jubilee Fleet Review for HM King George V.

Tiger: 1911 ESTIMATES

Design

The single battlecruiser provided for in the 1911 Estimates was to be the last battlecruiser laid down for the Royal Navy under the pre-war programme, and the last of its type for which Philip Watts was responsible as DNC.

The Board had originally required a vessel along the same lines as *Queen Mary*, but updated. Watts, however, was not content with the idea, and proposed three new sketch designs to the Controller on 31 July 1911. The essential features of the designs, compared to *Queen Mary*, were as shown in the table. The Committee met on 14 August to approve one of the proposed designs, and were quickly in favour of the 'A1' layout. Watts pointed out that in the 'A' and 'A1' designs, four turrets were disposed, two at each end of the ship, but in design 'C' the two after turrets were placed some distance apart as in *Queen Mary*. Because of the need to reposition bulkheads in order to accommodate the after torpedo room, it was found advantageous to place the centre turret abaft the funnels and masts where, incidentally, the arcs of fire would increase from 240° to 300° for that turret.

Both designs could be arranged for 6in or 4in anti-torpedo guns with a corresponding adjustment of displacement. In 'A' and 'A1', the protection for the secondary armament was given as 5in, but in 'C' the 4in guns had only 3in screens. 'A' and 'A1' had the lower edge of belt armour carried down to 2ft 6in below the main armour strake by a strip of 3in; this scheme had been adopted in all modern Japanese battleships as a result of experience gained during the Russo-Japanese War of 1904 where it had shown its value against the steeply diving shell, fired from long range. This 3in addition was not included in design 'C'. In all designs, the length was the same as in *Queen Mary*, but the beam had increased in 'A' and 'A1' from 87ft to 91ft – a 4ft increase over that vessel.

Eventually, design 'C' was rejected; having adopted a 6in secondary armament for battleships (*Iron Duke* class), the Board considered that this should be so for any proposed large and more vulnerable cruiser types under consideration. Of 'A' and 'A1', it was definitely 'A1' that was preferred, but with some reservations toward the 6in forward arcs of fire, which was considered to be the weak point in the design. At this point Watts proposed a slight modification to 'A1' and presented an additional design – 'A2'. Here the disposition of the main armament was the same as in *Queen Mary* but the centre turret ('Q') would be able to fire right

Below: *Tiger* fitting out at John Brown's in 1914.

aft, which was not possible in *Queen Mary.* The side armour was carried right up and gave additional protection to the secondary armament, offering a thickness of 5in to ten of the guns which were located on the upper deck level, the remaining two being fitted in casemates above them. 'A2' appeared to be very satisfactory and was submitted for approval on 18 August 1911.

By 12 December 1911 the sheer, midships section and final legend had been approved and invitations to tender were sent out on 21 December. On 2 March 1912, the tender from the John Brown Shipyard was accepted by telegram, the final letter of approval from the Admiralty being sent on 3 April. The contract was signed on 4 April 1912.

On 21 December 1911 a further modification was made when it was proposed to fit all available spaces in the double bottoms as oil tanks, bringing total fuel capacity up to a colossal 3,340 tons of coal and 3,800 tons oil. This was approved, but it was stressed that the normal capacity in peacetime would be 3,240 tons of coal and only 800 tons of oil. The modification had been made in the light of the intention of fitting the vessel as an all oil-fired ship, but because the design was well advanced, and being almost a repeat of the machinery fitted in *Queen Mary* (but with increased SHP), the arrangement for both coal and oil were kept. The principal alterations in the final design since first conceived in August 1911 were as shown in the table. The essential features of 'A2' compared with *Queen Mary* were:

1. Relocation of 'Q' turret abaft instead of before third funnel, where it had a considerably wider arc of fire.
2. Provision of a 6in instead of 4in secondary battery.
3. Addition of two extra torpedo tubes at stern.
4. Extension of belt armour at extremities, and slightly increased horizontal armouring.
5. Rearrangement of boiler rooms to accommodate new location of 'Q' turret.
6. Substitution of single pole mast for full tripod, suppression of mainmast, and an addition of derrick stump fitted close before third funnel.
7. Protection to secondary armament increased from 3in to 6in.
8. Designed speed increased from 27 to 29 knots.

As completed, *Tiger* represented a distinct improvement over *Lion* and *Queen Mary*, but the protection was still inadequate to withstand heavy-calibre shellfire, and when the ship was compared with the German battlecruiser *Derfflinger* in all-round efficiency, *Tiger* was not generally regarded as an equal, despite the heavier armament.

Armament

By grouping all boiler rooms together amidships, it had been found possible to relocate the centre main turret abaft instead of before the third funnel, and it was this feature that constituted one of the principal improvements over previous vessels of this type. At the same time, it was kept sufficiently far ahead of 'Y' turret to allow for direct astern firing without danger of blast effects, and eliminated the risk of both turrets being put out of action by a single hit (as occurred in the German battlecruiser *Seydlitz* at the Battle of Dogger Bank in January 1915).

Shortly after the 'A2' design was accepted, controversy began concerning the secondary armament – the usual debate about the heavier 6in shell against the 4in, which could be mounted in greater numbers. It was also suggested that crews of the 6in guns could manage just as well if halved so as to alleviate the congested gun positions.

A committee from the Department of Naval Ordnance met on 1 April 1912 and gave the matter much thought. The committee, which consisted of A. B. Brock, W. K. Hall and J. M. W. Ley, reflected that the idea of half crews manning the anti-torpedo battery dated back to 1901, when the threat of torpedo attack was not a very real one. At that time it was felt that as the guns were entirely unprotected, the men could not be kept at them, and it was likely that a good many of the guns might be knocked out anyway before the occasion to man them arose; therefore, half crews would suffice to man the surviving guns, for a short period, with some degree of success. Conditions by 1912, had changed entirely and it was now believed that a torpedo attack during a fleet action would be a certainty – and was, in fact, an integral part of German tactics.

The German torpedo craft had a heavy torpedo armament (4 tubes), reached speeds of up to 32 knots and invariably went to sea with the battlefleet where they would always deliver an attack. German capital ships, on the other hand, had a heavy and well-protected secondary battery whose special function was to demolish the unprotected secondary battery of an enemy battleship, to leave the ship vulnerable to torpedo attack. That the German battleships intended to close to near ranges was indicated by the large number of torpedo tubes they themselves carried.

Above: *Tiger*, as completed, leaves the Clyde in September 1914 for her basic sea trials.

TIGER: PRELIMINARY DESIGNS

	Queen Mary	'AI'	'A1'	'A2'	'C'
Displacement (tons):	27,000	28,450	28,100	28,200	27,250
Length (pp):	660ft	660ft	660ft	660ft	660ft
Beam:	89ft	91ft	91ft	90ft 6in	90ft
Draught:	28ft	28ft	28ft	28ft	28ft 3in
Sinkage (tons):	99	101	101	101	101
13.5in guns:	Eight	Eight	Eight	Eight	Eight
6in guns:	–	Sixteen	Twelve	Twelve	–
4in guns:	Sixteen	–	–	–	Sixteen
Belt above wl:	16ft	24ft 3in	24ft 3in	24ft 3in	24ft 3in
Belt below wl:	3ft6in	6ft	6ft	6ft	6ft
Coal (tons) min.:	1,000	1,000	1,000	1,000	1,000
Coal (tons) max.:	3,700	3,700	3,700	3,750	3,700
Oil (tons):	1,100	1,100	1,100	1,100	1,100
SHP:	75,000	80,000	79,000	82,000	79,000
Speed (knots):	28	28	28	28	28
Complement:	999	1,000	1,000	1,109	1,000
Hull (tons):	9,760	9,860	9,830	9,720	9,600
Armour (tons):	6,595	7,030	6,980	7,390	6,730
Machinery (tons):	5,460	5,780	5,720	5,500	5,500
Armament (tons):	3,352	3,860	3,650	3,600	3,450
Equipment (tons):	805	820	820	840	820
Cost:	£2,850,000	£2,235,000	£2,199,000	£2,199,000	£2,100,000

TIGER: ADDITIONS TO DESIGN WHILE UNDER CONSTRUCTION

1. Rearrangement of cabins, messes, etc., in order to berth most of the crew on the upper deck in daytime, and give the crew 2.2ft per man seating accommodation.
2. Additional lighting and ventilation to living spaces.
3. W.C. added near compass platform.
4. Position of torpedo control tower altered.
5. Wheels for working magazine flood valves grouped in watertight cabinets on main deck.
6. Deeper keels fitted amidships.
7. Struts added to foremast, and mast shifted further forward on account of director firing.
8. Police office added.
9. New arrangement for coding office.
10. Hawser pipe for stern anchor.
11. Modification of gun control tower, so as to have officer in fixed position.
12. Steel lockers instead of bags and sacks for mens' clothing.
13. Wood backing added behind battery armour.
14. Lifeboats stowed on shelter deck instead of forecastle deck.
15. Oil filling arrangements increased because of additional stowage.
16. Anti-torpedo nets deleted.
17. Position of searchlights altered.
18. Number of 3pdrs reduced from six to four.
19. Two 6in hoods added for officers controlling battery guns.

It was considered that in the design proposed ('A2'), the secondary battery could be worked to a satisfactory degree but not if the guns were served by half crews. It was generally accepted that a 6in Lyditte shell was the smallest that would stop a large torpedo-boat or destroyer type with a single hit, so the volume of fire would have to be at its maximum for long periods during the initial attack; therefore to serve the guns with half crews, who would soon tire, was utterly out of the question.

The committee recommended that this ship and any succeeding designs should definitely be fitted with a powerful 6in secondary battery, each gun of which should be manned by a full crew of nine men.

The disposition of the secondary battery in *Tiger* allowed for a concentration of fire ahead, instead of equally ahead and astern as with the 4in guns of the *Lion* class. The forecastle deck was carried well abaft 'Q' main turret, allowing the secondary battery to be well sited amidships, considerably farther aft than in the contemporary *Iron Duke* battleships, and allowing the guns an increased all-round fire, and less likelihood of being washed out by heavy, breaking seas.

Armour

The maximum armour thickness remained the same as in *Lion*, but was more widely distributed, the outstanding feature being the extension of the side armour up to forecastle deck level amidships, over the secondary battery position. There was also some alteration in the deck protection over previous classes. The principal modifications were:

1. Belt armour extended almost to the bow and stern.
2. Depth of 9in belt below water, was reduced from 3ft to 2ft 3in, but a 3ft 9in wide strip of 3in armour was added below the belt between outer faces of 'A' and 'Y' barbettes; this increased the total depth of armoured side on this section to 6 feet.

TIGER
Outboard profile, October 1914, as fitted

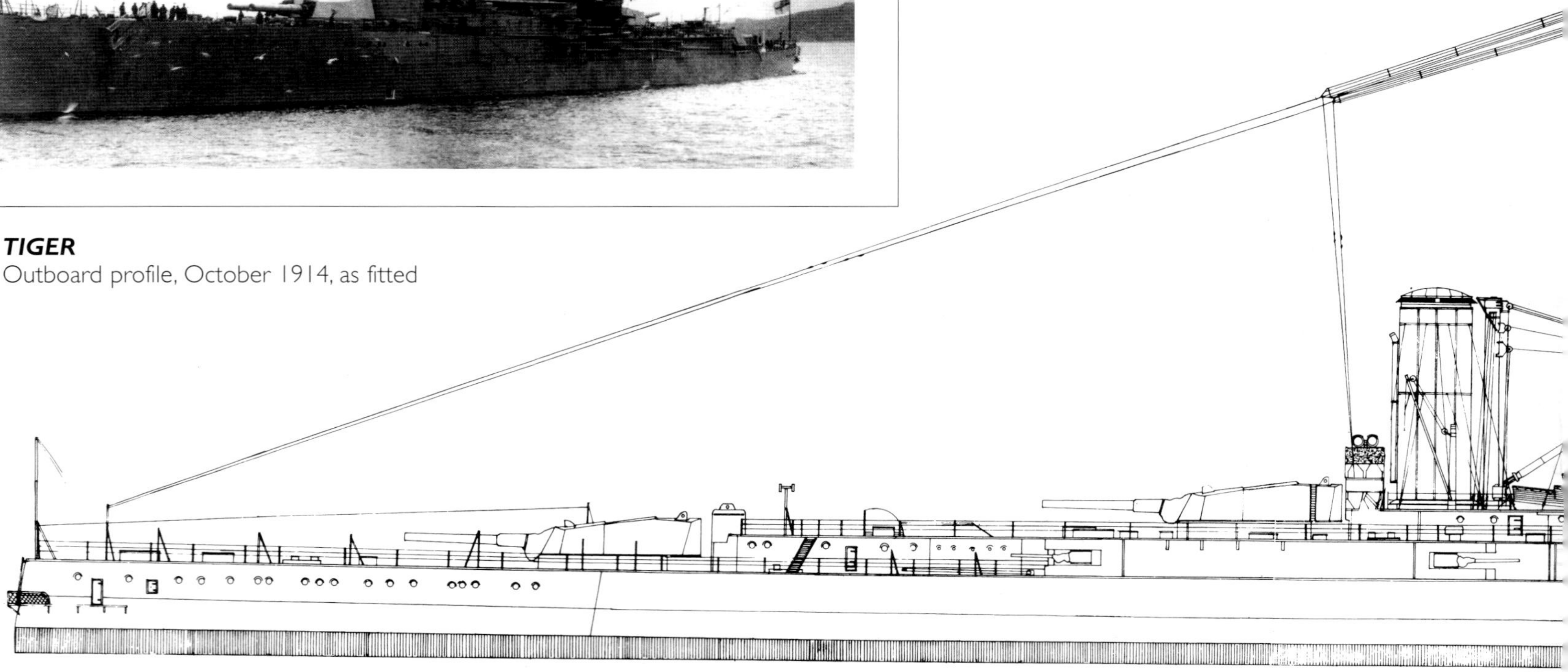

3. 6in battery armour added on side amidships between forecastle and upper decks, from inner face of 'A' to abaft 'Y' barbette, and terminated in a 5in bulkhead forward and 4in bulkhead aft.
4. Upper deck armour was suppressed within the area of the battery owing to the addition of side armour over this length.
5. 1in armour fitted to main deck forward, with length of the main deck armour abaft 'Y' turret increased.
6. Lower deck outside the forward bulkhead was increased from 2½in to 3in.
7. After extremities terminated 25 feet inside the stern instead of being complete.

The 3in strip below the armoured belt was an innovation in the Royal Navy, but it was only repeated in the later design (and final battlecruiser design) of *Hood* (1916 Estimates). Apart from the above quoted alterations, *Tiger* was armoured along similar lines to *Queen Mary*, but the outstanding feature was the 6in upper belt above the main strake (9in). This corrected a major deficiency in all earlier British battlecruisers in which the open forecastle deck side was very vulnerable and, in the absence of strong deck protection below, left the magazines and machinery especially exposed to long-range plunging shellfire.

Tiger's main 9in belt ran from abreast the conning tower to the inner face of 'Y' barbette: the upper edge was at main deck level, and the lower edge 2ft 3in below the water-line. The 5in to 4in forward extended to within 30 feet of the stem at the same height as the midships section. It was 5in to just beyond 'A' barbette, and 4in outside this. The 5in and 4in belt aft extended to within 25 feet of the stern at the same height as the midships section; 5in abeam 'Y' barbette, 4in abaft outer faces of 'Y' barbette. The 6in strake amidships ran over the same length as the 9in belt between upper and main deck levels.

The main bulkheads closed the forward extremities of 4in side armour, and then carried below this to the lower deck: the thickness was 4in between upper and main decks, and 2in from main to lower. Aft, the bulkhead closed the 5in side armour with the outer face of 'Y' barbette between lower and upper decks.

There was a forward bulkhead which closed the forward extremities of 4in belt armour between lower and main decks; this bulkhead was itself 4in thick. A similar bulkhead aft closed the after extremities of the 4in side armour and, again, this bulkhead was 4in thick.

The forecastle deck was 1in over the centre and 1½in at the sides, running over the 6in secondary battery. The upper deck ran from the forward main bulkhead to 'A' barbette, and from the after end of the battery to 'Y' barbette, all at 1in thickness. The 1in main

Above: *Tiger* at war, c.1915 (*Lion* class in distance).

Opposite: *Tiger* seen at Scapa Flow on joining the 1st BCS in October 1914.

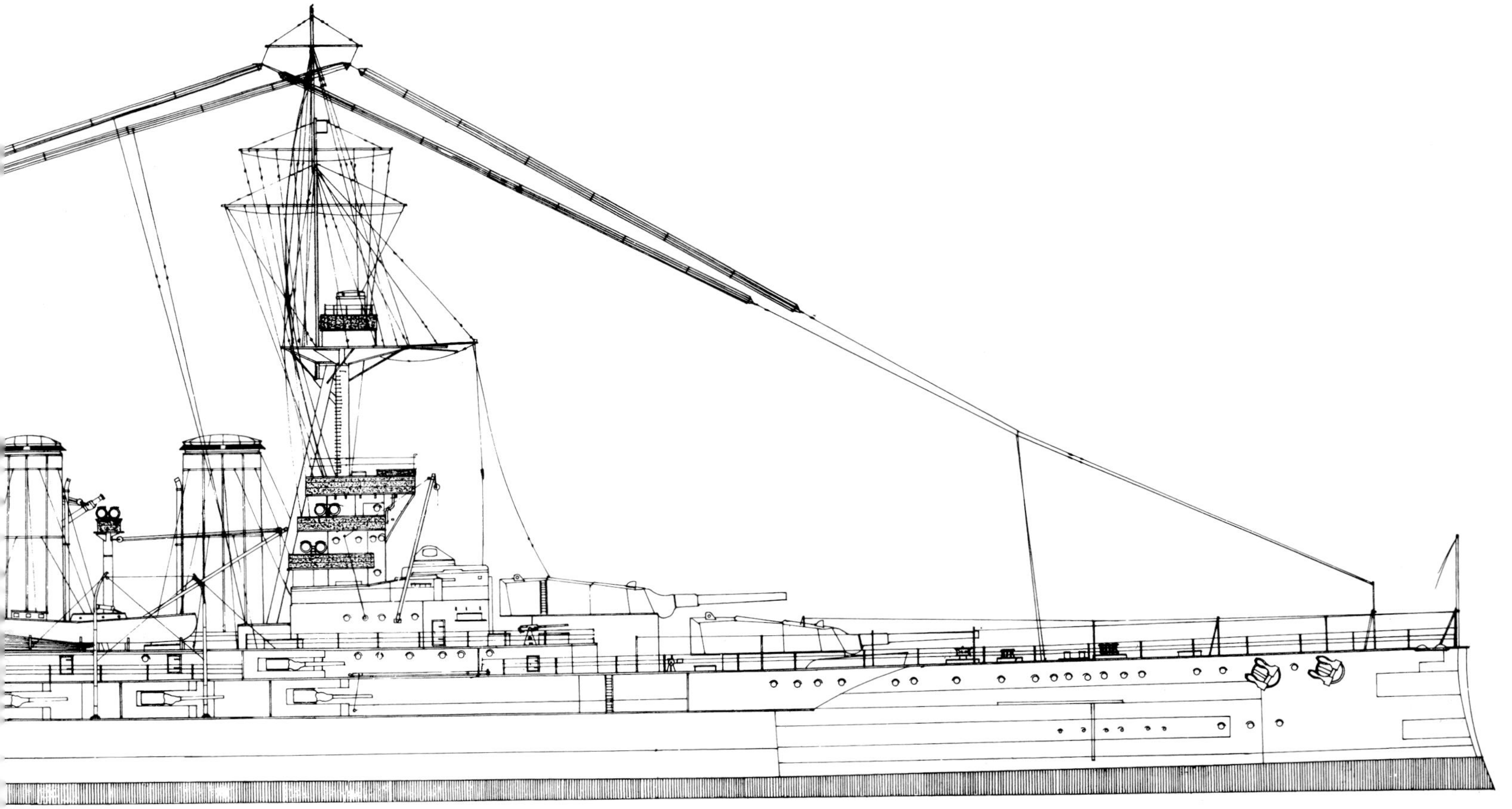

Opposite, top: *Tiger* on 29 January 1915, just a few days after the Dogger Bank action. Showing unusual camouflage (white stripes on funnels, and dark-grey panel on hull).

Opposite, bottom: Post-war view showing rear of aft funnel and 'Q' 13.5in turret of *Tiger* 1919.

deck ran from the forward bulkhead to the forward main bulkhead, and between 'Y' barbette and the after main bulkhead. The lower deck was 1in on the slope and flat, but increased to 3in right forward outside the forward bulkhead.

Barbettes varied in thickness according to location: 'A' barbette had 9in outer faces and sides above the upper deck, and then reduced to 4in once below this. Inner faces were 8in above the forecastle deck, reducing to 3in below where it passed the battery armoured strake. 'B' barbette had 5in outer and inner faces except for the top section where it was 9in uniform above the forecastle. 'Q' and 'Y' turrets were of similar application and thickness to 'A' barbette. The 6in battery guns were protected by a 6in strake which thinned to 5in at the extremities of the battery. The battery roof was 1in–1½in thick, formed by the forecastle deck. ¾in rear screens, fitted longitudinally port and starboard, were set well inboard throughout the whole length of the battery. 1in traverses were fitted near the forward pair of guns, between the second and third guns, and between the fourth and fifth guns.

The 6in sighting hoods were located between the second and third guns (port and starboard). The 6in gun casemates were 6in thick on the faces and had a 2in rear and 1in roof.

The conning tower was 10in on the sides, had a 3in roof and a base of 2in carried down to forecastle level, which was used as a distribution (signal) station and Intelligence office. The tube was

TIGER: PARTICULARS, AS COMPLETED

Construction
John Brown; laid down 20 June 1912; launched 15 Dec 1913; started trials Aug 1914; completed Oct 1914.

Displacement (tons)
28,100 (as designed), 28,800 (legend), 27,550 (light), 32,800 (load), 33,677 (deep).

Dimensions
Length: 660ft pp, 697ft 9in wl, 704ft oa
Beam: 90ft 6in
Draught: 28ft 3in (legend), 32ft (load), 32ft 3in (deep)
Height of 13.5in guns above wl: 'A' 33ft, 'B' 42ft 6in, 'Q' 31ft 9in, 'X' 23ft
Height of CT vision slits above lower wl: 50ft 3in
Height of fore funnel: 83ft
Height of lower foremasthead: 105ft
Depth of keel from battery deck: 44ft 6in.

Armament
Eight 13.5in 45cal Mk V; 80rpg peace, 130rpg war
Twelve 6in 45cal Mk VII; 120rpg
Two 3in QF; 150rpg
One 12pdr (8cwt)
Four 3pdr (saluting); 64rpg
Five Maxim MG
Ten Lewis guns
Four 21in torpedo tubes (beam, submerged); twenty torpedoes.

Director control
Gun director for main armament carried aloft in director tower and in alternative tower on superstructure aft; two directors for secondary armament. Follow-the-pointer gear on all sights and electrical control instruments.

Armour*
Main belt: 9in
Ends: 6in–5in–4in–3in
Transverse bulkheads: 4in–2in
Secondary battery: 6in
Splinter bulkheads: 1in
Barbettes: 9in–8in–4in–3in–1in
Turrets: 9in face, 8in rear, 3¼in–2½in roof
Conning tower: 10in side
Control tower: 6in
Communications tube: 4in–3in
Underwater protection: 2½in–1½in–1in
Decks: forecastle 1½in–1in, upper 1½in–1in, main 1in, lower 3in–1in.

Machinery
Brown Curtis impulse-type turbines, four propellers
Boilers: thirty-nine Babcock & Wilcox, working pressure 235psi
Five boiler rooms; four containing eight boilers, one containing seven
Heating surface: 170,008sq ft
Grate area: 4,501sq ft
Designed SHP: 85,000 = 28 knots
As completed SHP: 108,000 = 29 knots
Fuel: 450 tons coal, 450 tons oil min., 3,320 tons coal, 3,480 tons oil max. In service, coal and oil capacity generally did not exceed 4,900 tons
Radius of action: 2,800nm at 25 knots; 4,000nm at 22 knots; 4,500nm at 20 knots; 4,900nm at 18 knots; 5,200nm at 12 knots.

Ship's boats
Pinnaces (steam): two 50ft
Pinnaces (sail): one 36ft
Launches (sail): one 42ft
Cutters: two 34ft, two 32ft, one 30ft
Gigs: one 30ft
Whalers: three 27ft
Dinghies: one 16ft
Balsa rafts: one 13ft 6in.

Searchlights
Sixteen twin 24in: four middle bridge, four lower bridge, four derrick stump, four platform abaft third funnel. (Six 36in 1919.)

Rangefinder positions (1918)
Two 25ft ('A' and 'Q' turrets)
Three 15ft ('X' turret, gun control tower, torpedo control tower)
One 12ft (spotting top)
Three 9ft ('B' turret, gun control tower, above compass platform)
One 6ft 6in HA.

Battle signal stations**
Two enclosed stations in 6in battery on upper deck, port and starboard abreast fore funnel. Signal flag lockers fitted.

Anchors
Three 150cwt stockless (2 bower, 1 sheet), one 50cwt stern.

Wireless (1918)
Main office: Types 1–34, Type 16
Second office: Type 2
Third office: Type 9
Fire control office: Type 34.

Complement
1,109 (as designed); 1,112 (Sept 1914); 1,344 (May 1915); 1,459 (April 1918).

Cost
Admiralty estimate £2,100,000.

*See text for additions after Jutland.
**Two peacetime signal stations were provided on the conning tower platform near the foremast.

TIGER: WEIGHTS (TONS)

	1914	1924
Hull and Armour:	17,351	18,234
Machinery:	5,407	5,775
Armament:	2,737	2,764
Equipment:	354	351
Totals:	**25,849**	**27,124**

4in and 3in thick and ran down to the lower deck. The sighting hood over the conning tower was 3in.

The torpedo control tower was 6in on the sides and had a 3in roof. The tube of the torpedo control tower was 4in and ran down to the upper deck only. Longitudinal magazine screens, port and starboard, were fitted abreast the magazine from the keel to the lower deck: 2½in abreast the midships and after magazines; 2½in and 1½in abreast the forward magazine, with the outer ends of the forward and after screens being closed by 1in transverse bulkheads.

Machinery

To accommodate the rearrangement of 'Q' 13.5in turret as compared with *Lion*, the construction department had to group the boilers together in one block amidships instead of separating them in two groups with magazines between as in those ships; a much more satisfactory arrangement indeed.

When the ship was under construction the DNC, Eustace Tennyson D'Eyncourt commented that it might be possible to adopt the small tube boiler, which would raise the estimated SHP and save a great deal of weight. The engineering department was not prepared to accept such a radical change at that time, especially as large tube boilers offered certain advantages although at a considerable cost in weight and space.

Tiger was fitted with Brown Curtis turbines, the first of this type fitted in a British capital ship. The main propelling machinery was arranged in four watertight compartments and consisted of two sets of turbines arranged in two forward compartments, the condensers and auxiliary machinery generally being placed in the two after compartments, each set being divided by a longitudinal bulkhead on the centreline of the ship.

Four shafts were fitted, with the HP ahead, and LP ahead turbines being arranged on the inner shafts, and the impulse turbines located on the outer shafts.

Being rushed to completion at the outbreak of war, she was not put through a lengthy trial period, but nine days after her commissioning with 1st BCS on 14 October 1914, she ran the Polperro course:

1. 6 runs; 267 revolutions (mean); 91,103shp (mean); 23.38 knots.
2. 4 runs; 278 revolutions (mean); 104,635shp (mean); 29.07 knots.

Appearance Changes

Public and service opinion conceded that *Tiger* was one of the most graceful-looking warships of the day: the blend of three tall, round, equal-sized funnels grouped closely amidships, coupled with tripod and no mainmast, all made for an extremely handsome vessel later equalled only by *Renown*, *Repulse* and *Hood*. The derrick stump–searchlight combination was an especially distinctive feature, not fitted in any other British warship except the ex-Turkish battleship *Sultan Osman I* (later *Agincourt*).

1914/15 Control top enlarged immediately after Dogger Bank battle. Director control fitted for 6in secondary battery. Topgallant mast removed (late 1914). Camouflage painted on hull (black or dark grey strip with angled edges) and on funnel (horizontal stripes on all three).
1915 Camouflage painted out.
1916–17 Small rangefinder added over conning tower, and

medium rangefinder added at rear of 'Y' turret. Searchlights removed from lower bridge. One pair SL ex platform abaft funnel lamps remounted for short period on 'Q' turret. Improvements in armour plating after Battle of Jutland: 179 tons on decks over magazine spaces; 77 tons on turret tops, 24 tons over machinery, 15 tons for bulkheads to 6in battery. Extra platform added around tripod legs over bridge. Small raised platform added port and starboard abeam third funnel.

1917–18 Small rangefinder over conning tower removed.

TIGER: GM AND STABILITY

As inclined, 12 September 1914

	Displacement (tons)	Draught	GM	Maximum stability	Stability vanishes at
'A' Condition (= load)*	–	28ft 5in	5.2ft	43°	74°
'B' Condition (= deep)**	–	32ft 5in	6.1ft	43°	80°
'C' Condition***	–	34ft	6.7ft	44°	86°

*Fully equipped plus 450 tons coal upper, 450 tons double bunkers.
**Fully equipped plus 2,450 tons coal, 2,450 tons oil, water-tanks full.
***Experimental condition with 1,030 tons coal, 870 tons added to 'B' condition.

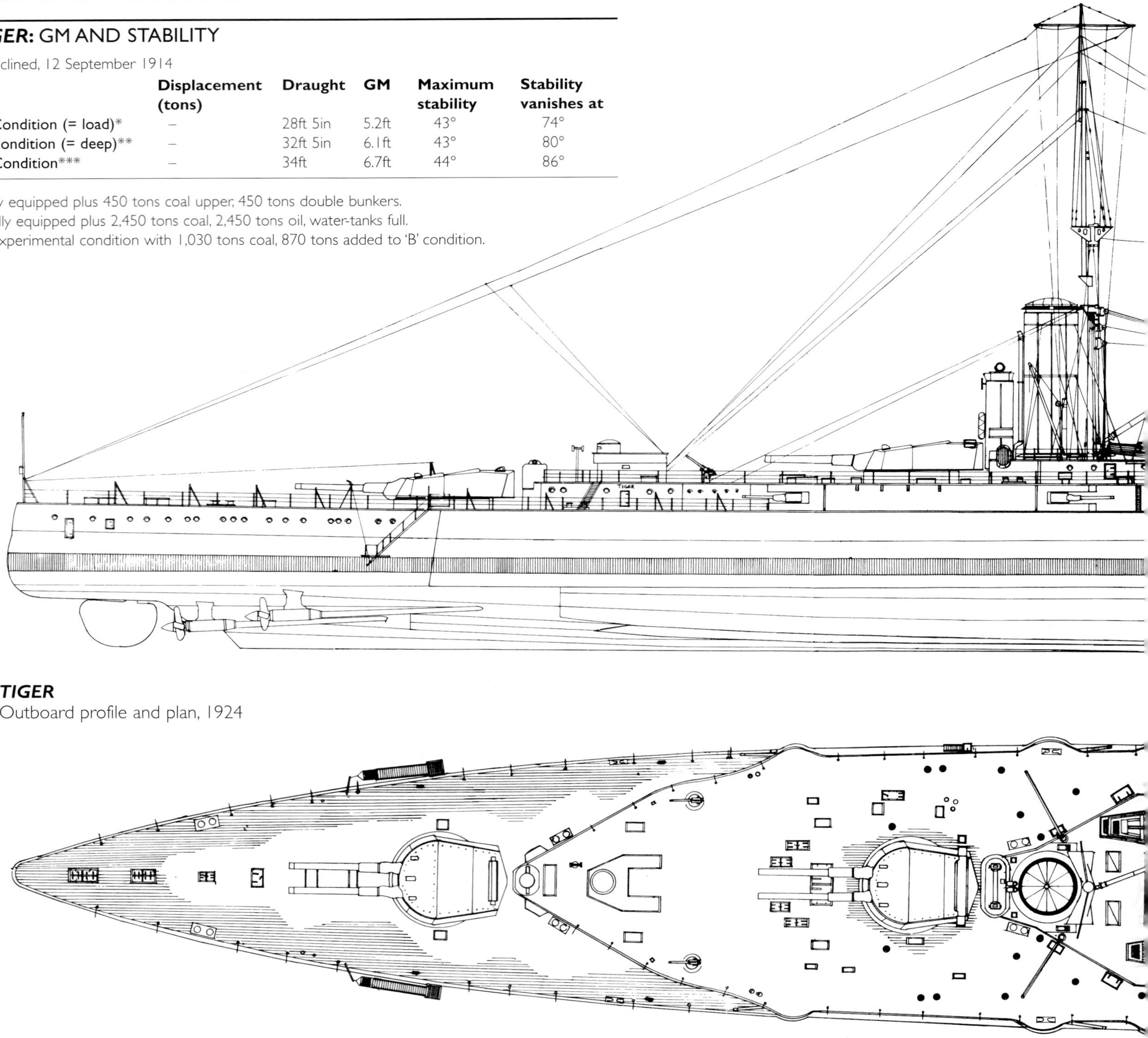

TIGER
Outboard profile and plan, 1924

Left: *Tiger* anchored in Scapa Flow in 1918, just before the end of the war. Note wind shield on 'X' turret (to protect aircraft).

Right: *Tiger* at sea with *Renown* in background, c. 1917/18.

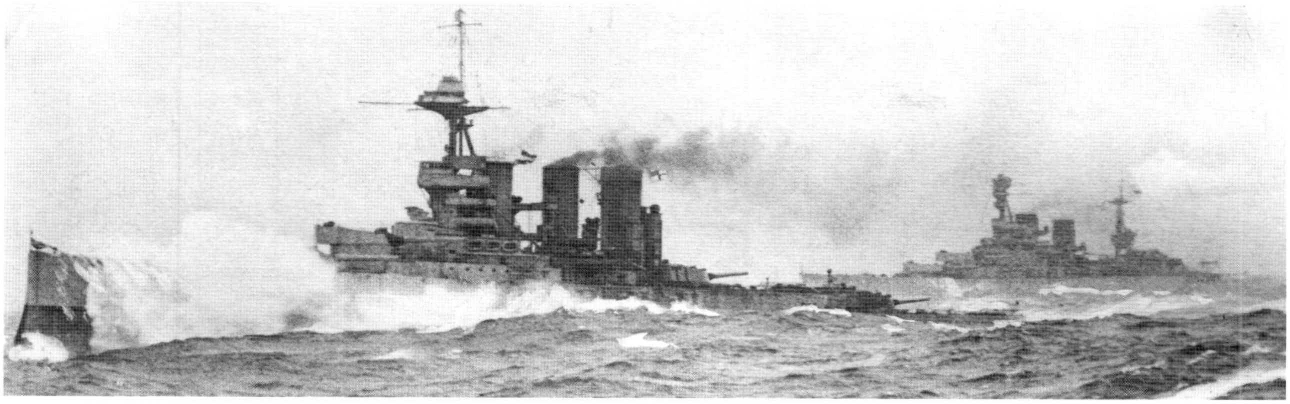

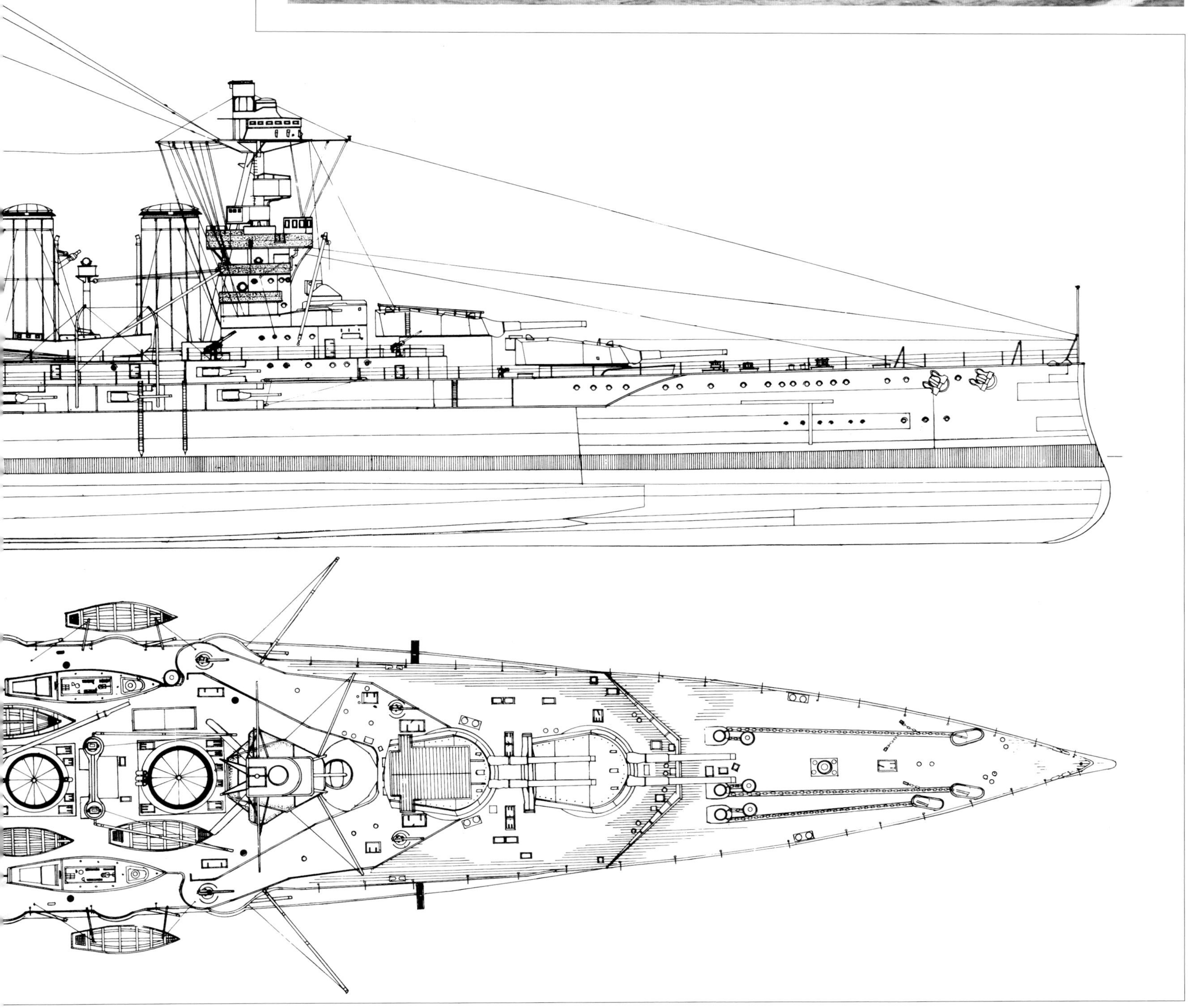

Above: *Tiger* at Devonport, c.1919/20. Note difference between aircraft runways on 'B' and 'X' turret tops.

Right: *Tiger*, 1916/17.

Below: *Tiger* leaves Scapa Flow, 1918/1919.

Left: *Tiger* early in 1917 showing identification letters on 'Q' turret.

Below: *Tiger* in Weymouth Bay, c.1923.

Bottom: *Tiger* leaves Portsmouth Harbour and passes Southsea beach, c. 1923.

Deflection scales painted on 'B' and 'Y' turrets. Small rangefinder on top of torpedo control tower replaced by medium-base rangefinder.

Searchlights redistributed for improved control: twin 24in lamps almost entirely replaced by single 36in lamps; control towers, with one 36in lamp in each, added at each side of third funnel; two 36in lamps mounted port and starboard on lower bridge; one 36in lamp added on each derrick stump platform between first and second funnel. All twin 24in removed except two pairs on middle bridge. Searchlight control positions below derrick stump enlarged.

Flying-off platforms added over 'Q' 13.5in turret. Panel-type dark camouflage on hull restored, but not quite the same as early (1915) scheme.

1918 Control top further enlarged. Medium-base rangefinder added over conning tower.

Right: *Tiger* in Weymouth Bay, c.1925.

Range clocks fitted to rear of searchlight tower abaft third funnel. High-angle rangefinder in shield added on control top (July 1918) raised well clear of the top. Torpedo control and concentration top fitted low on foremast. Camouflage painted out.

1919 Large-base rangefinder fitted at rear of 'A' turret. Range clocks fitted over torpedo control top. Deflection scales on turrets painted out. Flying-off platform fitted over 'B' turret.

1921–2 Searchlights removed from towers abeam third funnel.

1922–4 Large-base rangefinders fitted at rear of 'Q' and 'Y' turrets. Medium rangefinder on 'Y' removed. AA guns increased to four 4in. Original 3in AA guns abeam conning tower removed.

Below: *Tiger* in Weymouth Bay, c.1923.

Left: *Tiger.* Broadside view while at anchor in Weymouth Bay, 1923/24.

Below: *Tiger* spent her last few years serving as gunnery training ship at Portsmouth before being finally condemned by the Washington Treaty and placed in Reserve .Seen here during that period, 1925/6.

Right: *Tiger* in dry dock at Rosyth. Note the flying-off platform on 'Q' turret, range clock on SL tower and stern anchor.

Twin 24in searchlights removed from middle bridge. Flying-off platforms removed from 'Q' turret. Signal struts at starfish removed, but yard retained. Main derrick stump raised well above funnel height with starfish at head of this. The topmast to this was retained, and a topgallant added.

1925–6 Range clocks over torpedo control tower removed. After pair of 4in AA guns remounted abreast conning tower.

1929 4in abreast conning tower reverted to original position abaft 'Q' turret. Searchlight control positions on derrick stump between first and second funnels slightly enlarged. No further alterations were made after this.

History: *Tiger*

1914 *3 Oct* Commissioned at Clydebank for 1st BCS, and joined the Grand Fleet with construction staff aboard working day and night; with Grand Fleet until April 1919.

1915 *24 Jan* Dogger Bank action. She engaged *Blücher, Seydlitz* and *Moltke.* She was hit seven times; port gun in 'B' turret disabled; signal distributing office wrecked. One officer, nine ratings killed. Her performance at this action has been recorded as being far from satisfactory, which was probably because she had not fully worked up.

1916 *31 May* Battle of Jutland. She was hit fourteen times (at least ten large shells); port side of forecastle badly damaged, and holed above water-line with much internal damage. 'A' barbette hit by a 12in shell, but not penetrated; left gun in 'Q' turret temporarily disabled by 11in shell, loading gear of both guns damaged. Side and deck armour abaft 'Q' turret penetrated by 11in shell which burst inside, causing a bad fire with many casualties, and making it necessary to flood port 6in magazine. 24 killed, 37 wounded. Refitted at Rosyth.

2 July Rejoined the Fleet, temporary flagship BCS while *Lion* received repairs. Took part in the Heligoland operations with *Glorious, Courageous* and *Repulse.*

1919 *April* With Atlantic Fleet; temporary flagship of squadron while *Hood* worked up.

1920 *May* Sent to Baltic with *Hood* to reinforce operations against the Bolsheviks. Left Portsmouth on 30 May and proceeded via Sweden and Denmark.

The force was recalled, however, owing to the change in policy towards the Soviet regime, and the force visited Oslo, en route home.

1920 *Autumn* Collided with battleship *Royal Sovereign* at Portland; considerable damage to *Royal Sovereign.*

1920 *Dec* Under refit at Devonport.

1921 *22 Aug* Paid off into Reserve at Devonport.

1922 *March* Refit at Rosyth.

1924 *14 Feb* Recommissioned at Rosyth for service as gunnery firing ship at Portsmouth.

1926 April–June Refit at Portsmouth. Relieved by battleship *Iron Duke* and transferred to BCS Atlantic Fleet, replacing *Hood* for refit.

1929 *June* With Atlantic Fleet.

1931 *28 April* Withdrawn from BCS.

15 May Paid off into Reserve at Devonport.

26 July Paid off onto the Disposal list at Rosyth under the life duration clause of Washington naval treaty.

1932 *Feb* Sold to T. W. Ward, Inverkeithing.

22 March Dismantled at Rosyth and towed to Inverkeithing for demolition.

Erin: WAR PURCHASE

Design

In 1911, two battleships provisionally named *Reshad V* and *Reshad-i-Hamiss* were ordered from Vickers and Armstrong respectively, after a call from the Turkish Government for capital vessels that would equal any afloat. Rear-Admiral Sir Douglas Austin Gamble, who was a member of the British Naval Intelligence department, and naval adviser to the Turkish government from 1909 to 1911, acted quickly to secure the orders for British shipyards. With the help of Sir Richard Thurston at Vickers, the initial design was prepared, but the completed ship was the outcome of design work from Vickers, John Brown and Armstrong. *Reshad V* was laid down in the autumn of 1911, and work proceeded at a leisurely pace. Financially embarrassed in the wake of the Balkan War, the Turks cancelled *Reshad-i-Hamiss* at Armstrong; but at Vickers, *Reshad V*'s building was accelerated and her name changed to *Reshadieh*.

Basically a shorter, beamier version of the *Orion* class, *Reshadieh* had a secondary battery of sixteen 6in guns that were much superior to the 4in mounted in that class. Her protection qualities, however, were thought by many to be inferior to British layouts, but close comparison of thicknesses and distribution show that by and large she was on a par with most British battleships. The original and accepted sketch designs all showed twin tripods, the foremost fitted abaft the funnel (see sketch above); but later, during modifications (and with a close eye on the *Lions*, which were having their funnel/mast layout changed), this was altered to a single tripod ahead of the funnel and a single-pole mainmast for spreading the W/T aerials. The internal arrangements were designed to meet Turkish requirements and provided problems when the British Navy formally expropriated her and renamed

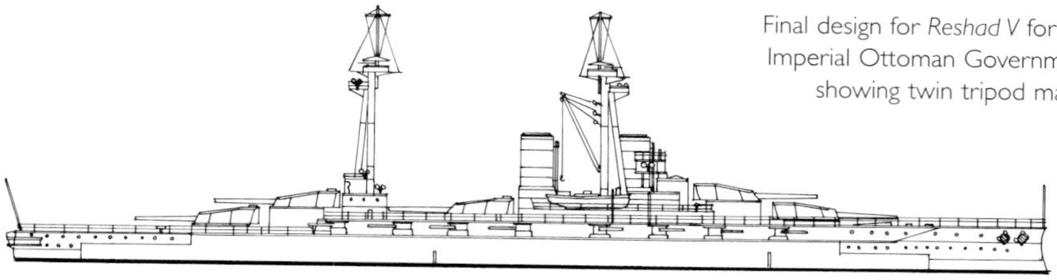

Final design for *Reshad V* for the Imperial Ottoman Government showing twin tripod masts.

Below: *Erin* fitting-out at Vickers, 3 June 1914. Note that mainmast is still in position (later removed). (*Emperor of India* on right.)

her *Erin* in 1914; accommodation was considerably cramped by British standards, showing features such as bathrooms and WCs opening direct into the junior officers' mess, and commander's, chief officers' and paymaster's cabins situated in the general mess spaces, with twenty beds fitted in them.

The completed ship not only compared favourably with *Orion*, but had a distinct advantage over the more recent *King George V* in sporting a superior 6in secondary armament. Differences from the British designs were:

1. Nominal displacement was the same as *King George V*, but on a shorter hull.
2. Freeboard forward and aft remained unchanged, but the forecastle deck was carried through considerably farther aft.
3. Extra beam meant that the ship could not be accommodated in any of the Royal docks, and would have to go into one of the private yards if necessary.

Comparison with *Iron Duke*, completed at about the same time as *Erin*, was favourable; beam and nominal draught in the former were greater, but on a displacement of some 2,000 tons less. *Erin's* stem curved outwards with a marked flare which made for increased dryness forward, and the fact that 'Q' turret had been placed a deck higher, and thus in a drier position than in British contemporaries, reflected great credit on the designers. Although internal construction of the Turkish ship was generally lighter than the usual British practice, there is no record of any sagging or hogging in the hull structure.

Armament

As was standard British practice, the main armament was disposed with all twin turrets on the centreline. The midships turret, however, was fitted a deck higher than in *Iron Duke*, which had been made practicable by the greatly extended forecastle.

The 13.5in guns were a Vickers 'special' and were classed as Mk VI (*Iron Duke* carried Mk V). Only ten were manufactured, all of which were mounted in the ship; it was claimed that replacements would be the usual Mk V. The Mk VI weighed 77 tons against 76 tons for the Mk V. The former differed from the latter in having a tapered inner 'A' tube, but generally, it was very much like the standard British gun.

The 6in secondary guns were well positioned, approximately twenty feet above the lower waterline, which made for a more suitable and dryer command; even so, the first three guns on each side were still prone to flooding in a swell. The ports for the 6in

ERIN
Outboard profile, 1914, as completed

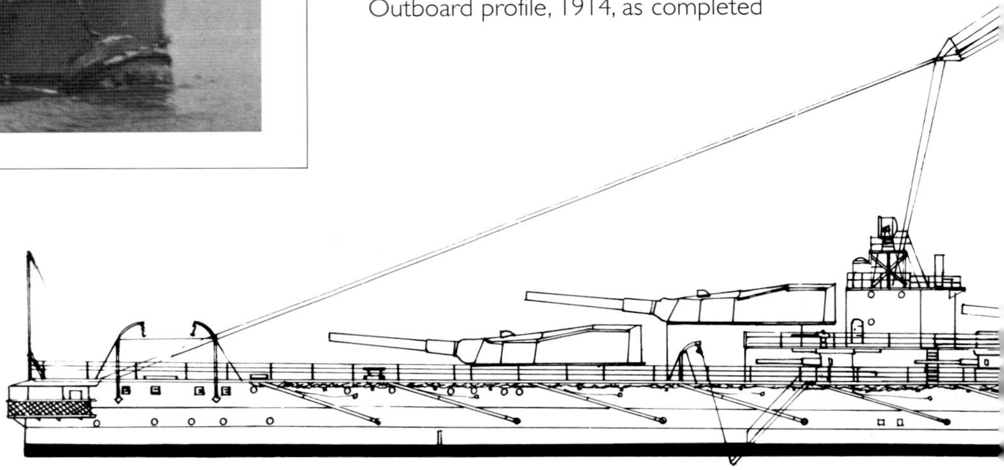

ERIN
Intboard profile, 1914, as fitted

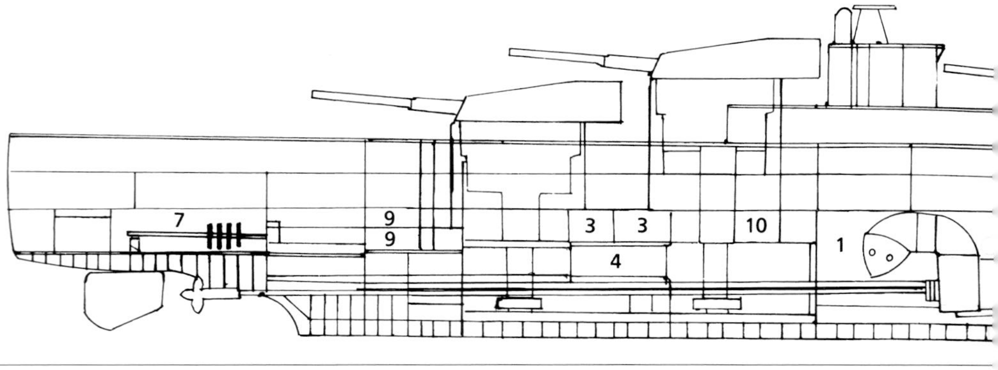

guns were not of the same standard as those fitted in *Iron Duke*, and were considered bad shell traps. They were another Vickers 'special' and allowed for extreme arcs of fire and a very good degree of elevation, slightly better than the Admiralty designs

Armour

The armour distribution was generally the same as in contemporary British designs and compared to *Iron Duke* and *King George V* as follows:

1. The 8in side armour was deeper and the 9in strake was shallower than in *King George V.*
2. The extensions to the belt, both forward and aft, were again shallower than in *King George V.*
3. Deck protection at the ends, outside the belt, were placed at middle instead of lower deck level, with the extremities of this middle deck sloping down to meet the lower deck.
4. Except for the outer faces of 'A' and 'Y' barbettes, the armour was thinner in these locations than in British ships.

Opposite: *Erin*, as completed summer of 1914, but prior to modification by Royal Navy.

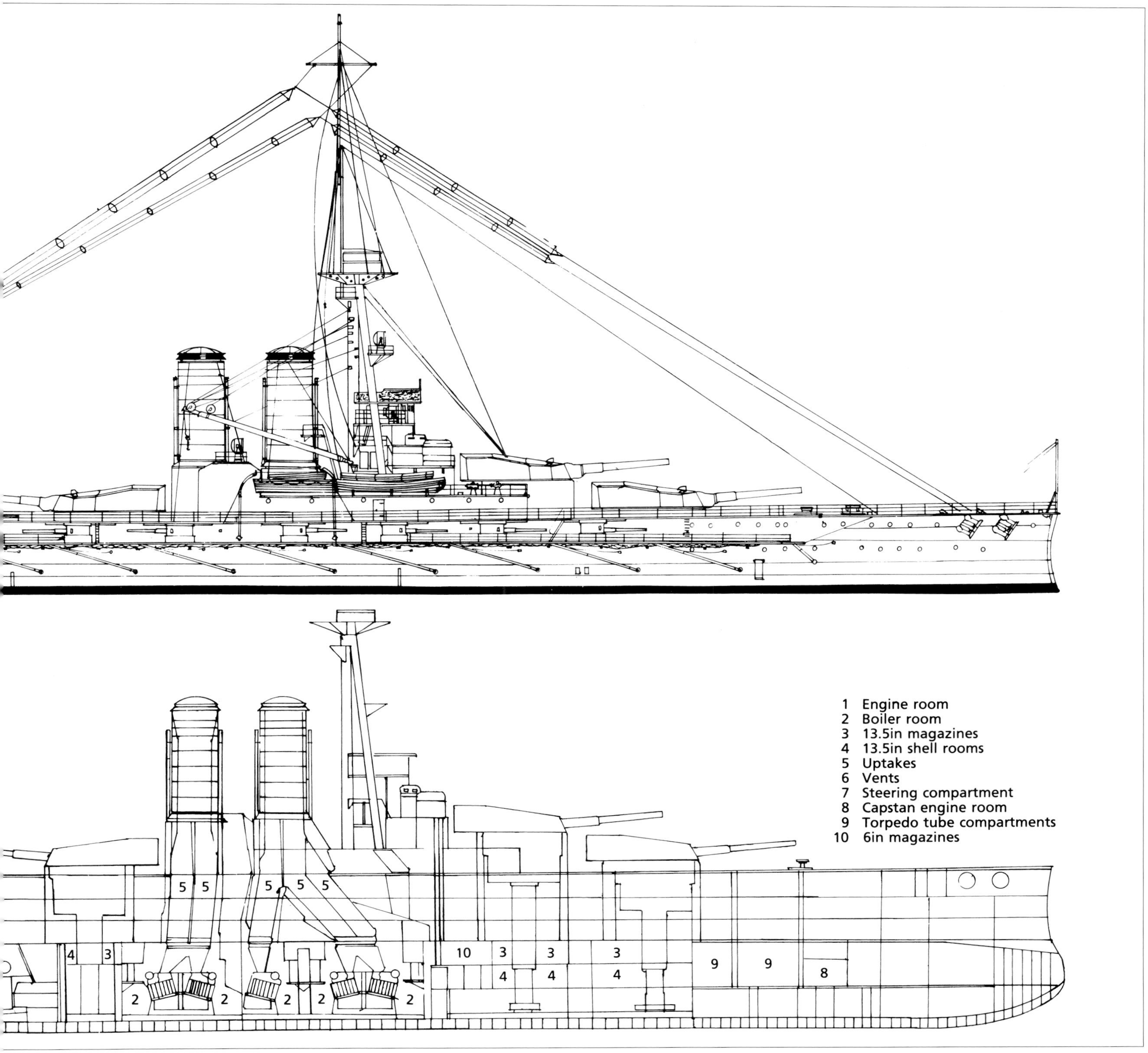

RESHADIEH: PARTICULARS AS COMPLETED

Construction
Vickers; laid down 6 Dec 1911; launched 3 Sept 1913; completed Aug 1914.

Displacement (tons)
22,780 (load), 25,250 (deep), 26,180 (extra deep).

Dimensions
Length: 525ft pp, 553ft wl, 559ft 6in oa
Beam: 91ft 7in
Draught: 28ft 5in (load), 30ft 11in (deep)
Height of 13.5in turrets above lower wl (at load): 'A' 29ft 3in; 'B' 38ft 9in; 'Q' 28ft 3in; 'X' 31ft 6in; 'Y' 22ft
Height of CT vision slits above lower wl: 48ft 6in
Height of fore funnel: 78ft
Height of lower masthead: 105ft
Depth of keel from upper deck: 44ft 6in.

Armament
Ten 13.5in 45cal Mk VI (Vickers 'Special'); 80rpg
Sixteen 6in 50cal; 150rpg
Two 12pdr (8cwt) field guns
Six 6pdr
Four 21in torpedo tubes; twenty torpedoes.

Director control
Main armament gun directors fitted in a tower aloft and in 'X' turret.

Armour
Main belt: 12in
Upper belts: 9in–8in
Ends: 6in–4in
Bulkheads: 8in–5in–4in
Barbettes: 10in–9in–5in–3in
Turrets: 11in–4in
Conning tower: 12in–4in
Tube: 6in
Hood: 6in–4in
Torpedo control tower: 4in
Anti-torpedo bulkheads: 1½in
Decks: forecastle 1½in, upper 1½in, main 1½in, middle 3in–1in
Total weight: 6,890 tons.

Machinery
Parsons direct-drive turbines, four propellers
Boilers: fifteen Babcock & Wilcox, normal working pressure 235psi
Designed SHP: 26,500 = 21 knots
Fuel: 900 tons coal normal, 2,120 tons coal max.
Radius of action: 3,400nm at 10 knots (coal only); 5,300nm at 10 knots (coal plus oil).

Ship's boats*
Pinnaces (steam): two 50ft
Pinnaces (sail): one 36ft
Launches (steam): one 45ft
Launches (sail): one 42ft
Cutters: two 32ft
Whalers: one 27ft
Gigs: one 30ft
Skiff dinghies: two 16ft
Punts: two 10ft.

Searchlights
Eight 36in: two fore bridge, two on platform low on tripod legs, two on platform between funnels, two after superstructure.

Rangefinder positions
Seven: one control top, one fore bridge, four in main turrets ('X' being master turret), one after island for HA guns when fitted.

Battle signal stations
Near foremast below main deck level.

Anchors
Three 140cwt (bower and sheet), one 40cwt stream (close stowing), two 16cwt kedge, one 8cwt. 450 fathoms 2⅞in cable.

Wireless
Main office: Mk III (fitted on takeover)
Type W/T 9 short-radius set (1914).

Complement
976 (7 Aug 1914); 1,064 (1915).

Cost
Estimated £2,500,000.

*On takeover boats' stowage was reduced to one 45ft steam pinnace, one 36ft sail pinnace, one 42ft launch, two 32ft life cutters, two 18ft dinghies.

Above: *Erin*, 1915. Note anti-rangefinder nets around foremast top.

5. Battery armour was generally 1in thinner than in *Iron Duke*.
6. Internal protection was slightly more complete, with continuous longitudinal bulkheads running from the end barbettes.

The main 12in armoured belt extended from abreast the end barbettes, with 3ft 8in below the water-line at normal draught, and the upper edge at middle deck level. The total height of protection, including all thicknesses, was 22ft 6in. The forward belts of 6in and 4in ran from the 12in strake, and was 6in for about 30 feet, reducing to 4in for another 15 feet. Aft, the same belt was 6in thick outside the end barbette, reducing to 4in beyond this. The 9in lower side belt extended over the same length as the 12in strake, but between middle and main deck levels. The 8in strake above this was also the same length as the 12in run, but at main and upper deck levels.

Main bulkheads of 8in and 5in ran obliquely inwards from the extremities of the 12in side armour to the outer faces of the end barbettes, this being at main and lower deck level; these bulkheads also picked up the 9in belt ends. There was a 4in forward bulkhead which closed the forward extremities of the 4in side armour between lower and middle deck levels. The 4in after bulkhead closed the extremities of the 4in side armour much in the same way as that for the forward bulkhead.

Barbette protection was somewhat thinner than in British ships, but still adequate if compared to *Agincourt* and *Canada*. 'A' barbette was 10in on the outer face above main deck level and reduced to 5in once below. The inner faces were 9in above the forecastle and reduced to 5in from the upper deck and 3in once below this. 'B' barbette had 9in plates on the outer face above the forecastle deck, with 5in from the upper to forecastle level and 3in below this. The inner face was 10in above forecastle level, otherwise the same as in 'A' barbette. 'Q' barbette was 10in on the face above forecastle level, with 5in from this level to upper deck, reducing to 3in once below this. 'X' barbette was 9in on the outer face with 10in on the

Above: *Erin* after the war, and laid up, *c.* 1920. Note aircraft runways over 'B' turret (also over 'Q') and general improvements to bridgework.

Below: *Erin*, 1916. Anti-torpedo nets temporarily replaced.

Above: A rare on–board view of *Erin* showing her forward 13.5in turrets and bridge layout. Note the twin boat derricks.

Left: *Erin* on steam trials, 1914.

inners, and all reduced to 3in once below the upper deck. 'Y' barbette was 10in on the outer face, with 5in on the main deck level. Inner faces were 9in above upper deck and 5in from main to upper, reducing to 3in below upper deck. Turrets were provided with 11in faces and sides and 3in–4in crowns.

The secondary battery had only 5in compared to the standard 6in in most British designs; this had been reduced because of the longer run of guns, and the provision of 1in traverses between each pair of guns within the battery. 3in sighting hoods were provided port and starboard for the 6in battery.

The main conning tower had 12in plates on the sides, a 4in roof and floor. The tube was 6in although a part of the base of the tube was not protected. The funnel uptakes were protected by 1in plates which extended above the middle deck right through to the shelter deck. Anti-torpedo bulkheads were 1½in thick and ran longitudinally, port and starboard, continuously from the end barbettes. They covered the engine rooms and machinery spaces, unlike *Iron Duke* and *King George V*, which were not covered by armour in this area.

The coal bunkers behind the armoured belt, above the middle deck and abreast the boiler rooms, afforded extra protection as in most British ships. Torpedo net protection was fitted, but later removed as in all capital ships during the war.

Deck protection was as follows: upper deck was 1½in amidships below the secondary battery; main deck was also 1½in, and was located at the ends outside 'A' and 'Y' barbettes between the forward and after main bulkheads; the 1in–3in middle deck ran the length of the ship, the ends sloping to meet the lower deck. The inclines and the flat were 1in with 3in on the slope to the lower deck at the ends.

Machinery

Nominal shaft horsepower was 500 tons less than that of *King George V*, but the designed speed was the same at 21 knots which, it is claimed, *Erin* attained during her builders' preliminary trials. (Unfortunately, no records are available.) Radius was slightly reduced because fuel stowage was considerably less than was normal practice, but it proved more than adequate in the North Sea when *Erin* was on patrol with the Grand Fleet.

Erin was fitted with Parsons direct-drive turbines, which turned four propellers: the HP turbines were located on the wing shafts, the LP were on the inner shafts. One HP ahead and one HP astern were fitted on each wing shaft, and the LP ahead and astern were fitted to the inner shafts in the same casing. Although full sets of steam trials were never carried out for the Royal Navy, it is almost certain that the ship easily made her designed speed of 21 knots. Admiralty books for this ship do not give any figures for trials, and the Ship's Book has been destroyed. Auxiliary machinery consisted of three steam-driven reciprocating generators, each of 250kW. There was also one 150kW oil-driven generator.

Appearance Changes

She was unique, quite unlike any ship in appearance. Her chief characteristics were:

1. Single tripod mast, legs reverse raked as in *Dreadnought*.
2. Small bridge structure, built up high around tripod legs.
3. Equal-sized and very round funnels with strongly ribbed sides.
4. Midships 13.5in turret was a deck higher than in British designs.
5. Extra-long 6in secondary battery extending from 'B' to 'X' turrets.
6. Strongly curved stem, quite unlike other vessels of her type.

1914–15 While fitting-out at Vickers she retained small pole

ERIN: GM AND STABILITY

Based on inclining experiments, 1914

	Displacement (tons)	Draught	GM	Maximum stability	Stability vanishes at
'A' Condition (= load)*	22,790	28ft 5in	6.15ft	32°	60°
B' Condition (= deep)**	25,250	30ft 11in (mean)	7.03ft	32°	62°

*Fully equipped plus 900 tons coal.

**Fully equipped plus 2,120 tons oil, 940 tons ammunition, 399 tons stores and provisions, 296 tons feedwater.

ERIN
Deck plans, showing gun arcs

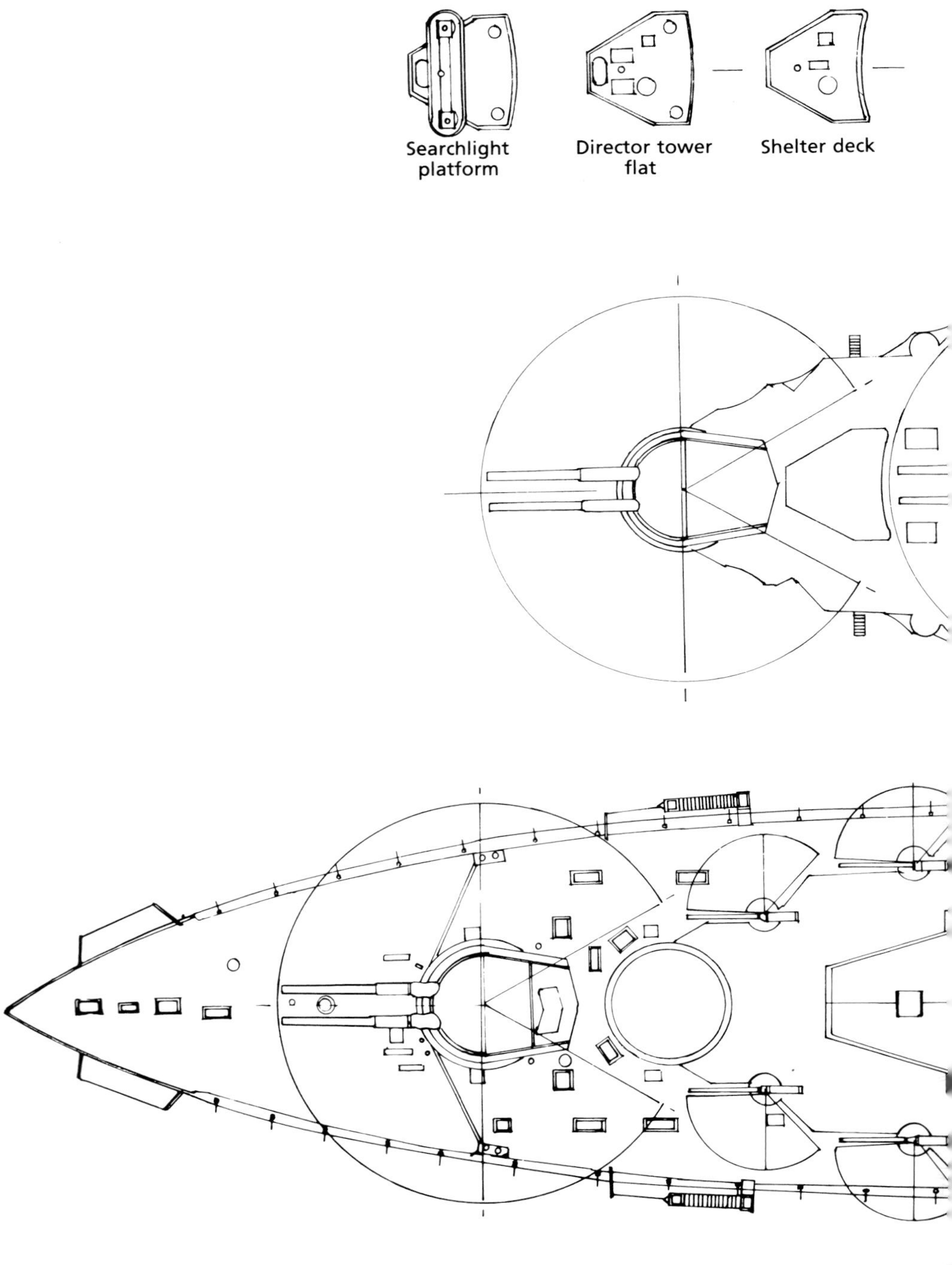

mainmast, but on takeover this was removed prior to entering service with RN.

SL removed from foremast and remounted at forward corners of after superstructure (platform retained). Signal struts fitted on starfish below control top. Large anti-rangefinding nets fitted around control top early in 1915, removed by August 1915.

1915–16 Both 3pdr quick-firing guns removed from after superstructure, as were two on forward superstructure. One 3in AA added on SL platform on after superstructure. SL ex platform over after superstructure remounted on top of superstructure. Anti-torpedo nets replaced temporarily. Topgallant mast removed by August 1915.

1916–17 Director control fitted for main armament. 13.5in director placed on platform below control top as usual. 6in secondary directors fitted port and starboard on ex SL platform on tripod legs. Control top modified and enlarged. Extra 3in AA fitted on platform over aft superstructure. Topmast further reduced.

1917–18 Deflection scales painted on 'B' and 'X' turrets. Range clocks fitted below main director platform and at rear of after superstructure. Searchlights redistributed and improved control

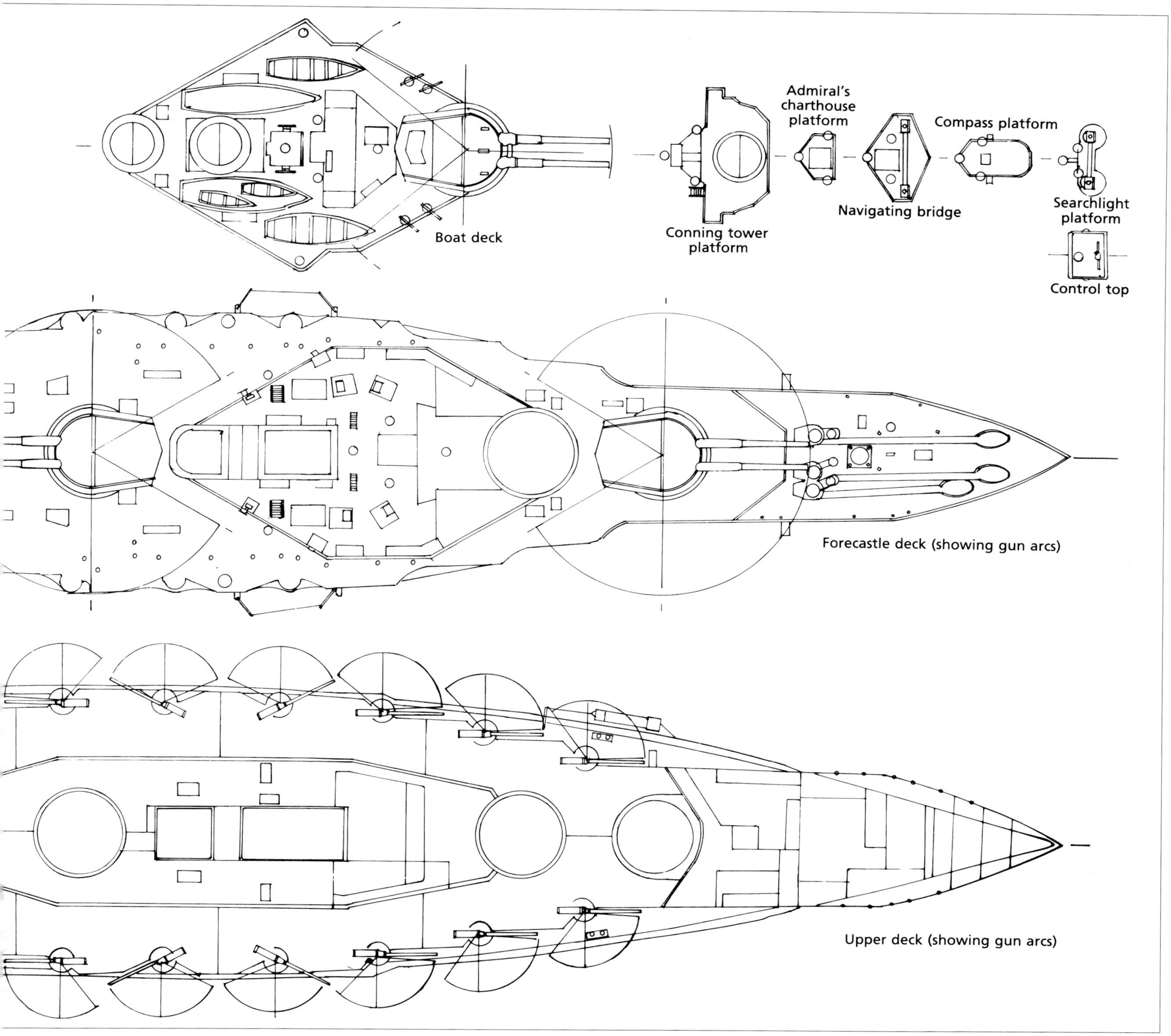

Erin in 1918, at the end of the war. Note the alterations and additions since completion: no nets, enlarged control top and director control improvements, range clock under director control, deflection scales on 'B' and 'X' turrets, 'coffee-box' SL towers around second funnel, improved arrangements in aft superstructure. Also note the director control for the 6in secondary battery just beneath range clock on mast (port and starboard).

Above, left: *Erin* in dry dock at Rosyth, early 1919. Left to right: the old battleships *Mars*, *Temeraire* and *Triumph*.

Above, right: Starboard broadside of *Erin* in Scapa Flow during a quiet period for the battlefleet. Time for a spell of leisure and rowing was always a favourite in the navy. Early 1917.

Below: Starboard quarter view of *Erin* in 1919. Note the 3in HA guns on the after superstructure.

facilities provided. 'Coffee-box'-type SL towers fitted abeam and abaft second funnel, one 36in lamp in each. After pair taller than forward towers. Two 24in signalling lamps added on bridge forward.

1918 High-angle rangefinder added in control top. Aircraft flying-off platforms fitted on 'B' and 'Q' 13.5in turrets. No external changes after this, and she retained this configuration to the end of her life, except that the deflection scales were painted out by 1920.

History: *Erin*

Ordered from Vickers as *Reshad V*, but later renamed *Reshadieh*. Completed shortly before the outbreak of war in August 1914, she was taken over by the Royal Navy on 22 August and renamed *Erin*.

1914 *5 Sept* Joined the Grand Fleet at Scapa Flow; 4th BS until October, then transferred to 2nd BS.
1916 *31 May* Battle of Jutland. No damage sustained.
1919 *March* With 3rd BS Home Fleet.
Oct In reserve at the Nore.
Dec Turret drill ship at Chatham.
1920 *March* Flagship at the Nore.
July Refit at Devonport (to Aug 1920). She was to have been retained under the provisions of the Washington Treaty of 1921, but her role as a seagoing training ship for cadets was instead taken by *Thunderer*.
1922 *May* Placed on the Disposal list.
19 Dec Sold to Cox & Danks.
1923 *Spring* Scrapped at Queenborough.

Canada: WAR PURCHASE

Design

In 1907, Brazil had placed orders with both Vickers and Armstrong for two large dreadnought-type ships, both to be armed with twelve 12in guns. On completion they would, without doubt, outclass anything that other South American Powers could muster at the time, and it was obvious that the ships would not be allowed to reach completion without a counter-bid of some kind. Sure enough, although a relatively poor country, Chile ordered ships to match the Brazilian threat, but not until the Brazilian pair had completed, and similar ships had been laid down for Argentina and Turkey in Great Britain and the United States.

Not content with her new ships, Brazil ordered from Armstrong a superdreadnought to carry the maximum possible number of guns. The design resulted in the *Rio de Janeiro* (later *Agincourt*), armed with fourteen 12in guns on a displacement of 27,500 tons. Shortly after this order had been placed, Chile ordered two large dreadnoughts from Armstrong to the design of J. R. Perret (who designed *Rio de Janeiro*), which would be capable of engaging any capital ship afloat.

The original design showed a displacement of 27,400 tons on a length of 620 feet and a beam of 92 feet. Armed with ten 14in guns, they were expected to be able match fourteen 12in at sea; the 14in shell was capable of penetrating *Rio de Janeiro*'s 9in side armour at ranges of less than 10,000 yards – the distance at which it was thought engagements would take place during a future war. The secondary armament was planned as twenty-two 4.7in guns, but before the final legend was accepted alterations were made to provide sixteen 6in guns, simply because the Brazilian ship carried a 6in secondary armament as did the latest battleships building for the Royal Navy. This addition increased nominal displacement by 600 tons which reduced the designed top speed of 23 knots by approximately half a knot.

The two ships, *Almirante Latorre* and *Almirante Cochrane*, were laid down in 1911. Work on *Almirante Latorre* began immediately, but the second ship had to wait because the Brazilian *Rio de Janeiro* was occupying the firm's second set of stocks and she was not scheduled to launch until late in 1912 or early 1913. *Almirante Latorre* was launched in 1913. *Almirante Cochrane* eventually commenced in February of that year, but work on both ships was stopped at the outbreak of war in August 1914. The Admiralty had planned to expropriate all warships building for foreign Powers and the Chilean pair fell into this category.

Above: *Canada* shortly after completion in 1915.

With *Almirante Latorre* in the fitting-out stage, she was approved for a quick completion, but her sister *Almirante Cochrane* would remain in a state of suspension for the time being. (She was launched in 1918, but converted to a full seagoing aircraft carrier for the Royal Navy.) The takeover of *Almirante Latorre* had been recommended by the British Cabinet on 5 September 1914. Very few alterations were needed to bring her into line for commissioning into the Royal Navy, renamed *Canada*. The limited modifications ordered were:

1. Remove twin derricks for boat-handling, and fit new single stump derrick similar to that in *Iron Duke*.
2. Slight modification of the forward bridge structure.
3. Alterations to the conning position.
4. Fitting of 14in and 6in director towers.
5. Alterations to wireless circuits, to be as in *Royal Sovereign*.

Left: *Canada* leaves Portsmouth, 1918, showing final wartime alterations and additions.

Opposite: *Canada* in Scapa Flow, April 1917.

6. Wireless installation to be enhanced, with Mk III range transmitter fitted.
7. Addition of extra voice pipes where necessary.
8. Slight modification to boat stowage.

Armament

Canada was armed with the 14in gun, which was unique within the Royal Navy. The gun was easily on a par with the British 13.5in; it was manufactured in much the same way, and its shooting qualities were excellent, but only fourteen were produced. The first ten were mounted in *Canada*, the remaining four being kept as spares. Official records show that these four were never used afloat and were scrapped in 1922. Several types of shell were made for the gun, including high-explosive, shrapnel, armour-piercing and common types. Shell weights ranged from 1,400lb to 1,586lb.

The secondary battery was placed considerably farther aft than in *Iron Duke*, although it was found that the after guns would have to be removed because of the blast from 'Q' 14in turret. The shields for the 6in guns were of a new Vickers pattern which allowed full elevation or depression at all arcs of fire. The wings of the side armour, being semi-circular in shape, formed the gun recesses. The anti-aircraft guns were originally to have been located on the forward superstructure abeam the bridge, but were repositioned in the after superstructure when the ship was taken over.

Armour

Like *Agincourt*, *Canada* was not protected on the same scale as British battleships. The 9in main belt was 3in thinner than that fitted in *Iron Duke* and was almost submerged in the deep load condition, when protection would depend entirely on the 7in upper belt – which would hardly keep out 11in and 12in shells.

In the normal condition the vertical protection was 16ft 6in

CANADA: GM AND STABILITY

Based on inclining experiments, 5 September 1915

	Displacement (tons)	Draught	GM	Maximum stability	Stability vanishes at
'A' Condition (= load)*	–	29ft (mean)	4.6ft	30°	56°
'B' Condition (= deep)**	–	31ft 1in	5.3ft	30°	58°

*Fully equipped plus 1,050 tons coal.
**Fully equipped plus 3,300 tons coal, 520 tons oil.

CANADA
Outboard profile and plan, 1915

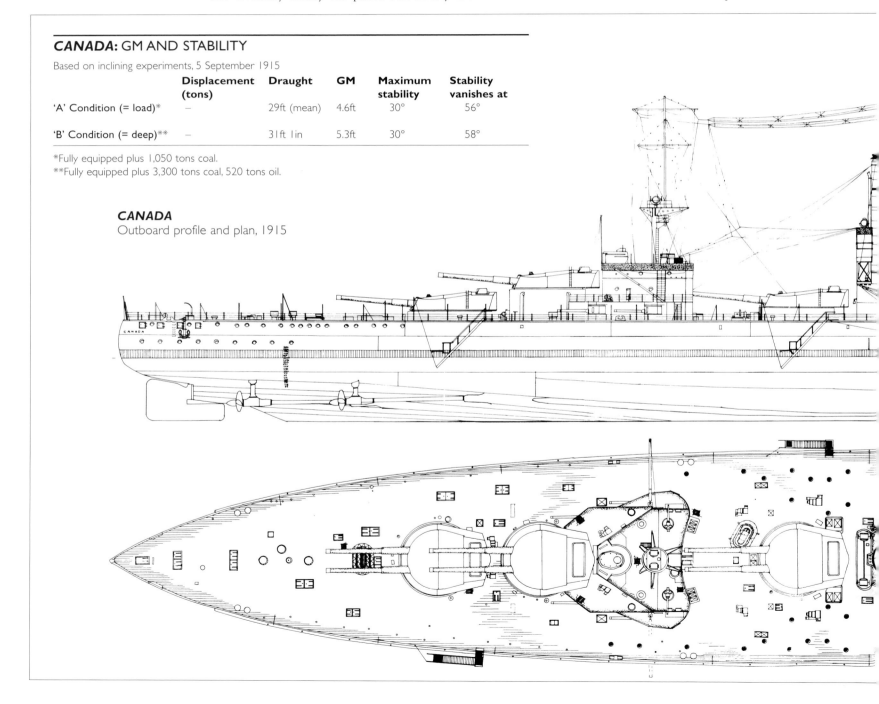

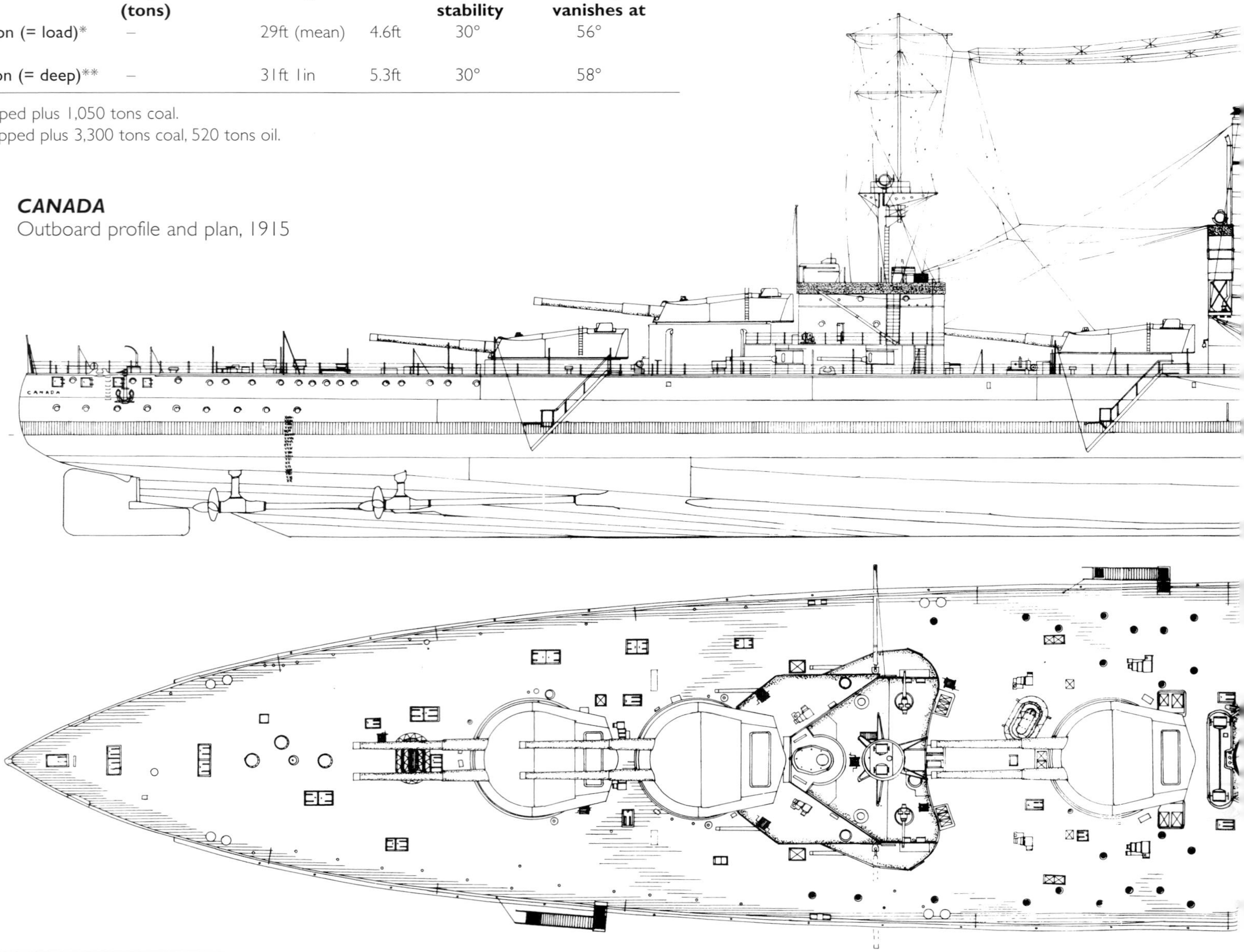

above the water-line and 4ft below. The uniform 9in belt extended to just outside the outer faces of 'A' and 'Y' barbettes, with the upper edge at middle deck level. The forward belt was 6in thick and ran for about 34 feet past the 9in belt before reducing to 4in which continued into the forward bulkhead. Aft, the belt was 4in thick, and ran from the 9in end to within 29 feet of the stern. Both of these end belts were on the same level as the amidships 9in strake. Above the 9in belt, a 7in thickness ran for the same length as the 9in, but at middle and main deck levels. Over this 7in run was another belt of 4½in which reduced to 4in at the forward extremities.

The main bulkheads were 3in forward and 4in aft. They both ran obliquely inwards from the lower edge of the 7in belt and joined the outer faces of 'A' and 'Y' barbettes respectively. A secondary 4in forward bulkhead closed the extremities of the side belt armour between lower and upper deck levels. Aft, the secondary bulkhead was of the same thickness and closed the

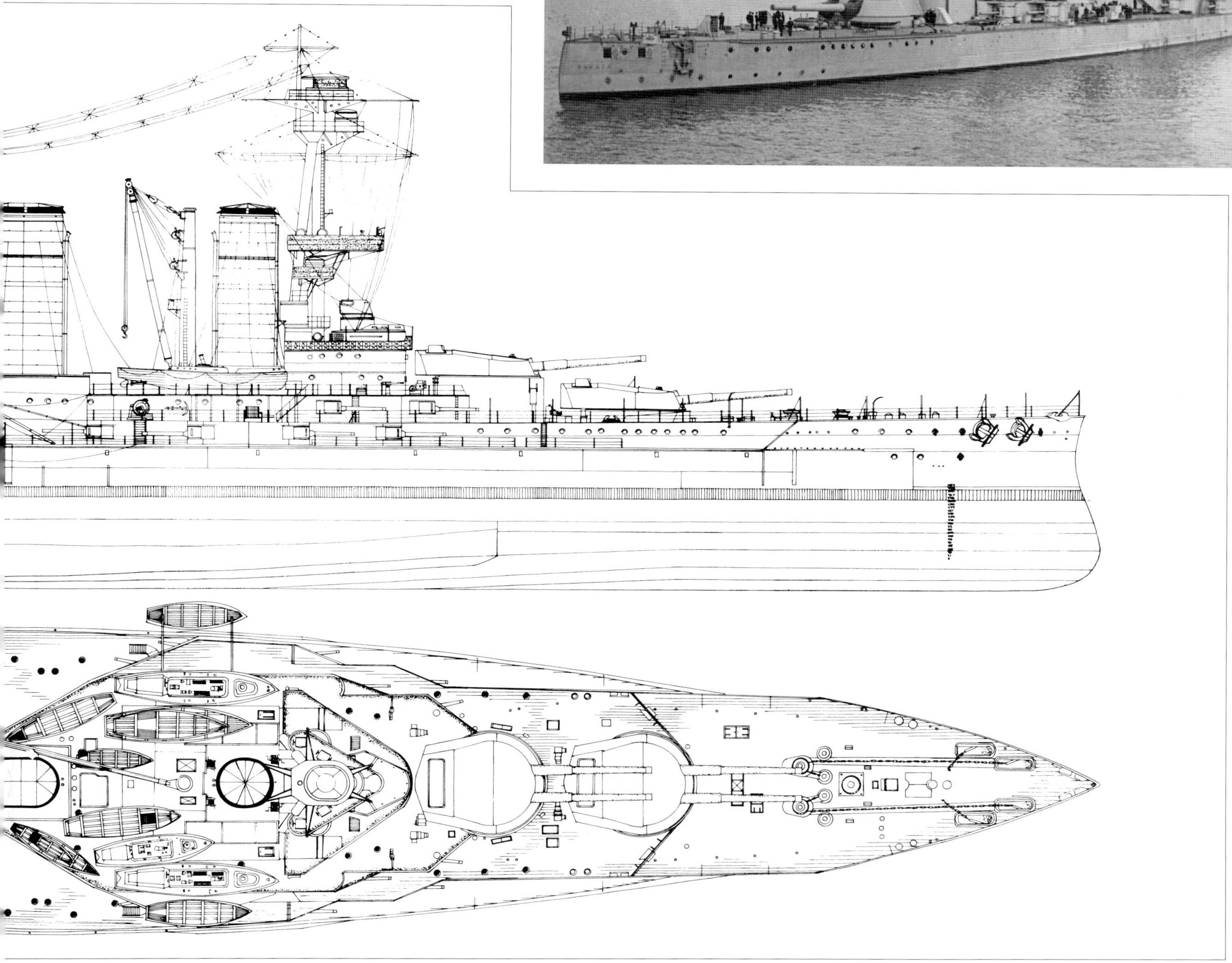

CANADA (EX-*ALMIRANTE LATORRE*): PARTICULARS, AS COMPLETED

Construction
Armstrong; laid down Dec 1911; launched 27 Nov 1913; completed Nov 1915.

Displacement (tons)
26,968 (light), 28,622 (normal), 32,188 (deep).

Dimensions
Length: 625ft pp, 654ft 10in wl, 661ft oa
Beam: 92ft
Draught (mean): 29ft 6in (normal), 31ft 11in max.
Freeboard: 27ft forward, 16ft amidships, 17ft 6in aft
Height of 14in guns above lower wl: 'A' 30ft 8½in; 'B' 40ft 8½in; 'Q' 24ft 11½in; 'X' 33ft 8½in; 'Y' 23ft 8½in
Height of CT vision slits above lower wl: 52ft 9in
Height of fore funnel above lower wl: 86ft
Height of fore topmast: 122ft
Depth of keel from upper deck: 43ft 9¾in.

Armament
Ten 14in 45cal Mk I; 100rpg
Sixteen 6in 50cal; 200rpg
Two 3in AA; 300rpg
Four MG (for boats); 5,000rpg
Four 21in torpedo tubes; twenty torpedoes.

Director control
On takeover office fitted, as in British ships, aloft just beneath control top. 'X' turret fitted as master turret.

Armour.
Main belt: 9in
Ends: 6in–4in
Upper side: 4½in–4in; lower side: 7in–6in–4in
Main bulkheads: 4½in–3in
Barbettes: 10in–6in–4in
Turrets: 10in–4in–3in
Decks: shelter, 1in, forecastle 1in, upper 1½in, main 1½in, middle 4in–1in, lower 2in
Secondary battery: 6in
Conning tower: 11in–3in
After torpedo control tower: 6in–2in
Tubes: 6in–3in
Magazine screens: 2in–1½in–1¼in.

CANADA
Inboard profile and upper deck plan, showing gun arcs, 1915

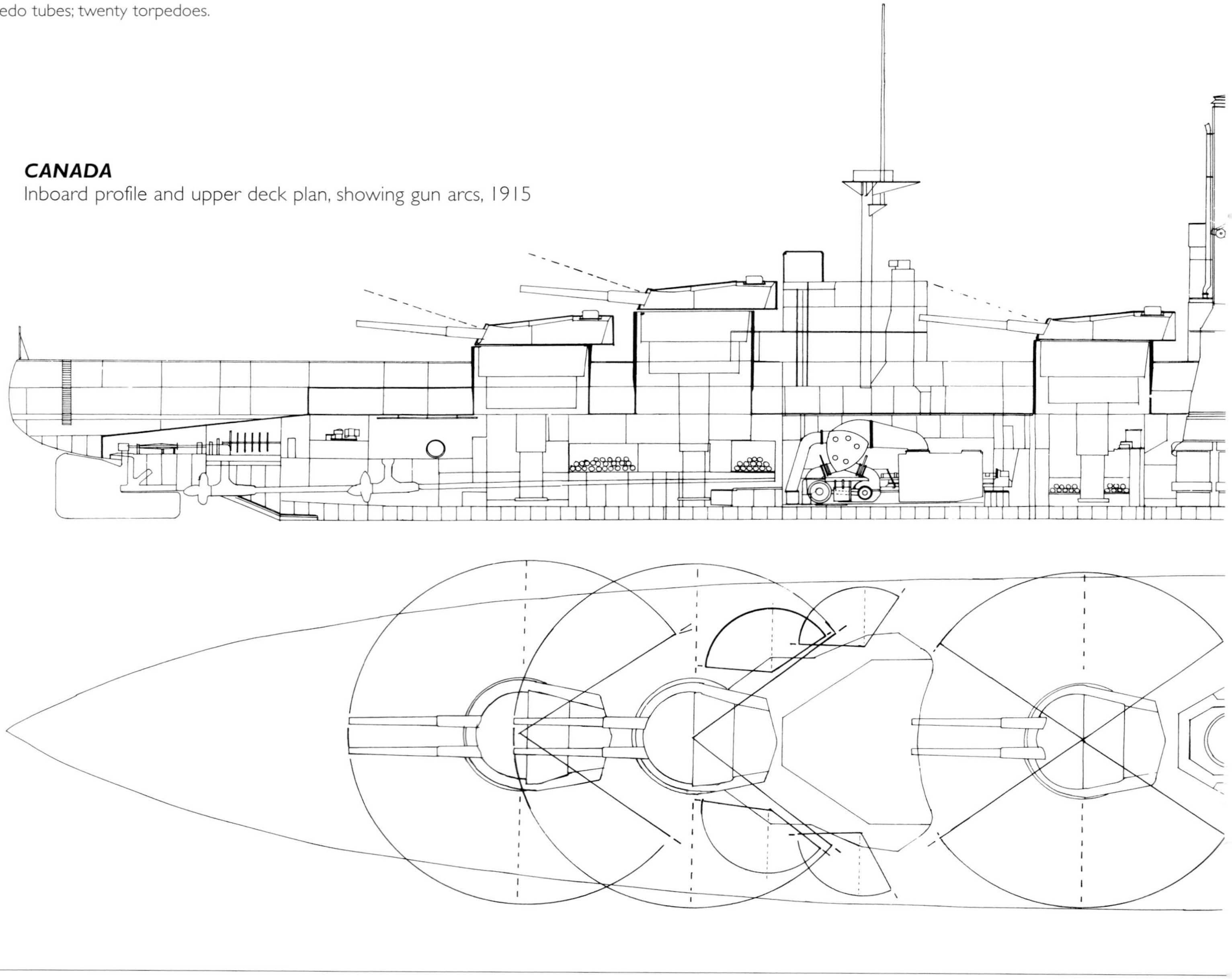

Machinery
Parsons and Brown Curtis turbines, four propellers
Boilers: twenty-one Yarrow large-tube, working pressure 250psi
Pressure at turbines: 225psi
Length of boiler rooms: (1) 68ft, (2) 64ft, (3) 56ft
Length of engine rooms: 70ft (divided into three compartments abreast two main condensers)
Cooling surface: 38,000sq ft
Heating surface: 11,020sq ft
Grate area: 2,303sq ft
Fuel: 1,050 tons coal min., 3,300 tons coal, 520 tons oil max.
Radius of action: 4,400nm at 10 knots. Could cruise at 13.5 knots with 6,540shp.

Ship's boats
Pinnaces (steam): two 50ft
Launches (steam): two 36ft
Launches (motor): one 36ft
Launches (sail): one 34ft
Dinghies (motor): one 23ft
Cutters: two 30ft
Gigs: one 30ft
Skiff dinghies: one 16ft
Rafts: two 14ft.

Searchlights
Eight 36in: two platform rear second funnel, two after superstructure, four upper bridge forward.

Rangefinder positions
One foremast, one each turret, one after director tower, one in revolving hood forward.

Anchors
Four 160cwt stockless (2 bower, 2 sheet).

Wireless
Main office: Types 1–16 fitted on takeover Type W/T 9 short-radius.

Complement
1,167–1,178.

Cost
Admiralty estimate £2,500,000.

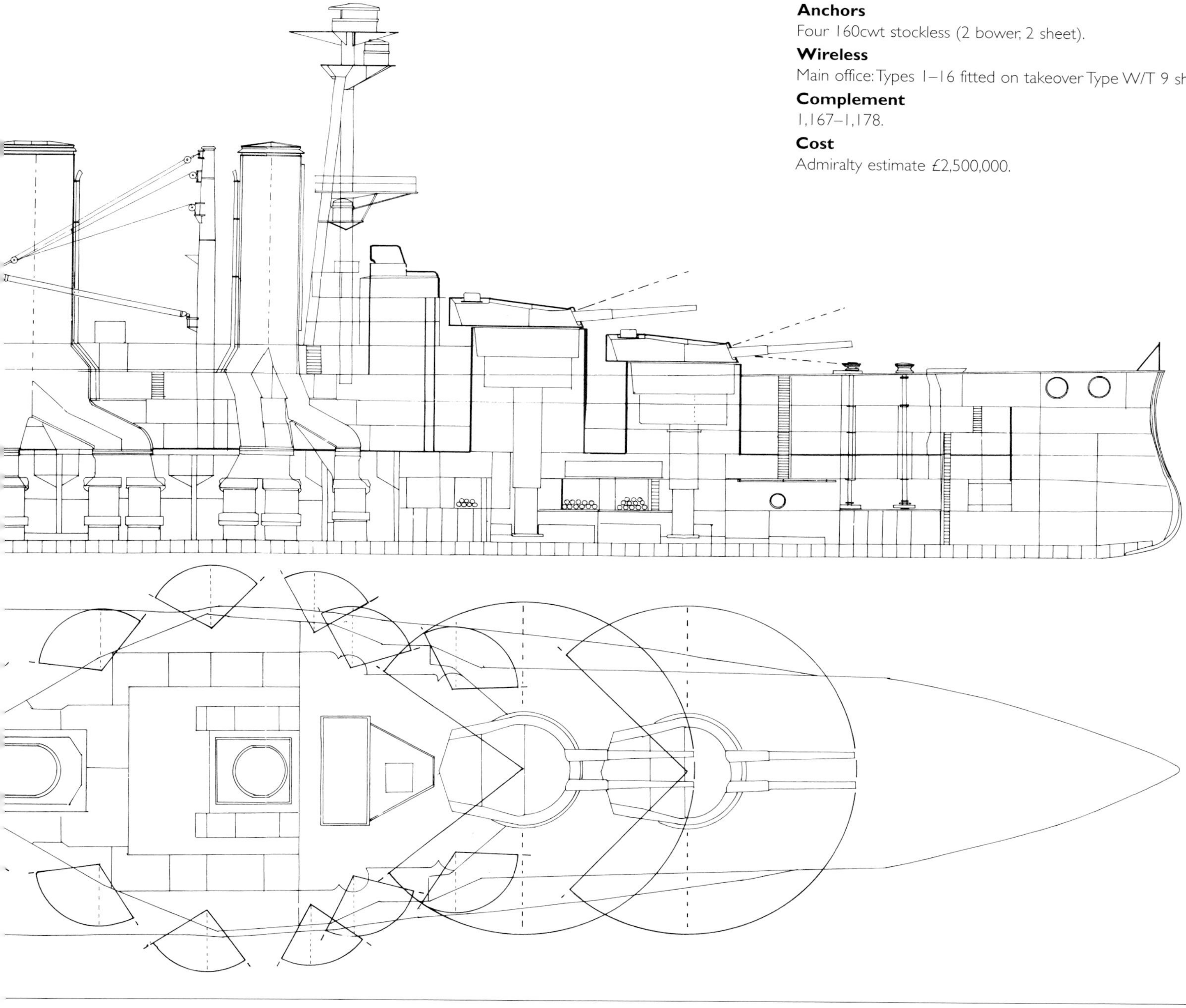

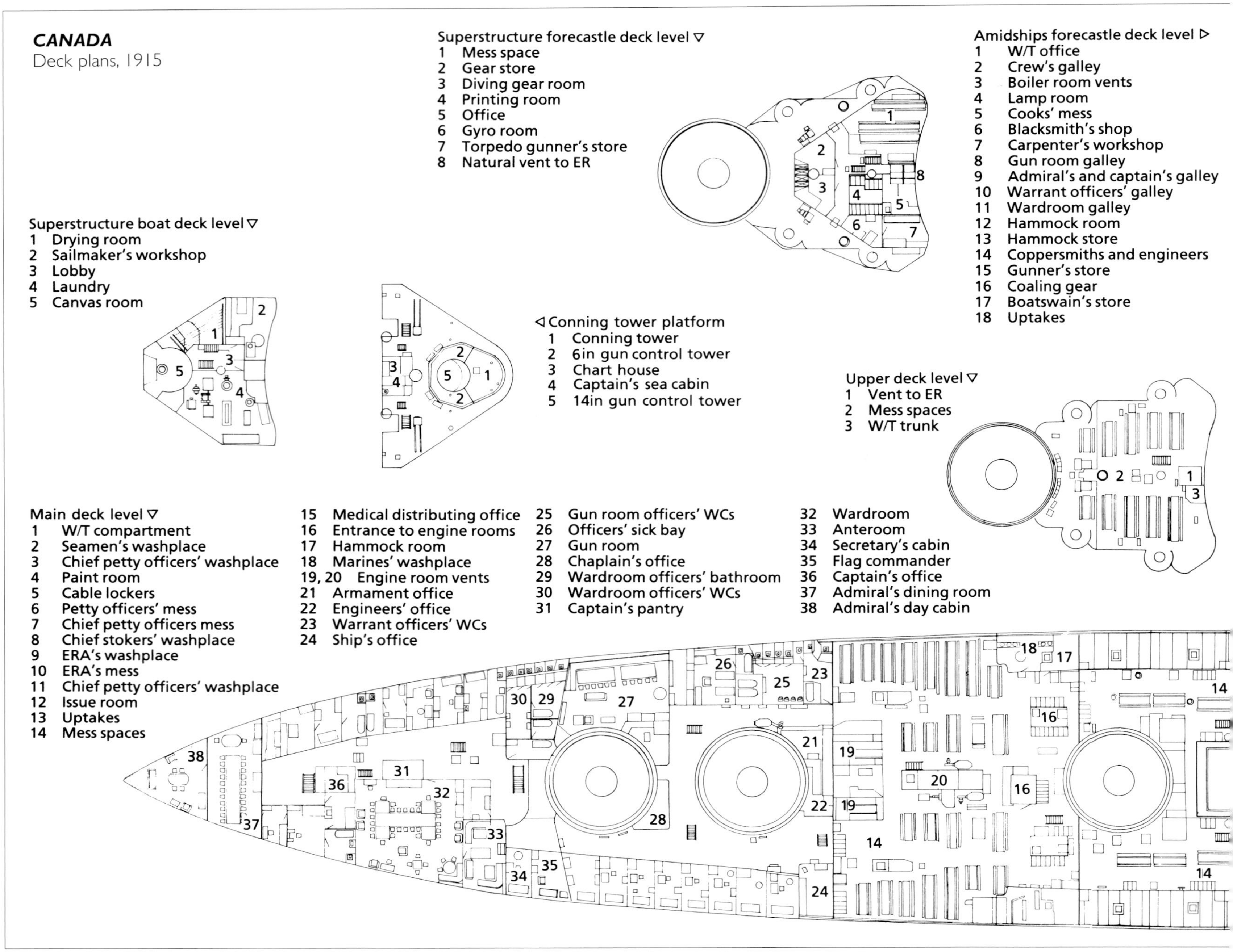

ends of the side armour between middle and main decks.

As usual, the barbettes varied in thickness: 'A' and 'Q' 10in above the upper deck, reducing to 6in from upper to main deck, with 4in below the main deck. 'B' and 'X' outer faces as in 'A'; inner faces were 10in above the shelter deck and 6in from shelter deck to upper deck; below this level the thickness reduced to 4in. 'Y' outer faces were 10in reducing to 4in below main deck level; inner faces were 10in above the upper deck, 6in upper to main and 4in below main deck level. Turrets were 10in on the face, 9in on the sides with a 4in roof. The forward and after battery were protected by 6in on the sides and a 1in roof. Sighting hoods over each battery, port and starboard, were a uniform 3in.

The conning tower had 11in sides, 6in base, 3in roof and its communications tube was 6in. The conning tower hood had 6in sides, and a 3in roof. The torpedo conning tower was given 6in sides and a 2in roof. Its tube was 6in reducing to 3in. The forecastle deck was 1in over the lower forward battery. The upper deck was 1½in between the forward bulkhead and the outer face of 'Y' barbette except over the forward battery. The main deck was protected by 1½in plates (aft only) and was outside 'Y' barbette between the lower side bulkhead and the after bulkhead. The middle deck ran from the forward bulkhead almost through to the stern, 1in thick on the flat and slope, increasing to 4in over the steering gear. The lower deck (forward only) sloped downwards from the base of the forward bulkhead to the stem of the ship. Magazine screens were fitted longitudinally, port and starboard, but abreast the magazines only. The forward magazines were protected by plates of 1¼in–1½in–1¾in–2in thickness. Midships, the screens were 1½in uniform, the after screens were 1½in–2in thick.

Machinery

The main machinery consisted of two sets of Brown Curtis and Parsons turbines, which were divided into three compartments. Abreast these were eight condensers which gave a cooling surface of 38,000 sq ft and two auxiliary condensers (7,000 sq ft).

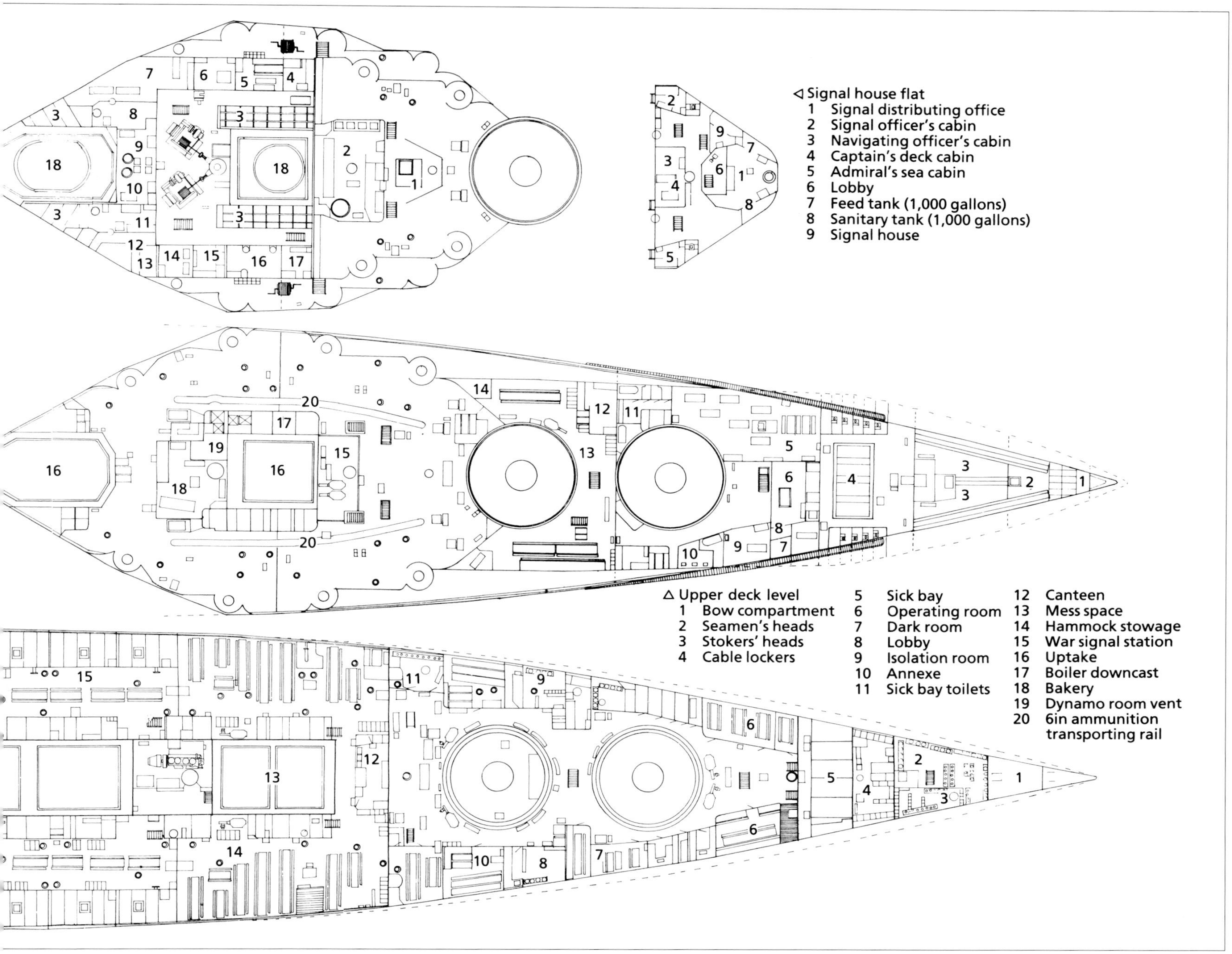

There were four shafts driving four propellers. The HP ahead and astern were located on the outer shafts, the LP ahead and astern were fitted to the inner shafts. Turbines of the reaction-type, direct drive were fitted, designed for a working speed of 300rpm. The machinery for *Canada* was very similar to that of *Emperor of India* in both arrangement and layout.

Pressure at the turbines was 226psi and *Canada* was able to maintain 13.5 knots with just 6,450shp. With a maximum speed of 23 to 24 knots, she was one of the fastest battleships to serve with the Grand Fleet.

A verbal request was sent by the DNC, Eustace Tennyson D'Eyncourt, to the Government of Chile in 1920, asking for basic details of the ship for Admiralty records, as it had not been possible to carry out any extensive trials during her period with the Royal Navy. The Chilean Government did not reply in any great detail, but merely sent a few notes on her metacentric height (GM), displacement and general dimensions. There were no steam trial figures.

CANADA: STEAM TRIALS

It being wartime, no speed trials were conducted. The following figures were recorded at sea on 16 May 1918.

303rpm	38,247shp	22.7 knots
310rpm	43,850shp	not recorded
335.5rpm	52,682shp	24.3 knots

Appearance Changes

Before commissioning into the Royal Navy, the original (much larger) bridge and charthouse were removed and replaced by two small open platforms built higher up around tripod legs, very exposed to the elements. The navigating platform was extended well forward, and no charthouse was provided. The heavy boats were stowed between the funnels, and were handled by the newly fitted single stump mast on the centreline close abaft the fore funnel.

Canada, 1918.

Left: Clear port-bow view of *Canada* coming into Portsmouth showing wartime modifications, 1918.

Below: *Canada* in the dockyard before being placed in the Reserve Fleet on the breakup of the Grand Fleet in April 1919.

The large tall funnels gave her a rather heavy profile, and she always looked low in the water, trimming by the bows.

1916–17 One bridge searchlight on each side was raised on small platform. After superstructure searchlights remounted on platform low on mainmast. Foretop mast reduced to stump. Signal struts fitted at starfish below control top, with unusually long strut forward. Yard below starfish was retained.

1917/18 Control top enlarged.

Medium-base rangefinder added over torpedo control tower replacing original small rangefinder. Deflection scales painted on sides of 'A' and 'Y' turrets. Range clocks fitted abaft torpedo control tower on after superstructure.

After pair of 6in guns removed from after battery because of blast damage from 'Q' main turret when fired on extreme bearing forward. Original SL position at rear of second funnel removed and replaced by new 'coffee-box' towers.

1918 Range clock added over control top. Aircraft platforms fitted over 'B' and 'X' turrets. Fore spotting top was given windows, enclosing that position.

1920 Handed back to Chile: no basic changes seen until her large refit at Devonport in 1929/31, which included: Improved fire control. Bridge structure remodelled. Foretopmast made taller, and extra yard fitted. Steam pipes on funnel enclosed. Searchlights on forward bridge removed. Secondary armament fire control fitted. Catapult for aircraft fitted on quarterdeck (1931). Tall topmast fitted on aft island, with small structure placed near base. Anti-torpedo bulges fitted, similar to those in British *Queen Elizabeth* class (in two parts). New wireless equipment fitted. 9ft rangefinder fitted in forward superstructure. After mast now only carried one yard. AA guns fitted in after island. Machinery completely renewed.

As *Almirante Latorre*, she kept this basic configuration (with the exception of increased AA guns during the Second World War) until scrapped in 1959. It is possible RDF installation was fitted during and after the war.

History: *Canada*

Ordered from Armstrong Whitworth by the Chilean Government. Laid down as *Valparaiso*, but name changed to *Almirante Latorre* just prior to her launch on 27 November 1913. Taken over by the British Government on 9 September 1914 for

Right: *Almirante Latorre* (ex-*Canada*), *c.* 1932/3, as a unit of the Chilean Navy. Note the modifications as fitted during 1929/31 refit. New bridgework, anti-torpedo bulges, improvements to SL arrangements, and AA guns.

service with the Royal Navy. Completed in 1915.

1915 *15 Oct* Commissioned for service with 4th BS Grand Fleet.
1916 *31 May* Battle of Jutland. Fired 42 rounds of 14in and 109 rounds of 6in, but was not hit herself.
12 June Transferred to 1st BS.
1919 *March* Reduced to reserve.
1920 *April* Re-purchased by Chilean Government.
27 Nov Formally handed over at Devonport and re-assumed name of *Almirante Latorre.* Few details of her service with the Chilean Navy, but she is known to have spent much time patrolling during the Second World War.
1959 Sold to a Japanese scrapping firm, the last surviving dreadnought to have served with the British Fleet at Jutland.
28 Aug Arrived at Tokyo Bay where she lay for some time before being broken up.

Below: *Almirante Latorre* (ex-*Canada*) seen in Devonport dockyard at the start of her long 1929–31 refit.

Agincourt: WAR PURCHASE

Design

The concept of this ship had its origin in the long and intense struggle between Argentina, Brazil and Chile to achieve supremacy in naval power. The Brazilian Government ordered from Armstrong a battleship greatly exceeding their requirements and financial means, and the vessel, to be named *Rio de Janeiro*, was laid down in September 1911. Three sketch designs were considered (Designs 1–3). The Brazilians, demanding that the ship carry the most powerful guns in existence, favoured Design 2 but asked for alterations to armour thickness so as to match British ships, which mostly had a 12in main strake. Armstrong's representative tried for an acceptance of the ship carrying 14in or 15in guns because a suitable 16in naval gun had not yet been manufactured; its procurement would involve a time-scale unacceptable to the Brazilians.

After much argument it was decided that the heaviest and beamiest ship (Design 1) should proceed and the contract was placed, against much foreign competition, with Armstrong. Within a few months, the Brazilian Government fell and financial restrictions were imposed until the new government could restore some semblance of order to the country. The contract was cancelled as being too large and too expensive, but an alternative design was asked for. A party, headed by Eustace Tennyson D'Eyncourt (who later would become DNC), was sent by Armstrong to Rio de Janeiro with alternative proposals by D'Eyncourt based on original sketches by J. R. Perret, Chief Constructor at Armstrong. This fourth design was a version of Design 3, of less imposing dimensions though carrying the same armament. The sketch design showed a vessel that was unique, rather large in size and carrying the largest number of heavy guns ever mounted in a battleship. It was accepted overnight.

In November 1913, only ten months after the ship's launch, financial problems in Brazil raised doubts about payment, and the ship was put up for sale. She was quickly purchased by the Imperial Ottoman Government for approximately £2,225,000, and was renamed *Sultan Osman I* while fitting out. At the outbreak of war she was formally expropriated by the Royal Navy and renamed *Agincourt* on 3 August 1914. Little alteration was needed to suit her to the requirements of British seagoing staff, but the following changes were made to bring her in line for commissioning in the Royal Navy:

1. Two 6in guns (port and starboard) were fitted in shields near the forward superstructure.
2. Anti-torpedo nets were removed.
3. Both topmasts and topgallants were removed.
4. Bridge wings were reduced in length.
5. The flying deck amidships was removed at the expense of reducing the lifeboat complement, but this was accepted in the interest of saving 82 tons.

RIO DE JANEIRO: PRELIMINARY DESIGNS

	1. Brazilian plan (Alexandrio)	2. Brazilian plan (de Bacellar)	3. British plan (Perret)	4. British plan (D'Eyncourt/Perret)
Displacement:	31,600 tons	30,500 tons	31,250 tons	27,500 tons
Length:	650ft	630ft	650ft	632ft
Beam:	92ft	90ft	90ft	89ft
Draught:	27ft	28ft	29ft	29ft
Speed:	22 knots	23 knots	23 knots	22 knots
Armament:	Twelve 14in Sixteen 6in Fourteen 4in	Eight 16in Six 9.4in –	Ten 15in* Fourteen 6in Four 3in	Fourteen 12in Eighteen 6in Twelve 3in
Armour:	12in–9in–6in belt 8in upper belt 6in battery 10in–12in turrets	9in main belt 10in–12in turrets	9in–6in–4in belt 9in upper belt 6in battery 12in turrets	9in belt 6in battery 9in turrets

*Or 16in if required.

DESIGN 685, JANUARY 1911
Displacement: 31,000 tons
Length: 650ft
Beam: 92ft
Armament: ten 16in, fourteen 6in

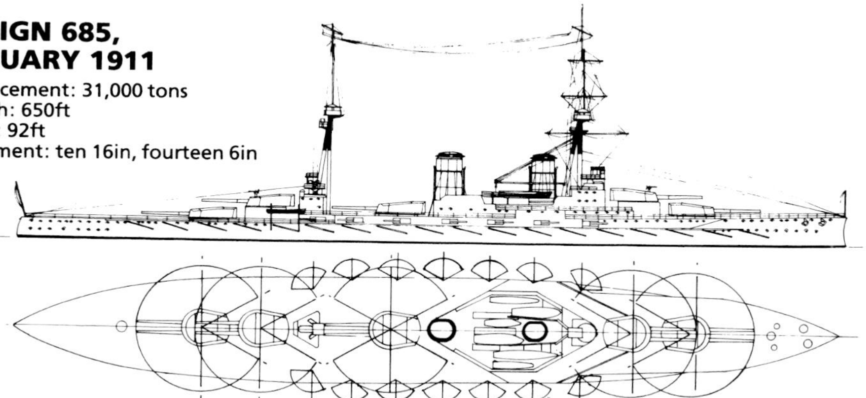

DESIGN 686
Displacement: 30,500 tons
Length: 630ft
Beam: 92ft
Armament: eight 16in, six 9.4in, fourteen 6in

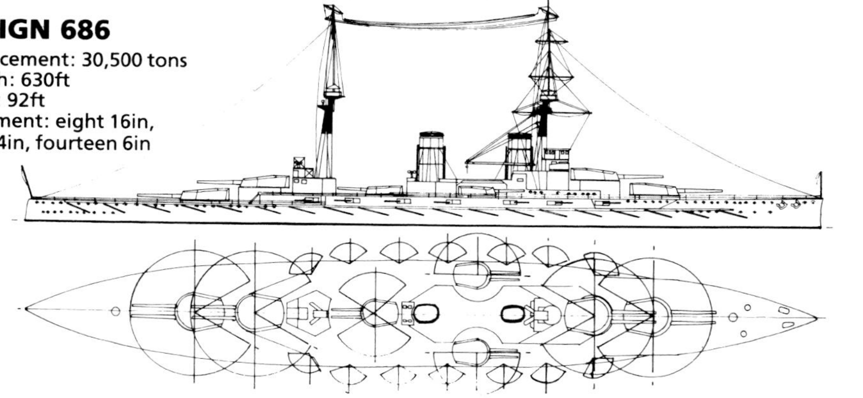

DESIGNS 685 AND 686
Armour layouts

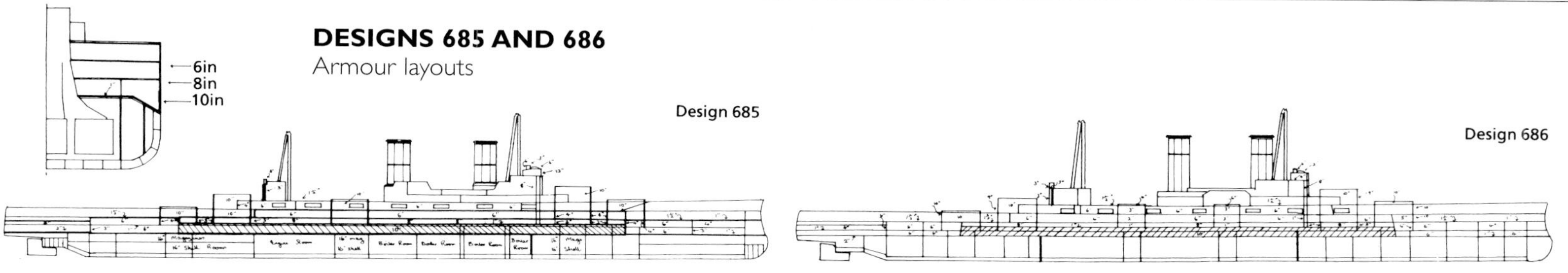

SULTAN OSMAN I: PARTICULARS, AS COMPLETED

Construction
Armstrong; laid down 14 Sept 1911; launched 22 Jan 1913; started trials July 1914; completed 20 Aug 1914.

Displacement (tons)
24,792 (light), 27,850 (load), 30,860 (deep), 31,620 (1918).

Dimensions
Length: 632ft pp, 668ft wl, 671ft 6in oa
Beam: 89ft
Draught: 29ft 10in (mean deep)
Height of 12in turrets above lower wl: 'A' 30ft 6in; 'B' 41ft; 'P' 30ft; 'Q' 30ft; 'X' 24ft; 'Y' 34ft 6in; 'Z' 24ft
Height of CT vision slits above lower wl: 49ft
Height of fore funnel: 76ft
Height of fore topmast: 108ft
Depth of keel from battery deck: 43ft.

Armament
Fourteen 12in 45cal (special mounting, Armstrong design)
Twenty 6in (eighteen as designed)
Ten 3in QF
Four 3pdr (saluting)
Three 21in torpedo tubes.

Director control
Fitted aloft in tower (similar to British practice); one turret fitted with directing gear.

Armour
Main belt: 9in amidships
Upper belt: 6in amidships
Main bulkheads: 3in forward and aft
Upper side bulkheads: 6in forward and aft
Forward bulkhead: 3in
After bulkhead: 6in–3in
Stern bulkhead: 2½in
Decks: forecastle 1½in, upper 1½in, main 1½in–1in, lower 2½in–1in
Barbettes: 9in–3in–2in
Turrets: 12in–10in–8in
Secondary battery: 6in, 1in traverses
Conning tower: 12in side, 4in roof
Communications tube: 8in–3in
Hood: 6in–4in
After CT: 9in–3in
Tube: 6in–2in
Magazine screens: 1½in–1in.

Machinery
Parsons direct-drive turbines, four propellers
Boilers: twenty-two Babcock & Wilcox, working pressure 235psi
Heating surface: 78,812sq ft
Grate area: 2,150sq ft
Designed SHP: 34,000 = 22 knots
Fuel: 1,500 tons coal normal, 3,200 tons coal max.; 620 tons oil
Radius of action: 7,000nm at 10 knots (official figure)
Auxiliary machinery: four steam-driven reciprocating dynamos.

Ship's boats*
Pinnaces (steam): two 50ft
Pinnaces (sail): one 36ft
Launches (steam): two 36ft
Launches (motor): one 36ft
Dinghies (motor): one 23ft
Launches: one 44ft
Cutters: two 30ft
Gigs: one 30ft
Dinghies: one 16ft
Rafts: two 14ft.

Searchlights
Six 36in: two upper bridge, two main derrick platform amidships, two on platform very low on main tripod legs (port and starboard). One 24in: on platform immediately below after control top.

Rangefinder positions
One on foremast, one in each turret.

Battle signal stations
Office near foremast.

Anchors
Three 150cwt stockless (2 bower, 1 sheet), one 50cwt stream, one 35cwt stream.

Wireless
Main office: Mk I (after takeover)
Second office: Types 2–34
Fire control office: Type 31.

Complement
1,109 (7 Aug 1914); 1,268 (1917).

Cost
Estimated £2,900,000.

*Original stowage showed one 56ft vedette, four 36ft steam pinnaces, two 30ft auxiliary motor cutters, one 25ft motor boat.

The outstanding balance of £690,000 from the Turkish Government's purchase price was paid to Armstrong by the British Government

Armament

The original designs called for armaments of: Design 1, twelve 14in in six twin turrets; Design 2, eight 16in in four twin turrets; Design 3, ten 15in or 16in in five twin turrets. The first two were at the insistence of the Brazilian Admiral de Bacellar; the third had been proposed by J. R. Perret, but complied with Brazilian wishes.

Design 1 was initially approved, but following the change of government it was rejected for reasons already mentioned; furthermore, a lobby was arguing for retention of a 12in calibre to conform to the existing battleships *Minas Geraes* and *São Paulo*. The accepted layout of fourteen 12in provided Brazil with a battleship having an exceptional volume of firepower, quite unmatched by any dreadnought afloat. The main guns, mounted in specially designed turrets and barbettes, could fire broadsides on either beam, although the problems of hull stress from such an unprecedented number of turrets were considerable. To counterbalance the colossal weight of the three twin turrets on the quarterdeck, special longitudinal girders were fitted beneath the supporting decks, consideration being given to the fact that stress and fatigue would be more of a problem when the guns fired full broadsides.

The massive secondary armament featured eighteen 6in guns protected by 6in armour. The forecastle was recessed before the battery to allow ahead fire for the forward pair of guns, and angled inwards aft, to permit a considerable degree of astern fire for the last two pairs. On takeover, however, two more 6in guns were added abeam the bridgework, and were given splinter shields for limited protection.

Armour

So much weight had been allocated to the armament that there was not much left for protective purposes, which resulted in a lower standard than was usual in British battleships. The distribution of the armoured strakes on such a large vessel was remarkably well laid out, but the thickness of the armour was inadequate, especially in the areas of the barbettes: the main 9in armoured belt ran for a length of 365 feet, extending from the outer face of 'B' barbette to abeam the centre of 'Y' (raised turret), with its upper edge at main deck level. Forward of this strake 6in armour ran

Opposite, top: The Turkish *Sultan Osman I* (*Agincourt*) in the Armstrong shipyard fitting out during the spring of 1914.

Opposite, bottom: *Sultan Osman I* bound for Devonport in July 1914 after being taken over by the Royal Navy (renamed *Agincourt* in August 1914).

AGINCOURT

Outboard profile, 3 August 1914, showing flying decks amidships

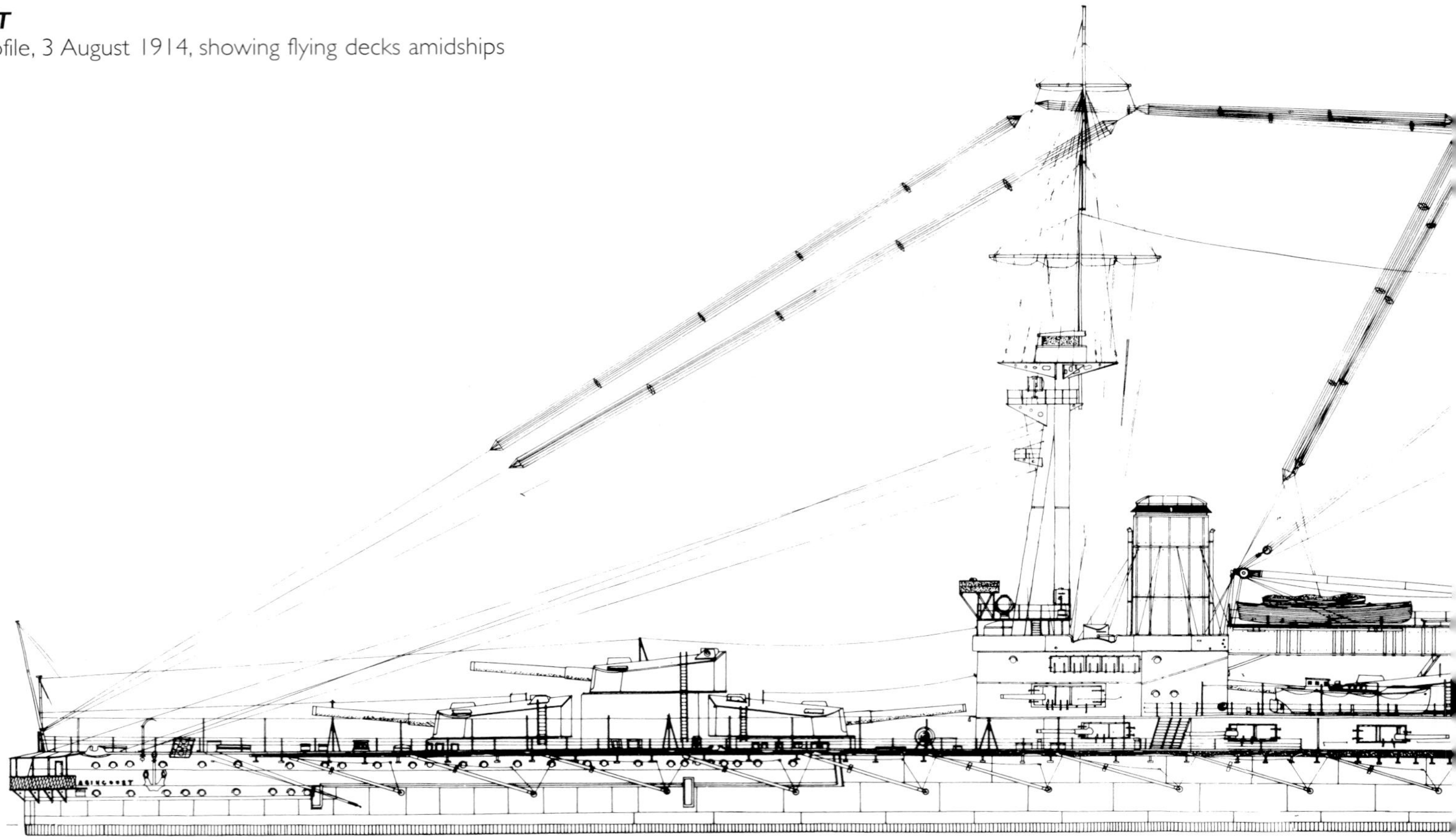

through at the same height for approximately 50 feet and then reduced to 4in which ran through to the stem of the vessel.

Aft of the 9in main belt the thickness again reduced to 6in, and ran approximately 30 feet past the after barbette where it reduced to 4in. This 4in run did not carry through to the stern, but was met by the end bulkhead. Above the 9in main belt amidships, ran the upper side belt which was 6in thick and ran from the inside of 'B' barbette to just beyond the inner face of the fifth barbette, and was located between the upper and main deck levels.

The main bulkheads were extended obliquely inwards from the forward and after extremities of the 9in main armoured belt, to the outer faces of the forward and after barbettes at a thickness of 3in. The upper side bulkheads extended from the same extremities, running obliquely inwards of the 6in upper belt armour and terminated in the same position as the lower bulkhead at the barbette faces.

AGINCOURT: GM AND STABILITY

Estimated by Armstrong, 1914

	Displacement (tons)	Draught (mean)	GM	Maximum stability	Stability vanishes at
'A' Condition (= load)*	–	27ft	4.2ft	35°	58°
'B' Condition (= deep)**	–	29ft 10in	4.9ft	35°	60°–65°

As inclined by Royal Navy, 6 July 1918

	Displacement (tons)	Draught (mean)	GM	Maximum stability	Stability vanishes at
Light	27,020			34°	56.8°
Legend	28,840			33.5°	59.8°
Deep	31,620			33.5°	61.7°

28,840 (legend), 31,620 (deep).

*Fully equipped plus 210 tons coal upper, 1,283 tons coal lower bunkers and 178 tons freshwater.

**Fully equipped plus 3,200 tons coal, 620 tons oil.

The deck protection was quite complicated in its layout: the forecastle deck amidships was 1½in thick and ran over the 6in battery; the upper deck was also 1½in and ran between the fourth and fifth barbettes over the engine and boiler rooms. The main deck was 1in–1½in and ran from the forward main bulkhead through to the stem; aft, this deck terminated at the after bulkhead having run from the main bulkhead face. The middle deck was 1½in on the slopes and 1in elsewhere; it ran from the forward barbette through to the stern; the lower deck was 1in forward and 2½in aft. Both lower-deck ends were below water.

Barbette protection was one of the ship's poor qualities. Ranging from 9in to 3in, it was certainly inadequate against 12in shells. On the foremost barbette there was a 9in uniform thickness of armour above the main deck level, but this reduced drastically to 3in once below. 'B' barbette had 9in on the outer faces until main deck level, and no armour at all after this, having thinned down to 3in from the forecastle to main deck level. The third and fourth barbettes were 9in thick above upper deck level, and 3in from upper deck to main deck, and had no armour after this. The fifth barbette was 9in above the upper deck, 3in from upper to main deck, reducing to 2in once below main deck level. The raised sixth barbette was 9in above the main deck, with 3in on the inner faces once past the main deck, and then no armour at all. That for the after barbette was identical with the fifth. Turret armour was 12in on the face, 8in sides and a 10in rear. Roof plates were 3in on the front and 2in at the rear.

The secondary battery was protected by a 6in strake at forecastle/upper deck level, which was met by 6in bulkheads at the ends. Sighting hoods for the secondary guns were located between the fifth and sixth guns and armoured with 3in plates.

The conning tower was protected by 12in plates on the sides, 4in roof and a 3in floor. The hood was 6in thick on the sides and

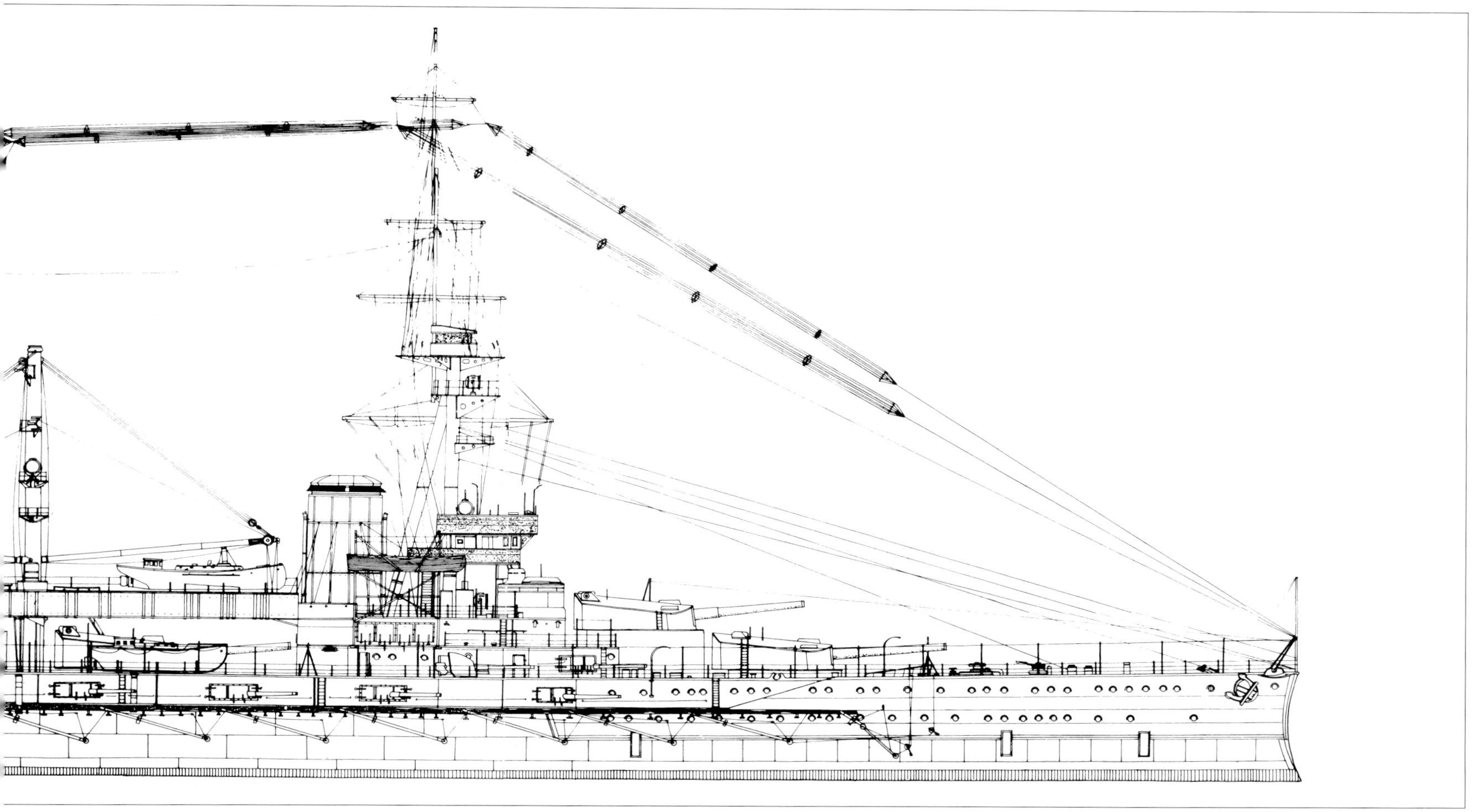

had a 4in floor. The after conning position sported 9in armour on the sides, with 3in roof and floor. The communications tube was 6in from the upper deck, reducing to 2in once below this level.

Magazine screens were longitudinal abreast magazines only, and had a thickness of 1½in outer and 1in inner abreast the forward magazine; the after screen was identical with the forward screen. Single 1½in and 1in screens were fitted abreast the midships magazines.

Reviewing these figures for *Agincourt*, it can hardly be claimed that she was a well-protected vessel, but she had been designed to rely on her massive weight of broadside for protective qualities.

Machinery

Parsons direct-drive turbines serving four propellers. The HP ahead and astern turbines were fitted on the wing shafts and the LP ahead and astern were on the inner shafts. Because of the great length of the ship, she was able to stow more fuel than was standard British practice (1,500 tons minimum), but maximum stowage was on a par with British contemporaries at 3,500 tons. Because her oil stowage was slightly less than usual, her estimated radius of action was somewhat reduced, but in practice gave figures in excess of most British designs.

War was declared at about the same time as the vessel was commissioned and full steam trials were not carried out by the Royal Navy, but she did undergo a series of tests for her builders off St Abb's Head on 17 July 1914 and produced the results detailed in the table.

Appearance Changes

Her appearance was very distinctive and impressive, especially as completed, with the large flying platform amidships. To a degree unequalled by any other capital ship, her profile gave an impression of great strength. The arrangement of the after 12in turrets was unique, and was never repeated. She was reported to be a most comfortable ship, especially well appointed internally, even after the special furnishings ordered by the Brazilian Navy had been removed.

Left: Port bow view of *Agincourt* in early 1915 showing her rather cluttered appearance with her two large tripods and central stump mast amidships. *Erin* follows.

SULTAN OSMAN I: BUILDER'S STEAM TRIALS, 17 JULY 1914

Off St Abb's Head
Wind: Force 3
Sea: Slight
Draught: 26ft 9in forward, 27ft 5½in aft
Propellers: 9ft 6in diameter; 3-bladed

	Outer		Inner	
Port	335rpm	7,238shp	326rpm	12,963shp
Starboard	332rpm	7,266shp	321rpm	12,622shp

Maximum speed on measured mile: 22.42 knots at 40,129shp
8-hour trial: 28,811shp gave speed of 20.61 knots at 308.5rpm (mean).

AGINCOURT: UNOFFICIAL PERFORMANCE NOTES, 8 SEPTEMBER 1914

Draught: 25ft 11in forward, 26ft 9in aft
Boilers in use: 10
SHP: 8,310 at 199.9rpm
Speed: not recorded
Coal consumption: 2.19lb per shp per hour for 32 hours
⅘ power: 27,200shp
⅗ power: 20,400shp
⅖ power: 13,600shp
⅕ power: 6,800shp.

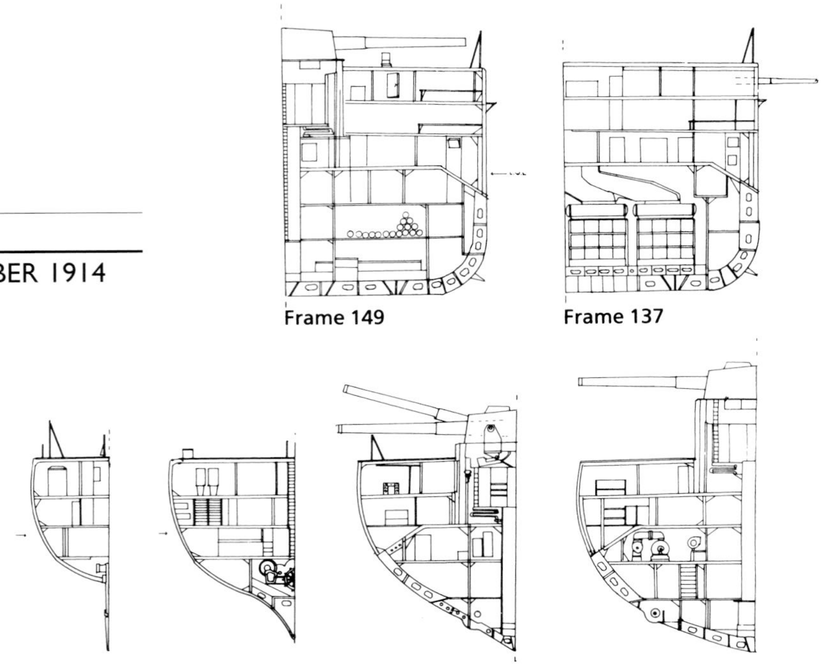

AGINCOURT
Inboard profile and sections, 1918

1. Engine room
2. Boiler room
3. 12in magazines
4. 12in shell rooms
5. Uptakes
6. Vents
7. Steering compartment
8. Capstan engine room
9. Torpedo tube compartments
10. 6in magazine

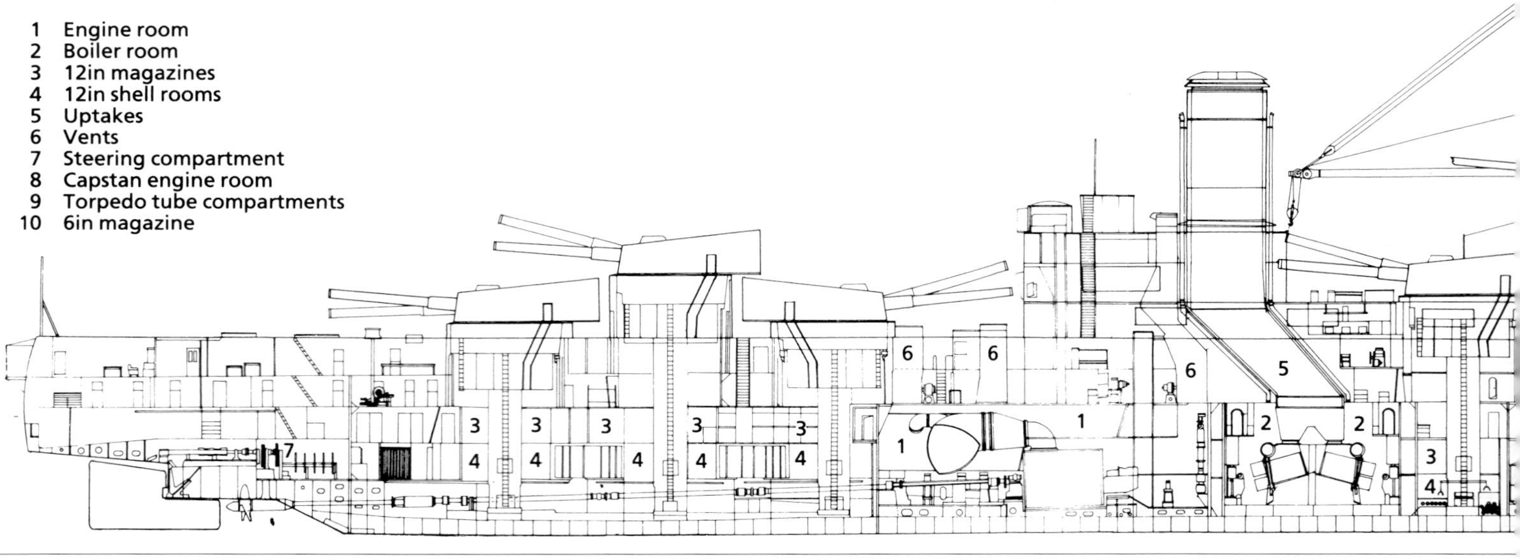

AGINCOURT: TURNING TRIALS, 22 SEPTEMBER 1914

Run	1	2	3	4
Angle of rudder	35°	35°	30°	15°
Advance (yards)	642½	602½	627½	677½
Tactical diameter (yards)	637	596	711½	851½
RPM	310.5	292.5	213	196
Speed (knots)	20.7	20	16	14.7
First 4 points turned in (secs)	52	46	63	82
Time in putting rudder over (secs)	9	16	10	6

1914 As modified for the Royal Navy on takeover, and prior to her commissioning for service:

1. Two 6in guns added in shields on superstructure forward.
2. SL removed from derrick standard (platform removed 1916).
3. Anti-torpedo nets removed.
4. Flying deck amidships removed.
5. Both topgallants removed from fore and mainmasts.
6. One derrick removed from standard amidships, but later replaced and then removed once more.

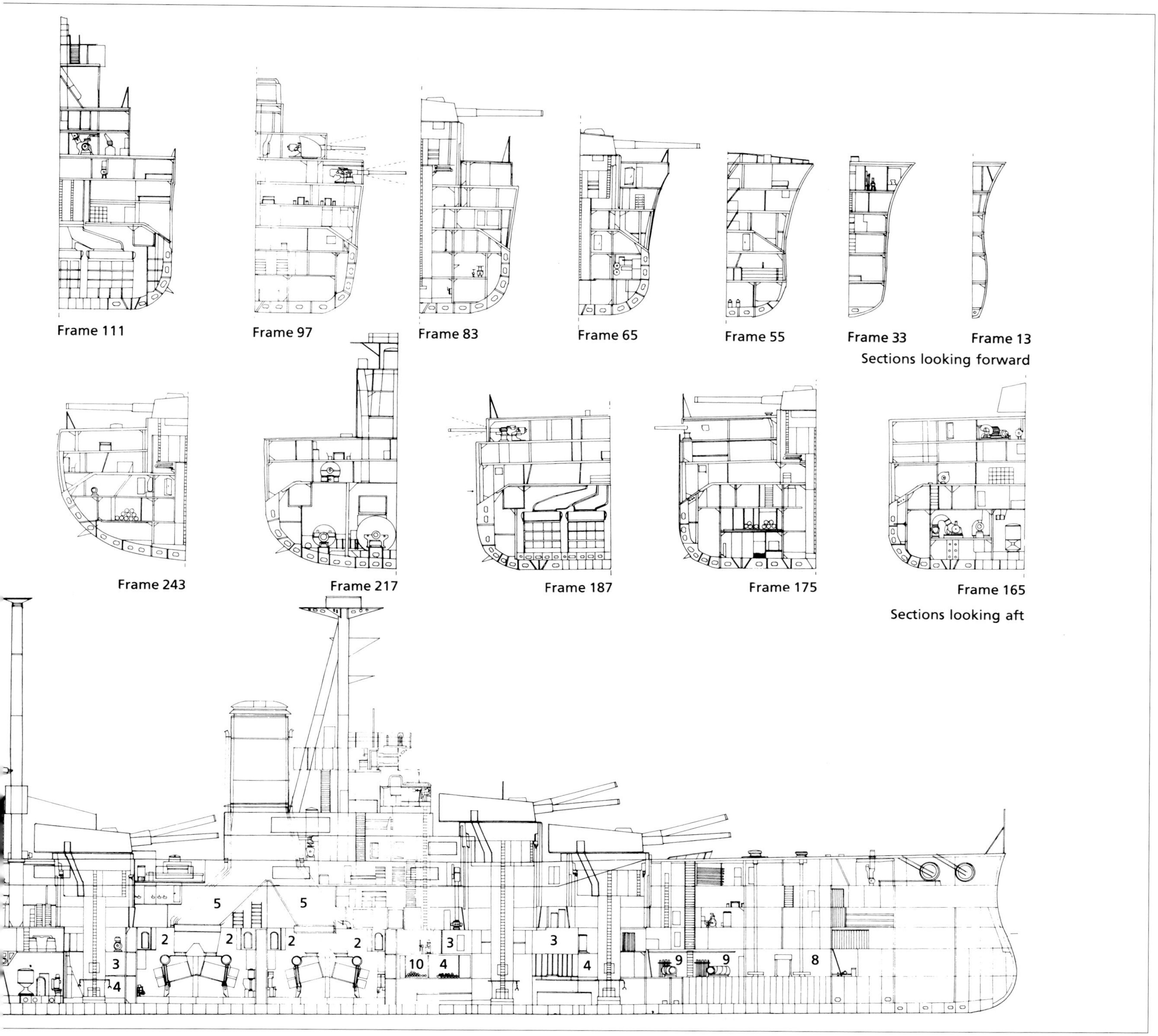

1914–15 24in signalling searchlights added on platform close below director platform on foremast. Extra platform placed on derrick standard.

1916 After control top removed. Bridge SL remounted on forward corners of after superstructure. 24in SL lamps removed from mainmast. Main tripod legs removed and short light pole fitted to mainmast.

1916–17 Fore control top improved and enlarged with narrow front. Director control fitted for 6in guns. 24in SL removed from position on foremast and remounted on lower bridge. Improvements in flash equipment and flooding arrangements made after the Battle of Jutland. Extra deck plating (high-tensile) added around magazine areas over main deck level (approx 70 tons). Foretopmast reduced in height. Mainmast removed and short topmast fitted to derrick standard.

1917–18 Small (9ft) rangefinder mounted on original SL platform on foremast. Deflection scales painted on 'B' and 'Y' turret. Range clocks fitted to rear of fore control top.

Two 3in AA guns added right aft on quarterdeck. SL

Left: *Agincourt* showing her teeth during manoeuvres, *c.* 1914/15.

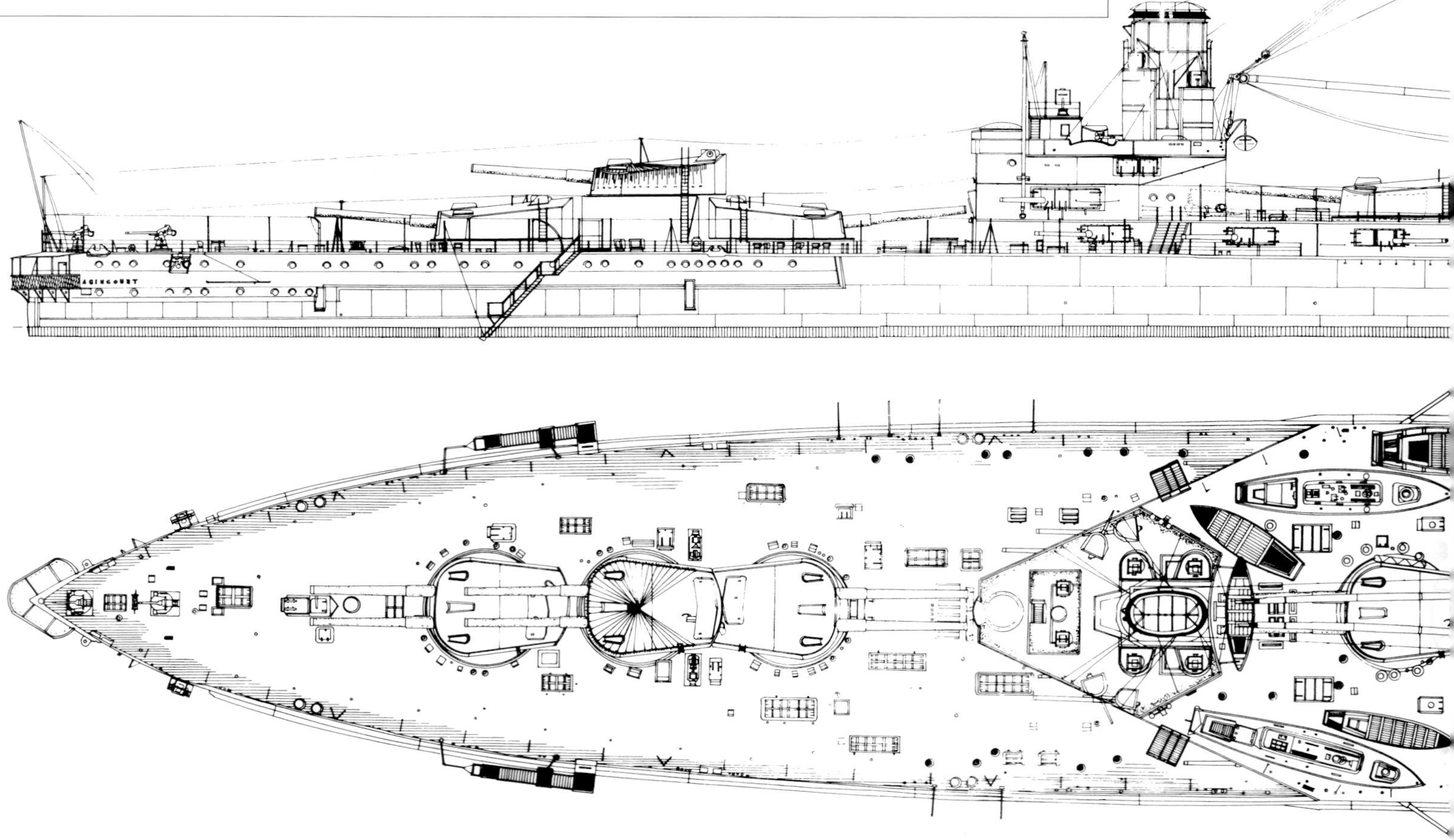

Left: *Agincourt*, c.1917. After mast removed.

AGINCOURT
Outboard profile and plan, March 1918

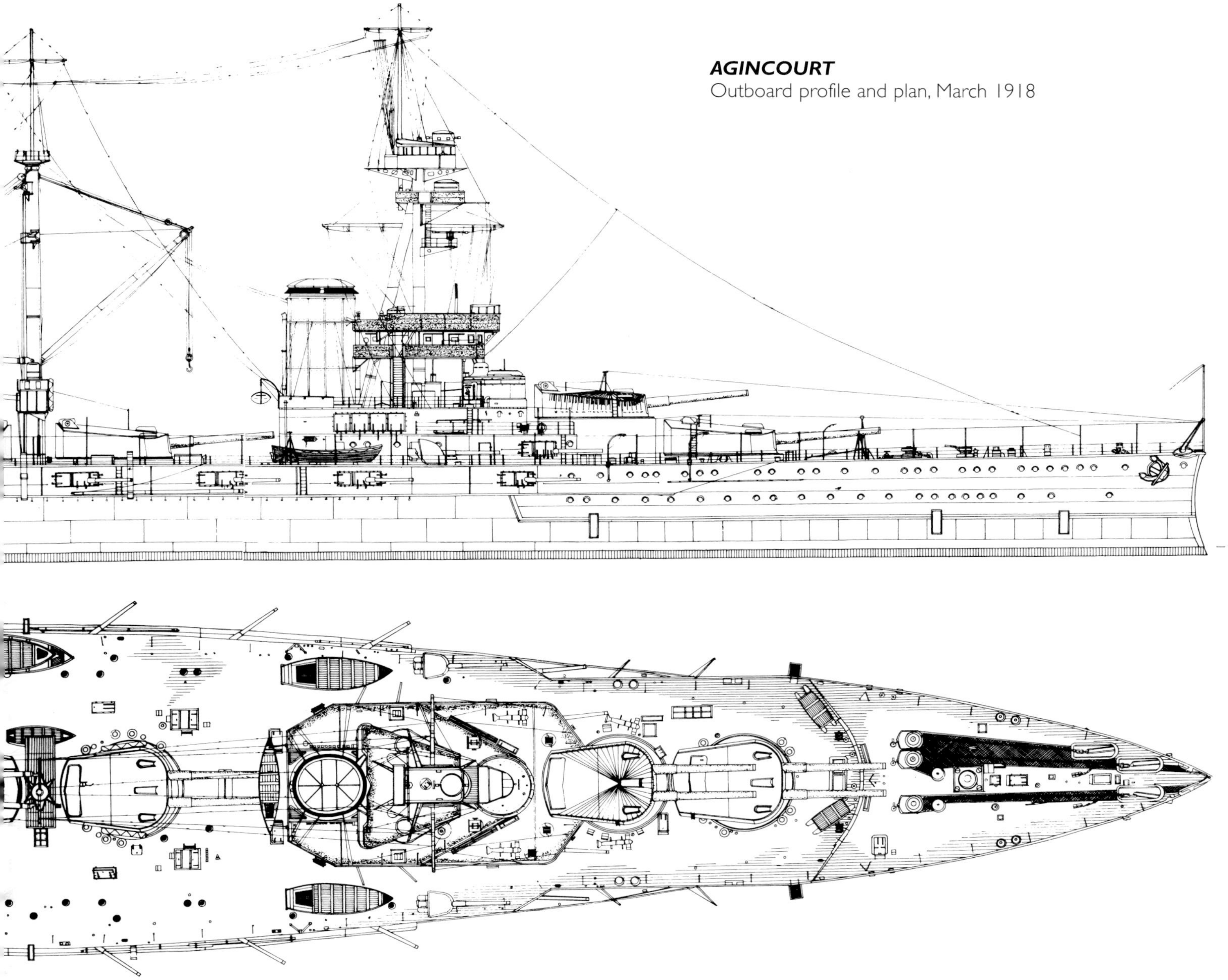

Above: *Agincourt.* 'A' and 'B' turrets and forward superstructure, *c.*1914/15.

Below: *Agincourt, c.* 1915.

partially redistributed with improved arrangements for control. After pair of SL towers fitted in summer 1917, but forward pair added later. SL removed from corners of the after superstructure.

1918 High-angle rangefinder added on fore control top. Retained this configuration until she was scrapped.

History: *Agincourt*

Laid down by Armstrong Whitworth & Co. as the Brazilian *Rio de Janeiro* and launched by Madame Huet de Bacellar, wife of the Brazilian Commissioner. December 1913, sold to Turkey, economic difficulties meaning that Brazil was now unable to afford such an expensive ship. Renamed *Sultan Osman I* and completed for trials in July 1914. On her completion, which had been delayed because of Turkish financial difficulties, she was placed under guard. The Turkish crew which arrived to board her were turned away with a variety of excuses. She was finally taken over by the Royal Navy in August 1914 and the Turkish crew were sent home. Renamed *Agincourt*, she completed her trials en route to Devonport.

1914 *7 Aug* Commissioned at Devonport still incomplete, some 12in guns not yet in place.
25 Aug joined 4th BS Grand Fleet.
1916 *31 May* Battle of Jutland. During the battle she fired 144 rounds from her 12in guns. Subsequently with Grand Fleet until November 1918.
1919 *March* Placed in Reserve Fleet at Rosyth (care and maintenance from March 1920).
1921 *April* Placed on Disposal list, but then used for experimental work.
1922 *19 Dec* Sold to Rosyth Shipbreaking Co. Still at Rosyth at the end of 1924 when, in order to comply with the naval treaties then in effect, she was cut in half and the two sections were floated out within 24 hours.

Queen Elizabeth Class: 1912/13 ESTIMATES

Design

Great importance had long been attached to the ability to bring a superior concentration of fire against the head of an enemy's battle line, a tactic that had been successfully employed by the Japanese Admiral Togo at the Battle of Tsushima in 1905. The Royal Navy had assigned this role to the large cruisers and battle-cruisers though it was appreciated that because of their inferior protection they could not be expected to engage the enemy's battleships successfully. What was required was a group of fast, well-protected battleships that could forcefully press home an attack on any type of ship.

The construction of such a revolutionary group of vessels had been strongly advocated by many leading officers of the day, including Sir Francis Bridgeman, the First Sea Lord, recently Commander-in-Chief of the Home Fleet. To this end, it was proposed that an appropriate design be formulated for the 1912 Programme for which funds for three battleships and one battle-cruiser had been allocated. It had been noted that many of the new capital ships building abroad (USS *New York*, IJN *Kongo*, etc.) were mounting gun calibres in excess of the 13.5in carried in the Royal Navy (14in), and it was thought advisable to provide an increase in calibre so as to match or even surpass these ships.

The DNC, Philip Watts, submitted three sketch designs (his last before leaving office) for approval. They were designated RIII, RIII* and RIV, and *Iron Duke* was used for comparative purposes. As the new ships were intended to form a fast battleship squadron, capable of operating around and against the head of an enemy line, they would have to embody maximum offensive power, adequate protection and a designed speed at least two or three knots faster than any other battleship extant; the figure of 25 knots being provisionally fixed by the war staff as the minimum. All three designs showed what was known as the '14in experimental' gun – in fact the new 15in – mounted in four twin turrets, and a secondary armament of sixteen 6in.

Sketch design RIII was closely based on *Iron Duke*, with provision to increase the main armoured belt by 1in, reduce the conning tower from 12in to 11in, increase the barbettes from 10in to 11in, and give the turret roofs 5in plates instead of 3in and 4in. Dimensions were 600ft pp; 90½ft; 28ft 6in, but otherwise the layout was much the same as that of *Iron Duke*. The preliminary sketch for RIII* was the same as RIII but with anti-torpedo bulkheads fitted; these were to run the whole length of the machinery spaces, and would be 1½in increasing to 2in outside those parts of the ship protected by the coal bunkers. This meant that the magazines and engine rooms were protected by the additional ½in.

In order to provide the extra weight allotted to these bulkheads, the main protective waterline belt would have to be slightly reduced to 12in, as in *Iron Duke*, but provision could be made for the thickness to remain at 13in as it passed the engine room spaces. Above the main belt, a 6in upper belt was proposed in place of the two-tier system of 8in lower and 6in upper in *Iron Duke*. With 10in barbettes and 11in turret faces, as in *Iron Duke*, it was generally thought in the DNC department that this was poor protection for a 15in-gunned ship, but it was accepted as adequate so long as the vessels were not opposed by ships armed with the same calibre.

Earlier a strong body of opinion (including Winston Churchill) had decided that the new ships should not have anti-torpedo nets; they were considered of little protective value, and if damaged in action would hang alongside the vessel and have dragging effect on speed; if they were omitted the weight saved could be used to improve the ship's internal underwater qualities. The Board agreed that the 120 tons saved should be used to provide an adequate internal screen; moreover, the 1½in advocated in the preliminary design could, if required, be increased to 2in throughout the length of the ship.

The layout for Design RIV was rather different from the first two: the principal alteration moved the third turret ('X') from just abaft the engine room to just before it, much as in *Iron Duke*. Also, it was proposed to fit the turret on the upper deck, thereby surrendering dead astern firepower, leaving only one turret ('Y') able to fire on this bearing – a feature that was considered a major fault in the design. With a displacement of 27,300 tons, RIV was 300 tons heavier than the other two, with an estimated increased cost of £30,000. Even so, after everything had been taken into consideration and despite 'X' turret's unfavourable position, the Committee felt that RIV was equally as good as RIII*. In the end, they chose RIII* as having the essential blend of requirements to suit the needs of the Royal Navy.

DESIGNS RIII AND RIV: PARTICULARS

	Design RIII		Design RIV
Displacement:	27,000 tons		27,300 tons
Length:	600ft pp		615ft pp
Beam:	90ft 6in		90ft
Draught:	28ft 6in (mean)		28ft 6in (mean)
Armament:	Eight 14in (experimental)		as RIII
	Sixteen 6in		
Armour:	Main belt 13in		as RIII
	Upper belt 8in, 6in		
	CT 12in		
	Barbettes 11in max.		
	Turrets 12in		
Weights (tons):	Hull	9,034	
	Armour	8,750	
	Armament	4,546	4,635
	Machinery	3.950	3,700
	Equipment	670	
	Fuel	650	
	Board margin	100	
GM (load)	6.1ft		

DESIGN RIII* (APPROVED DESIGN): FINAL LEGEND

Displacement (tons)
27,000.

Dimensions
Length: 600ft pp
Beam: 90ft 6in
Draught: 28ft 6in
Freeboard: 26ft forward, 16ft 6in amidships, 18ft aft
Sinkage: 95 tons.

Armament
Eight 15in
Sixteen 6in Mk XII
One 12pdr
Eight 6pdr
Four 3pdr(saluting)
Five MG
Four 21in torpedo tubes.

Armour
Main belt: 13ft 6in amidships
Ends: 6in forward, 4in aft
Barbettes: 10in–4in
Turrets: 11in–5in
Conning tower: 11in side
CT tube: 6in–4in.

Machinery
Fuel: 600 tons min., 3,500 tons max.
Designed SHP: 56,000 normal, 75,000 overload
Speed: 25 knots.

Weights (tons)

Hull:	8,900
Armour:	8,600
Armament:	4,550
General equipment:	650
Board margin:	100

Cost: Estimated £2,080,000 each ship.

Barham fitting out at John Brown's, 1915.

Right: *Queen Elizabeth* fitting out at Portsmouth, January 1915.

Below: *Queen Elizabeth* during the Dardanelles campaign. Looking aft over 15in gun turrets.

Invitations to tender were sent out for four ships in June 1912, and all four had been laid down by February 1913. Then a gift of a battleship was offered to the British Government by the Federated Malay States in November 1912, and it was decided to utilize it as a fifth unit of this new *Queen Elizabeth* class of battleships, and she was laid down in October 1913.

Although largely experimental, the ships turned out exceptionally well in service, and it was generally conceded that the design represented one of the most efficient and satisfactory battleship designs ever produced on the displacement. Their all-round fighting qualities were strikingly demonstrated throughout their long and distinguished careers, and they never failed to give a good account of themselves. There were weak points in the design, however. The 6in secondary battery was considered to be too cramped and placed too far forward; the guns had restricted all-round arcs of fire and were extremely difficult to fight in a head sea. Secondly, the thick armoured belt above the water-line was not high enough and there were no rear screens within the battery.

The 1921 Washington-London Treaty restriction on new capital ship construction meant that old ships would have to be modernized; all vessels of the class were given refits and varying degrees of modernization between 1924 and 1941, with *Warspite*, *Queen Elizabeth* and *Valiant*'s being more extensive than any other British battleships.

Armament

To prevent any delay in commencement, a decision had to be made whether or not to fit the new 15in gun, for secrecy's sake referred to as the '14in experimental gun'. To fit such a large and untried weapon in a capital ship before testing was certainly contrary to normal Admiralty practice, and the final decision had to take into account the possibility of its being a complete failure.

In the original design it had been suggested that the ships might carry ten such guns in twin turrets, disposed as in *Iron Duke*, but, as the DNC pointed out, the increase in length and the extra weight which the hull would have to carry would not leave a sufficient percentage of displacement to devote to the machinery, especially when such high speeds were envisaged. In fact, the adoption of the new gun was, without doubt, the outstanding feature of the design, and was one of the factors primarily responsible for the ships' success. After the RIII* design, which allowed for eight guns in four twin turrets, had been approved, the ideal arrangement had been reached, and it was to be the standard practice for many successive designs.

Although the new guns and turrets were considerably heavier than the twin 13.5in, by omitting the centre turret ('Q') it was found that the total weight of eight '14in experimental' guns and turrets was practically the same as five twin 13.5in, but with the advantage of an increased broadside of 1,360lb and nearly fifty percent greater destructive effect. With these figures before them, the Board's decision to fit the guns had been unanimous. As it turned out, in service the 15in gun exceeded all expectations and was one of the most efficient heavy-calibre naval guns ever produced.

The design called for a secondary armament of sixteen 6in guns as against the twelve fitted in *Iron Duke*, with an extra pair in the battery, and the others in casemates on the main deck level aft, two port and two starboard. *Queen Elizabeth* herself was completed with all these guns in December 1914, but the main deck guns aft were found to be practically useless because of their very low command, only about twelve feet above the water-line at normal load displacement. In May 1915 one pair were removed altogether and the other pair were mounted in shields on the forecastle deck abaft the second funnel, where they had an exceptionally high command and a good all-round arc of fire. The other ships were similarly modified while still fitting-out. In service, however, it was found that the remounted guns on the forecastle would have to be abandoned; the crews were inadequately protected and it was difficult to maintain an adequate supply of shells, no provision having been made for this in the original design.

The battery was located somewhat farther back than in *Iron Duke*, but because of the way the forecastle sides were recessed and the three foremost guns being 'stepped' to secure ahead fire, they proved very wet commands in all but a moderate seaway, and were no better off than preceding classes in regard to secondary gun location. In the *Iron Duke* class, the midships 13.5in turret and shorter forecastle had necessitated crowding the secondary battery well forward and, with the exception that the forward pair of guns were located abreast 'B' instead of 'A' turret, the same arrangement with its attendant disadvantages was followed in *Queen Elizabeth*, despite the longer forecastle which would have allowed the entire battery to be shifted farther back and the guns to be spaced more widely, but unfortunately this was not a feature of the design.

Armour

The scale of armouring was generally along the same lines as *Iron Duke*, but with provision for increased thickness at the water-line, lower deck, turrets and anti-torpedo bulkheads and reductions on

QUEEN ELIZABETH: LAUNCH FIGURES, 16 OCTOBER 1913

Displacement: 10,607 tons
Recorded weight of hull: 9,641 tons
Draught: 9ft 2in forward, 16ft 4in aft
Length: 600ft 5½in pp
Beam: 90ft 7½in
Beam as moulded: 90ft 5½in
Breakage at launch:
longitudinal in a distance of 468ft = 0 15/16in hog
transverse in a distance of 85ft 4in = nil
Launch weight (tons):
Barham 14,500; *Malaya* 14,585; *Warspite* 11,072.

VALIANT: GM AND STABILITY

Based on inclining experiments, September 1916

	Displacement (tons)	Draught	GM	Maximum stability	Stability vanishes at
'A' Condition (= load)*	30,030	30ft 11in	5ft	36°	65°
'B' Condition (= deep)**	33,260	33ft 7¼in	6.5ft	38°	75½°
	27,470 (light)				

*Fully equipped plus 130 tons coal (culinary), 100 tons oil double-bottom tanks, 500 tons wing tanks.
**Fully equipped plus 3,437 tons oil, all reserve and feed tanks full.

Below: *Queen Elizabeth*, c. 1916/17. Note anti-rangefinder baffles on foretopmast, between funnels and on mainmast.

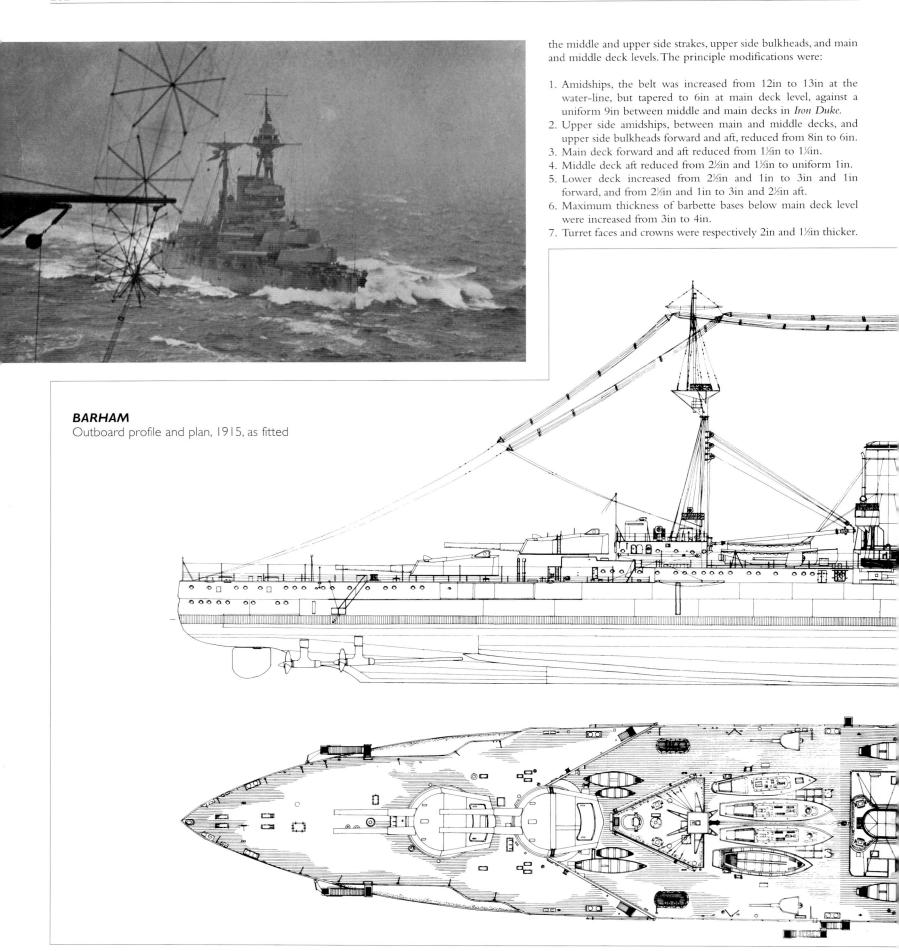

the middle and upper side strakes, upper side bulkheads, and main and middle deck levels. The principle modifications were:

1. Amidships, the belt was increased from 12in to 13in at the water-line, but tapered to 6in at main deck level, against a uniform 9in between middle and main decks in *Iron Duke*.
2. Upper side amidships, between main and middle decks, and upper side bulkheads forward and aft, reduced from 8in to 6in.
3. Main deck forward and aft reduced from 1½in to 1¼in.
4. Middle deck aft reduced from 2½in and 1½in to uniform 1in.
5. Lower deck increased from 2½in and 1in to 3in and 1in forward, and from 2½in and 1in to 3in and 2½in aft.
6. Maximum thickness of barbette bases below main deck level were increased from 3in to 4in.
7. Turret faces and crowns were respectively 2in and 1½in thicker.

BARHAM

Outboard profile and plan, 1915, as fitted

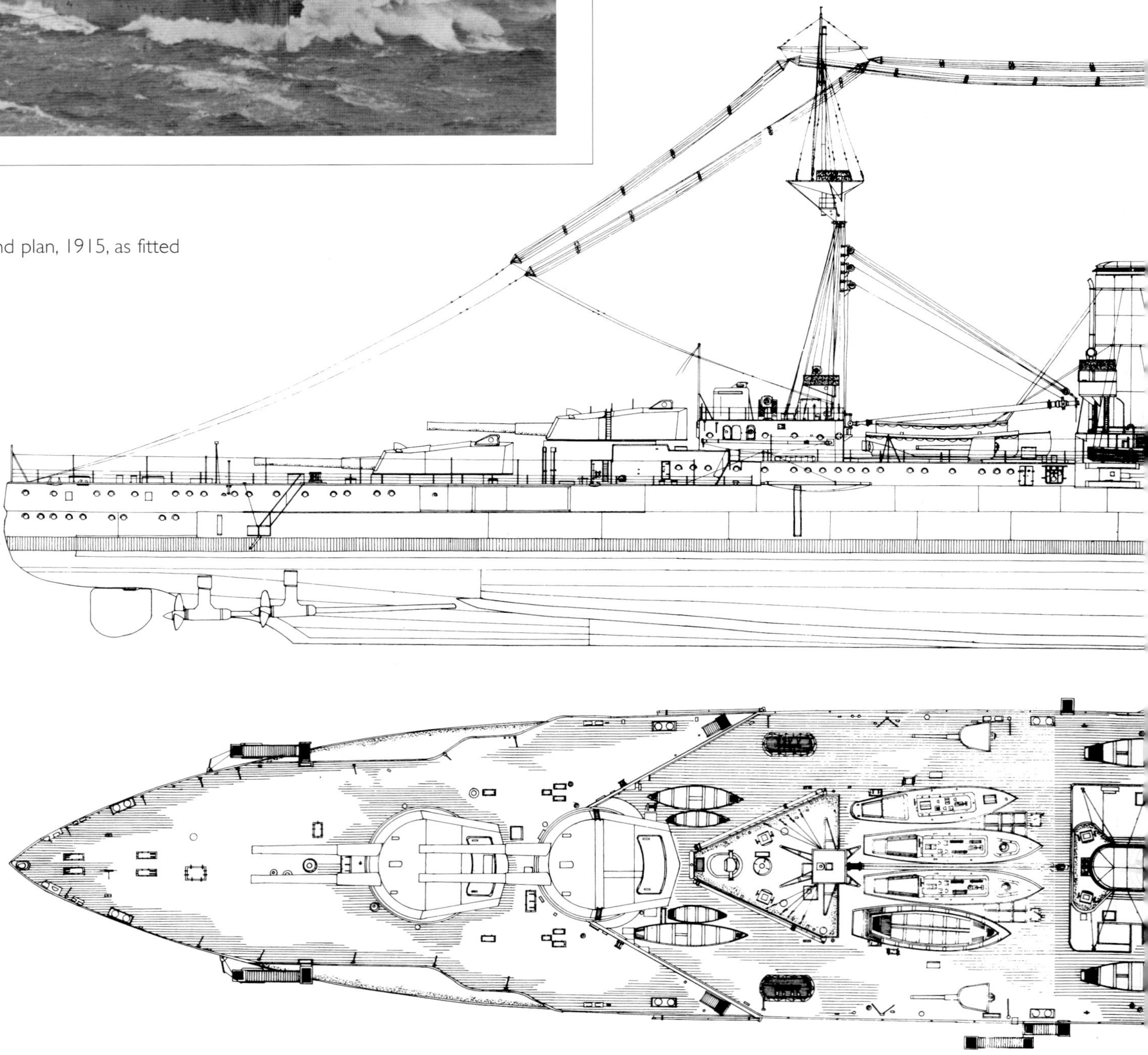

Left: *Warspite* at speed during the winter of 1917/18.

Right: *Warspite* dips her bows into swell during exercises in the North Sea, c. early 1918.

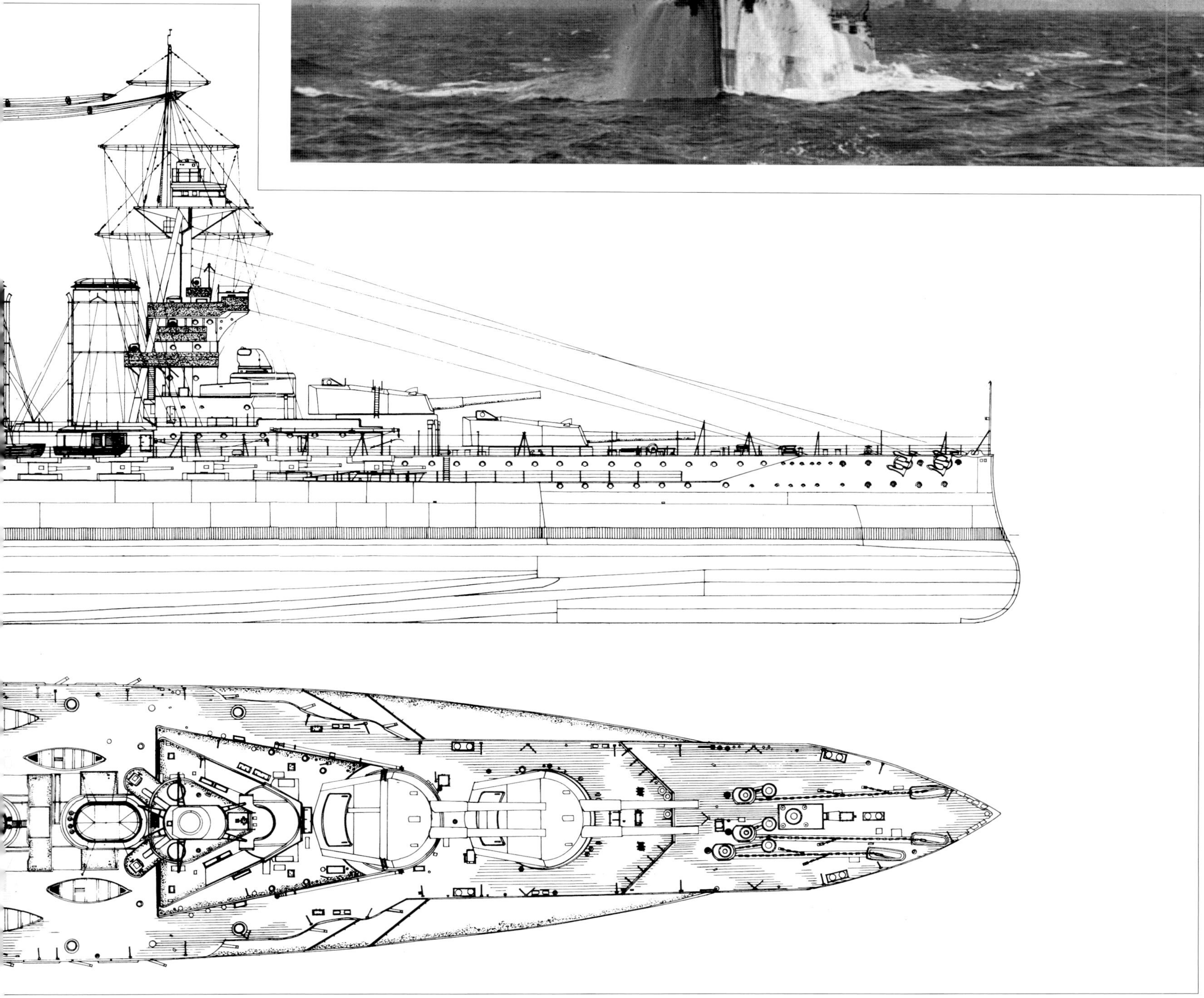

8. Anti-torpedo bulkheads were increased from 1in and 1½in to 2in uniform thickness, and extended completely between the forward and after magazines, whereas these bulkheads had been omitted in wake of the boiler rooms in *Iron Duke*.

The main protective strake of 13in and the upper strake of 6in gave a total width of 20ft 6in, with 15ft 1½in above the water-line, and 5ft 4½in below at normal displacement load. The 13in strip's top edge was at main deck level, and ran from abeam the centres of 'A' and 'Y' barbettes. At the lower edge the 13in reduced to 8in along the whole length. The upper 6in thickness ran over the same distance as the 13in, but reduced to 4in about 27 feet before 'A' barbette, and 20 feet abaft 'Y' barbette with 4in outside this. The upper side strake extended from abeam the centre of 'A' barbette to just beyond the inner face of 'Y' between main and upper deck level.

The main bulkheads were 6in thick at the forward location, which ran obliquely inwards from the forward extremity of the 6in upper side armour to the sides of 'A' barbette between the upper and lower deck levels, and at the same angle inwards from the after extremity of the 13in belt armour to the outer face of 'Y' barbette between the middle and main deck levels on the aft location. There was a 6in upper side bulkhead that ran obliquely inwards from the after extremities of the 6in upper side armour to the centre of 'Y' barbette between the main and upper decks. An after bulkhead of 4in thickness closed the 4in armour belt between middle and main decks, and another outer after bulkhead closed the 4in armour belt from keel to middle deck, being 4in above and 1½in below lower deck.

The forecastle deck was 1in thick over the secondary battery. The upper deck extended between 'A' and 'Y' barbettes and consisted of 1¼in–1¾in–2in plates. The main deck extended from 'A' barbette to the forward bulkhead, and from 'Y' barbette to the inner after bulkhead (4in), and had a thickness of 1¼in uniform.

QUEEN ELIZABETH CLASS: PARTICULARS, AS COMPLETED

Construction

	Dockyard	Laid Down	Launched	Completed for trials	Completed
Queen Elizabeth:	Portsmouth DY	21 Oct 1912	16 Oct 1913	1 Dec 1914	Jan 1914
Warspite:	Devonport DY	31 Oct 1912	26 Nov 1913	8 March 1915	April 1915
Valiant:	Fairfield	31 Jan 1913	4 Nov 1914	13 Jan 1916	Feb 1916
Barham:	John Brown	24 Feb 1913	31 Dec 1914	19 Aug 1915	Oct 1915
Malaya:	Armstrong	20 Oct 1913	18 March 1915	28 Jan 1916	Feb 1916.

Displacement (tons)
27,470 (light), 32,590 (load), 33,260 (deep) *Valiant*, 1916.

Dimensions
Length: 600ft 5½in pp, 634ft 6in wl, 639ft 9in oa (643ft 9in *Barham, Warspite*)
Beam: 90ft 6in (as designed), 90ft 7½in (actual)
Draught (mean): 29ft 6in–33ft (see Stability)
Height of 15in guns above lower wl: 'A' 30ft 9in; 'B' 40ft 9in; 'X' 33ft 3in; 'Y' 23ft 3in
Height of CT vision slits above lower wl: 50ft
Height of funnel: 80ft
Height of lower foremasthead: 113ft 2in
Depth of keel from battery deck: 46ft.

Armament
Eight 15in 42cal Mk I; 80rpg (100rpg 1917)
Fourteen 6in 45cal Mk XII; 130rpg
Two 3in AA; 150rpg
Four 3pdr (saluting); 64rpg
Five MG; 5,000rpg
Ten Lewis guns
Four 21in torpedo tubes (beam, submerged); twenty torpedoes Mk II or IV (forward tubes fixed at 80°, after tube at 100°; depression -2°).

Director control
Main armament directors aloft in tower and in armoured hood of conning tower, with 'X' as director turret; two directors for secondary armament in fore bridge. 'Follow the pointer' gear on all sights and flexible voice pipes for night firing.

Armour
Main belt: 13in, 8in lower edge
Ends: 6in–4in
Bulkheads: 6.4in
Decks: forecastle 1in, upper 2in–1½in–1¼in, main 1¼in, middle 1in, lower 3in–2in–1in
Barbettes: 10in–9in–7in–6in–4in
Turrets: 13in–11in–4¼in
Conning tower: 11in–6in–3in
Anti-torpedo screens: 2in
CT tubes: 4in
Secondary battery: 6in
Secondary gunshields: 3in
Uptakes: 1½in–1in.

Machinery
Parsons reaction turbines (Brown Curtis direct-drive *Valiant, Barham*), four propellers
Boilers: twenty-four Babcock & Wilcox (Yarrow *Warspite, Barham*), working pressure 235psi
Pressure at turbines: 175psi
Heating surface: 98,166sq ft (106,752sq ft *Warspite, Barham*)
Length of boiler rooms: 144ft
Length of engine rooms: 83ft 11½in
Propellers: 3-bladed
Propeller diameter: 12ft
Propeller pitch: 10ft outers; lift 2in inners (10ft 5in outers; 10ft 8in inners *Barham, Warspite*)
Designed SHP: 56,000 = 23 knots; 75,000 (overload) = 25 knots
Fuel: 650 tons oil normal, 3,400 tons oil max.; 100 tons coal
Radius of action: 1,600nm full power; 2,500nm at 22 knots; 3,800nm at 18 knots; 4,500nm at 15 knots; 5,000nm at 12 knots.

Ship's boats
Pinnaces (steam): two 50ft
Pinnaces (sail): one 36ft
Launches (motor): one 42ft
Cutters: three 32ft
Whalers: two 27ft
Gigs: two 30ft
Skiff dinghies: one 16ft
Balsa rafts: one 13ft 6in.

Searchlights
Six 36in: two lower bridge, two platform abaft second funnel, two after superstructure
Seven 36in *Queen Elizabeth*
Eight 36in *Warspite, Valiant, Malaya*
Two 24in *Barham.*

**Warspite* had 18ft rangefinder on spotting top platform, but no 9ft. *Valiant* had two 9ft on secondary director towers fitted experimentally in 1919.
**Each had signal locker and arrangements for flags to be hoisted on foremast through a trunk passing through the main deck.

The middle deck extended from 'A' barbette to the outer after bulkhead, and was given 1in on the flat, and 1¼in on the inclines. The lower deck extended from the outer base of 'A' barbette right through to the stem of the ship, with the forward extremity sloping downwards once outside the forward bulkhead. A thickness of 1in inside and 3in outside the forward bulkhead was provided. Aft, this deck extended from the after extremity of the 6in belt armour and continued to the stern of the ship, 2½in inside and 3in outside the inner after bulkhead.

Barbettes were: 'A' 10in on the face and sides above the main deck level reducing to 6in once below; 'B' face and rear was 9in above main deck level and 4in below; sides were 10in above and 4in below main deck level; 'Y' 10in sides above main deck, 4in below, face and rear 9in and 7in above and 6in below main deck. 'X' was almost the same as 'Y' except that it reduced to 6in and 4in from upper to main deck level and 4in below this. Turrets had 13in faces, 11in sides and 4¼in crowns.

The secondary battery was given 6in plates on the sides and a 6in–4in rear bulkhead. A 2in longitudinal bulkhead right through the centre of the battery, except in wake of the funnel uptakes, was provided, with 1½in traverses extending about 15 feet inboard between individual guns, and carried to the full height of the battery. Gunshields were 3in with 3in sighting hoods, and were located on the forecastle deck, port and starboard, between the fourth and fifth guns. The casemates had 6in faces, a 6in rear bulkhead and 3in shields.

The conning tower was 11in on the sides, 6in and 3in on the roof, the base was 6in on the sides with a 3in face and rear. The conning tower hood had a 6in face and sides, a 2in rear and 3in roof. The torpedo control tower was given 6in sides, 2in roof, 3in floor and 4in tube.

The funnel uptakes, which carried up to shelter deck level, were 1in from middle to forecastle deck, and 1½in from this level.

The anti-torpedo bulkheads were longitudinal, port and star-

Rangefinder positions (1918)*
Two 30ft: 'B', 'X' turrets
Three 15ft: 'A', 'Y' turrets, gun control tower
Two 9ft: spotting top, fore bridge platform abaft funnel
One 6ft 6in: fore bridge for HA.

Battle signal stations**
Two separate and enclosed, main deck level port and starboard abaft foremast.

Anchors
Three 150cwt Admiralty (bower, sheet), one 60cwt stockless stem, 16cwt Admiralty, one 12cwt Admiralty.

Wireless (1918/19)
Main office: Types 1–32, 35X *Queen Elizabeth*; Type 35X *Warspite*; Types 1–16 *Valiant*; Types 1, 2, 3, 34 *Barham*; Types 1–16 *Malaya*
Second office: Types 2–34
Third office: Type 9 short-radius
Fourth office: Type 9 (*Valiant* only)
Action office: Type 9 (*Malaya* only)
Fire control office: Type 31.

Complement
923–951 (as completed)
***Queen Elizabeth*:** 1,262 as flagship (1920)
***Warspite*:** 1,025 (1915); 1,220 (1920)
***Valiant*:** 919 (1915); 1,218 (1919)
***Barham*:** 1,016 (1916); 1,249 as flagship (1920)
***Malaya*:** 1,217 (1919).

Cost
***Queen Elizabeth*:** £3,014,103
***Warspite*:** £2,524,148
***Valiant*:** £2,537,037
***Barham*:** £2,470,113
***Malaya*:** £2,945,709.

Below: Work to be done 'up top' was accomplished by certain members of the crew who obviously had a head for heights. Being around 100ft up from the waterline to maintain rigging etc was no easy task. On *Valiant*, with *Barham* and *Malaya* astern. 1918.

board, and were set in about 6 feet from the ship's side; they extended completely from the forward to the after magazines, from keel to the middle deck level, the ends, outside 'A' and 'Y' barbettes, being closed by transverse bulkheads of the same thickness (2in).

Machinery

Admiralty requirements for a 'fast' battleship division made it necessary to provide an advanced type of propulsion plant that would enable the ships to manoeuvre around the High Seas Fleet if required. As a designed speed of 25 knots was intended the increase of 4 knots over *Iron Duke* meant that two-and-a-half times as much horsepower would be needed over the latter, an unprecedented class-to-class increase for battleships. It was estimated that with mixed coal and oil burning not more than 22 knots could be provided on the given displacement, except by sacrificing either offensive or defensive qualities. This could of course be done, but on a substantially increased size and cost, which neither the Board nor the DNC had in mind.

After much consideration the Board finally approved the vessels for burning all oil fuel, even though ships of such a size had never been tested with this type of fuel propulsion. The advantages were overwhelming:

1. The steaming radius was greater on a given weight of oil against coal.
2. Speed could be increased more rapidly and maintained much easier.
3. Simplified and faster refuelling, an end to arduous coaling.
4. A distinct lack of smoke from the uptake, making it easier to close the enemy without being seen.

The decision to make the vessels all-oil burning was not taken without considerable apprehension about maintenance of supplies during wartime, and the Board was subjected to some criticism on the grounds that it was undesirable to build ships whose mobility was entirely dependent on overseas fuel supplies. It was because of this that the class were only altered to burn all oil after the RIII design had long been accepted, and it was the primary reason why the succeeding class of *Royal Sovereigns* were fitted with mixed coal and oil fuel arrangements.

The machinery, as fitted, consisted of two sets of turbines arranged in three groups, each of watertight construction, divided by two longitudinal bulkheads. Direct-drive turbines were provided for all the ships of the class, but *Queen Elizabeth*, *Warspite* and *Malaya* were also given a separate cruising turbine, a new version of those which had been installed with little success in the *Dreadnought* and *Bellerophon* classes. However, the type fitted in these three, as built, gave superior consumption results over the two ships that were not fitted.

Each ship was given four propellers, the HP turbines being

Below: *Malaya* in 1918.

fitted on the wing shafts and the LP on the inners, one ahead and one astern turbine on each shaft. The separate reaction cruising turbines fitted in *Queen Elizabeth*, *Malaya* and *Warspite* were on the wing shafts, one in each wing compartment. The LP ahead and astern turbines were arranged in the same casing, and placed in the middle compartment. Two sets of screw gear were fitted for the steering, with the steering engine in duplicate located in the centre engine room. William Janney auxiliary steering gear was fitted to all ships of the class.

The fuel bunkers were about 30 feet high, and were located abreast the boiler rooms on both sides of the longitudinal anti-torpedo bulkheads; they extended vertically from the inner bottom up to the middle deck. The oil fuel was pumped into filling pipes, leading from the weather deck into the ship's fuel tanks, with a break in the form of a filter to relieve any pressure in the tanks and to filter the oil before it came into contact with the boilers. The oil fuel pumps themselves, were vertical steam reciprocating single-cylinder types, capable of delivering 12 tons of oil fuel per hour; the main feed pumps could deliver 47 tons per hour.

Appearance Changes

As completed, they were probably the best-looking battleships to date. Their principal characteristics were the large, well-balanced twin funnels; tripod foremast, well built up with different levels of bridgework, similar to *Iron Duke*'s, but upper levels extended farther back around the tripod; long forecastle carried right aft to 'X' turret; four twin 15in turrets, all making for a graceful profile. As built, they were very much alike and were quite difficult to tell apart. Individual differences were as follows:

Queen Elizabeth: Only unit to be completed with sternwalk. 6in guns in casemates on main deck aft as completed. Lowest yard on foremast at starfish below control top.
Warspite: Lowest yard on foremast at starfish level.
Valiant: Small control position on upper bridge. Lowest yard on foremast either at starfish or below heel of topmast.
Malaya: Small platform without searchlight, fitted very low on mainmast. Lowest yard on foremast very close below starfish.
Barham: Searchlight on upper bridge at foot of mast, and on small platform low on mainmast. Flagpole fitted to topmast (fore). Lowest yard on foremast as in *Queen Elizabeth*

1915 Large nets draped below control top (early form of anti-rangefinder baffles), false bow wave painted on *Queen Elizabeth* during her Dardanelles sortie (February 1915). Both items removed on her return to UK in May 1915.
1916–17 Secondary control position added low on mainmast. Various alterations and distribution methods applied to search-

QUEEN ELIZABETH: STEAM TRIALS

English Channel, 30 January 1915. It being wartime, full trials of the class were not carried out. The following figures are taken from surviving builders' preliminary trial contracts.
4-hour, full power
Draught: 32ft 5¾in forward, 32ft 1¾in aft
Number of boilers in use: 24
Steam pressure: 203psi at boilers, 178psi at turbines
Heating surface: 98,162sq ft
Oil temperature: 181°F
Oil pressure: 140psi
Propellers: 3-bladed
Diameter: 12ft
Pitch: 10ft outer, 11ft 1in inner
Speed: not recorded
Revolutions
Port: outer 294.9rpm; inner 267.3rpm
Starboard: outer 290.1 rpm; inner 255.4rpm
Total SHP: 57,133

BARHAM: STEAM TRIALS

Bute Sound, 6 July 1916
Draught: 32ft 6in (mean)
Displacement: 32,252 tons
Oil pressure: 145psi
Revs (mean): 293rpm outers; 293rpm inners
Speed (mean): 23.91 knots

	Outer	Inner	Speed
First run			23.61 knots
Port:	293.4rpm	290.4rpm	
Starboard:	296rpm	292.1rpm	
Second run			24.08 knots
Port:	292.4rpm	288.9rpm	
Starboard:	294.6rpm	289.8rpm	
Third run			23.72 knots
Port:	293.4rpm	296.8rpm	
Starboard:	294.3rpm	293.4rpm	
Fourth run			24.22 knots
Port:	294.1rpm	294.1rpm	
Starboard:	293.3rpm	294.9rpm	

Below: A need to keep the ships in top condition meant that they would often be in dry dock for hull cleaning and inspection etc. *Valiant* is shown here in 1918.

BARHAM

Inboard profile, sections, and upper deck and plan showing gun arcs, 1915

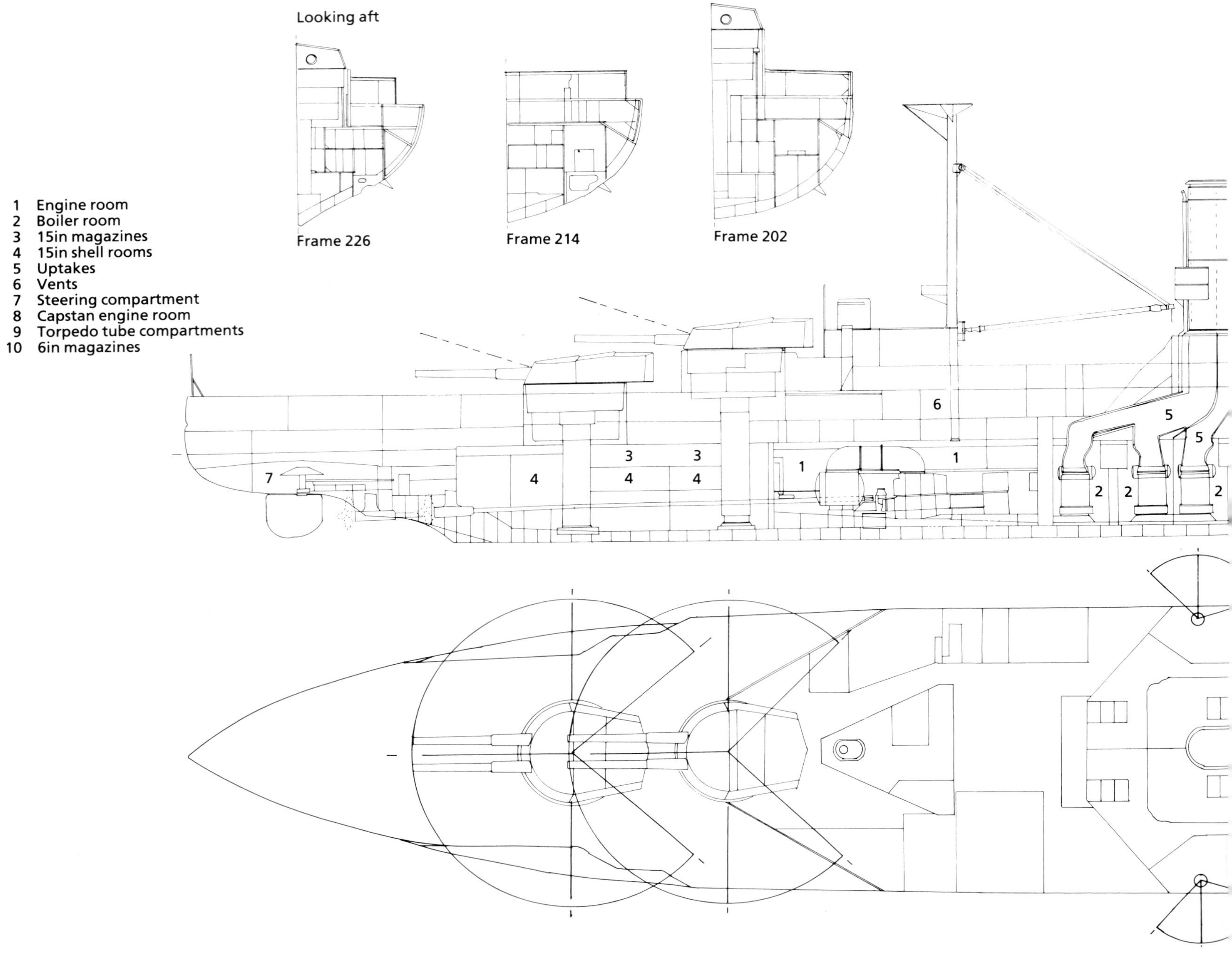

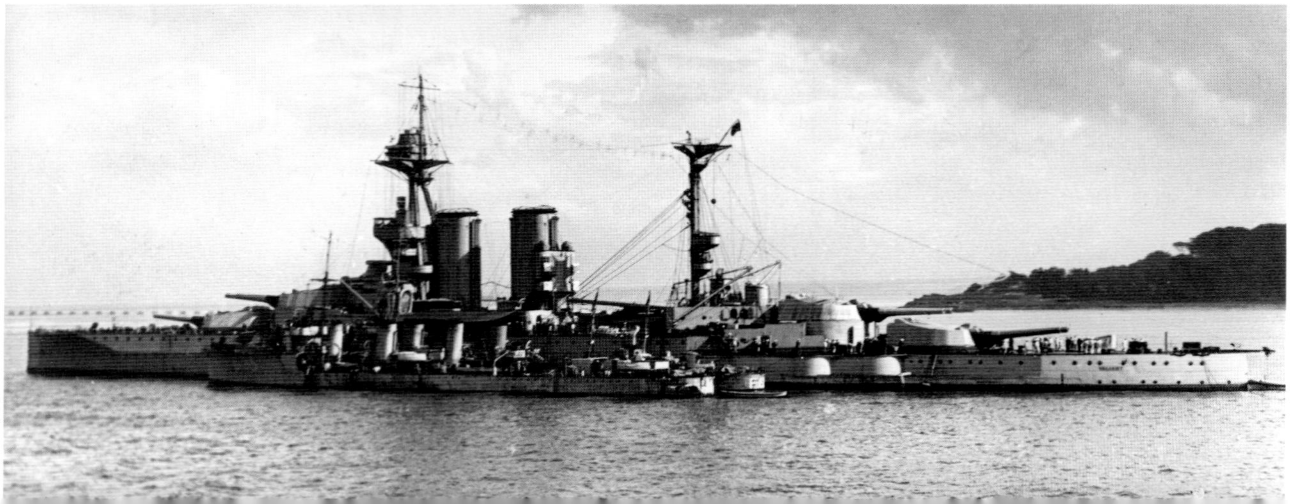

Right: *Valiant* in August 1917.

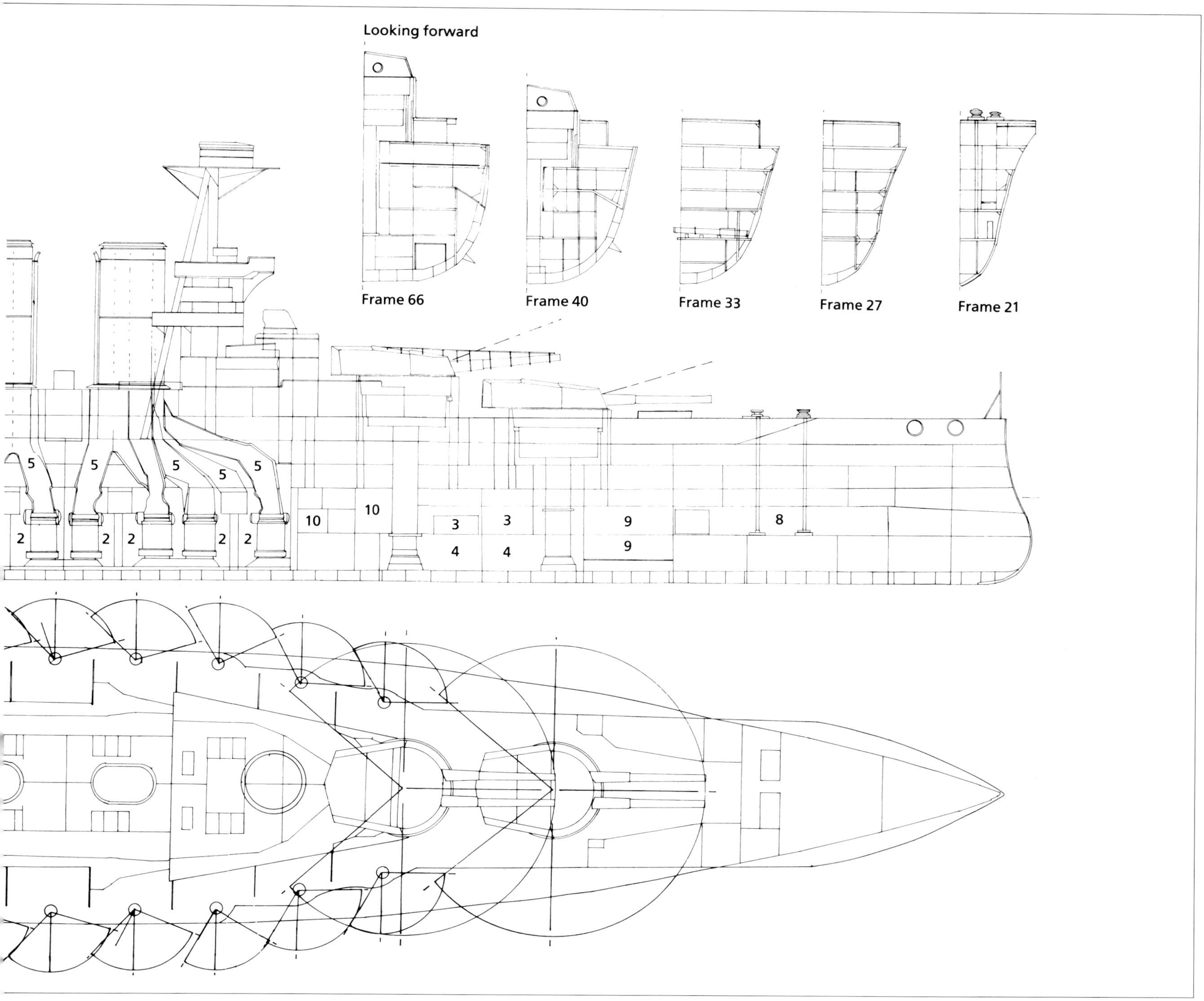

light systems. *Barham*: 36in lamp added on platform low on foremast. SL removed from sides of after superstructure. One remounted on platform in centre, the other on platform low on main mast. 24in removed from upper bridgework, remounted port and starboard on forward superstructure. *Malaya*: SL removed from middle bridge. After superstructure SL redistributed as in *Barham*. *Queen Elizabeth*: SL ex middle bridge remounted port and starboard on superstructure abaft second funnel. SL in centre of after superstructure raised on platform, one 36in lamp added on platform low on mainmast. Two 24in signalling lamps added on middle bridge. *Valiant*: SL removed from lower bridge. Single 36in SL mounted on 'B' turret for use in conjunction with turret and night-fighting experiments. *Barham* and *Warspite* fitted for towing kites. Improvements in protection made good after Jutland in May 1916. 1in plating added on middle deck around vicinity of magazines and extra 1in added to magazine bulkheads. Improved arrangements in isolation of shell and magazine rooms, extra valves fitted to service pipes and flooding gear. Sternwalk removed from *Queen Elizabeth*. Maintopmast removed in all except *Queen Elizabeth*. Very long forward struts in *Valiant*. Rangefinder baffles fitted to one, or both topmasts (see photographs).

1917–18 Deflection scales painted on 'A' and 'X' or 'B' and 'Y' turrets. SL arrangements again improved, 'coffee-box' towers added abeam and abaft second funnel. Many variations in SL locations, although SL tower positions were common to all ships of the class. Rangefinder baffles removed towards the end of the year.

Right: *Malaya* as completed, seen during her working-up period in early 1916.

Below: *Queen Elizabeth* anchored at the Forth Bridge, 20 April 1918. Compare with the photograph opposite. Rangefinder baffles are out, and 'coffee-box' SL towers have been added to second funnel.

QUEEN ELIZABETH: STEAM TRIALS (AFTER SHIP WAS BULGED)

Date	Wind Force	Sea	RPM	SHP	Speed (knots)
14 Sept 1927	2	slight	301	73,884	23.451
16 April 1928	4	good	285	75,230	22.8
29 Oct 1928	5	swell	284	72,840	21.8
9 April 1929	3	3	298	75,150	23.55
30 Oct 1930	4	3	295	75,517	22
28 April 1931	7	4-5	299	76,405	23.1
24 Oct 1931	6	3	293	75,768	22.75
20 April 1932	5	3	297	76,381	23
24 Oct 1932	2	swell	297	76,096	23.1
27 Feb 1933	2	swell	299	75,338	23.6
11 Oct 1933	calm	calm	301	75,973	23.4
26 April 1934	7		297	75,639	22
24 Oct 1934	3		296	76,527	23.5
13 April 1935	9		300	77,827	23.6
19 May 1936	9		299	71,880	23.5
29 Oct 1936	5-6		293	78,850	22
19 April 1937	1-2		300	79,518	23.7

The poor figures were taken when the ship's bottom was foul.

1918 Flying-off platforms fitted to 'B' and 'X' turrets in all except *Queen Elizabeth*.

1919 Fore control top enlarged in *Queen Elizabeth* and *Warspite*. Large-base rangefinder added at rear of 'B' and 'X' turrets in *Malaya*, *Queen Elizabeth* and *Warspite*. Deflection scales on turrets painted out. Number and location of range clocks varied from ship to ship. Sternwalk fitted to *Barham* and *Warspite*. Flying-off platform fitted to 'B' and 'X' turrets in *Queen Elizabeth* by February 1919. Foretopmast removed and maintopmast replaced in *Barham*, *Malaya*, *Valiant* and *Warspite*.

1921–2 Large-base rangefinder fitted at rear of 'B' and 'X' turrets in *Barham* and *Valiant*. Range clocks added over 'X' turret in *Valiant* and *Warspite*. Medium-base rangefinder fitted over torpedo control tower in *Valiant*, replacing original small rangefinder. Foretopmast replaced in *Barham*. Topgallant fitted to mainmast in *Barham*, *Malaya*, *Queen Elizabeth* and *Valiant*.

1922–3 SL removed from mainmast and after superstructure in all.

1924–6 After control top removed from *Barham*, *Queen Elizabeth* and *Valiant*. Small rangefinder over conning tower in *Valiant* remounted over bridge (1925/6). Range clocks removed from all positions except over 'X' turret in *Barham* and *Warspite*. 3in AA replaced by 4in AA in all. Flying-off platforms removed from 'X' turret in *Queen Elizabeth*. After superstructure built up and sternwalk replaced in *Queen Elizabeth*. Foretopmast replaced in *Valiant* and *Malaya*. Yard below control top removed from *Malaya*.

1926–34 *Warspite* reconstructed from Oct 1924 until April 1926. Improved bulges fitted, quite different from those in *Royal Sovereign* class. They were in two parts and some compartments were used for oil fuel. Others were filled with water or were just airtight. No tubes were fitted in these structures. Control top enlarged and modified, 15in director remounted on new platform well below this. After control top removed. Range clocks retained over 'X' turret only. Extra pair 4in AA guns added amidships on forecastle deck. After pair of torpedo tubes removed. Bridge structure enlarged and modified, upper and middle levels extending back around tripod legs. Fore funnel trunked into second to keep bridge and control tops relatively free from boiler gases. This arrangement was first introduced in the US *Indiana* class, which had been cancelled in 1921, and was later adopted in the Japanese cruiser *Yubari* in 1923. The arrangement was an efficacious but expensive expedient compared to the cowling and aft discharge uptakes which were developed a little later. Yard below control top removed, extra signal struts fitted on forward starfish.

1926 *Malaya* refitted: Control top enlarged and modified, director placed well below this as in *Warspite*. After control top removed. Extra pair 4in added as in *Warspite*. High-angle rangefinder added on control top. Foretopmast removed. SL platform removed from mainmast.

1926–7 *Queen Elizabeth* under refit (May 1926 to Aug 1927): Protective bulges as in *Warspite*. Control top, torpedo tubes aft, extra 4in HA RF, all as in *Warspite*. Torpedo control tower removed, small rangefinder on platform replacing this. RDF equipment fitted. DF cabinet at rear of director platform, with aerial over control top. 36in SL removed from bridge. Bridgework enlarged and modified, funnels trunked as in *Warspite*. Taller topgallant fitted to mainmast. Wide W/T yard fitted low on topgallant.

1927 *Valiant* under refit (April to July): Control top enlarged and modified, 15in director tower relocated. Range clocks retained over 'X' turret only. Extra pair 4in AA as in *Warspite*. HA RF added on control top. Foretopmast and yard below control top removed. Long forward struts fitted to starfish.

1928 *Barham* under refit (Feb to July): Control top and director as in *Warspite*. Extra 4in AA, HA RF, range clocks over 'X' turret, all as in *Warspite*. 24in signalling SL transferred from lower bridge to forward superstructure (now four 24in signalling on forward superstructure). Screen added around rear of after superstructure. Foretopmast and yard below control top removed.

1927–9 *Malaya* under refit (Sept 1927 to Feb 1929): Bulges, bridges, funnels, etc., as in *Warspite*. Two 24in signalling lamps added port and starboard on middle bridge. Yard added at starfish on mainmast.

Early 1930 (approx) *Queen Elizabeth*: Range clocks removed from over 'X' turret. HA RF replaced by HA director. Improved DF aerial fitted.

1929–30 *Valiant* under refit (March 1929 to Dec 1930): Bulges, bridgework, funnels trunked, after pair torpedo tubes removed, etc., all as in *Warspite*. HA RF replaced by HA director remounted in small tower over bridge. AA lookout positions added port and starboard below control top. DF equipment fitted as in *Queen Elizabeth*. 36in SL removed from bridge. Forward pair SL towers around funnel modified to bring SLs further away from funnel. Bridge enlarged, but upper bridge completely enclosed in addition. Training aircraft catapult fitted on quarterdeck, right aft, with a straight-arm crane abaft it. Flying-off platform removed from 'X' turret. (During 1921–2, a series of trials were carried out to select a suitable weapon for dealing with close-range aircraft attack, and the eight-barrel 2pdr produced by Vickers in 1927 had proved ideal; it was selected after it had been thoroughly tested in HM minelayer *Adventure*. The barrels of the guns were arranged so that they could fire independently of one another, which would ensure a constant stream of shells from each mounting. Later, the weapon was to prove itself extremely effective in breaking up dive-bombing attacks. *Valiant* was the first British capital ship to have this fitting; a multiple 2pdr eight-barrel pom-pom was mounted on the starboard side of the super-

QUEEN ELIZABETH CLASS: PARTICULARS, 1933

Displacement (tons) (deep)
Queen Elizabeth: 35,480
Warspite: 35,060
Valiant: 35,710
Barham: 35,970
Malaya: 35,380.

Beam
Increased to 104ft (average) outside bulges.

Draught (mean)
Warspite: 31ft 9in
Barham: 32ft 6in
Malaya: 31ft 11in.

Armament
Main: as built
Twelve 6in, all in upper deck battery
Four 4in AA
Sixteen 2pdr (2 × 8-barrel, *Barham*)
Eight 2pdr (1 × 8-barrel, *Valiant*)
Eight 0.5in MG (*Barham*)
Original MG and saluting guns in remainder.

Aircraft
Training catapult in *Barham* and *Valiant*
One Fairey III reconnaissance seaplane
Barham carried Walrus amphibian for short period in 1934.

Machinery
As built.

Searchlights
Four 36in in funnel towers
Two or four 24in (signalling).

GM
Average of 6.9ft–7.01ft at deep load for class.

Left: *Queen Elizabeth* anchored just past the Forth Bridge during the winter of 1917/18. Note range clock below control top.

QUEEN ELIZABETH CLASS: PARTICULARS, 1939–44

Displacement (tons)

Queen Elizabeth: 32,100 (load), 36,920 (deep) after reconstruction 1941; 37,984 (deep) 1944
Warspite: 31,320 (load), 36,096 (normal deep) after reconstruction; 36,974 (deep) 1943
Valiant: 32,008 (load), 37,006 (deep) after reconstruction; 37,400 (deep) 1944
Malaya: 37,154 (deep) 1944.

Armament

Queen Elizabeth:
Main armament unchanged, but turret ports altered for higher elevation
Twenty 4.5in DP
Thirty-two 2pdr
Sixteen 0.5in MG
Up to fifty-four 20mm added until 1944
No torpedo armament.

Warspite:
Main armament unchanged, but elevation increased
Eight 6in
Eight 4in twin mountings
Thirty-two 2pdr AA (4 x 8-barrel)
Sixteen 0.5in MG (4 x 4-barrel)
No torpedo armament.

Valiant:
Main armament unchanged except as in *Queen Elizabeth*
Twenty 4.5in DP
Thirty-two 2pdr AA
Up to forty-eight 20mm added throughout the war
No torpedo armament.

Barham:
Main armament unchanged
4in increased to eight in twin mountings.

Malaya:
Main armament unchanged
Eight 4in AA
Sixteen 2pdr AA
Eight 0.5in MG
No torpedo armament.

Armour: see Appearance Changes.

Machinery: see Appearance Changes.

structure abeam the bridge.) Arrangement of signal struts below control top modified.

1931 HA RF over control top replaced by HA director in *Malaya* and *Warspite*. Range clocks removed from 'X' turret in *Malaya* and *Valiant*.

1933–4 A point of particular interest to be found in the 'Ships' Covers' is a suggestion in 1933/34 to convert ships' boilers to burn coal instead of oil, it being feared that oil might be difficult to procure in a future war. The idea embraced not only this class, but the *Royal Sovereigns*, *Renown*, *Repulse* and the latest *Nelson* and *Rodney*. The scheme was not considered practicable, especially in view of the great cost: £50,000 for the *Royal Sovereigns*, £100,000 for *Renown* and *Repulse*, £50,000 for the new *Nelson* and *Rodney* and £60,000 for the *Queen Elizabeth* class.

1933–40 The class underwent their second modernization programme, which had been initiated with a view to bringing the ships more nearly in line with existing requirements for the modern capital ship, especially in respect of increased horizontal protection against plunging fire from bombs and shells, and against underwater attack, to which all the older battleships were vulnerable. *Malaya* and *Warspite* were taken in hand in 1934 and completed in 1936 and 1937 respectively. *Queen Elizabeth* (1937 to 1941) and *Valiant* (1939) were modernized along similar lines to *Warspite*.

Malaya (reconstructed Oct 1934 to Dec 1936): Extra deck armour added to middle deck over engine rooms by fitting 2½in plates of non-cemented armour; lower deck was increased to 4in over magazines. Twin 4in Mk VI replaced single 4in guns. Multiple 2pdr AA added port and starboard on high platform abeam funnel. Multiple 0.5in AA added port and starboard on 'X' turret. HA RF on control top replaced by HA director, and second director was added on after superstructure. Remaining torpedo tubes and torpedo control tower removed. MF/DF equipment added. 36in SL lamps replaced by 44in. Former SL control towers around funnel removed. Two aircraft

BARHAM
Outboard profile, 1934

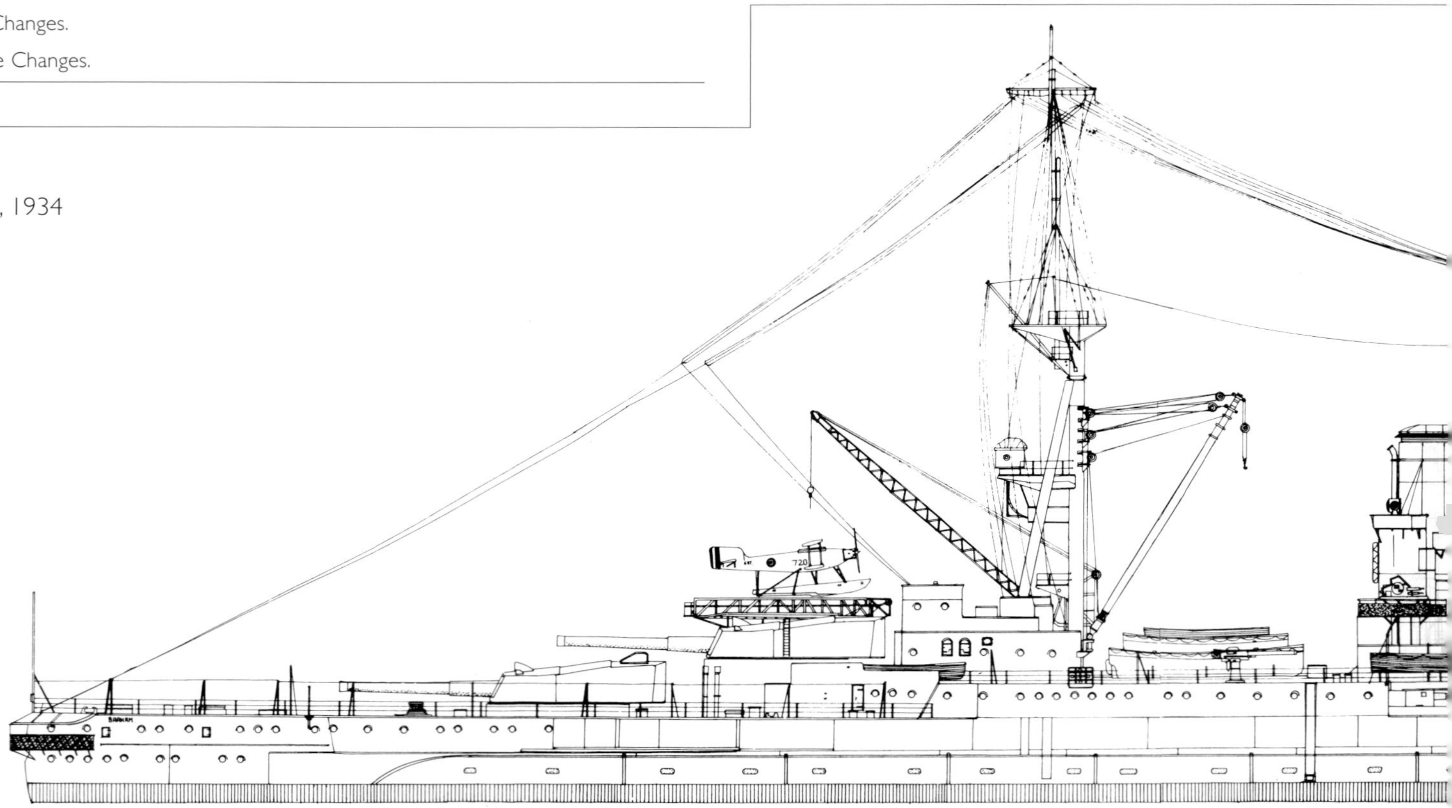

hangars abaft funnel provided, and straight-arm crane fitted at top of each hangar. Accommodation for four aircraft, either Swordfish T/S/R or Walrus amphibians. *Malaya* was the first battleship to have hangar accommodation for aircraft. No change in boilers or machinery except for overhaul of equipment. Ship reported to be capable of 23.7 knots before refit. A new type of completely open upper bridge was fitted, the design being otherwise adopted in *Royal Oak* only. After superstructure abaft mainmast enlarged.

Warspite (reconstructed March 1934 to June 1937): Former bridgework and conning tower replaced by new modern-type structure, watertight and gastight. Trunked funnel replaced by single, slim, much smaller funnel, affording space for additional AA armament with better, unrestricted arcs of fire. Tripod mainmast replaced by single, slightly lighter pole mast. Re-engined and re-boilered with Parsons single-reduction geared turbines and six Admiralty 3-drum high-pressure boilers, arranged in three compartments all grouped together. Boiler weight was reduced from 1,461 tons to 900 tons and machinery from 1,737 tons to 967 tons. Armament weight increased from 4,970 tons to 5,264 tons, armour protection from 5,431 tons to 5,980 tons, and general equipment from 1,287 tons to 1,420 tons. Hull and protective plating increased from 16,250 tons to 17,130 tons. Deck protection increased: main deck from 'A' barbette to forward bulkhead increased to 3in; middle deck increased to 5½in over magazines and 3½in over machinery and magazines. Weight was compensated by removal of heavy armoured conning tower, as already mentioned, and a protected navigating position with 3in plates was added in the lower portion of the new tower. The forward and after pair of 6in secondary guns were removed, and the main 15in turrets were enlarged at the ports to give increased elevation from 20° to 30°. 36in SL lamps replaced by 44in. Aircraft and hangars similar to those in *Malaya* were added.

Valiant (reconstructed March 1937 to Nov 1939): Along the same lines as *Warspite*, but slight differences of bridge structure, armoured plate thicknesses and secondary armament. 6in battery replaced by twenty 4.5in dual purpose. Special 'D' type armoured plates added to sides below forward group of secondary gun turrets. Main deck protection increased to 4½in around face of 'Y' barbette. Lower deck increased to 3½in outside forward bulkhead, otherwise same as *Warspite*. Internal subdivision increased substantially. Aircraft equipment as in *Warspite*, but bent-arm cranes added instead of straight-arm type as in that ship.

Queen Elizabeth (under reconstruction from August 1937 until January 1941): Almost identical with *Valiant*. Tripod legs added to mainmast.

1940–3 *Valiant* painted in unofficial camouflage scheme from 1941 until 1943. *Queen Elizabeth* completed her refit with Admiralty first disruptive camouflage. *Warspite* carried an unofficial scheme of two greys from 1941. Type 79Z radar fitted in *Valiant* in January 1940. Type 279 radar fitted in *Queen Elizabeth* January 1941. Radar-controlled main armament, Type 284, fitted in all except *Barham* by early 1941. Type 285 radar fitted

Above: *Valiant* at sea during the last months of 1918.

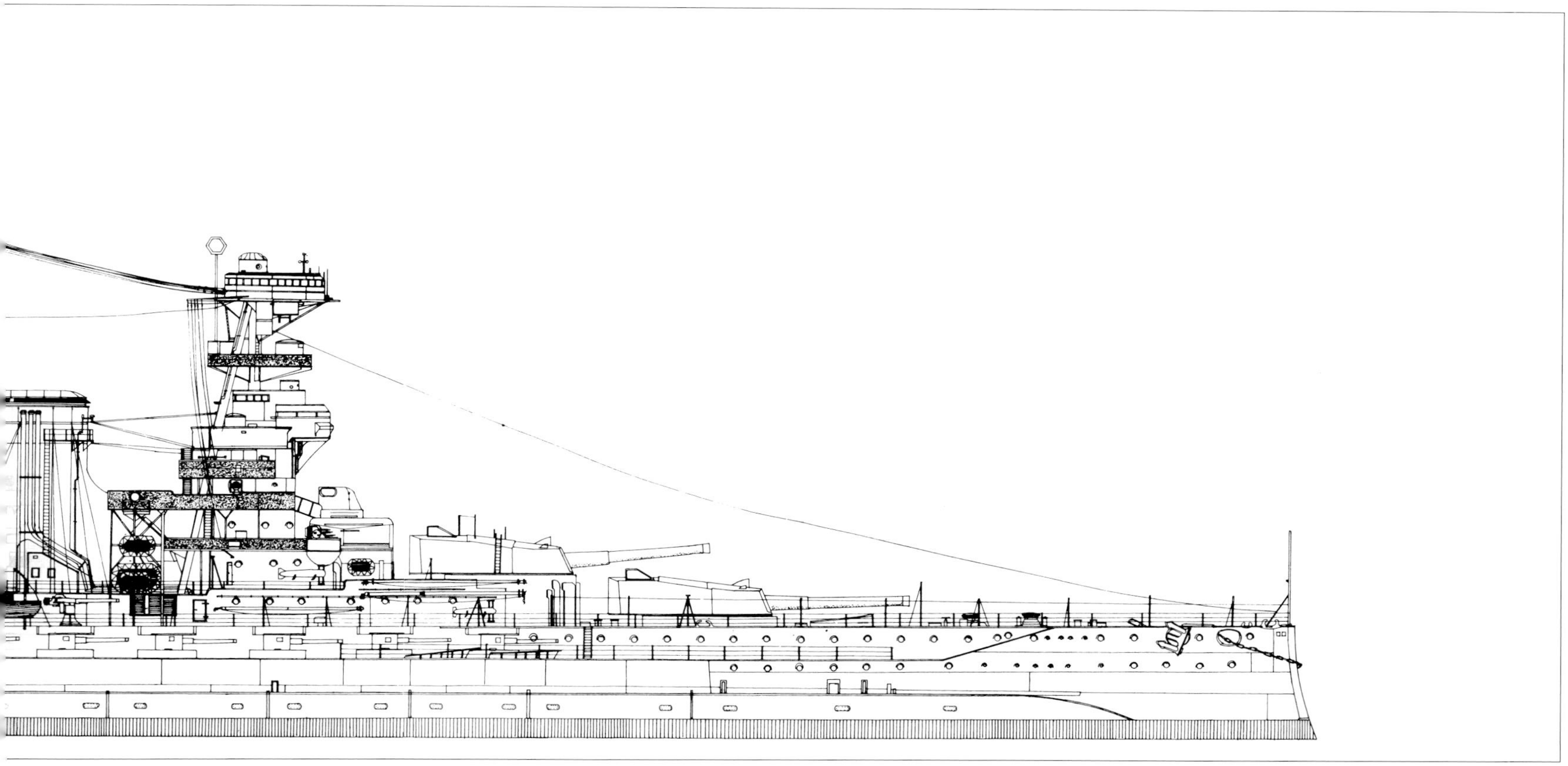

for 4.5in and 4in AA in all except *Barham*. Multiple 2pdr AA added on 'B' turret in *Barham* spring 1941. 0.5in AA varying in number throughout the war, and considerable difference in location throughout the class. Addition of 20mm AA for *Valiant* and *Queen Elizabeth* (see chart). Camouflage in *Barham* from the middle of 1940, but deleted at the end of the year. Repainted in an unofficial scheme of white and dark-grey, which she carried until loss. Type 282 radar fitted for close-range barrage fire for 2pdrs and twin 20mm AA. *Queen Elizabeth* fitted in June 1941. Air warning radar (Type 281) fitted in *Barham*, *Warspite* and *Malaya* during 1941. Improvements in DF equipment in all ships during 1942–3. *Malaya* carried unofficial camouflage scheme during 1940–1. Admiralty disruptive type camouflage painted in *Valiant* and *Queen Elizabeth* during 1943. *Malaya* also carried disruptive type from 1943 until scrapped. *Valiant* and *Queen Elizabeth* both painted in Admiralty standard scheme during 1944–5. *Warspite* carried almost same camouflage as in 1941, but with some minor variations. No aircraft carried from 1944. Improved radar proposed for *Queen Elizabeth* and *Valiant*, but only *Valiant* received such, during her refit of 1945–6. Type 284 replaced by Type 274 for main armament and Type 273 replaced by Type 277. Surface warning (navigational) and surface/air warning aerials (Type 293) also added.

Below: *Warspite* in dry dock showing her collision damage. Note 6in gun barrels. December 1915.

History: *Queen Elizabeth*

Queen Elizabeth was built at Portsmouth under a certain amount of secrecy, her fine hull lines being kept hidden while she was on the stocks. The old pre-dreadnought *Zealandia* was moored near the athwart slipway so as to conceal the launching ceremony to some extent, but many photographs were taken of her as she entered the water. It is said that a German officer aboard *Zealandia* was happily taking snaps! The pace of construction was slowed by labour problems, but work resumed swiftly on the outbreak of war in August 1914, and she was ready for preliminary sea trials in October of that year.

1914 *22 Dec* Commissioned for independent service at Portsmouth and was working-up until Feb 1915. She carried out gunnery trials en route from UK to Gibraltar, and was sent to the Dardanelles for special service. It was anticipated that her 15in guns would have good effect on the heavily protected forts hidden deep in the hills.

1915 *19 Feb* Arrived at the Dardanelles and went into action against the forts the same day. She took part in the bombardments of the Entrance and Narrows forts from Feb to March 1915.

During these operations she was hit by shore batteries, but did not sustain any substantial damage.

27 April Fired on the German battlecruiser Goeben, by indirect fire off Nagara, using a kite balloon for spotting.

It had long been realized that she was very vulnerable to mines and U-boat attack and, her 15in guns not proving as successful as at first hoped, Fisher ordered her home.

12 May Relieved from Dardanelles.

26 May Arrived at Scapa Flow.

May Joined the newly formed 5th BS Grand Fleet. Not present at Jutland, being in dockyard hands.

1916 *28 Nov* Admiral Beatty selected her as his flagship when he relieved Admiral Jellicoe as CinC Grand Fleet. She was refitted at Newcastle for this service from Nov 1916 to Feb 1917.

1918 *15 Nov* Terms of the naval armistice with Germany were arranged on board at Rosyth.

1919 *4 April* Grand Fleet being dispersed, became flagship Atlantic Fleet.

1924 *Nov* Transferred to Mediterranean Fleet with rest of class; flagship.

1926 *May* Reconstructed at Portsmouth.

1928 *2 Jan* Commissioned with Mediterranean Fleet.

1929 *Nov* Refit (to May 1930).

1930 *July* Sent to Alexandria with *Ramillies* to reinforce local forces during riots.

1932 *Nov* Under refit (until March 1933).

1935 *16 July* Senior flagship at Jubilee Fleet Review.

Oct At Alexandria until summer of 1936.

1937 *19 May* Coronation Review at Spithead.

Aug Under complete reconstruction until Jan 1941.

1941 *21 Feb* Commissioned to work up. 2nd BS Home Fleet.

May 1st BS Mediterranean Fleet.

1943 *June* Home Fleet.

1944 *Jan* Eastern Fleet.

Nov East Indies Fleet.

1945 *Aug* Placed in Reserve at Rosyth in Aug 1945.

Oct 2nd BS Home Fleet.

1946 *March* Reserve Fleet Portsmouth.

1948 *May* Sold to the British Iron & Steel Corporation and allocated to Arnott Young for scrapping.

Left: *Barham*. Close-up of range clocks/funnels etc 1918. Note the makeshift boards over the edge of the tower with paint pots at the ready.

Below: *Queen Elizabeth* commissioned at Portsmouth for trials on 22 December 1914, worked up her gunnery at Gibraltar January/February 1915 and then went straight to the Dardanelles (shown here arriving on 19 February 1915). She went into action for about 20 minutes on the same day. At this time, however, she had no HE ammunition and the hits, although spectacular, were not very effective.

7 July Arrived at Dalmuir to be scrapped; her hull later taken to Troon for final demolition.

History: *Malaya*

Built with funds supplied by the Federated Malay States.

1916 *April* Commissioned for service with 5th BS Grand Fleet.
31 May Battle of Jutland. Ship fired 215 rounds of 15in and 31 rounds of 6in. Hit several times by large shells, sustaining damage as follows. (1) Strike on lower tier of armour, armour pushed in slightly. (2) Strike on lower tier of armour, slight dent. (3, 4) Close together, inner and outer bottoms torn away just below armoured shelf. (5) Pierced forecastle deck and then exploded, causing cordite fire in starboard 6in battery, which resulted in 102 men suffering burns. (6) Strike on lower boom stanchion with damage to local superstructure. (7) Strike on middle roof plate of 'X' 15in turret, but did not pierce or cause much damage internally. Throughout action, 63 men killed, 33 wounded. Under repair at Cromarty until 24 June 1916.
1918 At end of war transferred to newly formed Atlantic Fleet.
1924 *Nov* Mediterranean Fleet.
26 July Fleet Review, Spithead.
1927 *Sept* Under reconstruction.
1929 *21 Feb* Recommissioned at Portsmouth for further service with Mediterranean Fleet.
Nov Transferred to Atlantic Fleet (renamed Home Fleet, March 1932).
1934 *Oct* Paid off for refit.
1937 *Jan* Mediterranean Fleet.
1939 *Oct* East Indies Fleet (Force 'J').
Dec North Atlantic Escort Force (3rd BS), based at Halifax.
1940 *May* 1st BS Mediterranean Fleet.
Dec Force 'H', based at Gibraltar, until March 1941.
1941 *July* 2nd BS, Home Fleet.

Right: *Malaya* leaving Portsmouth after refit, 27 September 1926. In evidence is the new large control top, modified 15in gun director located below top. SL platforms have been removed from mainmast and after superstructure.

Below: *Malaya* 1919. Close-up showing range clocks on compass platform, and back of 'coffee-box' SL towers.

27 Oct Rejoined Force 'H'.
1942 *May* North Atlantic Command.
Oct Home Fleet.
1943 *Dec* Paid off into Reserve.
1944 *March* Refit.
May Commissioned for operations with Home Fleet.
June Shore bombardment at Normandy invasion.
Oct Reserve.
1947 *June* Placed on Disposal list.
1948 *20 Feb* Sold to Metal Industries.
12 April Taken to Faslane for scrapping

History: *Warspite*

1915 *5 April* Commissioned at Devonport for service with 2nd BS Grand Fleet.
13 April Arrived Scapa Flow. With Grand Fleet.
16 Sept Grounded in the Forth, her bottom sustaining some damage. Under repair in the Admiralty floating dock until November.
24 Nov Rejoined Grand Fleet and transferred to the newly formed 5th BS.
3 Dec In collision with *Barham*.
1916 *31 May* Battle of Jutland. (5th BS temporarily attached to BC Squadron and were of great assistance to the battlecruisers.) *Warspite* was one of the most severely damaged ships in the action, but did great service throughout, firing 259 15in salvoes and a considerable quantity of 6in shells. She received 13 hits from large shells and damage was as follows. (1) Strike on the unarmoured side between main and middle deck level, starboard, the burst inside causing extensive damage. (2) Strike on unarmoured side between main and middle decks, on port side, in Captain's quarters, shell burst inside. (3) Strike through 6in armour above middle deck and burst inside. (4) Strike went through the upper deck and burst inside. (5) Another strike through the 6in armour between main and upper deck levels. (6) Hit on the 13in belt broke a piece off the top corner. (7) Another pierce on the 6in plate. (8) A shell went through the upper deck and caused a fire. (9) A shot went through the after funnel striking the gratings and deflected upwards, and then burst near the starboard side. (10) Hit on the upper deck exploded on impact and caused a small cordite fire. (11) Another hit passed through the after funnel, and was again deflected by the gratings, and passed through the shelter deck. (12) Strike on the deck edge of the forward shelter deck, shell burst inside and caused a fire. (13) An important strike on the after side of the communications tube which half-severed it; the shell then turned through 60° and burst. The shell that struck in the area of the Captain's cabin (2) caused difficulties in the steering compartment and the rudder became jammed. This caused the ship to turn in a large circle, and at one point she was steaming straight towards the enemy battle line, and was fired on and hit by many heavy shells. This phase of the action is referred to as 'Windy Corner'. At the critical point she was as close as 12,000 yards to the enemy, and it was reported that her own fire at the time was excellent. She was forced to leave the line and make her way back to Rosyth; she was able to raise steam and make 15, 19 and then 22 knots, before reaching Rosyth.
1 June Reached Rosyth, drawing 35ft 6in aft, but with no vital impairment to her fighting efficiency – a remarkable achievement. Under repairs until 20 July 1916.
23 July Rejoined the Fleet.
24 Aug Collided with *Valiant* and damaged; repaired by 29 Sept 1916. No further action during the war.
1919 *April* With Atlantic Fleet.
1924 *31 Oct* Paid off at Portsmouth for reconstruction.
1926 *6 April* Recommissioned at Portsmouth to relieve *Queen Elizabeth* as flagship Mediterranean Fleet.

Above: *Valiant* opens fire during a practice shoot, c 1919.

1928 *Sept* Under refit at Portsmouth.
1929 *Jan* Mediterranean Fleet.
1930 *May* 2nd Flagship, Atlantic Fleet (later Home Fleet) until Dec 1933.
1934 *March* Complete reconstruction.
1937 *29 June* Commissioned for Mediterranean Fleet.
1939 *28 Oct* Home Fleet.
1945 *Feb* Paid off into Reserve.
1946 *31 July* Laid up at Motherbank and placed on Disposal list, despite much talk of preserving her.
1947 Sold to Metal Industries.
18 April Left Portsmouth, bound for scrapyard; ran aground in Mounts Bay, Cornwall, and stuck fast. Scrapped in that position (to 1955).

History: *Valiant*

1916 *13 Jan* Commissioned on the Tyne for service with 5th BS Grand Fleet.
16 March Joined Grand Fleet after a short programme of sea trials.
31 May Battle of Jutland. She was the least damaged ship of the squadron, sustaining only splinter damage. Fired her 15in guns at both *Seydlitz* and *Derfflinger*, 288 15in and 91 6in shells being expended. She was ready for service again within a few days.
24 Aug Collided with *Warspite* in Scapa Flow and sustained considerable damage. Repaired at Cromarty.
18 Sept Rejoined Grand Fleet.
1919 *April* Transferred to newly formed Atlantic Fleet.

Below: *Warspite*. The 6in secondary battery opens fire during a practice shoot.

Right: *Warspite* after her first reconstruction. Having been in dockyard hands from October 1924, she emerged looking like this in April 1926. The bridge structure has been enlarged and modified; twin funnels have been trunked into one; anti-torpedo bulges of an improved type have been fitted, and an improved director control has been located below the new control top.

Right: *Warspite* at Malta in January 1938, showing her new lines after her reconstruction. Note the multiple 0.5in guns on 'B' and 'X' turret tops, multiple 2pdrs amidships, and twin 4in in shield amidships. Red, white and blue stripes on 'B' turret are identification marks painted during the Spanish Civil War.

Opposite, top left: *Barham*. An aircraft takes off from the runway on 'B' turret.

Opposite, top right: Units of *Queen Elizabeth* class put to sea for exercises during 1919/20. Taken from *Barham*, looking back on *Warspite*, *Valiant* and *Malaya*.

Opposite: Looking back from the forecastle over the 15in turrets and bridge of *Valiant* on Christmas Day 1917. Note the Christmas trees on the masts.

1924 *Nov* Transferred with the rest of her class to Mediterranean Fleet.
1927 *Feb* Refit at Portsmouth (to July 1927).
1929 *23 March* Paid off at Portsmouth for reconstruction.
1930 *2 Dec* Recommissioned with Atlantic Fleet.
1932 *March* Home Fleet.
1935 *July* Transferred to Mediterranean Fleet, exchanging stations with *Ramillies*. With 1st BS Mediterranean fleet.
1937 *March* Paid off into Devonport Dockyard control for total reconstruction (until Nov 1939).
1939 *30 Nov* Recommissioned and attached to the America and West Indies Fleet, working-up off Bermuda prior to joining Home Fleet.
1940 *Jan* 2nd BS Home Fleet.
June Force 'H' (Gibraltar).
Aug 1st BS Mediterranean Fleet.
1942 *June* South Atlantic Command.
1943 *Jan* West Africa Command (to Feb 1943).
June Force 'H' June (to Oct 1943).
1944 *Jan* Eastern Fleet.
8 Aug In dry dock at Trincomalee when her supports gave way and she collapsed into the dock sustaining great damage to her hull which was never the same again, even after repair. The collapse was blamed on a mechanical fault caused by bomb damage from Japanese aircraft in 1942, which had never been repaired properly. *Valiant* was 37,400 tons displacement in the deep load at the time of the incident. The blocks on the slipway were driven into the vertical keel plate at the bows and formed a trough-like depression about 18in deep at station 23, and extended to the bows. She was also pierced at station 27 for about 2½ft and the stern was 3½in into the blocks, this damage extending for approximately 50ft. The port rudder was damaged and the inner shafts were completely severed. The two damaged propellers were removed and the ship was patched up. She proceeded slowly at about 16–18 knots to the Suez Canal where it was found that her draught was too great to let her through. On 21 Oct she became grounded near the mouth of the Canal and remained firmly stuck for six hours. Freed, she left the Canal Zone bound for home via the Cape and Freetown, and finally reached Devonport on 1 Feb 1945.
1945 Under repair and refit for most of the year; it was considered that the repairs were adequate for a ship that would probably never fight again.
1946 *June* Placed in the Reserve, and attached to the training establishment HMS *Impérieuse* as a seagoing training ship.
1948 *Jan* Disposal list. Sold to Arnott, Young Ltd.
11 Aug Left for Devonport and arrived at Cairnryan on 16th for breaking up

History: *Barham*

1915 *19 Aug* Commissioned.
2 Oct Joined Grand Fleet. The 5th BS was constituted in November 1915, and the group had worked-up to full strength by March to May 1916; with the arrival of *Valiant* and *Malaya* they formed one of the most powerful battleship squadrons the world had ever seen.
3 Dec Collided with *Warspite* while on exercises, and was damaged. Repaired at Invergordon.

1916 *1 Jan* Rejoined Grand Fleet.

31 May Battle of Jutland. Damaged during the engagement as follows. (1) A large shell pierced the upper deck (starboard) and exploded between upper and main deck levels. (2) A shell pierced the upper deck and exploded between upper and main decks, a fragment entering the lower part of the conning tower. (3) A shell penetrated the starboard side of the superstructure and exploded on the forecastle deck. (4) A shell pierced the forecastle deck and exploded inside. (5) The side plating was pierced between the upper and main deck levels and exploded causing a fire. (6) Strike on the side armour on the port side, but this did little damage except drive the plate in about ¾in.

All of these hits were from 11in or 12in shells; they caused much superficial damage, but did little to impair the ship's fighting qualities. *Barham* did well, at one time engaging *Von der Tann* at 19,000 yards, and scoring hits. The majority of the hits on *Barham* were made when the class was turning north to join the main battlefleet when she was hit at least four times in ten minutes. She was also reported to have fired on *Seydlitz* and *Derfflinger*, causing considerable damage to both. *Barham* fired 337 15in and 25 6in shells during the battle.

4 July Rejoined the Fleet having been repaired at Cromarty. On demise of Grand Fleet in April 1919, joined Atlantic Fleet until November 1924.

1924 *26 July* Spithead Fleet Review.

1 Nov Class transferred to Mediterranean Fleet as 1st BS.

1929 *Nov* Atlantic Fleet.

1930 *Dec* Paid off at Portsmouth for refit until October 1933.

1934 *11 Jan* Recommissioned at Portsmouth for 2nd BS Home Fleet.

1935 *Aug* Mediterranean Fleet.

1939 *13 Dec* Rammed and sank the destroyer *Duchess* in the North Channel, en route for home.

Dec Home Fleet.

28 Dec Torpedoed in the bows by *U30* just off the Hebrides, but managed to reach Liverpool by the 29th under her own steam. Repaired by Cammell Laird, Jan to April 1940.

1940 *28 Aug* Detached for operations against Dakar.

Nov Mediterranean Fleet until Nov 1941.

1941 *27 May* Damaged by bomb off Crete. Refitted at Durban from June to July 1941.

25 Nov While patrolling off the Libyan coast with *Valiant* and a destroyer screen she was torpedoed by *U331* being hit at least three times in quick succession. She listed to port until the magazines exploded. She sank very quickly, taking with her 56 officers and 806 ratings.

Royal Sovereign Class: 1913 ESTIMATES

Design

When Phillip Watts resigned as Director of Naval Construction shortly after producing the excellent *Queen Elizabeth*-class battleships in 1912, his successor, Eustace Tennyson d'Eyncourt, was faced with the problem of drafting a design for a 15in-gunned version of *Iron Duke*, a ship which had been part of the 1911 Estimates. Furthermore, the Board of Admiralty had it in mind that the new ship should carry ten 15in guns, rather than repeat the layout of *Queen Elizabeth*, which carried eight mounted in four twin turrets.

The Board stated that they would like the vessel to have a speed of at least 21 knots, which was regarded as adequate for normal North Sea duties with the Grand Fleet. It was proposed that the new class revert to using coal and oil, the standard practice of the day, rather than copy *Queen Elizabeth*, which had been fitted to burn oil only, having been designed as a 'special fast battleship' capable of operating with the battlecruiser force if required.

D'Eyncourt and his staff were asked to develop a design along these guidelines for the 1913 Estimates and to experiment with a view to producing a triple turret for the new ships. Within a month or so, the Department of Naval Construction was able to forward to the Board for approval some of the designs they had conceived. The ten 15in-gunned ship had not materialized because the construction department had felt it impossible to produce a satisfactory layout on the limited displacement of the Board's initial specification. Furthermore, D'Eyncourt regarded as unnecessary the five twin mountings as arranged in *Iron Duke*; the amidships turret required a great increase in length and weight, to say nothing of the cost and time involved in procuring the extra armament and fittings. He was quick to point out that two extra guns was not generally viewed as a great improvement over the four twin mountings of *Queen Elizabeth* as regards firepower, and any thoughts of a triple turret would have to be abandoned for the time being because of lack of experience and the lengthy period of experimental work needed before such a radical change in British battleship construction could be realized. He also felt that in the event of a knockout blow to a turret, less firepower would be lost in a ship fitted with twin mountings.

The Board took these views into account before settling for a layout that showed only eight guns. They had approved the initial schematic layout by 31 March 1913 and the new class was designated Design 'T1' for a first-class battleship of the 1913 Estimates. As laid down the design differed from the *Queen Elizabeth* class in that:

1. Nominal displacement was reduced by approximately 1,750 tons with a reduction of 20ft in length, 2ft in beam, and 3ft on the designed draught.
2. Main armament remained unchanged but the 6in secondary battery was reduced from 16 to 14 guns. The battery was arranged so that a greater all-round arc of fire could be secured and by placing the guns further towards the midships section they were less likely to be washed out in a seaway. The 6in main deck, as first fitted in *Queen Elizabeth*, would now be discarded.
3. Protection to the middle and lower sides amidships would be increased with a uniform 13in of armour and not taper like

DESIGN 'TI': FINAL LEGEND

Displacement (tons)
25,750.

Dimensions
Length: 580ft pp
Beam: 88ft 6in
Draught: 28ft 6in
Sinkage: 91 tons
Freeboard: 26ft forward, 16ft amidships, 18ft aft
Height of 15in guns above load wl: 'A' 30ft 6in; 'B' 40ft 6in; 'X' 33ft; 'Y' 23ft.

Armament
Eight 15in
Sixteen 6in
Four 3in AA
Four 21in torpedo tubes.

Armour
Main belt: 13in (to extend 15ft 9in above wl, 5ft below)
Extensions: 6in–4in
Bulkheads: 6in–4in
Barbettes: 10in–4in
Turrets: 11in
Conning tower: 11in
Signal tower: 6in
Wood backing for main armour: 4in teak
Decks: forecastle 1in, upper 1½in–1¼in, main 2in–1½in–1in, lower aft 4in–3in.

Weights (tons)

Hull:	8,630
Armour and backing:	8,250
Armament:	4,570
Machinery:	2,550
Coal (min.):	900
General equipment:	750
Board margin:	100
Designed condition:	25,750

Below: *Resolution* fitting out at Palmer's shipyard, 17 June 1916. 'B' 15in turret is not in position at this date.

that of the *QE*. Behind this the protective deck was placed a deck higher than before (main deck level), and 6in thicker.
4. Nominal speed was to be 4 knots less, with a mixed fuel arrangement, but fuel capacity would remain the same.

The freeboard of the new ships was to be the same as in *Iron Duke* and was regarded by many of the construction staff as one of the ship's poorer qualities; they were thought of as wet ships even before they were laid down.

The forecastle level extended aft to 'X' 15in turret, as in *Queen Elizabeth*, although the sides before the secondary battery were less strongly recessed, the flare being unbroken as far aft as 'A' turret in *Revenge* and 'B' turret in the others. Placed farther back along the main deck level, the secondary battery had a light shelter deck placed above it.

One of the main features of the ships, named the *Royal Sovereign* class in the summer of 1913, was that the metacentric height had been lowered (two feet less than in *Iron Duke*) in order to gain a greater proportion of steadiness which made for a good gun platform. The ships would, of course, be stiffer, their stability would suffer; it was realized that if any considerable flooding took place as a result of action damage, they would not be able to maintain stability as well as previous designs. To counteract this to a certain extent a change in protection was adopted:

1. By raising the height of the protective deck to main deck level, the vessels had a better-protected freeboard well above the deep load water-line. Furthermore, the maximum thickness of armour was to be carried right up to the deck.
2. By providing armoured longitudinal bulkheads between the main and middle deck levels on each side amidships.

It was realized that the change in protection would result in a ship that would be prone to heavy, if slow, rolling, but this inconvenience was accepted; the greatly increased protection even when the ships rolled and exposed their sides (which would be a uniform 13in), far outweighed the disadvantages of stability.

REVENGE: LAUNCH FIGURES, 29 MAY 1915

	tons
Displacement:	11,954
Machinery:	363
Armour:	1,487
Ballast, equipment, men:	370
Recorded weight of hull:	9,734

Draught: 13ft 6in forward, 16ft 9¾in aft
Length: 580ft 0½in pp
Beam: 88ft 7in
Beam as moulded: 88ft 3in
Length of boiler rooms: (1) 38ft 0⅝in, (2) 38ft 1in, (3) 38ft 0¾in
Length of engine rooms: 69ft 11½in
Water density: 35.25cu ft
Breakage at launch:
longitudinal in a distance of 436ft 9in 1⅛in hog
transverse in a distance of 78ft 10in = 0 1/16 sag.

Armament

The main armament of *Queen Elizabeth* was continued in the *Royal Sovereigns* with four twin turrets mounted on the centreline, the only differences being:

1. Nominal height of forward and after turrets was reduced by approximately 1ft forward and 6in aft.
2. The director tower was placed on a platform just beneath the control top instead of on the roof.

On paper, the *Royal Sovereigns* were given wider arcs of fire for the 15in guns but in service the arcs were practically identical.

Consideration was given to securing a better position for the 6in secondary battery because in the *Iron Duke* and *Queen Elizabeth* classes it had been sited too far forward and was liable to be washed out in a seaway. So the battery was taken back closer to the midships section and approximately 238 feet from the bows; this was accepted as a notable improvement.

Below: *Royal Sovereign* completes her fitting-out at Portsmouth DY in March 1916.

In the original design, shell stowage was given as 80 rounds per gun, but later it was able to accommodate 100 rounds per gun. The magazines and shell rooms were situated at the foot of the central trunk, with the shell rooms one deck below the magazines. After the First World War consideration was given to placing the magazines above the shell rooms (1922), but after a short inquiry, this was seen as a bad move which would cause numerous problems: reduced rate of loading; reduced capacity for shell stowage; great expense; and the alterations would exceed the terms of the London and Washington Treaties.

Armour

Distribution was almost identical with that of *Queen Elizabeth*, but was 13in throughout and did not reduce to 8in below the water-line. The armour was rearranged to provide increased protection to the middle and lower side amidships with a greater height of armoured freeboard below the principal protective deck. The chief modifications over that of *Queen Elizabeth* were:

1. The main belt was uniform and not tapered.
2. Main belt's height above water: 13ft 9in (*Queen Elizabeth* 15ft 1½in); below water 7ft 13in (*Queen Elizabeth* 5ft 4½in of partly 8in).
3. The main belt was carried up to main deck level at 13in, whereas it reduced to 6in in *Queen Elizabeth* and 8in and 6in in *Iron Duke*.

Above: *Revenge* at full speed during steam trials, 24 March 1916. Seen in the Firth of Clyde on the Skelmorlie Mile, she attained a high of 22.140 knots with 43,080shp.

Below: *Revenge* during her steam trials on the Skelmorlie Mile, 24 March 1916.

ROYAL SOVEREIGN CLASS: PARTICULARS, AS COMPLETED

Construction

	Dockyard	Laid Down	Launched	Completed for trials	Completed
Ramillies:	Beardmore	12 Nov 1913	12 Sept 1916	5 May 1917	Sept 1917
Resolution:	Palmer	29 Nov 1913	14 Jan 1915	7 Dec 1916	30 Dec 1916
Revenge:	Vickers	22 Dec 1913	29 May 1915	1 Feb 1916	24 March 1916
Royal Sovereign:	Portsmouth DY	15 Jan 1914	29 April 1915	8 April 1916	May 1916
Royal Oak:	Devonport DY	15 Jan 1914	17 Nov 1914	1 May 1916	mid May 1916.

Displacement (tons)
Ramillies: 30,400 (load), 33,570 (deep)
Revenge: 29,590 (load), 32,820 (deep)
Royal Oak: 27,970 (load), 31,130 (deep).

Dimensions
Length: 580ft 3in pp, 614ft 6in wl, 620ft 6⅞in oa (*Ramillies*)
Beam: 88ft 6in (101ft 5½in *Ramillies*, after bulging)
Draught (mean): 30ft (load), 33ft 7in (deep)
Height of 15in guns above lower wl: 'A' 30ft 6in; 'B' 40ft 6in; 'X' 33ft; 'Y' 23ft
Height of conning tower vision slits above lower wl: 50ft
Height of fore funnel: 74ft
Height of lower masthead: 120ft
Depth of keel from battery deck: 44ft 6in.

Armament
Eight 15in 42cal Mk I
Fourteen 6in 45cal Mk XII
Two 3in AA
Four 3pdr
Five MG
Ten Lewis guns
Four 21in torpedo tubes (beam, submerged); twenty-one torpedoes Mk II, IV, IVHB (tubes fixed at 90° and -2°).

Director control
Fitted in a tower aloft and in an armoured tower, 'X' 15in turret fitted with director gear.
'Follow the pointer gear' fitted to all sights and flexible voice pipes fitted for night firing.

Armour
Main belt: 13in amidships
Forward: 6in–4in–1in
Aft: 6in–4in
Upper side amidships: 6in
Main bulkheads: 6in
Decks: forecastle 1in, upper 1½in–1¼in, main 2in incline, flat 2in–1½in–1in, middle 4in–3in–2in, lower ½in–1in
Barbettes: 10in–9in–7in–6in
Turrets: 13in–11in
Conning tower: 11in–3in
Uptakes: 1½in–1in
Anti–torpedo bulkheads: 1½in–1in.

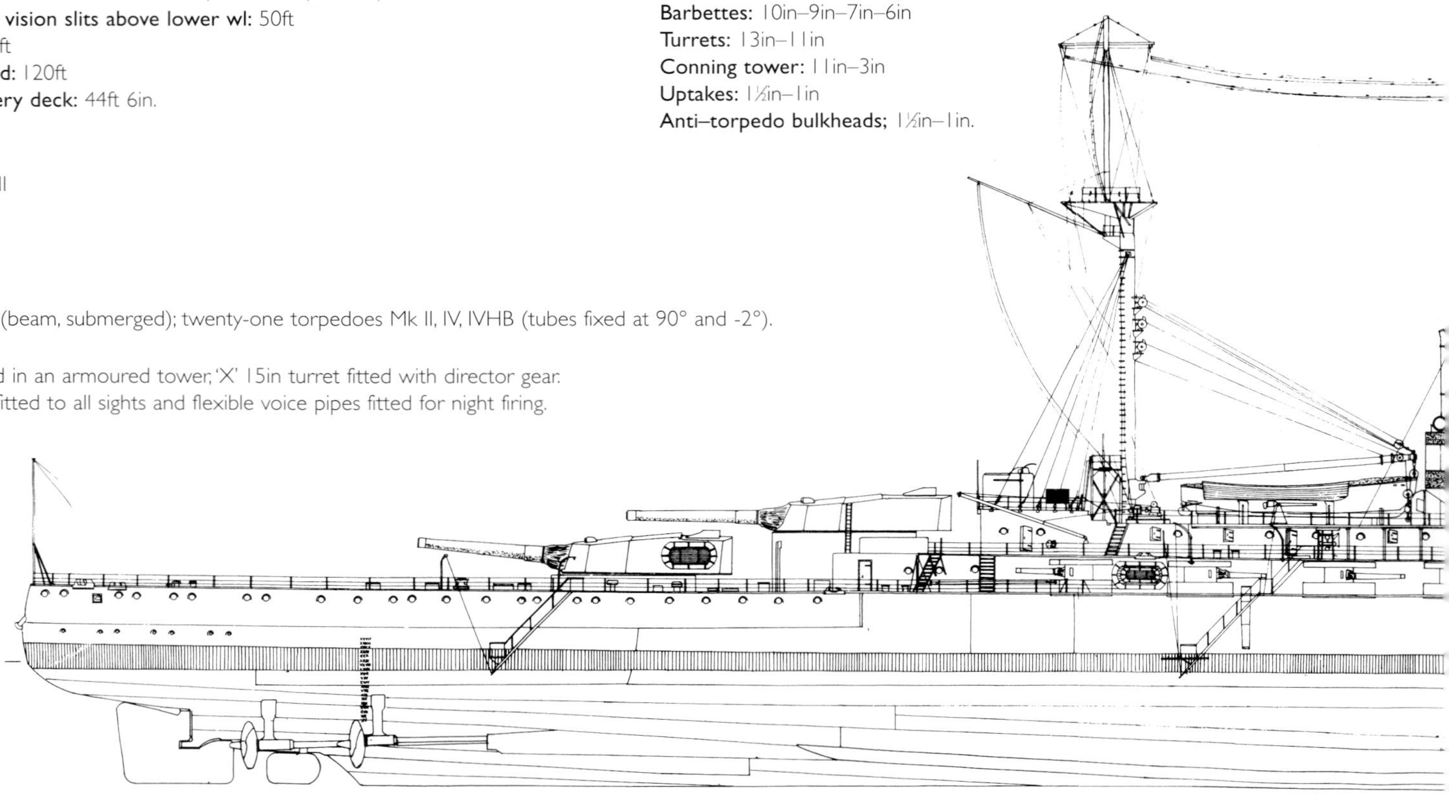

RESOLUTION
Outboard profile and plan, 1916, as fitted

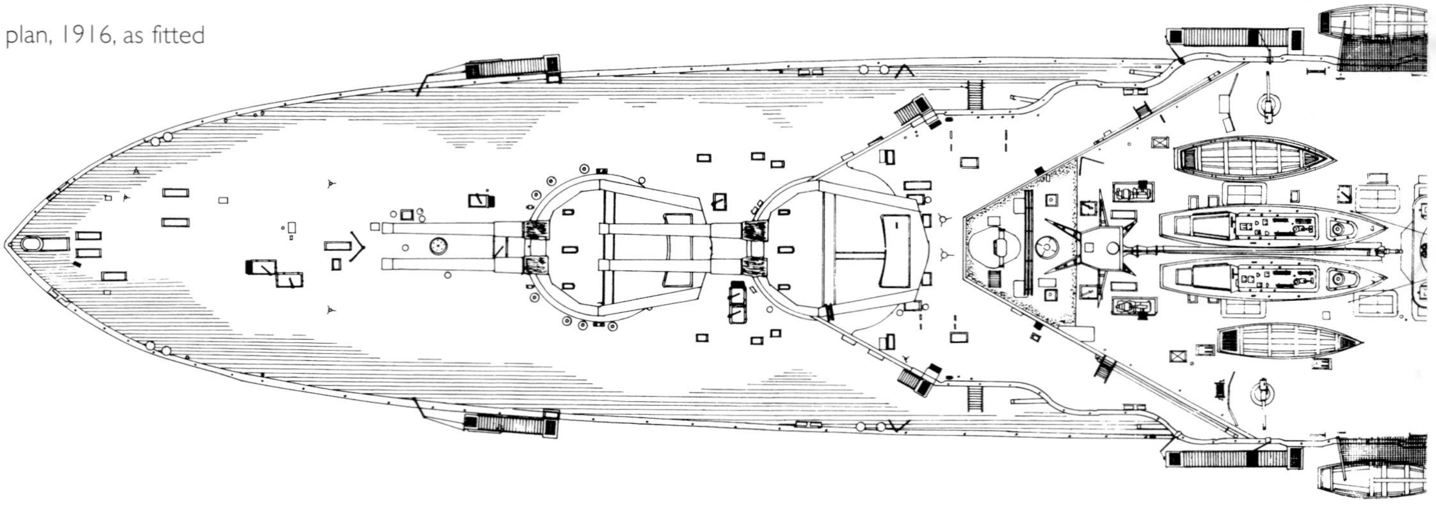

Machinery
Parsons reaction-type turbines, four propellers
Boilers: eighteen Babcock & Wilcox (Yarrow *Resolution*, *Royal Oak*), working pressure 235psi
Pressure at turbines: 200psi
Heating surface: 63,846sq ft (69,840sq ft *Resolution*, *Royal Oak*)
Propellers: 3-bladed
Propeller diameter: 9ft 3in outers; 10ft inners
Propeller pitch: 9ft 6in outers; 10ft inners (9ft 3in outers; 8ft 9in inners *Resolution*, *Royal Oak*)
Designed revs.: 300rpm
Designed SHP: 40,000 23 knots
Fuel: 900 tons oil min., 3,400 tons oil max.
Radius of action: 2,700nm full speed; 3,600nm at 18 knots; 7,000nm at 10 knots.

Ship's boats
Pinnaces (steam): two 50ft
Pinnaces (sail): one 36ft
Launches (steam): one 42ft*
Cutters: three 32ft
Whalers: two 27ft
Skiff dinghies: one 16ft
Balsa rafts: one 13ft6in.

Boat derricks
One 65ft–60ft at base of mainmast; two 35ft, two 32ft for light boats.

Searchlights
Eight 36in: four fore bridge, two base of funnel, two after superstructure
Two 24in signalling lamps
As completed *Ramillies* carried eleven 36in.

*Added 1919.

Rangefinder positions (1918)
Two 30ft: 'B', 'X' 15in turrets
Four 15ft: 'A', 'Y' turrets, gun control tower, torpedo control tower
One 12ft: spotting top
Two 9ft: fore bridge or platforms abreast funnels
One 6ft 6in: fore bridge.

Battle signal stations**
Two separate and enclosed, main deck level.

Anchors
Three 145cwt stockless (bower, sheet), one 60cwt Admiralty stern.

Wireless (1918)
Main office: Types 1–16
Second office: Types 2–34
Third office: Type 9
Fire control office: Type 31
Destroyer office in *Royal Oak*, *Revenge*, Type 9 (modified).

Complement
Ramillies: 936 (1917)
Resolution: 910 (1916); 1,012 (1923)
Revenge: 940 (1917)
Royal Sovereign: 1,240 (1921)
Royal Oak: 909 (1916).

Cost
Ramillies: £3,295,810
Resolution: £2,449,680
Revenge: £2,406,368
Royal Sovereign: £2,570,504
Royal Oak: £2,468,269.

**Each provided with lockers and arrangements for working signals through W/T trunks running through the decks.

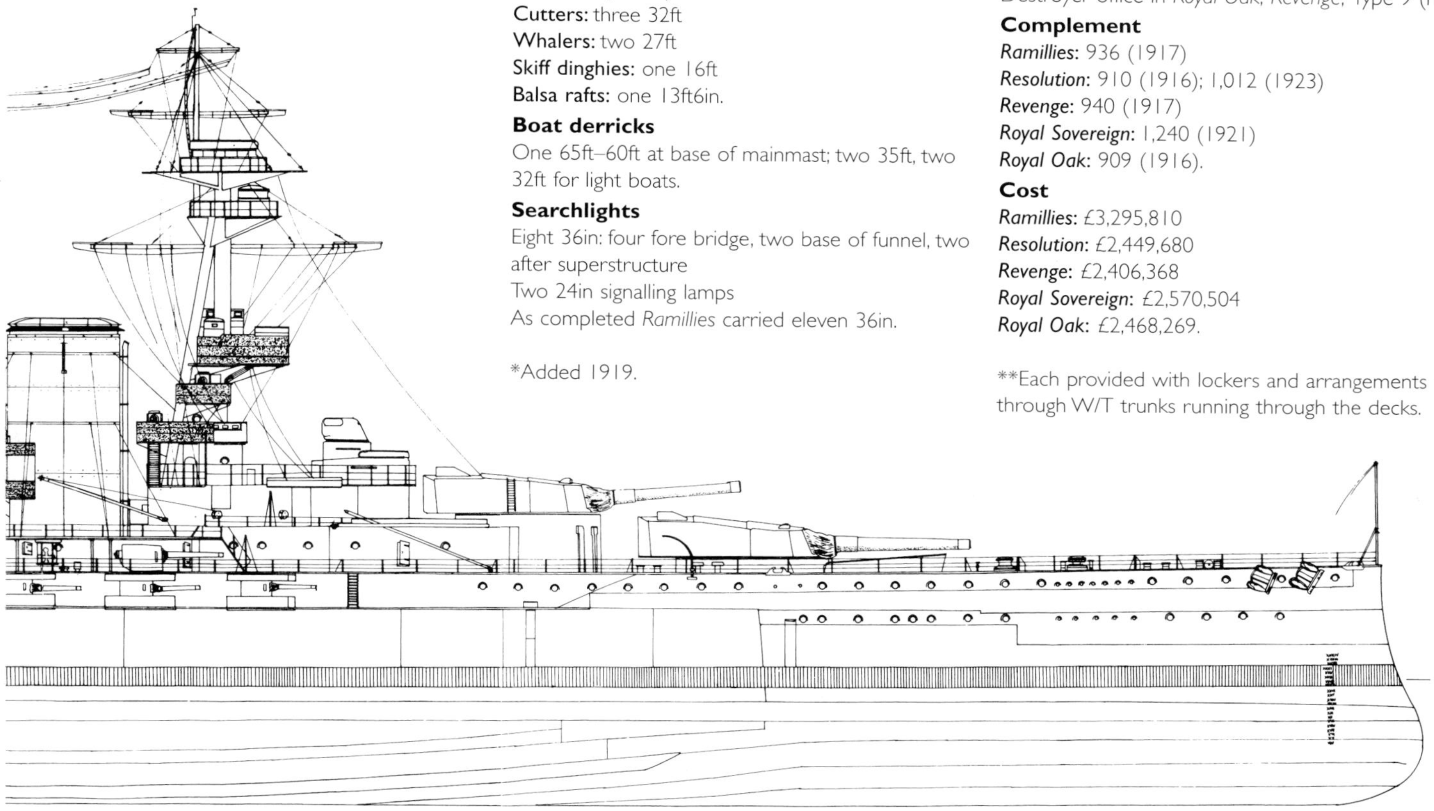

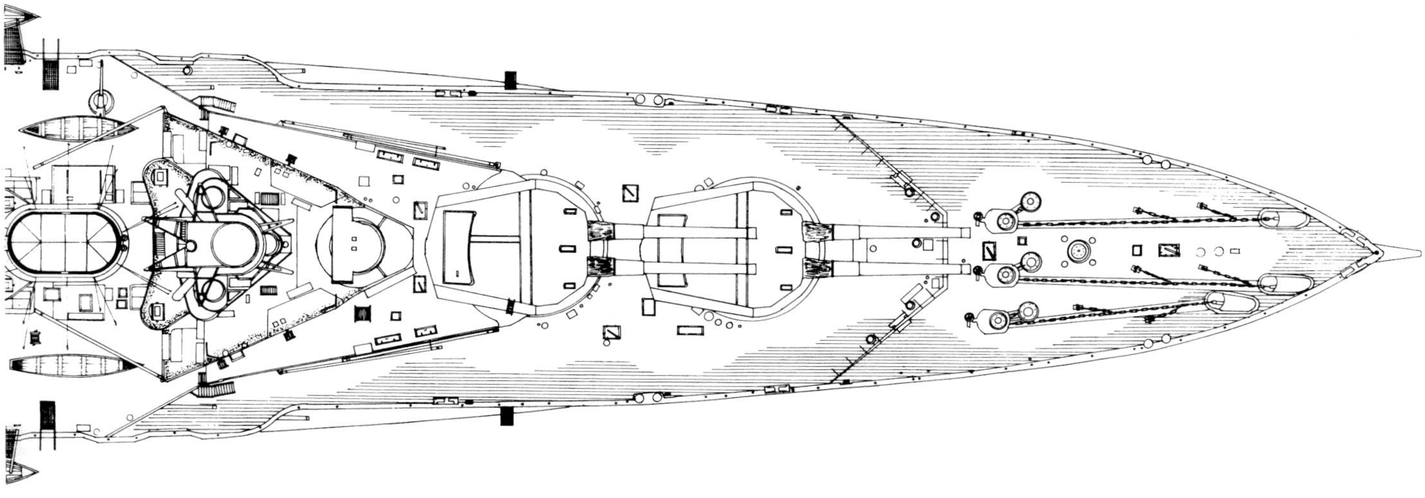

Above: *Ramillies*, November 1917. Her colours were quite different from those of *Revenge*, consisting of dark-blue, yellow, black, light-blue, green and mauve (deep pink).

Above, right: *Royal Sovereign* in the North Sea, *c.* 1916/17.

Right: *Ramillies* seen from the air in 1918. Painted grey once more, although there is still some of the lighter colours of her dazzle evident on the funnel and bridgework which suggests a date of March/April 1918.

Below: *Revenge* at anchor in Scapa Flow in March 1918 shortly before her dazzle was painted over with grey again. Anti-torpedo bulges have been fitted.

Left: Stern of *Royal Sovereign* (nearest) and *Resolution* during manoeuvres in the North Sea 1916/17.

4. The 6in extension belt forward was taken slightly higher up than before and ran right through to the bows where it reduced to 1in. The after extremities of the belt terminated in a bulkhead just before instead of after the rudder head.
5. The main belt and sloping deck armour between middle and main deck levels was reinforced by a ¾in longitudinal bulkhead set well inboard on both port and starboard sides. This bulkhead extended from 'A' to 'Y' barbettes and was originally to have been backed with coal protection before an all-oil policy was adopted.
6. An increase to 2in on the deck inclines and additional 2in thickness on the flat before thinning to 1in.
7. 1in armour added around the stemhead between forecastle deck and upper deck.
8. Anti-torpedo bulkheads were reduced from the uniform 2in thickness in *Queen Elizabeth* to 1½in and 1in.

This class were the first British battleships to revert to having armoured protection carried through to the extremities of the ship since *Neptune* (1911), but the 1in thickness at the bows was little more than a placebo.

The ships' armour weighed approximately 8,240 tons. All the main strakes were of the Krupps process, but the decks, centreline bulkheads, battery traverses, funnel uptakes and anti-torpedo bulkheads were of high-tensile steel.

The 13in belt amidships extended to abeam the centres of 'A' and 'Y' barbettes with the upper edge reaching main deck level about 7ft 9in above the load water-line. Forward of the belt was a 6in strake which extended for approximately 42 feet and reduced to 4in before terminating some 34 feet from the stem. The upper edge of the 6in run was carried slightly above main deck level, its bottom at the same height as the 13in run. Aft, the 13in run was met by a 6in strake which extended to about 50 feet from the stern and ran at the same height as the midships section. Outside this it reduced to 4in. Above the 13in belt was a 6in thickness which extended from 'A' to 'X' barbette between main and middle deck levels. The 1in forward strake was a short patch at the stem between the upper and forecastle deck levels.

The main bulkheads were 6in on the forward fitting which ran obliquely inwards from the extremities of the 13in belt and 6in side armour to the outer face of the side armour of 'A' barbette between lower and upper decks. The aft bulkhead was also given a 6in thickness and ran inwards much the same as that forward, meeting 'Y' barbette before it terminated. A stem bulkhead of 1½in closed the extremities of the short patch of side armour at the stemhead between forecastle and upper deck levels. A 4in bulkhead closed the ends of the 4in belt aft between lower and main deck levels. Special ¾in bulkheads ran longitudinally port and starboard from just outside 'A' to abreast 'Y' barbettes; these were set well inboard.

Deck protection varied in thickness according to location: the forecastle deck was 1in amidships over the 6in battery, while that of the upper deck ranged from 1¼in to 1½in and ran from 'A' to 'Y' barbettes. The main deck was 2in on the inclines which reached just on to the flat; after this it was reduced to 1in throughout the ship. The middle deck ran from the outer base of 'Y' barbette and was fitted with 2in–3in–4in plates which terminated at the stern. The after extremities once outside the after bulkhead sloped steeply to meet the lower deck at the stern. There was a 2in inner bulkhead with 4in and 3in outside it to cover the steering gear. The lower deck, which was forward, ran below water from the base of 'A' barbette to the stem where it was met by a bulkhead; the deck was 1in inside this bulkhead and 2½in outside.

The protection given to the barbettes varied a great deal: 'A' sported thicknesses from 10in to 6in. The outer face was 10in above main deck level with 6in below. Inner faces were 9in and 7in above upper deck level reducing to 6in through the upper level to the main deck. Sides were 10in above upper deck level and reduced to 6in from upper to main deck level. 'Y' was 9in on the face above main deck level and reduced to 6in below this, the rear being 9in and 7in with 4in below main deck. The sides were 10in above and 6in below main deck level. Turrets were given 13in on the face plates with 11in sides. Rears were also 11in and the roof consisted of 4¾in–5in plates.

The battery armour was 6in and ran amidships between upper and forecastle deck levels with a 4in bulkhead closing each end. The 2in centreline bulkhead, which ran the length of the 6in battery except in wake of the funnel uptakes, extended from the 4in bulkhead to 'B' barbette. The 1½in traverses, extending some 15 feet inboard, were situated between the 6in guns and were carried up to the full height of the battery. The 6in gunshields were 3in and the sighting hoods, also 3in, were located near the fourth and fifth guns on the forecastle deck level.

The main conning tower was 11in on the sides with a 3in roof, 4in floor, 6in base and a 6in communications tube. The torpedo CT had 6in sides, 4in tube and a 2in floor; uptakes were 1½in.

The 1½in–1in anti-torpedo bulkheads ran longitudinally port and starboard between the forward and after magazines. They reached down from middle deck to keel level and were met by transverse bulkheads.

Underwater Protection

Throughout the years leading up to the First World War, the subject of providing adequate underwater protection had been much debated, and during the early months of the war experiments were conducted in some of the old pre-dreadnoughts. Explosives were detonated against strategic bulkheads and certain parts of the hull and the effects were recorded. Much work was done at the Chatham Float test tank, where midship sections built to various scales were tested in the quest for a suitable method. By 1915 progress had been such that shaped steel plates had been made to withstand a 400lb charge of TNT with a certain amount of success. It was found that if tubes were used as a protective barrier the effects of a hit by a torpedo carrying a 400lb charge would be reduced, and inner bulkheads would remain intact. The DNC, Eustace Tennyson D'Eyncourt, told the Board, in a letter dated 7 September 1915, that it could safely be anticipated that any ship would be greatly improved regarding underwater defence if fitted with this latest and relatively easy method of protection.

It was decided to fit one of the new *Royal Sovereigns* then under construction, and *Ramillies* was chosen because her building was at an advanced stage and there was clear space available for launching. The scheme adopted for her was slightly inferior to that of the test-piece at Chatham, but was the only suitable method that could be applied to a ship on the stocks. Obviously, had the bulges been an integral feature of the original design, a better job would have been made of them. Fitting them at this stage presented many problems – which were overcome. The business was not made easier by the fact of the Board's insistence that the ship's building be not interrupted and that the launch take place on the builder's stipulated date.

The bulges (or blisters), approximately 220 feet long and 7ft 3in wide, were made from ½in plating, and were shaped to conform to the hull's configuration. Inside, there were watertight compartments, 18–20 feet long. The outer compartments were separated from the inner by a bulkhead backed by fir wood. The inner compartments were divided into top and bottom sections and were filled with tubes of ¾in steel, plugged at the ends by wooden bungs. These tubes were separated from one another by fir wood packing. The tubes in the top section were 9in in diameter, in the bottom 8in. They cost £150,000, excluding extras.

RAMILLIES
Bulge, showing tube protection, 1917

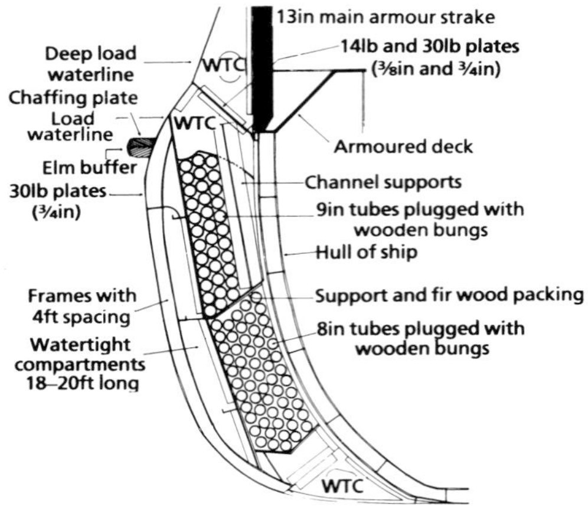

It was feared that the bulbous excrescences would reduce the ship's speed, and the DNC asked the experimental department at Chatham and Haslar to give a reliable estimate. A model was made and tested, and to everyone's surprise the speed loss was a mere 1–2 knots and the ship would still be capable of more than 21 knots in all weathers; an expected bonus was that the bulges would inhibit excessive rolling. *Ramillies* underwent a lengthy series of trials and was found to be little impaired by the bulges, and the other ships of the class were approved to be fitted with similar protection.

Revenge and *Resolution* were fitted during 1917–18, but as a result of further experimentation they received an improved type without tubes inside. The bulge was in two parts as before, but the bottom section was empty and watertight; the top section was filled with wood offal and cement. This was considered an improvement because of substantial saving in weight. *Royal Sovereign* was bulged during her long refit of 1920, but *Royal Oak* did not receive hers until as late her 1922–4 refit, when another improved type was fitted. This time, the bulges rose above the water-line and up the sides almost to the 6in battery. Another innovation had been to include water-filled compartments in the bulges, but it was stressed that if seawater got in they would be less effective. At their initial fitting they had at least 15–20 per cent of air in the compartments filled with fresh water. In 1927, *Ramillies* had her early, shallow bulges removed and was given a set almost identical with those of *Royal Oak*.

During 1924, bulge tests were carried out and it was found that 14rpm had been needed to make 14–15 knots; with bulges, however, it required only a 5 per cent increase to reach speeds of 12–20 knots.

After *Royal Oak* had been fitted with her full-bellied bulges, she was inclined, with the following results (2 June 1924):

'A' condition: Ship fully equipped with 900 tons oil on board, plus water protection in the bulges. Displacement: 29,160 tons. Draught: 28ft 3½in. GM: 6.3ft.
'B' condition: Ship as above, but with 3,300 tons oil on board (no water protection). Displacement: 32,300 tons. Draught: 30ft 11½in. GM: 6.3ft.
'C' condition: Ship as above plus reserve feed tanks full and water protection: Displacement: 32,800 tons. Draught: 31ft 4½in. GM: 6.3ft.
Light condition was at 27,920 tons and a GM of 6.2ft.

When *Resolution* was docked some years later on 26 August 1930, inspection of her bulges showed that considerable corrosion had taken place. The top part of the bulge where the wood offal was placed had let in water and the offal had rotted with the concrete being badly pitted. Not only had corrosion set in but the wood packing had been thrown in loosely and not placed in the correct order. Forward of frame 22, and abaft 228, the packing was so loose that it was of no practical use whatsoever and the seawater which filled the compartments had rendered the entire length of the bulge ineffective against a torpedo hit. Later, as other units of this and the *Queen Elizabeth* classes were found to be in the same state, much closer attention was paid to the packing and watertight joints.

Machinery

The main propulsion machinery consisted of two sets of turbines arranged in three watertight compartments divided by two longitudinal bulkheads. The two main and two auxiliary condensers were located near the main midships compartment but the auxiliary condenser and auxiliary machinery was in separate compartments on the wings. Each ship had four shafts.

The HP ahead and astern, plus the cruising turbine, were

REVENGE: STEAM TRIALS, 24 MARCH 1916

Preliminary 4-hour, full power
Skelmorlie, Firth of Clyde
Wind: light breeze, NNE
Sea: smooth
Ship's bottom: clean
Draught forward: 33ft 2in
Draught aft: 32ft 7in
Steam pressure, boilers: 220psi
Steam pressure, turbines: 204psi
Number of boilers in use: 18
Heating surface: 63,800sq ft
Fuel consumption: 1.19lb per shp, per hour
Oil pressure: 75psi
Oil temperature: 190°F
Propeller diameter: outer 9ft 3in, inner 10ft
Propeller pitch: 9ft 6in
Speed: 20.773 knots

Measured mile revolutions, four runs

	Outer	Inner	Speed (knots)
First run			20.966
Port:	312rpm	308rpm	
Starboard:	310rpm	300rpm	
Second run			20.665
Port:	312rpm	300rpm	
Starboard:	314rpm	302rpm	
Third run			20.85
Port:	310rpm	298rpm	
Starboard:	312rpm	302rpm	
Fourth run			20.667
Port:	316rpm	308rpm	
Starboard:	314rpm	308rpm	

Speeds recorded on overload
1. 43,080shp = 22.140 knots
2. 42,610shp = 21.710 knots
3. 42,350shp = 22.031 knots
4. 42,680shp = 21.898 knots.

ROYAL SOVEREIGN CLASS: STEAM TRIALS

It being wartime, full trials of the class were not carried out. These figures show that the best speed attained was a little over 21 knots.

Measured mile, full power
Revenge, 24 March 1916, 2-hour, full load 326rpm; 41,938shp; 21.9 knots
Royal Oak, 9 May 1916, 1½-hour, full load 328rpm; 40,360shp; 22 knots
Royal Sovereign, 22 May 1916, 2-hour, full load 320.4rpm; 41,112shp; 21.75 knots
Resolution, 30 Dec 1916, 2-hour, full load 317.75rpm; 41,405shp; ? knots
Ramillies, 1 Oct 1917, 2-hour, full load 325rpm; 42,414shp; 21.5 knots

Full power trials after bulges had been fitted
February 1921
Ramillies: bottom slightly foul; 37,710shp; 20.8 knots
Resolution: bottom foul; 40,306shp; 21 knots
Revenge: bottom foul; 40,940shp; 21.1 knots
Royal Oak (no bulge): bottom foul; 40,395shp; 21 knots

Trials in March 1921 when the bottoms were even worse (*Royal Oak* had been at sea for seven months without cleaning) produced the following figures:

Ramillies:	41,480shp	20.9 knots
Resolution:	40,196shp	20.5 knots
Revenge:	41,320shp	19.4 knots
Royal Oak:	40,498shp	20.8 knots

ROYAL OAK AND *RAMILLIES*: GM AND STABILITY

As inclined, 1917

Royal Oak	**Displacement (tons)**	**Draught**	**GM**	**Maximum stability**	**Stability vanishes at**
'A' Condition (= load)*	27,970	30ft (mean)	2.01ft	34°	53°
'B' Condition(=deep)**	31,130	33f 7in	3.4ft	33.5°	58°
'C' Condition (= light)***	26,750	–	1.14ft	–	–
Ramillies (differed because of bulges)					
'A' Condition	30,400	–	4ft	–	–
'B' Condition	33,570	–	4.5ft	–	–

*Fully equipped plus 900 tons oil, feed tanks full.
**As above, but oil 3,380 tons, plus reserve tanks full.
*** No oil fuel, minimum feed in tanks.

arranged on the outer shafts in each wing compartment; the LP ahead and astern turbines (in one casing) were located on the inner shafts in the middle compartment. Parsons reaction turbines with a designed 300rpm were fitted in all ships of the class.

As first designed the ships were given a mixed firing system of coal and oil but on his recall to the Admiralty, one of Lord Fisher's first moves was to convert the *Royal Sovereigns* to all oil burning. As a result the shaft horsepower was increased from 31,000 to 40,000, and speed increased from 21 to 23 knots. This conversion was approved in December 1914 by which time the ships were nearing the launching stage (in fact *Royal Oak* had already been launched in November), but apparently no problems ensued. Oil stowage was to be the same as an all-coal stowage which was almost identical with the *Queen Elizabeth* class at 3,400 tons maximum. Fuel arrangements were improved over the preceding class by fittings on the upper deck whence oil would be filtered before reaching the tanks, which made for easier refuelling. Because of the reduction in boilers it had now become practicable to fit one uptake only, which made them the only British battleships with one stack during the First World War.

Appearance Changes

The *Royal Sovereigns* were well-proportioned, finely balanced ships characterized by the single uptake which gave them a distinctive and most impressive appearance; bow-on, they seemed the very embodiment of the layman's idea of how battleships should look. The arrangement of the upper bridges away from the funnel, which differed in all ships, gave a rather unbalanced effect seen from the side. The upper bridge was carried slightly abaft the mast and the navigating bridge projected unusually forward. In *Ramillies* after completion, the bridge was shortened at the rear and did not extend behind as much as the others. In 1918 when operating together at sea, it was very difficult to tell them apart, especially from a distance. There were, however, some distinguishing features within the class as follows.

Ramillies: Tall searchlight tower fitted over upper bridge on foremast. Low searchlight towers fitted abeam mainmast. Low breastwork around upper pair of 6in guns. Lower yard on foremast at director platform level. Completed with shallow bulges, hidden from view when at deep load.
Resolution: No foretopmast in 1916/17. Very long gaff at starfish.
Revenge: Forecastle sides recessed from abaft outer face of 'A' barbette; abaft 'B' in the others. Very prominent caging to funnel. Two yards on foretopmast, one in others.
Royal Sovereign: Shorter gaff from heel of topmast.
Royal Oak: Flange high up between tripod legs (only ship with this). Very long gaff from heel of maintopmast.
No bulges in any ships except *Ramillies.*

1916–17 One, later two extra 36in lamps added in maintop in *Royal Oak* and one in *Royal Sovereign* over control top. *Revenge*

RESOLUTION

Deck plans, inboard profile and sections, 1917, showing bulge

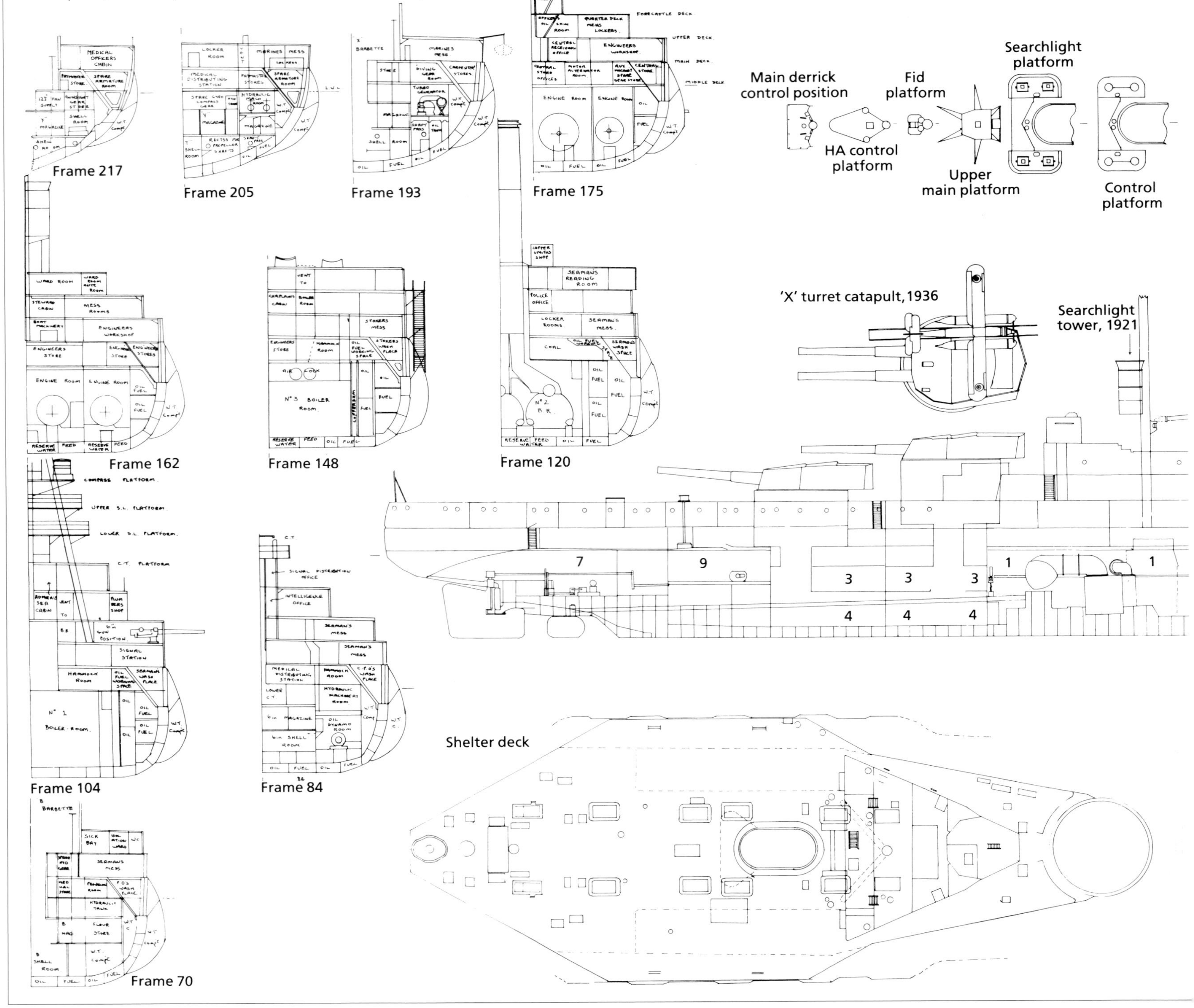

fitted for towing kite balloons. Extra fittings as a result of Jutland, but uncertain if any armour additions. Rangefinder baffles temporarily fitted to main top mast and funnel in *Royal Oak* and on funnel only in *Revenge*. These were removed by mid-1917.

1917–18 Control top enlarged. Deflection scales painted on 'A' and 'Y' or 'B' and 'X' turrets. Range clocks fitted to face of control top or on short pole over this and at rear of SL tower abaft mainmast. High-angle rangefinder fitted on roof of control top. Searchlight equipment in first four ships improved (all but *Ramillies*). Funnel platform replaced by two large 'coffee box'-type towers with two 36in lamps in each. After superstructure SLs were removed from *Royal Oak* and *Royal Sovereign* and remounted on new platform against after side of mainmast. SL transferred from lower bridge position to that of new SL towers around funnel. SL removed from tops in *Royal Sovereign* and *Royal Oak*. Armoured casemates fitted to upper deck 6in guns in *Resolution* and *Royal Sovereign* (1918). *Resolution*, *Revenge* and *Ramillies* fitted with below-water bulges increasing beam to 101–102ft.

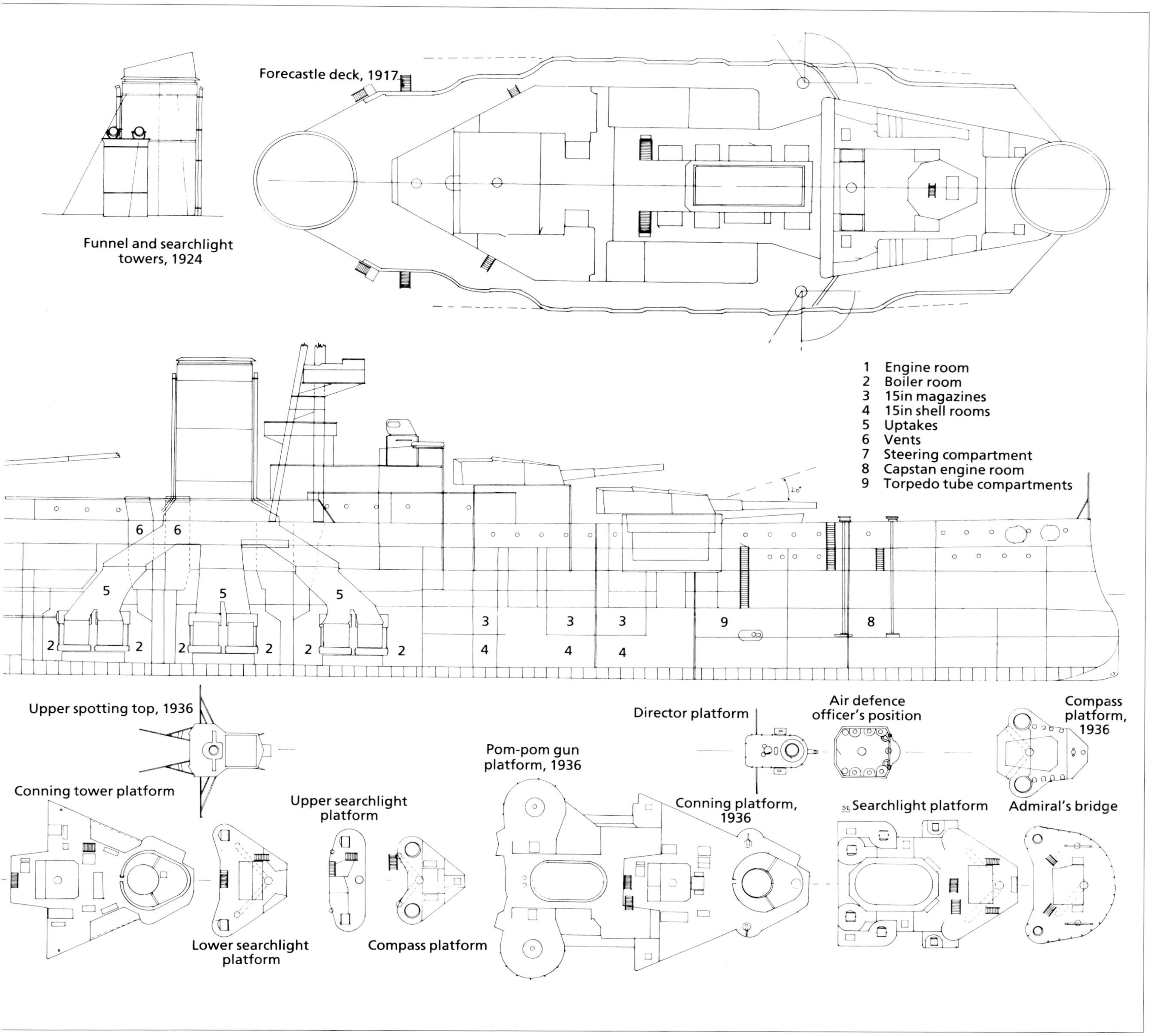

Resolution and *Revenge* during Nov 1917 to Feb 1918: Middle and lower bridges were extended aft and extremities connected by curved screens. Upper bridge in *Revenge* extended back almost to the funnel. Short topmast fitted in *Resolution* which had completed without this feature. Foretopmast in *Royal Oak* was temporarily removed in 1917. Removed also from *Royal Sovereign* but replaced later by foretopmast of same length. Signal struts fitted forward from starfish in *Ramillies* and below control top in *Royal Sovereign*. Norman Wilkinson-type dazzle camouflage painted on *Ramillies* and *Revenge*. Experimental painting was for the purpose of confusing rangefinding equipment, especially that of submarines. *Ramillies* sported her scheme of grey shades and six colours from November 1917 until March 1918, whereafter she was again painted in an all grey colour.

1918 Large-base rangefinder fitted at rear of 'B' and 'X' turrets in *Revenge*, but only on 'B' in *Ramillies* and *Resolution*. Small rangefinder added between SL towers at rear of funnel in *Royal Sovereign*, intended primarily for checking distances from the next ship astern during 'pair ship' concentration shoots, when

Right: A good view of *Ramillies* showing her dazzle on the starboard side (see colour plates for colours).

the leading ship was controlling fire of both ships. SL tower location was experimental with this class and various locations for lamps can be seen in photographs throughout this period.

Medium-based torpedo rangefinder fitted over TCT in *Resolution* which replaced original rangefinder. SL tower over bridge in *Ramillies* removed. Flying-off platforms fitted over 'B' and 'X' turrets in all.

1919–21 Deflection scales painted out by 1919. Large-base rangefinder added to rear of 'B' turret in *Resolution*, *Royal Oak*, *Ramillies*; *Royal Sovereign* had similar RF fitted to rear of 'X' turret. Two small rangefinders (one in *Resolution*) mounted between after pair of SLs on funnel in *Resolution*, *Revenge*, *Royal Oak*. 24in signalling SL removed from forward superstructure and remounted on middle bridge in *Revenge*. Sternwalk fitted in *Revenge*. *Royal Sovereign* fitted with bulges in Dec 1920. Long struts fitted to forward starfish in *Resolution* and *Revenge*.

1921–2 *Royal Sovereign* refitted (May 1921 to Sept 1922). Large-base rangefinder fitted at rear of 'B' turret. Rangefinder removed from between SL towers at rear of funnel. Range clocks added over 'X' turret with additional one over control top. High-angle rangefinder added on small tower over bridge. SL tower abaft mainmast removed. Other ships of the class had SL removed from towers abaft mainmast, but towers retained in some ships until 1924–5. Armoured casemates to upper 6in guns now fitted to rest of class.

1922–4 *Royal Oak* refit (Sept 1922 to June 1924). Large-base rangefinder fitted to rear of 'B' turret. Rangefinder clocks removed from between SL towers. Range clock added over 'X' turret. High-angle rangefinder added in small tower over bridge. Very prominent high anti-torpedo bulge fitted, extending almost up to 6in battery. Middle bridgework extended back to reach funnel. There was much modification

Below: Looking back from the quarterdeck of *Ramillies* over to *Resolution* as she passes under the Forth Bridge as the fleet leaves the anchorage at Rosyth (*Revenge* follows), winter 1917/18.

in the location of range clocks throughout the class. Rangefinders were removed from *Resolution* and *Revenge* in 1924. The SL were removed from the middle bridge in *Ramillies* and *Resolution* (July to October 1924 in *Resolution*). Clinker cap fitted to funnel during refit of 1924, making her very distinct from rest of class.

1924–5 Range clocks over control tower removed from *Resolution* and *Royal Sovereign* (by July 1925 in *Resolution*). Range clocks added over 'X' turret in *Ramillies* and *Revenge*. 36in lamps removed from middle bridge in *Revenge*, *Royal Oak* and *Royal Sovereign*. Two 24in signalling lamps on middle bridge in *Revenge* remounted in forward superstructure and extra pair of 24in temporarily mounted on 'B' turret, these being removed by spring 1926. Signal and distributing office was added at rear of upper bridge in *Revenge* and this served to identify that ship for many years to come.

1926–7 *Revenge*: Signalling SL transferred from the forward superstructure to lower bridge. Office at rear of upper bridge enlarged considerably. Taller topmast fitted to mainmast. *Ramillies* refit (Sept 1926 to April 1927): Control top modified and enlarged. Upper pair 6in guns removed, but casemates retained. Extra pair 4in AA guns added on shelter deck abeam funnel (3in AA had been replaced by 4in in all ships during 1924–5). HA RF mounted in small tower on bridge. 24in lamps remounted from forward superstructure to lower bridge. High, sloping, bullet-proof roof fitted to upper bridge. Foretopmast and lower yard removed. One feature *Ramillies* retained throughout her long life was the row of small scuttles just beneath her upper bridge, an excellent identification feature. *Resolution* refit (Dec 1926 to Dec 1927): Control top enlarged and modified. Range clocks added over 'X' turrets. Upper pair 6in guns removed but casemates retained. Extra pair 4in HA guns as in *Ramillies*. Training catapult (McTaggart type) with crane fitted on quarterdeck right aft. Foretopmast and yard below director removed. Extra signalling struts fitted to starfish below control top. Topgallant mast fitted to mainmast. *Revenge*: 24in lamps removed from middle bridges. One 24in lamp mounted on small platform very low before bridge.

1927 *Royal Oak* refit (March 1927 to June 1927): Control top enlarged and modified. Range clocks over control top removed. Upper pair 6in guns removed. Extra 4in HA AA guns added. Foretopmast and yard below director platform removed. Extra signal struts fitted on starfish below top. Topgallant added to main mast.

1927–8 *Royal Sovereign* refit (Oct 1927 to June 1928): Control top enlarged and modified. Upper pair 6in removed and this time casemate also. Extra pair 4in HA AA guns fitted. Foretopmast and lower yard removed. Extra signal struts as in *Royal Oak*.

Above: *Resolution*, c.1918, showing her layout.

Left: *Revenge* having left Devonport, April/May 1918. Note additional rangefinders to front of bridge, and on control top. Also kite balloon experiments are in progress.

Opposite, top: Late wartime view of *Royal Sovereign* during North Sea sweeps, 1918.

Opposite, lower: *Ramillies* in 1918.

1928–9 *Revenge* refit (Jan 1928 to Jan 1929): Control top enlarged and modified. Upper pair 6in guns and casemates removed. Extra pair 4in HA AA guns fitted. AA observation post fitted both port and starboard below director tower. RDF equipment fitted. DF cabinet located at rear of director platform, with aerial at rear of control top. Forward section of each SL tower enlarged to bring forward one pair of lamps in each. After section was raised along with lamps. Flying-off platforms removed from the turrets. Bridge enlarged. Flag signalling transferred from fore to mainmast. After superstructure enlarged to accommodate required staff. Taller topgallant added to mainmast. Signal yard at head of maintopgallant, close above starfish.

1930–1 *Resolution*: Forecastle deck 6in casemates removed (by March 1931). HA RF on control top replaced by HA director. After pair torpedo tubes removed (by March 1931). *Royal Sovereign*: HA RF on control top replaced by HA director.

1931 *Revenge* (May): HA RF replaced by HA director. Range clocks removed from 'X' turret. *Revenge* refit (May to Dec 1931): Multiple (8–barrel) 2pdr pom-pom fitted on raised platform on starboard side of shelter deck abeam funnel (none on port). Modified type of DF fitted. Base of SL towers on starboard side cut away to accommodate 2pdrs. 24in lamps removed from fore and remounted on small platform low on mainmast. Signal struts raked well aft and fitted below starfish below control top.

1931–2 *Ramillies*: Range clocks removed from 'X' turret. Upper deck casemates removed by July 1932. *Royal Oak*: Range clocks removed from 'X' turret by April 1932. Upper deck 6in casemates removed from April to July 1932. HA DF replaced by HA director.

1932 *Royal Sovereign* refit (Jan to Nov): Range clocks removed from 'X' turret. Multiple 2pdr pom-poms added on raised platform around funnel on both port and starboard. Platform cut away to accommodate pom-poms' arcs of fire. AA observation posts fitted each side of 15in director platform. After pair TT removed. New rectangular SL towers fitted around funnel, with after pair of lamps raised higher than those aft. Training catapult fitted on quarterdeck, right aft, with crane to serve this. Flying-off platforms removed from turrets. Bridge modified and enlarged. Deep supporting flanges added below navigating platform. Lower bridgework extended back around funnel base to meet new SL towers.

1933 *Resolution*: Range clocks removed from turrets. Starboard 4in AA guns replaced by experimental twin 4in AA mounting and a gastight turret. This was the prototype which was eventually fitted to *Queen Elizabeth* class shortly before Second World War. Multiple (4-barrel) 0.5in AA added abeam conning tower on shelter deck level. *Royal Oak*: After pair of TT removed. Flying-off platforms removed.

1933–4 *Ramillies* refit (Jan 1933 to Aug 1934): Multiple pom-poms added around funnel as in others. Multiple 0.5in AA added abeam conning tower. HA DF on control top replaced by HA director; after director added on platform on main tripod legs. Tripod legs fitted to mainmast. After pair TT removed. Torpedo control tower and rangefinder removed. Training catapult fitted to port side of 'X' turret with crane to serve this fitted on platform on after superstructure. Flying-off platforms removed from turrets. Bridge enlarged and modified. Roof over upper bridge made steeper, with prominent flanges for support placed below navigating platform.

1935 *Ramillies*: HA RF fitted to mainmast to support HA directors. *Royal Sovereign*: Multiple 0.5in AA added as in others. HA RF removed from bridge May to July 1935.

Below: *Ramillies*, late 1918. Note SL tower over compass platform has been removed.

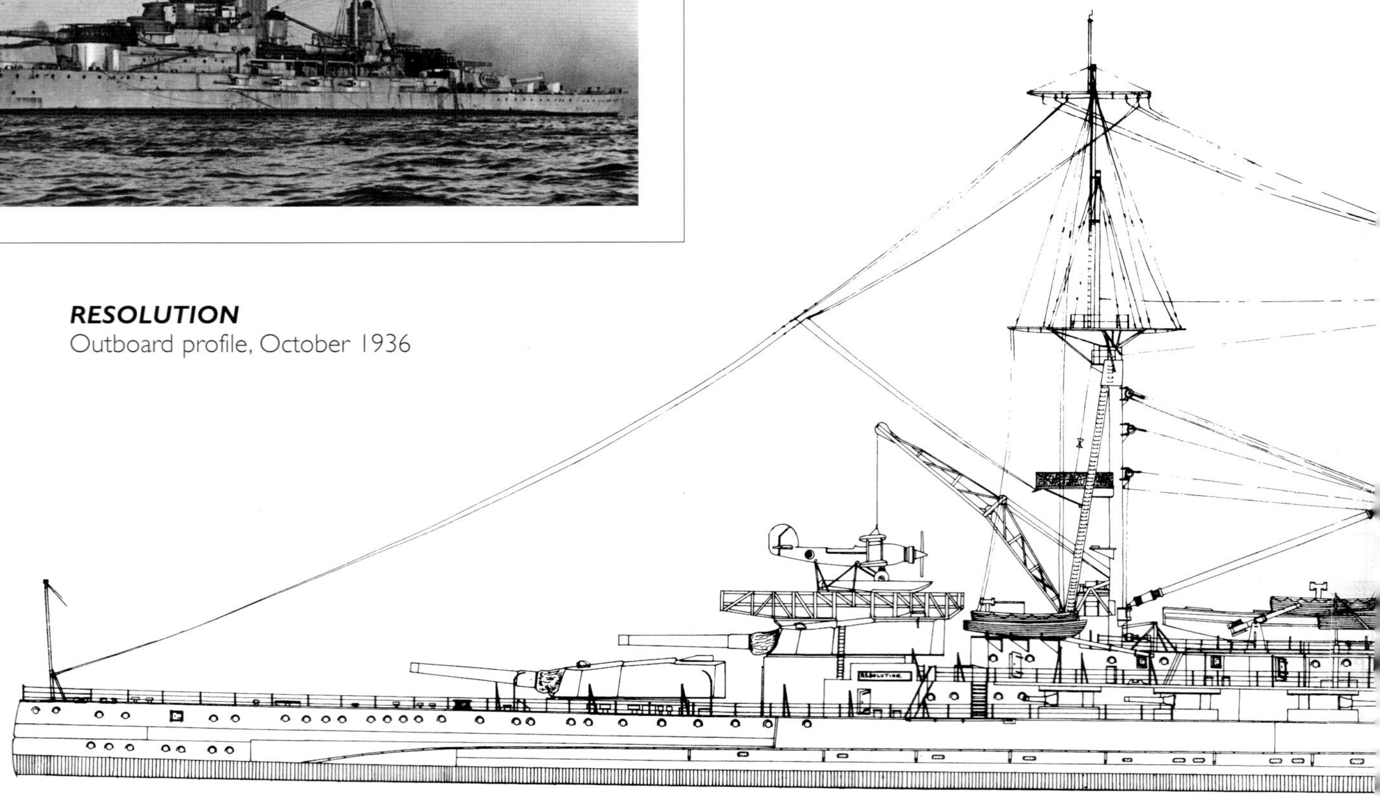

RESOLUTION
Outboard profile, October 1936

1934–6 *Royal Oak* refit (June 1934 to Aug 1936): 6in director towers relocated port and starboard on new platforms on foremast below 15in director. Single 4in AA replaced by larger mounted twin fittings. Multiple 2pdrs added around funnel as in others. Multiple 0.5in guns added around CT. AA RF removed from over bridge and from control top. HA director platform fitted on legs of tripod although director not yet fitted at this date. 4 x 21in torpedo tubes added (experimental) port and starboard, in recessed ports in forecastle before 'A' turret. Remaining forward pair TT removed. DF equipment fitted. 36in SL lamps replaced by 44in. Training catapult fitted as in *Ramillies*, but of different type. Upper part of bridge completely renewed with an open structure giving clear view all round. Tripod legs fitted to mainmast to support director. Maintopgallant removed and topmast reduced in height. Lower part of bridge extended back around funnel as in *Royal Sovereign*.

1935–6 *Resolution* refit (Dec 1935 to Sept 1936): As above in *Royal Oak*, but different face for bridgework.

1936–7 *Revenge* refit (July 1936 to March 1937): Torpedo rangefinder and tower removed. 36in lamps replaced by 44in.

1937 *Royal Sovereign* (March): Multiple 2pdrs temporarily removed. 36in lamps replaced by 44in. Catapult and crane removed. Catapult and base on quarterdeck retained. *Royal Oak* (April): HA director fitted on control top and on platform on tripod legs. Flagpole fitted to each mast. *Ramillies* (May): 36in lamps replaced by 44in. Tower over bridge replaced by large open platform which extended back around tripod legs. In 1937, red, white and blue recognition stripes were painted on 'B' turret in those vessels operating near Spanish waters. Also large letters were painted on turret tops to indicate ship's name: 'RA', *Ramillies*; 'RO', *Royal Oak*; 'RE', *Revenge, etc.*

1937–8 *Royal Sovereign* was under refit from June 1937 until Feb 1938 and was fitted much the same as the rest of the class (see *Royal Oak*).

1938 *Resolution* (Jan): 2pdr AA fitted to those mounts that had

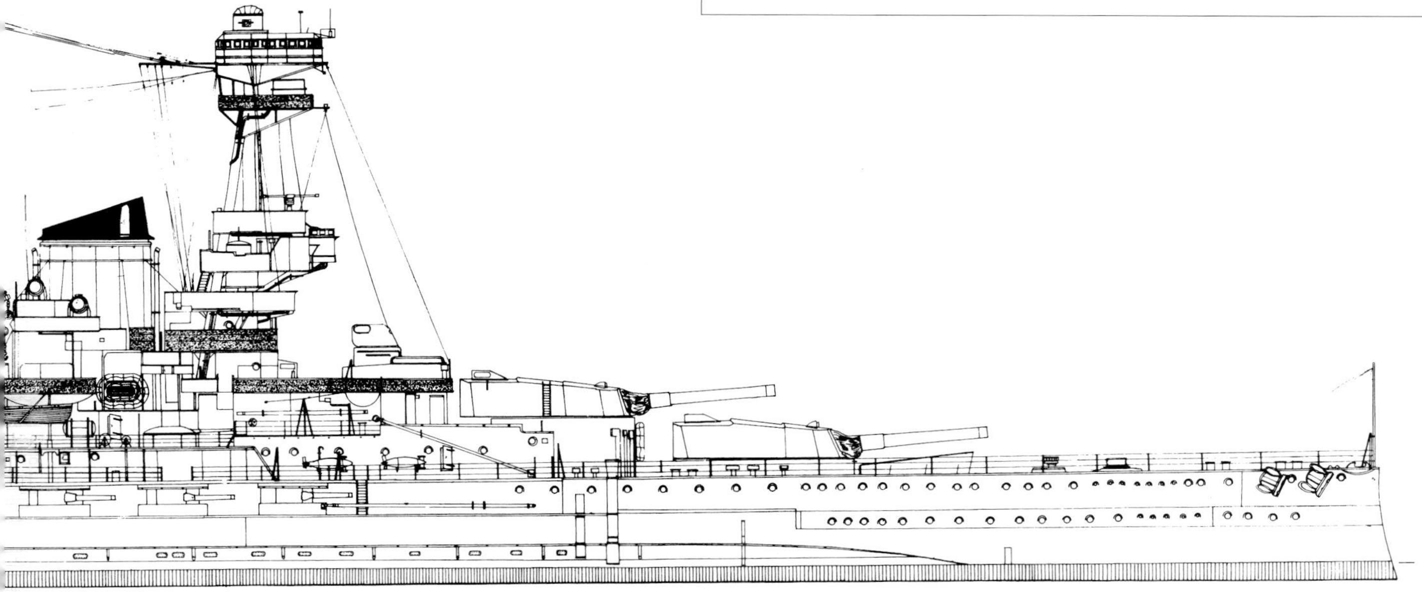

***ROYAL SOVEREIGN* CLASS: PARTICULARS, 1944**

Displacement (tons)
Ramillies: 30,507 (light), 34,032 (average action load), 35,507 (deep)
Resolution: 28,013 (light), 34,249 (deep)
Revenge: 31,875 (load), 33,230 (deep)
Royal Sovereign: 29,948 (light), 33,491 (average action load), 34,836 (deep).

Beam
101ft 4in (average) except *Ramillies* 102ft.

Draught
29ft 4⅛in (light) average, 33ft 6½in deep.

Armament
Main unchanged
Eight 6in
Eight 4in AA (twins)
Ramillies: twenty-four 2pdr AA; twelve to twenty-two 20mm AA
Resolution: twenty-four 2pdr AA; ten 20mm AA
Revenge: ten 20mm AA
Royal Sovereign: twenty-four 2pdr AA; up to forty-two 20mm AA
Quadruple pom-poms on turret tops (and quarterdeck *Resolution*) in all ships by 1942
Small-calibre AA removed from *Resolution*, *Revenge* on becoming trainings ships at Devonport.

Armour
Extra 2in over magazines at main deck level *Ramillies*, *Resolution*, *Royal Sovereign*.

Machinery
Radius reduced, speed decreased in wartime conditions
Average speed: 19 knots.

Complement
1,037–1,240.

been purposely fitted in 1936. *Ramillies* (June): Catapult removed but crane retained. Remaining pair TT removed. Single 4in AA replaced by twin fittings. Topgallant mast reduced in height.

1939 *Revenge* refit (early 1939 to Aug 1939): Single 4in AA replaced by twin mountings. Multiple 2pdr added around funnel. Multiple 0.5in AA added abeam CT. HA director added on control top, raised well clear of top. After HA added in place of torpedo director tower. DF aerial removed from over top. Modified aerial fitted at head of main topgallant. Base of SLs cut away to accommodate pom-poms. Signal and distributing office at rear of bridge removed. Clinker screen fitted to funnel. Signal yards removed from maintopmast.

1940–1 0.5in AA removed and eight–ten 20mm AA added on 'B' and 'X' turrets, superstructure, shelter deck forward, and quarterdeck at extreme ends. *Ramillies* painted in a one-off dazzle type of camouflage believed to have been blues and greys. Clinker screen to cap in *Ramillies. Revenge* and *Royal Sovereign* camouflaged with early versions of the dazzle theme: both were unofficial.

1941–2 Type 284 radar fitted for control of main armament. Type 285 radar fitted for control of 4in. Type 285 radar fitted for air warning, Type 79Y in *Ramillies* at first, Type 279 in *Revenge* and *Resolution*. Type 273 radar fitted for surface warning. Original DF aerials on masts removed. Modification of bridgework in *Ramillies*, *Resolution* and *Royal Sovereign*. Maintopgallant removed in *Ramillies*, *Revenge* and *Resolution*. Admiralty disruptive camouflage painted on *Ramillies* and *Resolution*. *Revenge* retained the same camouflage from 1942. *Royal Sovereign* was

Left: *Resolution* in early 1919.

camouflaged and refitted for special service with the Russian Fleet and was renamed *Archangelsk* (Archangel). All vessels fitted with funnel caps by 1942.

1942–3 Two foremost 6in guns (port and starboard) removed. Six twin 20mm AA added in *Royal Sovereign*. Type 282 radar fitted for 2pdrs. Directors for this were port and starboard abeam bridge.

1944 *Ramillies*: 1. Twin 20mm AA mounted on 'B' and 'X' turret and on quarterdeck right aft. 2. VHF equipment added before Normandy beach landings. 3. Special type of missile-jamming aerials mounted at base of main tripod, Type 650. Although there were no major alterations during these years, the ships became very heavy in appearance because of ever-increasing additions in AA defence.

History: *Ramillies*

Laid down and built by Beardmore on the Clyde. When launched on 12 Sept 1916 her bottom hit the underside of the runway and serious damage was done to her keel plating and rudders. No dock being available to take her length, she left for Gladstone Dock, Liverpool, to be repaired by Cammell Laird. Temporary repairs were carried out for the journey and she left her builders on 7 May 1917. She ran aground again, however, though being handled by eight tugs, and was not freed until 23 May.

1917 *Sept* Joined Grand Fleet, being the last major unit to do so during the First World War. Her weight at launch was recorded as 18,750 tons; those of her sisters were: *Resolution* 9,407 tons; *Revenge* 11,954 tons; *Royal Oak* 9,635 tons and *Royal Sovereign* 10,225 tons. The Board of Inquiry checked the supports of the launching runway, took into account the increased weight of the bulges (1,430 tons) and even took recordings of the tides, but they came up with no concrete evidence of neglect by the builders and the matter was dropped. She served with the Grand Fleet from Sept 1917 until April 1919 when the Grand Fleet was dispersed. With post-war reorganization, the Fleet was broken up into the new Atlantic, Mediterranean and Home Fleets.

1919 *April* With Atlantic Fleet. With 1st BS when it was attached to Mediterranean Fleet during operations against Turkish Nationalists at Constantinople and in the Black Sea from March to July 1920.

1920 *Aug* Rejoined Atlantic Fleet.

1921 *May* 1st BS and 2nd BS merged, *Royal Sovereign* class forming 1st Division, *Queen Elizabeth* class 2nd.

1922 *Sept* Again detached to Mediterranean with all her sisters except *Royal Oak* to reinforce Mediterranean Fleet during more troubles in the area. She was employed mainly in the Dardanelles and Sea of Marmora.

Nov Rejoined Atlantic Fleet.

1924 *June* Undergoing refit at Rosyth.

1 Nov *Queen Elizabeth* class transferred to Mediterranean as 1st BS, *Royal Sovereign* class remaining as Atlantic Fleet until 1926.

1926 *Sept* Extensive refit at Devonport.

1927 *1 March* Recommissioned.

Aug Transferred to Mediterranean Fleet.

1929 *Oct* Stationed at Jaffa during troubles in Palestine.

1932 *June* Paid off into Reserve at Devonport for refit until August 1934.

1933 Feb Extensive refit.

1934 *17 Sept* Recommissioned for Mediterranean Fleet.

1935 Early in the year it was decided to revert to the deployment of *Royal Sovereigns* and *Queen Elizabeths* adopted in 1924. The former would now become the Home Fleet and the latter would all join the Mediterranean Fleet.

July 2nd BS Home Fleet.

16 July Jubilee Fleet Review at Spithead.

Aug Exchanged roles with *Barham*.

31 Aug Collided with German steamer *Eisenach* in a gale off Dover, sustaining slight damage to bows.

1936 Seagoing training ship (boys and RNR officers) to Dec 1937.

1937 *May* Coronation Fleet Review in May 1937.

1938 *July* Refitted at Devonport.

1939 *22 Feb* Recommissioned at Devonport and transferred to Mediterranean Fleet.

July Transferred to Home Fleet as training ship.

9 Aug Review of Reserve Fleet by HM the King at Portland. Then left Clyde for Alexandria, via Gibraltar, and served on this station until October.

5 Oct Ordered to North Atlantic Escort Force (Halifax).

6 Oct Recalled to replace *Malaya* in Mediterranean Fleet. Later ordered to Indian Ocean to take part in search for the raider *Graf Spee*, then returned to Mediterranean Fleet.

Nov East Indies; 3rd BS, Aden.

1940 *May* Transferred via Suez Canal to Mediterranean Fleet because of threat of war with Italy. 1st BS Mediterranean Fleet.

15 Aug With *Malaya*, *Warspite* and the cruiser *Kent*, bombarded Bardia.

11 Nov With supporting force for attack on Italian Navy in Taranto by aircraft from *Illustrious*.

Opposite: *Ramillies* steaming into Grand Harbour, Malta, c. 1930/1, while serving with the Mediterranean Fleet. Note her massive anti-torpedo bulges.

Nov Transferred to North Atlantic Escort Force following reduction of Italian battleship strength as a result of the Taranto raid.
27 Nov Attached to Force 'H' on passage to Gibraltar, and was with this force during convoy action against Italian warships at Cape Spartivento though not herself engaged.
Dec At Devonport for refit.
1941 *12 Jan* Left for Halifax via the Clyde to escort a Middle East convoy in its initial stage.
Jan–Aug North Atlantic Escort Force; flagship RA 3rd BS based on Halifax. Escort ship on Bermuda–Halifax–UK convoy duty. Deterred German battlecruisers *Scharnhorst* and *Gneisenau* from attack on convoy.
23 May Detached to take part in the search for *Bismarck*.
Oct (to March 1942) accompanied her sisters to Colombo; 3rd BS, Indian Ocean.
Aug Refitted at Liverpool.
Dec 3rd BS Eastern Fleet. Attached to Force 'F' at Colombo.
1942 *7 May* Took part in bombardment and occupation of Diego Suarez and remained there until the surrender.
30 May During her stay she was attacked by Japanese midget submarines from their parent submarines *I16* and *I20*. A torpedo struck just forward of 'A' turret on the port bulge, and inflicted damage from frames 27 to 58. Extensive flooding occurred below the middle deck (frames 27 to 42), with the exception of certain wing compartments. Frames 42 to 58 below the main deck inboard of the incline were also flooded and many seams in the hull plating were found to be leaking. Although she was badly damaged, the crew were soon able to bring her under control and out of immediate danger. The explosion took place well inboard in a highly dangerous area near the shell and magazine rooms. The explosive materials were removed from these compartments to a safer position; the anchor was removed and its cable was laid on the quarterdeck. Divers reported that the torpedo had struck just before bulkhead 42, the explosion opening the bulge completely from frames 27 to 42 at the bottom of the lower compartment, down to the bilge. The damage extended inboard in the shape of a cone, sloping forward with its apex on the middle line at which point the bulkhead on the platform deck suffered a hole 4 feet in diameter. The ½in bulge plating was corrugated abaft frame 42 and curved well inboard. The 6in armour forward was slightly displaced and some of the support channels were damaged, but this was the extent of it. Although taking in tons of water the ship managed to right herself (weight unknown); her draught was now: port forward 39ft 3in; starboard forward 39ft 1in; port aft 3lft 3in; starboard aft 29ft 11in. The freeboard forward was approximately fourteen feet! After the bulkheads had been shored and local damage contained, she was able to proceed to Durban at a speed of 9–10 knots. The Constructor, H. S. Pengally, flew to Durban to inspect the damage and commented on the vessel very highly, saying: 'Although the vessel is now 26 years old and felt by most to be of little value owing to reduced size and slow speeds, the *Ramillies* is in exceptionally good shape, and I should wonder whether or not the capital ships of today (1943) with their lighter scantlings would survive a blow as well as this old girl, some 26 years after they were built.' She was temporarily repaired at Durban from June to Aug and then sailed for Devonport to complete there, being under refit until June 1943.
1943 *July* Rejoined Eastern Fleet at Kilindini (East Africa), the only battleship remaining at that station.
28 Dec Left Colombo for home. Refitted for shore bombardment.
1944 *Jan* Joined Home Fleet.
6–17 June During Normandy invasion she bombarded batteries at Villerville, Benerville and Houlgate, putting the latter battery out of action.
25 and 28 Aug Unit of the force which carried out shore bombardment in the south of France for the invasion there, bombarding shore batteries at Toulon.
1945 *31 Jan* Reduced to Reserve at Portsmouth. Attached as accommodation ship to the training establishment HMS *Vernon*, and was known as *Vernon III*.
1947 *Dec* Placed on the Disposal list.
1948 *2 Feb* Sold to British Iron & Steel Co. and allocated to Arnott, Young Ltd.
23 April Arrived at Cairnryan for scrapping

History: *Resolution*

Laid down and built by Palmer at Jarrow; launched on 14 January 1915.

1916 *7 Dec* Commissioned for service with Grand Fleet.
30 Dec Joined the Fleet at Rosyth. Except for minor differences her early life was much the same as that of *Ramillies*, the class usually operating as a group. See Appearance Changes for refit dates.
1939 *Aug* Assigned to Channel Force at Portland under the war organization.
1 Oct Ordered to join South Atlantic Command (Freetown) after sinking of SS *Clement* by German panzerschiffe *Graf Spee*, but orders cancelled.
5 Oct Transferred with her sister *Revenge* to North Atlantic Escort Force (Halifax). Left England carrying bullion to Canada.

Right: *Royal Oak* anchored in Weymouth Bay, *c.* 1937/38. Note her lines after reconstruction: new superstructure, enlarged control top, tripod mainmast, improved gunnery control and SL arrangements.

North Atlantic Escort Force; escorting convoys of Canadian troops coming to Britain in December 1939.

1940 *April* Rejoined Home Fleet for Norwegian campaign.

12 May Took part in capture of Bjerkvik during operations against Narvik, carrying tanks and motor craft for the landing. Attacked by aircraft and damaged by a bomb later in the month; two killed, 27 injured.

4 June Left Scapa.

28 June Joined Force 'H' (Gibraltar).

3 July With *Hood*, *Valiant*, *Ark Royal*, *Arethusa*, *Enterprise* and destroyer force, took part in attack on French Fleet at Mers-el-Kebir (Oran).

23–25 Sept With *Barham*, *Devonshire*, *Cornwall*, *Cumberland*, *Australia* and the carrier *Ark Royal*, bombarded Dakar. Engaged by the battleship *Richelieu* and shore batteries, receiving four hits.

25 Sept Torpedoed by French submarine *Beveziers*, sustaining considerable damage. The port engine room was flooded and she developed a serious list; draught forward reaching as much as 40 feet. Her speed dropped to 12 knots, and later to 5 and then 3 knots. Towed with great difficulty by *Barham* to Freetown and arrived there on the 29th. Temporary repairs carried out there and later she moved to Gibraltar.

1941 *March* Left Gibraltar, attacked by enemy aircraft but not hit and reached Portsmouth safely. Left Portsmouth for the USA as it was not safe for big ships to lie in dock because of frequent air attacks at this time.

April–Sept Completely repaired at Philadelphia Naval Dockyard.

Dec Hoisted flag of VA 3rd BS Eastern Fleet.

1942 *26 March* Arrived at Colombo.

1943 *Feb* She was a unit of the escort force convoying Australian troops from Suez to Australia in February 1943.

Sept Returned home. Under refit at Rosyth.

Oct Reduces to Reserve, at Southampton.

1944 *June* Transferred to Devonport as part of the stokers' training establishment HMS *Impérieuse*. Her main armament was removed as spares for *Warspite* and *Ramillies* which were bombarding the coast of Normandy.

1948 *Feb* Paid off on to the Disposal list, sold to The British & Iron Steel Co. and allocated to Metal Industries Ltd.

13 May Arrived at Faslane for scrapping

History: *Royal Oak*

Laid down and built at Devonport Royal Dockyard, 1913–16.

1916 *1 May* Commissioned at Devonport for 4th BS Grand Fleet.

31 May Battle of Jutland. She engaged German battlecruiser *Derfflinger* at a range of 14,000 yards and obtained several hits, firing 38 15in shells.

Her subsequent history was very similar to that of *Ramillies* (refit dates in Appearance Changes).

1936 *Aug* 2nd BS Home Fleet.

1938 *Nov* Conveyed the body of Queen Maud of Norway from UK to Norway after her death.

1939 *7 June* Commissioned at Portsmouth on 7 June 1939 for service with the Mediterranean Fleet, but never joined, staying with Home Fleet on reorganization in August 1939. Based at Rosyth and Scapa Flow during the early months of the war.

14 Oct While at anchor in Scapa Flow on the night of the 14th she was attacked and sunk by *U47*. She was taken completely by surprise; the U-boat having squeezed through the under-water defences at Hoxa Sound entrance. One torpedo had been fired without effect at approximately 01.00, and it is

Above: No rest for the crew, as they go about their daily tasks even in wartime. Scrubbing the decks was routine and a job that had to be done. Lads on *Royal Oak* are shown here in mid-1918.

Right: *Royal Sovereign* leaves Philadelphia Navy Yard after refit, 14 September 1943. Note additions to rear of main superstructure, radar on mainmast (2735W) Types 282 for the 20mm AA on directors abeam bridge, Type 284 for the main armament on rangefinder over conning tower; also extensive aerials on masts. Four of her 6in secondary battery guns (2 port and 2 starboard) have been removed to improve internal accommodation, but the AA defence has been greatly increased. Note extensive pom poms and 20mm.

thought that it struck the anchor chain. *U47* reloaded her tubes and fired at least two more which tore the bottom out of the ship. She turned turtle and sank within thirteen minutes, taking with her 24 officers and 809 men. She lies beneath the waters of Scapa Flow to this day, having been designated a war grave despite frequent demands to have her raised and sold for scrap.

History: *Revenge*

Laid down and built by Vickers from 22 Dec 1913 until Feb 1916.

1916 *1 Feb* Commissioned at Barrow and joined 1st BS Grand Fleet.
31 May Battle of Jutland. She engaged the battlecruisers *Von der Tann* and *Derfflinger* at 11,000 yards. She fired a total of 102 15in shells, but received no hits herself. She relieved *Marlborough* as flagship of 1st BS after that ship was hit by a torpedo during the action.
See *Ramillies* for inter-war periods.
1939 *9 Aug* Reserve Fleet Review at Portland.
Aug Channel Force.
Oct North Atlantic Escort Force, orders to join South Atlantic Escort Force with sister *Resolution* having been cancelled.
1940 *Aug* Transferred to Plymouth Command as Base Ship, in view of threatened German invasion of Britain.
Oct Bombarded Cherbourg coastline from 15,700 yards.
Nov Rejoined Atlantic Escort Force.
1941 *23–27 May* Took part in search for *Bismarck*, leaving Halifax for this operation.
1942 *April* Selected for the newly formed Eastern Fleet and based at Colombo. She was employed mainly on Australian troop convoy duties in the Indian Ocean.
1943 *31 Sept* Returned to the Clyde and reduced to Reserve for subsidiary service until March 1948. This early retirement was partly because of her poor condition which had been reported as early as 1936. Her electrical layout was in a very bad state, many of the main cables being overdue for replacement. Her hull, too, was showing signs of stress and she was in need of an extensive refit.
1944 *Jan* Transferred to Portsmouth Command at Southampton.
17 Dec She was employed as a stokers' training ship at Devonport, but was later detached to take Winston Churchill to the Cairo–Teheran Conference.
1948 *March* Placed on Disposal list.
July Sold to British Iron & Steel Co. and allocated to T. W. Ward Shipbreaking Co.
5 Sept Arrived at Inverkeithing to be scrapped

History: *Royal Sovereign*

Laid down and constructed at the Portsmouth Royal Dockyard, from 1913 until 1916.

1916 *18 April* Commissioned.
25 May Joined Grand Fleet. Absent from Jutland because of machinery troubles.
See *Ramillies* for inter-war period and see Appearance Changes for refit times.
1935 *April* Home fleet.
1939 *Oct* Transferred to North Atlantic Escort Force.
Dec Refit at Devonport.
1940 *May* Transferred to 1st BS Mediterranean Fleet on threat of war with Italy. With *Warspite* and *Malaya* in action off Calabria against Italian battle squadron while on convoy duty from Malta to Alexandria.
Aug Left Mediterranean to rejoin North Atlantic Escort Force via Suez, Aden, Durban, Capetown and Gibraltar.
Sept–Oct Under refit at Durban.
Dec Arrived at Halifax. North Atlantic Escort Fleet.
1941 *Feb* Escorted Canadian troops to UK.
May–June Under refit at Norfolk Navy Yard, USA. Selected for East Indies (see *Ramillies*).
Aug Refit in Glasgow.
Oct Eastern Fleet.
1942 *Sept* Detached for refit in USA; proceeded via Capetown and Freetown.
Oct Under refit at Philadelphia Naval Yard, USA.
1943 *Oct* Withdrawn from Eastern Ocean duties after refit and returned home.
5 Nov Paid off into care and maintenance at Rosyth. In Reserve at Rosyth until May 1944.
1944 *17 Aug* Sailed for Murmansk on loan to USSR, where she was renamed *Arkhangelsk*. This loan was a response to the Russians' demand for a portion of the Italian Fleet and was surrounded by much secrecy. Little is known of the ship's activity while with the Soviet Fleet. She was still in Russian hands well after the war, and her return was procured only after great difficulties.
1949 *15 Jan* Left Murmansk.
4 Feb Arrived at Rosyth and immediately placed on the Disposal list. Sold to British Iron & Steel Co., being allocated to T. W. Ward.
18 May Arrived at Inverkeithing, the last unit of the class to reach the scrapyard; all but one having served for more than thirty years.

Renown and *Repulse*: 1914/15 ESTIMATES

Design

The ships were laid down under the normal 1914 Programme as two units of an improved *Royal Sovereign*-class battleship. Four ships were provided under these estimates: *Renown*, *Repulse*, *Resistance* and another, to be built along the lines of *Queen Elizabeth*. The three improved *Royal Sovereign* type would incorporate all the latest improvements and developments since that design, and in a letter to the DNC, from the Chief Constructor at Portsmouth, W. Gard, proposals were suggested for the new ships' final legend.

1. The 1½in protective wing bulkheads would be carried at full thickness throughout the whole depth: i.e. an increase of ½in for the upper part so as to enable the bulkhead to be more homogeneous with connecting plates, and take into consideration the results of the experiments with underwater explosions carried out in the old pre-dreadnought *Hood*.
2. An enlarged torpedo control tower.
3. An enlarged conning tower with the armour rearranged for better access.
4. Provision for a protected spotting position in the bows.
5. The vertical keel to be fitted in two parts, and the width of the flat keel increased so as to provide a more rigid structure amidships to resist stress on docking, etc.
6. Stowage for 100 rounds per gun for the 15in shells instead of a normal capacity of 80.
7. Suggested legend dimensions for new ships were 25,750 tons; 580ft x 88ft 9in x 28ft 6in. 31,000 shaft horsepower would be sufficient to give a speed of approximately 21 knots.

Acting upon this information, more calculations were made by the DNC's department, and a final legend was approved within four or five weeks, on 13 May 1914. It was agreed that two of the ships for the years' estimates would be built in the Royal Dockyards, with *Resistance* at Devonport, the *Queen Elizabeth*-type ship at Portsmouth and *Renown* and *Repulse* put out to tender. *Renown*'s order was placed with Fairfield, and *Repulse*'s at Palmers Shipyard.

The first ten plates were laid down for *Repulse* on 30 November 1914, but building for both *Repulse* and *Renown* was very slow because labour and materials were being concentrated on such heavy ships as could be hastened to completion (*Royal Sovereign* and the remainder of the *Queen Elizabeth* class, now nearing completion) during the six months it was thought hostilities would last. It was not until 19 December 1914, however, that the first intimation reached the DNC about the required battlecruiser type. They were to be armed with 15in guns, have a speed of 32 knots and to be built with the utmost speed, even if it meant cannibalizing other ships under construction.

The design stemmed from experience gained in the Heligoland Bight action on 28 August 1914, and as a direct result of the Battle of the Falklands on 8 December 1914, both of which demonstrated the value of high speed, combined with a powerful armament and wide radius of action. They were to be lightly armoured – on the same scale as a conventional cruiser in fact; the *Indefatigable*'s 6in main belt and 7in barbettes were to be taken as a yardstick. The DNC made it clear at the time that it was undesirable to apply such thin protection to ships of such great proportions, but he agreed that features of such magnitude could only be reached if the protective qualities were indeed scanty.

It was Fisher's intention to employ the ships in connection with his Baltic project, which envisaged an invasion of the Pomeranian coast (some 80 miles from Berlin) by a British or Russian landing force, supported by a large force of specially designed ships with a large cruising radius, long-range guns, and an extremely shallow draught.*

Progress was remarkably swift.

31 Jan 1915: Both firms supplied with sufficient drawings for preparing all main structural drawings, i.e.: hull specification; midships section; part profile and deck flats; sections of protective deck; sketch of armour plating.
15 Feb: 250 feet of the keel on the blocks and a further 4,000 tons of material ordered.
28 Feb: All drawings almost complete.
15 March: 375 tons on blocks, 3,000 ton of steel on premises.
30 March: Hull specification complete, 800 tons on blocks.
12 April: All drawings complete, 1,200 tons on blocks.
8 Jan 1916: *Repulse* launched.
15 Aug: First seagoing trials.

Thanks to Admiral Fisher's drive and a high degree of co-operation between the Construction Department and the contractors, the ships were at sea within nineteen or twenty months, which was thought to be a world record for ships of such size and novel design. A typical wartime product, the hastily conceived design departed radically from the recognized procedures in line of development, and took the battlecruiser type to the limit; Fisher's dictum 'speed is armour' and the sacrificing of thick armour were

RENOWN AND REPULSE: FINAL LEGEND, 2 APRIL 1915

Displacement (tons)
26,500.

Dimensions
Length: 750ft pp, 794ft oa
Beam: 90ft
Draught: 25ft 6in (mean).

Armament
Six 15in Mk I
Seventeen 4in Mk IX
Two 3in AA.

Armour
Main belt (9ft deep): 6in
Barbettes: 7in
Turrets: 9in–7in–4¼in
Bulkheads: 4in and 3in
Conning tower: 10in
Uptakes: 1½in
Decks: forecastle 1½in, armoured 1in flat, 2in inclines, lower 2½in.

Machinery
Designed to develop 110,000–120,000shp for 31–32 knots.
Boilers laid out as in *Tiger*, but burned oil fuel only.

Weights (tons)

Machinery:	5,660
Armour:	4,770
Armament:	3,335
General equipment:	685

* This idea, of 'outflanking' the Germans, received support from both Churchill and Lloyd George (then Chancellor of the Exchequer) in November and December 1914. However, it was soon brushed aside as Churchill poured his enthusiasm into an alternative 'outflanking' naval operation – the Dardanelles campaign.

REPULSE
Outboard profile, 1916, as completed

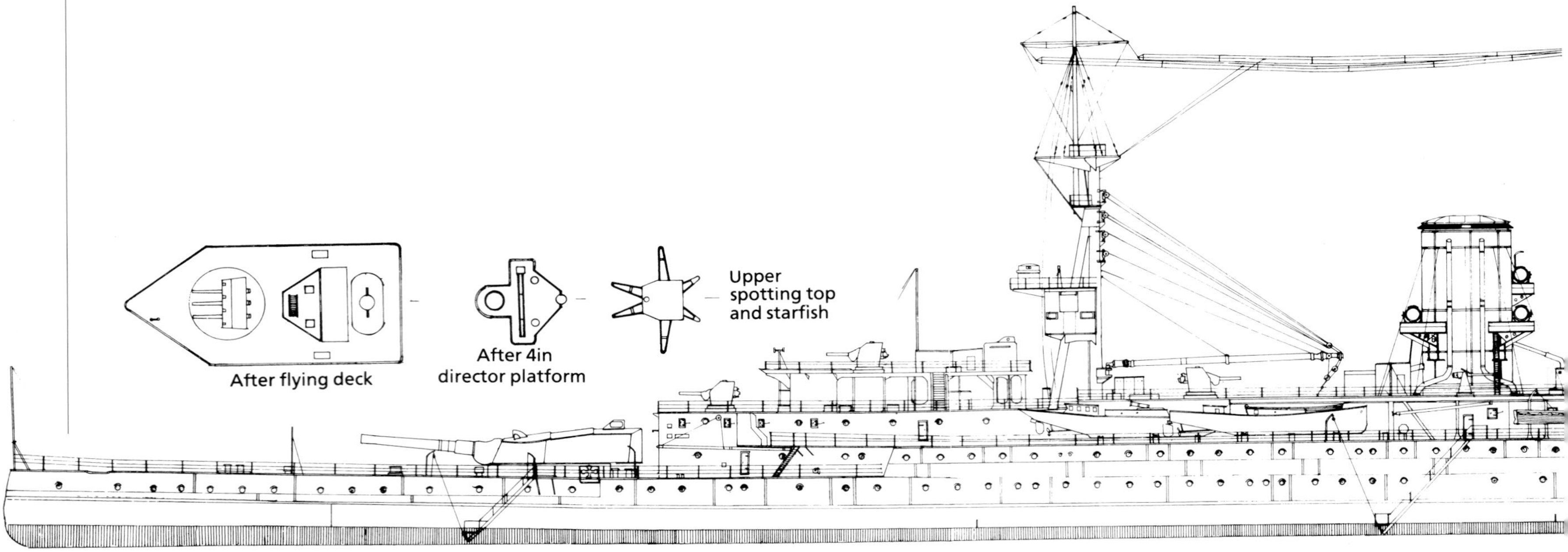

REPULSE
Inboard profile, 1916

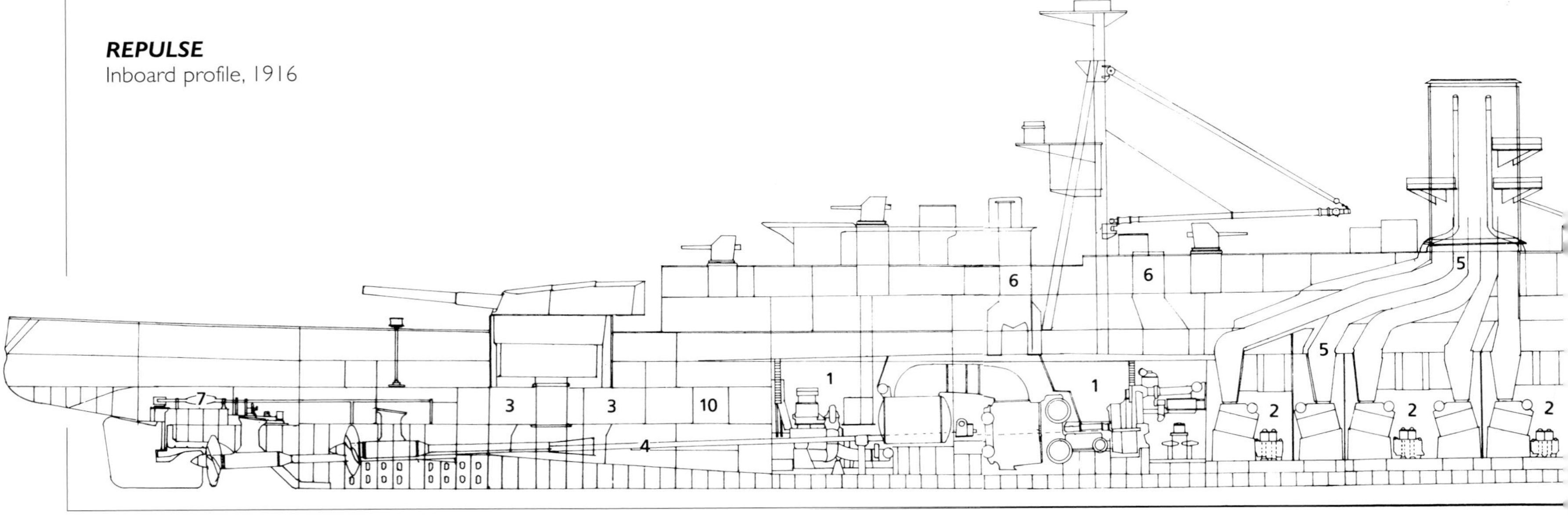

embodied to an even greater degree than in the *Indefatigable* class, which had already been dubbed 'tin cans'. On completion, however, both ships turned out very well, staying within the design limits and conforming exactly to Admiral Fisher's requirements. He, unfortunately, left office before their trials were completed, and before his so-called 'Baltic Plan' could materialize. The exact nature of the role *Renown* and *Repulse* should now play was not known, though they were ideal for long-range bombardment and troop support.

Armament

Admiralty requirements, for which Fisher was directly responsible, called for the maximum possible number of 15in guns on a moderate displacement commensurate with a speed of 32 knots. In view of the demand for a completion within fifteen months, which was paramount so far as Fisher was concerned, the design had to be based on the number of 15in guns and turrets available. Although it was appreciated that eight guns would make for better salvo firing and fire control, only six guns per ship could be procured at that time, so the layout was based on three twin turrets.

As Fisher had always been opposed to a heavy secondary armament in capital ships, an unhappy return was made to the 4in gun. However, the triple mountings chosen for the ships were an innovation in this and the following *Courageous* classes, being designed to secure the maximum concentration of fire, the guns being placed at the most advantageous points to achieve freedom from

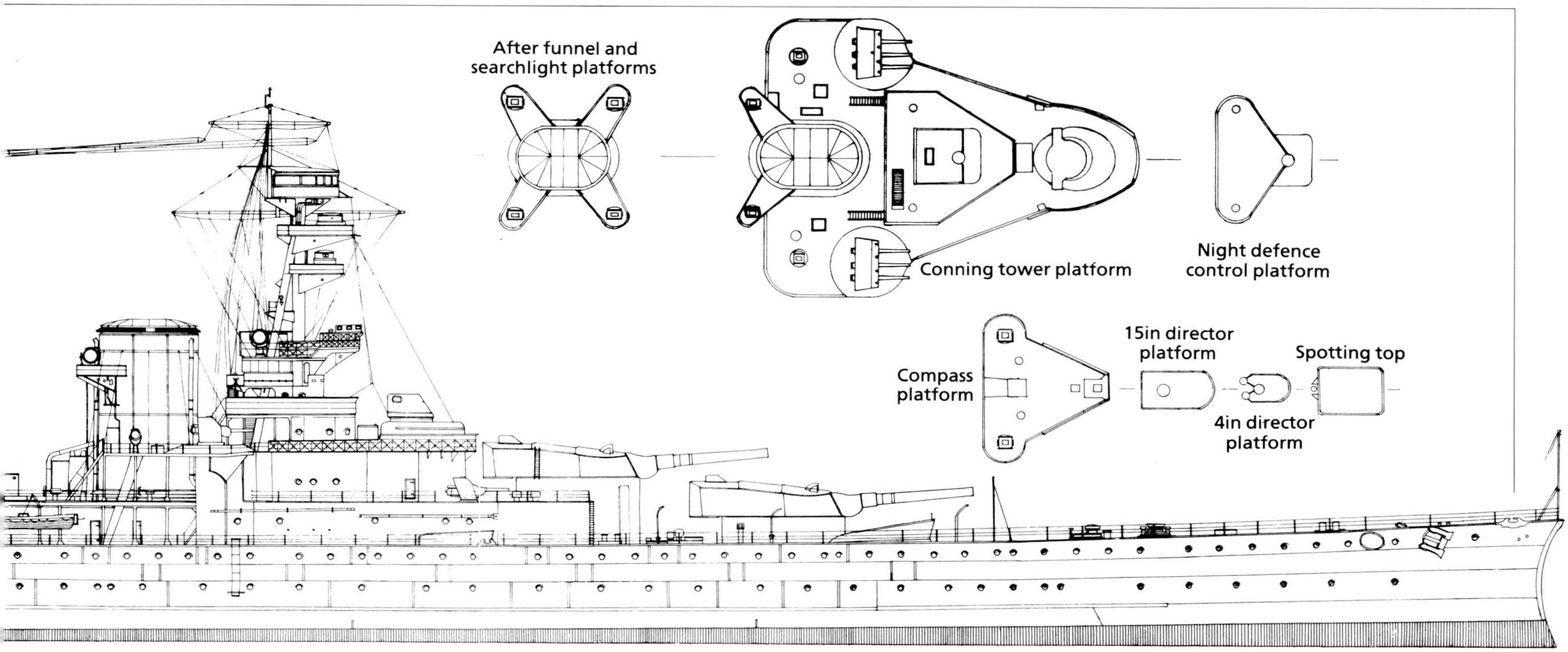

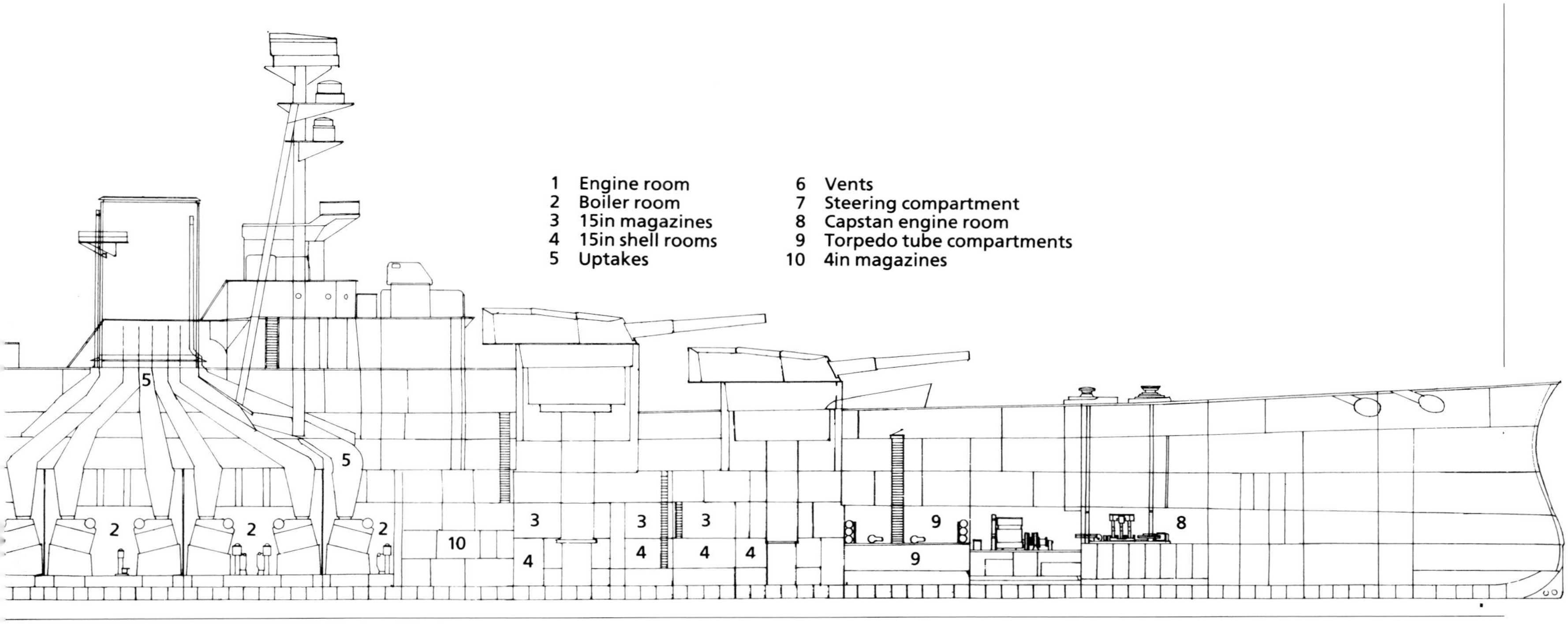

Left: *Renown* early in 1917, showing raised fore funnel and even level of SL platforms around second funnel.

Right: *Renown*, showing her forward 15in guns and bridge in 1917. During 1917 there were experiments with a flying-off platform across the forecastle. A steel girder runway was erected from the front of 'A' 15in turret through to the bow of the ship. Little is known about the experiments but the apparatus was soon removed.

interference. The guns in each mounting had a common training, but they were not mounted in one sleeve and their breech mechanism allowed each to be loaded, elevated and fired independently. Director control towers were fitted: one on the foremast below the 15in director, the other on a platform fitted to the main tripod legs.

As fitted, the triple 4in looked very good on paper, providing excellent saturation of fire on all bearings, but in practice the mountings proved clumsy, because of the close proximity of the breeches, and the 23 loaders per triple mounting were apt to obstruct one another which brought the rate of fire well down from what had been expected.

Armour

Because the armour scale of protection was based on that of *Indefatigable*, *Renown* and *Repulse* were lightly protected. The main belt was 462 feet long and 9 feet wide, with a thickness of 6in. This standard, which had been embodied in the original design, was undoubtedly inadequate, both in extent and thickness, and any suggestion that the completed ships should ever oppose enemy capital ships was out of the question.

After the Jutland experience, more armour plating was worked into the ships, as it was in the rest of the battlefleet; the battle having proved that nearly all the battlecruisers suffered very badly because of inadequate deck protection. An extra inch of high-tensile plating was added to the main deck on the flat, but only in those areas covering the magazines, so it remained inadequate.

After *Renown* and *Repulse* joined the Grand Fleet in September 1916, they were recalled almost immediately for a further refit to enhance their protective qualities: it being thought ridiculous to put these two monsters in the front line, only to receive similar punishment as had *Invincible*, *Indefatigable* and *Queen Mary*. The Commander-in-Chief, Admiral Jellicoe, suggested in a letter to the DNC that the crowns of the magazines should receive special attention, and felt that it was a pity that something could not be done to improve the vertical armour, although realizing that this was quite impracticable at that time. The suggestions were quickly approved and the work was carried out at Rosyth from 10 November 1916 to 29 January 1917 for *Repulse*, and from 1 February 1917 to mid April 1917 for *Renown*. Main deck protection was increased to 3in over machinery; lower deck was increased to 2in over magazines, and 3½in over the steering gear. Total weight of the additions was approximately 504 tons. Despite

REPULSE: LAUNCH FIGURES, 8 JANUARY 1916

Displacement: 15,156 tons
Hull not weighed
Draught: 14ft 11in forward, 17ft 8¼in aft
Length: 750ft 1⅛in pp
Beam as moulded: 89ft 7½in
Depth of keel from forecastle deck: 49ft 1in
Breakage at launch:
longitudinal in a distance of 581ft = 1¾in hog
transverse in a distance of 80ft = 2⅝in sag
Length of boiler rooms: *Repulse* 192ft 11¼in, *Renown* 193ft
Length of engine rooms: *Repulse* 110ft, *Renown* 109ft 10in.

RENOWN: LAUNCH FIGURES, 4 MARCH 1916

Displacement: 16,065 tons
Estimated hull weight: 11,620 tons
Draught: 14ft 8in forward, 18ft 9in aft
Length: 750ft 2in pp
Beam as moulded: 89ft 9¾in
Depth of keel from forecastle deck: 41ft 1½in
Breakage at launch:
longitudinal in a distance of 577ft = 2 3⁄16in hog
transverse in a distance of 83ft 3in = nil.

Left: *Repulse* in the summer of 1917.

RENOWN AND REPULSE: PARTICULARS, AS COMPLETED

Construction

	Dockyard	Laid Down	Launched	Completed
Renown:	Fairfield	(as battlecruiser) 25 Jan 1915	4 March 1916	Sept 1916
Repulse:	John Brown	(as battleship) 30 Nov 1914		
		(as battlecruiser) 25 Jan 1915	8 Jan 1916	14 Aug 1916.

Displacement (tons)
Renown: 27,320 (legend), 32,220 (deep)
Repulse: 26,854 (legend), 31,592 (deep).
Seagoing displacement (tons) (Sept 1917)
Renown: 32,740
Repulse: 32,140.

Dimensions
Length
Renown: 750ft 2in pp, 787ft 9in wl, 794ft 1½in oa
Repulse: 750ft 1⅛in pp, 787ft 9in wl, 794ft 2½in oa
Beam
Renown: 90ft 1¾in
Repulse: 89ft 11½in
Draught
Renown: 25ft 0½in forward, 27ft aft (legend); 30ft 2in forward, 30ft 1in aft (deep)
Repulse: 25ft forward, 26ft 7in aft (legend); 29ft 9in forward, 29ft 7in aft (deep)
Height of 15in guns above load wl: 'A' 35ft; 'B' 45ft; 'Y' 23ft
Height of CT vision slits above lower wl: 55ft
Height of fore funnel: 88ft
Height of lower foremasthead: 115ft 6in.

Armament
Six 15in 42cal Mk I; 120rpg
Seventeen 4in 44cal Mk IX; 200rpg
Two 3in QF HA; 150rpg
One 12pdr (8cwt) field gun
Four 3pdr (saluting)
Five Maxim MG
Ten Lewis guns
Ten 21in torpedo tubes (2 beam submerged); ten torpedoes Mk IVHB, sixteen torpedoes Mk IVSL.

Armour
Main belt: 6in
Ends: 6in–3in
Bulkheads: 4in–3in
Barbettes: 7in–4in
Turrets: 9in face, 7in side, 11in rear, 4¼in roof
Conning tower: 10in–6in
Communications tube: 3in
Decks: forecastle 1⅛in–¾in, main 1in, slopes 2in, lower 2in–1¾in
Uptakes: 1½in–1in.

Machinery
Brown Curtis impulse-type turbines, four propellers
Boilers: forty-two Babcock & Wilcox, pressure 275psi
Total heating surface: 157,206sq ft
Designed SHP: 112,000 = 31.5 knots
Fuel: 1,000 tons oil normal, 4,289 tons oil max. (4,243 tons *Repulse*)
Radius of action: 2,700nm at 25 knots; 4,000nm at 18 knots; 4,700nm at 12 knots.

Ship's boats
Pinnaces (steam): two 50ft
Pinnaces (sail): one 36ft
Launches (motor): one 42ft
Cutters: three 32ft
Whalers: two 27ft
Gigs: three 30ft
Dinghies: one 16ft
Balsa rafts: one 13ft 6in
***Repulse* as flagship carried, in addition:** one 45ft Admiral's barge, one 30ft gig, one 16ft dinghy.

Searchlights
Eight 36in
Two 24in (signalling).

Rangefinder positions (1918)
Renown
Two 30ft: 'Y' turret, back of armoured tower
Four 15ft: 'A', 'B' turrets, torpedo control tower, armoured tower
One 12ft: spotting top
Two 9ft: fore bridge
One 6ft 6in HA
Repulse
Three 30ft: 'A', 'Y' turrets, back of armoured tower
Three 15ft: 'B' turret, armoured tower, torpedo control tower
One 12ft: spotting top
Two 9ft: fore bridge
One 6ft 6in HA.

Battle signal stations
Two: separate, enclosed with lockers, one each side of main deck near foremast.

Anchors
Three 145cwt stockless (bowers, sheet), one 60cwt stern.

Wireless

	Renown	*Repulse*
Main office:	Types 1–16	Types 1–16, 34
Second office:	Type 2	Type 2
Third office:	Type 9	Type 9
Fire control office:	–	Type 31.

Complement
Renown: 953 (as completed); 1,223 (1919)
Repulse: 967; 1,057 (1917); 1,222 (1919).

Cost
Renown £3,117,204
Repulse £2,829,087.

Above: *Repulse* in 1917, when camouflage was first given to her. Note the dark panel on hull forward.

this refit, however, the armouring on the two ships remained relatively weak, and they were subjected to a good deal of criticism when they eventually became operational in 1917.

Internal subdivision was quite good, reliance having been placed on this feature to localize any damage that might occur. The upper side armour, which was 1½in, was laid in two thicknesses, and intended to serve a dual purpose: as shell plating, and to provide light armour protection, the latter being negligible, it being so liberally pierced by rows of scuttles. The designed total weight of protection had been 4,770 tons, but after many improvements had been made this had increased to 5,274 tons, and was later increased again to 5,700 tons.

The main belt amidships was 6in thick, and extended from 'A' to 'Y' barbettes. Forward it was met by a thickness of 4in which ran to within 100 feet of the stem at the same width as the midships section. Aft, the thickness was only 3in, and extended to within approximately 75 feet of the stern. The upper sides of 1½in extended to just beyond 'A' and 'Y' barbettes between forecastle and main deck levels, except that the after extremity, above the upper deck, terminated 68 feet short of 'Y'.

The main bulkheads were: outer forward, 4in, which ran obliquely and closed the forward extremities of the 4in side armour, and carried above this to upper deck level. The inner forward bulkhead of 3in ran obliquely abreast 'A' barbette between the forecastle and main decks. The after inner bulkhead of 4in closed the after extremities of the 6in side armour to the outer face of 'Y' turret, between main and lower decks. The after outer bulkhead of 3in ran transversely, closing the after extremities of the 3in side armour, between the main and lower deck levels.

The decks, as completed after the refits of 1916–17 were: forecastle deck was ½in before 'A' barbette, ¾in around 'A' and 'B' barbettes, 1¼in amidships, increasing to 1½in at edges. 1½in right aft over magazines. The upper deck was 7⁄16in from 'Y' barbette, increasing to ½in around and abaft this. The main deck, which extended from between the forward and after belt bulkheads, was ¾in forward of 'A' barbette, 2in over the forward magazine, 1in amidships over boilers, 3in over machinery, 2in over and abaft the after magazines, with the inclines being a uniform 2in. The lower deck was 2in over the forward magazines, 2½in and ¾in between the outer face of 'A' barbette and the forward outer bulkhead. A uniform thickness of 2½in was fitted outside this. Aft, the lower deck ran from well inside 'Y' barbette to the stern, covering the after magazine, 2in over the magazines, 3½in outside the after outer bulkhead.

'A' barbette was 7in uniform above the main deck, then the outer face reduced to 4in, the inner face having no armour at all. 'B' barbette was 7in uniform above the forecastle deck, reducing to 4in from forecastle to main. 'Y' had 7in uniform above, and 4in below the main deck levels. Turrets had 9in faces, 7in sides and 4¼in special-quality steel roof plates. The rears were 11in.

The conning tower was provided with 10in sides, a 3in roof and a 6in floor. Conning tower tube was 3in and the sighting hood was given a 6in face and sides with a 3in rear. The torpedo control tower had 3in sides, 1½in roof, a 1in floor and no tube. Funnel uptakes were 1in–1½in between forecastle and shelter deck levels.

No anti-torpedo bulkheads were fitted, the ships' relying on the newly introduced integral anti-torpedo bulges. These were approximately 14 feet inboard and three feet outboard of the hull, and extended over the magazines, machinery spaces and boiler rooms. *Renown* and *Repulse* were the first British warships, other than the monitors, to be fitted with integral anti-torpedo bulges. The first trials had been carried out from late 1913, when different types were fitted experimentally to one side of the old pre-dreadnought *Hood* (1893). Further experiments were carried out during 1914/15 when vessels other than battleships were fitted with this type of protection: gigantic bulges were fitted to the monitors *Earl of Peterborough*, *Abercrombie* and the *Marshal Soult* class; later, the monitors *Erebus* and *Terror* were also fitted in this way, as completed in 1916. Similar bulges were added in four of the old *Edgar*-class cruisers which were employed on special bombardment duties during the Dardanelles campaign in 1915. Special detachable bulges were fitted to the sides of the old pre-dreadnought *Redoubtable* (ex-*Revenge*, 1893) for her deployment to bombard the Belgian coast during the winter of 1914. Official experiments were also being carried out at the Chatham Float, and in some cases at private yards during the early months of 1915.

The bulges for *Renown* and *Repulse*, however, were of a modified type intended to replace the anti-torpedo bulkhead and screens of previous designs. Excessive increase in beam was avoided, the protective structure being kept outside the hull proper. The system employed an outer cellular skin which held a wide cushion of oil and was separated from the hull compartments by a narrow, cellular air space – quite different from the system fitted to the battleship *Ramillies*, then under construction.

Machinery

As a result of their greater length and finer hull lines, a 2½-knot nominal increase over *Tiger* was obtained with only 4,000 extra shaft horsepower; with the exception of *Glorious* and *Courageous*, they were the fastest capital ships in existence until the arrival of *Hood* in 1920.

Right: *Repulse*, showing camouflage, 1918.

REPULSE AS COMPLETED: STEAM TRIALS

Tail of the Bank, Arran, 23 August 1916
Average displacement: 29,900 tons

	Outer	Inner	SHP	Speed (knots)
First run				
Port:	125rpm	133rpm	11,660	15.34
Starboard:	129rpm	133rpm		
Second run				
Port:	127rpm	133rpm	12,450	16.07
Starboard:	128rpm	133rpm		
Third run				
Port:	169rpm	179rpm	29,630	21.43
Starboard:	179rpm	181rpm		
Fourth run				
Port:	171rpm	179rpm	27,600	21.39
Starboard:	176rpm	177rpm		
Fifth run				
Port:	211rpm	221rpm	56,960	25.34
Starboard:	219rpm	223rpm		
Sixth run				
Port:	212rpm	224rpm	55,000	26.18
Starboard:	212rpm	220rpm		
Seventh run				
Port:	244rpm	256rpm	101,400	29.63
Starboard:	259rpm	272rpm		
Eighth run				
Port:	256rpm	268rpm	101,700	31.12
Starboard:	259rpm	269rpm		
Ninth run				
Port:	268rpm	277rpm	118,800	31.31
Starboard:	271rpm	281rpm		
Tenth run				
Port:	269rpm	253rpm	119,250	32.14
Starboard:	271rpm	281rpm		

Because of the demand for a rapid completion, the machinery of *Tiger* was repeated, but provision for three extra boilers was made so as to produce the required speed for the special purpose for which they were primarily built, the Baltic project. The main propulsive unit was arranged in four watertight compartments and consisted of two sets of Brown Curtis turbines in the two forward compartments, with the condenser and auxiliary machinery in the two after compartments, each set being divided by a longitudinal bulkhead on the ship's centreline. The ships were fitted with four shafts, the HP ahead and LP ahead and astern turbines being arranged on the inner shaft, the HP astern and LP ahead being located on the outer shafts. One steering engine was placed in each condenser room, with Williams Janney steering gear provided as an auxiliary.

It had been thought that the excessive flare of the hull at the bows might be detrimental to performance, but the commanding officer during *Repulse*'s first service cruise claimed that 'the ship handles very well, even in a considerable swell, and has an even motion'. He was of the opinion that *Repulse* made more progress against heavy seas than ships without the flare.

Appearance Changes

The hull was beautifully shaped, with a graceful upwards sheer at bow and stern. The strongly curved stem, the first of its type to be fitted to any of the British dreadnoughts, was a feature not seen since the old ironclads of 1867. They were exceptionally fine-looking ships, with a rather piled up superstructure forward and very odd searchlight platforms placed around the funnel. As completed, they were extremely hard to tell apart, but *Renown* had an enclosed navigating platform, while *Repulse*'s was open; also *Repulse* had taller steam pipes to the second funnel.

Above: Quarterdeck of *Renown* as she passes under the Forth Bridge during 1918. Note the 'Etna' strips on the deck.

1916 Fore funnel raised approximately ten feet after trials because of heat and smoke problems.

1917 Deflection scales painted on 'Y' turret. High-angle rangefinder fitted to control top.

Individual searchlight platforms on second funnel of *Renown* replaced by single platforms which encircled the funnel at low level. Flying-off platforms fitted over 'Y' turret in both ships. Flying-off platforms on turrets, with or without runways over the guns, were fitted during the latter part of 1917 to enable high-performance aircraft to be carried within the Grand Fleet for attacking Zeppelins which shadowed the Fleet and reported their movements.

Repulse was the first ship to be fitted with this equipment, in

Above: *Renown*, winter 1916.

Sept 1917, and by early 1918 all battlecruisers and *Courageous* and *Glorious* were similarly equipped. The platforms fitted in *Renown* and *Repulse* were an early experimental type fitted only in *Lion*, *Princess Royal*, *Tiger*, *Courageous* and *Glorious*. They were large and well clear of the turret; the total runway length was 17 feet. Their adoption had been suggested by Lieutenant-Commander Gowen, who had been associated with the fitting of one over the forecastle of the cruiser *Yarmouth* in July 1917. On 24 August 1917, a Sopwith Pup was flown off this ship and brought down Zeppelin *L23* off the Danish coast. The first flight from *Repulse*'s turret top was on 1 October 1917. The upper bridge in *Renown* was extended aft, and the rig was reduced in both ships. Various forms of camouflage were painted, but the most notable was that for *Repulse*: an apparently one-off scheme which extended down to the hull. *Renown* was given a dark band around her fore funnel.

1918 Range clocks fitted to the face of the control top in *Renown* facing the 15in gun director platform. Deflection scales painted on 'A' turret. Searchlights redistributed with improved control arrangements. Platforms on second funnel replaced by four control towers, two each side of funnel, with a single searchlight in each. Searchlights removed from forward funnel and placed on platform on main tripod legs. Upper bridge SL transferred to lower bridge. Upper bridge in *Repulse* was extended aft, almost reaching the funnel. Stump foretopmast fitted in *Renown* at the end of 1918. Funnel camouflage and hull markings painted out, but *Repulse* retained the stripes on the funnels until the end of December.

Dec Repulse under refit (to Oct 1920).

1919 Deflection scales on turrets painted out. *Renown* fitted for Royal Tour in June 1919. Flying-off platforms removed from turrets. Tall flagpole for Royal Standard and Ensign fitted to each topmast.

1920 *Jan–March Renown* under refit. Large-base rangefinders added over control position on conning tower and at rear of 'Y' turret.

1920 *March Renown* on second Royal Tour to New Zealand and Australia (to October 1920), and had the following special modifications carried out: After triple 4in mounting and both 3in AA guns removed to allow extra accommodation and promenade deck. Large deckhouse added port and starboard on shelter deck between funnels. These accommodated a squash court on the port side, and a cinema on the starboard side. Promenade deck built over the after superstructure, and spaces made internally for the Prince of Wales and his staff.

Repulse refit Dec 1918–1920: Main armoured belt removed from original position and placed at higher level from main to upper decks. A new 9in strake was added in the old position, fitted from 'A' to 'Y' barbettes. Wider anti-torpedo bulges fitted, which increased beam by 12ft 8in, and draught by 1ft 4in. The bulge was similar to that of the battleship *Ramillies*, and was filled with crushing tubes. Extra high-tensile plating was worked into the main deck, with 1in added on the flat and 2in on the inclines. The lower deck received an extra 1in of plating over the magazine. Extra weight amounted to approximately 4,300 tons. Searchlights removed from after pair of funnel towers, but towers were retained. Maintopmast was replaced with topgallant. Eight 21in above-water torpedo tubes added in four twin mountings, on upper deck: 2 port, 2 starboard.

1922 Range clocks removed from *Renown* by June.

1923 *July Renown* under refit (to Sept 1926): 6in armoured belt replaced by 9in belt, adding 1,430 tons. Wider bulges fitted, but unlike those of *Repulse* being rather similar to those in the

RENOWN AND *REPULSE*: GM AND STABILITY

Based on inclining experiments in *Renown*, 2 September 1916

	Displacement (tons)	Draught (mean)	GM	Maximum stability	Stability vanishes at
'A' Condition (= load)*	–	26ft 3in	35ft	43°	64°
'B' Condition (= deep)**	–	30ft 1½in	6.2ft	44°	73°

*Fully equipped 1,000 tons oil, reserve tanks empty.
**Fully equipped, 4,289 tons oil, 112 tons coal, all tanks full.

REPULSE
Outboard profile, October 1927

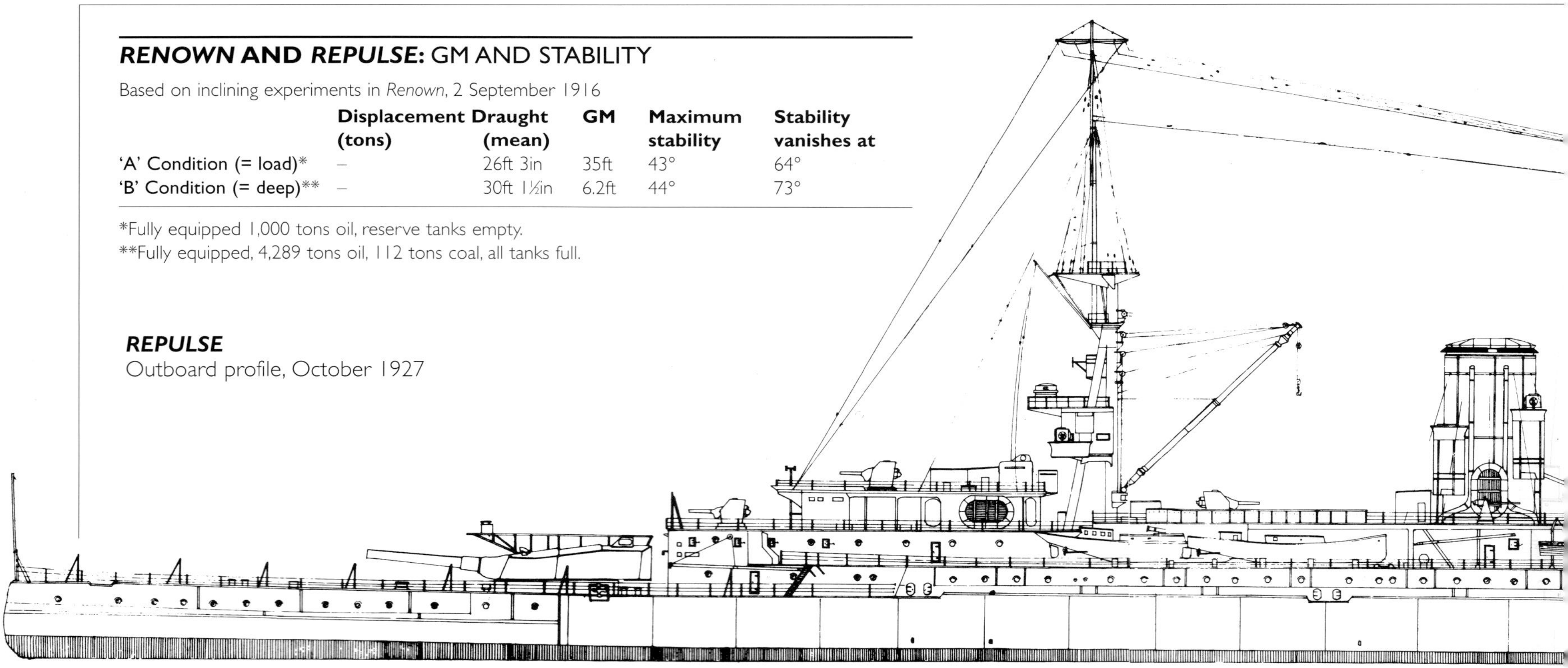

Queen Elizabeth class. 2in of high-tensile plating added over main deck in the vicinity of magazines (flat and slopes). Elsewhere on main deck, an extra 1½in was worked in. Plates of 2½in were added from tops of inclines, extending to ship's sides, over boiler and machinery spaces. Total of 1,020 tons added in deck protection. Single range clock fitted over 'Y' turret. After triple 4in mounting again fitted. New square-type control top, considerably larger than the original. AA guns increased as in *Repulse*. Searchlights removed from after pair of towers. Flying-off platform replaced on 'B' turret. Upper bridge improved and modified with a signal distributing office fitted at rear. Foretopmast removed. Topgallant mast fitted to mainmast.

1924–5 *Repulse*: Single 4in guns on shelter deck abeam conning tower replaced by 4in AA guns in *Repulse*. Original 3in AA were replaced by 4in AA to make AA armament four 4in. Navigating platform enclosed. Squash court platform added for Royal Tour March 1925.

1926 *Repulse*: New type of control top fitted as in *Renown*. Signal distributing office added at rear of upper bridge as in *Repulse*. Foretopmast removed and signal struts added.

1927 *Jan Renown*: Short flagpole fitted abaft control top, and to main topmast for Royal Tour (Jan to June). Deckhouse replaced on port side of shelter deck amidships. Deckhouse in *Repulse* removed during this period.

1930–1 *Renown*: Range clock removed from 'Y' turret.

1932 *Sept Renown* under refit (to June 1932): Midships triple 4in removed to accommodate aircraft catapult (fitted later). Multiple 2pdr AA added on starboard side of superstructure abeam forward funnel. High-angle rangefinder on control top replaced by high-angle director. Flying-off platform removed from 'B' turret. After pair of SL removed from abeam second funnel.

1932–3 *Renown* fitted with McTaggart aircraft catapult. One Fairey 111D seaplane carried. No special aircraft crane carried, aircraft being handled by the boat derrick.

1933 *April Repulse* given the largest refit (to May 1936) she would ever receive. Reconstruction involved about 50 per cent of the structure, and improvements were made by adding more deck protection. 1in plating was removed from the main deck over the magazines, and replaced by 3¾in non-cemented plates. 3½in plates were fitted over the main deck abaft 'Y' turret on top of original plates, giving a maximum thickness of 4¼in. Over the engine room there were already three 1in plates, but two of these were removed, and replaced by a new thickness of 2½in non-cemented armour. Forward of the ship, the lower deck was given new thick plates of 3½in over magazines, after the original 1¾in high-tensile plates were removed. Crushing tubes were removed and watertight compartments and bulge supports in the upper section of the bulge were improved. Midships 4in triple mounting was removed to make way for aircraft catapult. 4in guns in two twin and four single mountings were added, plus sixteen 2pdrs and eight 0.5in machine-guns. Two gastight twin turrets were mounted (one port, one starboard) on the shelter deck abreast the mainmast. These were experimental and data obtained from them was used in the construction and fitting of the 4.5in secondary armament in *Renown*, *Queen Elizabeth* and *Valiant* later on. New medium-frequency direction-finding equipment was fitted at the head of the topgallant mast and a new D/F cabinet fitted on the maintop. Searchlights were redistributed: two on platform over lower bridge, two on platform before forward

Above: *Renown*, c. 1918, showing her wartime alterations and additions.

RENOWN: GM AND STABILITY, 1 JULY 1939

	Draught (mean)	GM	Maximum stability	Stability vanishes at
'A' Condition*	29ft 10¼in	4ft	37°	67°
'B' Condition**	31ft 7¼in	4.8ft	39°	73°

***Renown*, 1943**

Displacement (tons) average 32,240, 37,600 deep

Draught: 29ft 11½in forward, 29ft 9in aft

GM: 4.4ft average, 5.1ft deep.

*Average action condition: 2,510 tons oil, 320 tons coal.

**Extreme deep condition: 4,810 tons oil, 320 tons water protection.

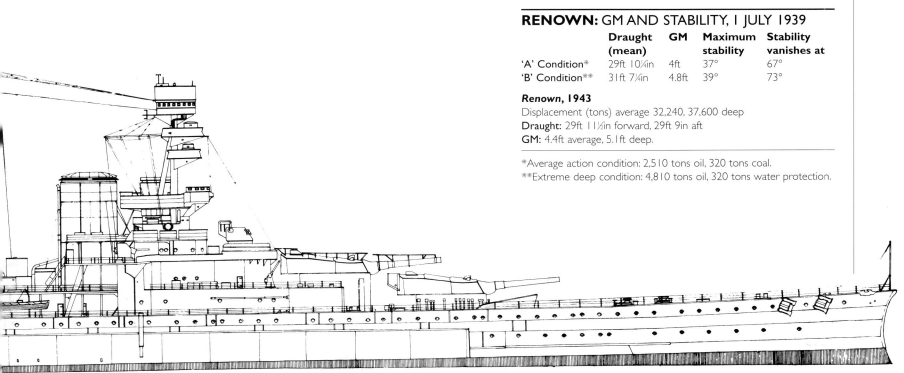

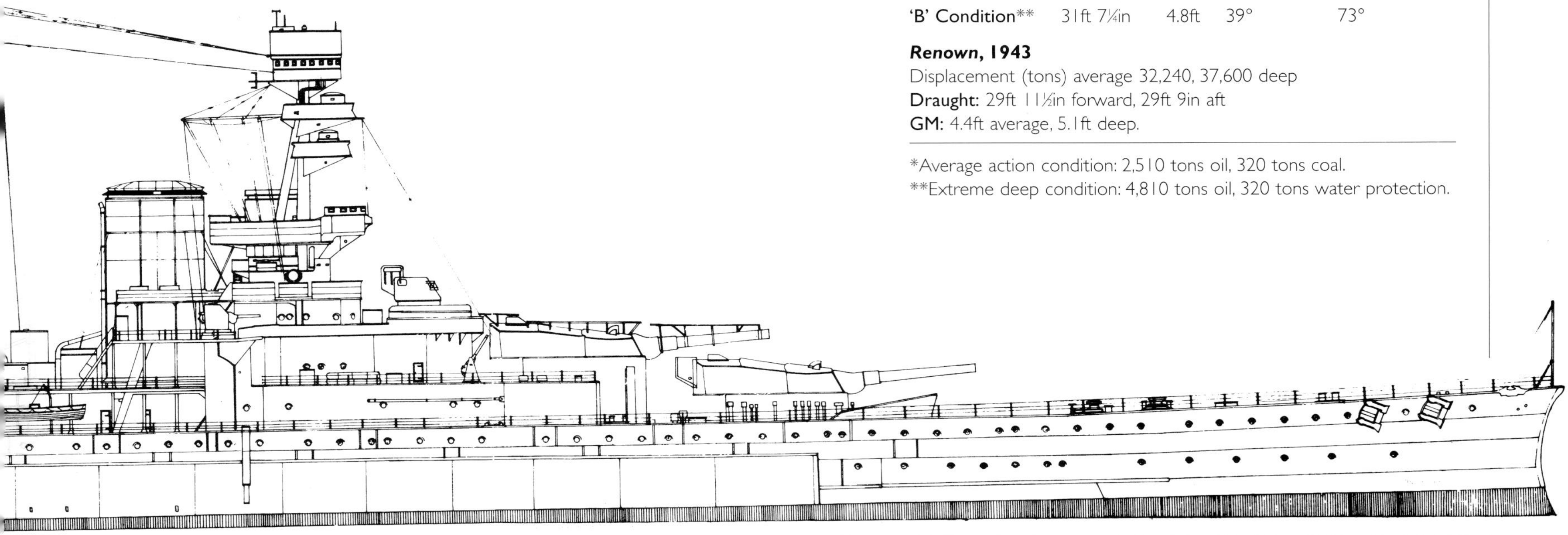

funnel, two on platform low on main tripod legs; the 24in signalling lamps on lower bridge were retained. Two aircraft hangars were provided in the superstructure abaft the second funnel, with the opening at the rear. A straight-arm electric crane was fitted on top of each hangar. A fixed, athwartships catapult, was provided on the upper deck abaft the hangars, the shelter deck being cut away to accommodate it. Provision was made for four aircraft, two in hangars, one on deck outside and one on catapult. The high superstructure containing the hangars was built around the second funnel; the lifeboats were stowed on top of this and were all handled by the aircraft cranes. The main boat derrick was suppressed.

1935 *Renown*: Multiple 2pdrs added on port side of superstructure abeam fore funnel.

1936 *Sept Renown* reconstructed on a scale never before attempted in a British capital ship, excepting only *Queen Elizabeth* and *Valiant*. She was under dockyard control until Aug 1939 and the total cost of her reconstruction was £3,008,008, only £29,000 less than her original cost in 1916. The reconstruction involved about 90 per cent of entire structure, the main theme being the improvement of the armour protection and a better secondary armament. Elevation of the 15in guns was increased to 30° and provision was made for an improved shell with a better calibre radius head. The original 15in gun director was replaced by a new and larger pattern located on top of the new control tower. The armoured control and rangefinder position over the conning tower was removed to the after shelter deck abaft the mainmast, the large-base rangefinder formerly in this position being suppressed. The original 4in triple mountings were all removed, and ten light twin turrets were mounted on the shelter deck in two groups: the forward group of three turrets were fitted on each side abeam the forward funnel, with the second group of two turrets abeam the mainmast. The turrets of each group were very closely spaced and they carried two 4.5in Mk III guns. High-angle control systems with Mk IV directors (4) were fitted on top of the superstructure forward and abeam the mainmast. The light AA guns were increased from sixteen to twenty-four 2pdrs in three eight-barrelled mountings, two on large raised platforms between the funnels and one on the centreline at the extremity of the after shelter deck immediately before 'Y' turret. The original 21in submerged torpedo tubes were removed and eight 18in above-water tubes were fitted in four twin mountings (new 18in Mk XI were carried). The 36in searchlights were replaced by 44in, with improvements in distribution. Horizontal armouring was improved considerably: forecastle and upper deck armour was reduced, but main deck increased from ¾in to 3in outside 'A' barbette, to 4in over forward main magazines and 5in over forward secondary magazines. 1in–2½in over boiler spaces and from 3in to 3½in over machinery, 5in and 4in over after magazines, and from 2in to 2½in over the strip outside 'Y' barbette. The lower deck was also increased to 4in over forward magazine, 4in over boilers and 3½in to 5in over machinery, with 4in plates over main and secondary magazines. Most of this plating was non-cemented, but a 2in thickness fitted on the sides between forecastle deck and shelter-deck below each group of secondary turrets, and 1½in fitted around above water torpedo positions, was of special 'D' steel. The original conning tower was replaced by an armoured lower navigating position, located high up in the face of the new large control tower, protected by 3in plates on the sides and 2in plates at the rear. This additional armour plating was the maximum that could be provided on the displacement, and was considered adequate for the day (1939), but by 1944, experience would show that no existing deck armour could withstand modern high-power bombs. *Renown* was given new machinery, which consisted of eight new Admiralty 3-drum boilers and new Parsons geared turbines which increased the shaft horsepower output to 120,000 for a nominal speed of 29 knots. Internal subdivision of the ship was improved, and longitudinal bulkheads of special plating were fitted abreast the machinery and boiler spaces. The original bridgework and conning tower were replaced by a large splinter and gas-proof control tower, similar, with variations in detail, to that fitted in *Warspite*, as reconstructed in 1937. This type of structure represented a further development of the type first introduced in *Nelson* and *Rodney* of 1927, which had been designed to meet the requirements of a fleet flagship, and to accommodate fire and control positions which had formerly been located on the foremast. Many levels were fitted within the tower, and from the base upwards these were: accommodation and recreation level; sea cabins for Admiral and other officers; armoured lower navigating position, signal, direction-finding and cypher offices; charthouse, remote control and plotting offices. The navigating platform and main secondary directors were located on the top and searchlight and lookout platforms at the sides. The tower itself was relocated farther forward than the original bridge structure, and was well away from the fore funnel, which had been shifted slightly aft to reduce smoke and heat interference to bridge and control positions. The original forward superstructure was replaced by a high superstructure which contained aircraft hangars; the structure was built up and around the second funnel. Most of the lifeboats were stowed on top of this hangar as in *Repulse*, the seaboats being carried in davits on the upper deck amidships. New, streamlined, ovoid narrow-backed funnels were fitted, set closer together than the original two. Accommodation, ventilation, and general equipment was all modernized or improved. No other modifications were made until war broke out in 1939.

1937 Red, white and blue stripes painted on 'B' turret of *Repulse* during the Spanish Civil War.

RENOWN AND REPULSE: PARTICULARS, 1932*

Displacement (tons)
Renown: 31,870 (light), 34,540 (legend), 37,630 (deep)
Repulse: 32,130 (light), 34,880 (legend), 38,100 (deep).

Beam
102ft 8in.

Draught (mean)
Average 27ft–31ft 7in.

Armament
Main unchanged
Twelve–fifteen 4in triple mountings
Single 4in mountings in both ships
Midships triple mounting removed from *Renown*
Four 4in AA
Eight 2pdr AA (1 × 8-barrel *Renown*)
Original TT *Renown*; eight 21in above-water *Repulse*.

Searchlights
Six 36in
Two 24in (signalling).

Aircraft
Renown: one Fairey III F reconnaissance seaplane (catapult)
Repulse: flying-off platforms (aircraft carried for exercises only).

Protection
See Appearance Changes.

Bulges
Renown fitted with improved type as in *Queen Elizabeth* class.

Machinery
Speed reduced since 1918; top speed approx. 29–30 knots.

*Both fitted as flagship.

RENOWN AND REPULSE: PARTICULARS, 1939

Displacement (tons)
Renown: 31,424 (load), 36,080 (deep)
Repulse: 34,600 (load), 38,311 (deep).

Draught (mean)
Average 26ft 9¾in–31ft 3in.

Armament
Renown:
Main unchanged
Twenty 4.5in DP (ten twin turrets)
Twenty-four 2pdr AA (3 x 8-barrel)
Eight 18in TT, above water.
Repulse:
Main unchanged
Twelve 4in triple
Six 4in Mk XV AA
Sixteen 2pdr AA (2 x 8-barrel)
Sixteen 0.5in AA (4 x 4-barrel)
Eight 21in TT, four above-water twins.

Aircraft
Two hangars with fixed athwartships catapult amidships capacity for four Swordfish TSR or Walrus amphibians.

Protection
See Appearance Changes.

Machinery
Eight Admiralty 3-drum boilers, 300psi
SHP: 120,000 = 29 knots
Radius of action: 6,580nm at 18 knots (4,860 tons oil).

Searchlights
Four 44in
Four 24in (signalling).

1938 *Sept Repulse* under refit (to Jan 1939): Twin 4in AA turrets replaced by single 4in AA in open mountings. Eight 0.5in machine-guns added on director platform on main tripod legs. Special accommodation provided for Royal Tour to Canada and USA. (This was not actually used, as it was later decided that the King and Queen should travel in SS *Empress of Australia* and have *Repulse* as an escort.)
1940 *May* Degaussing equipment fitted.
1941 *Renown*: Radar fitted for main and secondary armament. Type 284 for main, Type 285 for 4.5in. Multiple (4-barrelled) 2pdr pom-poms fitted on 'B' turret. Type 282 radar for AA guns fitted. Type 281 air, and Type 271 surface warning radar fitted. Improved DF equipment fitted, with aerial on face of control tower. Tripod legs fitted to mainmast for extra support for Type 281 radar. Admiralty first disruptive type camouflage painted late in 1941.
Aug Repulse: Type 284 radar fitted for 15in guns; originally proposed in November 1940 and approved in February 1941. 4in triple mountings on superstructure abaft mainmast removed. Single 4in AA port and starboard on forecastle deck amidships remounted on top of hangar. Multiple 8-barrel 2pdr AA guns mounted on after superstructure in place of 4in (by July 1941). Single 20mm AA added port and starboard on 'Y' turret. Unusual, semi-official camouflage painted up which comprised dark-grey patches over medium-grey: everything above forecastle deck abaft fore funnel was dark-grey; everything before it, including the fore funnel, was medium-grey. There were further proposals for *Repulse*, which had not been carried out before she was sunk in December 1941. In Dec 1940, however, the Commanding Officer had suggested that the lengthening of the fore funnel or the fitting of a cap, like those in the 'R' class, would be a considerable help in preventing gases and smoke from reaching personnel working on the bridge levels. This was suggested in Jan and again in June 1941, but approval was not given until July 1941. Also, further proposals were made for fitting more radar sets and replacing the existing 4in triple mountings for a new twin-mounted 4in Mk XVI. In Dec 1941 it was recommended that she should be fitted with an extra 3in of plating on the lower deck aft, but none of these proposals were carried out. The improvements would not have saved her from her fate on 10 Dec 1941.
1942 *July Renown* underwent certain modifications until Aug 1943. Seventy-two 20mm AA were added in twenty-three twin and twenty-six single mountings. Additional Type 282 light AA directors were fitted on superstructures amidships and aft. Catapult was removed, but aircraft cranes were retained for handling boats. Hangar spaces converted for use as offices, etc. Aircraft no longer carried. Boat stowage rearranged on catapult deck. Camouflage altered to Admiralty intermediate disruptive type.
1944–5 20mm AA removed from 'B' turret only. Camouflage changed to Admiralty standard type in March 1945.
1945 *July* Armament reduced after ship had passed into Reserve. Forward group of 4.5in turrets (12 guns) removed, presumably for one of the aircraft-carriers. All AA guns removed, but mountings retained. No other visible changes.

RENOWN, AFTER RECONSTRUCTION: STEAM TRIALS

Measured mile, Tolland, 11, 24, 25 July 1939
Displacement: 30,948–32,252 tons

Runs	Mean revs	Mean SHP	Speed (knots)
First	87.5rpm	3,742	9.877
Second	137rpm	13,061	15.633
Third	162rpm	22,128	18.530
Fourth	176rpm	29,209	20.115
Fifth	188.5rpm	35,264	21.121
Sixth	223rpm	57,242	25.332
Seventh	–	120,951	29.962

History: *Renown*

Laid down in Jan 1915 and launched on 4 March 1916. Trials from 12 Sept 1916 after which she left Govan for Scapa on the 18th, arriving on the 20th. Taken in hand at Rosyth for improvements and did not join the Grand Fleet, operationally, until Jan 1917 when she hoisted the flag of Rear-Admiral 1st BCS.

1917 *12 Dec* With other units of the fleet put to sea to intercept the German 3rd Half Division (destroyers) which had attacked the Scandinavia convoy, and covered return of damaged destroyer *Pellew*.
1918 *21 Nov* With 1st BCS at German surrender at Rosyth.
1919 *7 April* Joined BCS Atlantic Fleet on abolition of Grand Fleet.
5 Aug Detached to carry HRH The Prince of Wales to Newfoundland and Canada. Afterwards cruised to West Indies and South American ports, and visited New York for ten days.
1 Dec Left for Portsmouth. Under refit early in 1920.
1920 *16 March* Carried HRH The Prince of Wales to Australia and New Zealand. Called at Barbados, Panama Canal, Honolulu, Suva, Auckland, Melbourne, Sydney, Albany, Adelaide, Hobart, Trinidad, Grenada, St Lucia and Bermuda before returning to Portsmouth on 11 Oct.
11 Nov Paid off at Portsmouth.
1921 *26 Oct* Carried HRH The Prince of Wales to India and Japan, calling at Malta where the proclamation declaring the island an independent Dominion was read.
1922 *2 June* Arrived at Plymouth.
July Reduced to Reserve.
1923 *19 July* Paid off into dockyard hands for refit. Began refit trials from July 1926.
1926 *3 Sept* Recommissioned for service with BCS Atlantic Fleet.

Above: *Renown* after her complete reconstruction (1936 to 1939). Although many thought that she was of modern appearance, there were others that thought the sleek lines of a battlecruiser had vanished.

Remained with Atlantic Fleet until January 1927.

1927 *Jan* Detached service until July 1927.

Sept Atlantic Fleet until Sept 1931. Atlantic Fleet renamed Home Fleet and consisted of *Hood, Renown* and *Repulse* (BCS) only from 1932.

1932 *Jan* Home Fleet Jan 1932 until Jan 1936.

1935 *16 July* Jubilee Fleet Review at Spithead.

1936 *Jan* Transferred to Mediterranean Fleet until May.

June Returned to Home Fleet.

Sept Paid off at Portsmouth for extensive refit.

1939 *Aug* Home Fleet (BCS).

2 Oct Detached as a unit of Force K (with *Ark Royal*) to take part in search for *Graf Spee.*

1940 *March* Home Fleet (BCS), relieving *Hood* as flagship of Vice-Admiral BCS.

9 April In action with German battlecruisers *Scharnhorst* and *Gneisenau* in the Narvik area, she scoring three hits on *Gneisenau* and forcing both ships to retire. *Renown* was hit twice during the action, before the enemy escaped in the bad weather.

Aug Transferred to Force H (Gibraltar), relieving *Hood* as flagship.

1940 *27 Nov* Part of Force H at indecisive action at Spartivento against units of the Italian Fleet.

1941 *21–23 July* Malta Convoy.

Nov Joined Home Fleet (2nd BS).

1942 *6–10 March* With 2nd BS, providing cover for outward and homeward bound Russian convoys and possible chance to intercept *Tirpitz.*

May Based at Hvalfjord (until June).

Oct Returned to Force H. Employed in covering initial British invasion force in North Africa and follow-up convoys against attack by Italian or Vichy French forces.

1943 *7 Feb* Arrived at Rosyth for refit.

June Home Fleet.

Dec Transferred to Eastern Fleet as flagship of Vice-Admiral 1st BS.

1944 *Nov* With East Indies Fleet.

Dec Refit at Durban until Feb 1945.

1945 *March* Recalled home to reinforce Home Fleet against any possible last sortie by German heavy units.

15 May Reduced to Reserve at Portsmouth.

1948 *1 June* Placed on disposal list.

Aug Sold to Metal Industries Ltd, Faslane.

Below: *Repulse* showing her clean, graceful lines as she is seen arriving at Scapa Flow in 1916.

History: *Repulse*

Laid down in January 1915 and launched on 8 Jan 1916. Began sea trials on 15 Aug 1916. Completed steam trials on her way north to join Grand Fleet.

1916 *21 Sept* Joined Grand Fleet at Scapa to work up. Joined 1st BCS Grand Fleet relieving *Lion* as flagship.

1917 *17 Nov* Detached from 1st BCS to cover retirement of light cruisers, penetrating minefields in their support. At 09.00 was in action with enemy light forces and scored a hit on the cruiser *Königsberg.* The shell passed through three funnels and exploded in a coal bunker where it started a serious fire. At 09.30 she was unsuccessfully attacked by a U-boat. From 10.00 to 10.46 she came under fire from German battleships *Kaiser* and *Kaiserin* and was forced to retire.

1918 *21 Nov* Flagship of BCS at German surrender off Rosyth.

17 Dec Paid off at Portsmouth for extensive refit.

1921 *1 Jan* Recommissioned for service with BCS Atlantic Fleet.

1922–31 BCS Atlantic Fleet. With Special Service Squadron on world cruise (*Hood* and LCS in company), 27 Nov 1923 to 29 Sept 1924. Carried HRH The Prince of Wales to West Africa, South Africa and South America 1 May 1925 to 29 July 1925.

1926 Under refit.

8 July Commissioned at Portsmouth for further service with BCS Atlantic Fleet.

1931 *Sept* Mutiny at Invergordon.

1933 *April* Paid off at Portsmouth for extensive refit.

1936 *14 April* Completed to full complement after refit. Mediterranean Fleet until 1938.

1937 *July* Fleet Review. Joined Home Fleet early in 1939.

1939 *16 Oct* At Rosyth during the first air raid there and sustained splinter damage.

7–12 Sept With *Nelson, Rodney* and *Ark Royal* carried out patrol off the Norwegian Coast.

8–10 Oct Took part with *Hood, Sheffield, Aurora* and four destroyers in search for *Scharnhorst* and *Gneisenau.*

21 Oct Detached with *Furious* to America and West Indies Command to cover Halifax to UK convoy.

Dec Home Fleet (BCS).

1941 *Oct* East Indies Command.

11 Nov Transferred to special striking force of new Eastern Fleet; ordered to meet *Prince of Wales* at Colombo, and joined that ship on 28 Nov, where the force was given the codename of Force Z.

1941 *2 Dec* Reached Singapore. In company with *Prince of Wales* and the destroyers *Electra, Express, Tenedos* and *Vampire*, left Singapore for Singora to support the Army's flank and prevent seaborne landings in their rear.

9 Dec Spotted by Japanese reconnaissance aircraft during the evening. Without air cover, the force turned back towards Singapore. From 11.30 to 12.30 subjected to high-level bombing, and torpedo attacks. Hit by one bomb and four torpedoes which reduced her to a sinking condition. She listed 60°–70° to port and hung there for several minutes before capsizing and sinking. A total of 42 officers (including Captain) and 754 ratings were picked up by the destroyers. Twenty-seven officers and 486 ratings lost.

Courageous, *Glorious* and *Furious*: 1915 ESTIMATES

Design

Their design was formulated by Admiral Fisher, who required two ships for his so-called 'Baltic Plan'. On 23 February 1915 the DNC wrote that in accordance with Fisher's instructions he had drawn up a design for an improved light cruiser of which the chief characteristics were:

1. Sufficient displacement to ensure maintenance of speed in moderate weather.
2. Draught restricted to allow operations in shallow waters at entrance of Baltic. Restriction of draught was to be approximately 5ft 6in less than the average for a capital ship, and all other factors would be subordinated to this.
3. A powerful armament.
4. High speed (at least 32 knots) so as to outsteam any enemy light cruiser. (It was anticipated that the ships would be operating mainly in waters too shallow for heavy ships.)
5. Protection to be on light cruiser standard, with 3in from water-line to forecastle deck.
6. Below water bulges for a considerable length amidships, and protected machinery and boilers kept as far inboard as possible and placed behind triple bulkheads.

The DNC went on to argue his case, saying that the new ships would present a smaller target against torpedo attack, and because of their extremely shallow draught would be able to navigate passages denied to our larger ships or large enemy ships, while carrying the largest calibre of guns available.

The design was, in general, a reduced edition of *Renown*, with 'B' turret suppressed and less protection. It was, in fact, the embodiment of Fisher's tactical ideas for a combination of the heaviest possible gun with a very high speed and light protection. At that date, it was the only example of an attempt to mount capital ship guns in a light cruiser.

An obstacle to Fisher's plans came in the shape of the Chancellor of the Exchequer's sanctions for further construction during 1915, which stipulated nothing larger than light cruisers. However, as the Chancellor had not said how big light cruisers might be, and as Fisher was very determined to carry his project through, he went ahead and laid down two 'whoppers, both of which would be armed with 15in guns, capable of annihilating any light cruiser in existence'. (Had it been possible to obtain sanction for further armoured vessels, they would have been a modified edition of *Renown*.)

COURAGEOUS: ORIGINAL LEGEND

Displacement (tons)
17,400.

Dimensions
Length: 735ft pp
Beam: 80ft
Draught: 21ft
Freeboard: 30ft 6in forward, 18ft 6in aft
Gun heights: 33ft forward, 23ft aft.

Armament
Four 15in
Sixteen 4in
Two 3in HA
Two 21in torpedo tubes (submerged).

Armour
Main belt: 3in, 2in aft
Forward bulkhead: 2in
After bulkhead: 2in
Barbettes: 7in–6in
Conning tower: 7in
Uptakes: ¾in.

Machinery
SHP: 90,000 = 32 knots.

Weights (tons)

Hull:	8,500
Armour:	2,800
Machinery:	2,350
Armament:	2,250
Oil:	750
General equipment:	650
Board margin:	100
Total:	**17,400**

A model designated 'VY' was made and tested at Haslar, and within a few weeks the first ship was laid down at Armstrong, and the second two months later. Because of the abnormal nature of their design, and the secrecy surrounding them, the ships became known as the *Outrageous* class or 'Hush-Hush' ships. They were extravagantly over-gunned for light cruiser work; the objection being that end-on fire (two 15in guns) when in chase, was too slow and would have only a fair chance of securing hits on small, fast-moving targets such as light cruisers, although it was admitted that one salvo on target would probably prove conclusive. As a covering force they had possibilities, but they were an expensive luxury, and conversion of the later *Furious* before she was completed indicates that no great value was placed on the type for employment as cruisers. In view of the restrictions under which it was produced, however, the design can only be regarded as a 'next best thing', rather than one carefully calculated to fill naval requirements, and it should be judged in this light.

Further to the Baltic idea, another ship designated 'WE', was proposed during the spring of 1915. Admiral Bridgeman, the Third Sea Lord, wrote to the DNC saying that his only objection to the design was the secondary armament. In his view, the 4in

Below: *Glorious* from the air showing her original battlecruiser layout. Note that flying-off trials are underway. 1918.

Above: *Courageous*, December 1916. As completed, and showing off her fine lines.

Opposite: *Glorious* at anchor in Scapa Flow, May 1917. Port quarter view.

scheduled for the other two new ships was inadequate, but any suggestion that the 6in be adopted was out of the question on grounds of weight. However, a 5in gun had been designed recently and was thought very suitable, but it would not be in production soon enough. Bridgeman went on to say that ships building in British yards for Greece, and which had been requisitioned, were to carry 5.5in guns of which at least sixteen were available; here was a golden opportunity to increase the new ships' secondary armament without greatly exceeding the weight of the Board margin.

The design was generally along the same lines as the first two except for the following modifications:

1. Provision for main armament to be two 18in (one forward and one aft), with an allowance to accommodate four 15in if the 18in proved unsatisfactory.
2. Increased displacement, increased beam, and slightly less draught. The final legend was approved on 23 May 1915 and *Furious* was laid down at Armstrong on 8 June 1915.

On learning details of *Furious*, the former DNC, Philip Watts, drew up a rather lengthy report on why he did not like the design, and went even further by proposing his own broader, better, but unsuitable design for Fisher's requirements. The main change, on which Watts was so insistent, was to the hull for which he proposed a flat-shaped configuration instead of the strongly curved, bulbous-bulged hull of the DNC's design. However, Bridgeman wrote to Watts arguing the case for the original design and stating that Watts' design was completely out of the question.

Great speed and low draught was stipulated, especially the latter, which must be maintained even if the ship were pitching and rolling in bad weather. This precluded the idea of a square bilge because of the draught increasing as the ship heeled. In order

COURAGEOUS
Outboard profile and plan, 1916, as completed

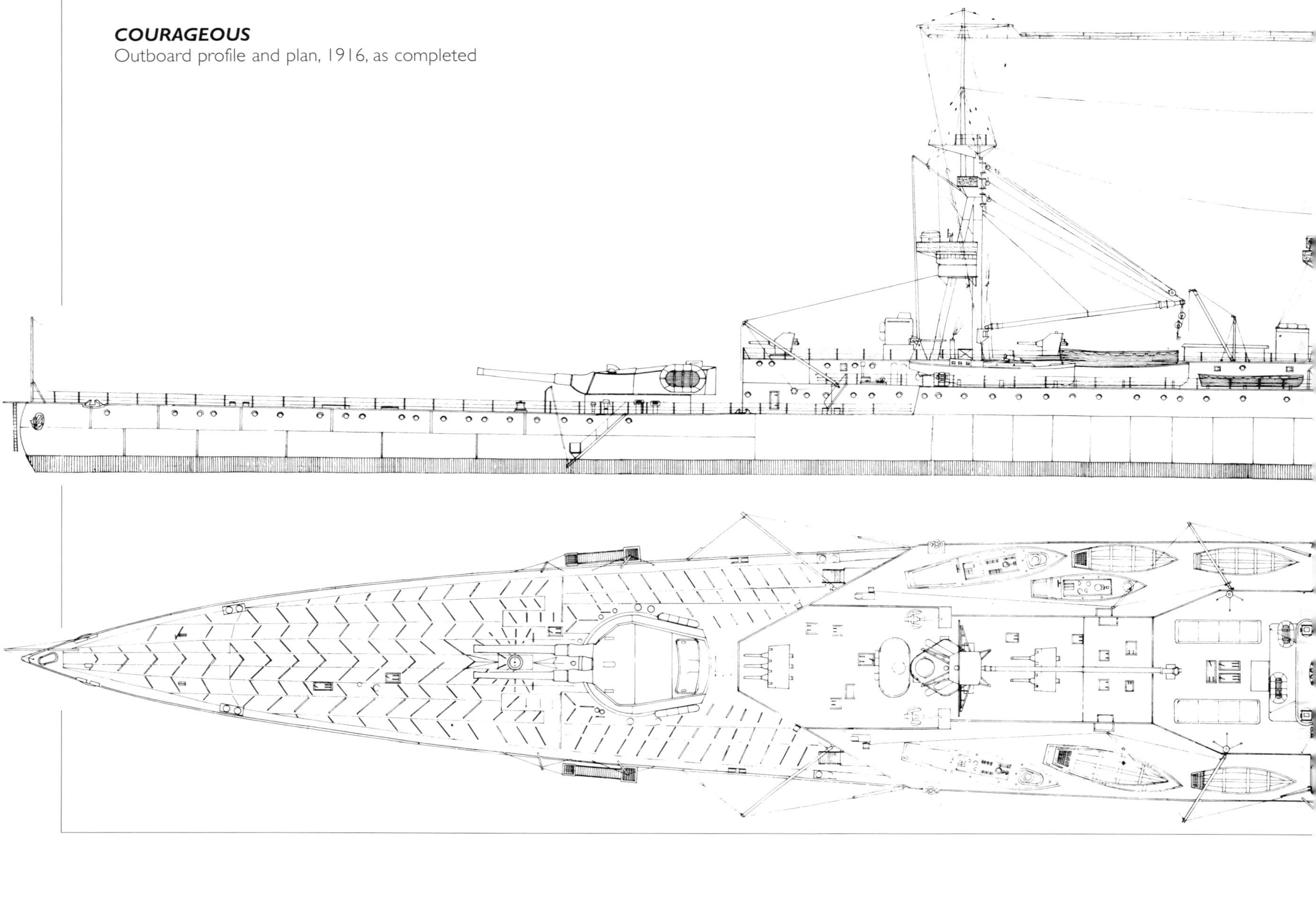

to provide such a low draught, weights had to be kept to a minimum, and the section shown by Watts, with added armour and large water chambers for protection, added considerable weight and reduced speed. Recent experiments had shown that better results were obtained against underwater explosions if the bulge were entirely external to the hull, and this was one of the features of D'Eyncourt's design. Watts's design allowed the explosions to take part inside the ship; he suggested that the light decks between the vertical sides would blow upwards and act as a vent.

In June 1916, while under construction, it was proposed that both *Glorious* and *Courageous* be converted to seaplane-carriers, and a letter was sent to the constructors asking what would be involved in cost, time and difficulty. In reply, they listed the items requiring alteration: cutting away the existing shelter deck forward; doing away with the CPO and PO ready rooms; raising the forward 4in guns; building new shelter deck and fitting watertight doors to the openings in the screen bulkheads for the passage of seaplanes. Bridgeman rejected the idea because of the delay involved. The first intimation that the ship might be converted to a seaplane-carrier came in March 1917 while ship No. 896 (*Furious*) was under construction. Board requirements were that she be able to carry four 2-seat reconnaissance aircraft and four single-seat fighters; an additional 14 officers and 70 ratings to handle the equipment; workshops for aircraft maintenance; net

COURAGEOUS: LAUNCH FIGURES, 5 FEBRUARY 1916

Displacement: 11,474 tons
Recorded weight of hull: 9,290 tons
Draught: 12ft 10¼in forward, 17ft 9½in aft
Length: 735ft 0 ⅝in pp
Beam: 81ft 2in
Depth of keel from upper deck: 36ft 1¼in
Breakage at launch:
longitudinal in a distance of 608ft = 2 1/16in hog
transverse in a distance of 70ft = nil

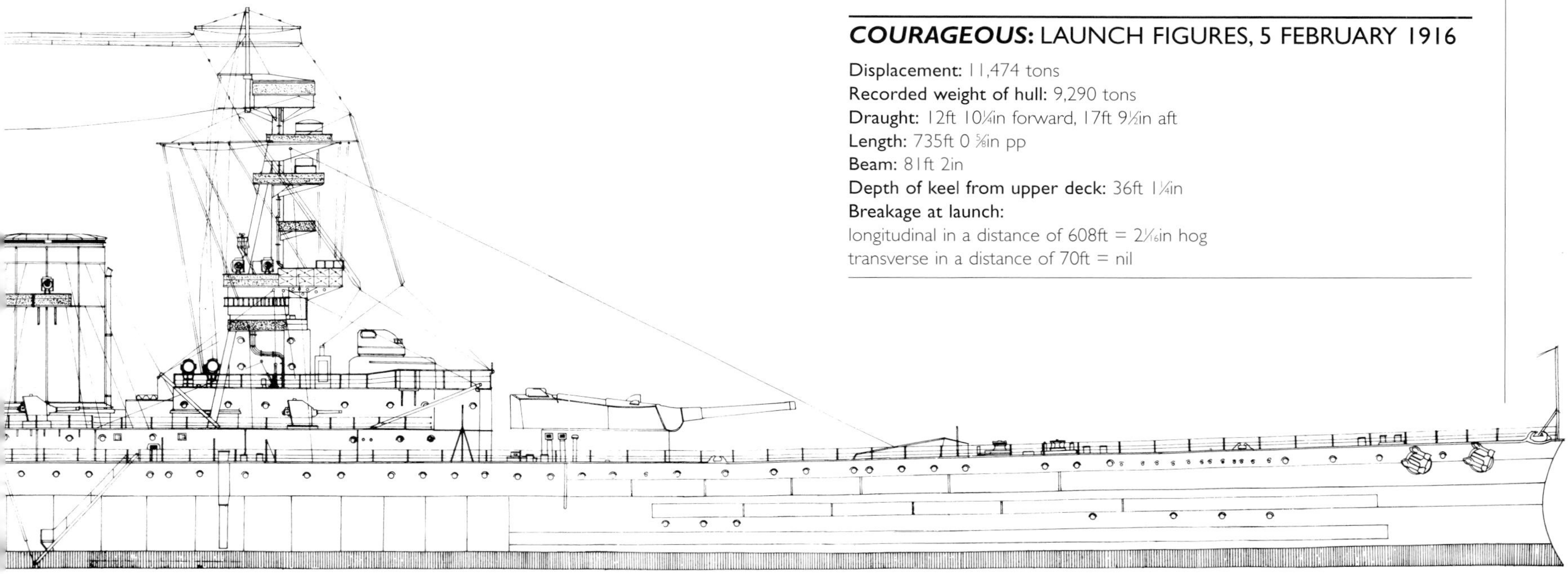

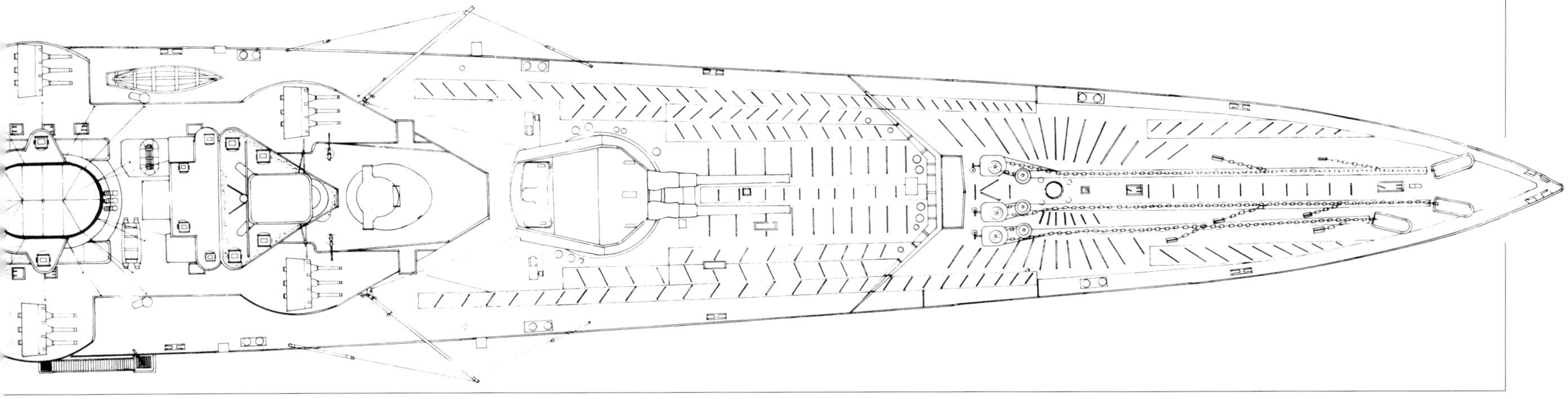

Below: *Glorious* as completed at Harland & Wolff during the winter of 1916/17. Note triple 4in, and 'Etna' deck stripping applied to weatherdeck (quarterdeck). These thin strips were introduced because of the ship's special design and corresponding light draught; no wood decking was to be fitted to save weight (*Renown* and *Repulse* fitted with the same).

defences to be removed. Experienced RFC officers to advise during conversion at Armstrong. After concluding their calculations, Armstrong sent a letter to the Board, listing the following:

1. Remove gun and mounting from 'A' position, plus the ring of armour above the forecastle deck, and make large new seaplane hangar and flying-off platform forward with workshops and equipment nearby.
2. Fit minelaying arrangements aft if required (this had been originally proposed in the legend, but rejected at that date).

3. Stop work on all anti-torpedo nets and remove what had been fitted.

They undertook to complete all these modifications without any considerable delay to completion which was provisionally scheduled for June 1917.

After visiting the ship at Belfast on 22/23 September 1917, the Assistant DNC, Stanley Goodall, wrote to the DNC saying that extra girders must be worked into the ship's bows to relieve stress from the additional weights of the flying-off deck, and although this was agreed in principle, it is doubtful if it was ever carried out; one of the stipulations made to her first Commander was that she should not be driven hard into a seaway at speed for fear of damaging her bows.

Armament

The decision to mount four guns of the heaviest calibre had resulted from the Admiralty stipulation for a very powerful armament, and the need for utilizing guns and mountings readily available. Both *Renown* and *Repulse* were still under construction at this time, which earmarked six mountings and twelve 15in guns; realizing this, the DNC made provision for the first two large cruisers to have four 15in guns in twin mountings, even though the Director of Naval Ordnance pointed out that with only four large guns, spotting and range taking would be difficult. However, because the 15in gun and mounting was in such short supply at this time, it was agreed that the original concept of four guns be accepted.

It has often been stated that when the ships underwent their initial gunnery trials, the hulls showed signs of strain, but there is no mention of this in official documents. *Courageous* carried out her gunnery trials on 16 November 1916, and although cracks appeared in several cabins after firing had ceased, no damage was done to the boats (a frequent occurrence in these particular trials) or to anywhere else; the ship behaving very well under the vibration of her own gunfire, and proving steady at all times.

Courageous and *Glorious* were given the same 4in Mk IX gun as fitted in *Renown* and *Repulse*. The original provision had been for sixteen guns, but with careful planning it proved possible to fit six triple mountings on the shelter deck, two each side abeam bridge, two each side abeam funnel, and one before and abaft mainmast on the centreline, making eighteen in all (see *Renown* notes for details of this triple mounting).

18in Gun in *Furious*

The ever-increasing gun sizes fitted to capital ships reached their peak when it was proposed to fit two 18in single mountings in *Furious* as designed. Trials of the gun were carried out throughout 1916 by Armstrong. At a weight of approximately 150 tons each, the guns proved difficult to manufacture; nevertheless, it had always been paramount that *Furious* should have the guns, and it was at Fisher's insistence that fitting should proceed rather than give her twin 15in as a substitute. The turret for the single gun was a modified 15in twin mounting with further modifications to the working chamber and loading systems. Provision for an elevation of 30° and depression of 5° were allowed, which in theory would fire the 3,320lb shell to a distance of approximately 30,000 yards.

Furious, with her single massive 18in gun aft, was something of a novelty, and was viewed by many with great misgivings. During her trials, the huge gun shook the ship considerably, but the hull bore the excessive weight (827 tons for entire revolving turret and gun) quite well. Only three guns were ever manufactured: two for fitting in the ship and one spare. After she was converted to a carrier the guns were later used in the monitors *Lord Clive* and *General Wolfe* for shore bombardment, in which they proved very successful.

Secondary armament was originally eight 5.5in but again, as in

Left: *Furious* fitting-out at Armstrong in 1917.

Left: *Furious*. The monster single 18in gun and turret as mounted on the quarterdeck. Note the 'Etna' stripping on weatherdeck.

Courageous and *Glorious*, careful arrangements led to the fitting of eleven guns all mounted in single fittings.

Armour

Fisher's requirements for protection to light cruiser standards left the ships far short of any standard that would justify inclusion in any category of 'armoured ship'. The cherished 'Baltic Plan' came to nothing, and by the time the ships were completed it was difficult to find a suitable role for them. In view of their freakish nature it was decided to deploy them as 'light cruiser destroyers' which effectively denied them any opportunity of proving themselves in their original role.

The main strake affording protection to the ship's hull consisted of just 2in of high-tensile steel, covered with a 1in skin to give the published figure of 3in which would scarcely withstand the lightest shellfire. The belt ran from between the end barbettes and was 23 feet above the water-line and a mere 18 inches below at normal draught condition. Forward was a 2in strake running from the forward barbette to the forward bulkhead between the lower and upper deck levels. The 2in forward bulkhead ran obliquely, closing the side armour, and was entirely internal. A 3in bulkhead ran outwards from 'A' barbette, to the ship's side at upper to lower deck levels. This fitting was exactly the same at 'Y' barbette. Another bulkhead aft closed the after extremities of the 3in side armour, and was itself 3in thick.

Barbettes were 7in and 6in above the upper deck in 'A', reducing to 6in and 4in from upper to main, and then 3in on the outer face only from main to lower deck. 'Y' barbette had 7in and 6in above the main deck and 3in from the main to lower decks. Turrets had 9in faces, 7in sides, 11in rears and 4¼in roofs. The conning tower was 10in on the sides and 2in on the lower sides; the roof was 2in, tube 3in, and floor 3in. The sighting hood was 6in on the insides, with a 3in roof. A torpedo control tower was provided, having 3in on the sides, ¾in to 1½in on the roof and a 2in tube. Funnel uptakes were 1in to 1½in from forecastle deck up.

The forecastle deck was given ¾in to 1in abaft the forward barbette, and then ran back to 'Y' barbette, but amidships this was only at the edges and did not cover the whole of the forecastle deck area. The upper level was 1in from the forward bulkhead, and around the aft barbette; there was nothing between. The main deck was 1in on the. slopes and ¾in on the flat. After the experience of Jutland, the main deck thickness on the flat was increased to 1¾in–2in around the magazines only, and added 116 tons to the displacement (see additions in Appearance Changes). The lower

COURAGEOUS CLASS: PARTICULARS, AS COMPLETED

Construction

	Dockyard	Laid Down	Launched	Completed
Courageous:	Armstrong	28 March 1915	5 Feb 1916	28 Oct 1916
Glorious:	Harland & Wolf	20 April 1915	20 April 1916	14 Oct 1916
Furious:	Armstrong	8 June 1915	18 Aug 1916	26 June 1917.

Displacement (tons)
Courageous: 18,180 (light), 19,180 (legend), 22,560 (deep)
Glorious: 19,180 (legend), 22,360 (deep)
Furious: 18,480 (light), 19,513 (legend), 22,890 (deep).

Dimensions
Length:
Courageous: 735ft 0⅛in pp, 786ft 9in oa
Glorious: 735ft 1½in pp, 786ft 9in oa
Furious: 735ft 2¼in pp, 786ft 9in oa
Beam:
Courageous: 81ft (as moulded)
Glorious: 81ft (at deck), 81ft 5¼in (at bulge)
Furious: 88ft 0⅝in
Draught:
Courageous, *Glorious*: 22ft 8in–25ft 10in
Furious: 21ft 6in–24ft 7in (see Stability).

Armament
Courageous, *Glorious*:
Four 15in 42cal Mk I; 120rpg
Eighteen 4in Mk IX; 150rpg
Two 3in HA
Two 3pdr
Two 21in torpedo tubes (abeam 'A' barbette, submerged); ten torpedoes
Furious:
One 18in 40cal Mk I
Eleven 5.5in 50cal Mk I
Two 3in HA
Two 3pdr
Two 21in torpedo tubes (near 'A' barbette, submerged); ten torpedoes.

Director control
Main armament directors in a tower aloft and in the armoured hood.

Armour
Main belt: 3in
Bulkheads: 3in–2in
Barbettes: 7in–6in–3in
Turrets: 11in–9in–7in–4¼in
Decks: forecastle 1in, upper 1in, main 1¾in–1in, lower 3in–1in
Conning tower: 10in–6in–3in
Uptakes: 1½in.

Machinery
Courageous:
Parsons geared turbines, four propellers
Boilers: eighteen Yarrow small tube, 235psi
Length of boiler rooms: 39ft 11⅞in forward, 40ft amidships, 40ft aft
Length of engine rooms: 42ft 1in forward, 42ft 0¾in aft
Designed SHP: 90,000 = 32 knots
Fuel: 750 tons as designed, 3,160 tons max.
Fuel consumption: 1,031 tons oil per 24 hours at full speed
Radius of action: 6,000nm at 20 knots.
Furious:
Brown Curtis geared turbines, four propellers
Boilers: eighteen Yarrow small tube, 235psi
Length of boiler rooms: 39ft 11⅝in forward, 39ft 11⅝in amidships, 40ft aft
Length of engine rooms: 41ft 11¾in forward, 41ft 11¼in aft
Designed SHP: 90,000 = 31.5 knots
Fuel: as *Courageous*
Fuel consumption: 1,014 tons oil per 24 hours at full speed
Radius of action: as *Courageous*.

Ship's boats (*Furious*)
Motor launches: two 36ft
Service boats: two 35ft
Life cutters: two 32ft
Cutters: two 30ft
Whalers: two 27ft
Gigs: two 30ft
Dinghies: two 16ft
Balsa rafts: two 13ft 6in.

deck was 1in forward and ran from the forward bulkhead to the stem: aft, it was 1in from the after barbette to the stern, increasing to 3in over the rudder, and 1½in and 2in on the slopes.

The internal sub-division and special protection consisted of underwater bulges (12 feet deep inboard) over machinery and magazine spaces, and 1½in anti-torpedo bulkheads running longitudinally for the same distance, and rising vertically from the keel to the main deck: these bulkheads were closed by 1in traverses rising to the main deck forward, and upper deck aft.

Below: *Glorious* at Scapa Flow, May 1917.

Machinery

Admiralty requirements called for speed of not less than 32 knots to enable them to outsteam anything that Germany could deploy against them. In service, however, they required more than 90,000shp to drive them to their full designed speed, although this did not prove difficult (see trial figures).

As the DNC pointed out, the ships could not only outrun any large warship in existence, but could also outrun a German torpedo-boat destroyer in anything other than very calm water – a condition seldom seen in the North Sea. It was finally decided to fit the vessels with small-tube boilers, and they provided an increase of at least 30 per cent in power over the large-tube boilers on the same weight. They were the first large warships to have geared turbines.

Courageous left Walker at 04.00 on 16 November 1916 for steam trials. Draught was 25ft 5in forward, 25ft 8in aft; displacement 22,100 tons, which meant that she was four feet deeper than designed legend load. At 06.00 the tugs left and she proceeded out of the river at about 20 knots. By 09.00 she had worked up to full power, estimated at 91,200shp on open exhaust. It was considered that the machinery could easily develop at least 110,000shp which, theoretically, would drive the ship at about one knot faster than the designed speed. The 91,200shp developed with 323rpm mean was estimated by log for a speed of 30.8 knots. There was some stripping on the face of the propellers and some disturbance within the shaft seating, but on the whole the trials were successful. However, on subsequent runs, she sustained structural damage from head seas when working up for her full power runs

Searchlights
Courageous:
Six 36in: two bridge, four funnel
Glorious:
Eight 36in: four bridge, four funnel
Furious:
Nine 36in: one under foretop, four abaft CT, four on platform around mainmast.

Rangefinder positions
Courageous:
Three 15ft: 'A', 'Y' turrets, control tower
Two 9ft: torpedo control tower, spotting top
One 6ft 6in HA: fore bridge
Furious:
Two 15ft: 'Y' turret, control tower
Two 9ft: torpedo control tower, spotting top
One 6ft 6in HA: fore bridge.

Battle signal stations
Two separate, enclosed, all ships.

Anchors
Three 150cwt Admiralty, one 60cwt stern.

Wireless
Main office: Types 1–16
Second office: Type 2.

Complement
Courageous: 787
Glorious: 768
Furious: 726 (as designed); 737 (as completed).

Cost
(initial building costs to 23 Nov 1916)
Courageous: £2,038,225
Glorious: £1,967,223
Furious: £1,050,000 (hull).

GLORIOUS: STEAM TRIALS

She left Belfast at 13.30 on 30 December 1916 making for the Tail of the Bank, where she anchored at about 19.00. Weather fine, sea smooth. Draught was 24ft 1½in forward, 25ft 9in aft; displacement 21,670 tons.

	Outer		Inner		Speed (knots)
First run					
Port:	203rpm	5,170shp	204rpm	4,450shp	19.67
Starboard:	204rpm	5,060shp	203rpm	5,670shp	
Second run					
Port:	208rpm	5,430shp	206rpm	5,000shp	20.59
Starboard:	207rpm	5,080shp	206rpm	5,730shp	
First run					
Port:	258rpm	10,850shp	253rpm	9,200shp	24.06
Starboard:	254rpm	9,350shp	254rpm	10,000shp	
Second run					
Port:	254rpm	10,350shp	253rpm	9,200shp	24.80
Starboard:	254rpm	9,800shp	253rpm	9,950shp	
Third run					
Port:	318rpm	–	300rpm	18,740shp	29.60
Starboard:	306rpm	–	313rpm	18,650shp	
Fourth run					
Port:	318rpm	20,450shp	314rpm	19,820shp	30.08
Starboard:	313rpm	–	314rpm	19,900shp	

Mean speed: 29.84 knots with 313rpm and 76,700shp.

On 1 January 1917 further runs were attempted, but thick mist and rain squalls reduced visibility to the point where the marker posts could not be seen and the trials were abandoned. The first run was completed, however, and the following figures were recorded. Displacement was 21,300 tons.

First run					
Port:	324rpm	21,960shp	328rpm	22,450shp	31.25
Starboard:	330rpm	21,500shp	328rpm	22,700shp	
Second run					
Port:	328rpm	22,550shp	332rpm	23,150shp	31.58
Starboard:	334rpm	23,900shp	332rpm	24,180shp	

Mean SHP: 93,780–94,450.

Furious
No steam trials carried out, but builder made preliminary runs to test machinery. No figures available.

just off May Island. At the time of the incident, the sea was stated to be moderate, and the speed reached at the moment when the damage occurred was approximately 30 knots. The forecastle deck between the breakwater and 'A' turret was deeply buckled in three places, with the after buckle extending to the turret on the starboard side. Rivets were sheared in the vertical flange of the angle-iron securing the deck armour. The side plating was visibly buckled on both sides at stations 50 and 56 between the forecastle and upper decks. The upper deck was also buckled by about 2 inches in the sick bay. Water had entered the submerged torpedo room, and the wings in the area showed signs of strain. A full investigation was carried out, and the findings were sent to the Third Sea Lord. It was suggested that the ships should not be driven at such high speeds in view of their rather light construction, and that extra frames, Z bars and shoring were needed. The Third Sea Lord did not agree, and asked whether or not the officers in charge on that day had any regard for the care of the ship; the NE wind was reported to be at gale Force 6 to 8, and the sea very rough. A Court of Inquiry was convened and both ship and officers were cleared, but further information as to what actually caused the damage has not been discovered.

Appearance Changes

The ships were quite distinctive, and unlike any other contemporary ships. The hull form was especially graceful and they could be easily identified by the large single uptake, and single turrets forward and aft.

Individual differences, as completed, were that *Courageous* had her searchlight platforms all on one level around the funnel, whereas *Glorious* had hers on two levels (*Courageous* shows SL on two levels in builders' original drawings). The only other major difference was the gaff, which was at the heel of the topmast in *Courageous* and at the starfish in *Glorious*.

Below: *Furious* in her original as-completed condition at sea during her trials period, 1917.

COURAGEOUS: GM AND STABILITY

As inclined, 8 October 1916

	Displacement (tons)	Draught	GM	Maximum stability	Stability vanishes at
'A' Condition (= load)*	19,180	22ft 8¼in	4ft	44°	85°
'B' Condition (= deep)**	22,560	25ft 10in	6ft	40°	94°

*Fully equipped plus 750 tons oil.
**Fully equipped plus 3,250 tons oil.

FURIOUS: FINAL LEGEND

Displacement (tons)
19,000.

Dimensions
Length: 735ft pp
Beam: 88ft
Draught: 20ft 6in forward, 22ft 6in aft
Freeboard: 30ft forward, 16ft amidships, 14ft aft
Sinkage: 88.5 tons
Turret heights: 35ft forward, 28ft aft.

Armament
Two 15in*
Eight 5.5in
Two 3in AA
Four 3pdr
Five MG
Two 21in torpedo tubes (submerged).

Armour**
Side: 3in amidships, 2in forward
Bulkheads: 3in
Barbettes: 7in–6in
Conning tower: 10in
Torpedo control tower: 3in.

Machinery
SHP: 90,000 = 31.5 knots.

Weights (tons)

Hull:	8,345
Armour:	3,780
Machinery:	3,030
Armament:	2,420
General equipment:	775
Oil:	750
Board margin:	100
Total:	**19,200**

*Actually 18in, but always referred to as 15in.
**23ft above lower wl; 4ft 6in below.

After Jutland, extra deck protection was worked in while the pair were still under construction, and amounted to 116 tons in weight (mainly around magazines).
Other modifications included:

	tons
Extra cabins and boats, when acting as flagship	45
Additional frame supports forward	28
Paravanes	20
40lb plating (1in) added under director tower	10
Increased ready-use stowage of ammunition	10
Charthouse and compass platform	10
Steel strips (Etna) and coconut matting to weather decks and other positions as applicable	9
Protective mattresses around bridge, etc.	8
Additional workshops	5
Extra kit lockers and mens' gear, etc.	17
Extra engineers' spaces	5
Torpedo office	3
Submarine lookout	5
Forge spaces in forecastle deck	4
Disinfection house	1
Engine room ventilation	5
Flash protection	5
Total	**306**

1917–18 *Courageous* and *Glorious*: The torpedo armament was increased by adding six 21in tubes above water: one pair port and starboard on the upper deck abeam the mainmast, and two pairs on quarterdeck abeam 'Y' turret. *Courageous* was temporarily fitted as a minelayer, with mine rails laid along the quarterdeck, and shutes on each quarter (never actually employed as minelayer). *Glorious* not fitted as minelayer.

Range clocks fitted to control tops on fore and mainmast. Deflection scales painted on turrets. High-angle rangefinder added in top during the winter of 1917/18. 36in SL on bridge remounted high on mainmast, and original SL platforms around funnel replaced by new towers, two on each side with a single 36in lamp in each.

1918 Flying-off platforms fitted over each turret. Mine chutes removed from *Courageous*.

Furious was completed as part carrier, with just one 18in gun and turret ('Y') on quarterdeck. Flying-off platform forward (see conversion notes). Original SL mountings redistributed by builders before being commissioned. Converted to complete aircraft carrier.

Aircraft Carriers

As completed, *Courageous* and *Glorious* were accepted into the ranks of the Grand Fleet with reservations, but *Furious*, with her flying-off deck forward, proved to be something of an achievement, and was viewed as such. Many experiments with aircraft were carried out on her forward deck, and she proved herself much more capable than the old *Empress*, *Campania*, *Engadine* and *Riveria*, all of which had been converted to suit the purposes of the aircraft provided on them. Each of these vessels was fitted with a hangar and carried up to 4 or 5 seaplanes, but there were no proper flying-off platforms fitted, and the procedure could only take place in calm weather with a smooth sea.

Furious, however, was to change all that, but not without extensive tests. She joined the Grand Fleet in July 1917, and from her forward deck, measuring 228ft 3in x 50ft, she constantly flew off her Short seaplanes and Sopwith Pups with much success. In August, the first successful landing was made by Squadron Commander E. H. Dunning, DSC, who was subsequently killed while making attempts to land.

Furious was taken in hand in November 1917 for further conversion. Her aft 18in gun, mainmast and torpedo control tower were removed, and a flight deck was fitted aft; to connect the flying-off platform (forward) with the landing platform (aft), a narrow strip of decking (11ft wide) was provided on each side of the superstructure. In 1922 it was again decided to remove the funnel and superstructure and convert her to a fully-fledged aircraft carrier. The results of the many experiments carried out in *Furious* throughout her long career resulted in the construction of the carriers that served during the Second World War, and were models for all other navies.

After a limited success in their cruiser role, *Courageous* and *Glorious* were finally earmarked for conversion to aircraft carriers although they would be reconstructed completely, and not in stages like *Furious*. *Glorious* was taken in hand for conversion in February 1924 and the work, which lasted until 1930, was carried out in Devonport Royal Dockyard, cost: £2,137,374. Armour remained unchanged except for the provision of modified and rather large underwater bulges. *Courageous* was reconstructed in the same way as *Glorious* and both proved to be very successful.

FURIOUS AS AIRCRAFT CARRIER, 1922

Displacement: 23,130 tons (normal load); 26,800 tons (deep load)
Length of flying deck (forward): 150ft
Length of landing deck: 576ft
Length of upper hangar: 530ft
Width of upper hangar: 50ft
Area of upper hangar: 26,000sq ft
Length of lower hangar: 550ft
Length of hull: unchanged
Beam: 107ft at navigating bridge
GM: 3ft (normal load), 3.6ft (deep load)
Complement: 1,132 (increasing to 1,194).

Above: *Furious*. Looking down on her forward flight deck which is covered with aircraft. Note the wooden windbreaks around the aircraft (1918).

Opposite: *Furious*. Starboard quarter, as completed, 1917.

History: *Glorious*

Laid down in May 1915 and launched on 20 April 1916. Commissioned for sea trials 23 October 1916.

1917 *Jan* Commissioned for service.
16 Oct With *Courageous* on the Scandinavia trade route patrol with 2nd LCS.

COURAGEOUS AND *GLORIOUS* AS AIRCRAFT CARRIERS

Displacement: 22,500 tons (normal load); 26,500 tons (deep load)
Length of flight deck: 591ft
Beam of flight deck: 100ft
Draught: 27ft 3in (mean)
Armament: sixteen 4.7in HA/LA; three 2pdr; twenty quadruple MG

Aircraft
1926: 12 F III F, 12 Ripon, 18 Flycatcher
1933: 24 F III F, 12 Ripon, 9 Nimrod
1937: 36 Swordfish, 9 Nimrod, 3 Osprey
1939: 36 Swordfish, 9 Gladiator.

FURIOUS: GM AND STABILITY

As inclined, 25 May 1917

	Displacement (tons)	Draught	GM	Maximum stability	Stability vanishes at
'A' Condition (= load)*	19,513	21ft 6in	3.75ft	44°	81°
'B' Condition (= deep)**	22,890	24ft 7in	5.33ft	44°	93°

*Fully equipped plus 750 tons oil.
**Fully equipped plus 3,393 tons oil.

FURIOUS
Outboard profile and plan, 1917, as completed

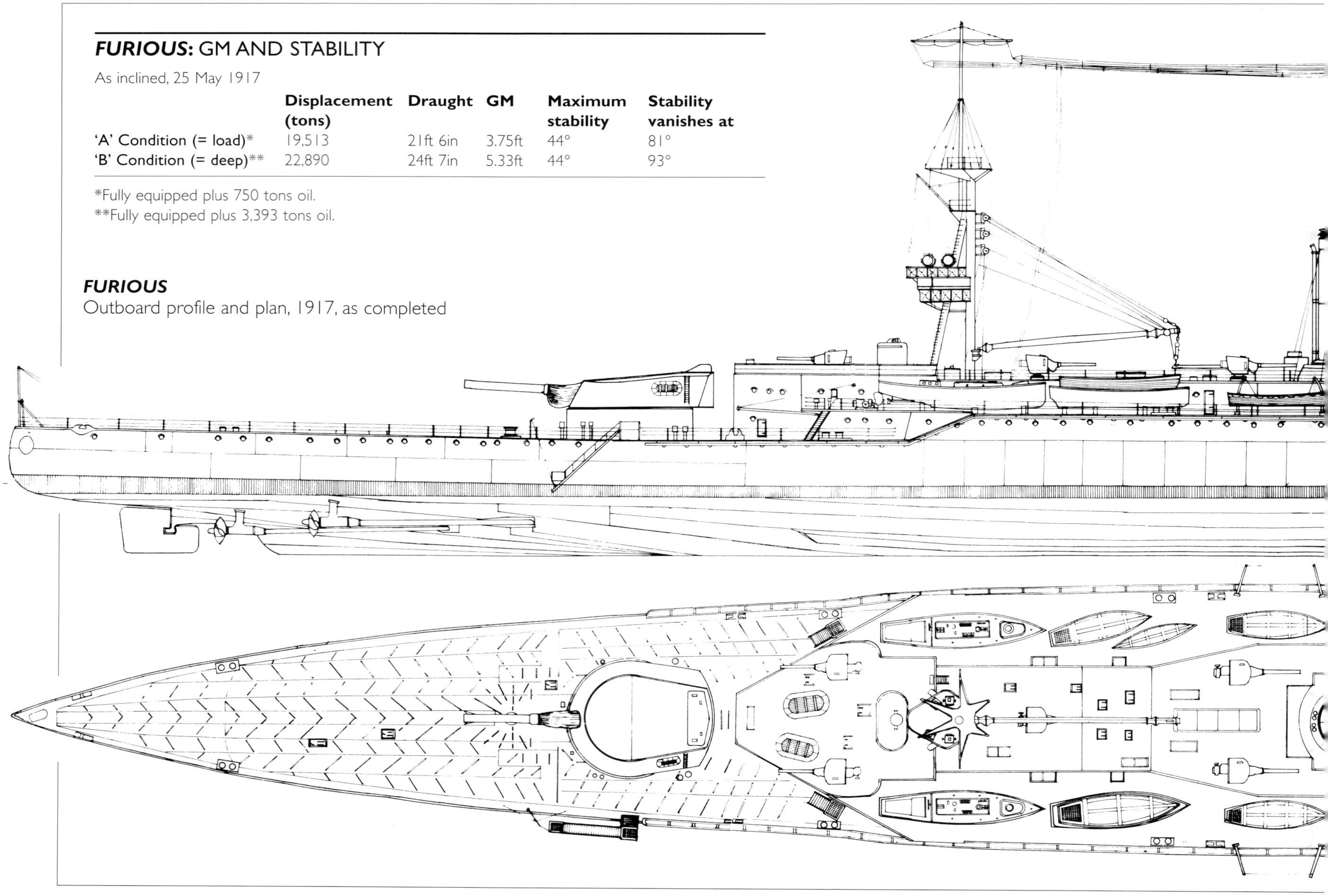

Left: *Courageous* and *Indomitable* at Devonport, late 1918.

Right: *Glorious* and *Courageous* anchored alongside each other after the war (*Glorious* nearest), late 1918.

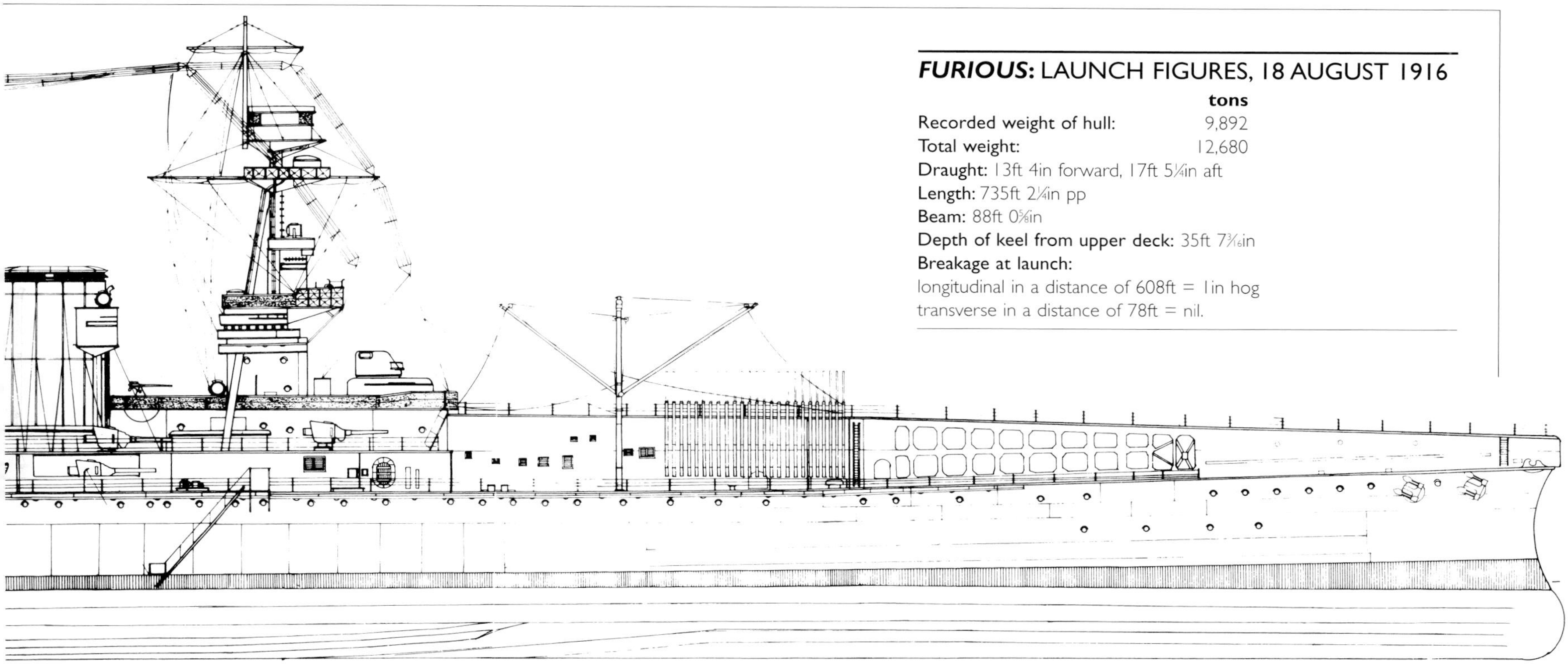

FURIOUS: LAUNCH FIGURES, 18 AUGUST 1916

	tons
Recorded weight of hull:	9,892
Total weight:	12,680

Draught: 13ft 4in forward, 17ft 5¼in aft
Length: 735ft 2¼in pp
Beam: 88ft 0⅝in
Depth of keel from upper deck: 35ft 7³⁄₁₆in
Breakage at launch:
longitudinal in a distance of 608ft = 1in hog
transverse in a distance of 78ft = nil.

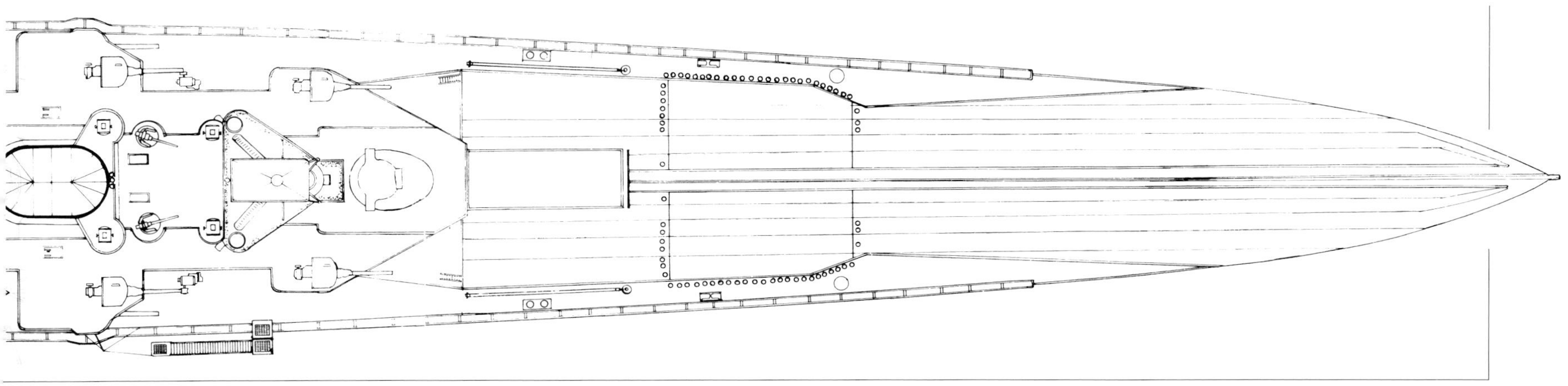

Above: *Glorious*, 1918.

Below: *Furious*, 14 July 1935, after more modifications.

17/18 Oct Action off Heligoland Bight. With other units attempted to bring the raiders *Bremse* and *Brummer* (German light cruisers) to action. From 07.30 to 09.32, with *Repulse* and *Courageous*, light cruisers and destroyers, was in action with German fleet off the Kattegat while making a sortie against German minesweepers clearing a passage along the fringe of the British barrage. Like her sister *Courageous*, her decks were damaged by the blast of her own gunfire.

1918 *21 Nov* With 1st LCS at the German surrender.

1919 *1 Feb* Reduced to Reserve at Rosyth and became tender to the battleship *Hercules*.

1920 *Dec* Turret drill ship at Devonport.

1921–2 Flagship Rear-Admiral Commanding the Reserve at Devonport.

1923 *Sept* Parent ship in the Reserve at Portsmouth.

1924 *14 Feb* Paid off at Rosyth to prepare for reconstruction as aircraft carrier. Served successfully in this role.

1940 *8 June* While evacuating RAF aircraft from Norway, she was spotted off Jan Mayen Island by the German battlecruisers *Scharnhorst* and *Gneisenau* and sunk by gunfire. More than 1,200 killed and injured.

History: *Courageous*

Laid down in March 1915 and launched on 5 February 1916. Further sea trials in January 1917.

1917 *16 Oct* As for *Glorious*.

17/18 Oct Action off Heligoland Bight: see *Glorious*.

1918 *21 Nov* Flagship LCS at German surrender. As *Glorious* until

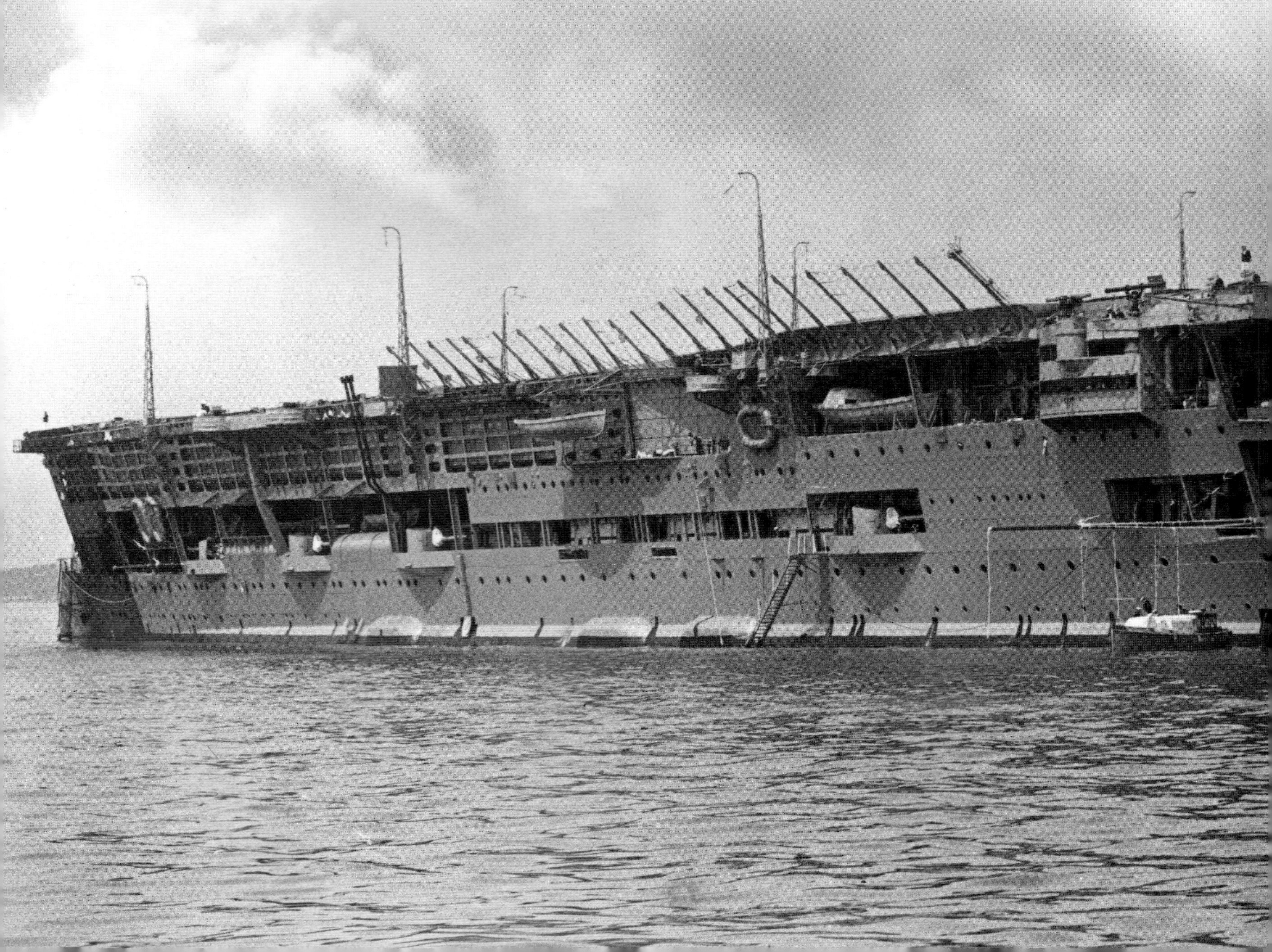

March 1920 when she became Flagship Rear-Admiral Commanding Reserve.

1924 *29 June* Taken in hand at Devonport for conversion to an aircraft carrier, estimated cost £2,025,800. Served successfully in this role, carrying out many experiments towards successful aviation at sea.

1939 *17 Sept* Torpedoed by *U29* off the Irish coast, the first major unit to be lost at sea during the Second World War, 509 killed.

History: *Furious*

Laid down June 1915 and launched on 15 August 1916. Shortly before completion as cruiser, was converted to a semi-aircraft carrier and began trials in this role on 26 June 1917.

1917 *4 July* Joined Grand Fleet. During the winter of 1917/18 was again converted, this time to full aircraft carrier. Experimental trials during March 1918.

1922–5 Underwent complete reconstruction.

1925 *1 Sept* Commissioned at Portsmouth and served as one of the most successful of the fully converted aircraft carriers. Served with distinction during the Second World War. Placed in Reserve at Portsmouth after the war.

1948 *15 March* Sold to T. W. Ward Shipbreakers and scrapped at Dalmuir.

Above: *Furious*, showing her Norman Wilkinson 'dazzle' camouflage, 1918.

Conclusion

By the end of the war, the Grand Fleet had proved itself supremely in command of the seas. Its ships and crews were the most battle-experienced in the world, and much had been learned during the four years of conflict. However, the price had been high, in both money and lives. And the impression lingers in the popular mind to this day, fostered by the frustratingly incomplete results of Jutland, that German ships were generally superior to their British counterparts.

When the new era of naval shipbuilding was inaugurated in 1906 with the arrival of *Dreadnought*, drastically departing from traditional ideas and designs, it was widely held that Germany had neither the financial resources nor the technical experience necessary to construct all-big-gun ships of the dreadnought type. Events proved the sceptics wrong. Germany's first attempts (the *Nassau* and *Helgoland* classes) were none too successful, but with the laying down of the first German battlecruiser, *Von der Tann*, in 1907, the British superiority was reduced considerably.

Although in 1914 it was generally agreed that the Royal Navy could defeat a German force at sea because of its numerical superiority, it was noted that individual German ships were being fitted with thicker main armoured belts than their British counterparts. To do this, they sacrificed seagoing qualities, however. An interesting case file of the time shows the perceived relative merits of each successive year's naval construction programme, and it highlights the thought patterns during those years:

1906: In both countries, displacements were approximately equal, the British ships being slightly ahead in speed and armament.
1907: The programme showed no relative change.
1908, 1909: In both years, British ships were still considered to be ahead.
1910: A complete change was discerned, it being generally accepted that some aspects of the German armouring system were superior.
1911: Hardly any change from 1910, but speed was now equal, while British armament was considered superior.

General comparisons on paper of one battleship against another do not really prove anything, however; naval actions were affected critically by weather, sea conditions, visibility and leadership. Ship for ship, the German battlecruisers were better than their British counterparts in armour protection only; in armament, machinery and seakeeping, the British ships had the edge. British battleships, meanwhile, compared very favourably with German ships. Much of the criticism of British capital ships of this period stem from the failure of the Grand Fleet to annihilate the German High Seas Fleet in the first year of the war, and from the failure of the battlecruisers at Jutland in 1916. But the opportunities for pure battle fleet actions were few and far between; attention had to be focused on the menaces of torpedo and mine.

The British battleships of the dreadnought period could claim the following attributes; while no figures can be found to show that any foreign fleet could surpass the combination they represented:

1. Adequate armour protection in most parts of the ship.
2. Excellent main armament.
3. Reliable machinery and speeds equal to any rival.
4. Unmatched seagoing qualities regardless of weather.

The less satisfactory aspects of the British battlefleet have been much publicized, though with scant regard for the facts. Perhaps the words of Commander E. S. Land, USN, provide a suitable perspective on the argument:*

> In my country they have a soap advertisement which claims for its product '99.44 per cent pure'. Personally, I am fed up with this ivory soap purity of everything pertaining to war material that bears the label 'Made in Germany'. We Anglo-Saxons are too prone to think the other fellow's goods are superior to our own.

* *Transactions of the Institute of Naval Architects*. 1921.

Right: Admiral Beatty's famous flagship and 'splendid cat' *Lion* now makes her inglorious last journey to the scrapyard, 1924.

These notes are taken from tables compiled by the National Intelligence Department (N.I.D.) and are, therefore, approximate. When compared to figures in the Ships' Books captured after the war, however, they prove remarkably accurate. The notes have been left unchanged so that the reader can follow the Admiralty's view in 1910–14.

NASSAU CLASS: PARTICULARS AS COMPLETED

Construction

	Dockyard	Laid Down	Launched	Completed
Rheinland:	A. G. Vulkan, Stettin	1 June 1907	26 Sept 1908	30 April 1910
Posen:	Friedrich Krupp Germaniawerft, Kiel	11 June 1907	12 Dec 1908	31 May 1910
Nassau:	Kaiserliche Werft, Wilhelmshaven	22 July 1907	7 March 1908	1 Oct 1909
Westfalen:	A. G. Weser, Bremen	12 Aug 1907	1 July 1908	16 Nov 1909

Displacement (tons)
18,600 (as designed); 18,569 (normal load); 20,210 (deep load).

Dimensions
Length: 451ft 9in pp; 478ft wl
Beam: 88ft 4in
Draught: 26ft 7in mean as designed
Freeboard at normal load: 22ft forward; 17ft 9in amidships; 19ft 6in aft.

Armament
Twelve 11in 45cal, mounted in pairs in electrically controlled turrets; 80rpg
Twelve 5.9in 45cal (1902/6 design)
Sixteen 3.4in 45cal 1906 design
Two 7pdr 21cal guns mounted in boats
Two machine-guns
Six 17.7in torpedo tubes (all submerged).

Armour
Main belt: 11.42in, tapering to 4¾in at lower edge
Ends: 6in forward, 4in aft
The main belt is complete except for about five feet before the stern. The depth of the belt is about five feet below the water-line at normal load.
Bulkheads: 7¾in
Battery: 6½in closed by bulkheads of the same thickness
Turrets: 11in faces
Barbettes: 11in–8in
Conning tower: 12in sides with 16in strake at the fore
The conning tower is roughly semi-circular in transverse section, the internal dimensions being 16ft athwartships and 13ft longitudinally. In shape it is an inverted truncated cone which is built into the forward part of the superstructure.
Aft conning tower: 8in–2in and is 8ft in diameter
Torpedo bulkheads: 1in–1⅛in approximately 6ft 7in from the ship's side
Decks: Armoured deck extends the whole length of the vessel with 2in on the flat and 3in on the inclines. At each end the deck slopes downwards.

Machinery
Three sets of engines. all abreast in separate watertight compartments, all situated under the mainmast. Triple expansion type (vertical) driving three screws.
Designed SHP 20,000 for 19–20 knots.
Boilers: Schulz Naval type located in three separate transverse rooms, each containing four boilers. Two uptakes each about 80ft in height.
Bunkers: Ten wing bunkers on each side of the ship which extend up to the armoured deck.
Speed trial results:

Rheinland	SHP: 27,498	Speed: 20.03 knots
Posen	SHP: 28,117	Speed: 20.12 knots
Nassau	SHP: 25,850	Speed: 20.6 knots
Westfalen	SHP: 27,477	Speed: 20.3 knots

Radius of action: 3,540 nautical miles at 18 knots with 14,000shp; 8,000 nautical miles at 10 knots with 2,500shp
Fuel: 935 tons coal normal, 2,658 tons maximum plus 197 tons liquid fuel.

Boat derricks
Two large cranes for hoisting boats.

Searchlights
Eight 43in electrically controlled from bridge, with driving motors below.

Anchors
Three stockless bowers, two fitted on starboard side and one to port, there is also a light stern anchor.

Wireless
Wireless room located on the battery deck abaft the second funnel; type unknown.

Complement
966 as private ship except *Westfalen* (957). Full crew for a turret, magazine and shell room 54 men and 4 officers.

These ships were Germany's answer to *Dreadnought*, and although they were strong, it was felt that they were badly cramped and over-gunned for their size. Displacement was on a par with *Bellerophon* with 6ft greater beam on 1ft less draught. The ships were known to be handy but also very unwieldy. Accommodation was poor. Broadside comparable with *Dreadnought*.

VON DER TANN: PARTICULARS

Construction
Blohm & Voss; laid down 25 March 1908; launched 20 March 1909; completed 1 Sept 1910.

Displacement (tons)
19,100 (normal load).

Dimensions
Length: 562ft 8in (wl)
Beam: 87ft 3in
Draught: 27ft 7in (mean).

Armament
Eight 11in 45cal mounted on Drehscheiben-Lafette C/06 type, and in pairs
Ten 5.9in 45cal on CP mountings. C/02/06, in central battery
Sixteen 22pdrs, 45cal, semi-automatic
Two 7pdrs in boats
Two machine-guns
Four 17.7in torpedo tubes (all submerged).

Armour
Main belt: 9.84in, complete except for about ten feet near the stern where closed by a 4in bulkhead
Ends: 6in and 4in
Bulkheads: 7in and 4in
Barbettes: 9in
Battery: battery and bulkheads in this area are reported to be 5in
Casemates: 1in
Turrets: 9in fronts, 3in roofs
Torpedo screens: unknown, but probably the same as in *Nassau*
Decks: uncertain, but known to be better than in *Invincible*.

Machinery
Four sets of turbines driving four screws
Boilers: Schulz Navy type. Eighteen in three sets
Designed SHP: 41,000 for 24/25 knots
Two uptakes, each about 75 feet from the waterline
Speed trials: up to 28 knots reported, but it is uncertain what SHP was used to attain this figure, if true at all
Fuel: 984 tons coal normal; 2,760 tons maximum stowage; 200 tons oil.

Boat derricks
Two cranes fitted, one on each side of the after funnel.

Searchlights
Eight 43in electrically controlled from bridge.

Anchors
Three stockless bowers: two on starboard side, one on port.

Wireless
The same installation as in *Nassau* class.

Germany's answer to *Invincible* was viewed with much respect by British naval constructors, and the vessel made a big impression at the Coronation Fleet Review at Spithead in 1911.

While under construction the ship was fitted with Frahms anti-rolling tanks because of reports about the *Nassau* class rolling so badly, but as the tanks were placed further from the ship's sides than would have been the case if they had been part of the original design, their effectiveness was unsatisfactory. With 231 tons of water in the tanks, the roll was reduced from 17 to 11 seconds which compared favourably with *Invincible* at 14 seconds. *Von der Tann* was more than a match for both *Invincible* and *Indefatigable* as regards armour protection. Her armament and machinery were on a par as regards installation, and it was because of these figures that the British battlecruisers of the 1909/10 programme (*Lion* class) had greater weight devoted to their protection.

Below: *Von der Tann*, Coronation Fleet Review, 1911

Bibliography

Unpublished Sources

Public Record Office

Ships' Books:

Dreadnought
Invincible
Revenge
Queen Elizabeth

Ships' Logs:

Ajax
Barham
Bellerophon
Benbow
Collingwood
Dreadnought
Furious
Glorious
Hercules
Indefatigable
Inflexible
Iron Duke
King George V
Lion
Neptune
New Zealand
Orion
Princess Royal
Queen Elizabeth
Ramillies
Renown
Repulse
Royal Sovereign
St Vincent
Superb
Temeraire
Thunderer
Tiger
Vanguard
Warspite

Admiralty Papers; ADM series:
Designs for new battleships, 1906
Battleships' construction, 1906–21
Dreadnought, trials and acceptance, 1907
Loss of *Audacious*, 1914. Board of Inquiry
Method of firing used by *Invincible* and *Inflexible* at Falklands, 1914
Warship design, 1914
Warships' movements, 1914–18
Loss of *Vanguard*, 1917. Board of Inquiry
Jutland Dispatches
Dogger Bank Dispatches
Haslar designs and experiments
Post-war fleet, 1919
Battleships' and battlecruisers' construction, 1921
Monarch, shell and bomb trials, 1925
Tiger, conversion to all-oil firing, 1925
Emperor of India, shell and bomb trials, 1931
Flash trials in *Marlborough*, 1931
Camouflage experiments
Loss of *Royal Oak*, 1939, Board of Inquiry
Damage to *Valiant* and *Queen Elizabeth* at Alexandria, 1942
Damage to *Valiant* at Trincomalee, 1943, Board of Inquiry
War records

Admiralty Library

Battleships and battlecruisers, histories
Warship construction, 1914–18
German warship construction
German war material
The Technical series
The Pink lists
National Intelligence files (NID)
Admiralty gunnery manuals

National Maritime Museum

Ships' Covers:

Agincourt
Bellerophon
Canada
Colossus
Courageous
Dreadnought
Erin
Furious
Indefatigable
Invincible
Iron Duke
King George V
Lion
Lord Nelson
Neptune
Orion
Queen Elizabeth
Queen Mary
Renown
Repulse
Royal Sovereign
St Vincent
Tiger

Published Sources

Attwood, E. L. *Warship Construction*. Longman, 1911.
Bywater, H. C. *The Searchlight on the Navy*. Constable, 1935.
Churchill, W. S. *The World Crisis*. Thornton-Butterworth, 1923.
Fawcett, H. W. and Hooper, G. W. W. *The Fighting at Jutland*. 1921.
Hase, Commander G. von. *Kiel and Jutland*. Skeffington.
Hough, Richard. *Dreadnought*. Michael Joseph, 1966.
Jellicoe, Admiral Lord. *The Grand Fleet 1914–16: Its Creation, Development and Work*. Cassell, 1919.
Marder, A. *From the Dreadnought to Scapa Flow*. Oxford, 1961–70.
Parkes, Dr Oscar. *British Battleships*. Seeley Service, 1957.
Raven, A. and Roberts, J. *Battleships of World War II*. Arms & Armour Press, London; Naval Institute Press, Annapolis, 1976.
Scheer, Admiral von. *The German High Seas Fleet in the World War*. Cassell, 1921.
Wood, Walter. *Battleship*. Kegan Paul, 1912.
Young, Filson. *With the Battlecruisers*. Cassell, 1921.
Jane's Fighting Ships. 1904, 1906, 1908, 1910, 1914.
Brassey's Naval Annual. Clowes, 1902, 1906, 1916, 1919, 1924, 1932, 1939.
Navy Lists. 1906, 1910, 1911, 1914. Sampson Low, Marston.
The Narrative of Jutland. HMSO, 1924.
Transactions of the Institute of Naval Architects. 1900–21.

Index

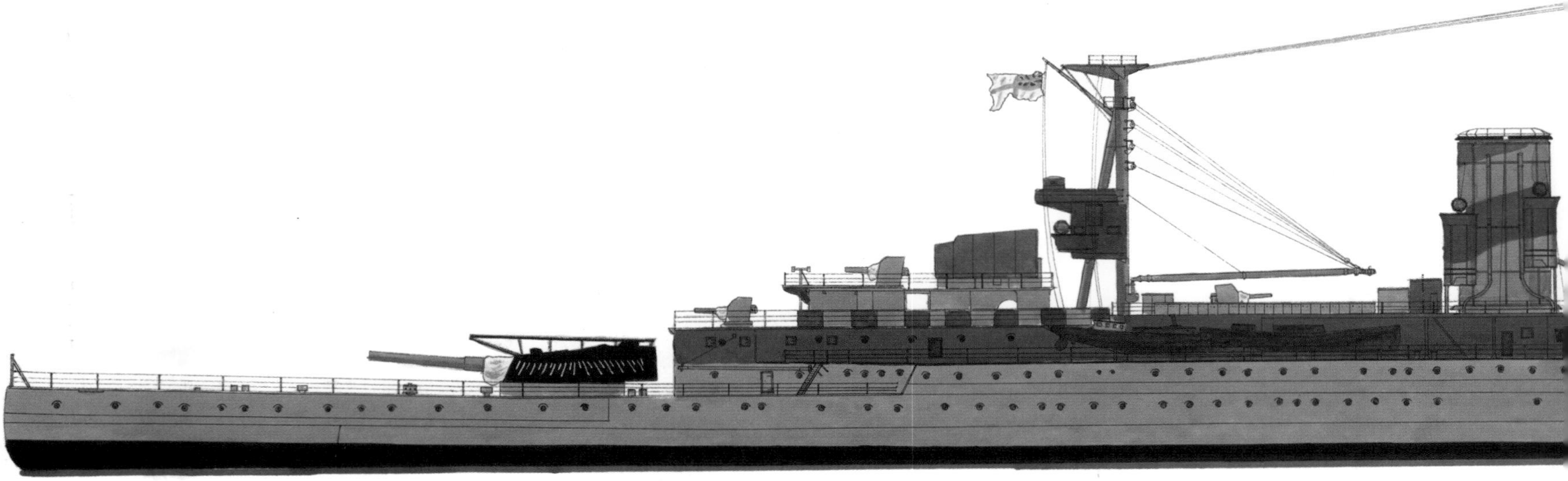

REPULSE 1917 TO THE END OF 1918.
A much-experimented scheme with changing ideas being painted up with the use of dark grey over light grey. The grey dash near the bow was only painted up for a short period but the funnels and bodywork for quite a long time.

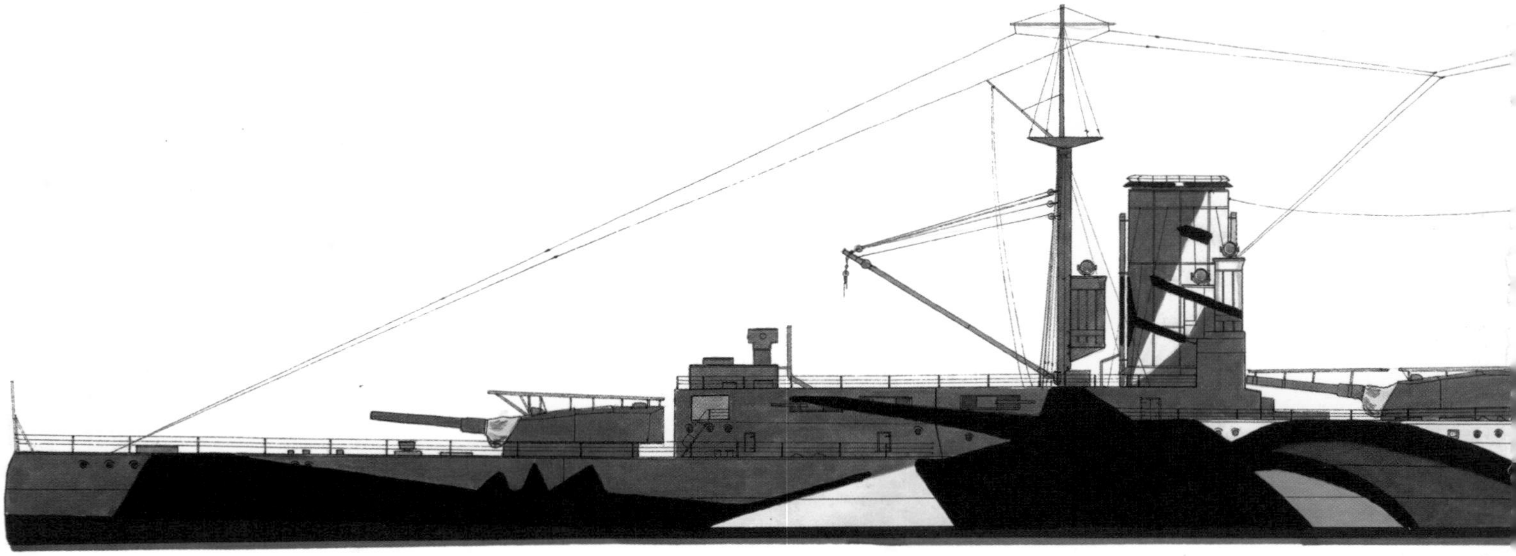

LION 1918 DAZZLE LAYOUT.
An extreme colour contrast scheme drawn up for *Lion* but never applied. The port side was very different as in the case of all dazzle layouts.